MICRO–
ECONOMICS

MICRO-ECONOMICS

Third Edition

ROGER N. WAUD

University of North Carolina, Chapel Hill

1817

HARPER & ROW, PUBLISHERS, New York
Cambridge, Philadelphia, San Francisco,
London, Mexico City, São Paulo, Singapore, Sydney

Photo Credit: Smith, p. 14, Culver Pictures.

Sponsoring Editor: John Greenman
Project Editor: Ellen Meek Tweedy
Text Design Adaptation: North 7 Atelier Ltd.
Cover Design: DanielsDesign Inc.
Text Art: Vantage Art, Inc.
Production: Debra Forrest
Compositor: Donnelley/ROCAPPI Inc.
Printer and Binder: R. R. Donnelley & Sons Company

MICROECONOMICS, Third Edition

Library of Congress Cataloging-in-Publication Data

Waud, Roger N., 1938–
   Microeconomics.
   Includes index.
   1. Microeconomics. I. Title.
HB172.W38   1986   338.5   85–21994
ISBN 0–06–046947–1

85 86 87 88 9 8 7 6 5 4 3 2 1

To Heather and Neil

Brief Contents

Detailed Contents

Preface

Since its inception, this book's primary objective has been to demonstrate how principles of economics are used to analyze real-world events and problems. To meet this objective in a new way, a major feature has been added to the third edition—a series of discussions about contemporary economic problems and policies for dealing with them. Each chapter has from one to four such sections, called "Policy Perspectives." They are directly related to the chapter's content and, because they deal with real-world situations, they enhance students' understanding of important economic issues.

Ultimately, a basic education in economics should attempt to develop a facility, indeed a habit, for disentangling and making sense of important economic issues encountered daily in the popular press and on television. The third edition's Policy Perspectives demonstrate how to do this, while at the same time exploring matters of concern to most citizens. As a chapter unfolds, the Policy Perspectives provide effective vehicles for showing beginning students *why* the study of economics is useful.

The third edition contains a number of significant substantive changes. In addition, all related data and graphs have been updated and, in a number of instances, new statistical information and graphs have been added. Every chapter has been reexamined with an eye to improving exposition and presentation, and no chapter has remained unchanged as a result of this process.

MICROECONOMIC THEORY AND APPLICATIONS

A main objective of the third edition, like that of the second, is to develop the standard tools of microeconomic analysis while showing how they may be applied to contemporary economic problems. The addition of the Policy Perspectives, one or more of which appears in every micro chapter, has further bolstered this objective in the third edition.

Chapter 11, "Oligopoly and Market Concentration," expands the discussion of barriers to entry to include an examination of the role of capital requirements, the control of input supplies, and government regulation of entry. The Policy Perspective titled "The OPEC Cartel—International Collusion in Oil" provides a good real-world example of the benefits (to the colluding parties) and problems associated with collusive behavior.

Chapter 12, "Market Structure, Public Policy, and Regulated Markets," has been extensively revised. There is an updated discussion of recent research on the types of industry structures which seem to best promote technological change and innovation, and on the role played by profits and advertising as determinants of industrial concentration. The discussion of the evolution of antitrust policy in the United States has been updated to take account of: the implications of such recent cases as the IBM and the AT&T cases; recent evidence on the extent of merger activity and the government's apparent lack of success at slowing conglomerate merger activity; and recent developments in policy pertaining to regulation of market conduct and business practices, as exemplified in the 1983 FTC ruling on price-fixing and price discrimination charges against Du Pont and the Ethyl Corporation. A new section on regulated industries has been added to this chapter. It focuses on the pros and cons of such regulation and the consequence of deregulation in such areas as trucking, airlines, and railroads. The Policy Perspective, "Is the U.S. Economy Becoming More, or Less, Competitive?," provides evidence from recent research on a major question that goes to the heart of the main subject of this chapter.

There are certain areas of microeconomics where my own teaching experience has found other principles texts wanting. I have taken particular care to bolster these areas in this book. Such areas include the comparison between pure competition and monopoly, the presentation of the factors pertaining to welfare loss from monopoly, and the discussion of the various sources of monopoly—all in Chapter 9; the discussion of oligopolistic market structures and the incentives for and consequences of price cutting and nonprice competition, Chapter 11; the evidence on the relationship between oligopoly and technological progress, and the relationship between market structure and antitrust policy, Chapter 12; the relationship between market structure and wage determination, Chapter 15; and the treatment of income distribution, poverty, and welfare policy, Chapter 17.

Why, in students' minds, should microeconomics always play the role of the ugly stepsister to the sexy Cinderella, macroeconomics? I am convinced that it's because we economics teachers have not exploited the abundance of real-world problems that naturally lend themselves to microeconomic analysis. If students can be shown real-world applications of market supply and demand, elasticity, and marginal analysis, their enthusiasm for microeconomics can be kindled. In putting together the Policy Perspectives used in this book, I was struck time and again by the abundance of policy problems and issues that are grist for microeconomic analysis. Indeed, the Policy Perspective approach seems a natural way to give vitality to the study of microeconomics.

On Explaining Things

It may seem an odd pitch to make about a textbook, but this book places an emphasis on explanation. In recent years many economics principles texts seem to put a premium on being terse—even to the point of being "slick." But there is a trade-off between brevity and explanation. Given the need to explain, the ideal is to be as brief as possible but not briefer than necessary. As a practical matter, books typically and unavoidably end up somewhat to one side or the other of the ideal. I have decided that if I am condemned to err, I would opt for explaining too much rather than too little. Every effort has been taken to make the book as understandable as possible. Numerous examples are provided to give concreteness to difficult concepts.

MORE ABOUT THE POLICY PERSPECTIVES

Each Policy Perspective has been selected because it illustrates an economic problem and concept directly related to the economic principles developed in a particular chapter. A Policy Perspective typically has two questions at the end that are intended to challenge the student to think (and hopefully encourage discussion) about the problems and issues raised. In addition to engaging the student's attention in a relevant way, the Policy Perspectives show how and why economic analysis is a powerful and useful tool. The following lists the Policy Perspective titles and page numbers.

- "Why Economists Disagree—The Role of Ideology," Chapter 1, p. 17.
- "Defense Spending—How Much Does It Cost?," Chapter 2, p. 34.
- "Should Profit Be the Only Objective of Business?," Chapter 3, p. 52.
- "Math and Science Teachers in Short Supply," Chapter 4, p. 84.
- "Energy Consumption and the Price of Energy—Adjusting to Energy Shocks," Chapter 4, p. 85.
- "A Sales Analysis of the Demand for Wine," Chapter 5, p. 100.
- "Oil Demand Adjustment to Price Change," Chapter 5, p. 105.
- "Oil Supply Adjustment to Price Change," Chapter 5, p. 108.
- "Farm Support Programs and the Surplus Problem," Chapter 6, p. 137.
- "Can Excise Taxes Stop People from Smoking?," Chapter 6, p. 142.
- "Acid Rain—A Spillover Cost or What?," Chapter 6, p. 148.
- "Economies and Diseconomies of Scale and the Number of Firms in an Industry," Chapter 7, p. 173.
- "Is Perfect Competition an Ideal?—The Pros and Cons," Chapter 8, p. 208.
- "The Monopoly as Cartel—Why Taxi Rides Can Be Expensive," Chapter 9, p. 234.
- "How Do You Keep Costs Down?—Fooling the Utility Commission," Chapter 9, p. 240.
- "How Important Is Advertising to Economic Prosperity?," Chapter 10, p. 256.
- "The OPEC Cartel—International Collusion in Oil," Chapter 11, p. 281.
- "Is the U.S. Economy Becoming More, or Less, Competitive?," Chapter 12, p. 289.
- "Controversy Over Benefit-Cost Analysis—How Much Is Human Life Worth?," Chapter 13, p. 323.
- "Air-Traffic Controller 'Burnout'—Working Conditions Versus Product Safety," Chapter 13, p. 328.
- "Will Robots Replace Workers?," Chapter 14, p. 351.
- "Have Unions Increased Wages?," Chapter 15, p. 381.
- "Subsidized Job Training Versus Labor's Economic Rent," Chapter 16, p. 394.
- "Who Gets Ahead?," Chapter 17, p. 417.
- "The Negative Income Tax—Give the Money to the Poor and Cut Out the Bureaucracy," Chapter 17, p. 430.

OTHER PEDAGOGICAL FEATURES

Checkpoints

Checkpoints appear in every chapter, generally at the ends of major sections. At each Checkpoint the student is signaled to stop and answer a series of questions about concepts just presented—to stop and check on his or her progress and grasp of the material. Questions and problems placed at the ends of chapters are too often easily ignored, like so much litter at the back of a closet that one is rarely forced to face. The Checkpoints are intended to surmount this problem by helping the student reconsider what has just been read—to assure the student's understanding of concepts as they are encountered. Answers to the Checkpoints appear at the back of the book to provide immediate feedback for the student who uses the Checkpoints. Frequently, the Checkpoints also provide grist for class discussion.

Learning Objectives

Learning objectives are listed and set off from the main text at the beginning of each chapter. They outline a plan of study for the chapter, as well as provide an overview of what's to be done. After completing the chapter, the student can also use the list of learning objectives as a quick check to see whether he or she has mastered the material in the chapter.

Economic Thinkers

Economic Thinkers essays are not so much personal biographies as studies in the history of economic thought. Their major purpose is to highlight the development of economic thinking on major problems and concerns while indicating the significant role that particular individuals have played in this development.

Key Terms and Concepts

Terminology is unavoidably abundant in economics. In addition, words that have several meanings in common everyday usage often have a more precise meaning when used in economics. Such words, along with other important economic terms, appear in boldface type when they are first introduced and defined in the text. The "Key Terms and Concepts" list at the end of each chapter highlights the new terminology presented in the chapter. These terms and concepts are defined again in the glossary at the back of the book.

Summaries

The summaries at the end of each chapter are fairly comprehensive. They tie together the main concepts developed in the chapter as well as alert the student to areas that may require rereading.

Questions and Problems

Questions and problems are also located at the end of each chapter. They are generally more complex and extended than the questions found in the Checkpoints. Some are almost case studies. Many may be readily used for class discussion. Answers to all end-of-chapter questions and problems are provided in the *Instructor's Manual.* The Checkpoints together with the end-of-chapter questions and problems and Policy Perspective questions provide significantly more in-text questions and problems than are offered by most other economic principles texts currently available.

Figures, Graphs, and Tables

Liberal use of real-world data is made in tables and figures throughout the book. Quite often, tables containing hypothetical data are used to illustrate particularly difficult concepts. The captions describing each graph and figure generally begin with a brief summary statement followed by a reasonably complete description of what is portrayed.

SUPPLEMENTS AND TEACHING AIDS

The text is supplemented by the following learning and teaching aids: a student study guide, an instructor's manual, transparency masters, and an expanded computerized test bank designed and constructed along lines recommended by the Joint Council on Economic Education.

Study Guide

The student *Study Guide* was written by Professor John E. Weiler of the University of Dayton. Each chapter in the study guide corresponds to a chapter in the textbook. At the beginning of each study guide chapter there is a summary of the corresponding chapter in the textbook. Then a set of basic problems follows, with at least one problem for each basic concept developed in the textbook chapter. The problems are aimed at helping the student use the economic principles developed in the text to quantitatively analyze a specific issue. The basic problem set is followed by a set of multiple-choice questions, a set of true-false questions, and a set of problems, questions, and exercises on matching terms. Each of the sets of problems, questions, and exercises is designed to give complete coverage to each major concept developed in the textbook chapter. The answers to all problems, questions, and exercises are given at the back of the study guide.

Instructor's Manual

Three suggested outlines for a one-semester course appear at the beginning of the *Instructor's Manual.* Each chapter of the manual first gives a summary of the corresponding textbook chapter along with a discussion of important chapter concepts and learning objectives. The manual contains answers to all the end-of-chapter textbook questions and problems.

Test Bank

The test bank has been expanded for the third edition. The test bank contains over 2,000 questions. The test bank is also available on MICROTEST, Harper & Row's computerized testing service. Contact your local Harper & Row representative for further information about the MICROTEST system for PCs.

The test bank, designed in accordance with guidelines suggested by the Joint Council on Economic Education, contains questions constructed to provide a balanced coverage, both by concepts and by the levels at which each concept might be tested. This is done in the following systematic way. In each test bank chapter, a table identifies, for each question, the principal concept which that question tests and the level at which the concept is tested. The concepts tested are closely coordinated with the learning objectives listed at the beginning of each textbook chapter. *A real effort has been made to include questions that test the student's ability to use a concept in a variety of settings.* Questions at the level of application are typically underrepresented in other test banks. This is not true of this test bank. Many of the questions in the test bank have been used at the University of North Carolina, Chapel Hill, where they have been subjected to statistical test item analysis.

Transparency Masters

All important graphs, roughly 90 in number, are available to adopters as a set of transparency masters.

ACKNOWLEDGMENTS

Many people have provided helpful comments and contributions to this book throughout the course of its development. I would like especially to thank the reviewers of the third edition of the book (starred names), as well as those of the earlier editions:

*Phillip Allman,
University of the Pacific

*Fred M. Arnold,
Madison Area Technical
College

Alan Batchelder,
Kenyon College

Arthur Benavie,
University of North
Carolina, Chapel Hill

Charles A. Bennett,
Gannon University

Dennis M. Byrne,
University of Akron

H. Richard Call,
American River College

Anthony J. Campolo,
Columbus Technical
Institute

Robert C. Dauffenbach,
Oklahoma State University

David Denslow,
University of Florida

Richard Froyen,
University of North
Carolina, Chapel Hill

*Philip Gilbert,
Mira Costa College

Jack B. Goddard,
Northeastern State
University

Roger S. Hewett,
Drake University

*Robert Jerome,
James Madison University

*William E. Kamps,
South Dakota State
University

David B. Lawrence,
Drake University

*Patrick M. Lenihan,
Eastern Illinois University

John L. Lewis,
Northern Illinois
University

*Patrick Litzinger,
Robert Morris College

John G. Marcis,
Kansas State University

*Ken McCormick,
University of Northern
Iowa

*Robert K. Miller,
Pennsylvania State
University, Beaver
Campus

*Walt Mitchell,
College of the Mainland

Henry K. Nishimoto,
Fresno City College

Martin Oettinger,
University of California at
Davis

John Rapp,
University of Dayton

*R.K. Russell, Southwestern
Oklahoma State University

*Timothy P. Ryan,
University of New Orleans

Michael Salemi,
University of North
Carolina, Chapel Hill

James A. Skurla,
University of Minnesota at
Duluth

*John A. Sondey,
University of Idaho

Izumi Taniguchi,
California State University,
Fresno

Helen Tauchen,
University of North
Carolina, Chapel Hill

*Robert Turner,
Colgate University

*Lawrence A. Waldman,
College of St. Benedict

Samuel Williamson,
University of Iowa

Edgar W. Wood,
University of Mississippi

*Allan Harris Zeman,
Robert Morris College

ROGER N. WAUD

To the Student

You don't have to have had a course in economics to be aware of economic problems. Newspapers, radio, and television bombard you with them daily. You no doubt are well aware of inflation, unemployment, and budget deficits. Paying tuition bills, finding a job, and just getting a few bucks to spend on a favorite pastime already have given you experience at economic problem solving. In short, you're not a novice to the subject of economics in the same way you might be to college physics. Nonetheless, economics is a rigorous subject. It should be studied in the same way that you would study a course in one of the sciences—a little bit every day.

Before reading a chapter, always look at the learning objectives that are set out at the beginning. They will give you a brief outline of what you are about to read and of the author's aims. At various points in the chapter your attention will be drawn to a Policy Perspective (a discussion of some economic problem or policy) where basic economic principles are developed to enable you to understand such topics. You will find that the economic way of thinking, which at times may seem somewhat abstract, is a powerful tool for analyzing real-world problems. Also, after completing a chapter, you should go back and see how well you have accomplished the learning objectives set out at the beginning. Doing so will provide a self-check on your grasp of the concepts and principles developed in the chapter.

When reading this book, read for understanding, not speed. Each chapter is broken into major sections that focus on important concepts. At the end of a major section, you will encounter a Checkpoint—a brief series of questions that enable you to test your understanding of what you have just read. You should always stop and measure your progress by trying to answer the questions in these Checkpoints. The answers to the Checkpoint questions appear at the back of the book to give you feedback as you study.

Economics is a problem-analyzing discipline. In order to give you more practice, further questions are provided at the end of each chapter. Try your hand at these as well. Discuss them with fellow students and your instructor whenever you feel unsure about the answers. Further problems and questions designed to supplement this book are contained in John E. Weiler's *Study Guide*. The *Study Guide* will give you considerable practice at economic problem solving and aid your understanding of important economic principles.

Finally, bear in mind that the concepts and principles studied in each chapter are typically used again and again in subsequent chapters. Mastering the material as you go makes the chapters that follow that much easier.

I wish you success in your study of economics.

ROGER N. WAUD

MICRO-ECONOMICS

ONE

Introduction

1

Economics and Economic Issues

═══════════

AFTER READING THIS CHAPTER, YOU WILL BE ABLE TO:

1. Define the terms *economy* and *economics*.

2. List and define the basic economic terms used most often in economic discussions.

3. Distinguish between and give examples of positive and normative statements.

4. Identify the basic elements that make up any economic theory.

5. Construct a simple graph from data given in a table.

6. Define the terms *macroeconomics* and *microeconomics*.

7. Define and give examples of the three major fallacies that may be found in statements of economic theory or analysis.

8. Explain the role of economic theory and analysis in economic policymaking.

It has been said that there are three kinds of people: those who make things happen, those who watch things happen, and those who wonder what happened. If you sometimes find yourself among the last group, the study of economics is for you.

How can the study of economics help you? Most importantly, a knowledge of economics will help you to analyze economic issues that are reported daily in the press and on television. Although the laws of economics may not be as absolute as the law of gravity, they will help you deal with facts and opinions about economic issues. As a result, you will be able to come to intelligent, informed conclusions when faced with both day-to-day problems and questions of national policy.

ECONOMY AND ECONOMICS

The word **economy** typically brings to mind ideas of efficiency, thrift, and the avoidance of waste by careful planning and use of resources. We might say that some job was done with an "economy of motion," meaning that there was no unnecessary effort expended. The word comes from the Greek *oikonemia*, which means the management of a household or state. In this sense, we often speak of the U.S. or the Chinese economy; of a capitalist, socialist, free-market, or planned economy; or of industrialized and underdeveloped economies. We use the term in this last sense when we refer to *a particular system of organization for the production, distribution, and consumption of all things people use to achieve a certain standard of living.*

The term **economics**, on the other hand, is not so simple. It covers such a broad range of meaning that any brief definition is likely to leave out some important aspect of the subject. Most economists would agree, however, that economics is a social science concerned with the study of economies and the relationships among them. *Economics is the study of how people and society choose to employ scarce productive resources to produce*

goods and services and distribute them among various persons and groups in society. This definition touches upon several important concepts—choice, scarcity, resources, production, and distribution—with which we will be concerned both in this chapter and throughout the book.

Before reading any further you should understand that, whatever it is, economics is not primarily a vocational subject such as accounting, marketing, or management. Nor is it primarily intended to teach you how to make money, though it may help. Economics studies problems from society's point of view rather than from the individual's. Nevertheless, it is likely you will find the study of economics helpful in whatever career you choose. Moreover, it should make you a more knowledgeable and able citizen.

THE LANGUAGE OF ECONOMICS

As is the case with many subjects, the words used in economics often seem strange to the beginner. Physicists talk about neutrons, quarks, and hysteresis; football coaches talk about fly patterns, look-in patterns, and flex defenses. To make sense of a typical news item about economic issues you must be familiar with the language of economics. Economists frequently use common words to mean something more precise than is generally expected in everyday conversation. For instance, when you say someone has a lot of money, common usage suggests that you mean a person who owns a lot of things such as cars, houses, buildings, bonds, stocks, cash, and so on. In economics, however, we generally accept that "money" means one's holdings of currency and demand deposits at a commercial bank. When we mean something else, we always spell out exactly what other items we mean to include in our definition of money. Certain basic terms, such as money, will come up again and again throughout this book. The following definitions will help you to understand and use them correctly.

Economic Goods

An economic good is any item that is desired and scarce. In general, economic goods may be classified as either commodities or services. Commodities are tangible items such as food or clothing. (*Tangible* means, quite literally, able to be touched.) Commodities do not have to be consumed when they are produced; that is, they may be stored. Services are intangibles (that is, nontouchables) such as shoeshines or haircuts. They cannot be stored or transferred. For example, I cannot give you my haircut (a service), but I can give you my coat (a commodity). Such distinctions are not always clear-cut. For example, the economic good electricity might be called a service by some who say it is intangible and a commodity by those who note that it can be stored in a battery. Most often, an economic good is simply referred to as a good. You may have heard of the output of the economy referred to as "goods and services." This is done largely to remind us of the existence of services.

Whether they are commodities or services, all economic goods share the quality of being **scarce**. That is, there is not enough of them to supply everyone's needs and desires. As a result, people have to pay to obtain them. What they have to pay is called the **price** of the good. As we will see in Chapter 4, price is determined to a large extent by the number of people who desire and are able to pay for a particular good, together with what it costs producers to provide it.

People desire economic goods because these goods provide some form of satisfaction. A refrigerator provides satisfaction by keeping food cold. A stereo system provides satisfaction by giving us entertainment. Because an economic good gives us satisfaction, we say that it is useful to us. As a result, economists sometimes refer to the satisfaction a good yields as its utility. The creation of goods that have utility is called production. Production is carried out through the use of economic resources.

Economic Resources

Economic resources, also called the factors of production, are all the natural, man-made, and human resources that are used in the production of goods. These resources may be broken down into two broad categories, nonhuman resources (capital and land) and human resources (labor).

Capital

Capital is an example of a term that is used to mean one thing in everyday conversation and another in economics. We often speak of capital when referring to money, especially when we are talking about the purchase of equipment, machinery, and other productive facilities. It is more accurate to call the money used to make the purchase financial capital. An economist would refer to this purchase as investment. An economist uses the term capital to mean all the man-made aids used in production. Sometimes called investment goods, capital consists of machinery, tools, buildings, transportation and distribution facilities, and inventories of unfinished goods. A basic characteristic of capital goods is that they are used to produce other goods. For example, electricity is produced with capital goods consisting of boilers, turbines, fuel storage facilities, poles, and miles of wire. Capital is scarce relative to the desire for the output of goods and services made with the use of capital.

Land

To an economist, *land* is all natural resources that are used in production. Such resources include water, forests, oil, gas, mineral deposits, and so forth. These resources are scarce and, in many cases, are rapidly becoming more scarce.

Labor

Labor is a very broad term that covers all the different capabilities and skills possessed by human beings. Labor is scarce relative to the desire for the output of goods and services made with the help of labor. Labor consists of welders, carpenters, masons, hod carriers, dentists, scientists, teachers, managers, and so forth. The term *manager* embraces a host of skills related to the planning, administration, and coordination of production. A manager may also be an entrepreneur (or enterpriser). This is the person who comes up with the ideas and takes the risks that are necessary to start a successful business. The founders of companies are entrepreneurs, while those running them are more accurately called managers.

The Firm

These economic resources of land, capital, and labor are brought together in a production unit that is referred to as a business or a *firm.* The firm uses these resources to produce goods, which are then sold. The money obtained from the sale of these goods is used to pay for the economic resources. Payments to those providing labor services are called wages. Payments to those providing buildings, land, and equipment leased to the firm are called rent. Payments to those providing financial capital (those who own stocks and bonds) are called dividends and interest.

Gross National Product

The total dollar value of all the final goods (as distinguished from goods still in the process of production) produced by all the firms in the economy is called the *gross national product* (GNP). In order to make meaningful comparisons of the GNP for various years, economists often use real GNP—GNP adjusted so that it only reflects changes in quantity of output, not changes in prices. When the real GNP goes down, we say the economy is in a state of recession. A severe recession is called a depression, although there is no general agreement as to how to decide exactly when a recession becomes a depression.

Inflation and Unemployment

The economic health of the nation, of which GNP is one measure, is directly affected by two other important factors, *inflation* and *unemployment.* Inflation is an ongoing general rise in prices. The steeper this rise, the faster the decline of a dollar's purchasing power. The unemployment rate measures the percentage of the total number of workers in the labor force who are actively seeking employment but are unable to find jobs. The higher the unemployment rate, the more the economy is wasting labor resources by allowing them to stand idle. However, it is generally believed that a decrease in the unemployment rate will lead to an increase in inflation, all other things remaining the same. ("All other things remaining the same" is an important phrase in economics that we will look into later in this chapter.)

Positive and Normative Statements

Intelligent discussion of economic issues requires that we distinguish between positive and normative statements. In the previous paragraph we made the statement that "a decrease in the unemployment rate will lead to an increase in inflation." This is a statement of fact that may be supported or refuted by examining data. As such, we can say it is a **positive statement**. *Positive statements tell us what is, what was, or what will be. Any disputes about a positive statement can be settled by looking at the facts.* "It rained last Thursday" and "the sun will rise in the east tomorrow" are positive statements.

But now let's change our statement about inflation and unemployment slightly. Let's say that "it is *better* to decrease unemployment and live with the resulting increase in inflation than to allow a large number of people to go without jobs." This is a **normative**

statement—*an opinion or value judgment.* Those of you who are looking for jobs would probably tend to agree with this statement. But your grandparents who are retired and living on fixed incomes would be likely to disagree. Since they are not seeking employment, an increase in the number of jobs available would in no way compensate them for a rise in prices. As far as they are concerned, it would probably be better to slow the rise in prices. This, of course, would lead to an increase in unemployment, which would make all job-seekers very unhappy. The dispute between these two groups cannot be settled by facts alone.

Normative statements tell us what should be (*normative* means establishing a norm or standard). *Although normative statements often have their origin in positive statements, they cannot be proven true or false by referring to objective data.* For example, I may make the normative statement, "You shouldn't drink and drive." This statement has its origin in the positive statement, "Drinking alcoholic beverages slows down one's ability to react." We could disagree forever over the first statement, but statistical studies could be brought to bear on any dispute over the second.

In any discussion about economic issues, as soon as voices rise you can almost be certain that the discussion has shifted from logic and fact to value judgment and opinion. However, don't forget that value judgments and opinion often parade in the clothes of logic and fact.

CHECKPOINT* 1-1
Pick out a short news item in today's paper and make a list of all the positive statements and a list of all the normative statements. Examine the normative statements and try to determine what kinds of positive statements they may be based on.

*Answers to all Checkpoints can be found at the back of the text.

ECONOMIC REALITY AND ECONOMIC THEORY

Economic reality—making a living, paying the rent, shopping for food, paying taxes, and so forth—forces us to deal with a large and confusing swarm of facts, figures, and events. The activities of households, firms, and federal, state, and local governments all have a direct effect on our economic lives. In order to make some sense out of the world around us we all have formulated some economic theories, even without being aware of doing so.

How to hold down inflation is a topic about which practically everyone has a theory. One individual, having just filled out an income tax return, might say, "If we don't curb all this government spending, inflation will get worse." The owner of a small business, on the other hand, feels that "if something isn't done to break up the big unions and big corporations, we'll never bring inflation under control." Based on observations of the way certain groups, organizations, and institutions function, each individual has focused on the relationship that appears to be most relevant to an explanation of inflation. From these examples, we can say that *an* **economic theory** *is an attempt to describe reality by abstracting and generalizing its basic characteristics. Economists often refer to an economic theory as a law, principle, or model.* Each of these terms may be taken to mean the same thing.

Observations and Predictions: The Scientific Method

The inflation-control theories of the individuals above share two common features: (1) each is based on observation of facts or events, and (2) each makes a prediction about the consequences of certain events. We can now add to our definition of an economic theory by saying that *an economic theory provides an explanation of observed phenomena that may be judged by its ability to predict the consequences of certain events.*

Although economics is not a science like chemistry or physics, it does make use of the scientific method in arriving at and testing theories. The aspects of the **scientific method** that we are most concerned with here are induction and deduction. **Induction** *is the process of formulating a theory from a set of observations.* **Deduction** *is the process of predicting future events by means of a theory.* The predictions made by deduction are then tested by once again observing facts or events to see if what was predicted actually takes place. If not, the theory will have to be changed to conform with reality, and the whole process begins again. For example, suppose there is an increase in government spending, the crucial event in the first individual's theory, but we do not observe the predicted increase in inflation. Following the scientific method, we must either modify or discard the theory because of its failure to predict correctly. The process of induction and deduction is never-ending, since all theories must be continually retested in light of new facts and events.

Constructing a Theory

Our income-tax payer and our small-business owner, needless to say, did not really use the scientific method in drawing up their theories. But now let's see how an economist would go about formulating a theory. As an example, we will analyze the law of demand, a theory that will be referred to many times throughout this book.

Elements of Economic Theory

Every formal statement of a theory has four basic elements:

1. a statement of specific variables;
2. a set of assumptions about other variables that may be relevant;
3. a hypothesis about the way the specific variables are related;
4. one or more predictions.

The law of demand states that the quantity of a good demanded per unit of time will increase as the price of the good decreases, all other things remaining the same. Let's break this statement down into the four elements listed above.

Variables.   The law of demand is concerned with two variables, price and quantity demanded. We call these variables because they can vary, that is, they are subject to change. As we noted in our discussion of the language of economics, price is the amount that must be paid to obtain a good. Quantity demanded is the amount of that good that people want and can pay for per unit of time.

Assumptions.   The law of demand makes the assumption that, except for price, all other variables that might influence demand will remain the same. This assumption, which is a feature of all economic theories, is often referred to as *ceteris paribus*. Logically enough, that's Latin for "all other things remaining the same." This assumption is important when we come to the point of testing our theory. Real-world events may not turn out as the theory says they should. We must be sure to find out whether this is because the theory is wrong or because something other than just price has changed, thus violating the *ceteris paribus* assumption.

Hypothesis.   A hypothesis is a statement of the way we think the variables in question relate to each other. Our hypothesis in the law of demand is that as price decreases, quantity demanded will increase. This is known as an **inverse relationship**, since the variables are changing in opposite ways. If the variables change in the same way (an increase in one leads to an increase in the other), we say they have a **direct relationship**.

Prediction.   Here we move directly into the realm of the real world. Armed with our theory, what can we say will likely happen if the manager of our local clothing store reduces the price of Irish knit sweaters from $45 to $35? While customers might not break down the doors to get in, our theory tells us that we can safely bet that the number of sweaters they want to buy will increase. Historically, the development of the automobile is a good example of the validity of the law of demand. The original cars, which were made on an individual basis, were so expensive that only the rich could afford them. Then Henry Ford developed the assembly-line method of production, which made cars less costly to produce. As a result of using this method, he was able to reduce prices. The quantity demanded soared.

How Exact Is Economic Theory?

Since economic theory tries to explain and predict human behavior, you probably wonder how it is possible to be very exact. Economic theory cannot be as exact as Newton's three laws of motion. But economic behavior is on average more predictable than the behavior of many subatomic particles currently studied in high energy physics. If economic behavior weren't predictable, stores wouldn't hold sales, banks wouldn't need vaults and security guards, and traffic tickets wouldn't carry fines. If you don't think economic behavior is predictable, drop a pail of quarters in a public swimming pool some summer afternoon. Make a practice of this and see if you notice a predictable pattern of behavior.

The law of demand is a good predictor because people's behavior on average is such that they will buy more of a good the lower its price is. True, there is the occasional person who will buy more of a good the higher its price because of "snob appeal." But this is unusual. When we look at the behavior of a large group of individuals, the on-average similarity of the behavior of the majority of them dominates the unusual behavior of the few.

CHECKPOINT 1-2
During the Arab oil embargo of 1973–1974, people waited in long lines to fill up their gas tanks. What does the law of demand suggest to you about a

way in which those lines could have been shortened?

Theories into Graphs

So far, we have been using words to explain how the law of demand works. But when we come to the point of relating the theory to data obtained through research, it is time to use pictures. In economics, the pictures we use take the form of graphs. Let's construct a graph from data about electricity use.

Basic Elements of a Graph

An ordinary graph starts out with two lines, which are called axes. One of the lines is drawn vertically, the other horizontally. The point at which they meet is called the origin and has a value of zero (see Figure 1–1). The value along each axis increases as we move

---

FIGURE 1-1 Basic Elements of a Graph

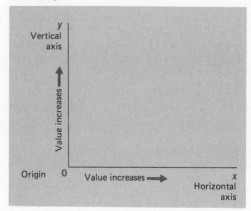

Every graph starts out with two lines. One is called the vertical (or *y*) axis. The other is called the horizontal (or *x*) axis. The point at which they meet is called the origin and has a value of 0. The value of the variable being measured on each axis increases as you move farther away from the origin. This means moving up along the vertical axis and to the right along the horizontal axis.

away from the origin. This means moving up along the vertical axis and to the right along the horizontal axis.

In the case of the law of demand, we noted that we would be looking at two variables, price and quantity demanded. In economics, it is customary to use the vertical axis to measure price. Quantity demanded, therefore, is measured along the horizontal axis. What does this mean in terms of our investigation into the demand for electricity? We now have to find out what numbers to use on each axis. In other words, we must determine how much electricity is demanded at various prices. Let's suppose that our research into electricity demand in one city comes up with the data given in Table 1-1.

Constructing a Graph

Returning to our graph, we can now label the vertical axis "Price per kilowatt-hour" and the horizontal axis "Kilowatt-hours demanded (in millions per month)," as shown in Figure 1-2. (These labels correspond to the column headings in Table 1-1.) We di-

TABLE 1-1 Demand for Electricity at Different Prices (Hypothetical Data)

	Price per Kilowatt-Hour	Kilowatt-Hours Demanded (in Millions per Month)
(a)	$.06	15
(b)	.05	17
(c)	.04	20
(d)	.03	25
(e)	.02	35
(f)	.01	50

This table tells us how much electricity will be demanded per month at various prices. If the price is $.06 per kilowatt-hour, the quantity demanded will be 15 million kilowatt-hours per month (combination a). If the price is $.03 per kilowatt-hour, the quantity demanded will be 25 million kilowatt-hours (combination d).

vide the vertical axis evenly into units representing $.01 increases in price. We divide the horizontal axis evenly into units representing 10-million kilowatt-hour increases in quantity demanded. Our next task is to find the points on the graph corresponding to the quantity demanded per hour figure and the price per kilowatt-hour figure for each of the six pairs of numbers given in Table 1-1. (We have labeled these pairs of numbers a, b, c, d, e, and f in our table.)

For combination a, we first move right along the horizontal axis to a point equal to 15 million kilowatt-hours. We then move directly upward from that point until we are opposite the point on the vertical axis that represents a price of $.06. We label the point at which we have arrived a, since it corresponds to combination a on our table. We use the same procedure to locate points b, c, d, e, and f. Our graph now looks like Figure 1-2.

If we draw a line connecting points a through f, we have what is called a demand curve. Our graph now looks like Figure 1-3. In this case, we see that the demand curve slopes downward and to the right. This tells us that as price decreases (moves down along the vertical axis), quantity demanded increases (moves right along the horizontal axis).

Thinking back to our discussion of the elements of a theory (pp. 8-9), you will remember that we called this type of relationship between two variables an inverse relationship. All inverse relationships (one variable increasing while the other is decreasing) produce this type of downward, rightward-sloping curve. It is one of the major purposes of a graph to show us, without our even having to read the specific numbers involved, what the relationship between the variables is. When we compare the picture of demand provided by our graph with our theory, we see that the theory is consistent with the facts. The downward, rightward slope of the demand curve shows us that as price decreases, quantity demanded increases.

Finally, it should be emphasized that an

FIGURE 1-2   **Demand for Electricity at Various Prices**

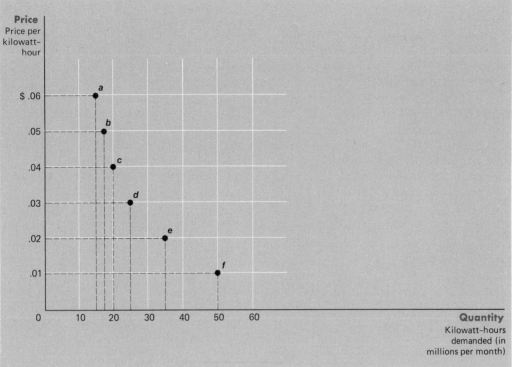

Using the data obtained from Table 1–1, we are able to locate points on the graph that represent the various price-quantity demanded combinations for electricity. To locate combination c, for example, we move right along the horizontal axis until we come to 20 million kilowatt-hours. We then move directly upward from this point until we are opposite the $.04 mark on the vertical axis. The same procedure is used to find the other combinations listed in Table 1–1.

economic theory can be (1) stated in words, (2) represented in a table (Table 1–1), and (3) illustrated in the form of a graph (Figure 1–3).

CHECKPOINT 1-3

Suppose that utility companies say they are finding it difficult to produce all the electricity their customers are demanding. Keeping in mind the graph in Figure 1-3, let us suppose we were able to obtain information on electricity demand in another city. In this case, let us suppose that the data indicate that the demand in this other city is less sensitive to changes in price than the demand in the city we've been looking at so far. What sort of shape do you think the demand curve for electricity would have compared with the one shown in Figure 1-3? In which city would an increase in price most relieve the strain on the utility companies? Why?

FIGURE 1-3 Demand Curve for Electricity

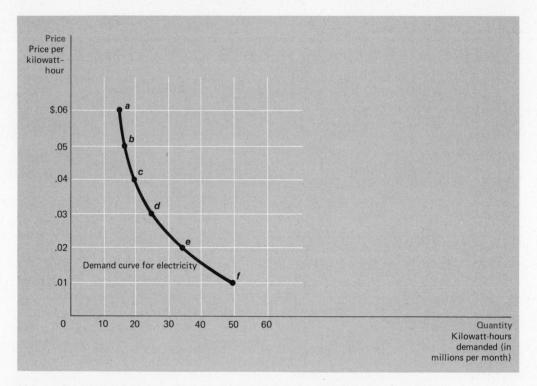

After we have located all the points that correspond to the price-quantity demanded combinations in Table 1–1, we draw a line connecting them. This line is called the demand curve. In this case, because the relationship between price and quantity demanded is an inverse relationship, the curve slopes downward and to the right.

MACROECONOMICS VERSUS MICROECONOMICS

Economists often use the terms *macroeconomics* and *microeconomics* to distinguish between different levels of economic analysis.

In **macroeconomics** we are concerned with the workings of the whole economy or large sectors of it. These sectors include government, business, and households. For the purposes of analysis, the smaller groups that make up these large sectors are often lumped together and treated as one unit. For example, the consumer sector may be treated as though it were one large household. The business sector might be considered to be one large business. Macroeconomics deals with such issues as economic growth, unemployment, recession, inflation, stagflation, and monetary and fiscal policy.

Microeconomics, on the other hand, focuses on the individual units that make up the whole of the economy. Here we are interested in how households and businesses behave as individual units, not as parts of a larger whole. Microeconomics studies how a household spends its money. It also studies the way in which a business determines how much of a product to produce, how to make best use of the factors of production, what pricing strategy to use, and so on. Microeconomics also studies how individual markets and industries are organized, what patterns of competition they follow, and how these patterns affect economic efficiency and welfare.

ECONOMIC REASONING: COMMON PITFALLS

In order to analyze an economic issue or problem correctly, we must avoid certain common pitfalls of economic reasoning. One of the most common fallacies arises from the difficulty of distinguishing between cause and effect. Another is commonly known as the fallacy of composition.

Cause and Effect

As we have seen in our analysis of the law of demand, a key interest of economics is to determine how events in the real world can be explained and even predicted. In other words, we are looking for causes. We want to be able to say with reasonable certainty that if A happens, B will be the result. Having analyzed the law of demand, we are able to say that if price is decreased, quantity demanded will increase, all other things remaining the same. Unfortunately, it is not always easy to tell if some event was the cause of another event or if it just preceded it in time. The situation is especially tricky when event B regularly follows event A.

In economics there are many times when it is very difficult to tell whether A caused B or B caused A. Perhaps there is no causal relationship between B and A at all, but both occur together because event C always causes both A and B to happen. A fire causes smoke and light, but smoke doesn't cause light and light doesn't cause smoke. People in high-income brackets tend to have better health and more education than people in low-income brackets. Possibly they were born with a hardier constitution and more than the average amount of energy. These factors would enable such people to attend school more

regularly and have a greater capacity for work. If so, it is possible that high income and education are no more causally related than smoke and light, but that being born with a hardy constitution causes both. On the other hand, it may be that higher education causes higher income, which makes it possible to afford a better diet and better medical care.

The rather common fallacy of concluding that A caused B simply because A occurred before B is known as the **fallacy of false cause.**

Fallacy of Composition

Common sense will tell you that if you find yourself in a burning building, you should get out as fast as you can. However, if the burning building is a crowded movie theater and each individual in it tries to get through the door at the same time, the results are likely to be tragic. What is good advice for you as an individual is not good advice for the group as a whole. *The false assumption that what is true for a particular part of the whole is also true for the whole itself is called the* **fallacy of composition.** (The whole is made up, or composed, of two or more individual parts.)

We can see how this fallacy works on an economic level if we consider the following example. If you are unemployed and have a mortgage on your house, you might be wise to sell the house. You can use the money obtained from the sale to pay off the mortgage and buy a cheaper house. In this way you can eliminate the burden of monthly mortgage payments. But if everyone on your block decides to do the same thing, the glut of houses on the market may drive prices down so low that you may not be able to get enough money to pay off the mortgage and buy a new house. What makes good economic sense for the individual does not necessarily make good economic sense for the whole economy. We will see other examples in this book where what is true at the microeconomic level is not necessarily true at the macroeconomic level.

ECONOMIC THINKERS

Adam Smith — 1723-1790

Adam Smith is often thought of as the father of modern economics, although his great work, *An Inquiry into the Nature and Causes of the Wealth of Nations* (1776), would not look very much like a modern economics textbook to today's reader.

One of Smith's most significant contributions to economic thought was his explanation of the importance of the division of labor and its relationship to the development of the economy. In his famous description of operations in a pin factory, Smith shows how output can be greatly increased by dividing tasks into small segments, each performed by specialists who require little training.

Smith's central theme was the value of enlightened self-interest, and he preached the doctrine of laissez faire. In Smith's view, the role of government should be minimized, in contrast with the power governments had exercised over all types of commerce in the past. Beyond maintaining national security, preserving internal order, and undertaking a few tasks such as public education, government was, according to Smith, to exercise little power. An advocate of economic freedom, Smith generally accepted the idea of "natural order" taught by the Scottish philosopher Francis Hutcheson, which implied the removal of restrictions of all kinds. Such a theory well suited the rising commercial class in Western Europe, particularly in England, which found government regulations irksome. Freedom allowed the natural instincts provided by a wise providence (in other words, self-interest) to prevail and provide the drive to turn the wheels of trade and commerce.

As Smith saw it, it would be foolish to assume that people satisfy the needs of others simply as a result of feelings of altruism. On the contrary, the baker, the brewer, and the candlestick maker each undertakes to satisfy the needs of others as a means of satisfying his or her own needs. By seeking to fulfill personal needs, each individual is helping to increase the wealth of society:

He generally, indeed, neither intends to promote the public interest nor knows how much he is promoting it. By preferring the support of domestic to that of foreign industry, he intends only his own security; and by directing that industry in such a manner as its produce may be of the greatest value, he intends only his own gain; and he is in this, as in many other cases, led by an invisible hand to promote an end which was no part of his intention.

FOR FURTHER READING

Clark, John J., and others. *Adam Smith, 1776–1926.* University of Chicago Press, 1928.

Smith, Adam. *An Inquiry into the Nature and Causes of the Wealth of Nations.* Modern Library ed. New York: Random House, 1937.

In judging what is true for the whole of society, we must not go to the opposite extreme and assume that what is true for the whole is also true for the individual parts. Such an assumption is known as the **fallacy of division**. For example, while it is true that society as a whole may benefit from a highly competitive marketplace, some individual firms with weak management skills may go bankrupt.

CHECKPOINT 1-4

Think of some examples where confusions about cause and effect might arise. Can you think of a fallacy

of composition that frequently occurs when a crowd watches a football game?

ECONOMIC POLICY

Economic theories have by and large evolved as responses to problems. In other words, necessity has been the mother of invention. But theory is only a tool, a way of looking at economic reality. It does not provide ready-made solutions to problems. John Maynard Keynes, a highly regarded policymaker as well as theorist, put it this way:

> The theory of economics does not furnish a body of settled conclusions immediately applicable to policy. It is a method rather than a doctrine, an apparatus of the mind, a technique of thinking, which helps its possessor to draw correct conclusions.

Economic policy *is concerned with finding solutions to economic problems.* While policymakers use economic theory to help them, they must go beyond it as well. They must consider the cultural, social, legal, and political aspects of an issue if they are to formulate a successful policy. In the end, making economic policy involves making value judgments such as those we explored when we looked at the conflict between unemployment and inflation. And an economist has no special claim over anybody else to making these judgments.

Economic Analysis and Economic Policymaking

While economic theory and analysis may not always be able to tell policymakers what they should do, it usually can tell them what they shouldn't do. An understanding of economic principles can keep us from both pursuing unwise policies and chasing conflicting goals. A few examples will illustrate how this is so.

An Unwise Policy

The printing of money by a government in order to finance its expenditures has long been considered by economists to be an unwise move. Despite their warnings, however, history is a graveyard of fallen governments that have yielded to this temptation. Somehow it always seems easier to turn on the printing press than to raise taxes. After World War I, the German government printed money at such a clip that the rate of inflation reached several thousand percent per week! At this point the deutsche mark ceased to have any value at all as a medium of exchange. No one would accept it in payment for goods or services. Faith in the government's ability to manage was seriously shaken. The resulting political instability probably contributed in some degree to the rise of Adolf Hitler and the Nazi party.

Conflicting Goals

In the conflicting goals category, an election year is often marked by talk of achieving full employment and reducing inflation—both at the same time. Full employment today is usually defined as an unemployment rate of roughly 6 percent. Almost everyone would agree that a 1 percent rate of inflation is low. But almost any economist will tell you that these two goals conflict with each other. A 6 percent unemployment rate goal is probably not compatible with a 1 percent inflation rate goal. Research findings, while not final or always clear-cut, might indicate that a 6 percent unemployment rate is possible only if we are willing to accept a 9 percent inflation rate. On the other hand, in order to cut inflation to 1 percent, we might have to live with an unemployment rate of 10 percent. This serves to remind us that an economy's behavior can only be modified within limits. (You can't expect a large bus to take corners like a sports car, or a sports car to carry 50 passengers.) Economic analysis can help us to form realistic policy objectives that don't conflict with one another.

The conflict between goals can be illustrated further by looking at the case of a retail clothier. Suppose the clothier stocked a large number of winter coats—the goal, to make money from their sale. But suppose the winter season is drawing to a close and the clothier still has a large number of winter coats on hand. The clothier has another goal—to make room for new spring fashions. Economic analysis, in particular the law of demand, tells the clothier to lower prices, in other words, to have a sale. But this may mean that the coats will have to be sold for less than what they cost the clothier. As a policymaker, the clothier has to choose between making money on winter coats and making room for the new fashions.

Economic Policy, Special Interests, and the Role of the Economist

Making economic policy forces us to choose among alternatives that have different consequences for different groups. Each of us is a member of one or more special interest groups. As students and educators, we might find it in our interest to pay special attention to any proposed legislation that affects education and institutions of learning. Similarly, labor unions are concerned about legislation on right-to-work laws and the powers and rights of unions to help one another enforce strikes and deal with strikebreakers. Business interests are also concerned with labor legislation, but their stands on such matters are usually opposed to those of labor. Farmers and consumers are both concerned with agricultural policy, but once again their interests are often in conflict. Resolution of these conflicts typically involves choices such as those we have discussed in connection with the inflation-unemployment trade-off. That is, we must make choices that are matters of value judgment. As we have noted, economists have no special calling to make subjective judgments as to what particular group should gain at another's expense. Economists probably do their greatest service to policymaking when they take the goals of all parties concerned as given and confine themselves to exploring and explaining which goals are compatible and which conflict, and what economic consequences will result from different policy actions.

Major Economic Policy Goals in the United States

A list of economic policy goals that most economists, policymakers, and citizens feel are important in the United States would probably look like this:

1. *Price stability:* in recent years this has meant checking inflation.
2. *Full employment:* in recent years most economists would take this to mean keeping the unemployment rate down around 6 to 6.5 percent.
3. *Economic growth:* continued growth in the standard of living for the average citizen.
4. *Environmental standards:* more control over the pollution and wastes that our production processes produce and impose on the environment.
5. *Economic security:* provision of an adequate standard of living for those who are unable to work either because of age, illness, and other handicaps beyond their control or because there are simply not enough jobs for all who want them.
6. *An equitable tax burden:* people, especially the middle-income groups, have shown increasing concern that our tax system favors those, typically in higher income brackets, who are in a position to take advantage of various loopholes in our tax laws to avoid or greatly reduce their "fair share" of the tax burden.
7. *Economic freedom:* the idea that businesses, consumers, and workers should be given much freedom in their economic activities.

We have already pointed out how economic experience has suggested that goals 1 and 2 may not be compatible, and that there seems to be a trade-off between the achievement of one at the expense of the other. The same may be true of goals 3 and 4 and of

POLICY PERSPECTIVE

Why Economists Disagree—The Role of Ideology

Put two economists in the same room and what do you get? An argument, or so it would seem to most people. Why do economists seem to disagree so much? How can the Nobel prize be awarded in economics and how can economics be regarded as a science if different economists can come up with such dissimilar answers when confronted with the same policy issue? The problem is that economics, unlike chemistry and physics for example, deals with human beings, the societies they live in, and the questions of who shall get what and how. Such questions invariably raise issues of value judgment about what is a "good" and "just" society, that is, issues of political ideology. The way different economists view an issue and the nature of their policy recommendations are usually colored by their particular ideological orientation. At the risk of oversimplification, there are three broadly recognizable political ideologies that provide different viewpoints on almost any economic issue. These different viewpoints may be termed conservative, liberal, and radical.

The Conservative View

Modern conservative ideology is rooted in two basic propositions. First, individual rights and the freedom of consenting parties to enter into private contracts (such as between buyer and seller) must be preserved to the greatest extent possible. Second, a competitive market system is central to the proper organization of society. Conservatives oppose any "unnatural" interference in the marketplace, and view the growth of big government as the greatest threat to economic progress and individual freedom. The government's proper role is: to maintain law and order;

to define and preserve property rights; to see that contracts are enforced; to provide a legal system to settle disputes; to promote competition by preventing the growth of monopoly power; to provide services not naturally provided by the market, such as national defense; to deal with problems not naturally solved by markets alone, such as environmental pollution; and to supplement private charity and the family to aid children and others handicapped for reasons beyond their control. In short, conservatives believe that government, the ultimate monopoly, should not do for people what they are capable of doing for themselves. Where government goes beyond these bounds, not only is individual freedom threatened, but otherwise well-intended government policies can cause or worsen economic problems. For example, conservatives would claim that minimum wage laws intended to improve the lot of low-paid workers actually hurt them in general. Conservatives argue that a government-enforced minimum wage higher than that otherwise determined by the market provides greater income for some workers but reduces the quantity demanded of those workers who are poorest, typically the unskilled and disadvantaged.

The Liberal View

A national opinion poll has suggested that Americans tend to associate the word "liberal" with big government, labor unions, and welfare. However, compared to conservatives and radicals, liberals are somewhat more difficult to pin down to a representative position. The liberal spectrum on public policy positions ranges from those who favor a moderate level of government intervention to those who advocate broad government planning of the economy. While liberals are defenders of the principle of private property and private enterprise, they do not view these as endowed with categorical rights to the extent conservatives do. Compared to conservatives, liberals are more prone to believe that individual property rights and the right to act freely in the marketplace must be constrained by concern for the general social welfare. Hence, government intervention in the economy, and even occasional direct regulation of certain industries and markets, is more acceptable to liberals than to conservatives. Liberals would argue that the benefits to the whole society of such intervention outweigh the infringements on individual liberties and property rights which government action might entail. Liberal economists and conservative economists both rely on the same tools of supply-and-demand analysis to explain markets and the behavior of the economy. They don't always differ so much on how to describe what is happening as they differ over how and whether government should intervene to affect the outcome.

The Radical View

To understand the representative radical position it is necessary to recognize the central role played by Marxist analysis (though there are some radicals who would reject a close association with Marxism). While it is impossible to do justice to the Marxist critique of capitalism in this short space, in brief, Marx essentially viewed capitalism as a system by which those who own the means of production, the capitalist class, are able to dominate and exploit the working class. According to Marx, the dominant capitalist class shaped private values, religion, the family, the educational system, and

political structures all for the purpose of production for private profit. Marxist analysis does not separate economics from politics and society's value system. The bourgeois democracies of the Western world are viewed as simply the tools for the dominant capitalist interests. For a Marxist, the problem with the capitalist system is the system itself, and no resolution of the problem is possible without changing the system. Coupled with this Marxist heritage, modern radicals are motivated by what they see as the failings of present-day liberalism. Liberal pursuit of policies for general social improvement are viewed as attempts to protect only some interest groups. And those who *really* benefit under liberal programs are seen as being those who have always gained. Corporate power continues to grow and the same elitist groups rule who have always ruled. Furthermore, liberal goals to improve the national well-being are also perceived as contributing to the exploitation of less-developed nations, continuing the cold war, and increasing the militarization of the economy.

When considering any economist's analysis of an economic issue it is always helpful to know his or her ideological orientation—to know "where he or she is coming from."

Questions

1. What do you think a Marxist would say about the conservative view of minimum wage laws?

2. Among the seven major economic policy goals, how do you think conservatives and liberals would differ in the relative importance they would attach to achieving those goals that we argued tend to conflict with one another?

goals 4 and 7. Goals 2, 3, and 5 all seem compatible in the sense that if we achieve 2 and 3, we will very likely enhance economic security, goal 5. With respect to goal 6, some would argue that certain of the so-called loopholes are important as a spur to risky business ventures and that without the tax breaks for these activities there would be less of the sort of enterprising activity essential to economic growth and full employment, goals 2 and 3. They would contend that goal 6, therefore, may not be compatible with goals 2 and 3.

Economic Analysis and the Economist

The examples we have considered illustrate why economic analysis is useful in formulating economic policy. In sum, economic analysis (1) helps to predict what the consequences of any policy action are likely to be, (2) indicates from among several ways to achieve a given goal which ones are most efficient in that their side effects are least detrimental, or possibly even helpful, to the achievement of other goals, (3) suggests which goals are compatible with one another and which are not, and (4) indicates what the likely trade-offs are between goals that are not mutually compatible.

If economic analysis does nothing else but keep policymakers from pursuing foolhardy policies, this alone is justification for its use as a policy tool. When economists go beyond the exercise of economic analysis summarized by points 1 to 4, they join the ranks of the various parties to any policy dispute. Their opinions and programs are then properly treated as those of a special interest group. Since economists, just like everyone else, usually do have opinions on matters of value judgment, they often use their economic expertise in support of a cause. In the end, therefore, the burden of separating objective economic analysis from value judgment must rest with you, the citizen. This fact alone should justify the time you devote to the study of economics.

SUMMARY

1. Economics is a social science concerned with the study of how society chooses to use its scarce resources to satisfy its unlimited wants. Economics studies the many issues and problems associated with this process from an overall point of view.

2. Goods are produced by using economic resources. Economic resources are of two basic kinds—human resources (labor) and nonhuman resources (capital and land). Economic resources are also referred to as the factors of production.

3. Discussions of economic issues make use of two kinds of statements. Positive statements are statements of fact. Normative statements, which may be based on positive statements, are statements of opinion.

4. In an effort to explain "how things work," economic analysis makes use of the scientific method. This method uses induction to formulate a theory from observation of facts and events. The theory is then used to predict future events (deduction).

5. Every economic theory has four basic elements: (1) a statement of variables, (2) a set of assumptions, (3) a hypothesis, and (4) one or more predictions about future happenings. Economic theories may also be called economic laws, principles, or models. Economic theory is exact to the extent that economic behavior is predictable.

6. Economic theories, such as the law of demand, may be represented graphically.

7. Economic analysis has been divided into two broad areas. Macroeconomics is concerned with the functioning of the whole economy or large sectors within it. Microeconomics focuses on individual units such as households and firms.

8. In economics, it is important to determine whether one event is the cause of another event or simply preceded it in time.

9. The assumption that what is true of the parts is true of the whole is known as the fallacy of composition. The assumption that what is true of the whole is true of the parts is known as the fallacy of division.

10. Economic policymakers use economic theory and analysis to help them formulate ways in which to solve the problems posed by economic reality. In most cases, the solution to these problems involves resolving a conflict between special interest groups. Such a resolution usually depends upon value judgments, and economists are no more qualified than anyone else to make such judgments. Economic analysis is most useful in determining the possible consequences of various policies.

KEY TERMS AND CONCEPTS

ceteris paribus
deduction
direct relationship
economic policy
economics
economic theory
economy
fallacy of composition
fallacy of division
fallacy of false cause
induction
inverse relationship
macroeconomics
microeconomics
normative statement
positive statement
price
scarce
scientific method

QUESTIONS AND PROBLEMS

1. Why is economics called a social science instead of a social study?

2. Why is it that economists, who supposedly use scientific methods when analyzing economic issues, are so often in disagreement?

3. Pick out a story from the financial and business section of today's newspaper and find instances in which a concept or subject is mentioned or discussed that is related to one or more of the economic terms introduced in this chapter.

4. Open today's newspaper to the financial and business section. Pick a story at random and calculate the ratio of positive statements to the total number of statements in the story. Now go to the financial and business *editorial* section and do the same.

5. *Think* about the following experiment. Suppose you were to run an ad in your local paper this week stating that you own a vacant 1-acre lot and that somewhere on the lot is buried a metal box containing $10. You state that any and all are welcome to come dig for it and that you will give the $10 to whomever finds it during the coming week. How many people do you think will show up to dig? Suppose, instead, you had said the box contained $30 instead of $10. How many diggers do you think would show up during the same week? Estimate how many would show up during the same week if the reward were $60, $120, or $150. Now construct a graph that measures dollars of reward on the vertical axis and number of diggers on the horizontal axis. Find the points representing each combination of dollars and diggers and draw a line connecting them.

a. Is the relationship you observe between the size of the dollar reward and the number of diggers an inverse relationship or a direct relationship?

b. What led you to hypothesize the relationship you did between the size of the dollar reward and the number of diggers?

c. If you actually ran the ads over the course of a year and tabulated the number of diggers who showed up for each reward, plotted the results, and found a relationship opposite to the one you had predicted, what would you conclude about your theory? Might the season of the year during which you ran each ad have had something to do with the difference between your theory and what actually happened? Suppose when you ran the $150 reward ad it rained for the whole week the offer was good. Suppose when you ran the $120 reward ad it was sunny the first day of the week and rained the next six. Suppose for the $90 reward ad it was sunny for the first two days and rained the next five. Suppose for the $60 reward ad it was sunny for the first three days and rained the next four. Suppose for the $30 reward ad it was sunny the first five days and rained the next two. Finally, for the $10 reward ad suppose it was sunny the whole week. How do you think the curve obtained by plotting the combinations of dollar reward and number of diggers might look now? Looking back at the first curve you drew, how important do you think your "other things remaining the same" assumption was?

d. Suppose your original curve was based on the assumption that it was always sunny. If instead it was always raining, where would the curve be—to the left or to the right of the original curve?

e. What would you predict would happen if you raised the amount of the reward money to $1,000?

f. Can you, as my economic policy advisor, recommend how I might clear off and dig up a 1-acre lot that I own in town?

g. Can you, as my economic policy advisor, tell me how to deal with the racial tensions that might arise between the people who show up to dig on my lot?

h. Do you think people respond to economic incentives?

i. Do you think human behavior is predictable?

6. The following item appeared in the *Wall Street Journal* of September 14, 1976:

Election Returns: Who holds the presidency "has an effect on the workers' ability to organize into unions," the AFL-CIO argues in its analysis of the past 16 years. It cites figures showing that in the Kennedy-Johnson years 57 percent of workers voted for unions in NLRB [National Labor Relations Board] elections, while only 44 percent favored unions in the Nixon-Ford years.

a. What do you think of the merits of this cause-and-effect argument?

b. Are there other explanations that might be offered for these facts?

2

Scarcity, Choice, and the Economic Problem

AFTER READING THIS CHAPTER, YOU WILL BE ABLE TO:

1. Explain why the combination of scarce resources and unlimited wants makes choice necessary.

2. Define the term *economic efficiency* and distinguish between unemployment and underemployment of resources.

3. Explain the concept of the production possibilities frontier and show why when an economy is on the frontier, it can have more of one good only by giving up some of another.

4. Demonstrate why the selection of an output combination on today's production possibilities frontier affects the location of tomorrow's frontier.

5. Formulate the basic questions posed by the fundamental economic problem that every economy must answer.

6. Distinguish among pure market economies and command economies.

In this chapter we will focus on the basic economic problem that has always confronted human beings and the fundamental questions it poses. Then we will look into the ways economies may be organized to answer these questions. The answers are related to the fundamental issues of how well people live, how hard they work, and how choices about these matters are to be made.

THE ECONOMIC PROBLEM

The basic **economic problem** *that underlies all economic issues is the combined existence of scarce resources and unlimited wants.* Ben Franklin put it this way: "The poor have little,—beggars none; the rich too much,—enough not one." As we noted in Chapter 1, the economic resources of land, labor, and capital exist only in limited amounts. Consequently, there is a limit to the quantity of economic goods that can be produced with these scarce resources. But unfortunately, people's desires for goods are really unlimited for all intents and purposes of economic analysis. While in theory it may be possible to attain a level of abundance that would satisfy everybody's appetites for all things, no such state has ever existed. And at this time, the prospects of achieving such a state seem remote to nonexistent. One only has to consider the standard of living in the world's richest nation, the United States, to realize that there is hardly a person who couldn't draw up a list of wanted goods that far exceeds his or her means to obtain them. Ask yourself, or anyone else, what you would do with an additional hundred dollars. If you felt completely without want, you might say that you would give it to a charity. But why does charity exist? Because some other group or person has unsatisfied wants.

Opportunity Cost and Choice: A Simple Example

Scarcity and unlimited wants force us to make choices. Let's consider a simple example.

Suppose a settler named Clyde lives alone in the wilds of Alaska. Clyde has to be self-sufficient. He produces only two goods: corn (for food) and wood (for heat). Clyde's scarce resources are his own stamina and his ability to grow corn and cut wood. Clyde will always try to produce the most he can with his scarce resources. He only has a fixed amount of resources and so he will try not to waste them.

The Production Possibilities Frontier

The nature of Clyde's economic problem can be illustrated by the use of a **production possibilities frontier.** *A production possibilities frontier is a curve representing the maximum possible output combinations of goods that can be produced with a fixed quantity of resources.*

Suppose Clyde's production possibilities frontier is the downward-sloping straight line in Figure 2–1. It shows the *maximum possible* combinations of quantities of corn and wood that Clyde can *choose* to produce in a year if he *fully utilizes* his fixed resources in the *most efficient* way he knows. By maximum we mean that Clyde cannot produce any combination of corn and wood represented by points lying to the right of or above his production possibilities frontier, the line from *a* to *e* in Figure 2–1. For example, he cannot choose to produce a combination of 27 bushels of corn and 15 cords of wood, point *f* in Figure 2–1. He simply doesn't have enough resources. On the other hand, Clyde can produce any combination lying to the left or below the frontier—for example, a combination consisting of 15 bushels of corn and 5 cords of wood, point *g*. But he would not want to do so because that would be an inefficient use of his fixed resources. Efficient resource utilization will always enable him to produce more of both goods than he gets at a point such as *g*.

Opportunity Cost

Clyde will always choose to produce a combination of goods represented by a point on

FIGURE 2-1   Clyde's Production Possibilities Frontier

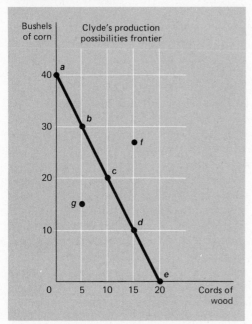

Clyde's production possibilities frontier is represented by the downward-sloping straight line *ae*. Each point on the frontier represents some maximum-output combination of bushels of corn and cords of wood that Clyde can choose to produce annually if he fully utilizes his fixed resources as efficiently as possible.

Clyde cannot produce any combinations represented by points to the right or above the frontier, such as *f*. He simply doesn't have enough resources—stamina and ability to grow corn and chop wood. Clyde can produce any combination represented by points to the left or below the frontier, such as *g*. But he wouldn't want to because that would entail an inefficient utilization of his resources.

his production possibilities frontier. (Later we will see that the frontier may not be a straight line.) Five of these possible combinations are indicated by points *a*, *b*, *c*, *d*, and *e*. For example, if Clyde chooses combination *b*, he will grow 30 bushels of corn and chop 5 cords of wood during the coming

year. Alternatively, he may choose combination *c*, consisting of 20 bushels of corn and 10 cords of wood. All he has to do is devote less of his fixed resources to corn growing and use the resources released from that activity to chop more wood. If Clyde chooses to produce combination *c* instead of *b*, he has to give up 10 bushels of corn (the difference between 30 and 20). However, he gains 5 cords of wood (the difference between 10 and 5). Conversely, if he chooses combination *b* instead of *c*, he gives up 5 cords of wood and gains 10 bushels of corn.

In general, if Clyde wants to produce more of one kind of good, he must of necessity produce less of the other. We say he must pay an **opportunity cost.** *The opportunity cost equals the amount of one good that must be given up in order to have more of another.* We see from Clyde's production possibilities frontier in Figure 2–1 that he has to *give up* 2 bushels of corn in order to get an additional cord of wood (a move downward along his production possibilities frontier). Conversely, he has to *give up* half a cord of wood in order to get an additional bushel of corn (a move upward along his production possibilities frontier). Hence the opportunity cost of a cord of wood is 2 bushels of corn. The opportunity cost of a bushel of corn is half a cord of wood.

Choice

When Clyde uses his fixed resources efficiently, he can choose to produce any output combination on his production possibilities frontier. Whenever he considers the choice between one combination and another along the frontier, however, he is always forced to choose between a combination with more wood and less corn and a combination with less wood and more corn. If he could have more of both or more of one without having to sacrifice any of the other, there would be no "hard" choice because nothing would have to be given up. Unfortunately, Clyde's limited or scarce resources always force him to give up something—to pay an opportunity cost—whenever he makes a choice. A choice requires that one opportunity be given up to gain another.

The concept of a production possibilities frontier, the existence of opportunity costs, and the need for choice are just as relevant for an entire economy as they are for Clyde. Let's see why.

Scarcity, Production, and Efficiency

Given that resources are limited and people's wants are unlimited, the problem that faces any economy is how to use scarce resources and organize production so as to satisfy to the greatest extent possible society's unlimited wants. This means that the available resources must be used as efficiently as possible. In other words, the maximum output must be obtained from the resources at hand.

There are two major problems that can prevent a society from achieving **economic efficiency**. These are **unemployment** and **underemployment**, or **resource misallocation**.

Unemployment

Maximum economic efficiency cannot be achieved if available resources are not fully used. This holds true for both human and nonhuman resources. As long as there are workers looking for work and unable to find it, or if plant capacity remains unused, maximum economic efficiency cannot be achieved. Notice that we stress that in order to have economic efficiency all *available* resources must be employed. Some parts of the population may not seek employment. By custom and law some people, such as children and the aged, may be prevented from working. Certain kinds of land are prohibited by law from use for certain types of productive activity. However, whenever there are available resources standing idle, there are fewer inputs into the economy's productive process. As a result, there is a lower output of goods to satisfy society's wants.

Underemployment, or Resource Misallocation

If certain available resources are used to do jobs for which other available resources are better suited, there is underemployment, or misallocation of resources. For example, if cabinetmakers were employed to make dresses and seamstresses were employed to make cabinets, the total amount of cabinets and dresses produced would be less than if each group were employed in the activity for which it was trained. Similarly, if Florida's orange groves were planted with wheat while Minnesota's farms were planted with orange trees, the same total land area would provide the country with substantially less of both crops than is the case with the conventional arrangement. Resource underemployment also results whenever the best available technology is not used in a production process. A house painter painting with a toothbrush and a farmer harvesting wheat with a pocketknife are both underemployed. A 10-ton bulldozer is underemployed when used to clear a half-acre yard once a week. *Whenever there is resource underemployment, or misallocation, a reallocation of resources to productive activities for which they are better suited will result in a larger output of some or all goods and no reduction in the output of any.*

Production Possibilities Trade-off

When an economy's available resources are fully employed (that is, there is no unemployment or underemployment), we say that economy is producing its maximum possible output of goods. Given that resources are limited, the maximum possible output level is, of course, limited too. Therefore, as in Clyde's world, producing more of one kind of good will of necessity mean producing less of another. Again, the amount of reduction in the production of one good that is necessary in order to produce more of another is called *opportunity cost*.

Let us illustrate this concept by focusing

on the issue of the cost of cleaning up environmental pollution. Suppose that the output of an economy may be divided into two categories—scrubbers and bundles of all other goods. (A scrubber is an antipollution device that removes pollutants from factory smokestack emissions.) One bundle will contain one of each and every good produced in the economy *except* a scrubber. A bundle may be thought of as a good—the composite good. The issue to be illustrated here is of more than academic interest. If we are to have a cleaner environment, we will need to use scrubbers in many production processes that cause pollution. How do we measure the cost to society of providing these devices?

Production and Choice

In answering this question we will make certain assumptions, as follows:

1. The existing state of technology will remain unchanged for the period in which we are examining this issue.
2. The total available supply of resources (land, labor, and capital) will remain the same. However, these resources may be shifted from producing scrubbers to producing bundles of all other goods and vice versa.
3. All available resources are fully employed (there is no unemployment or underemployment in the economy).

Given the existing supply of resources and level of technology, society must make choices. Should its fully employed resources be devoted entirely to the production of bundles of all other goods? Or should it reduce its output of bundles and use the factors of production released from that activity to produce scrubbers? If so, what combinations of bundles and scrubbers can it produce, given that its resources are fully employed? Clearly, the more scrubbers the economy produces, the more resources will have to be devoted to their production. Fewer resources

will then be available for the production of bundles. Given that resources are fully employed, whatever combination of bundles and scrubbers the economy might think of producing, any other combination will necessarily contain more of one and less of the other. If the economy wants to produce more scrubbers, it will have to give up a certain number of bundles. If it wants to produce more bundles, it will have to give up a certain number of scrubbers.

Just as in Clyde's world, something must be given up in order to gain something. In short, you can't get something for nothing. You have to pay an opportunity cost.

Choices for Pollution Control

Some of the possible combinations of bundles and scrubbers that the economy we have been considering can produce per year when all resources are fully employed are listed in Table 2–1. If this economy were to devote all of its resources to producing bundles of all other goods, it would be able to produce 80 million bundles per year and no scrubbers (combination *A*). Although it seems very unrealistic and highly unlikely, the economy could devote all of its fully employed resources to producing scrubbers and go without all other goods (combination *E*). Such a choice would certainly carry environmental considerations to the extreme, in the sense that the cost would amount to giving up the production of all other goods. However, at the other extreme, combination *A* would probably not be very desirable either. With this combination, the economy would not be doing anything at all about pollution. If it were deemed desirable to do something about pollution, the economy could be moved away from point *A* toward point *E*. *To do this, resources would have to be shifted out of the production of bundles and into the production of scrubbers.* How much of a shift in this direction society chooses to make will depend upon the degree of concern about pollution. A cleaner environment will cost

TABLE 2-1 Possible Combinations of Scrubbers and Bundles of All Other Goods That May Be Produced in a Full-Employment Economy (Hypothetical Data)

Product	Production Possibilities (Output per Year)				
	A	B	C	D	E
Scrubbers (in thousands)	0	50	80	100	110
Bundles of all other goods (in millions)	80	60	40	20	0

something. Suppose society's concern is such that it chooses to produce combination B instead of combination A. The cost of the 50,000 scrubbers it will now have is the 20 million bundles of all other goods it must give up to achieve this combination. If society has an even greater concern about pollution, combination C or even combination D could be chosen. However, to have the greater quantities of scrubbers associated with combination C or combination D requires that society forgo the production of more bundles of all other goods.

The Opportunity Cost of Choice

In summary, because economic resources are scarce, a full-employment economy cannot have more of both bundles and scrubbers. To have more of one, it must give up some of the other. The cost of having more of one is the opportunity cost, or the amount of the other, that must be given up. By choosing combination B in Table 2-1 *instead* of combination A, society must forgo the opportunity of having 20 million bundles of all other goods (the difference between 80 million and 60 million). The opportunity cost of the 50,000 scrubbers is therefore 20 million bundles. The opportunity cost of choosing combination C *instead* of combination B, or the opportunity cost of having an additional 30,000 scrubbers, is another 20 million bundles. The opportunity cost of choosing C *instead* of A, or the opportunity cost of having

80,000 scrubbers, is 40 million bundles, the difference between the number of bundles associated with combination A and the number associated with combination C.

Whenever scarcity forces us to make a choice, we must pay an opportunity cost. This cost is measured in terms of forgone alternatives. All costs are opportunity costs (often simply referred to as costs). If you buy a note pad for a dollar, you forgo the opportunity of spending that dollar on something else. Since the pad cost you a dollar, you now have a dollar less to spend on all other goods, unless you have an infinite supply of money, which is impossible. There is no free lunch.

CHECKPOINT* 2-1

What is the opportunity cost to Clyde of choosing combination d instead of combination c in Figure 2–1? Of choosing combination b instead of combination d? Of choosing combination d instead of combination b?

*Answers to all Checkpoints can be found at the back of the text.

The Economy's Production Possibilities Frontier

To derive our hypothetical economy's production possibilities frontier, let's plot the data from Table 2-1 on a graph. On the horizontal axis we measure the number of scrubbers. On the vertical axis we measure the number of bundles. As we did in Chapter 1, we now locate all the points on the graph that represent the possible scrubbers-bundles combinations listed in our table. If we draw a line connecting the points, the result looks like Figure 2-2. The curve slopes downward because when the available resources are fully employed, more scrubbers can be produced only by producing fewer bundles.

On and Off the Frontier

The curve we have drawn by connecting all the points on the graph is our hypothetical

FIGURE 2-2   The Production Possibilities Frontier

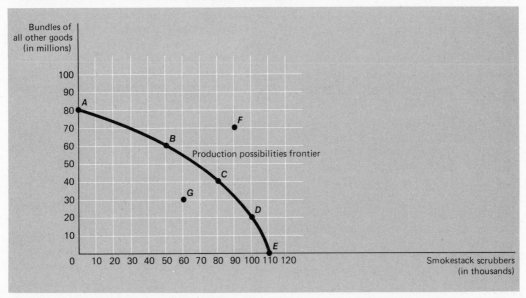

Each point on the downward-sloping curve represents some maximum-output combination for an economy whose available resources are fully employed. In this case, the output consists of scrubbers and bundles. Because no combination to the right or above the curve is possible, it is called the production possibilities frontier.

Point *G* represents a combination of scrubbers and bundles produced when the economy is operating inefficiently. Unemployment or underemployment of economic resources has resulted in a smaller output than is actually possible. Point *F*, on the other hand, represents a combination that cannot be produced given available resources and technology. This point can only be achieved if the production possibilities curve shifts outward as a result of economic growth.

economy's production possibilities frontier. *Each point on a production possibilities frontier represents a maximum output combination for an economy whose available resources are fully employed.* The term *frontier* is used because it is not possible for the economy to produce any combination of scrubbers and bundles represented by a point above or to the right of the curve. For example, a combination of quantities of scrubbers and bundles represented by the point *F* in Figure 2–2 is not possible.

What if the economy's available resources are not being used efficiently (they are either unemployed or underemployed)? Then the economy cannot produce any combination of scrubbers and bundles represented by any

point on its production possibilities frontier. It will only be able to produce output combinations represented by points inside the frontier, such as point *G*.

The Law of Increasing Costs

Figure 2–2 illustrates how graphs plotted from economic data can make the relationship between two economic variables immediately obvious. In Figure 2–2 we are struck at once by the change in the trade-off between bundles and scrubbers as we move from combination *A* to *B* to *C* and so on to *E*. When we move from *A* to *B*, a sacrifice (or cost) of 20 million bundles allows us to have 50,000 scrubbers. However, a move from *B* to *C*, which costs another 20 million bundles, allows us to have only an additional 30,000 scrubbers. The additional quantity of scrubbers obtained for each succeeding sacrifice of 20 million bundles continues to get smaller as we move from *C* to *D* to *E*. The reason for the deteriorating trade-off is that economic resources are more adaptable to some production processes than others. As more and more resources are shifted from the production of bundles into the production of scrubbers, we are forced to use factors of production whose productivity at making scrubbers is lower and lower relative to their productivity at making bundles. For example, when we move from *A* to *B*, a large number of engineers and scientists might be moved from bundle production to the highly technical production of scrubbers. As we continue moving from *B* to *E*, it becomes harder and harder to find labor resources of this nature. When moving from *D* to *E*, only the labor least suited for producing scrubbers will be left—poets, hod carriers, and so forth.

The decrease in the number of additional scrubbers obtained for each additional sacrifice of 20 million bundles as we move from *A* to *E* is a common economic phenomenon. It is sometimes called the **law of increasing costs**. To illustrate this law more clearly, divide the number of bundles that must be sacrificed by the additional number of scrubbers obtained by moving from one combination to the next. In the move from *A* to *B*, it costs 20 million bundles to obtain 50,000 scrubbers, or 400 bundles per scrubber. In the move from *B* to *C*, it costs 20 million bundles to obtain 30,000 scrubbers, or 666.6 bundles per scrubber. The move from *C* to *D* costs 1,000 bundles per scrubber. The move from *D* to *E* costs 2,000 bundles per scrubber. We are accustomed to measuring costs in dollars—so many dollars per unit of some good. Since dollars merely stand for the amounts of other goods they can buy, we have simply represented the cost of scrubbers in terms of bundles of other goods. *The law of increasing costs says that when moving along the production possibilities frontier, the cost per additional good obtained measured in terms of the good sacrificed rises due to the difference in productivity of resources when used in different production processes.*

Economic Growth

The production possibilities frontier in Figure 2–2 is based on a given state of technology and a fixed quantity of resources (land, labor, and capital). What happens if there is a change in technology or in the quantity of resources? The potential total output of the economy will change. Hence the production possibilities frontier will shift position.

The economy's population and labor force tend to grow over time. So too does its stock of capital—the quantities of machines, buildings, highways, factories, and so forth. In addition there are advances in the state of technology. *The growth in the economy's resources and improvements in technological know-how cause* **economic growth,** *an increase in the economy's ability to produce output.* This shifts the economy's production possibilities frontier outward (up and to the right) as shown in Figure 2–3. As a result the economy can produce more of both scrubbers and bundles when its available resources are fully employed.

Ecology's Price Tag

Some people are wondering whether the cost of protecting the environment is outrunning the benefits of doing so. The production possibilities frontier shows us the nature of the choices and the associated costs that must be considered when answering this question. The economist can objectively say that society would be making an inefficient use of resources if it decided to produce a combination of goods inside the frontier. Similarly, an economist can objectively say that a combination above or to the right of the frontier is not possible. But the following also needs to be said. In an economy such as that summarized in Table 2–1, it must be pointed out to those who would like to produce 80,000 scrubbers that they cannot produce 80 mil-

FIGURE 2-3 **Economic Growth Means That the Production Possibilities Frontier Shifts Outward**

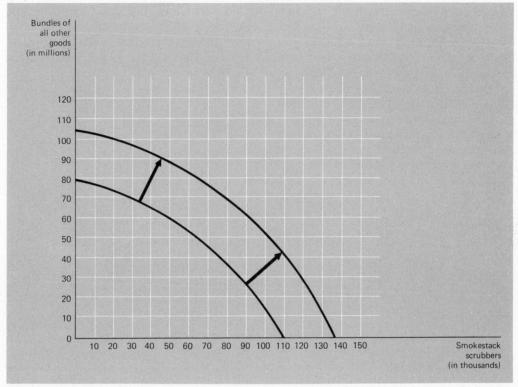

Growth in the economy's available resources and technological know-how shifts the production possibilities frontier outward. This allows the economy to produce more of both scrubbers and bundles—to have economic growth.

lion bundles as well. Almost everyone is for God, mother, and country—and environmental protection. The question is, How much are we willing to pay for it, *in terms of other goods and services not produced?*

Choice of Product Combination: Present Versus Future

We are all aware that choices made today are an important determinant of the choices available to us tomorrow. Therefore it should not surprise us that *an economy's pre-sent choice of a point on its production possibilities frontier influences the future location of that frontier.*

To demonstrate why this is so, suppose we divide the total output of an economy into two categories—consumption goods and capital goods. Consumption goods are such things as food, clothing, movies, tennis balls, records, and so forth. Capital goods are such things as machinery, tools, and factories; they enable us to produce other goods, including machinery, tools, and factories. An increase in the quantity and quality of capital goods contributes to economic growth, the expansion of the economy's capacity to produce all goods. Suppose the production possibilities frontier for our economy in 1986 is as shown in Figure 2–4—capital goods are measured on the horizontal axis, consumption goods are measured on the vertical axis.

If the economy chooses point *a* on its 1986 frontier, it will produce an output combination consisting mostly of consumption goods. Alternatively, if it chooses point *b* on the frontier, the economy will produce a combination predominantly made up of capital goods. All other things remaining the same, we can expect the economy's future (1990) production possibilities frontier to be farther

out if it chooses point *b* on its 1986 frontier than if it chooses point *a*. That is, the choice of point *a* on the 1986 frontier will give rise to 1990 frontier *a*, whereas choosing point *b* will give rise to 1990 frontier *b*. The reason is that choice *b* produces more capital goods, the kind of goods that contribute to economic growth, whereas choice *a* produces fewer of such goods. We hasten to add, however, that this does not mean *b* is a better choice than *a*. After all, remember that choice *b* means having fewer consumption goods to enjoy in 1986 relative to the number resulting from choice *a*.

FIGURE 2-4 Present Choices Affect Future Production Possibilities Frontiers

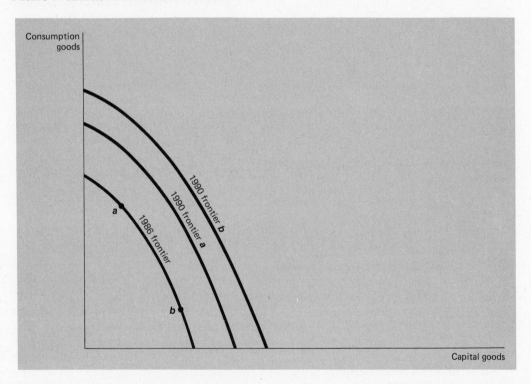

If the economy chooses point *a* on its 1986 frontier, it emphasizes consumption goods production; if it chooses point *b*, it favors capital goods production. Therefore choice *a* gives rise to less economic growth or a smaller outward shift in the frontier (to 1990 frontier *a*) than does choice *b* (to 1990 frontier *b*).

CHECKPOINT 2-2
In Table 2–1 what is the opportunity cost of choosing combination *C* instead of *D*; *B* instead of *C*; or *A* instead of *D*? Consider the movement from *E* to *A* in Figure 2–2 and represent the law of increasing cost measured in terms of scrubbers.

BASIC PROBLEMS FOR ANY ECONOMY

Given an economy's available resources and technology, we have seen how the production possibilities from which it may choose can be characterized by a production possibilities frontier. A frontier can be determined for any economy, whatever its form of government. A knowledge of what is possible is necessary in order to answer a number of important questions or problems that any economy, be it that of the Soviet Union or the United States or Pakistan, must solve. These questions confront socialist, communist, and capitalist countries, developed and underdeveloped economies alike. These questions are:

(1) What and how much to produce?
(2) How should production be organized?
(3) For whom should goods be produced?

What and How Much to Produce

We could draw up an incredibly large list of goods that could be produced in the United States, including everything from needles and thread to space vehicles and kidney dialysis machines. Some of the goods on the list, while possible to produce, might not be desired by anybody. Other goods, such as various kinds of food, might be desired by nearly everyone. If we were to draw up a list of goods that could be produced by one of the less developed countries in the world, it would probably be considerably shorter. Nevertheless, given its respective list, each country would have to decide what goods and how much of each to produce.

In the economy summarized in Table 2–1, the answer to the question, "What to produce?" was scrubbers and bundles of all other goods. The question, "How much?" really asks what point on the production possibilities frontier would be selected. The answer to this question must be decided by society's tastes and priorities. The answer is thus a value judgment. As we noted in Chapter 1, an economist's value judgment has no superior claim over anyone else's. It may be that a relatively underdeveloped country seeking rapid economic growth and industrialization would feel little concern about the environmental impact of these processes. It might not want to divert resources to producing scrubbers. However, a country such as the United States, having experienced growth and industrialization, might be more aware of their adverse environmental impact. It therefore might be more willing to divert a larger share of resources to producing scrubbers. Whether the cost of protecting the environment is outrunning the benefits will depend on who is assessing the benefits.

Who makes the decisions about what and how much to produce? The answer to this question varies greatly from one economy to another. In countries such as the Soviet Union or Communist China, these decisions are made by a central planning bureau of the government. In the United States, Canada, and Western Europe, a large portion of the decisions about the allocation of resources is made by the pricing system, or market mechanism. However, the political process has legislated government intervention in some decisions. In the United States, for example, electric utility companies set rates subject to approval by government regulatory agencies. Similarly, decisions about pollution control have to a considerable degree been made through congressional action. Government intervention seems desirable in certain cases because society has decided that

POLICY PERSPECTIVE

Defense Spending—How Much Does It Cost?

In recent years there has been an increasingly heated debate about whether or not the United States is spending enough on defense. An important aspect of this debate is the cost of national defense.

As with any good or service, we can only have more defense goods and services (more guns, missiles, and the services of soldiers) by giving up nondefense goods and services (such as automobiles, golf carts, and the services of house painters). The opportunity cost of more defense is measured by the amount of the necessary sacrifice of nondefense goods and services. This is illustrated by the economy's hypothetical production possibilities frontier in Figure P2–1 which shows the maximum-output combinations of defense and nondefense goods and services the economy can choose to produce when available resources are fully employed. If point *A* is chosen the economy would produce the quantities OD for defense (horizontal axis) and ON for nondefense (vertical axis). However if policymakers decide that more defense is needed, say an additional amount equal to *DD'*, then it will be necessary for the economy to move to point *B* by giving up a quantity of nondefense goods and services equal to *NN'*—that is the (opportunity) cost of the increased defense. *The additional cost NN' is the additional "spending" on increased defense.*

Some perspective on the actual cost of national defense in the United States is provided by measuring defense spending as the percentage of GNP (gross national product), the economy's total annual output of final goods and services. Such a percentage tells us what portion of the dollar value of total output is given over to the production of defense goods and services. In terms of opportunity cost, it is the portion of total output that otherwise could have gone into the production of nondefense products—the goods and services given up in order to produce defense products. In 1960, defense spending amounted to 9.7 percent of GNP (on a fiscal year basis). By 1970 it had declined slightly to 8.4 percent and, due largely to the ending of the Vietnam War, it declined more noticeably to 5.2 percent by 1980. Since 1980 defense spending has increased to an estimated 6.7 percent of GNP in 1984 and has been projected to rise further to around 7.6 to 7.8 percent by 1989.

Here we have focused on the economic way to measure the cost of national defense. How much national defense we should have depends on one's views of international tensions and their implications for war and peace, and thus the potential

---

FIGURE P2-1 Production Possibilities Frontier for Defense and Nondefense Goods

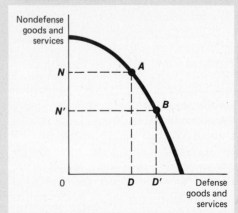

benefits of national defense. But that is a different, and more controversial, issue.

Questions

1. What would the opportunity cost be of choosing point *A* instead of point *B* in Figure P2–1?

2. Why might it be said that economic growth would reduce the intensity of the debate between those who want more defense spending and those who don't?

the resource allocations made by free markets have been unsatisfactory in some areas. Pollution control is one of these. National defense is another.

How Should Production Be Organized?

In discussing the production possibilities frontier, we emphasized that to be on the frontier it is necessary to use economic resources in the most efficient way. Once society has determined what goods to produce, the amount of each of those goods it will be able to produce will depend on how available resources are allocated to various productive activities. If we try to grow oranges in Minnesota and raise wheat in Florida, we are not going to have as much of either as we would if those land resources were used the other way around. In addition, even when resources are allocated to their most productive activities, the most efficient known productive processes must be used. Harvesting wheat in Minnesota with pinking shears and making orange juice in Florida by squeezing the oranges by hand is still not going to give us as much wheat or orange juice as is technologically possible. Ideally, *society should allocate available resources to productive activities and use known productive techniques in such a way that no reallocation of resources or change of technique could yield more of any good without yielding less of another. This is true of any combination of goods represented by any point on the production possibilities frontier.*

This ideal is easy enough to understand and describe. But it may have struck you by now as a little like being told that the way to make money on the stock market is to buy low and sell high. You can understand that perfectly and wouldn't disagree a bit. But only a moment's reflection will lead you to ask the inevitable question: "Yes, but how do I *know* when a stock is at its low and when it is at its high?" Similarly, an economy doesn't have a big television screen up in the sky with a picture of its production possibilities frontier and a white dot that can be moved around by turning knobs until society has got itself right at the desired spot on the frontier. Society can't "see" the economy's production possibilities frontier, nor is it a simple matter of turning a few control knobs to "move" onto it. So how should an economy go about organizing its available resources in order to use them most efficiently? How will the most efficient production techniques be determined? What regulating mechanisms or management techniques can be used to ensure that the appropriate kinds and necessary amounts of resources will be directed to industries producing desired goods? Any economy, be it centrally planned or completely market oriented, wants to be on its production possibilities frontier. The question is, How does it get there?

For Whom to Produce

For whom should the output of the economy be produced? Put another way, how should the economy's total output be distributed among the individual members of the economy? Should it be distributed to individuals according to their productive contribution to the making of that output? Or should we take from each according to his or her ability and give to each according to his or her need? If people receive strictly according to their productive contribution, it's clear some people are going to be terribly poor. On the other hand, if there is no relationship between an individual's productive contribution and the reward received for it, what will be the incentive for hard work? If the able and productive members of society do not have incentives to work hard, the total output of the economy will not be as large. If the total pie is smaller, there simply will be less to go around. All societies must wrestle with this problem. They must decide how to distribute output in such a way as to encourage the productive members to work up to their ability and at the same time try to maintain a minimum standard of living for all. In short, they must decide what degree of income inequality can be tolerated given these conflicting goals. The range of opinion on this is wide indeed and can fire the most heated debates. It is a matter of politics, cultural values, and moral issues.

In addition to solving this problem, all economies must decide how much of the total output should go to government, how much to business, and how much to households. This, of course, raises questions about how taxes should be levied and who should pay them. It raises questions about how much of the decision-making process for allocation of resources should be in the hands of the government rather than of the private sector (households and businesses). In wartime, any society is likely to give to the government whatever portion of output it needs to ensure survival. In peacetime, without the pressure of such a common goal, decisions about how to distribute total output are not usually made with such a consensus.

Full Utilization of Resources

In our discussion of economic efficiency and the problem of how to organize production, we emphasized that *an economy can fall short of its production possibilities frontier if resources are misallocated or if the best-known production techniques are not used. Another kind of economic inefficiency, also noted earlier, occurs whenever available resources are allowed to stand idle. This kind of inefficiency will also keep an economy from operating on its production possibilities frontier.*

In twentieth-century capitalist economies, such as that of the United States, there have been frequent periods of recession, which means that significant amounts of labor and other available resources have been idle, or unemployed. During the depression of the 1930s, the measured unemployment rate was around 25 percent. Economists estimate that the actual rate of unemployment may have been considerably higher than this. (The reason is that some of the unemployed were not reported.) In capitalist economies we often refer to the recurring pattern of increasing and decreasing unemployment associated with decreasing and increasing output as **business fluctuations** or **business cycles**. Centrally planned economies such as those of the Soviet Union, Communist China, and the Eastern European nations are not free from the problem of fluctuations in their production of output. The underlying reasons why they have these difficulties are different, and for ideological reasons they describe the problem differently. An economist visiting the United States from the central planning bureau of an Eastern European country was asked if they experienced anything like our business fluctuations. He said, "Oh, no." The question was then rephrased, "Well, don't you ever experience fluctuations in production?" He responded, "Oh, you mean 'technical cycles'!"

In the industrialized economies of the

Western world, the problem of eliminating or reducing unemployment of labor and other available resources is a high priority of economic policy. In the United States, Congress passed the Employment Act of 1946, declaring that it shall be the continuing policy and responsibility of the federal government "to promote maximum employment, production, and purchasing power."

Unemployment of economic resources is similar in its effects to the underemployment of economic resources that results from their misallocation to inappropriate activities or when the best-known techniques of production are not used. Both unemployment and underemployment cause the economy to produce at a point inside its production possibility frontier. However, the appropriate ways to deal with these two problems are quite different. *The underemployment problem requires an answer to the question of how to organize production.* Remedies there require establishing ways to see to it that Minnesota is planted with wheat and not oranges, and that harvesting machines instead of pinking shears are used to cut it. These kinds of problems are generally studied in microeconomics.

Remedies for the unemployment problem generally take the form of ensuring that there is enough demand for goods and services to require the full utilization of all available resources to meet that demand. You might think it strange that resources could be idle at all, and that it could be due to a low demand for goods. After all, don't people work in order to earn income to buy goods? Unfortunately, in a money-using economy producing many kinds of goods, a person's offer of labor services in one place is quite removed from his or her desired purchase of goods in another. A line of unemployed job-seekers at a steel mill's gate does not mean that each wants to work in direct exchange for a ton of cold-rolled steel to be carried home at the end of the day. The mill manager's plans to produce steel and hire workers are affected quite differently by a line of job-seeking, unemployed steelworkers than they are by a line of customers wanting to place orders. It is not obvious that if workers were employed in the back, customers would materialize out front to purchase their output. This is true even though the workers would most likely use their earned money to buy a multitude of items requiring steel. All firms in the economy producing all kinds of goods are in the same situation as the steel mill. Clearly when there are unemployed laborers and other resources in the whole economy, it is a result of the totality of these situations. The remedies for this sort of problem are studied in macroeconomics.

Change, Stability, and Growth

All economies are subject to change. The underlying causes of change are sometimes quite predictable. Population growth and the increase of technological know-how are a main impetus to economic growth. These kinds of change are fairly steady and ongoing. Population growth in underdeveloped countries is typically higher than in more industrialized countries. It is so high, in fact, that it poses a problem for those economies. Namely, it makes it very difficult to increase the standard of living. The growth in the number of people to be fed makes it difficult to divert resources from agricultural production to the capital formation needed for industrialization. This applies not just to the formation of physical capital but to the investment in human capital needed to provide the level of literacy and know-how required of the labor force in an industrialized economy. In other countries, such as Australia, it is felt that the rate of population growth is too low to spur the kind of economic growth desired. Depending on the particular economy, the level of population growth can pose a problem by being either too high or too low. In India, birth control measures are a primary policy concern. In Australia, population policy has been aimed at creating incentives to encourage immigration from abroad and the settlement of the vast interior of the continent.

Other kinds of change are often less predictable and pose severe problems for maintaining stable economic processes in a country. The abrupt onset of the energy shortage in the United States in 1973 and 1974 was not widely predicted or anticipated. It is felt by most economists that it was a major contributing factor to the recession that began in late 1973 and lasted through the first quarter of 1975. At that time this was the severest recession in the United States since the depression of the 1930s.

Often, drastic institutional and political changes, even when well intended, can cause severe economic problems for an economy. After the Communists took over in China in 1949, they instituted a new agricultural and industrialization program. This program increased grain production from 108 million tons in 1949 to 182 million tons in 1956 and steel production from 360,000 tons in 1950 to 3.32 million tons by 1956. Then in 1958 the Chinese leadership attempted to institute what they called the Great Leap Forward. They constructed backyard steel furnaces throughout the country, mandated 18-hour workdays, and transferred half a billion peasants into giant communes. All this, combined with three years of bad weather, proved to be too much change for the economy to adapt to. In some places, there was near starvation for the first time since the Communist takeover. Production dropped sharply and economic progress may have been set back by as much as a decade.

A major cause of instability in industrialized Western economies in recent years has been increases in the general levels of prices. This phenomenon is more commonly referred to as inflation. Since World War II, the general direction of prices in the United States has been continually upward. But during the 1970s the rate of increase of prices rose considerably. Perhaps of equal concern from the standpoint of stability has been the variation in the rate of increase. For example, during the recession lasting from November 1973 through March 1975, the consumer index rose at a compound annual rate of 10.9 percent. During the subsequent year of recovery, it rose at a compound annual rate of 6.1 percent. In 1980 the inflation rate peaked at 13.5 percent and then declined during the largely recessionary years of the early 1980s, falling to a 3.2 percent rate by 1983. This kind of variation creates uncertainty among consumers and businesses. Consumers often become more cautious about making major purchases, such as of housing and automobiles. Businesses and labor unions spend more time haggling about cost-of-living clauses in contracts. Economists are in broad agreement that price instability is a most undesirable source of change in the economy.

Every economy has to contend with various kinds of change at one time or another. Some are thought to be desirable, such as the growth in technological knowledge. In industrialized economies of the West, change in consumer tastes and an economy's ability to adapt to meet those changes is generally considered desirable. Other kinds of change, including inflation, recession, and external shocks to the economy, such as that caused by the Arab oil embargo, are on everybody's bad list. About some forms of change we have mixed feelings. A prime example in the United States in recent years is economic growth. We like it to the extent that it provides employment and an increase in goods and services. On the other hand, we don't like the accompanying increase in pollution, congestion in urban areas and on highways, and what many feel is a growing rootlessness and depersonalization of our way of life.

A major problem to be solved by an economy is how to adapt to various kinds of change so as to maximize the benefits derived from the desirable aspects of change and minimize the losses caused by the undesirable.

CHECKPOINT 2-3
Do you think the questions of what to produce and for whom to produce it are of a normative or a positive nature? Why?

THE VARIETY OF ECONOMIC SYSTEMS

There is a wide variety of ways of organizing an economy to answer the basic questions we have discussed in this chapter. How an economy deals with the basic problem of scarcity—the questions it poses—is also an expression of its vision of the relationship between the individual and society. The way in which a society chooses to organize its economy is therefore to a large extent a reflection of its cultural values and political **ideology**. It was in recognition of this fact that the subject of economics was originally called political economy. Almost any debate over the relative merits of various types of economic systems cannot avoid dealing with the different political ideologies on which they are based. In this section we will consider two basic types of economic systems without dwelling at any length on their political and ideological implications. Nonetheless, it should be kept in mind that these implications are usually regarded as matters of considerable importance.

Pure Market Economy, Laissez Faire Capitalism

Laissez faire is a French expression that means "let [people] do [as they choose]." Especially in matters of economics, it means allowing people to do as they please without governmental regulations and controls. *The ideological basis of such an economic system is the belief that if each economic unit is allowed to make free choices in pursuit of its own best interests, the interests of all will be best served.*

What are the main features of a **pure market economy** based on laissez faire **capitalism**? The means of production are privately owned by private citizens and private institutions. Private property is the rule. Government ownership is generally limited to public buildings and other facilities needed by the government in order to provide such things as national defense, a judicial system, police and fire protection, and public schools and roads. There is freedom of choice for consumers, businesses, and all resource suppliers. Consumers may purchase what they want subject to the limits of their money incomes—there is consumer sovereignty. Businesses are free to purchase and utilize resources to produce whatever products they desire and sell them in markets of their choice—there is free enterprise. Suppliers of resources such as labor, land, and financial capital are likewise free to sell them in whatever markets they please. The major constraint on businesses and resource suppliers is imposed by the marketplace, where consumer sovereignty decides what goods and services can and cannot be produced and sold profitably. Freedom of choice and all market activities are subject to the broadest legal limits consistent with maintaining law and order and with enforcing contracts freely entered into by consenting parties.

The Market Mechanism

The mechanism that serves to coordinate the activities of consumers, businesses, and all suppliers of resources is the market. A **market** is defined as an area within which buyers and sellers of a particular good are in such close communication that the price of that good tends to be the same everywhere in the area. The answers to the questions of what and how much to produce are determined by the signals communicated between buyers and sellers via the interacting network of markets and prices. The potential buyers of a good make contact with the sellers or suppliers in the market. Then a price must be determined such that suppliers will provide just the quantity of the good that buyers wish to purchase. On the buyers' (demand) side of the market, the level of the price determines who will buy the good and how much will be bought. On the suppliers' side of the market, the price level determines who will supply the good and how much will be supplied. If buyers want more than is being supplied at the prevailing price, they will signal their desires for more by bidding up the price. Suppliers will then respond by providing more of the good. If at the prevailing price sellers are providing a larger quantity of the good than buyers demand, prices will be bid down. This will be a signal to sellers to reduce the quantity of the good they supply to the market. In this way prices serve as the communicating link between buyers and sellers in a market economy.

Markets Determine What, How, for Whom

The markets for different goods are interrelated because the alternative to using one good is to use another. If the price of beef were felt to be too high, one alternative would be to buy poultry. And if the price of poultry were likewise thought to be too high, another alternative might be to buy ham. Hence the amounts of these goods buyers will demand will depend on the price of beef relative to the price of poultry and ham. Similarly, suppliers will be induced to supply those goods that are selling for the highest prices relative to the prices of other goods. Changes in the price in one market will set up a chain reaction of adjustments in quantities demanded and supplied in related markets. For example, other things being equal, an increase in demand for new housing will cause an increase in the price (wages) of architects, bricklayers, carpenters, furniture sales personnel, and so on. This will induce labor resources to move from other activities into those that now appear relatively more rewarding. All markets in the economy are interrelated with one another to varying extents in this way. It is the "invisible hand" of the marketplace that determines the allocation of resources, *what* goods will be produced, and *how much* of each.

Competition among suppliers of goods and labor services will ensure that the most efficient and productive will charge the lowest price for any good and thus make the sale to shopping buyers. Hence the forces of the marketplace will cause labor and other resources to flow into those occupations and uses for which they are best suited. This is the way a market economy determines *how production should be organized.*

For whom are goods produced in a market economy? Obviously, for whomever is able to pay the price for them. And who are these people? Those who are able to sell their labor services and any other resources they own that can be used in the production of other goods. The emphasis is on competition and a reward structure oriented toward the most efficient and productive. The vision of the individual's relation to society that underlies pure market, laissez faire capitalism has sometimes been characterized as an ideology of the survival of the fittest. All are free to go into any line of work or business they choose, to take any risks at making as much or losing as much money as they care to. The individual is entitled to all the rewards of good decisions and must bear the full consequences of bad ones.

Resource Utilization

How fully do pure market systems utilize their available resources? This is difficult to evaluate, because history provides few, if any, examples of a pure market economy without any form of government intervention. However, many of the industrialized economies of the Western world have a significant portion of their economic decisions determined by market forces. This was even more so in the nineteenth century and the twentieth century prior to World War II. The Great Depression, which afflicted these nations during the 1930s, together with the record of previous decades, suggests that pure market economies have difficulty keeping their available resources fully employed all the time.

Change, Stability, and Growth

As to change, stability, and growth, economies that most closely approximate pure market, laissez faire capitalism have achieved some of the highest standards of living in the world. Such systems seem particularly well suited to responding to the changing tastes of consumers. They are also able to develop new products and bring new technologies to the everyday use of the masses. From the standpoint of stability, fluctuations in economic activity as measured by GNP, employment, and the behavior of prices have always been a source of concern in such economies.

Obviously, one would be hard pressed to find a pure form of this type of economy today. In the late eighteenth century at the beginning of the Industrial Revolution, England and the United States came pretty close. Nonetheless, there are still many economies today where markets play a dominant role. Moreover, *the concept of pure market, laissez faire capitalism may be viewed as one extreme on a spectrum of ways of organizing an economy.*

The Command Economy

In the **command economy,** also called the planned economy, the government answers the questions of how to organize production, what and how much to produce, and for whom. These answers take the form of plans that may extend for as far as 10 to 20 years into the future. In such a planned economy, the government literally commands that these plans be carried out.

Government Domination

Typically, the government owns the means of production, as in the Soviet Union or Communist China, but this is not always so. In Nazi Germany the government controlled and planned the economy, but ownership remained largely in private hands. *In economies where planning is the most centralized and complete, the government must be very authoritarian. Therefore, it is often a totalitarian regime—ideologically committed to communism or to fascism.* Even in these economies the government may allow markets to operate in certain areas of the economy if it is consistent with, or helpful to, the achieve-

ment of other planning objectives. The Soviet Union allows this to some extent in its agricultural sector, for example. In a command economy all forms of labor, including management, are essentially government employees. The state is the company store, the only company.

Planning What, How, and for Whom

The underlying rationale for a command economy is that the government knows best what is most beneficial for the entire economy and for its individual parts. In a command economy there are differences between what consumers may want and what the planners have decided to produce. If planners do not want to devote resources to television sets, consumers simply will go without. Once the plan for the entire economy has been drawn up, each producing unit in the economy is told *what* and *how much* it must produce of various goods to fulfill its part of the plan. This determines each unit's need for labor, capital equipment, and other inputs. Obviously it is not easy to centrally coordinate all the component parts of the plan to ensure that the right kinds and amounts of labor, capital, and other inputs are available to each producing unit so that each may satisfy its individual plan. *How to organize production* is quite a task for central planners overseeing the economy of an entire nation. Managing General Motors, AT&T, or IBM pales in comparison.

For *whom* is output produced? Centrally planned economies typically provide for all citizens regardless of their productive contribution to the output of the economy. However, planners cannot avoid the fact that human nature does respond to material incentives. As a result, government-determined wage scales vary from one occupation or profession to the next, depending on where planners feel there are shortages or surpluses of needed labor skills. This, of course, depends on how authoritarian the government wants to be in allowing people to pick and choose their occupation or profession. For example, it appears that Communist China is more authoritarian in this regard than some of the Eastern European countries.

Resource Utilization

Full utilization of available resources presumably does not pose a problem in a command economy. Remember that by full utilization we mean that there are no available resources standing idle. This is a different issue from whether or not resources may be underemployed due to poor planning. In the Soviet Union planners seem to have continual difficulty in meeting their agricultural goals. If they think their goals are reasonable, their relatively frequent shortfalls from these goals suggest that the resources devoted to agriculture may not be as efficiently employed as possible, even allowing for setbacks caused by bad weather.

Change, Stability, and Growth

How do planned economies deal with *change* and *growth?* Obviously, in a planned economy growth and many kinds of change can be engineered by the central planning bureau to a large extent. If the government wants more economic growth, the central planning agency will draw up plans devoting a larger share of the economy's resources to the production of capital goods. On the other hand, critics argue that authoritarian control, large bureaucratic structure, and centrally dictated goals put a damper on individual initiative and innovation. Because of this it is argued that technological discovery and change are inhibited. This is considered a major factor in economic growth, a factor that critics feel is weak in planned economies. The *stability* of planned economies depends on how well the government is able to set realistic goals and structure the appropriate plans to attain them. If goals are too ambitious, and if the amount of reorganization in the economy is too great for the time allowed, the loss of economic stability can be severe. This was the case with Communist China's ill-fated Great Leap Forward discussed earlier.

Summing Up

The planned, or command, economy may be viewed as representing the other extreme on the spectrum of economic organization from that of pure market, laissez faire capitalism. No two economies in the world are exactly alike, but each may be thought of as lying somewhere on the spectrum between the two extremes we have described. Most fall under the very broad category of the **mixed economy,** which represents all the in-betweens. All economies have to grapple with the economic problem posed by scarcity, unlimited wants, and the consequent need for choice. In the next chapter we will examine the nature of the mixed economy.

CHECKPOINT 2-4

Describe the likely process of selecting a point on the production possibilities frontier of Figure 2–2 (that is, the combination of scrubbers and bundles) for a pure market economy and a planned, or command, economy. For each of these two kinds of economies, what difference do you think it makes, in terms of the point chosen on the frontier, if they are industrially underdeveloped as compared to the likely outcome if they are industrially advanced?

SUMMARY

1. While available economic resources are limited, human wants are virtually unlimited. This creates the fundamental problem of scarcity, which makes it necessary to make choices.

2. Economic efficiency requires that there be no unemployment or underemployment of resources. Unemployment exists whenever some available resources are idle. Underemployment (or resource misallocation) exists if certain available resources are employed to do jobs for which other available resources are better suited. It also exists whenever the best available technology is not used in a production process.

3. When there is no unemployment or underemployment of available resources, an economy is able to produce the maximum amount of goods possible. When producing this maximum, the economy is said to be on its production possibilities frontier. This frontier is a curve connecting the maximum possible output combinations of goods for a fully employed economy. In this situation, the production of more of one kind of good is possible only if the economy produces less of another. The cost of having more of one good is the amount of the other that must be given up. This cost is often called the opportunity cost of a good.

4. Economic growth occurs when an economy's available supply of resources is increased or when there is an increase in technological know-how. As a result, the production possibilities frontier expands outward. The output combination chosen on today's frontier affects the amount of capital goods that will be available tomorrow. Therefore, today's choice will affect the location of tomorrow's production possibilities frontier.

5. Any economy, whatever its political ideology, must answer certain questions that arise because of the basic economic problem of scarcity. Every economy must decide what goods to produce, how much to produce, how to organize production, and for whom output is to be produced. The answer to the question of what to produce determines the nature and location of the production possibilities frontier. The answer to the question of how much to produce determines the point chosen on the frontier. How to organize production determines whether the chosen point on the frontier will be reached. For whom to produce is largely determined by ideological orientation as to the proper mix of free markets, government regulation, and central planning.

6. Every economy must concern itself with maintaining full employment of its resources (avoiding unemployment). This has frequently been a problem for the industrialized economies of the West. Every economy must also deal with change. The stability of an economy depends very much on how well it is able to adjust to change. An important kind of change is economic growth, and economies are often judged on how well they promote economic growth.

7. There are two basic kinds of economies, or ways of organizing the process of deciding what and how much, how, and for whom to produce. Each kind presumes a particular relationship between the individual and the state. They are basically distinguished by the amount of government intervention they permit in the decision-making process of the economy.

a. *Pure market, laissez faire capitalism.* Individual economic units are given free choice in all economic decisions, which are completely decentralized. There is no interference by government in the form of regulations or controls. Markets and prices are the sole coordinating mechanisms for allocating resources and organizing production.

b. *Command, or planned, economy.* An authoritarian government decides what and how much, how, and for whom to produce. Government typically owns the means of production, plans economic activities, and commands that these plans be carried out. The underlying rationale is that the government knows best what is most beneficial for the entire economy and its individual parts.

KEY TERMS AND CONCEPTS

business cycles
business fluctuations
capitalism
command economy
economic efficiency
economic growth
economic problem

ideology
laissez faire
law of increasing costs
market
mixed economy
opportunity cost
production possibilities frontier
pure market economy
resource misallocation
underemployment
unemployment

QUESTIONS AND PROBLEMS

1. Think about the following situation in terms of the concept of opportunity cost. If you choose not to go to college, suppose your best alternative is to drive a truck for $12,000 per year. If you choose to go to college, suppose that you must pay a tuition fee of $2,000 per year and buy books and other school supplies amounting to $400 per year. Suppose that your other living expenses are the same regardless of which choice you make. Suppose you choose to go to college. What is the opportunity cost of your college diploma?

2. The following is a production possibilities table for computers and jet airplanes:

Product	Production Possibilities				
	A	B	C	D	E
Computers (in thousands)	0	25	40	50	55
Jet airplanes (in thousands)	40	30	20	10	0

a. Plot the production possibilities frontier for the economy characterized by this table.

b. Demonstrate the law of increasing costs using the data in this table.

c. Suppose technological progress doubles the productivity of the process for making computers and also of that for making jet airplanes. What would the numbers in the production possibilities table look like in that case? Plot the new production possibilities frontier.

d. Suppose technological progress doubles the productivity of the process for making computers but there is no change in the process for making jet airplanes. What would the numbers in the production possibilities table be now? Plot the new production possibilities frontier.

e. Suppose technological progress doubles the productivity of the process for making jet airplanes but there is no change in the process for making computers. What would the numbers in the production possibilities frontier be now? Plot the new production possibilities frontier. Why is it that, despite the fact that there is no change in the productivity of producing computers, it is now possible at any given level of production of jet airplanes to have more computers?

3. Consider a production possibilities frontier for consumer goods and capital goods. How would the choice of a point on that frontier affect the position of tomorrow's frontier? Choose three different points on today's production possibilities frontier and indicate the possible location of tomorrow's frontier that is associated with each.

4. Construct your own production possibilities frontier by putting a grade point scale on the vertical axis to measure a grade in your economics course and the number of waking hours in a typical day (say 16) on the horizontal axis. Out of those 16 hours per day, how many do you think you would have to give up to get a D? a C? a B? an A? Plot the frontier determined by these combinations.

5. Compare and contrast the ways in which the two types of economies we have discussed deal with the five basic questions or problems any economy faces.

3

The Nature of
the Mixed Economy

AFTER READING THIS CHAPTER, YOU WILL BE ABLE TO:

1. Explain why markets exist.

2. Explain how money makes trading much easier and therefore promotes specialization and trade.

3. Define *normal profit*.

4. Define the role of profit in the creation and allocation of capital.

5. State the nature and rationale of government intervention in a mixed economy.

In a mixed economy the answers to the questions what and how much to produce, how to organize production, and for whom to produce are determined by a mixture of government intervention, regulation, and control in some areas of the economy, coupled with private enterprise and a reliance on markets in other areas.

In some mixed economies, government intervention extends even to the ownership of certain industries—such industries are called **nationalized industries.** In Great Britain, for example, the steel, the airline, and the railroad industries are nationalized. The public by and large felt that these industries would operate better under complete government control than under private ownership subject to varying degrees of government regulation, as is the case with the railroads and airlines in the United States. Hence, a mixed economy may involve not only a mixture of private and public decision making but a mixture of private and public ownership as well.

The role of government varies from one mixed economy to the next, reflecting the varying opinions on this issue in different countries. Nonetheless, there are certain characteristics common to all. They all have markets where the exchange of goods and services takes place using money as the medium of exchange. They all have had a strong tradition of capitalism stemming from their history of economic development, particularly the fact that they experienced the Industrial Revolution.[1] They all have felt the need to modify capitalism and the workings of free markets through government intervention.

In this chapter we will get a brief overview of some of the main characteristics of mixed economies like our own. Much of the analysis in the rest of this book will focus on mixed economies. This chapter will also briefly explore the role of markets, money, profits, and government in such an economic

---

[1] Countries that most commonly come to mind are the United States, Great Britain, Canada, the Scandinavian countries, France, West Germany, Italy, Australia, New Zealand, and Japan.

system. Of course a good deal of what we say about each of these subjects is true whether or not we are speaking of a mixed economy.

MARKETS AND MONEY

Specialization gives rise to the need for trade, and trade creates markets. Money makes trade easier and therefore encourages specialization and a more extensive development of markets. Let's consider the truth of each of these statements in turn.

Specialization and Markets

Why do markets exist in the first place? Why are goods traded? What is it that leads people to go to market? The answer lies in the fact that each of us is better at doing some things than at doing others. We often refer to our best skill as "my thing," "my bag," or my "long suit." We tend to specialize in that thing we are best at. We "trade on it." Have you ever heard it said of movie stars that "they trade on their good looks"?

When each of us specializes in that particular thing he or she is best at, the whole economy is able to produce more of everything than if each of us tries to be self-sufficient. Of course when each specializes in producing one thing, each is dependent on others for the production of everything else. With specialization most of what one produces is a surplus that must be traded for the other things that one wants. Hence the more **specialization of labor** there is in an economy, the greater is the need for trade. And as trade becomes more important to the functioning of an economy, markets in all kinds of goods and services become more commonplace.

The Role of Money

A prominent characteristic of markets with which you are familiar is that goods are traded for money. In a **barter economy** goods are traded for goods. The more an economy is characterized by specialization of labor, the less likely it is that we will observe goods being traded directly for goods. What led people to start using money in the first place? The fundamental reason for the invention and existence of money is that it makes specialization and trade much easier. This is most obvious if we consider the difficulties of trade in a barter economy.

Trade in a Barter Economy

Suppose you are a member of an economy in which each individual specializes in the production of a particular good. Like everyone else, you produce more of your particular good than you need for yourself and trade the surplus for other goods. Suppose you specialize in chopping wood and today you decide to go shopping for a pair of sandals. Lugging your wood on your back, you go in search of a sandal maker. Finding one at last, you are disappointed to find that the sandal maker has no need for chopped wood. No trade takes place, and so with aching back and sore feet you continue on your quest. Your problem is twofold. You must first find someone who has sandals to trade. Second, while you may encounter several such people, you must find among them one who wants to acquire chopped wood. In other words, you are looking for an individual who coincidentally has sandals to trade *and* also wants chopped wood. In order to have a trade, it is necessary to have a **coincidence of wants**.

At this point you might ask, is it not possible that someone who has sandals to trade, but no need for chopped wood, might accept the wood and then trade it for something he or she does want? Yes, it is possible, but very inconvenient. If that person accepts the wood, the problem of finding a coincidence of wants has really just been transferred from you to him or her.

In sum, *the difficulties involved in finding a coincidence of wants tend to discourage specialization and trade in a barter economy.* Given the effort and time that must be spent just to find a coincidence of wants, many individuals in a barter economy would find it easier to be more self-sufficient and produce more items for their own consumption. To this extent, the gains from specialization and trade cannot be fully realized.

Money as a Medium of Exchange

How does the use of money allow us to get around these difficulties? *Money eliminates the need for the coincidence of wants.* If the economy uses money to carry on trade, you can sell your chopped wood to whomever wants it and accept money in exchange. Whether the purchaser makes something you want is now irrelevant. As long as you can use the money received to buy what you want you are satisfied. You can use the money to buy a pair of sandals or whatever. Similarly, the sandal maker will accept your money even though he or she may have no need for your chopped wood. We say money serves as the medium of exchange.

At different times and in different societies, the medium of exchange used as money has taken many forms—from hounds' teeth to precious stones to gold coin to currency, checks, and credit cards. Whatever its form, *money's common characteristic is that it must be acceptable to people because they know they can use it as buyers. Because money eliminates the need for coincidence of wants, it promotes specialization and trade and thereby makes possible the gains that stem from specialization and trade. The incentive for societies to use money in exchange derives from these gains. The introduction of money into a barter economy essentially causes that economy's production possibilities frontier to be shifted outward.*

CHECKPOINT* 3-1

Suppose there are three people, A, B, and C, and that A specializes in growing corn, B in catching fish, and C in growing wheat. A has a surplus of corn, B a surplus of fish, and C a surplus of wheat. Suppose A would like to get some wheat from C, but C doesn't have any desire for A's corn. Suppose that C would like to get some

fish from B, but B doesn't want any of C's wheat. And suppose that B would like to get some corn from A, but A doesn't want any of B's fish. Each wants something from one of the others, but has nothing to offer in exchange. What is lacking here? Further, suppose each lives alone on an island 20 miles from each of the others and that each has a boat. Describe how trade would have to be carried on under a barter system, if it were carried on at all. By comparison, describe how trade would be carried on if A, B, and C used money.

*Answers to all Checkpoints can be found at the back of the text.

MARKETS AND PROFITS

A money-using economy with extensive markets fosters specialization among workers and in the methods of production. This specialization leads to the development of more sophisticated production processes, which typically require large amounts of investment in capital goods. In a capitalistic economy where the productive units or firms are privately owned either by those who run them or by shareholders, sizeable amounts of funds, or financial capital, must be raised by the owners in order to acquire the capital goods. Whether or not it is worthwhile to commit funds to such investments depends on that controversial thing called profit. And the amount of profit is determined by the markets where the goods produced by the capital goods are sold. Another key role played by profit in a capitalistic economy is to provide an incentive for entrepreneurial activity. The entrepreneur described in Chapter 1 is a key factor in the creation and organizing of new production techniques and the founding of firms that employ these techniques to satisfy the demands of new and continually changing markets.

What Is a Normal Profit?

Profit is one of the most controversial and least understood concepts in economics. For some people the mere mention of the word conjures up images of exploitation and robber barons carving out their pound of flesh from the downtrodden. But what is a "reasonable" profit, or what economists call a **normal profit**? When we say that a firm is earning a normal profit, what must be the relationship between its total sales revenue and its total costs?

In order to answer these questions, recall that we emphasized in the previous chapter that all costs are opportunity costs due to the fact that resources are scarce and have alternative uses. Our discussion of the production possibilities frontier indicated that if resources are used to produce one good, they are not available to produce other goods. The cost of the one good is thus the alternative goods that must be forgone in order to produce it. This notion of cost is directly applicable to the individual firm. All the resources, including financial capital and entrepreneurial skills, that a firm needs in order to produce its product have alternative uses in the production of other products by other firms. Hence *the costs of production for a firm are all those payments it must make to all resource suppliers in order to bid resources away from use in the production of alternative goods. When the firm's total sales revenue is just sufficient to cover these costs, all resources employed by the firm are just earning their opportunity costs.* In particular, *the financial capital and the entrepreneurial skills used by the firm are being compensated just enough to keep them from leaving and going into some other line of productive activity. That amount of compensation is called a normal profit.*

Profit and the Allocation of Resources

Changes in the level of profits that are earned in different markets play an important role in the efficient allocation of resources in a dynamic, changing economy. Suppose that a market for a new product develops or that there is a sudden increase in demand for an existing product. Firms already in the market or those first to enter will find they can earn more than normal profits or above-normal profits. This happens because demand so exceeds the existing capacity to meet it that prices considerably in excess of cost can be charged. Above-normal profits serve as a signal to entrepreneurial skills and financial capital in other areas of the economy that they can earn more by moving into the new and expanding markets. Resources will continue to move into these areas so long as above-normal profits exist. Eventually, enough resources will have moved into these markets and increased capacity sufficiently that above-normal profits will no longer exist. In this way *above-normal profits serve to allocate resources to those areas of the economy where they are most in demand. Similarly, of course, below-normal profits in one area of the economy will cause entrepreneurial skills and financial capital to move out of that line of productive activity and into those where they can earn their opportunity cost.*

Controversy About the Role of Profit

Anytime you read something or hear a discussion about profit, you should ask yourself how the term is being used. There is a good deal of misunderstanding about the nature of profit in mixed economies.

Early Views on Profit

Suspicion of profit is an ancient theme in Western culture. A sixteenth-century French thinker, Michel de Montaigne, wrote an essay entitled "The Profit of One Man Is the Damage of Another." His thesis was that "man should condemn all manner of gain." However, with the dawn of the era of capitalism two centuries ago, the profit motive found an able defender in Adam Smith—the renowned author of *The Wealth of Nations.* In this book, published in 1776, Smith argued that profits are the legitimate return for risk and effort. He put forward the notion that the "invisible hand" of market forces turns private greed into productive activity, which provides goods for the benefit of all. A century later, Karl Marx argued the opposite view. He maintained that labor, not capital, was the ingredient that added value to goods or raw materials in the production process. He asserted that profit was the "surplus value" that the capitalist unjustifiably added on to the real worth of the product.

Twentieth-Century Views on Profit

In the early part of the twentieth century, the Fabian socialists argued that profits should be "taxed into oblivion" to create a new socialist order. If they meant above-normal profit, they might have a good case in certain circumstances. In the mixed economy of the United States, public policy has recognized that due to the technology of producing certain kinds of goods and due to the size and nature of certain kinds of markets, one firm can become dominant and exclude any others from the market. In that case, the monopoly position of the firm allows it to charge high prices and earn above-normal profit because consumers who want the product have no alternative but to buy it from that firm. Electric power companies, telephone companies, and gas companies are examples. Without some type of government intervention, such firms could go on earning above-normal profits until technological innovation provided some substitute good not yet existent. Because of this, utility companies are subject to government regulation of the prices they can charge. In this way, profit in excess of normal profit, frequently called monopoly profit, is supposed to be taxed into oblivion. Most economists, policymakers, and the general public feel this procedure is justified in such "natural" monopoly situations. In practice such regulation has not always been able to achieve the desired goal.

Suppose the Fabians' expressed desire to tax profits into oblivion were meant to apply to normal profits. This would effectively remove any return to financial capital and entrepreneurial skill. It would, therefore, remove the incentive for anybody to provide the financial capital necessary for the creation of physical capital goods or the innovative effort necessary to create new technology and supply new markets. When an economy ceases to build capital goods, the growth in its capacity to produce other goods stops. If the Fabians meant by profits normal profits, taxing profits out of existence would certainly be an extreme position. There would definitely be a new social order.

The taxation of profits will undoubtedly always be a much debated issue in mixed capitalistic economies. Unfortunately, much of the debate is often the result of misunderstanding over the meaning or meanings of the word profit.

Profit in Today's Economy

Today the average individual directly or indirectly owns a sizeable portion of the shares (or stock) of corporations in the United States. The dividends paid on these shares derive directly from the profits of the corporations. Nearly half of all corporate shares, measured in dollar value, are owned by institutions such as pension funds, insurance companies, college endowments, and churches. Hence, for millions of Americans such things as the assurance of a retirement income, the soundness of an insurance policy, and the availability of a college scholarship are heavily dependent on the continued profitability of U.S. corporations. When profits go down or turn into losses, the average person in the street often has as much cause for concern as the corporate board of directors. It should be said, however, that above-normal profits derived from situations where competition in the marketplace is nonexistent or inhibited are generally considered not to be in the economy's best interest.

CHECKPOINT 3-2

Samuel Gompers (1850–1924) was an American labor leader. He was the first president of the American Federation of Labor, a position he held from 1886 until his death (except for one year, 1895). He once said, "The worst crime against working people is a company which fails to operate at a profit." What do you suppose he meant by this? Like Gompers, Marx championed the working class. How do their views on profit seem to differ?

GOVERNMENT'S ROLE IN THE MIXED ECONOMY

As with profits, there is always a good deal of controversy over the appropriate role of government versus that of markets in determining what, how, and for whom to produce. "Be thankful you don't get all the government you pay for" say some who are skeptical of what government does and how efficiently it does it. A critic of the market system once said, "Competition in the marketplace brings out the best in products and the worst in people."

Government, whether it is local, state, or federal, performs four main functions in a mixed economy: (1) it provides the legal and institutional structure in which markets operate; (2) it intervenes in the allocation of resources in areas of the economy where public policy deems it beneficial to do so; (3) it redistributes income; and (4) it seeks to provide stability in prices, economic growth, and economic conditions generally. Of course, government actions in any one of these spheres almost invariably have implications for the others.

Legal and Institutional Structure for Markets

Even in pure market, laissez faire capitalism, the government must provide for legal definition and enforcement of contracts, property rights, and ownership. It must also establish the legal status of different forms of business organizations, from the owner-operated small business to the large corporation. It must provide a judicial system so that disputed claims between parties arising in the course of business can be settled. Government also provides for the supply and regulation of the money supply, the maintenance of a system of measurement standards, and the maintenance of a police force to keep order and protect property.

You will find little disagreement anywhere as to the need for government to provide this basic legal and institutional structure. Since the turn of the century, however, the legal sanctions and constraints on the functioning of markets and the economic relationships between business, labor, and consumers have become more complex. In the United States the government has taken an active role in trying to maintain competition in markets. We have already noted how government regulates pricing activities in the utilities industries, where technological and market conditions do not naturally encourage competition. In an attempt to maintain competitive conditions in all markets, Congress has enacted a number of antitrust laws, which are essentially aimed at preventing market domination by one or a small number of large firms. Starting with the Sherman Act of 1890, these laws also make it illegal for firms in any particular market to collude in setting prices or conspire to restrict competition. Legislation such as the Taft-Hartley Act of 1947 was enacted to impose legal constraints on the way unions are organized and run and on collective bargaining procedures. These laws also prescribe how strikes that threaten the general well-being of the nation are to be handled. Government intervention to protect consumers has been the subject of legislation throughout the twentieth century, starting with the Pure Food and Drug Act of 1906. More recently the government has actively intervened in the area of pollution control. In

1969 Congress established the Environmental Protection Agency in order to develop quality standards for air and water with the assistance of state and local governments.

Government intervention in the marketplace through creation and change of certain aspects of the legal and institutional structure has often proved beneficial. In other instances, it has not. One of the most disastrous examples was the Volstead Act passed in Congress in 1919. It prohibited the production and sale of alcoholic beverages. The act became so unpopular that Congress repealed it in 1933. Many observers feel that it provided a tremendous economic windfall to the underworld, which did a thriving business in the illicit production and sale of the liquor that a thirsty public would not do without. This is felt to have laid the foundation for modern organized crime as a big business.

Resource Allocation

Government affects resource allocation in our economy through its spending activities, its tax policies, and its own production of certain goods and services.

Government Spending

In the United States about 70 percent of all output is produced and sold in markets. The quantity and variety of goods and services represented by this 70 percent of total output is the result of decisions made by numerous firms and consumers—the private sector of our economy. The other 30 percent of the economy's output is the result of government (public sector) expenditure decisions. This includes all levels of government—state, federal, and local. Though much of this output of goods and services is produced by private businesses, it is done under government contract and reflects government decisions about what to produce and for whom—highways for motorists, schools, and military hardware for national defense are just a few examples.

POLICY PERSPECTIVE

Should Profit Be the Only Objective of Business?

Do businesses have obligations to society beyond making profit? There is considerable disagreement over the appropriate answer to this question. On one side of the issue it is argued that the *only* responsibility of business is to make profits because by pursuing that goal alone society's interests are best served. Alternatively, the other side of the issue holds that businesses should act according to higher moral principles to prevent damage to society that might otherwise result from a single-minded pursuit of profit. In the extreme, this view holds that it amounts to "murder for profit" when businesses produce and advertise cigarettes, market automobiles that are not "adequately crash-proof," and dump toxic wastes in rivers. Are there not moral principles that should inhibit such behavior even at the cost of forgone profit opportunities?

The "Only Profits" View

The view that profit should be the sole objective of business points out that corporate managers in today's world are responsible to the corporation's stockholders (the owners) who expect them to do everything within the law to earn the owners a maximum return (profit) on their investment. The "only profits" view argues that if a corporate executive takes an action that the executive feels is "socially responsible" and that action reduces profit, then the executive has spent (in effect, stolen) the owners' money. This violates a fundamental tenet of our political-economic system that no individual shall be deprived of property without his or her permission. Corporate executives who want to take socially responsible actions

should use their own money, supporting special interest groups, charities, or political parties and causes that promote the social actions they desire. However, to the extent that executives sacrifice profit to such actions, they effectively deprive stockholders of the right to spend the sacrificed higher profits (which otherwise belong to stockholders) on social actions of the stockholders' choosing, and on anything else for that matter. If corporate executives and stockholders choose to spend their *own* money to support (in whatever way) social actions to regulate business behavior, so be it.

The "Profits Plus Other Concerns" View

The point of view that business should not pursue profit to the complete exclusion of other social concerns argues that the sole pursuit of profit tends to give rise to immoral, if not illegal, business behavior. According to this view business firms do have a moral responsibility not to design products or engage in behavior (for example, deceptive advertising) that they have reason to believe will seriously injure or possibly kill people. Business's willingness to do what is clearly immoral for the sake of profit conflicts with an old moral precept (going back at least to Aristotle) that money is a means to an end, in itself not the sort of end that justifies acting immorally to get it. The "profits plus other concerns" view also argues that if profit is the sole objective of business then the associated abuses and immoral behavior that result will lead the public to impose greater government regulation on business activity. Increased government intrusion in the private sector will cause economic inefficiency as well as pose potential threats to individual freedoms. Therefore, it is argued, it is in the long run in the best interest of business (and all of us) to pay heed to moral principles while pursuing profit. Otherwise society will increasingly use the government and political processes to correct perceived abuses.

How Do You Get Socially Responsible Business Behavior?

Is it really possible for firms to be "socially responsible" and survive in a competitive market? Firms that incur additional costs to make a safer product or avoid polluting the environment, say, may put themselves at a competitive disadvantage vis-a-vis less socially responsible rival firms. Will the more socially responsible firms not be driven out of business, leaving only those motivated solely by profit, thus making the greater government regulation predicted by the "profits plus other concerns" view inevitable? It depends on the nature of the socially responsible behavior firms engage in. Firms that make products that get a reputation for being unsafe, for example, will lose sales to the safer products of rivals—they will be disciplined by the market while the more socially responsible firms will be rewarded.

On the other hand, socially responsible firms that voluntarily incur costs to prevent environmental pollution are likely to lose out to less socially responsible rivals because pollution control efforts don't show up in product quality where they will be rewarded by the market. Therefore government regulation to protect the environment may be the only solution to pollution control problems, while the discipline of the market may be a more reliable and efficient way to enforce product safety. Even on the issue of product safety however, the question is "how many injuries and lost lives does it take for the market to react against an unsafe product?" Where the public has answered "too many," government regulation has been called for, giving rise to such regulatory bodies as the Food and Drug Administration and the National Transportation Safety Board.

The Role of Human Nature

What if human nature is such that it is only realistic to expect that the main objective of business *is* profit, as Adam Smith believed (see Adam Smith, p. 14)? Then the relevant questions are: (1) What kinds of socially irresponsible business behavior will be curbed by the discipline of the market, and what kinds will not? (2) Where market discipline is of questionable effectiveness, are the costs of government regulation (in terms of increased threat to individual freedom as well as increased tax cost) less than the costs (such as injury and loss of life) that trigger market discipline?

Some perspective on answers to the last question is provided by the following examples. Despite the fact that lower speed limits are known to reduce highway fatalities, there is no public outcry for lower speed limits. The public values reduced travel time more than reduced fatalities. (People do put a price on life!) Similarly, there is a limit to what people will pay for a "crash-proof" car. A business that tried to produce them, out of a sense of social responsibility, would probably go bankrupt because only a few people would be willing to pay a price that would cover the cost of making them. If the public is unwilling to pay for such a level of product safety, it would hardly seem justifiable to many citizens for the government to impose it by subsidizing production of such cars with taxpayers' money. It would also be misleading to assume the absence of such cars is due to automakers' lack of social conscience and singular pursuit of profit.

might you expect a helmet manufacturer to differ from a motorcycle company on the two views about profit in this case?

Questions

1. In some states motorcyclists are required to wear crash helmets. Why

2. In the United States it is legal to sell alcoholic beverages but not marijuana. How *might* this distinction be justified?

Taxation

Another way in which the government affects the allocation of resources is through its power to levy taxes. For example, we have already noted how changes in profit affect the incentive to create new capital goods. From our discussion of the production possibilities frontier in the previous chapter, we know that there is a trade-off between producing capital goods and producing goods for present consumption. In order to produce more of one kind of good, it is necessary to obtain the resources to do so by cutting back on production of the other. That is, it is necessary to reallocate resources from one line of productive activity to another. By changing the rate of taxation of profit, the government changes the incentive to produce capital goods relative to the incentive to produce goods for current consumption. For instance, suppose the government increased taxes on profits. This would discourage the production of capital goods relative to consumer goods. Some resources would therefore be reallocated from capital goods production to consumer goods production. This is but one example of the way in which the government can affect the allocation of resources through tax policy.

Government Production of Goods and Services

Another way that the government affects resource allocation is by producing goods and services itself. There are certain kinds of

goods and services that would not be produced at all if the choice were left up to the market mechanism, even though it might be acknowledged by everybody that such goods provide benefits for all. Such goods are **public goods**.

An essential feature of a public good is that it cannot be provided to one person without providing it to others. If the government provides a dam to protect your property from floods, the benefits accrue to your neighbor as well. Public goods are *not* subject to the so-called **exclusion principle**. *Any good whose benefits accrue only to those who purchase it is said to be subject to the exclusion principle.* Those who do not buy the good are excluded from its benefits. The exclusion principle almost invariably applies to goods produced and sold in a market economy. When producers cannot prevent those who don't pay for the good from having it, the exclusion principle does not hold for that good. If one can have a good without paying for it, then there is no way for producers to charge and receive a price to cover the costs of producing it. Hence there will be no incentive for firms to produce it in a market economy. If I build a lighthouse, there is no way I can exclude any ship at sea from benefiting from its beacon. Hence there is no way I can charge ships at sea for its service, so I won't build it, despite the fact that shipping companies all agree that it cuts down their economic losses due to shipwrecks. Similarly, it is difficult to privately produce and sell the services of a dam, national defense, cloud seeding, and clean air.

Another feature of a public good is that once it is provided for one citizen, there is no additional cost to providing it for others. This is really just another aspect of the fact that when a public good provides benefits to one, it unavoidably provides them to others. It costs no more to protect one ship at sea than to protect several with the same lighthouse.

Of course, there are many goods that are not by nature public goods that the government provides anyway. Examples of goods and services that can be privately produced and sold in markets but are provided by state, local, or federal government are education, police and fire protection, certain kinds of preventive medical treatment, sewage treatment, garbage collection, bridges, toll roads, and air shows financed by the government through the Defense Department. In most of these cases, it is usually argued that there are substantial social benefits, and that if their provision were left strictly to private producers and markets, less of these goods would be produced than is desirable.

Income Redistribution

In virtually all modern, industrialized, mixed economies there are specific government policies aimed at alleviating the hardships of poverty. If people cannot earn some minimal standard of living in the marketplace, it is generally agreed that they should be given economic assistance in some form. Whatever form it takes, this assistance makes it necessary to redistribute income from those judged to have enough to those who do not. One obvious way to do this is for the government simply to levy heavier income taxes on people in higher income brackets and transfer the money collected to those in lower brackets.

Many government transfers of income and wealth between citizens do not necessarily redistribute from the rich to the poor. Social security payments to retired persons are financed by social security taxes paid by all those citizens presently working as well as by their employers. Any retired citizen over 62 years of age, even a multimillionaire, is eligible for these benefits. And even the lowest-paid worker is obliged to pay the social security taxes used to finance these benefits.

Government has played a growing role in income redistribution since World War II. This is illustrated in Figure 3-1, which shows that an increased share of federal government outlays takes the form of payments to individuals. The payments to individuals are transfer payments in the form of Medicare and social security benefits to retired workers and the disabled, unemployment benefits, and payments to those eligible for various welfare and special assistance programs. The payments to individuals are often referred to as income maintenance programs because they effectively maintain minimum income levels for the recipients. They represent an income redistribution from taxpayers to those receiving the payments. The share of total federal government outlays accounted for by payments to individuals grew from 12.3 percent in 1953 to 41.5 percent in 1983.

A good deal of the transfer of income and wealth among citizens takes the form of government provision of goods and services at zero or below cost to the citizens who use them. These are not included in "payments to individuals." The costs of providing such goods and services are covered by tax revenue, much of which is collected from citizens who may not themselves use these governmentally provided goods and services. Public education, parks and recreation areas, public libraries, and a partially subsidized postal service are but a few examples. Again, a wealthy person might choose to use these facilities while someone with a much lower income might use them little or not at all, even though he or she pays taxes used to subsidize the government provision of such goods and services.

Another way in which the government affects income distribution is by direct intervention in the marketplace. Well-known examples of this are governmentally enforced

FIGURE 3-1 Percentage Shares of Major Components of Total U.S. Federal Government Budget Outlays

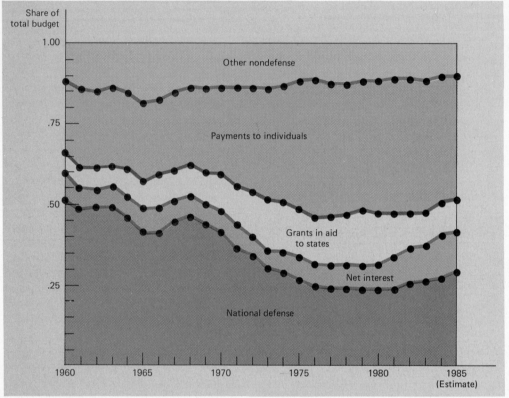

Federal budget outlays reflect increased emphasis on income redistribution in the form of payments to individuals.

price supports in agricultural markets and minimum-wage laws in labor markets. Farm price supports reflect a desire to maintain the income levels of farmers. Minimum-wage laws supposedly reflect a desire to see to it that laborers' wage levels ensure some minimum standard of living. In the case of agriculture such direct market intervention has been criticized for unjustly favoring special interests and distorting resource allocation. It has also been charged that minimum-wage laws aggravate unemployment and contribute to poverty rather than alleviate it. Some argue that minimum-wage laws reflect the desire of skilled or unionized workers to diminish the competition they face from low-wage workers.

Economic Stabilization

In the previous chapter we noted the difficulties that market-oriented economies have avoiding recessions in economic activity, fluctuations in employment and GNP, and unacceptable levels of inflation. In most capitalistic, mixed economies, we observed that a good deal of responsibility for avoiding these difficulties has been vested in the government—witness the Employment Act of 1946 in the United States. Governmental efforts to carry out the spirit of that act are an example of how the exercise of a government responsibility in one area invariably affects other areas. Fiscal policy—government expenditure and tax changes aimed at smoothing out fluctuations in economic activity—unavoidably affects resource allocation, income distribution, and even the competitive market structure of industries in which the government buys goods and lets contracts for public projects. By changing the levels of interest rates, monetary policy has similar effects on resource allocation and income distribution.

Controversy About the Role of Government

In recent years there has been a growing skepticism about the ability of government to provide services to the public, direction to the economy, and solutions to a number of social problems. This has led to a critical examination of how government functions in our economy, a search for the reasons why once-optimistic expectations about the government's role have often not been fulfilled.

Efficiency in Government

Many critics point out that government bureaucracies by their very nature do not have the built-in incentives for efficiency that exist in the typical business firm. The reward of profit and the threat of loss are absent. Moreover, it is typically difficult to measure either output or performance. It is often impossible for a government bureaucrat to show how and where he or she has saved the taxpayers money. How can one tell how efficiently the Department of the Interior, the local library, or a city school system is being operated? If efficient performance is hard to demonstrate, it is likely to be unrecognized and unrewarded, so why try so hard? Similarly, an inefficient performance is equally hard to detect. Neither the carrot nor the stick is much in evidence under these circumstances. In short, because the relationship between taxpayer dollars and benefits produced is hard to

establish, the incentives for efficiency are weak.

Special Interest Legislation

Special interest groups often push hard for legislation that provides special benefits for them and possibly little or no benefit for anyone else. Special interest groups often get their way even when it may not serve the broader public interest. Why?

Suppose some special interest group presses for a program that will cost each individual taxpayer only a dollar. The total cost of the program may be tens of millions of dollars. But as far as the individual taxpayer is concerned the extra dollar of taxes will hardly be noticed. For the individual taxpayer it is scarcely worth the effort to become informed about the program. However, those in the special interest group may stand to benefit substantially, so that they have very strong feelings about whether the program is approved or not. Consequently a politician who doesn't vote for the special interest group's program stands to lose the group's vote in the next election and quite likely a helpful financial contribution to his or her campaign as well. On the other hand, a vote for the program will probably cost the politician few if any votes among the other largely uninformed voters. Consequently the politician votes for the special interest group's program, even though it may not be in the broader public interest.

For example, you are a member of Congress from a district where a large company dumps toxic wastes into a river. Downstream the river runs through heavily populated areas, creating a health hazard and requiring costly water treatment plants. Suppose the citizens downstream are ill-informed about the source of their dirty water. An antipollution law is proposed in Congress that would require offending companies, such as the one in your district, to clean up their toxic wastes. The company and its employees, who fear a loss of jobs, are a special interest group on this issue. You can't afford to lose their vote and so you vote against the legislation, to the detriment of the larger but ill-informed public downstream.

Consumer Preferences and the Bundle Problem

When you buy goods in the marketplace, you shop for them on an item-by-item basis. You are able to be very selective. Your selection of governmentally provided goods and services is much more limited because you must select them through an intermediary, the candidate for political office. Each candidate really represents a bundle of public goods and services, the ones that the candidate will support and vote for if he or she is elected. Your choice of bundles is limited by the number of candidates running for an office. Each candidate may have certain goods and services in his or her bundle that you want and others that you don't want. You vote for the candidate whose bundle most closely matches your preferences. Even then you are forced to take some public goods and services you don't want in order to get those that you do want.

For example, you choose to vote for candidate A because A supports the construction of a dam that you want very much. The candidate may also be in favor of price supports for wheat and corn, which you don't want, but you don't feel as concerned about price supports as you do about the dam. Candidate B is against the price supports but does not favor the dam either. You vote for A instead of B. Even though A's bundle of goods and services doesn't match your preferences perfectly, it comes closer than the alternative bundle represented by B.

Bias Toward Current Benefit, Hidden Cost Projects

Because politicians must worry about getting reelected, there is a natural tendency for them to favor projects and programs that have immediate, highly visible benefits and less visible costs. An objective economic analysis of project A might show it to be more worthwhile than a number of other projects. But suppose project A's benefits are spread over a distant future, while tax increases will be required to cover its immediate costs. Project A is therefore likely to lack support, while other economically less worthwhile projects that have more immediate benefits and less visible costs will be pushed forward.

It should be emphasized that none of these criticisms of the way government functions to provide goods and services is a criticism of politicians and government bureaucrats. They respond to rewards and incentives just like people in other walks of life. Given that, these criticisms are directed at the ways in which the reward and incentive structures of our political and governmental institutions are not always geared to provide goods and services in the most economically efficient manner.

Resource Utilization

How good are mixed economies at maintaining a *full utilization of their available resources?* The Great Depression of the 1930s, which plagued the industrialized economies of the West, led these countries to call for more government intervention in the future. In this way, these economies hoped to avoid another episode of such dramatic underemployment of resources. The ideas put forward at that time by the British economist John Maynard Keynes provided a rationale for how government intervention could prevent such a calamity. Income tax reductions and stepped-up government expenditures to offset the fall in expenditures by businesses and consumers were among the recommended measures to be used. Most economists today are of the opinion that such government intervention would be appropriate and effective in averting another Great Depression. However, there is considerable debate and skepticism among economists as to whether such intervention has been either practicable or effective in alleviating the recessions that have occurred in the United States since World War II.

Change, Stability, and Growth

Mixed economies justify government intervention, at least in part, as a means of promoting stability and growth and those kinds of change that are considered desirable. How well mixed economies have succeeded is a matter of continual debate among economists.

In the United States some economists think that the antitrust activities of the government on the whole have helped to prevent the growth of monopoly and thereby promoted competition in some areas of the economy. It is felt that more competition better serves changing consumer tastes and leads to more innovation in products, which is a spur to economic growth. On the other hand, the government has intervened to save large faltering corporations from bankruptcy, as in the case of Chrysler. Many critics feel that this interferes with the beneficial working of the marketplace, which serves to weed out inefficient producers, a form of change felt to be desirable. Furthermore, they ask, why should the government prop up certain large failing corporations when many smaller businesses fail every day because they are unable to meet the rigors of the marketplace?

With regard to economic growth and stability, many economists argue that in the United States greater growth and stability have been promoted by government intervention. Others say, not so, that the increasing growth of government has stifled the private sector with heavy personal income and corporate profits taxes. In addition, they argue that government policies have been a major cause of inflation. The reply to these criticisms is often "Well, even if there is some truth to that, at least we have not had another Great Depression." Debates over the pros and cons of mixed economies and the appropriateness or folly of government intervention in different areas of the economy are unending. We will encounter these issues again and again throughout this book.

CHECKPOINT 3-3
Explain how the government's power to enforce contracts contributes to the development of markets. Is the postal service a public good or not? Why or why not? Is the military draft a form of government transfer of income or wealth? Why or why not? It appears that sometimes when a government agency isn't working very efficiently, its budget is increased. What happens when a private business doesn't operate very efficiently? In order to eliminate some of our present political system's shortcomings for providing governmentally produced goods and services, it has been suggested that limits should be placed on the number of terms that politicians can remain in office. Explain why you think this might or might not help.

SUMMARY

1. Individuals have different abilities for performing different tasks. Because of this, individuals have an incentive to specialize in production and to trade the surplus of their output in excess of their own need for the other goods they want but don't produce themselves. This incentive stems from the fact that specialization and trade make possible a larger output of goods and services than is possible if each individual tries to be self-sufficient—that is, if there is no specialization and trade.

2. There is an incentive to use money as a medium of exchange because it eliminates the need for the coincidence of wants, which is necessary for trade to take place in a barter economy. Because of this, money promotes specialization and trade and hence makes possible a larger output of goods and services than is possible within the context of a barter system of trade.

3. A firm's costs are all those payments it must make to all resource suppliers in order to bid resources away from use in alternative lines of production of goods. Among the resources used by the firm are financial capital and entrepreneurial skills. When they are being compensated just enough to keep them from leaving and going into some other line of productive activity, we say they are earning a normal profit.

4. Above-normal profits will draw resources to those areas of the economy where they are most in demand. Below-normal profits in one area of the economy will cause entrepreneurial skills and financial capital to move out of that line of productive activity and into those where they can earn their opportunity cost.

5. At minimum in any economy, government typically has basic responsibility for maintaining law and order, providing for the nation's money supply, its national defense, the judicial system, and a uniform standard of time, weight, and measurement. In mixed economies government: reallocates resources in instances where it is felt the market mechanism gives unacceptable or undesirable outcomes; often strives to maintain competitive conditions in markets not naturally conducive to them; redistributes income in accordance with some norm of equity and concern for those who can't work or earn a minimally adequate income; and attempts to maintain economic stability with reasonably full employment of resources.

6. There are several reasons why the government is not a very efficient producer of goods and services. Government bureaucracies have a weak incentive structure due to the difficulty of measuring their output and judging their performance. Politicians often support special interest legislation because it wins them votes from special interest groups without losing the votes of an often ill-informed public. A voting citizen must choose from a limited number of candidates, each representing a particular bundle of goods and services that typically does not accurately match the voter's preferences. Politicians are subject to an incentive structure biased toward the adoption of projects and programs with highly visible immediate benefits and well-hidden costs.

7. Government policies are likely to be effective in preventing another Great Depression. There is less agreement as to how effective government policies are at avoiding the periodic bouts of unemployment associated with post-World War II recessions. Controversy also surrounds the government's intervention in the marketplace, which is sometimes intended to promote competition through antitrust policy and occasionally to rescue large corporations from bankruptcy. There is also ongoing debate about the government's effect on economic growth and inflation.

KEY TERMS AND CONCEPTS

barter economy
coincidence of wants
exclusion principle
nationalized industries
normal profit
public goods
specialization of labor

QUESTIONS AND PROBLEMS

1. We have discussed specialization in terms of its economic advantages. From the laborer's standpoint, what are some of the disadvantages of specialization often heard about in the modern industrialized world?

2. We have noted that it might be possible that someone who has sandals to trade, but no need for chopped wood, might nonetheless accept the chopped wood and trade it for something else. In a situation such as this, where there is a lack of coincidence of wants, do you think the sandal maker would be more, or less, willing to accept strawberries than chopped wood (given that the sandal maker wants neither and must trade them for something he or she does want)? Why? Compared to a situation where there is a coincidence of wants between woodchopper and sandal maker, how do you think the terms of the exchange (the amount of wood needed to purchase a pair of sandals) would be different if the woodchopper wanted sandals but the sandal maker didn't want chopped wood?

3. Elaborate on the following statement: "Profits can, of course, be immoral—if they are exploitive, for example, or result from price-fixing schemes or monopolies. But most profits . . . are an essential and beneficial ingredient in the workings of a free-market economy."

4. Describe the nature of the role of profit that the author of the following statement must have in mind. "Today profits, far from being too high, are still too low to ensure the nation's continued economic health. Among the top 20 industrialized countries, the United States in recent years has fared badly in terms of new industrial investment per capita. . . ."

5. A perhaps overly cynical view of government is that the function of government is to distribute money, that the effectiveness of government is measured by the sums dispensed, and that the worth of politicians is weighted by how much they are able to get the federal government to spend in their districts. It is illegal for a politician to slip a derelict $5 for a vote, but a politician can buy office by legislating billions of dollars. As a result of this situation, a number of critics of Congress claim there is much more government spending than can be justified on objective economic grounds.

One suggested way of dealing with this problem is to require that Congress establish some sort of total spending ceiling at the beginning of each new term.

a. Why might this force members of Congress to make more economic choices?

b. Why might this curb the "you vote for my pet project and I'll vote for yours" type of logrolling among members of Congress? Why is it such logrolling leads to ever higher levels of government spending?

4

Demand, Supply, and Price Determination

AFTER READING THIS CHAPTER, YOU WILL BE ABLE TO:

1. Formulate and explain the law of demand and construct its graphical representation, the demand curve.

2. Enumerate the determinants of demand.

3. Demonstrate the significance of, and recognize the difference between, shifts in the position of a demand curve and movements along a fixed demand curve.

4. Formulate and explain the law of supply and construct its graphical representation, the supply curve.

5. Enumerate the determinants of supply.

6. Show how demand and supply interact to mutually determine equilibrium price and quantity (also called market equilibrium).

7. Demonstrate how changes in the determinants of demand and supply disturb the existing market equilibrium and result in the establishment of a new market equilibrium.

In this chapter we will focus on the laws of demand and supply. We will examine in some detail the notion of the demand curve and the supply curve. And we will consider how demand and supply interact to determine the equilibrium price at which the quantity of a good or resource supplied is just sufficient to satisfy demand for it. We will see how all of this is necessary for a better understanding of how markets work and how prices function to allocate resources.

DEMAND AND DEMAND CURVES

You have already met the notion of demand and its graphical representation, called the demand curve, in Chapter 1. There it was presented as an example of an economic theory or law. Here we want to examine in more detail the law of demand and how the demand curve is determined. We will see how individual demand curves can be combined to give the aggregate demand curve representing the entire market demand for a particular product, resource, or service. Finally, we will examine the very important distinction between shifts in the position of a demand curve and movements along it.

Law of Demand

As we saw in Chapter 1, the **law of demand** is a theory about the relationship between the amount of a good a buyer both desires and is able to purchase per unit of time and the price charged for it. Notice that we emphasize the ability to pay for the good as well as the desire to have it. Your ability to pay is as important as your desire for the good, because in economics we are interested in explaining and predicting actual behavior in the marketplace. Your *unlimited* desires for goods can never be observed in the marketplace because you can't buy more than you are *able* to pay for. At a given price for a good, we are only interested in the buyer's

demand for that good which can effectively be backed by a purchase.

The law of demand hypothesized that the lower the price charged for a product, resource, or service, the larger will be the quantity demanded per unit of time. Conversely, the higher the price charged, the smaller will be the quantity demanded per unit of time—all other things remaining the same. For example, the law of demand predicts that the lower the price of steak, the more steak you will desire and be able to purchase per year—all other things remaining the same. As we noted in Chapter 1, the law of demand is confirmed again and again by observed behavior in the marketplace. Businesses have sales (cut prices), and the amount of goods they sell per period increases. If the price of steak goes up, the amount purchased per unit of time decreases. Why is this? For most goods there are other goods that may be used to satisfy very nearly the same desires. When the price of steak goes up, if the prices of pork chops, lamb chops, and hamburger remain unchanged, then all these kinds of meats are now relatively cheaper compared to steak. Hence, buyers will purchase more of them and less of steak. These kinds of meats are *substitutes* for steak. Although not exactly the same as steak, they are another kind of meat that will do.

Individual Demand

The inverse relationship between the price of a good and the quantity of the good demanded per unit of time can be depicted graphically as we demonstrated in Chapter 1. Suppose we consider an individual's demand for hamburger. Table 4–1 shows the number of pounds of hamburger that the individual will demand per month at each of several different prices. Note that the higher the price, the smaller the quantity demanded per month. Conversely, the lower the price, the greater the quantity that will be demanded per month. Why? Again, because the higher the price of hamburger, the greater the incentive to cut back on consumption of it and

TABLE 4-1 **An Individual's Demand for Hamburger** (Hypothetical Data)

Price per Pound	Quantity Demanded (Number of Pounds per Month)
$5	1.0
4	2.0
3	3.0
2	4.5
1	6.5

price of hamburger rises. Conversely, more hamburger will be demanded when successively lower prices are charged for it because it will become less and less expensive relative to other kinds of meat.

If we plot the price and quantity combinations listed in Table 4–1 on a graph, we obtain the **demand curve** *DD* shown in Figure 4–1. (If you need to brush up on how to plot data on a graph, refer back to pp. 9–10.) Economists almost always represent the demand for a good, resource, or service by use of a demand curve. Verbal descriptions or tabular descriptions such as Table 4–1, while useful, are not typically as readily understood. This is an instance where a picture is worth a thousand words.

eat other kinds of meat instead—assuming their prices and all other things remain the same. *Relative* to hamburger, other kinds of meat simply become cheaper to eat as the

FIGURE 4-1 **An Individual's Demand Curve for Hamburger**

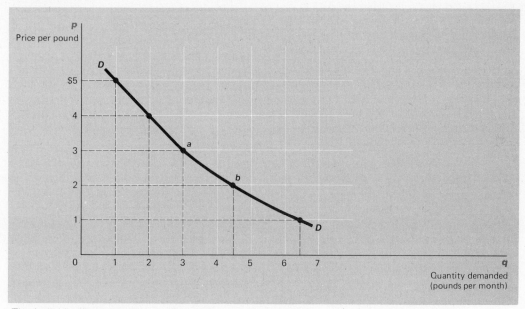

The individual's demand curve for hamburger is plotted here using the data from Table 4–1. It slopes downward from left to right reflecting the inverse relationship between the quantity demanded and the price of the good. It illustrates the law of demand, which says that individuals will demand more of a good the lower is its price. A change in the price of the good causes a change in the quantity demanded, and is represented by a movement along the demand curve. For example, if price changes from $3 per pound to $2 per pound, the quantity demanded increases from 3 to 4.5 pounds per month. This is represented by the movement from *a* to *b* along the demand curve *DD*.

Demand Determinants: The Other Things That Remain the Same

When we draw a demand curve such as that in Figure 4–1, we emphasize the way in which the price charged for a good determines the quantity of it demanded. The price of the good is thereby singled out as the determining factor, and all other things are said to be equal, or remain the same. (If you prefer Latin, you may say *ceteris paribus*.) The important point is that *movement along the demand curve means that only the price of the good and the quantity of it demanded change. All other things are assumed to be constant or unchanged.* What are these other things? They are (1) the prices of all other goods, (2) the individual's income, (3) the individual's expectations about the future, and (4) the individual's tastes. A change in one or more of these other things will change the data in Table 4–1. Therefore the position of the demand curve in Figure 4–1 will be shifted. Such a shift in the demand curve is called a *change in demand*. A movement along a fixed demand curve is referred to as a *change in the quantity demanded*.

Prices of All Other Goods

We may classify all other goods according to their relationship to the good for which the demand curve is drawn, say good X. Other goods are either substitutes for X, complements of X, or basically unrelated to X.

Substitute good: *A good is a substitute for X to the extent that it can satisfy similar needs or desires as X.* Different substitute goods will, of course, vary in the extent to which they satisfy the needs or desires that X does. T-bone steak is a closer substitute for sirloin steak than are lamb chops, although both T-bone steak and lamb chops typically would be regarded as substitutes for sirloin steak. *When the price of a substitute good for good X rises, the demand curve for good X will shift rightward.* This is so because when the price of the substitute *rises*, it becomes cheaper to use X instead of the substitute good.

For example, suppose initially the demand curve for hamburger is DD in Figure 4–2. Now suppose the price of a substitute, chicken, rises. This will cause the individual's demand curve to shift rightward from DD to D_1D_1. This means that at *any* given price of hamburger (measured on the vertical axis of Figure 4–2), the quantity of hamburger demanded (measured on the horizontal axis) will now be larger as a result of the increase in the price of chicken.

The opposite of the above is also true— *when the price of a substitute for good X falls, the demand curve for good X will shift leftward.* This happens because when the price of the substitute *falls*, it becomes relatively more expensive to use X instead of the substitute good. For example, a fall in the price of chicken causes a leftward shift of the demand curve in Figure 4–2, such as from DD to D_2D_2.

Complementary good: *A good is a complement, or complementary good, to good X to the extent it is used jointly with good X.* For example, gasoline and tires are complements to each other. So are football shoes and football helmets, records and phonographs, and salad dressing and lettuce. *When the price of a good that is a complement to good X falls, the demand curve for good X will shift rightward.* This happens because the complementary good is now less expensive to use and therefore more of it will be demanded. More of good X will be demanded as well, because it is used jointly with the complement. For example, a complementary good to hamburger is hamburger buns. If the price of the buns falls, the cost of a hamburger in a bun will be less. This will cause the demand curve DD for hamburger to shift to the right in Figure 4–2—to a position such as D_1D_1 for instance. At *any* given price of hamburger, the quantity of hamburger demanded will be greater.

The opposite is also true. *When the price of a good that is complementary to good X rises, the demand curve for good X will shift leftward.* The complementary good is now more expensive to use and therefore less of it will be demanded. Less of good X will be demanded because, again, it is used jointly with

FIGURE 4-2 **Shifts in an Individual's Demand for Hamburger**

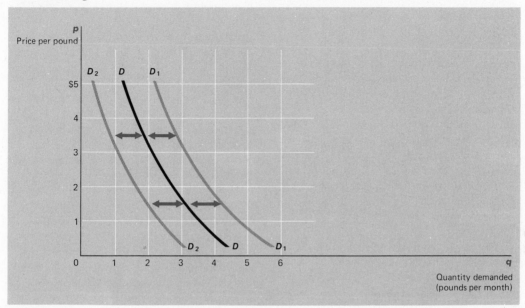

The position of the demand curve is given by the determinants of demand. These are the prices of all other goods, the individual's money income, the individual's expectations about the future, and the individual's tastes. Changes in any of these will cause a change in demand, which is represented by a shift in the demand curve either rightward or leftward. A shift of the demand curve to the right represents an increase in demand. A shift of the demand curve to the left represents a decrease in demand. *Warning:* Do not confuse the concept of a *change in demand*, represented by a shift in the demand curve, with the concept of a *change in the quantity demanded*, represented by movement along a fixed demand curve such as that described by the movement from *a* to *b* in Figure 4–1.

the complement. In Figure 4–2 a rise in the price of hamburger buns will cause *DD* to shift leftward to a position such as D_2D_2.

Finally, some goods are basically *unrelated* to good X in that it would be very difficult to classify them as either substitutes or complements for X. In this sense toothpaste seems basically unrelated to garden clippers, or pears to combs, or tennis balls to ball-point pens.

Income

Another thing assumed equal or constant when we move along an individual's demand curve is the individual's money income.

How does a change in the individual's in-

come affect the individual's demand curve for a particular good? The answer depends on the nature of the good. Basically we may distinguish between two types of goods in this respect: normal goods and inferior goods.

Normal good: A normal good is one that most people typically want more of as their income goes up. Such things as food, clothing, and medical services are examples. *An individual's demand curve for a normal good will shift rightward when the individual's income rises. Conversely, when the individual's income falls, the demand curve will shift leftward.*

Inferior good: An inferior good is one that an individual will want more of at lower income levels than at higher income levels. For example, it has been observed that poor people tend to eat more potatoes and bread than do people in higher income brackets. Evidence suggests that people tend to cut back on their consumption of such foods as their income rises above a certain level. *An individual's demand curve for an inferior good will shift rightward as income rises only at very low levels of income, and then shift leftward as income rises to higher levels.* Conversely, as an individual's income falls, the individual's demand curve for an inferior good will shift rightward until income reaches some low level of income at which point a further fall in income will cause the demand curve to shift leftward.

Suppose the individual in Figure 4–2 is a student and that hamburger is a normal good. If the student's income were to rise as a result of an increase in a scholarship stipend, the student's demand curve for hamburger would rise from DD to D_1D_1.

Expectations

Among the other things assumed equal or constant when we move along an individual's demand curve are the individual's expectations about all things relevant to his or her economic situation. For example, suppose there is suddenly an upward revision of what the individual expects the price of hamburger to be in the future and the individual therefore wants to buy more now to avoid paying a higher price for it later. As a result the demand curve DD shifts rightward to a position such as D_1D_1 in Figure 4–2.

Tastes

Tastes are another thing assumed equal or constant when we move along an individual's demand curve. If a person suddenly develops a sweet tooth, that person's tastes have changed. This will be reflected in a rightward shift in that person's demand curve for candy. Conversely, several painful sessions at the dentist might cause you to lose your taste for candy. In that event your demand curve for candy would shift leftward.

Market Demand: The Sum of Individual Demands

The **market demand curve** for a good is obtained by summing up all the individual demand curves for that good. To illustrate in the simplest possible case, suppose there are only two individuals who have a demand for hamburger. The first individual's demand is that given in Table 4–1. These numbers are repeated in Table 4–2, along with the second individual's demand for hamburger at each of the five prices listed. The market demand, or total demand, for hamburger is the sum of the quantities demanded by each individual at every price. The sums obtained in this way at each of five of these prices are shown in the last column of Table 4–2. Using the data from Table 4–2, we construct the individual demand curves in Figure 4–3, along with the market demand curve, which is the summation of these individual demand curves.

Because market demand curves are the sum of individual demand curves, they are subject to the same determinants and are affected in the same way by changes in those determinants as the individual curves. There is one additional determinant of a market demand curve, however, and that is the number of individual demand curves or buyers that enter into the summation. *An increase in the number of buyers in the market will cause the market demand curve to shift rightward. Conversely, a decrease will cause it to shift leftward.* In sum, the other things that are assumed to remain the same as we move along a market demand curve are (1) prices of all other goods, (2) money income, (3) expectations, (4) tastes, and (5) the number of buyers.

Changes in Quantity Demanded Versus Shifts in Demand

Warning: One of the most common areas of confusion in economics concerns the distinction between movement along a demand curve versus shifts in the position of the demand curve.

Movement along a demand curve represents

TABLE 4-2 The Market Demand for Hamburger:
Two Individual Buyers (Hypothetical Data)

Price per Pound	Quantity Demanded per Month					
	First Individual's Demand (Pounds per Month)		Second Individual's Demand (Pounds per Month)		Total Market Demand (Pounds per Month)	
$5	1.0	+	.5	=	1.5	
4	2.0	+	1.5	=	3.5	
3	3.0	+	2.5	=	5.5	
2	4.5	+	3.5	=	8.0	
1	6.5	+	4.5	=	11.0	

a change in the price of the good under consideration and the associated change in the quantity of the good demanded, and nothing else. All other determinants of demand are assumed to remain the same. For example, when the price of hamburger is changed from $3 to $2 per pound in Figure 4–1, the quantity of hamburger demanded increases from 3 pounds to 4.5 pounds per month. This is represented by the movement from point *a* to point *b* along the demand curve *DD*. By convention, when we simply refer to *a change in the quantity of a good demanded*, we mean *a movement along a fixed demand curve*, such as that from *a* to *b* in Figure 4–1, unless we say otherwise.

In contrast, a change in one or more of the five determinants of demand discussed above will cause the position of the demand curve to change in the manner shown in Figure 4–2. By convention, when we simply refer to a *change in demand* we mean a *shift in the position of the demand curve*, unless we say otherwise. *When the demand curve for a good shifts rightward, more of that good will be demanded at every possible price. When the demand for a good shifts leftward, less of that good will be demanded at every possible price.*

FIGURE 4-3   The Sum of the Individual
Demand Curves Gives the Market Demand Curve

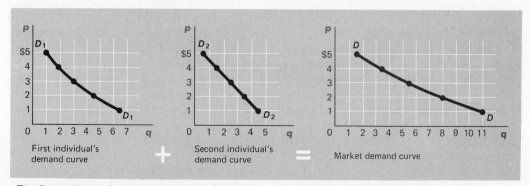

First individual's demand curve   +   Second individual's demand curve   =   Market demand curve

The first individual's demand curve D_1D_1 and the second individual's demand curve D_2D_2 are constructed from their individual demand data in Table 4–2. The market demand curve *DD* is equal to the sum of the individual demand curves and is constructed from the total market demand data in Table 4–2.

A change in demand results from a change in one or more of the five determinants of demand.

CHECKPOINT* 4-1

If the price of peas were to rise, what do you think this would do to the demand curve for lima beans? If the price of pretzels were to fall, what do you think this would do to the demand curve for beer? What would it do to the demand curve for pretzels? Would we say there is a change in the demand for pretzels or a change in the quantity of pretzels demanded? If the price of hamburger buns went up, what do you think this would do to the demand curve for hamburgers?

*Answers to all Checkpoints can be found at the back of the text.

SUPPLY AND SUPPLY CURVES

Given that there are demands for goods, what is the nature of the process that determines how those demands will be met? To answer this question we must have an understanding of the law of supply and the concept of a supply curve and its determinants.

Law of Supply

The law of supply is a statement about the relationship between the amount of a good a supplier is willing and able to supply and offer for sale per unit of time and each of the different possible prices at which that good might be sold. That is, if we said to the supplier, "Suppose the good can be sold at a price of such and such dollars per unit. How many units of the good would you be willing and able to produce and offer for sale per unit of time?" We write down the answer along with the price we quoted to the supplier. Then we repeat the question exactly *except* that now we quote a somewhat higher price. We observe that the higher the price, the larger the quantity the supplier is willing and able to supply for sale per unit of time. And, of course, the lower the price, the smaller the quantity that is offered. This observed relationship is the **law of supply**, which *says that suppliers will supply larger quantities of a good at higher prices than at lower prices.*

The Supply Curve

Suppose the supplier whom we have been questioning produces hamburger. Table 4-3 lists some of the answers that the supplier gave in response to our questions. If we plot the data of Table 4-3 on a graph, we obtain this supplier's supply curve. As in Figure 4-1, we measure the price per unit (a pound) on the vertical axis and the number of units (pounds) on the horizontal axis. The resulting curve SS is shown in Figure 4-4. We have plotted only the five price-quantity combinations. At all the possible prices in between, we presumably could have filled in the whole curve as shown by the solid line connecting the five plotted points. You may view the **supply curve** in different ways. *It indicates the amount of the good the supplier is willing to provide per unit of time at different possible prices.* Or alternatively, you may say *it shows what prices are necessary in order to give the supplier the incentive to provide various quantities of the good per unit of time.*

The shape of the supply curve clearly shows that as the price of the good rises the supplier supplies more of the good; as the price falls the supplier supplies less of the good. Why is this? Just as with a demand curve, *such movement along a supply curve always assumes that all other things will remain the same.* Among other things, the prices of all other resources and goods are assumed to remain the same, including the prices of the inputs used by the supplier. Thus the profit that can be earned from producing a good will almost certainly increase as the price of the good rises. The supplier has a greater incentive to produce more of the good. This is one basic reason why a supply curve slopes upward to the right. An-

TABLE 4-3 An Individual Producer's Supply of Hamburger (Hypothetical Data)

Price per Pound	Quantity Supplied (Number of Pounds per Month)
$5	1,200
4	1,100
3	900
2	600
1	200

other is the fact that beyond some point most production processes run into increasing production costs per unit of output. This is because certain inputs such as plants and equipment cannot be increased in a short period of time. Hence as the producer increases output by using more of the readily variable inputs,

such as labor and materials, fixed plant and equipment capacity causes congestion and bottlenecks. Productive efficiency drops, and the cost of additional units of output rises. Therefore producers must receive a higher price to produce these additional units.

Consider the individual producer's supply curve for hamburger shown in Figure 4-4. Assuming the prices of all other resources and goods are constant, if the price per pound is raised from $1 to $2, it becomes relatively more profitable to produce hamburger. In this instance, the price increase is just sufficient to make it worthwhile to employ the additional resources necessary to increase production from 200 pounds per month to 600 pounds per month. This is indicated by the move from point *a* to point *b* on the supply curve. Similarly, successively

FIGURE 4-4 An Individual Producer's Supply of Hamburger

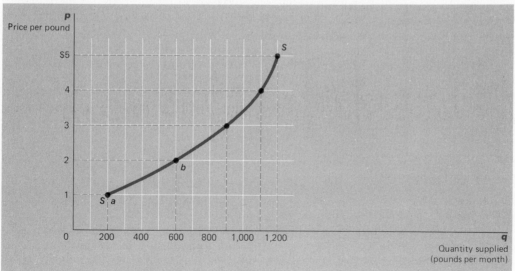

An individual producer's supply curve for hamburger is plotted here using the data from Table 4–3. It slopes upward from left to right reflecting a direct relationship between the quantity of the good supplied and the price of the good. It illustrates the law of supply, which says that suppliers will supply more of a good the higher is its price. A change in the price of the good causes a change in the quantity supplied and is represented by a movement along the supply curve. For example, if price changes from $1 per pound to $2 per pound, the quantity supplied increases from 200 pounds per month to 600 pounds per month. This is represented by the movement from *a* to *b* along the supply curve *SS*.

higher prices make it even more profitable to produce hamburger, and the supply of hamburger will be even larger.

Suppose that there are 100 producers of hamburger, each of whom has a supply curve identical to that of Figure 4–4. At each price per pound listed in Table 4–3, the quantity of hamburger supplied by the sum of all producers is simply 100 times the amount supplied by one producer. Using these data, Figure 4–5 shows the market or industry supply curve SS for hamburger. Note that the units on the horizontal axis of Figure 4–5 are a hundred times larger than those on the horizontal axis of Figure 4–4.

Supply Determinants: The Other Things That Remain the Same

When we draw a supply curve such as SS in Figure 4–5, we emphasize the way in which the price of the good determines the quantity of it supplied. As with a demand curve, the price of the good is singled out as the determining factor and all other things are assumed to be unchanging. These other things are (1) the prices of resources and other factors of production, (2) technology, (3) the prices of other goods, (4) the number of suppliers, and (5) the suppliers' expectations. If one or more of these things change, the supply curve will shift.

1. Prices of Resources

As we saw in Chapter 1, all production processes require inputs of labor services, raw materials, fuels, and other resources and goods. These inputs to a production process are frequently referred to as the **factors of production**. The supplier of a good has to purchase these factors in order to produce the good.

Suppose now that the price of one or more of the factors of production should fall—that is, one or more of the input prices that were assumed to be constant when we drew SS

now changes to a lower level. Hence at each possible price of the good suppliers will find it profitable to produce a larger amount of the good than they were previously willing to supply. The supply curve will therefore shift rightward to a position such as S_1S_1 in Figure 4–5. Conversely, if one or more of the input prices should rise, the cost of production will now be higher and producers will not be willing to supply as much at each possible price of the good. The supply curve will therefore shift leftward to a position such as S_2S_2 in Figure 4–5.

For example, if producers could sell hamburger for $2 a pound, they would be willing to supply 60,000 pounds of hamburger per month. This price-supply combination is represented by point a on the market supply curve SS in Figure 4–5. Suppose that the price of one or more inputs falls so that the market supply curve shifts rightward to S_1S_1. Now a price of $1.50 per pound is sufficient to induce suppliers to produce 60,000 pounds of hamburger per month, as indicated by point d on S_1S_1. Because they are receiving $2 per pound, however, they are encouraged to expand output even more until they have moved up the supply curve S_1S_1 from point d to point b. Here they are producing 80,000 pounds per month. At point b, the price of $2 per pound is just sufficient to induce producers to supply this quantity of hamburger per month.

Alternatively, suppose the price of one or more inputs should rise so that the supply curve shifts leftward from SS to S_2S_2. Now a price of $2.80 per pound is sufficient to induce suppliers to produce 60,000 pounds of hamburger per month, as indicated by point e on S_2S_2. However, if they are receiving only $2 per pound, they will reduce output until they have moved back down the supply curve S_2S_2 from point e to point c, where they will produce 30,000 pounds per month. Once again, at point c the price of $2 per pound is just sufficient to induce suppliers to produce this level of output and no more.

FIGURE 4-5   Shifts in the Market Supply Curve for Hamburger

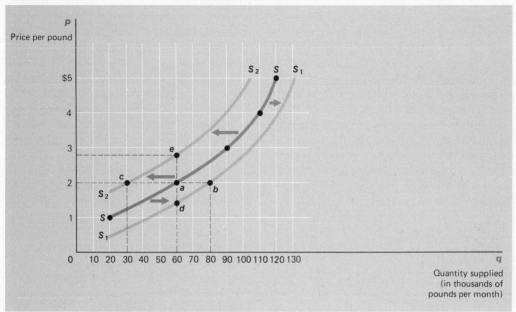

The position of the supply curve is established by the determinants of supply. These are the prices of factors of production, technology, the prices of other goods, the number of suppliers, and the suppliers' expectations about the future. Changes in any of these will cause a change in supply, which is represented by a rightward or leftward shift in the supply curve. A rightward shift represents an increase in supply. A leftward shift represents a decrease in supply. *Warning:* Do not confuse the concept of a *change in supply,* represented by a shift in the supply curve, with the concept of a *change in the quantity supplied,* represented by movement along a fixed supply curve such as that described by the movement from *a* to *b* in Figure 4–4.

2. Prices of Other Goods

Along a fixed supply curve, it is also assumed that the prices of other goods are unchanged. Why do we distinguish between the prices of other goods and the prices of factors of production? The prices of factors of production refer only to the goods used in the production of the good for which the supply curve is drawn. The prices of other goods we now refer to are all the other goods not used in the production of the good for which the supply curve is drawn.

Factors of production are attracted to those production activities where they are paid the highest prices. The higher the price the producer gets for the good produced with those inputs, the greater his or her willingness to pay high prices for those factors. Hence, if the price of milk rises relative to the price of hamburger, farmers will use less of their pastureland for grazing beef cattle in order to make it available for grazing dairy cattle. The opportunity cost of using pasture to produce the beef used in hamburger has effectively risen because the value of that pasture in its alternative use of producing milk has risen. Factors must be paid their opportunity cost if they are to be used in a particular productive activity. That is, the price that must be paid a factor input must be at least as high as what it could earn in an alternative activity. Since the price of pastureland will go up because of its increased value in milk production, the cost of using it in beef production will rise. The supply curve for hamburger will then shift leftward, such as from SS to S_2S_2 in Figure 4-5. To induce hamburger producers to supply any given quantity of hamburger, the price of a pound of hamburger will have to be higher. Why? To cover the increased cost of pastureland, which is now more expensive to use because of its increased value in milk production due to the rise in the price of milk. Again we are reminded that the economic problem is how to allocate scarce resources to alternative uses.

3. Technology

Any production process uses some form of technology, whether it involves tending a rice paddy with a handmade sickle in Southeast Asia or making synthetic fibers in a large plant in Wilmington, Delaware. The term **technology** *refers to the production methods used to combine resources of all kinds, including labor, to produce goods and services.* The history of the human race is in no small way a history of the advancement of technology.

This advancement has been characterized by an increase in the ability of humans to produce goods and services—that is, by an increase in productivity. Often productivity is measured as output produced per labor hour used in the production process. Increases in productivity are then taken to mean increases in output per labor hour. *Because technological advance increases productivity, it lowers the cost of producing goods.* Suppose, for example, that there is a technological advance in the technique used to produce hamburger—such as the development of electric meat grinders. This lowers the cost of producing hamburger. Suppose the position of the supply curve in Figure 4-5 is

at SS before the technological advance. The advance will cause the supply curve to shift rightward to a position such as S_1S_1. At every level of output the price necessary to induce suppliers to produce that output level will now be lower, because costs will be lower.

Circumstances that reduce productivity can arise as well. A drought will reduce the productivity of land and cause crop yields to be less. Such adverse developments essentially require the application of additional production techniques if output levels are to be maintained—the construction of irrigation ditches, for example. But these new techniques add to the cost of production. If the crop were corn, a rise in the cost of production would cause the supply curve for corn to shift leftward.

A news item on rising farm prices might note that "the weather in much of the farm belt was bad for crops this summer." Bad weather tends to decrease the productivity of the land. For example, the grass on pastureland will grow less rapidly, and so fewer cattle can be raised per acre. Since the output per unit of input falls, the cost per head of beef cattle rises. This will raise the cost of producing hamburger, so that the supply curve of hamburger will shift leftward, such as from SS to S_2S_2 in Figure 4-5. The price required to induce hamburger producers to supply any given quantity of hamburger will now be higher.

Remember that whenever we speak of movement along a fixed supply curve, the state of technology is assumed to be unchanged.

4. Number of Suppliers

When we constructed the market or industry supply curve SS in Figure 4-5, we did it by assuming there were a hundred identical individual suppliers, each with a supply curve like that shown in Figure 4-4. Summing the individual supply curves horizontally gave us the market supply curve SS. If there had been more suppliers, the market supply curve would have been further to the right at a position such as S_1S_1. It follows from these observations that when more suppliers enter the industry, the aggregate supply curve will shift to the right. When suppliers leave the industry, it will shift to the left. When we speak of movement along an aggregate supply curve, it is assumed that the number of suppliers does not change.

5. Suppliers' Expectations

This term refers to the expectations suppliers have about anything that they think affects their economic situation. For example, if garment manufacturers expect a strike to stop their production in a few months, they may attempt to supply more now so that stores can build up their inventories to tide them over—the garment industry's supply curve would shift rightward. If suppliers of a good expect its price to be higher in a few months, they may hold back supply now in order to sell it at higher prices later—the industry's supply curve would shift leftward. Changes in expectations can cause the supply curve to shift in either direction depending on the particular situation. However, for any movement along a supply curve, expectations are assumed to remain unchanged.

In sum, the other things that are assumed to remain unchanged when we move along a supply curve are (1) the prices of resources and other factors of production, (2) the prices of other goods, (3) technology, (4) the number of suppliers, and (5) the suppliers' expectations. When one or more of these things change, the supply curve shifts.

Changes in Quantity Supplied Versus Shifts in Supply

Warning: Along with our earlier warning about the demand curve, another common confusion in economics concerns the distinction between movement along a supply curve versus shifts in the supply curve.

Movement along a supply curve represents a change in the price of the good under con-

sideration and the associated change in the quantity of the good supplied. All other things are assumed to be unchanged. By convention, when we simply refer to a *change in the quantity of a good supplied,* we mean a *movement along a fixed supply curve,* such as that from d to b in Figure 4–5, unless we say otherwise.

A change in one or more of the five determinants of supply discussed above will cause the supply curve to shift in the manner shown in Figure 4–5. By contrast, movement along a fixed supply curve always assumes these five things remain unchanged. By convention, when we simply refer to *a change in supply,* we mean *a shift in the position of the supply curve,* unless we say otherwise. *When the supply curve for a good shifts rightward, more of that good will be supplied at every price. When the supply curve shifts leftward, less of that good will be supplied at every price. A change in supply results from a change in one or more of the five determinants of supply.*

CHECKPOINT 4-2
If wages go up, what effect will this have on the supply curve *SS* in Figure 4–5? If someone develops an improved process for fattening cattle to be used to make hamburger, what effect will this have on the supply curve *SS* in Figure 4–5? Suppose the price of lamb were to rise. Would we refer to the effect of this on *SS* in Figure 4–5 as a "change in the supply" or a "change in the quantity supplied" of hamburger? Explain the economic process by which farmland used to produce corn becomes converted into factory property for the production of CB radios.

MARKET EQUILIBRIUM: INTERACTION OF SUPPLY AND DEMAND

As any armchair economist knows, supply and demand are what economics is all about.

Like the blades of a scissors, supply and demand interact to determine the terms of trade between buyers and sellers. That is, supply and demand mutually determine the price at which sellers are willing to supply just the amount of a good that buyers want to buy. The market for every good has a demand curve and a supply curve that determine this price and quantity. When this price and quantity are established, the market is said to be in equilibrium. In equilibrium there is no tendency for price and quantity to change.

Equilibrium Price and Quantity

In order to see how equilibrium price and quantity are determined in a market, consider again our hypothetical example of the market demand and supply for hamburger. Table 4–4 contains the market supply data (usually called the market **supply schedule**) on which the market supply curve *SS* of Figure 4–5 is based. It also contains the market demand data (usually called the market **demand schedule**) that determine the market demand curve for hamburger. In this case, the market demand schedule has been obtained by supposing that there are 20,000 individual buyers in the market. Each of these buyers is assumed to have an individual demand schedule like that given in Table 4–1.

(That table contained the data for the individual demand curve of Figure 4–1.) The market quantity demand data of Table 4–4 thus equals 20,000 times the individual quantity demand data given in Table 4–1.

Market Adjustment When Price Is Above the Equilibrium Price

Observe in Table 4–4 that at a price of $5 per pound suppliers would supply the market 120,000 pounds of hamburger per month (column 2). Buyers, however, would only demand 20,000 pounds per month (column 3). At this price, there is an excess of supply over demand, or a *surplus* of 100,000 pounds of hamburger (column 4). A price of $5 per pound serves as a relatively strong incentive to suppliers on the one hand, and a relatively high barrier to buyers on the other. If suppliers should produce the 120,000 pounds, they will find they can sell only 20,000. They will be stuck with 100,000 pounds. This surplus will serve notice to suppliers that $5 per pound is too high a price to charge. They will realize that the price must be lowered if they want to sell more hamburger (column 5), as the law of demand would predict. If they continue to produce 120,000 pounds per month in the belief that they can sell that much for $5 per pound, unwanted invento-

TABLE 4-4 **Market Supply and Demand for Hamburger** (Hypothetical Data)

(1)	(2)	−	(3)	=	(4)	(5)
Price per Pound	Total Number of Pounds Supplied per Month		Total Number of Pounds Demanded per Month		Surplus (+) or Shortage (−)	Price Change Required to Establish Equilibrium
$5.00	120,000	−	20,000	=	+100,000	decrease
4.00	110,000	−	40,000	=	+ 70,000	decrease
3.00	90,000	−	60,000	=	+ 30,000	decrease
2.50	78,000	−	78,000	=	0	no change
2.00	60,000	−	90,000	=	− 30,000	increase
1.00	20,000	−	130,000	=	−110,000	increase

ries will grow due to the continuing surplus. Competition among suppliers will cause the price to be bid down as each tries to underprice the others in order to sell their individual surpluses.

As a result of suppliers' attempts to correct this undesirable situation through competitive price cutting, the price eventually falls to $4 per pound. Now suppliers will produce a lower total quantity of hamburger, 110,000 pounds per month (column 2), and buyers will increase quantity demanded to 40,000 pounds per month (column 3). At this price, the quantity supplied will still exceed the quantity demanded, however. Though smaller, the surplus amounts to 70,000 pounds of hamburger per month (column 4). Again, if suppliers continue to produce 110,000 pounds per month in the belief that they can sell that much for $4 per pound, unwanted inventories will continue to grow due to the continuing surplus. This situation will cause individual suppliers to continue to try to underprice one another in their competitive attempts to get rid of their individual surpluses. The price in the market will therefore continue to fall (column 5).

At $3 per pound, the quantity supplied will still exceed the quantity demanded, but the surplus that cannot be sold will have fallen to 30,000 pounds of hamburger (column 4). Nonetheless, this will still signal that price must fall further (column 5). Only when price has been reduced to $2.50 per pound by the competition among suppliers will they be induced to produce and supply a quantity that is just equal to the quantity that will be demanded at that price, 78,000 pounds per month (columns 2 and 3). No unsold surplus will be produced (column 4), and there will be no incentive to change price any further (column 5). Market equilibrium will prevail. **Market equilibrium** *is established at the price where the quantity of the good buyers demand and purchase is just equal to the quantity suppliers supply and sell. The price and quantity at which this occurs are called the* **equilibrium price** *and* **equilibrium quantity**. In equilibrium the forces of

supply and demand are in balance. Price and quantity will have no tendency to change. They are at rest.

The process just described and the equilibrium achieved are readily visualized with the aid of a market demand curve and a market supply curve. Using the supply and demand schedule data given in Table 4–4, the market supply curve and demand curve for hamburger are constructed in Figure 4–6. This is done in exactly the same manner used to obtain the demand and supply curves drawn in the previous figures in this chapter. Indeed the supply curve *SS* in Figure 4–6 is the same one shown in Figure 4–5 as *SS*. Both the quantity demanded and the quantity supplied are measured on the horizontal axis in Figure 4–6. Equilibrium occurs at the point where the market demand and supply curves intersect. The equilibrium point corresponds to the equilibrium price of $2.50 and the equilibrium quantity of 78,000 pounds of hamburger bought and sold per month. It is readily apparent from the diagram that at prices above $2.50 supply exceeds demand. Competition among suppliers attempting to underprice one another in order to get rid of their surpluses will cause the price to be bid down. This price cutting will cease when the equilibrium price is reached—the price at which quantity demanded equals quantity supplied.

Market Adjustment When Price Is Below the Equilibrium Price

Suppose that we consider an initial price below the equilibrium price, say $1 per pound. The situation in the market for hamburger is now reversed. The price inducement for suppliers to produce hamburger is relatively low, and so they produce relatively little. Because the price barrier to buyers is relatively low, the quantity demanded is relatively high. From Table 4–4 the total quantity supplied is 20,000 pounds per month (column 2), while the total quantity demanded is 130,000 pounds per month (column 3).

FIGURE 4-6 The Market Demand and Supply Determine the Equilibrium Price and Quantity for Hamburger

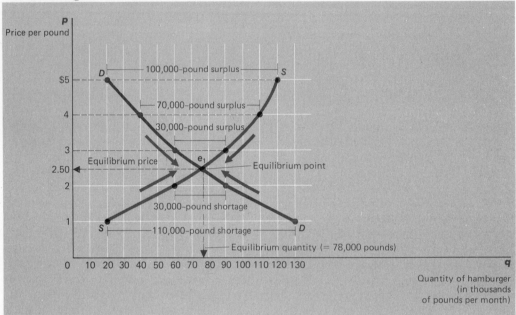

The determination of the equilibrium price and quantity is indicated by the intersection of the market demand curve DD and the market supply curve SS at e_1. The equilibrium price is $2.50 per pound and the equilibrium quantity is 78,000 pounds. At prices above the equilibrium price, there will be surpluses as indicated. These surpluses will cause a competitive bidding down of price, thereby reducing the quantity supplied and increasing the quantity demanded until they are equal and equilibrium is achieved. At prices below the equilibrium price, there will be shortages as indicated. These shortages will cause a competitive bidding up of price, thereby increasing the quantity supplied and decreasing the quantity demanded until they are equal and equilibrium is achieved.

Hence there is now an excess demand for hamburger. Buyers cannot purchase as much as they want at this price. The shortage amounts to 110,000 pounds (column 4).

There is not enough hamburger "to go around" at $1 per pound. Buyers begin to bid up price (column 5) as they compete with one another by letting suppliers know they are willing to pay more to get the inadequate supply increased. As the price of hamburger is bid up, suppliers are encouraged to devote more resources to the production of hamburger, in accordance with the law of supply.

At the same time, as price rises, buyers will begin to reduce the quantity of hamburger that they demand, in accordance with the law of demand. When price has risen to $2 per pound, suppliers will be encouraged to increase production to 60,000 pounds per month (column 2). The quantity demanded will be reduced to 90,000 pounds per month (column 3). The quantity demanded still exceeds the quantity supplied, but the shortage has been reduced considerably—to 30,000 pounds (column 4). Nonetheless, there is still a shortage. Buyers will continue to bid price up (column 5) as they compete with one another for a supply of output inadequate to satisfy demand. Only when price has been bid up to $2.50 per pound will the quantity demanded be equal to the quantity supplied—78,000 pounds per month (columns 2 and 3). Market equilibrium will prevail. The shortage has been eliminated. All buyers who demand hamburger at $2.50 per pound will be able to get it. All suppliers who are willing to supply it at $2.50 per pound will find they can sell exactly the quantity they desire to supply. There will be no further incentive for price to be changed.

This process of adjustment to equilibrium is illustrated in Figure 4–6. At prices below $2.50 per pound, quantity demanded clearly exceeds quantity supplied and a shortage will exist. Competitive bidding by buyers attempting to secure some of the inadequate supply will cause price to rise. As price rises suppliers are induced to buy more inputs and produce more hamburger. The quantity demanded, on the other hand, will fall as buyers are increasingly discouraged from purchasing hamburger as the price rises. Again, this process will eventually lead to the equilibrium point where the demand and supply curves intersect to determine the equilibrium price and quantity.

The Nature of Market Equilibrium

Whether price is initially above or below the equilibrium level, market forces operate to cause adjustment to the same equilibrium point. If the process starts from above the equilibrium price level, we may envision buyers moving down the demand curve DD and suppliers moving down the supply curve SS as adjustment takes place. If the process starts from below the equilibrium price level, buyers move up DD and suppliers up SS. There is only one price at which the quantity supplied is equal to the quantity demanded. At that price every buyer will be able to buy exactly the quantity each demands, and every supplier will be able to sell exactly the quantity each desires to supply. *At the equilibrium*

price the demand intentions of buyers are consistent with the supply intentions of suppliers. When these intentions are actually carried out in the form of buyers' bids to purchase and suppliers' offers to sell, they mesh perfectly. *In equilibrium, the decisions of buyers are not frustrated by shortages and the decisions of sellers are not frustrated by surpluses.* Since shortages lead to price rises and surpluses to price reductions, *the absence of shortage or surplus will mean price will neither rise nor fall.* The market is in equilibrium.

Changes in Supply and Demand

Suppose the market for hamburger is initially in the equilibrium position depicted by the intersection of the demand and supply curves shown in Figure 4–6. These curves are reproduced as DD and SS in Figure 4–7. We know from our discussion of the determinants of supply and demand that any change in one or more of these determinants will cause either the supply curve or the demand curve or both to shift. Such a shift will undo the existing market equilibrium at e_1 and establish a new equilibrium position in the market.

A Change in Demand

Consider first the effect of an expected decrease in beef supplies. Such an expectation would very likely cause people to change their expectations about the future price and availability of hamburger. In particular, people are now likely to expect that the future price of hamburger will be higher. Therefore, they will want to buy more hamburger now and "stock up" on it in order to avoid paying a higher price for it later. Hence the market demand curve for hamburger will shift rightward to D_1D_1 as shown in Figure 4–7. At every possible price the quantity demanded is now larger.

In particular, at the initial equilibrium price of $2.50 per pound the quantity demanded will increase from 78,000 to 120,000 pounds per month. At this price the quantity

FIGURE 4-7 An Increase in Demand for Hamburger

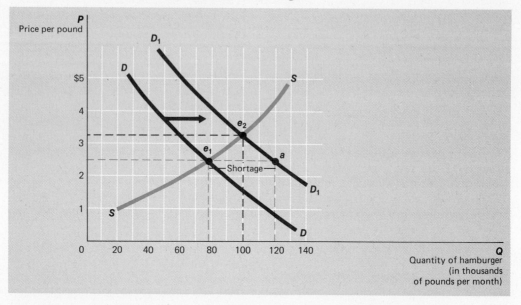

The market is initially in equilibrium where market demand curve *DD* intersects market supply curve *SS* at e_1. At this point, the equilibrium price is $2.50 per pound and the equilibrium quantity is 78,000 pounds. The increase in demand is indicated by the rightward shift of the market demand curve from *DD* to D_1D_1. This initially gives rise to the shortage of 42,000 pounds indicated. Competitive bidding among frustrated buyers pushes the price up until market equilibrium is established at e_2. The new equilibrium price is $3.30 per pound and the new equilibrium quantity is 100,000 pounds.

demanded will now exceed the quantity suppliers are willing to provide. Specifically, there is now a shortage amounting to 42,000 pounds of hamburger. This shortage is the difference between point *a* on D_1D_1 and the initial equilibrium point e_1 on the supply curve *SS* in Figure 4–7. As a result of this shortage, buyers will tell sellers they are willing to pay a higher price for hamburger in order to get some. When price is eventually bid up high enough, equilibrium will once again be established. Now equilibrium is found at point e_2 where the demand curve D_1D_1 intersects the supply curve *SS*. The new equilibrium price is $3.30 per pound, and the new equilibrium quantity bought and sold is 100,000 pounds per month. Hence *an*

increase in demand, represented by a rightward shift in the demand curve, will increase both price and quantity assuming other things remain the same. (Supply is one of the things that remain unchanged, as represented by the unchanged position of the supply curve.)

It is interesting to note that the expectation of an increase in the price of hamburger is in fact sufficient to cause an actual price increase. Eventually price rises enough to ration or cut back the quantity demanded (a movement from *a* to e_2 along D_1D_1) while at the same time causing an increase in the quantity supplied (a movement from e_1 to e_2 along *SS*). This increase in quantity supplied is sufficient to restore equilibrium in the market and eliminate the shortage.

A Change in Supply

For the moment set aside the effect of a change in expectations on the market. In our discussion of the determinants of the supply curve, we noted that adverse weather conditions cause the supply curve to shift leftward. In addition, we know from our earlier discussions that increases in the prices of inputs will also cause the supply curve to shift leftward. Again consider the initial equilibrium as shown in Figure 4–8. (The demand curve *DD* and the supply curve *SS* are in exactly the same position as *DD* and *SS* in Figure 4–7.) Suppose both the onset of bad weather and a rise in farmers' costs conspire to reduce

supply or shift the market supply curve leftward from *SS* to S_1S_1. At every possible price, suppliers will now reduce the quantity of hamburger they are willing to supply. In particular, at the initial equilibrium price of $2.50 per pound, they are now only willing to supply 50,000 pounds of hamburger per month. At this price buyers will continue to demand 78,000 pounds per month, however. The quantity demanded therefore exceeds the quantity supplied and there is now a shortage amounting to 28,000 pounds, represented by the distance between points *b* and e_1. Again this causes the price to be bid up. When the price reaches $3 per pound, the quantity demanded will again equal the

FIGURE 4-8   A Decrease in the Supply of Hamburger

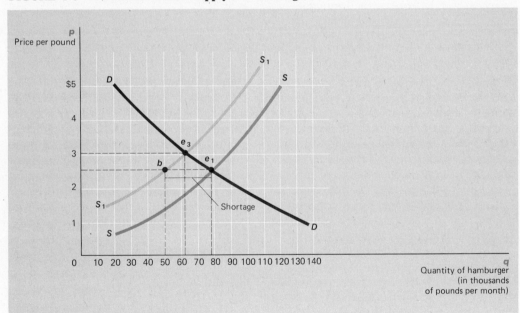

The market is initially in equilibrium where market demand curve *DD* intersects market supply curve *SS* at e_1. This gives an equilibrium price of $2.50 per pound and an equilibrium quantity of 78,000 pounds. The decrease in supply is indicated by the leftward shift of the market supply curve from *SS* to S_1S_1. This initially gives rise to the indicated shortage of 28,000 pounds, represented by the distance between points *b* and e_1. Competitive bidding among frustrated buyers pushes the price up until market equilibrium is established at e_3. The new equilibrium price is $3 per pound, and the new equilibrium quantity is 62,000 pounds per month.

quantity supplied. Equilibrium in the market will once more be restored. The equilibrium point is now at the intersection of DD and S_1S_1 indicated by e_3. At the new equilibrium price of $3 per pound, the equilibrium quantity bought and sold is 62,000 pounds per month. Hence *a decrease in supply, represented by a leftward shift in the supply curve, will increase price and decrease quantity assuming other things remain the same.* (Demand is one of the things that remain the same, as represented by the unchanged position of the demand curve.)

Both Supply and Demand Change

Suppose that in fact the expectations affecting hamburger demand and the events affecting hamburger supply have all occurred at about the same time. To analyze the consequences for the market for hamburger we must consider the rightward shift in the demand curve of Figure 4–7 together with the leftward shift in the supply curve of Figure 4–8. This combination of shifts is shown in Figure 4–9. Again the market supply curve SS and the market demand curve DD are the same as shown in Figures 4–7 and 4–8, and the initial equilibrium point determined by their intersection is again shown as e_1. The rightward shift in the demand curve from DD to D_1D_1 caused by the changed expectations is exactly the same as that shown in Figure 4–7. The leftward shift in the supply curve from SS to S_1S_1 caused by the bad weather and rising farmers' costs is exactly the same as that shown in Figure 4–8. At the initial equilibrium price of $2.50 per pound, the quantity demanded increases from 78,000 to 120,000 pounds per month. At the same time, the quantity suppliers are willing to supply falls from 78,000 to 50,000 pounds per month. The shortage now is equal to the sum of the shortages shown in Figures 4–7 and 4–8. Specifically, there is now a shortage amounting to 70,000 pounds of hamburger, the difference between point a on D_1D_1 and point b on S_1S_1. To restore equilibrium, price will have to be bid up until the quantity of hamburger demanded once again equals the quantity suppliers are willing to provide. This occurs where the demand curve D_1D_1 intersects the supply curve S_1S_1 at e_4. The new equilibrium price is $3.80 per pound, and the equilibrium quantity bought and sold is now 80,000 pounds of hamburger per month.

Note that when the leftward shift of the supply curve is considered together with the rightward shift of the demand curve in Figure 4–9, the resulting rise in price is greater than when either shift is considered alone, as in Figures 4–7 and 4–8. This is readily apparent from Figure 4–9. When only the demand shift was considered, the new equilibrium point was e_2. When just the supply shift was considered, the new equilibrium point was e_3. When the effect of both shifts is considered, the new equilibrium point is e_4, which occurs at a higher price than at either e_2 or e_3.

In general, when demand increases and supply decreases, as in Figure 4–9, it is possible for the new equilibrium quantity bought and sold to be either larger or smaller than that of the initial equilibrium position. Whether it is larger or smaller depends on the relative size of the shifts in the two curves. In the hypothetical example of Figure 4–9, the relative sizes of these shifts are such that the new equilibrium quantity associated with e_4 is slightly larger than the initial equilibrium quantity associated with e_1. If the leftward shift of the supply curve had been somewhat larger, or the rightward shift of the demand curve somewhat smaller, or both, the new equilibrium quantity might have been somewhat less than the initial equilibrium quantity.

CHECKPOINT 4-3

If the price of hot dogs should fall, what do you predict would happen to the equilibrium price and quantity of hamburger? If the price of hamburger buns falls and the wage rate that producers of hamburger must pay labor also falls, what do you predict would happen to the equilibrium price

**FIGURE 4-9   Combined Effects of an Increase
in Demand and a Decrease in Supply for Hamburger**

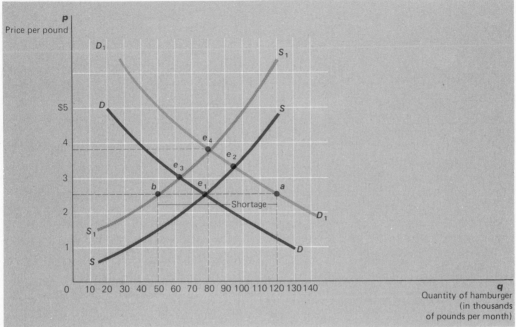

The combined effects of the increase in demand in Figure 4–7 and the decrease in supply in Figure 4–8 are shown here. Starting from the initial equilibrium determined by the intersection of *DD* and *SS* at e_1, the market demand curve shifts rightward to D_1D_1 while the market supply curve shifts leftward to S_1S_1. The initial shortage amounts to 70,000 pounds, the sum of the initial shortages indicated in Figures 4–7 and 4–8. Competitive bidding among frustrated buyers pushes the price up until market equilibrium is established at e_4. At that point, the new equilibrium price is $3.80 per pound, and the new equilibrium quantity is 80,000 pounds per month. Notice that the new equilibrium price is higher than that established when either the increase in demand or decrease in supply is considered separately, as in Figures 4–7 and 4–8. The new equilibrium quantity is larger given the relative sizes of the demand and supply curve shifts shown here. Had the leftward shift of the supply curve been larger or the rightward shift of the demand curve been smaller, or both, the new equilibrium quantity could have been smaller than the initial equilibrium quantity at e_1.

and quantity of hamburger? If the price of electricity rises and the rent rate for office space used by the producers of hamburger also rises, what do you predict would happen to the equilibrium price and quantity of hamburger? If someone told you that the price of hamburger had risen but gave you no other information, what would you be able to say about the quantity of it bought and sold? If you were told that the price of shoes had increased and the quantity bought and sold had decreased, what would you make of a newspaper story that claimed consumers' income was increasing? (*Hint:* What do you think an increase in consumers' income would do to shoe demand?)

POLICY PERSPECTIVE

Math and Science Teachers in Short Supply

In recent years over 40 states have reported shortages of math and physics teachers. Moreover, a survey by the National Science Teachers Association revealed that about a quarter of math and science teachers surveyed said they were planning to leave teaching for better paying jobs in industry. The shortage is aggravated by teachers unions' traditional opposition to pay differentials among teachers who teach different subjects.

The problem can be illustrated in terms of the hypothetical demand and supply curves for math teachers shown in Figure P4–1. Suppose teachers' unions prohibit schools from paying math teachers more than $20,000 per year. This annual wage (vertical axis) corresponds to point *a* on the demand curve *D* for math teachers. At point *a* schools demand the annual services of 2 million math teachers (horizontal axis). However only 1 million math teachers are willing to work for the schools at this wage, corresponding to

point *b* on the supply curve *S*. The shortage of math teachers equals the difference between points *a* and *b*, so that at an annual wage of $20,000 a million more math teachers are demanded than are supplied. If the union prohibition against paying math teachers a higher wage were lifted, schools would bid the wage of math teachers up to $30,000 corresponding to the intersection of the demand and supply curves at point *c*. Here the number of math teachers willing to teach, 1.5 million, would just equal the number schools want to hire. The shortage would be eliminated.

Why is it necessary to pay math and science teachers more than other teachers? Because those with math and science training can work for higher wages in other sectors of the economy. If schools want to eliminate the shortage of math and science teachers they will have to change their wage policies to recognize that in the marketplace society places different values on different kinds of labor skills, just as it places different values on different kinds of goods.

Questions

1. What is true of the opportunity cost of math and science teachers relative to the opportunity cost of other kinds of teachers?

2. How would an increase in scholarship aid to college students majoring in math and science affect Figure P4–1?

FIGURE P4-1   Demand and Supply for Math Teachers

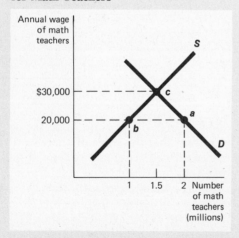

POLICY PERSPECTIVE

Energy Consumption and the Price of Energy— Adjusting to Energy Shocks

Throughout the 1950s and 1960s, the price of energy increased less rapidly than the prices of most other goods. This means that the *real* price of energy—its price in terms of other goods—was gradually falling. This pattern continued into the early 1970s. The falling real price of energy encouraged people to use more of it, as the law of demand would predict. Consumers bought ever more powerful gas-guzzling cars, and the per capita consumption of gasoline rose year after year. Electrical appliances were used increasingly to do household chores previously done by hand. Homes were heated to higher temperatures in winter and cooled to lower temperatures in summer. Natural

gas was so cheap that oil producers often burned it as a nuisance by-product of oil production.

The Era of Cheap Energy

The decline in the real price of energy and the rise in U.S. energy consumption from 1960 to 1973 can be explained in terms of changes in the demand and supply for energy, as illustrated in Figure P4-2, part a. The demand curve for energy was shifted rightward by increasing population and economic growth between 1960 and 1973. But over this period the supply curve for energy was shifted rightward an even greater amount by oil and natural gas discoveries, improved oil-

FIGURE P4-2 **Interaction of the Demand and Supply for Energy**

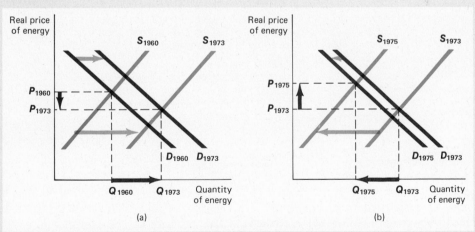

From 1960 to 1973 the demand curve for energy shifted rightward, but by a smaller amount than the rightward shift in the supply curve (part a). Consequently, the real price of energy fell while the quantity consumed increased.

From 1973 to 1975 the demand curve for energy shifted leftward, but by a smaller amount than the leftward shift in the supply curve (part b). Therefore, the real price of energy increased while the quantity consumed decreased.

FIGURE P4-3   Energy Consumption and the Real Price of Energy

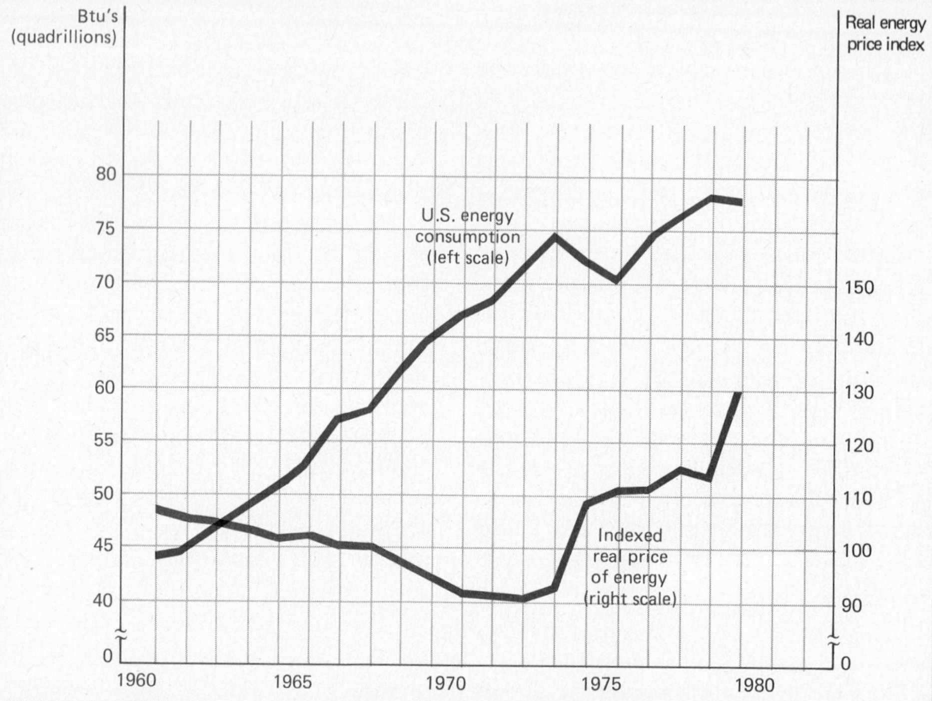

The gradual decline in the real price of energy until 1973 encouraged the steady increase in U.S. energy consumption. The Arab oil embargo of 1973 caused a sharp rise in the real price of energy, which led to a decline in energy consumption from 1973 through 1975. A similar episode, caused by the Iranian revolution in 1979, halted a similar, later rise in U.S. energy consumption.

SOURCE: U.S. Department of Labor, Bureau of Labor Statistics; U.S. Energy Information Administration, *Annual Report to Congress,* Vol. II.
[a] The real price of energy is a composite real price index that includes the prices of fuel oil, coal, bottled gas, piped natural gas, electricity, gasoline, motor oil, coolant, and so on.

drilling and natural gas pipeline technology, and increased efficiency in electric power generation. As a result the real price of energy fell from P_{1960} to P_{1973}, and the quantity consumed increased from Q_{1960} to Q_{1973} in Figure P4–2, part a.

The Arab Oil Embargo

The Arab oil embargo of 1973 abruptly reversed the downward trend in energy

prices. The real price of energy rose about 22 percent between 1973 and 1975, and energy consumption fell a bit more than 5 percent, as can be seen from Figure P4–3. This behavior can be explained in terms of the changes in demand and supply shown in Figure P4–2, part b. The demand curve for energy was shifted leftward during this period as the economy experienced the most severe recession since World War II. But the Arab oil embargo caused the supply curve to shift leftward by an even greater amount. The net result was that the quantity of energy consumed fell from Q_{1973} to Q_{1975} while the real price of energy rose from P_{1973} to P_{1975} in Figure P4-2, part b.

The Iranian Revolution

From 1975 to 1978 the real price of energy rose only slightly (somewhat more than 3 percent), and U.S. energy consumption resumed its upward climb. However, consumption did not regain its 1973 level until 1976 (Figure P4-3). The Iranian revolution of 1979 abruptly interrupted world oil supplies once again. The real price of energy rose sharply (by about 12 percent) and again the upward climb in U.S. energy consumption ceased (Figure P4-3).

In sum, *experience shows the extent to which U.S. energy consumption is sensitive to the real price of energy*. The rise in the real price of energy has encouraged energy conservation—fuel-efficient cars, better-insulated houses, reuse (rather than dumping) of process heat by industry, and increased energy efficiency in appliances and heating and air-conditioning systems. It has also made feasible the development of alternative, but previously prohibitively expensive, sources of energy.

Questions

1. What could you say about the change in the price of energy and the quantity of energy bought and sold if a major oil discovery occurred at the same time as a breakthrough in solar heating technology?

2. Similarly, what could you say about the change in price and quantity of energy if there were a severe winter coupled with another oil embargo?

SUMMARY

1. The law of demand asserts that the lower (higher) the price charged for a good, the larger (smaller) will be the quantity demanded—all other things remaining the same. This law may be represented graphically by a demand curve that slopes downward left to right on a graph with price measured on the vertical axis and quantity measured on the horizontal. Any point on a demand curve tells us the quantity of a good buyers desire to purchase per some specified unit of time at the price associated with that point.

2. In addition to the price of the good for which the market demand curve is drawn, the other determinants of market demand are (1) the prices of all other goods, (2) money income, (3) expectations, (4) tastes, and (5) the number of buyers in the market. A change in one or more of these determinants will cause the market demand curve to shift either rightward (an increase in demand) or leftward (a decrease in demand). A shift in the demand curve is referred to as a change in demand. It is to be distinguished from a change in the quantity demanded, which refers to a movement along a fixed demand curve. The latter can only occur because of a change in the price of the good for which the demand curve is drawn.

3. The law of supply asserts that suppliers will supply larger quantities of a good at higher prices for that good than at lower prices—all other things remaining the same. This law may be represented graphically by a supply curve that slopes upward left to right on a graph with price measured on the vertical axis and quantity measured on the horizontal axis. Any point on a supply curve tells us the quantity of a good suppliers are willing to produce and desire to sell per some specified unit of time at the price associated with that point.

4. Along with the price of the good for which the supply curve is drawn, the other determinants of supply are (1) the prices of resources and other factors of production, (2) the prices of other goods, (3) technology, (4) the number of suppliers, and (5) the suppliers' expectations. A change in any of these determinants will cause the supply curve to shift either rightward (an increase in supply) or leftward (a decrease in supply). Such a change is called a change in supply. It is to be distinguished from a change in the quantity supplied, which is a movement along a fixed supply curve due to a change in the price of the good for which the supply curve is drawn.

5. Supply and demand interact to adjust price until that price is found where the quantity of the good demanded is just equal to the quantity supplied. This is the equilibrium price and quantity, which is determined by the intersection of the supply and demand curves. When this point of intersection is established, we have market equilibrium.

6. Changes in supply and demand, represented by shifts in the supply and demand curves, will upset equilibrium and cause either shortages or surpluses. This will set in motion competitive price bidding among buyers and sellers that will ultimately restore market equilibrium, most typically at new levels of equilibrium price and quantity.

7. An increase (decrease) in demand will lead to an increase (decrease) in equilibrium price and quantity—other things remaining the same. An increase (decrease) in supply will lead to a decrease (increase) in equilibrium price and an increase (decrease) in equilibrium quantity—other things remaining the same. When both supply and demand change, the effect on equilibrium price and quantity depends on the particular case.

KEY TERMS AND CONCEPTS

complementary good
demand curve
demand schedule
equilibrium price
equilibrium quantity
factors of production
inferior good
law of demand
law of supply
market demand curve
market equilibrium
normal good
substitute good
supply curve
supply schedule
technology

QUESTIONS AND PROBLEMS

1. Classify each of the following goods according to whether *in your opinion* it is a normal (essential) or inferior good: shoes, beer, leather gloves, life insurance, auto insurance, stereo equipment, pet dog, four-ply tires.

2. Classify each of the following pairs of goods according to whether you think they are substitutes, complements, or basically unrelated to each other: ham and eggs, meat and potatoes, Fords and Chevrolets, ice skates and swimsuits, coffee and tea, butter and margarine, apples and oranges, knives and forks, saltshakers and hats.

3. Suppose today's weather forecast states that chances are 9 out of 10 there will be rain all during the coming week. What effect do you think this will have on the demand curve for each of the following: umbrellas, baseball tickets, electricity, taxi rides, parking space in shopping centers, camping equipment, books, and aspirin?

4. What do you predict would happen to the market demand curve for oranges in the United States as a result of the following:

a. a rise in average income;

b. an increase in the birthrate;

c. an intensive advertising campaign that convinces most people of the importance of a daily quota of natural vitamin C;

d. a fall in the price of orange juice;

e. a fall in the price of grapefruit juice?

5. What will happen to the supply of cars if each of the following should occur? Explain your answers.

a. an increase in the price of trucks;

b. a fall in the price of steel;

c. introduction of a better assembly-line technique;

d. an increase in the desire of auto manufacturers to be highly esteemed by the nation rather than to earn as much money as possible;

e. an increase in the price of cars?

6. If goods are expensive because they are scarce, why aren't rotten eggs high priced?

7. What will be the effect on the supply curve of hogs of a fall in the price of corn? What will be the effect on the supply curve of corn of a fall in the price of hogs?

8. What effect do you think an advertising campaign for coffee would have on each of the following—other things remaining the same: the price of coffee, the price of tea, the quantity of sugar bought and sold, the price of doughnuts, the quantity of sleeping pills bought and sold, the price of television advertising time on the late show?

9. Suppose you read in the paper that the price of gasoline is rising along with increased sales of gasoline. Does this contradict the law of demand or not? Explain.

10. Suppose there is a strike in the steel industry. Other things remaining the same, what do you predict will happen to the price of steel, the price of automobiles, the quantity sold and the price of aluminum, the price of aluminum wire, the price and quantity of copper wire sold, and the price of electricity? At each step of this chain spell out your answer in terms of the relevant shift in a demand or supply curve. What do you think of the characterization of the economy as a chain of interconnected markets?

11. Suppose we were to look at some industry data on the buggy whip industry collected at about the time the automobile industry was rapidly moving out of its infancy. What would you make of the finding that many buggy whip manufacturers were getting out of the business, yet the price of buggy whips was not falling? Demonstrate your analysis diagrammatically.

12. During the energy crisis of late 1973 and early 1974 it was not uncommon to see automobiles lined up for blocks waiting to buy gas.

a. Demonstrate diagrammatically what happened in the gasoline market when the energy crisis hit.

b. Given the long lines of cars observed waiting to buy gas, do you think the equilibrium price of gas was established at that time?

c. If gasoline prices haven't risen that dramatically since early 1974, what would explain the disappearance of the lines of waiting motorists at gasoline stations since that time?

TWO

The Price System and the Organization of Economic Activity

5

Elasticity of Demand and Supply and Further Topics in Demand Theory

AFTER READING THIS CHAPTER, YOU WILL BE ABLE TO:

1. Define the concept of elasticity and show how it is measured.

2. Explain the relationship between total revenue and elasticity along a demand curve.

3. List the determinants of the elasticity of demand.

4. List the determinants of the elasticity of supply.

5. Explain the theory of utility and show how it explains the existence of a downward-sloping demand curve based on the law of diminishing marginal utility.

In this chapter we will examine the important concept of elasticity, which helps us to measure the responsiveness of quantity to price change in demand and supply analysis. We will then build on the tools of supply and demand analysis that we first developed in Chapter 4 in order to analyze some familiar but controversial economic issues.

BRIEF REVIEW OF SUPPLY AND DEMAND

Before beginning our discussion of elasticity, let's briefly review the basics of demand and supply developed in Chapter 4. The *law of demand* says that in general people will demand a larger quantity of a good at a lower price than at a higher price. The law of demand is represented graphically by a downward-sloping demand curve, such as D_0 in Figure 5-1, part a. The *law of supply* says that in general a larger quantity of a good will be supplied at a higher price than at a lower price. The law of supply is represented graphically by an upward-sloping supply curve such as S_0 in Figure 5-1, part a.

The intersection of the market demand curve D_0 and market supply curve S_0, part a of Figure 5-1, determines the equilibrium price p_e and quantity q_e. At the equilibrium price the market is said to be in equilibrium because the quantity demanded is exactly equal to the quantity supplied. At any price above the equilibrium price, the quantity supplied exceeds the quantity demanded, so that there is a market surplus. This surplus will push the market price down to the equilibrium level. At any price below the equilibrium level, the quantity demanded exceeds the quantity supplied and there is a market shortage. The shortage will push the market price back up to the equilibrium level.

Movement along a demand curve means that only the price of the good and the quantity of it demanded change. All other things are assumed to be constant, or unchanged. Among these other things are (1) the prices of all other goods, (2) income, (3) expectations, (4) tastes, and (5) the number of buyers in the market. A movement along a demand curve is referred to as a *change in the quantity demanded*. If one or more of the other things change, then the demand curve will shift in the manner shown in part b of Figure 5-1. Such a shift in the demand curve is called a *change in demand*. Note that when demand increases, the demand curve shifts rightward, such as to D_1, thereby increasing both the equilibrium price and quantity. When demand decreases, such as to D_2, both equilibrium price and quantity decrease.

As with a demand curve, movement along a supply curve means that only the price of the good and the quantity of it supplied change. Among all other things assumed to be constant, or unchanged, are (1) the prices of resources and other factors of production, (2) technology, (3) the prices of other goods, (4) number of suppliers, and (5) expectations. Movement along a supply curve is referred to as a *change in the quantity supplied*. If one or more of the other things change, the supply curve will shift as shown in part c of Figure 5-1. This is referred to as a *change in supply*. An increase in supply is represented by a rightward shift in the supply curve, such as to S_1, thereby reducing equilibrium price while increasing equilibrium quantity. When supply decreases, such as to S_2, equilibrium price rises while equilibrium quantity decreases.

ELASTICITY—THE RESPONSIVENESS OF QUANTITY TO PRICE CHANGE

What does it mean when someone says that "the public has demonstrated that it's very responsive to price changes"? In other words, how responsive is "very" responsive? In economic analysis, we find it helpful to use a specific quantitative measure of the degree of responsiveness of quantity demanded to a change in price. We call this measure the **elasticity of demand**. Similarly, the **elasticity of supply** is used to measure the degree of responsiveness of quantity supplied to a change in price.

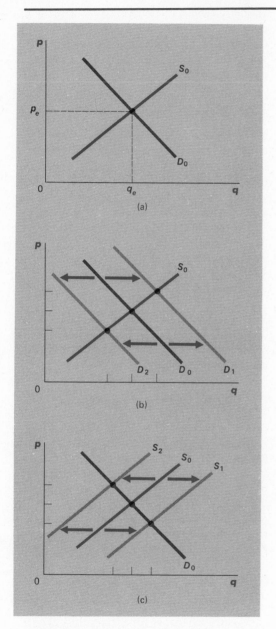

(a)

(b)

(c)

FIGURE 5-1   Demand and Supply Determine Equilibrium Price and Quantity in the Market

The intersection of the supply and demand curves S_0 and D_0, respectively, determine the equilibrium price p_e and quantity q_e in the market, part a.

A rightward shift of the demand curve to D_1, part b, increases both the equilibrium price and quantity. A leftward shift to D_2 decreases equilibrium price and quantity.

A rightward shift of the supply curve to S_1, part c, reduces equilibrium price and increases equilibrium quantity. A leftward shift of the supply curve to S_2 reduces equilibrium quantity and increases equilibrium price.

The elasticity of demand, or supply, is measured as the ratio of the percentage change in quantity demanded, or supplied, to the percentage change in price. Elasticity therefore measures the percentage change in quantity (demanded or supplied) per 1 percent change in price.

ELASTICITY OF DEMAND

The responsiveness of the quantity of a good demanded to a change in its price is reflected in its demand curve. This is illustrated in Figure 5–2. At a price of p_1 the quantity demanded is q_1. Suppose the price is lowered

FIGURE 5-2 **Change in Quantity Demanded in Response to a Price Change**

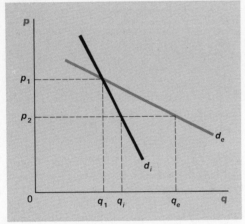

Suppose the price of a good is initially p_1 and the quantity demanded is q_1. If the demand curve is d_e, the quantity demanded increases from q_1 to q_e in response to a fall in price from p_1 to p_2. However, if the demand curve is d_i, the quantity demanded increases by a smaller amount, from q_1 to q_i. For the exact same change in price the change in quantity demanded is greater for the demand curve d_e than it is for d_i. This reflects the fact that the demand curve d_e is more "stretched out" than the demand curve d_i. For this price change we say that the demand curve d_e is more elastic than the demand curve d_i.

from p_1 to p_2. If the demand curve looks like d_e, the quantity demanded increases from q_1 to q_e. On the other hand, if the demand curve looks like d_i, the quantity demanded only increases from q_1 to q_i. For the exact same change in price the change in quantity demanded is greater for the demand curve d_e than it is for d_i. The reason is that for this price change the demand curve d_e is more "stretched out" than the demand curve d_i. Hence for this price change we say that the demand curve d_e is more "elastic" than the demand curve d_i. Our graphical example of Figure 5–2 gives us a feel for the origin of the term elasticity. But a precise measure of

elasticity cannot be obtained by looking at a demand curve or a supply curve. Indeed, we shall see that the appearance of such curves is not a reliable indicator of the elasticity of demand or supply.

Coefficient of Elasticity

By measuring the responsiveness of quantity demanded to a change in price in percentage terms, we avoid the confusion that can arise from differences in the choice of units. The number arrived at as a result of these calculations is called the **coefficient of elasticity** (e_d). We can obtain this number with the formula:

$$e_d = \frac{\text{percentage change in quantity demanded}}{\text{percentage change in price}}$$

The sign of the coefficient of elasticity of demand is negative because the sign of the change in price is opposite to the sign of the associated change in quantity along a demand curve. (This is so, remember, because price and quantity demanded are inversely related according to the law of demand.) By convention the minus sign is usually ignored.

Armed with the coefficient of elasticity, we may now give a much more precise meaning to the concept of elasticity by defining the terms elastic and inelastic. **Elastic demand** *exists when the coefficient of elasticity (e_d) is greater than 1.* Put another way, we can say that *demand is elastic if a given percentage change in price results in a larger percentage change in quantity demanded.* Conversely, **inelastic demand** *exists when the coefficient of elasticity is less than 1.* We can also say demand is inelastic *if a given percentage change in price results in a smaller percentage change in quantity demanded.* Suppose the price of salt per pound increased from $.10 to $.12 and the quantity demanded decreased from 500 lb per month to 450 lb per month. The coefficient of elasticity would be .5. A 20 percent increase in price resulted in only a 10 percent decrease in quantity demanded. In the special in-between case where the percentage change in price results in an equal percentage change in quantity demanded, we say that demand is **unit elastic** or of *unitary elasticity*. In this case the coefficient of elasticity equals 1. Put another way, if the price of a good falls by 1 percent and the quantity demanded increases by 1 percent, demand for that good is unit elastic.

The elasticity of demand for most goods falls between two extremes. At one extreme, the quantity of a good demanded does not change at all in response to a change in price. In this case we say demand is **perfectly inelastic,** and the demand curve for the good is perfectly vertical. At the other extreme is a good for which demand is zero when price is above a certain level, but unlimited when price is at or below that level. We then say the demand for that good is **perfectly elastic,** and the demand curve is perfectly horizontal at that price level.

Calculating Elasticity

Suppose we wanted to calculate the elasticity of demand for tickets to the Rose Bowl game on New Year's Day. The demand curve for tickets is shown in Figure 5-3. Let's begin by computing the elasticity for the price change between points *a* and *b* on the demand curve. At point *a* the price of $6 per ticket has an associated quantity demand of 50,000 tickets. We will use this as our base point. At point b, the price of $5 per ticket has an associated quantity demand of 60,000 tickets. We must therefore compute the percentage change corresponding to a $1 change in the price of a ticket and the percentage change corresponding to the associated 10,000 ticket change in the quantity of tickets demanded. Using the formula for the coefficient of elasticity, our calculations for the elasticity of demand would be

$$e_d = \frac{\dfrac{10,000}{50,000}}{\dfrac{1}{6}} = 1.2$$

Alternatively, suppose we use point *b* as our reference point. Five dollars per ticket and 60,000 tickets would be the base price and

quantity from which we would compute the percentage change corresponding to a $1 change in the price of a ticket and the percentage change corresponding to the associated 10,000 ticket change in the quantity of tickets demanded. Our calculations for the elasticity of demand would now be

$$e_d = \frac{\dfrac{10,000}{60,000}}{\dfrac{1}{5}} = .83$$

These two calculations result in considerably different values of the elasticity of demand despite the fact that they are based on the same change along the same demand curve. Moreover, in this particular instance, the first calculation indicates that demand is elastic, while the second indicates it is inelastic. This conflict is clearly an unsatisfactory state of affairs. How can we resolve it?

The Midpoints Formula Variation

The conventional way around this difficulty is to use the averages of the two quantities and the two prices as base points when computing the percentage changes in quantity and price used to calculate the coefficient of elasticity. The average of the two quantities associated with points *a* and *b* is (50,000 + 60,000)/2, which equals 55,000. The average of the two prices is (6 + 5)/2, which equals 5.5. The percentage change in quantity is therefore (10,000/55,000) × 100, or 18.2. The percentage change in price is (1/5.5) × 100, or 18.2. The calculation of the coefficient of elasticity is now

$$e_d = \frac{\dfrac{10,000}{55,000}}{\dfrac{1}{5.5}} = \frac{18.2}{18.2} = 1$$

In general then, we may restate our formula for the coefficient of elasticity so that it reads

$$e_d = \frac{\text{change in quantity}}{\dfrac{\text{sum of quantities}}{2}} \div \frac{\text{change in price}}{\dfrac{\text{sum of prices}}{2}}$$

This new formula is sometimes called the **midpoints formula variation** in elasticity

FIGURE 5-3 Demand for Tickets to the Rose Bowl

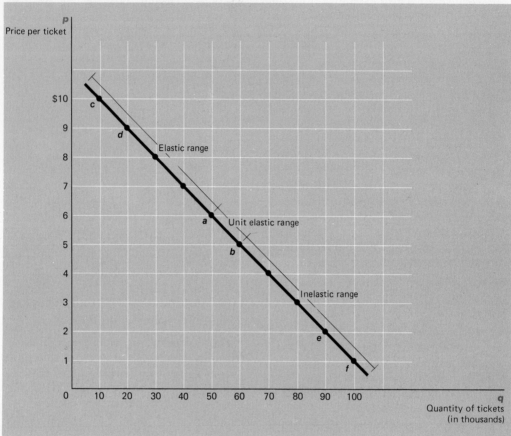

The elasticity of a demand curve is typically different over different ranges. For this hypothetical demand curve for tickets to the Rose Bowl, the coefficient of elasticity is 6.33 over the range c to d and gets progressively smaller as we move down the curve from left to right. It is unit elastic over the range a to b and becomes progressively more inelastic below this range. The coefficient of elasticity over the range e to f is .16.

Note, however, that the *slope* of this demand curve is the same over all ranges, because the curve is linear (a straight line). From this example, we can see why the slope of the curve over any range is not a good indicator of the elasticity over that range.

along a demand curve. It is also sometimes called the arc elasticity.

Variation in Elasticity Along a Demand Curve

At this point you should be warned against thinking that the elasticity of demand is the

same over all ranges of a demand curve. Although it is possible to construct demand curves where the coefficient of elasticity is the same over all ranges, such curves are not typical.

Consider again the demand curve in Figure 5–3, which *is* fairly typical. Using the midpoints formula, we can determine the coefficient of elasticity for the range c to d by making the following calculations:

$$e_d = \frac{10,000}{\frac{30,000}{2}} \div \frac{1}{\frac{19}{2}} = 6.33$$

We have already seen that for the range a to b, e_d has a value of 1. The value of e_d over the range e to f is

$$e_d = \frac{10,000}{\frac{190,000}{2}} \div \frac{1}{\frac{3}{2}} = .16$$

It is apparent that the demand curve is very elastic at the highest price levels and becomes less and less elastic as we move to lower price levels. At price levels below the a to b range, the demand curve is inelastic and becomes more so as we move to yet lower price levels. Elasticity is higher in the upper-left part of the demand curve because the base quantity level from which the percentage change in quantity is computed is small. On the other hand, the base price from which the percentage change in price is computed is large. When we compute the coefficient of elasticity, a relatively large percentage change in quantity is divided by a relatively small percentage change in price. This gives an elastic demand over this range. In the lower-right part of the demand curve, the situation is just the opposite. The base quantity level from which the percentage change in quantity is computed is large, while the base price level from which the percentage change in price is computed is small. When we compute the coefficient of elasticity, a relatively small percentage change in quantity is divided by a relatively large percentage change in price to give a coefficient of elasticity less than 1. This indicates an inelastic demand.

Slope and Elasticity

Obviously the elasticity of demand typically will be different at different parts of the demand curve. It is easy for beginning students of economics to confuse the slope of a demand curve over some range with the elastic-

ity of demand over that range. Slope and elasticity are different concepts. *The* **slope of the demand curve** *over some range is defined as the change in price over that range divided by the associated change in quantity demanded.* This is obviously not the same as the coefficient of elasticity.

For a straight-line demand curve, such as that in Figure 5–3, the slope is the same over its entire length. For every $1 change in price, the associated change in quantity of seats demanded is always 10,000. We have already seen, however, that the elasticity is decidedly different between the ranges c to d, a to b, and e to f, for example. This illustrates how misleading it can be to judge the elasticity of demand by looking at the slope. While the slope of the demand curve can be readily observed from the appearance of the demand curve over any range, the elasticity cannot. Consider the demand curve in Figure 5–4. The slope over the range a to b is clearly steeper than that over the range c to d. The slopes over both of these ranges are clearly steeper than the slope over the range e to f. Yet this demand curve has been constructed so that it is unit elastic throughout its length. The coefficient of elasticity is always equal to 1, whether it is calculated for the range a to b, b to c, c to d, d to e, or e to f.

Elasticity and Total Revenue

The **total revenue** *received from the sales of a good is equal to the quantity of the good sold multiplied by the price per unit.* There is a definite relationship between total revenue and the elasticity of demand. The way total revenue changes as we move along a demand curve tells us how elasticity changes along the demand curve. And conversely, the way elasticity changes along a demand curve tells us how total revenue changes.

Consider again the demand curve in Figure 5–3, reproduced in Figure 5–5. At point c, total revenue is equal to the price per ticket of $10 multiplied by the 10,000 tickets demanded at that price, or $100,000. At point d, total revenue is equal to $9 per ticket times

POLICY PERSPECTIVE

A Sales Analysis of the Demand for Wine

The concept of elasticity can be a practical tool in the business world for providing useful information about markets. Suppose, for example, that you are a consultant hired by a California grape growers association to anaylze the wine sales of an especially large local winery. The members of the association are always keenly interested in how their large customer is doing in general, and in what kind of sales policies association members should adopt in dealing with the winery in particular. The grape growers want you to give them some idea of the degree of their customer's wine sales responsiveness to price change.

In the course of researching the problem you discover that the winery recently cut the price of its prestigious red table wine from $3.50 a bottle to $2.36 a bottle. You also find out that before the price cut the wine had been selling at a rate approximately equal to 1,000 cases per month. After the price cut sales climbed to more than 4,000 cases per month.

You decide to use the midpoints formula variation to calculate the coefficient of elasticity of demand. The average of the two sales quantities is $(1,000+4,000)/2$ which equals 2,500. The average of the two prices is $(\$3.50 + \$2.36)/2$ which equals $2.93. Using these two pieces of information you now calculate the percentage increase in the quantity (number of cases) of wine sold per month, and the percentage reduction in the price per bottle that led to the increase in wine sales. Since you are using percentages it makes no difference whether you measure the quantity in terms of cases or bottles, or price as price per case or price per bottle. The percentage change in quantity is therefore $(3000/2500)100$, or 120. The

percentage change in price is $(1.14/2.93)$ 100, or 38.9. The calculation of the coefficient of elasticity of demand is

$$e_d = \frac{\dfrac{3000}{2500}}{\dfrac{1.14}{2.93}} = \frac{120}{38.9} = 3.13$$

You now interpret your findings for the grape growers association by telling them that wine sales of the winery's prestigious red table wine increase 3.1 percent for each 1 percent reduction in the price of the wine. You also point out that the winery must have increased its total revenue by lowering the price of its red table wine from $3.50 to $2.36 per bottle. Why? Your calculated coefficient of elasticity of demand for this price change is greater than 1. Therefore the demand curve for the red table wine is elastic over the range corresponding to this price cut, and hence total revenue must have increased. A calculation of total revenue from the rough quantity data also shows that this is so. At a price of $3.50 per bottle roughly 1,000 cases of wine were sold per month. Assuming 12 bottles to the case, total revenue was $42,000 per month (equal to 12 × 1,000 × $3.50). When price was lowered to $2.36 per bottle, the total quantity sold increased to 4,000 cases per month and total revenue increased to $113,280 per month (equal to 12 × 4,000 × $2.36).

Questions

1. What should your findings suggest to the grape growers association about the likely significance of the effect on the demand for grapes by the winery as a consequence of the winery's

decision to lower the price of its red table wine?

2. Do you think your reported findings would encourage, or discourage, the

members of the association from lowering the price they charge the winery for grapes in an attempt to increase the sales revenue from grape sales? Why?

20,000 seats, or $180,000. Hence, if price is lowered from $10 to $9 per ticket, total revenue increases. We have already observed that demand is elastic over this range, which means that the percentage change in quantity is greater than the percentage change in price. In other words, when the price of tickets is lowered from $10 to $9, the loss in revenue due to the reduction in price is more than offset by the gain in revenue due to the increase in the quantity of tickets sold. Conversely, if the price per ticket is raised from $9 to $10, total revenue falls because the gain in revenue due to the increase in price is more than offset by the loss in revenue due to the reduction in the number of seats sold. Hence, *in the elastic portion of a demand curve, a change in price, up or down, results in a change in total revenue in the opposite direction.*

Now consider the behavior of total revenue over the range *e* to *f* on the demand curve of Figure 5–5. At point *e* total revenue is equal to the price per ticket of $2 multiplied by the 90,000 tickets demanded at that price, or $180,000. At point *f* total revenue is equal to $1 per ticket times 100,000 tickets, or $100,000. Therefore, if price is lowered from $2 to $1 per seat, total revenue decreases. Recall that demand is inelastic over this range, which means that the percentage change in quantity is less than the percentage change in price. Hence, when the price is lowered from $2 to $1 per ticket, the loss in revenue due to the reduction in price is larger than the gain in revenue due to the increase in the quantity of tickets sold. Conversely, if the price per ticket is raised from $1 to $2, total revenue rises from $100,000 to $180,000 because the gain in revenue due to

FIGURE 5-4 Unit Elastic Demand Curve

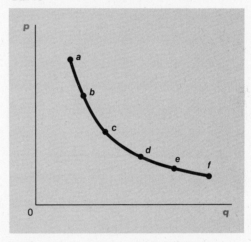

This demand curve is unit elastic (the coefficient of elasticity equals 1) throughout its length. However, the slope varies throughout its length. The slope is very steep over ranges along the upper-left portion of the curve, such as *a* to *b*, and becomes progressively flatter as we move down along the demand curve from left to right. This again illustrates why it is misleading to judge the elasticity of a demand curve over any range by its slope over that range.

the increase in price more than offsets the loss in revenue due to the decrease in the number of tickets sold. Therefore, *in the inelastic portion of a demand curve, a change in price, up or down, results in a change in total revenue in the same direction.*

Over the range *a* to *b* the demand curve of Figure 5–5 is unit elastic. At point *a* total

FIGURE 5-5   Relation Between Elasticity of Demand and Total Revenue

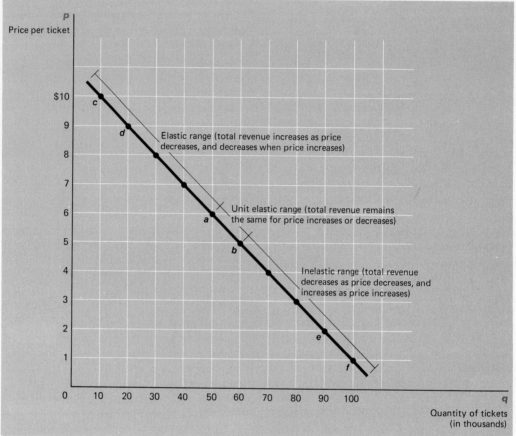

Total revenue (equals price per ticket times the number of tickets demanded at that price) gets progressively larger as we move down the demand curve from left to right over the elastic range. Total revenue reaches its maximum over the unit elastic range and gets progressively smaller as we move down the demand curve over the inelastic range. As we move up the demand curve from right to left, total revenue rises to a maximum at the unit elastic range and then falls continuously thereafter.

   Use the numbers in the diagram to convince yourself of the validity of these statements. Also note in Figure 5–4 that because the demand curve has the same elasticity throughout its length, total revenue is the same at all points on it.

revenue is $300,000, which is determined by a price of $6 per ticket multiplied by 50,000 tickets. Total revenue is also $300,000 at point *b*, where the price of $5 per ticket is multiplied by 60,000 tickets. Thus, whether price is lowered from $6 to $5 or raised from $5 to $6, total revenue remains unchanged.

This is so because the percentage change in price in one direction is exactly the same as the percentage change in quantity in the other. The change in revenue due to the change in the price per seat is exactly offset by the change in revenue due to the change in the opposite direction of the quantity of seats sold. *In that portion of a demand curve that is unit elastic, a change in price, up or down, has no effect on total revenue.* Because the demand curve of Figure 5–4 is unit elastic throughout its length, total revenue remains the same no matter what price is charged.

Usually the easiest way to estimate whether a demand curve is elastic, inelastic, or unit elastic over a certain range is to examine the change in total revenue as price and quantity vary over that range. Always remember that *along the elastic portion of a demand curve, total revenue and price move in the opposite direction. Along the inelastic portion of a demand curve, total revenue and price move in the same direction.* With these rules in mind, in Figure 5–5 you should be able to convince yourself that total revenue from Rose Bowl ticket sales is at a *maximum* when tickets are priced at either $5 or $6. Note that this would mean the stadium would be only about half full!

What Determines Elasticity of Demand?

There are three main determinants of the elasticity of demand for a good: (1) the degree of substitutability with other goods, (2) the size of the portion of buyer's income typically devoted to expenditure on the good, and (3) the length of time over which demand conditions are considered.

1. Degree of Substitutability

In Chapter 4 it was argued that the demand curve for a good typically slopes downward from left to right because there are other goods that to varying degrees can be used as substitutes for the good. Hence, if the price of a good goes up, it becomes more expensive relative to its substitutes. Therefore, less of that good and more of the substitute goods will be demanded. Conversely, if the price of a good goes down, it becomes less expensive relative to its substitutes. In this case, more of that good and less of its substitutes will be demanded. The demand curve for a good

will be flatter the more close substitutes it has and the more perfect is their degree of substitutability for that good. Conversely, the demand curve for a good will be steeper the fewer close substitutes it has and the less perfect is their degree of substitutability for that good. How is the degree of substitutability related to the elasticity of demand?

Before answering this question we should first be clear about the terminology commonly used to describe the degree of steepness, or slope, of a demand curve. Recall that you cannot judge whether a demand curve is elastic or inelastic over a certain range simply by looking at it. However, when *comparing* slopes of demand curves (those shown in Figure 5–2, for example), it is common practice to say that the steeper demand curve is "less elastic" than the flatter demand curve. Or alternatively, we can say the flatter demand curve is "more elastic" than the steeper demand curve. The terminology "more," or "less," "elastic" is often used even when comparing two demand curves over a price range where they are both inelastic. The use of this terminology is accurate as long as it is understood to mean that the "more elastic," or flatter, demand curve has a higher coefficient of elasticity than the "less elastic," or steeper, demand curve over the same price range. This means that the comparison is only valid for a change in price away from a point of intersection of the demand curves. For example, for the price change from p_1 to p_2 in Figure 5–2, demand curve d_e is more elastic than d_i.

In sum, abiding by these conventions of usage, the following statements can be made about the appearance of demand curves. We can say that the flatter a demand curve is over any given price range, the more elastic is demand over that range. Conversely, the steeper a demand curve is over any given price range, the less elastic is demand over that range. It follows that *the more close substitutes a good has and the more perfect is their degree of substitutability for that good, the greater is the elasticity of demand for that good. Conversely, the fewer close substitutes a good has and the less perfect is their degree of substitutability for that good, the smaller is the elasticity of demand for that good.*

There are many fairly close substitute wines for the red table wine discussed in the Policy Perspective. It is not surprising that our calculations of the coefficient of elasticity based on the numbers cited should suggest that demand for that wine is fairly elastic. By contrast, there are few, if any, substitutes for an artificial heart valve. Therefore, demand for artificial heart valves is probably quite inelastic.

2. Size of Expenditure

If you went to the store to buy a number of things, chances are the number of books of matches you might purchase would be little affected by whether they cost \$.02 or \$.03 a book. If they were \$.03 and you were pretty sure they could be had elsewhere for \$.02, you probably wouldn't feel it was worth the hassle and cost (the opportunity cost of your time, for example) to make a special trip just to buy a few books of matches for \$.02 apiece instead of \$.03. This is probably true even though the latter price is 50 percent higher than the former. For this reason your demand for matches is probably fairly inelastic. On the other hand, suppose you were shopping for a new automobile. Price differences of a few hundred dollars among similar models would likely send you shopping all over town, even though such differences might amount to less than 10 percent of the purchase price. Therefore your demand for a particular model and make of automobile is probably fairly elastic—almost certainly more so than your demand for matchbooks. What this illustrates is that *in general the demand for a good will tend to be more elastic the larger is the portion of your income required to purchase that good.*

3. Time

It is costly and time consuming for buyers to gather information about the prices and types of different goods and the degree to which they may serve as substitutes for one another. As a result, it takes time for buyers to adjust their consumption habits in re-

FIGURE 5-6 **Effect of Time on the Elasticity of Demand**

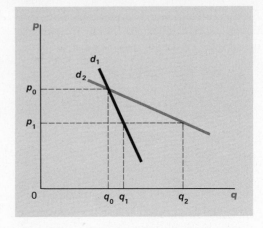

When the price of a good changes, it takes time for all buyers to become aware of the change (time to shop around, for example) and to adjust their consumption habits. The demand curve d_1 for a particular good holds for a shorter period of time, say a week, than the demand curve d_2, which holds over a longer period of time, say a month. The demand curve d_2 is more elastic than d_1. When price falls from p_0 to p_1, the quantity of the good demanded increases from q_0 to q_1 after a week according to the demand curve d_1, but by the larger amount from q_0 to q_2 after a month according to the demand curve d_2.

sponse to price changes that alter the relative expensiveness of different goods. For example, if the price of one brand of toothpaste is lowered significantly relative to that of other brands, there may be little switching away from other brands to the cheaper brand the first day after this price change. However, as time passes and knowledge of the new price difference spreads among buyers, the quantity demanded at the new lower price of the cheaper toothpaste will increase. Hence, the demand curve for this toothpaste will be flatter in the long run than in the short run. This means that the long-run demand curve will be more elastic throughout its length than the short-run demand curve. Suppose that d_1

POLICY PERSPECTIVE

Oil Demand Adjustment to Price Change

The price of oil has risen nearly twentyfold since the 1973 OPEC (Organization of Petroleum Exporting Countries) oil embargo. We might expect such a large price increase to reduce the demand for petroleum products substantially. But how much time does it take?

Prior to 1973, 2 decades of falling real prices (prices in terms of other goods) for oil and petroleum products led firms and consumers to acquire large stocks of energy-using durable goods—houses, factories, commercial buildings, motor vehicles, and machinery and equipment. The large increase in the price of oil in 1973 and 1974 suddenly made existing stocks of housing and building much more costly to heat and stocks of motor vehicles and machinery and equipment much more expensive to operate. However, American firms and consumers were stuck with these durable goods in the short run, no matter what the price of the oil. *In the short run the demand for oil is quite inelastic.* It took years to complete the adjustment to substitute sources of energy and to replace existing durable goods with more energy-efficient durable goods.

The elasticity of demand for oil, like that of other goods, is larger in the long run than in the short run. Over the long run, oil consumers have more time to seek out alternative energy sources, develop and build more energy-efficient durable goods, and generally change their energy consumption habits. Hence, as illustrated in Figure P5–1, the short-run demand curve for oil D_s, is less elastic than the long-run demand curve D_l. Therefore, if OPEC raises the price of oil from p_e to p_o, for example, the quantity of oil demanded falls from Q_e to Q_s, a short-run adjustment corresponding to a move from point a to point b on D_s. *However, as time passes and buyers are able to make all the oil-saving adjustments to the higher price p_o*, the demand curve shifts from D_s to D_l and the quantity of oil demand falls from Q_s to Q_l, corresponding to point c on D_l.

There is some evidence on how long the adjustment process might take.[1] For example, most studies of gasoline demand find the estimated 1-year elasticity of demand to lie between .2 and .4. That is, a 10 percent rise in the real price of gasoline causes a 2 to 4 percent reduction in con-

---

[1] This evidence was reported in the *Economic Report of the President,* 1980, p. 108; 1981, p. 91.

FIGURE P5-1 The Elasticity of Demand for Oil Increases with Passage of Time

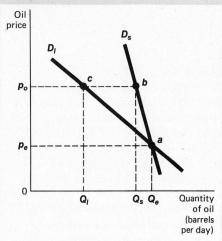

With the passage of time the elasticity of oil demand increases and the demand curve shifts from the short-run position D_s to the long-run position D_l. Therefore, when the price of oil is increased from p_e to p_o, demand for oil decreases from Q_e to Q_s in the short run but by a larger amount from Q_s to Q_l in the long run.

sumption after 1 year—perhaps due mainly to such factors as increased car pooling and shorter vacation trips. The estimated 5-year elasticities are higher, ranging between .6 and .8. Over a 5-year period, consumer appears to adjust by buying more fuel-efficient cars, moving closer to work, and generally changing fuel consumption habits. The result is that a 10 percent gasoline price rise reduces consumption about 6 to 8 percent. Note, however, that even the 5-year elasticity of demand is still inelastic. This suggests that the ultimate adjustment to OPEC oil price increases may take considerably longer, perhaps a decade or more.

Questions

1. What do the elasticity estimates for gasoline demand imply about the behavior of gasoline sales revenue when gasoline prices increase?

2. Do you think the demand for oil would be more or less elastic for an oil price decrease compared to the response for an oil price increase? Why?

in Figure 5–6 represents the demand curve for a good that holds for a week and d_2 represents the demand curve that holds for a month. It is obvious that a fall in price from p_0 to p_1 results in a larger increase in the quantity demanded after a month (q_0 to q_2) than after a week (q_0 to q_1). In general, *the elasticity of demand for a good is greater in the long run than in the short run because buyers have more time to adjust to a change in price.*

CHECKPOINT* 5-1

We have already calculated the coefficient of elasticity for the ranges c to d, a to b, and e to f along the demand curve in Figure 5–3. Using the midpoints formula, calculate the coefficient of elasticity along this demand curve for the ranges $9 to $8, $8 to $7, $7 to $6, $5 to $4, $4 to $3, and $3 to $2. What do you observe about the elasticity of demand as we move down the demand curve from left to right? The Rose Bowl game is usually "sold out." Let's assume that total revenue is at its maximum. Where do you think the demand curve actually is—to the right or left of the hypothetical demand curve shown in Figure 5–2? Could the elasticity of the demand curve in the range lying directly above the 100,000-seat point on
the horizontal axis be inelastic? Why or why not?

* Answers to all Checkpoints can be found at the back of the text.

ELASTICITY OF SUPPLY

The notion of elasticity is also applicable to supply. The midpoints formula used to calculate the elasticity of demand may also be used to determine the elasticity of supply. *Supply is more elastic the larger is the change in the quantity of output produced by suppliers in response to a change in price.* Figure 5–7 shows an inelastic supply curve S_i and an elastic supply curve S_e. Consider a change in price from p_0 to p_1. The increase in quantity supplied would be from q_0 to q_1 for the inelastic supply curve S_i, a smaller increase than from q_0 to q_2 for the elastic supply curve S_e. **Elastic supply** *exists when the coefficient of elasticity is greater than 1.* **Inelastic supply** *exists when the coefficient of elasticity is less than 1. It is unit elastic if the coefficient equals 1.*

What Determines Elasticity of Supply?

There are two main determinants of the elasticity of supply of a good: (1) the degree of

FIGURE 5-7 Elasticity of Supply

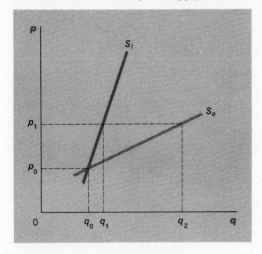

The greater the elasticity of supply, the larger the quantity-change response to a change in price. If price increases from p_0 to p_1, the increase in quantity supplied will be from q_0 to q_1 for the inelastic supply curve S_i. The same price increase will result in a larger increase in supply, from q_0 to q_2, for the elastic supply curve S_e.

substitutability of factors of production among different productive activities, and (2) time.

1. Degree of Substitutability

When the price of a good rises, it becomes profitable to produce more of it. We examined the reasons why this is so when we discussed the law of supply and the nature of the supply curve in Chapter 4. The increase in the quantity of a good that can be supplied in response to an increase in its price depends, in part, on the ease with which needed factors of production can be induced away from other uses. And this in turn will depend on how readily factors may be adapted from use in other lines of production to production of the good in question.

For example, land that can be used equally well to produce oats or wheat will be easily converted from wheat to oats production if there is an increase in the price of oats (assuming the price of wheat remains unchanged, of course). The greater the degree of substitutability of land between wheat and oats production, the larger will be the increase in the quantity of oats supplied in response to any given increase in its price. Consequently, the supply curve for oats will be flatter, or more elastic. Similarly, if the price of oats should fall, land will be readily taken out of oats production and converted to wheat production. The quantity of oats supplied will be noticeably reduced. On the other hand, if the price of handcrafted artwork were to rise, the quantity produced might increase very little because of the difficulty of finding additional craftspersons. The substitutability of labor between other activities and this one is low. Similarly, a fall in the price of artwork might lead to little reduction in the quantity supplied because the craftspersons like their work so much they are willing to take a considerable cut in wages rather than do something else. The supply curve for handcrafted artwork might therefore be quite steep, or inelastic. In general, *the greater the degree of substitutability of factors of production between the production process of one good and the production processes of other goods, the greater the elasticity of supply of that good.*

2. Time

The relationship between time and the elasticity of supply is closely related to the degree of substitutability. The more time there is, the more factors of production can be shifted from one productive activity to another. In the oats-wheat example, if the price of oats rises, it will not be possible to increase the quantity of oats supplied during the first week. After the price rise, time will be needed to convert the land to growing oats. As time passes, it will be possible to convert more and more land and other resources to oats production.

In general, in economics we distinguish

POLICY PERSPECTIVE

Oil Supply Adjustment to Price Change

An increase in the price that domestic producers receive for oil should lead to stepped-up oil exploration and drilling efforts. This is certainly suggested by Figure P5-2, which shows the sharp rise in drilling activity that accompanied the price increase caused by the OPEC oil embargo of 1973–1974. However, the process of discovering and producing oil requires time. It takes time to explore for potential oil fields, to drill a sufficient number of wells to tap new oil fields once they are found, and to build pipelines and refineries to process more oil into products such as gasoline and heating oil.

Higher oil prices will also encourage

FIGURE P5-2 Oil Price Increases Lead to Increased Drilling Activity

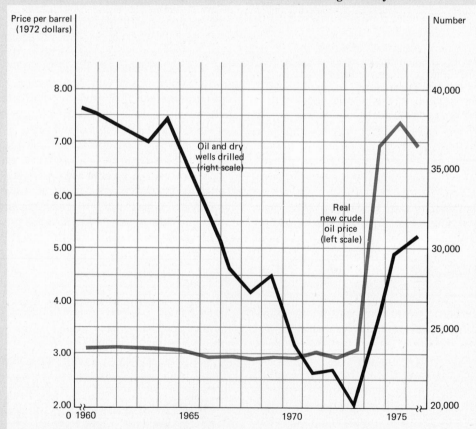

The oil price increases caused by the OPEC oil embargo of 1973–1974 led to increased oil drilling activity in the United States.

SOURCE: U.S. Department of Energy, U.S. Department of Labor, and American Petroleum Institute, as reported in the *Economic Report of the President*, 1978, p. 183.

more intensive utilization of existing oil fields. Typically an oil field is abandoned after only a portion (sometimes only 20 to 30 percent) of its oil has been extracted—the cost of getting the rest out is too high. But increased oil prices make it worthwhile to employ the more costly techniques needed to extract a higher proportion of the oil from a field. Still, it takes time to build and install the equipment that such techniques require.

The elasticity of the domestic supply of oil will thus increase with the passage of time, just like the elasticity of supply of other goods, as illustrated in Figure 5–8.

Questions

1. Why might the import quotas (government limits on the amount purchased from abroad) on oil during the 1960s, coupled with the existence of cheap foreign oil, have contributed to the decline in oil drilling in the United States during those years, as shown in Figure P5–2? (*Hint:* What would happen if import quotes were suddenly removed?)

2. How would the development of solar energy affect the elasticities of demand and supply for oil?

between the **short run** and the **long run**. *In the short run, the quantities of at least some of the factors of production available for the production of a good are given, or fixed.* Hence, the short run is a period of time that is not long enough to allow the quantities of all factors of production to be changed. *A short run during which none of the factors of production can be changed is sometimes called a* **market period**. At the other extreme, *in the long run there is sufficient time to change the quantities of all factors of production.*

Since none of the factors of production can be changed during a market period, it is not possible in this period to change the quantity of output supplied in response to a change in price. Therefore, the supply of a good for a market period is perfectly inelastic. The vertical supply curve of a good in a market period appears as S_m in Figure 5–8. In the short run, some factors of production can be changed, and therefore it is possible, to some extent, to change the quantity of output supplied in response to a price change. Supply may still be inelastic, but it is not perfectly inelastic as in the market period. The supply curve for a good in the short run appears as S_s in Figure 5–8. In the long run, all factors of production may be changed. Thus, the change in quantity of the good supplied in response to a price change can be much greater than in the short run. Supply is more elastic and the supply curve appears as S_l in Figure 5–8. In sum, if price rose from p_0 to p_1 in Figure 5–8, the quantity of the good supplied would remain at q_m in the market period, would increase from q_m to q_s in the short run, and would increase from q_m to q_l in the long run.

CHECKPOINT 5-2
When we calculate the coefficient of elasticity for the change in quantity supplied that results from a change in price, we automatically get a positive number. Hence we don't need to adopt a convention of ignoring the minus sign as we do when we calculate the coefficient of elasticity for demand. Why is there this difference between the coefficient of elasticity for supply and that for demand?

FIGURE 5-8 The Effect of Time on the Elasticity of Supply

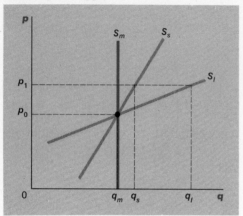

The more time suppliers have to respond to a change in price, the greater will be the change in the quantity of output they supply. Suppose price rises from p_0 to p_1. In the very short run, or market period, all factors of production are fixed and it is therefore not possible to change the quantity produced and supplied. Hence, the supply curve is perfectly inelastic, or vertical, like S_m. In the short run, some factors of production, such as plant and equipment, are fixed. But some, such as labor, may be changed. Therefore, the supply curve is more elastic, like S_s, and the quantity of output supplied can be increased from q_m to q_s. In the long run, all factors of production can be changed and the supply curve is even more elastic, like S_l, and the quantity of output supplied can be increased an even larger amount from q_m to q_l.

CONSUMER UTILITY AND DEMAND THEORY[1]

Up to now we have based our assumption that demand curves slope downward from left to right on simple common sense and casual observation of the economic world around us. If pushed further, we might rea-

[1] This section may be skipped without disturbing the continuity of the text.

son that if the price of a good is reduced, it will now take a smaller portion of our money income to buy the same quantity of it. This means that more of our money income is now available to purchase more of other goods, as well as more of the good whose price has fallen. In this sense, a price reduction has the same effect on demand for the good as an increase in real income (purchasing power). This demand-increasing aspect of a price reduction is termed the **income effect**. In addition to this effect, we would also expect demand for the good whose price has fallen to increase because that good is now cheaper relative to all other goods. Hence, consumers would substitute more of that good for others. This demand-increasing aspect of a price reduction is termed the **substitution effect**.

In general, any change in the price of a good (up or down) may be said to have a substitution effect and an income effect on the demand for that good—all other things, such as the consumer's tastes and money income, remaining the same. The substitution and income effects of a change in price on the demand for a particular good provide a somewhat fuller explanation of why the demand curve for a good slopes downward from left to right.

Yet another explanation for the shape of a demand curve is based on the concept of utility.

The Concept of Utility

In Chapter 1 we noted that people desire goods because they provide some sort of satisfaction or service. A movie provides entertainment, which gives satisfaction. An apple or a glass of milk provides not only satisfaction but nourishment, which serves to sustain life. The service or satisfaction a good yields is often referred to as the **utility** that the consumer gets from the good. Utility is not to be confused with "usefulness." A record may not be considered as "useful" as a screwdriver, but one may feel there is more utility in the form of satisfaction associated with the former than with the latter.

It is not possible to compare the utility I get from eating a candy bar with the utility you get from eating one. The issue of how much more you enjoy a candy bar than I do is not something that can be settled by objective measurement, as is the case in a dispute over which one of us is taller, for example. However, the concept of utility has been used by economists to provide an explanation for the shape of a consumer's demand curve for a good. This can be done because it is possible to envision an individual consumer making comparisons of the different levels of utility that he or she associates with different kinds and quantities of goods.

Total Utility

Suppose we consider the utility that a particular (hypothetical) individual gets from eating chocolates over some given period of time, say a day. This is known as total utility. Assume that this utility, or satisfaction, is measured in units called utils. The relationship between the amount of chocolates consumed and the amount of associated utility is shown in Table 5-1. The utility associated with eating the first chocolate is 10 utils. If the individual eats another chocolate, the total utility from eating the two chocolates is 19 utils. If the individual were to eat 10 chocolates, the total utility would amount to 55 utils. The data for total utility and chocolate consumption from Table 5-1 are plotted in Figure 5-9, part a. This graph clearly shows that total utility increases as the number of chocolates eaten increases. However, total utility reaches a maximum at 10 chocolates. If the individual eats 11 chocolates, the total utility doesn't change. The last chocolate neither adds to nor subtracts from satisfaction. If a twelfth chocolate is consumed, it doesn't go down so well and total utility decreases to 54 utils.

Marginal Utility

A more useful consideration from an economist's point of view is the way total utility changes with the consumption of each addi-

TABLE 5-1 One Individual's Total Utility and Marginal Utility from Eating Chocolates During a Day (Hypothetical Data)

Number of Chocolates per Day	Total Utility (Utils)	Marginal Utility (Change in Utility per Additional Chocolate)
1	10	
		9
2	19	
		8
3	27	
		7
4	34	
		6
5	40	
		5
6	45	
		4
7	49	
		3
8	52	
		2
9	54	
		1
10	55	
		0
11	55	
		−1
12	54	

tional chocolate. *The change in total utility that occurs with the consumption of an additional unit of a good is the* **marginal utility**. It refers to the increment, or addition, to total utility associated with the additional, or marginal, unit of the good consumed. The marginal utility associated with chocolate eating for our hypothetical individual is shown in the third column of Table 5-1. For example, if the individual has had one chocolate already, the additional, or marginal, utility associated with eating a second is 9 utils. This brings the total utility to 19 utils. The additional, or marginal, utility of a third chocolate is 8 utils, which brings the total to 27 utils, and so forth. Observe that as the consumer eats more chocolates, the marginal utility associated with eating one more chocolate gets smaller and smaller. This is

FIGURE 5-9   Total Utility and Marginal Utility

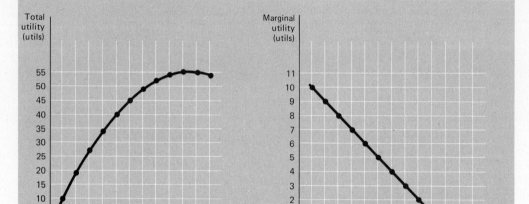

The data on total utility associated with the individual's daily consumption of chocolates from Table 5–1 are graphed in part a. Part b is a graph of the data on marginal utility from the same table. Total utility clearly rises as the individual eats more chocolates, but at a diminishing rate. The slowdown is clearly shown by the graph of the additional, or marginal, utility (part b) that the individual realizes from each additional chocolate eaten. The fact that it slopes downward from left to right illustrates the *law of diminishing marginal utility*. This law states that the marginal utility associated with the consumption of any good over a given period of time will eventually begin to fall as more and more of the good is consumed. It reflects the widely observed fact that typically the more a person has of a good, the less satisfaction, or utility, is derived from having one more unit of the good.

clearly seen in the graph of the marginal utility in Figure 5–9, part b.

Law of Diminishing Marginal Utility

The important thing to note about marginal utility is that it decreases as more of the good is consumed over a given period of time. It is, of course, possible that the second or third unit of a good consumed may add more to total utility than the first. (For some choco-late eaters this may be true.) But for almost any good one can think of, marginal utility will eventually begin to fall as more and more of the good is consumed over a given period of time and one's appetite for that good becomes satiated. Even the marginal utility associated with the consumption of salted peanuts eventually begins to fall.

Economists believe this observation about the behavior of marginal utility to be so universal that they call it the **law of diminishing marginal utility**. *This law states that,* *given the consumer's tastes, the marginal utility associated with the consumption of any good over a given period of time will eventually begin to fall as more and more of the good is consumed.* This law is demonstrated by the downward-sloping marginal utility curve in Figure 5-9, part b, for example. The law simply reflects the widely observed fact that the more a person has of a good, the less satisfaction or utility is derived from having one more unit of the good.

How the Consumer Allocates Expenditures Among Goods

No consumer has an unlimited budget. Therefore it is necessary to make choices—more of one good can be obtained only by purchasing less of another. Given a limited budget, the individual consumer's problem is how to allocate expenditure of that budget among goods so as to make total satisfaction, or total utility, as large as possible. Given a limited budget, how does a consumer determine what combination of goods should be purchased in order to realize the greatest possible satisfaction? A simple example will

help us to understand the answer to this question.

Determining the Utility-Maximizing Combination of Goods: A Simple Example

Let's consider a consumer who has a total daily income of $11. Suppose there are only two goods, X and Z. (We could consider many goods, but exactly the same principles apply as in the simpler case of two goods.) The utility that our consumer gets from the two goods is shown in Table 5-2. Column 2 gives the total utility obtained from the consumption of the quantity of good X indicated in column 1. Column 3 shows the marginal, or additional, utility derived from the consumption of each successive unit of good X. Similarly, columns 5 and 6 show the total and marginal utility, respectively, derived from the consumption of good Z. For each good the law of diminishing marginal utility is reflected in the fact that marginal utility declines (columns 3 and 6) as more of the good is consumed.

The consumer's preferences or feelings

TABLE 5-2 Utility, Marginal Utility, and Marginal Utility per Dollar Obtained from Goods X and Z[a]
(Hypothetical Data)

(1)	Good X: Price = $1			Good Z: Price = $2		
	(2)	(3)	(4)	(5)	(6)	(7)
Quantity of Good	Total Utility from X (Utils)	Marginal Utility (Utils)	Marginal Utility per Dollar (*MU*/Price)	Total Utility from Z (Utils)	Marginal Utility (Utils)	Marginal Utility per Dollar (*MU*/Price)
1	10	10	10	22	22	11
2	19	9	9	42	20	10
3	25	6	6	58	16	8
4	29	4	4	70	12	6
5	31	2	2	78	8	4
6	30	1	1	80	2	1

[a] It is assumed that the marginal utility of either good is unaffected by the quantity of the other good consumed.

about goods X and Z, as reflected in the utility data of Table 5–2, combined with the prices of the two goods, will determine the combination of X and Z that maximizes the consumer's total utility, given a fixed budget of $11 per day. In order to see how the consumer chooses this combination, the marginal utility data of columns 3 and 6 must be expressed as marginal utility per dollar spent. This makes it easier to compare the additional utility obtainable by spending a dollar on one of the goods with the additional utility obtainable by spending that dollar on the other good. Suppose the price of a unit of X is $1, while that of a unit of Z is $2. The marginal utility per dollar spent on X, column 4, is found by dividing the marginal utility data in column 3 by $1. Similarly the marginal utility per dollar spent on Z, column 7, is found by dividing the data in column 6 by $2.

We can now see how our consumer will go about spending a daily income of $11 on X and Z. Remember, the consumer's objective is to allocate expenditures on X and Z in such a way as to achieve the highest possible level of utility. Comparing columns 4 and 7, the consumer should first purchase 1 unit of good Z because its marginal utility of 11 utils per dollar is higher than X's. The consumer still has $9 to spend. At this point the consumer could get the same marginal utility per dollar, 10 utils, from 1 unit of X or 1 unit of Z. So the consumer buys both of them. The consumer now has 1 unit of X, 2 units of Z, and $6 yet to spend. Comparing columns 4 and 7 again, the consumer next should buy a second unit of X since its marginal utility per dollar is greater than that of a third unit of Z. Having done this, observe that the marginal utility per dollar of a third unit of Z exceeds that of a third unit of X. Hence a third unit of Z is purchased. Now the consumer has 2 units of X, 3 units of Z, and $3 left to spend. The consumer is indifferent as to the choice between a third unit of X and a fourth unit of Z since each yields 6 utils per dollar spent. However, the consumer has just enough money left to buy each of them.

The consumer has now spent the whole daily income of $11 to obtain a combination consisting of 3 units of X and 4 units of Z. Note that this combination is such that the marginal utility derived from the last dollar spent on each good is the same. This combination gives the consumer the highest total utility possible, given a budget of $11. Total utility equals 95 utils, the sum of the 25 utils derived from the 3 units of X, column 2, plus the 70 utils derived from the 4 units of Z, column 5. There is no other combination that can be purchased for $11 that will give the consumer as much total utility. For example, $11 could purchase a combination consisting of 1 unit of X and 5 units of Z— total utility equals 88 utils. Or $11 could buy 5 units of X and 3 units of Z, giving a total utility of 89 utils. Notice that for either of these combinations it is *not true* that the marginal utility derived from the last dollar spent on each good is the same.

The rule that emerges from our example of picking the combination of goods that maximizes total utility is: *To maximize total utility the consumer should spend a given money income to buy that combination of goods such that the marginal utility derived from the last dollar spent on each good is the same.*

Why the Rule Works

We can get additional insight into why the rule works by restating it more concisely. The marginal utility (MU) per dollar spent on X is equal to the MU of good X divided by the price of X, column 4 of Table 5–2. The marginal utility (MU) per dollar spent on Z is equal to the MU of good Z divided by the price of Z, column 7 of Table 5–2. The utility-maximizing rule says that the consumer should spend a given money income to buy that combination of X and Z that makes the marginal utility of the last dollar spent on X equal to the marginal utility of the last dollar spent on Z or, more concisely,

$$\frac{MU \text{ of good X}}{\text{price of X}} = \frac{MU \text{ of good Z}}{\text{price of Z}}$$

For the optimum combination of 3 units of X and 4 units of Z in Table 5–2, obtained by spending the $11 of money income, this equality is met:

$$\frac{6 \text{ utils}}{\$1} = \frac{12 \text{ utils}}{\$2}$$

If this equality is not satisfied, it is always possible to increase total utility by buying less of the good having the lower marginal utility per dollar and buying more of the good with the higher marginal utility per dollar.

For instance, suppose our consumer in Table 5–2 spent the $11 money income to buy a combination consisting of 5 units of good X and 3 units of good Z. Then the marginal utility derived from the last dollar spent on X is 2 utils (column 4 of Table 5–2), which is less than the marginal utility of 8 utils (column 7 of Table 5–2) derived from the last dollar spent on Z. The equality is not satisfied:

$$\frac{2 \text{ utils}}{\$1} \neq \frac{16 \text{ utils}}{\$2}$$

The consumer's total utility could be increased if he or she purchased a smaller amount of X and a larger amount of Z. To see why, suppose the consumer reallocates expenditures by taking $2 away from expenditure on X and instead spending that $2 on more Z. This reduces consumption of X by 2 units (from 5 units to 3 units) and the utility derived from X by 6 utils, the sum of 2 utils plus 4 utils in column 3 of Table 5–2. The additional $2 of spending on Z increases consumption of Z by 1 unit (from 3 units to 4 units), and the utility derived from consumption of Z rises by 12 utils, column 6 of Table 5–2. The net gain in total utility resulting from this reallocation of expenditures is 6 utils—total utility increases from 89 utils (equal to 31 utils, column 2, plus 58 utils, column 5) to 95 utils (equal to 25 utils, column 2, plus 70 utils, column 5).

The utility-maximizing rule works because whenever the marginal utility derived from the last dollar spent on good Z is greater than that derived from the last dollar spent on X, the increase in utility obtained by consuming more Z is greater than the decrease in utility that results from consuming less X. The marginal utility per dollar spent on Z declines as the consumer moves down Z's diminishing marginal utility curve, and the marginal utility per dollar spent on X increases as the consumer moves up the diminishing marginal utility curve of X. As the consumer continues to reallocate expenditures from X to Z, at some point the marginal utility of the last dollar spent on X is brought into equality with the marginal utility of the last dollar spent on Z. The rule is satisfied. At this point total utility cannot be increased more by any further reallocation of expenditure.

Why a Demand Curve Slopes Downward

We are now in a position to see how utility theory explains why a demand curve slopes downward, from left to right.

Recall that movement along a fixed demand curve means that only two things change—the price of the good and the quantity of the good demanded. All other things remain unchanged, including the consumer's income and all other prices. Assume that the consumer whose preferences are reflected in the utility data of Table 5–2 is maximizing the total utility obtainable from a daily income of $11 by purchasing 3 units of X and 4 units of Z. Hence we already have one point on the consumer's demand curve for Z: given an income of $11 and a price of $1 per unit of the other good X, the quantity of Z demanded at a price of $2 is 4 units.

Suppose now that the price of Z is lowered to $1 per unit, all other things remaining unchanged. This means that the data for the marginal utility per dollar in column 7 will double. In fact these data will be identical to the data in column 6. The combination of 3 units of X and 4 units of Z no longer gives the consumer the largest possible total utility. Applying the utility-maximizing rule, the consumer will now purchase the combination consisting of 5 units of X and 6 units of Z. Here the marginal utility derived from the last dollar spent on X will equal the marginal utility derived from the last dollar spent on Z, 2 utils per dollar. Lowering the price of Z from $2 per unit to $1 per unit has caused the quantity of Z demanded to increase from 4 units to 6 units.

This analysis based on utility theory gives the basic proposition of the law of demand. *A decrease in the price of a good will result in an increase in the quantity of that good demanded by the consumer, given that the consumer's budget and the prices of all other goods are held constant.* If this is true for each consumer, it will also be true for all of them taken together. Hence, the market demand curve will slope downward, from left to right.

CHECKPOINT 5-3
Suppose that

$$\frac{MU \text{ of } X}{\text{price of } X} > \frac{MU \text{ of } Z}{\text{price of } Z}$$

Explain why and how the consumer's expenditures out of a fixed budget will be reallocated until

$$\frac{MU \text{ of } X}{\text{price of } X} = \frac{MU \text{ of } Z}{\text{price of } Z}$$

Why can we expect the demand curve for X to slope downward?

SUMMARY

1. Elasticity of demand is the degree of responsiveness of the quantity of a good demanded to a change in its price. It is measured by the coefficient of elasticity, which is the percentage change in quantity divided by the percentage change in price.

2. When the coefficient of elasticity is greater than 1, demand is said to be elastic. When the coefficient is less than 1, demand is said to be inelastic. The quantity demanded is less responsive to price change when demand is inelastic than when it is elastic.

3. The elasticity of demand is typically different over different parts of a demand curve. Therefore it can be very misleading to judge the elasticity of demand along a certain part of a demand curve by the slope, or flatness or steepness, of the demand curve along that part.

4. Whether a demand curve is elastic or inelastic along a certain part can be determined by observing how total revenue changes along that part as price changes. If total revenue moves in the opposite direction to price, demand is elastic; if total revenue moves in the same direction as price, demand is inelastic.

5. The main determinants of the elasticity of demand for a good are the degree of substitutability with other goods, the size of the portion of a buyer's income that must be devoted to expenditure on the good, and the length of time over which demand conditions are considered. Demand will usually be more elastic the greater is the degree of substitutability with other goods, the larger is the portion of a buyer's income that must be devoted to expenditure on the good, and the longer the length of time over which demand conditions are considered.

6. The concept of elasticity is also applicable to supply. Supply is more elastic the larger is the change in the quantity of output produced by suppliers in response to a change in price. The greater the degree of substitutability of factors of production among different productive activities and the longer the time period over which supply is considered, the more elastic is supply.

7. Income and substitution effects of price changes provide explanations for the law of demand. By the income effect, when the price of a good declines, the consumer's money income can buy more of the good whose price has fallen, as well as more of all other goods. By the substitution effect, we would also expect demand for the good whose price has fallen to increase because that good is now cheaper relative to all others. The income and substitution effects of a price increase cause the demand for the good whose price has risen to fall.

8. Another explanation for the law of demand is provided by the theory of utility. This theory assumes that the amount of utility a consumer gets from a good can be measured. This measurement is the basis for the law of diminishing marginal utility, which says that the more of a good a consumer has, the smaller the addition to total utility provided by an additional unit of the good.

9. The law of diminishing marginal utility can be used to show how the consumer's total utility is maximized when the consumer spends a given size budget in such a way that the marginal utility derived from the last dollar spent for each good is the same. Assuming that the consumer's budget is spent in accordance with this principle, it is possible to derive a downward-sloping demand curve for each good.

KEY TERMS AND CONCEPTS

coefficient of elasticity
elastic demand
elasticity of demand
elasticity of supply
elastic supply
income effect
inelastic demand
inelastic supply
law of diminishing marginal utility
long run
marginal utility
market period
midpoints formula variation
perfectly elastic
perfectly inelastic

short run
slope of the demand curve
substitution effect
total revenue
unit elastic
utility

QUESTIONS AND PROBLEMS

1. Classify the following goods and services according to whether you think the demand for them over a period of a year is elastic or inelastic: gasoline, margarine, kidney machines, Budweiser beer, haircuts, electricity, chocolate ice cream, appendectomies, trash disposal, fire insurance, funeral services, medical doctors, and postal service.

2. Classify the following goods and services according to whether you think the supply of them over a period of a year is elastic or inelastic: Rembrandt paintings, advice, soft drinks, suspension bridges, medical doctors, car salespersons, corn, ivory, matches, cactus plants, 5-year-old wine, and oil tankers.

3. Suppose you owned a lake that had fish in it and could charge people a daily fee for the privilege of fishing in your lake. That is, payment of the fee, or price, for a daily fishing right would entitle anyone to fish all day for 1 day with 1 fishing pole.

a. If you knew that the demand for fishing rights was unit elastic, how would you decide what price to charge for a fishing right—a price that would result in the sale of 1 right, 2 rights, more, or none at all? Why?

b. Suppose neighbors down the road also own a lake. Observing your activity, they decide to start selling fishing rights to their lake. How will this affect the elasticity of the demand curve for fishing rights in your lake? Will you raise or lower the price you charge for a fishing right?

4. In the early part of 1977, there was a severe cold spell and parts of the country experienced gas shortages. Suppose the price of natural gas had been free to rise at this time.

a. What would you predict would happen to the dollar volume of gas sales relative to the number of cubic feet of gas actually sold?

b. Suppose you had read in the paper that households were reported to be keeping their thermostats at 72 degrees but that many businesses and factories had cut back operations considerably. What would you have concluded about the household demand for gas relative to the commercial demand?

5. Suppose the demand curve for a good shifts rightward while the supply curve shifts leftward. Rank the following sets of conditions according to the size of the change in price you would predict as a result of the shifts: demand curve elastic and supply curve inelastic, demand curve inelastic and supply curve inelastic, and demand curve elastic and supply curve elastic.

6. Suppose the demand curve for a good shifts rightward and the supply curve remains fixed. Rank the following sets of conditions according to the size of the change in quantity you would predict as a result of the shift: supply curve inelastic and demand curve inelastic, supply curve elastic and demand curve inelastic, and supply curve inelastic and demand curve elastic.

7. Suppose the supply curve for a good shifts leftward and the demand curve remains fixed. Rank the following sets of conditions according to the size of the change in quantity you would predict as a result of the shift: supply curve elastic and demand curve inelastic, supply curve inelastic and demand curve elastic, and supply curve inelastic and demand curve inelastic.

8. I buy caviar each month at a price of $2 per ounce and pay monthly for water at a price of $.01 per 30 gallons. I get 2,000 utils from the last ounce of caviar I eat and 50 utils from the last 30-gallon bath I take. Am I maximizing my utility or should I change the combination of caviar and water I consume per month? If so, how should I reallocate my expenditures between these two goods?

9. Suppose a consumer gets the following utility, shown in the table, from drinking beer and eating nuts:

Cans of Beer	Total Utility (Utils)	Bags of Nuts	Total Utility (Utils)
1	12	1	10
2	30	2	19
3	46	3	27
4	58	4	34
5	68	5	40
6	76	6	45
7	83	7	49
8	88	8	52
9	91	9	54
10	92	10	55

a. What are the marginal utilities associated with drinking beer and eating nuts?

b. If the price of beer is $1 per can and the price of nuts is $.50 per bag, what combination of beer and nut consumption will maximize the consumer's utility from consuming beer and nuts, given that the consumer has $8 for such expenditures? What if the consumer has $9.50?

c. If the price of nuts falls to $.25 per bag and the price of beer remains $1 per can, what is the optimum combination of beer and nut consumption given that the consumer has $4.75 to spend?

d. If the price of beer falls to $.50 per can and the price of nuts remains at $.25 per bag, what is the optimum combination of beer and nut consumption given that the consumer has $3.25 to spend?

e. What is the optimum combination of beer and nut consumption if the consumer has an unlimited expense account for such consumption activities?

There is a fundamental objection to using the law of diminishing marginal utility to explain the existence of downward-sloping demand curves. It is the fact that utility can't be measured in the way we measure distance, weight, and temperature. An alternative explanation of demand curves that doesn't require measurement of this nature is based on the concept of a consumer's indifference curves.

THE CONCEPT OF AN INDIFFERENCE CURVE

Suppose there are two goods, A and B, and we want to find out how a particular consumer feels about consuming various combinations of these two goods. We might begin by saying to the consumer, "Suppose you have 10 of B and 2 of A. Tell us what other combinations of B and A would give you exactly the same satisfaction." Another way of putting this would be to say, "What other combinations of B and A would leave you feeling no better off and no worse off than you do when you have 10 of B and 2 of A?" Yet another way of saying exactly the same thing would be, "Tell us those combinations of B and A about which you would feel *indifferent* as to whether you have one of them or the combination consisting of 10 of B and 2 of A."

In response, suppose this particular consumer gives us five other combinations of B and A. These combinations together with the combination of 10 of B and 2 of A are listed in Table A5-1. They are also plotted as the points *a*, *b*, *c*, *d*, *e*, and *f* in Figure A5-1. The consumer could list many more combinations until there is a continuum of points forming the curve connecting points *a* through *f*. This curve is called an **indifference curve**. The list of all the combinations represented by the points on this curve is called an **indifference schedule**. Table A5-1 lists six of the combinations from this schedule. The essential characteristic of an indifference schedule is that the consumer feels indifferent as to which particular combination of B and A is consumed. This is because the consumer gets exactly the same satisfaction from any one combination as from any other. Correspondingly, *the consumer gets equal satisfaction at any point along an indifference curve.*

Marginal Rate of Substitution

There is a particularly important point to note about the indifference schedule and its graphic representation, the indifference curve. Starting from any combination or point, if the consumer is given an additional amount of one good, a certain amount of the other must be taken away if the consumer's level of satisfaction is to remain unchanged. The amount taken away is the minimum amount of the one good that the consumer is willing to part with in order to have an addi-

TABLE A5-1 A Consumer's Indifference Schedule for Two Goods, A and B

Combination	Indifference Schedule (Combinations of B and A)	Marginal Rate of Substitution Between B and A
a	10B, 2A	
		3/1 = 3.0
b	7B, 3A	
		2/1 = 2.0
c	5B, 4A	
		1/1 = 1.0
d	4B, 5A	
		1/2 = .5
e	3B, 7A	
		1/3 = .3
f	2B, 10A	

tional unit of the other good. It is just the amount that will leave the consumer feeling as well off as, but no better off than, before. *The rate at which the consumer is just willing to substitute good B for good A so as to leave his or her level of satisfaction unchanged is called the* **marginal rate of substitution**. For the consumer of Table A5-1, the marginal rates of substitution between the combinations *a* through *f* are shown in the third column. For example, between the combinations *a* and *b*, the consumer would be just willing to give up 1 unit of A in exchange for 3 units of B—a move from *b* to *a*. Or alternatively, the consumer would be just willing to give up 3 units of B in exchange for 1 unit of A—a move from *a* to *b*.

Diminishing Marginal Rate of Substitution

Another important characteristic of the indifference schedule and the indifference curve is that the marginal rate of substitution between B and A gets smaller the larger is the amount of A the consumer has relative to the amount of B. For example, suppose the consumer initially has combination *a*. If the

consumer is given one more unit of A, it is necessary to take away 3 units of B to maintain the same level of satisfaction. Then the consumer has combination *b*. Continuing in the same fashion from point *b* to *c*, *c* to *d*, *d* to *e*, and *e* to *f*, observe that to maintain the same level of satisfaction the amount of B that the consumer is willing to give up per additional amount of A becomes less and less. This characteristic of the behavior of the marginal rate of substitution along an indifference curve is sometimes referred to as the **diminishing marginal rate of substitution**. It reflects the fact that the more of good B a consumer has *relative* to good A, the more of good B the consumer is willing to part with in order to get an additional unit of good A. It plays a role in indifference theory very similar to the role played by the law of diminishing marginal utility in utility theory.

The Consumer Has Many Indifference Curves

The indifference curve of Figure A5-1 represents only one of a family of indifference curves that characterize the particular consumer's feelings of satisfaction derived from consumption of the two goods A and B. All points on it represent combinations of the goods A and B that give the consumer the *same* level of satisfaction—a level of satisfaction that is but one among many possible levels of satisfaction. Each of the other possible levels of satisfaction also has an associated indifference curve.

This is illustrated in Figure A5-2. The indifference curve I_1 is exactly the same one as in Figure A5-1. We are talking about the same particular consumer. Assume the consumer is at point *e* on I_1, a combination consisting of 7 units of A and 3 units of B. Suppose the consumer was given 4 more units of B while still keeping 7 units of A. The consumer would then have combination *h*, consisting of the same amount of A as combination *e* but more B. Since at *h* the consumer has more of the one good and the same

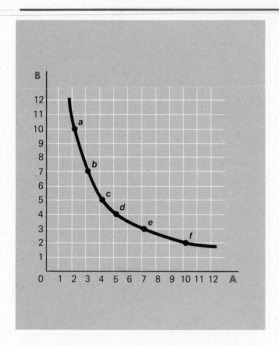

FIGURE A5-1 A Consumer's Indifference Curve

The consumer's indifference curve represents all possible combinations of the goods A and B that give the consumer equal satisfaction.

The points *a* through *f* are plotted from Table A5-1. The curve through these points is the indifference curve—the consumer is indifferent between the various combinations of A and B on it. In other words, each combination on the curve gives the same satisfaction as every other combination on the curve. Any point above and to the right of the curve is a preferred combination to any point on the curve. Any point on the curve is a preferred combination to any point below or to the left of the curve. Movement along the indifference curve requires the consumer to give up a certain amount of one good for every unit acquired of the other. This represents the rate at which the consumer is just willing to substitute good A for good B so as to leave his or her level of satisfaction unchanged—it is called the *marginal rate of substitution*. This rate diminishes with movement down the indifference curve, reflecting the fact that the consumer is willing to give up less B for an additional unit of A the smaller the quantity of B the consumer possesses relative to the quantity of A.

amount of the other as at *e*, the consumer must feel better off (or feel a higher level of satisfaction) at *h* than at *e*. Since the consumer experiences the same level of satisfaction at all points on I_1 as at *e*, it follows that the consumer feels a higher level of satisfaction at point *h* than at any point on the curve I_1.

Now suppose we again ask the consumer to tell us other combinations that give exactly the same level of satisfaction as that at point *h*. We would then be able to derive the indifference curve I_2 in exactly the same way that we derived the indifference curve I_1. Because the level of satisfaction associated with point *h* is greater than that associated with any point on I_1, it follows that any point on I_2 represents a higher level of satisfaction than any point on I_1.

Proceeding in this manner, it would be possible to derive an unlimited number of indifference curves, or the **indifference map**, for this particular consumer. *Each indifference curve represents a unique and different level of satisfaction. Therefore, they can never intersect with one another.* If they did, we would have the logical absurdity that the consumer experiences two different levels of satisfaction at the same point. *Any indifference curve represents a higher level of satisfac-*

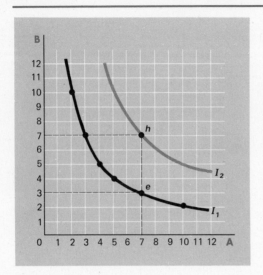

FIGURE A5-2   The Consumer's Indifference Map

The consumer has an unlimited number of indifference curves, each of which represents a different level of satisfaction.

These curves make up the consumer's indifference map. Two from among this unlimited number are shown here. All points on a particular indifference curve, such as I_1, represent alternative combinations of the goods A and B that give the consumer equal satisfaction. The farther out an indifference curve lies from the origin, the higher the level of satisfaction it represents. Hence I_2 represents a higher level of satisfaction than I_1. For example, the consumer must feel better off at point h than at point e because combination h contains the same quantity of good A as combination e, but a greater quantity of good B.

tion than the curves that lie to the left and below it.

In the example shown in Figure A5-2, I_2 represents a higher level of satisfaction than I_1. Note, however, that it is not necessary to measure something like utility to establish this. The consumer simply *prefers* combinations on I_2 to those on I_1, because the consumer feels better off on I_2 than on I_1. All that is involved is an ordering. Combinations on I_2 are ranked above those on I_1. No mention is made or need be made about a measure of *how much* better combinations on I_2 are than those on I_1.

If we chose another consumer and established that consumer's indifference map in the same way, we would find that it looks somewhat different from that for the consumer of Figures A5-1 and A5-2. As with fingerprints, no two consumers' tastes are perfectly identical.

THE BUDGET CONSTRAINT

The consumer's indifference curves reveal how he or she *feels* about having different quantities of the goods A and B. The question of what combinations of A and B the consumer can actually have is a wholly separate issue. Its answer depends entirely on the size of the consumer's budget and the prices of the goods A and B.

Suppose, for example, that the consumer has a budget of $50 and that the price of A is $10 per unit, while the price of B is $5 per unit. The budget constraint, or limit, that this puts on the consumer is depicted in Table A5-2 and in Figure A5-3, part a. If the consumer's entire budget of $50 is spent on A, 5 units of A can be purchased—line f in Table A5-2 and point f in Figure A5-3, part a. At the other extreme, if the consumer spends the entire $50 on B, 10 units of B can be purchased—line a in Table A5-2 and point a in Figure A5-3, part a. The consumer can, of course, spend the $50 so as to have some of both goods. For example, the consumer could purchase 8 units of B and 1 unit of A (line b and point b), or 6 units of B and 2 units of A (line c and point c), or 4 units of B and 3 units of A (line d and point d), or 2 units of B and 4 units of A (line e and point e). If the two goods can be pur-

TABLE A5-2 Budget Constraint and Possible Combinations of A and B Purchased

Combination	p_A × Units of A	+ p_B × Units of B	= Budget Constraint
a	$10 × 0	+ $5 × 10	= $50
b	$10 × 1	+ $5 × 8	= $50
c	$10 × 2	+ $5 × 6	= $50
d	$10 × 3	+ $5 × 4	= $50
e	$10 × 4	+ $5 × 2	= $50
f	$10 × 5	+ $5 × 0	= $50

chased in fractions of a unit, then any combination of A and B lying along a straight line connecting these points can be purchased. This line is called the **budget constraint** or budget line.

The budget constraint is a straight line representing all possible combinations of goods that a consumer can obtain at given prices by spending a given size budget. Note that the slope of this line is just equal to the price p_A of the good on the horizontal axis divided by the price p_B of the good on the vertical axis (ignoring the negative sign):

$$\text{slope of budget constraint} = \frac{p_A}{p_B}$$

In the example of Figure A5–3, part a, this slope is calculated as

$$\frac{\$10}{\$5} = 2$$

If the price of good A decreased from $10 to $5, the slope of the budget constraint would then equal 1. The budget constraint would be pivoted counterclockwise about point *a* to the position depicted in Figure A5–3, part b, by the straight line connecting the points *a* and *f′*. Whatever combination of goods the consumer selected on the old budget constraint, he or she can now select combinations on the new budget constraint that contain more of both goods. For example, if previously the consumer selected point *c*, he or she can now select a combination anywhere between *b′* and *c′* on the new budget constraint.

If the consumer's budget doubled from $50 to $100, the budget constraint in Figure A5–3, part a, would shift outward to a position parallel to its initial position. It would connect the point at 10 on the horizontal axis to the point at 20 on the vertical axis. Similarly, in part b of the figure, the new budget constraint would connect the point at 20 on the horizontal axis to the point at 20 on the vertical axis. In either case, the consumer can buy twice as much as previously.

In sum, *for a given size budget, decreases (increases) in the price of a good cause the budget constraint to pivot outward (inward) about the point on the axis of the good whose price has not changed.* A price decrease allows the consumer to buy more goods, a price increase fewer. *For given prices, a budget increase (decrease) causes the budget constraint to shift outward (inward) parallel to itself.* A budget increase (decrease) means the consumer can buy more (fewer) goods.

The Consumer's Optimum Combination

The consumer's objective is to purchase a combination of A and B that puts him or her on the highest possible indifference curve, given the size of his or her budget. By doing this, the consumer will achieve the highest possible level of satisfaction.

The consumer's indifference map reveals how he or she feels about various combinations of quantities of the goods A and B. It is a *subjective* matter reflecting the consumer's tastes. On the other hand, the consumer's

FIGURE A5-3   The Budget Constraint

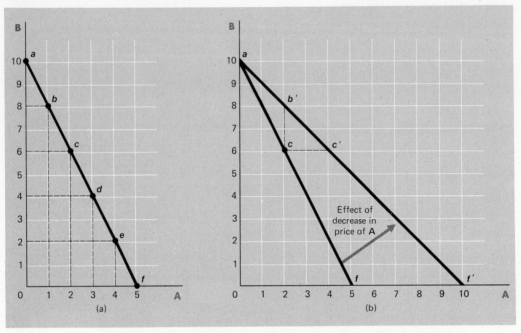

The budget constraint shows all the possible combinations of the goods A and B that the consumer may purchase with a given size budget and for given prices of A and B.

In part a the consumer is assumed to have a budget of $50. The price of A is assumed to be $10 per unit and the price of B is assumed to be $5 per unit. The points a through f represent the combinations of goods A and B listed in Table A5–2 that may be purchased with this budget at these prices. The slope of this line is just equal to the price of good A on the horizontal axis divided by the price of good B on the vertical axis (ignoring the minus sign). In this example, the slope equals 2.

In part b the effect on the budget constraint of a change in price of good A is shown. When the price of good A is reduced from $10 per unit to $5 per unit, the budget constraint pivots counterclockwise about point a from position af to position af'. Whatever combination of A and B was purchased before the price reduction, the consumer may purchase a combination containing more of both goods after the price reduction. For example, if combination c were purchased before, the consumer may now purchase any combination between b'c' on the new budget constraint af'.

An increase in the size of the consumer's budget causes the budget constraint to shift outward parallel to itself. For example, if the budget were doubled, from $50 to $100, the budget constraint in part a would shift out until it connected the horizontal axis at 10 units with the vertical axis at 20 units.

budget constraint reflects the *objective* facts of the world that impinge on the consumer's decisions—the amount of money available for expenditure and the prices of the goods. These constraints cannot be ignored—like them or not. They tell what is possible as opposed to what is desirable.

To reconcile the consumer's tastes and desire with what is possible, the consumer's budget constraint and indifference map must

FIGURE A5-4 The Consumer's Optimum Purchase Combination

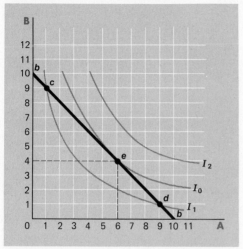

If the consumer has a budget of $50 and the price of both A and B is $5 per unit, the consumer can purchase any combination given by the budget constraint *bb*. For example, the consumer could spend the $50 to purchase combination *c* or *d*. The level of satisfaction associated with *d* is represented by the indifference curve I_1. The consumer can do better than this, however, by selecting the combination of 6 units of A and 4 units of B represented by point *e*. Point *e* lies on the highest indifference curve it is possible to reach by moving along *bb*. It is therefore the combination of goods A and B that gives the consumer the highest level of satisfaction allowed by his or her budget constraint.

be brought together. In this way the consumer determines from among all the possible combinations of A and B the one that is most desirable in the sense that it maximizes his or her feeling of satisfaction. How this is done is shown in Figure A5-4, which combines the consumer's indifference map with the budget constraint of Figure A5-3, part b. The price of both good A and good B is $5 per unit, and the consumer is assumed to have a budget of $50. Of the unlimited num-

ber of indifference curves that make up the consumer's indifference map, three are shown in Figure A5-4.

Of all the possible combinations of the two goods A and B along the consumer's budget constraint *bb*, which one will the consumer choose? For example, if either combination *c* or *d* were chosen, the consumer would experience the level of satisfaction associated with the indifference curve I_1. However, since the consumer's objective is to achieve the greatest level of satisfaction possible, neither of these combinations would be the optimum choice. The reason is that it is possible to get to a higher indifference curve. If combination *e* is chosen, the consumer will be on the highest *possible* indifference curve I_0, and thereby achieve the highest *possible* level of satisfaction. It is the highest possible given the budget constraint.

Note that the optimum combination *e* is the point where *bb* and I_0 touch each other. This is known as the point of tangency. All indifference curves below I_0 have two points in common with the budget constraint *bb*. Only the highest possible indifference curve has only one point in common with it—the point of tangency. Any combination of A and B on an indifference curve above I_0, such as I_2, is unattainable given the budget constraint.

In sum, *the point of tangency of an indifference curve with the budget constraint determines the optimum purchase combination. It is optimum in that the consumer realizes the highest possible level of satisfaction.* In Figure A5-4 this combination consists of 6 units of A and 4 units of B.

FROM INDIFFERENCE CURVES TO DEMAND CURVES

Figure A5-5 shows again the consumer's budget constraint *bb* and the two indifference curves I_0 and I_1 from the consumer's indifference map. If the consumer has a budget of $50 and the prices of A and B are each $5 per unit, the consumer will buy combination *e* consisting of 6 units of A and 4 units of B.

FIGURE A5-5 Effect of a Price Change

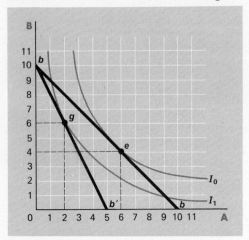

If the consumer has a budget of $50 and the prices of A and B are each $5 per unit, the consumer's optimum purchase combination is e (6 units of A and 4 units of B). If the price of A were to rise from $5 to $10 per unit, the budget line would pivot clockwise about point b from the position bb to bb'. The consumer's optimum purchase combination would then be g (2 units of A and 6 units of B). Conversely, if the price of A had fallen from $10 to $5 per unit, the quantity of A purchased would increase from 2 units to 6 units, while the quantity of B purchased would decrease from 6 units to 4 units.

Suppose the price of A rises from $5 per unit to $10 per unit, while the price of B remains $5 per unit and the consumer's budget is still $50. The budget constraint would pivot clockwise from bb to bb'. The consumer is now constrained to purchase one of the possible combinations along bb'. That combination of A and B that maximizes the consumer's satisfaction by putting him or her on the highest possible indifference curve is at point g. At g the consumer will purchase 6 units of B and 2 units of A. Hence, the doubling of the price of A, with the price of B and the size of the consumer's budget staying

the same, has caused the consumer to reduce his or her demand for A from 6 units to 2 units.

Suppose we plot the price of A (p_A) on the vertical axis and the quantity of A demanded (q_A) on the horizontal axis as in Figure A5–6. Given the price of B of $5 per unit

FIGURE A5-6 Derivation of a Demand Curve

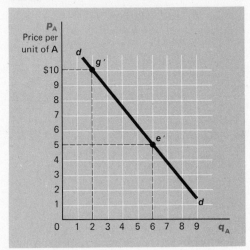

The demand curve dd is derived from the points of tangency between the consumer indifference curves and budget constraints of Figure A5–5. The price per unit of good A is measured on the vertical axis and the number of units of good A on the horizontal axis. Given that the consumer has a budget of $50 and that the price of good B is $5 per unit, when the price of good A is $5 per unit, we see from point e in Figure A5–5 that the consumer demands 6 units of A. This is plotted here as point e'. If the price of good A is raised to $10 per unit, we see from point g in Figure A5–5 that the consumer demands 2 units of A. This is plotted here as point g'. By varying the price of A in this fashion, it is possible to derive the entire demand curve dd from the points of tangency between the budget lines and indifference curves in Figure A5–5.

and the consumer's budget of $50, if the price of A is $5 per unit, the quantity of A demanded is 6 units, point *e* in Figure A5-5. Corresponding to point *e* in Figure A5-5, we have point *e'* in Figure A5-6. If the price of A is increased to $10 per unit and the price of B and the consumer's budget remain the same, the quantity of A demanded decreases to 2 units, point *g* of Figure A5-5. Corresponding to point *g* in Figure A5-5, we have point *g'* in Figure A5-6. If we continued to vary the price of A while holding the price of B and the consumer's budget constant in Figure A5-5, we could derive the entire demand curve *dd* for good A in Figure A5-6.

Thus, by the use of indifference curves, we can explain the existence of a downward-sloping demand curve. Unlike the utility theory approach, it is not necessary to measure *how much* a consumer likes a certain quantity of a good. All that is required is that the consumer be able to tell which combinations of goods are regarded as equivalent and which combinations are preferred to others. The indifference curve approach thereby gets around the problem that utility cannot be measured. This problem is the major shortcoming of the utility theory approach in explaining why a demand curve slopes downward left to right.

SUMMARY

1. Indifference curves reflect the consumer's tastes or feelings about goods. They are therefore subjective. The size of the consumer's budget and the prices of goods are objective facts that determine the consumer's budget constraint or budget line.

2. By bringing the consumer's indifference map, which consists of all the consumer's indifference curves, together with the consumer's budget constraint, it is possible to determine the optimum purchase combination of goods. This combination is optimum in the sense that it is the one, from among all *possi-ble* combinations, that gives the consumer the greatest satisfaction.

3. By varying the price of one good while holding the size of the consumer's budget and the price of the other good fixed, it is possible to derive the demand curve for a good from the tangency points of the consumer's indifference curves and budget constraints. Hence, the existence of a downward-sloping demand curve can be explained without resorting to the measurement of utility—an exercise that is not practicable.

KEY TERMS AND CONCEPTS

budget constraint
diminishing marginal rate of substitution
indifference curve
indifference map
indifference schedule
marginal rate of substitution

QUESTIONS AND PROBLEMS

1. Draw one of your possible indifference curves between the following goods:

   a. brand X salt and brand Y salt;

   b. right-hand gloves and left-hand gloves;

   c. red apples and yellow apples;

   d. bread and water.

2. Suppose there is a change in the tastes of a consumer, one of whose indifference curves is shown in Figure A5-1. Suppose this consumer develops a stronger preference for good A relative to good B. How do you think this will change the indifference curve shown in Figure A5-1?

3. Consider again the consumer budget constraint shown in Figure A5-3, part a. Show how each of the following will affect the budget constraint:

   a. The consumer's budget is reduced from $50 to $30.

b. The consumer's budget is increased from $50 to $80.

c. The price of B is increased from $5 per unit to $10 per unit.

d. The price of A is reduced from $10 per unit to $5 per unit and the consumer's budget is reduced to $35.

4. In Figure A5-1, suppose the consumer's tastes change in such a way as to increase the consumer's preference for good B relative to good A.

a. How would this affect the optimum combination purchased by the consumer?

b. Using Figure A5-5, show how this would affect the position of the demand curve in Figure A5-6.

5. Suppose the consumer's budget were increased from $50 to $60. Using Figure A5-5, show how this would affect the position of the demand curve in Figure A5-6.

6

Applications of Demand, Supply, and Elasticity

AFTER READING THIS CHAPTER, YOU WILL BE ABLE TO:

1. Describe the problems of enforcing price ceilings and show how price ceilings affect resource allocation.

2. Explain how price supports are maintained and demonstrate their effect on resource allocation.

3. Demonstrate the relationship between the concept of tax incidence and the elasticity of demand and supply.

4. Explain the concept of market externalities and the external, or spillover, costs and benefits they cause.

In the previous two chapters we have developed the fundamental concepts of supply and demand. These concepts can be used to examine a wide variety of economic issues. In this chapter we will apply these concepts to an analysis of how government price regulation affects markets, in particular as illustrated by price ceilings on natural gas, wartime price ceilings, rent controls, and price supports in agriculture. We will also examine how the existence of sales and excise taxes affects markets and how the burden of paying these taxes is distributed between buyers and sellers. Finally, we will consider the consequences of the fact that some of the costs and benefits associated with certain goods are not always borne solely by those who directly buy and sell them.

PRICE REGULATION— PRICE CEILINGS

Price regulation occurs whenever the government establishes laws imposing an upper limit or a lower limit on the price at which a particular good or service can be bought or sold. An upper limit is called a **price ceiling**. Price ceilings are often referred to as price controls. A legally imposed lower limit on a price is called a price support, or a price floor. When a price ceiling is placed below the equilibrium market price or a price support is placed above it, serious economic consequences follow. You should understand these consequences because they are often prevalent in the economy around you.

Price Ceilings on Natural Gas

Federally imposed price ceilings on natural gas have been a major issue of debate and controversy in our economy. Let's examine how such ceilings affect the way a market functions. The price regulation of natural gas provides a ready, and highly relevant, example.

Consider the effect of the price ceiling imposed by the Federal Power Commission on the market for natural gas that is bought and sold across state lines. The demand curve D and the supply curve S for that market are shown in Figure 6–1. (The data are hypothetical, except for the fact that up until recent years the price ceiling was set at $1.44 per thousand cubic feet.) If the market forces created by the interaction of buyers and sellers are allowed to work, equilibrium will be established at point e. This point is determined by the intersection of D and S. The equilibrium price would be $2.40 per thousand cubic feet and the equilibrium quantity would be 700 million cubic feet per month. However, the government-imposed price ceiling on natural gas shipped across state lines makes it illegal to sell it at a price greater than $1.44 per thousand cubic feet. At this price, suppliers will only be willing to supply 500 million cubic feet per month while buyers will want to purchase 1,000 million cubic feet per month. The shortage amounts to 500 million cubic feet per month, the difference between point a on D and point b on S.

Because the price cannot be higher than $1.44 per thousand cubic feet, there is no way to induce suppliers to devote more resources to the production of a larger quantity of natural gas. If price is not allowed to rise above $1.44 per thousand cubic feet, there is no way to cut back the quantity of natural gas that buyers will want to purchase. The rationing effect of a rising price is not allowed to work. Buyers know how much they want to purchase at that price and there is no effective way of changing their minds if price is not allowed to rise. Given the behavior of sellers and buyers, the market is stuck with a shortage. We can see why a newspaper reported that "Producers of natural gas, along with many of the nation's energy experts, now claim that the Federal Power Commission set gas prices artificially low. The result of these low price levels has been to discourage producers from drilling for gas while at the same time leading to a surge in consumers' demand for gas."

FIGURE 6-1 Effect of a Price Ceiling on the Market for Natural Gas (Hypothetical Data)

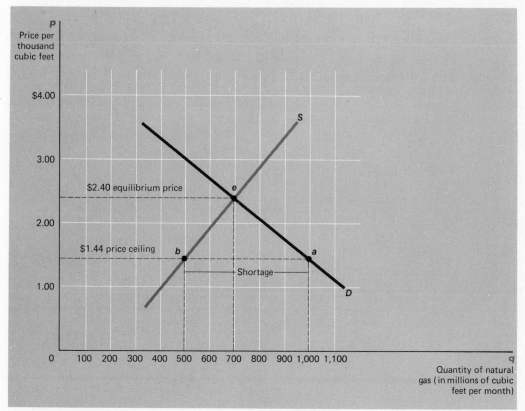

The demand curve *D* and supply curve *S* determine an equilibrium price of $2.40 per thousand cubic feet for natural gas bought and sold across state lines. However, if a price ceiling of $1.44 per thousand cubic feet is imposed, market forces created by the interaction of buyers and sellers are not allowed to work. The equilibrium price of $2.40, corresponding to the intersection of *D* and *S* at point *e*, will not be achieved. At the ceiling price of $1.44 per thousand cubic feet, suppliers are willing to supply only 500 million cubic feet, while buyers will want to purchase 1,000 million cubic feet. Market forces will be prevented from eliminating the resulting shortage (equal to 500 million cubic feet, the horizontal distance between points *a* and *b*) because buying and selling at prices above the ceiling is prohibited by law.

Price Ceilings and Nonprice Rationing

Price ceilings have been used in the United States extensively during wartime. At such times the government has had to divert a vast amount of resources to producing war goods, such as weapons and equipment and supplies,

to support troops. At the same time the civilian labor force is typically fully employed, working long hours and making high wages. The economy is on its production possibilities frontier.

If the civilian labor force is allowed to spend the high wages in the marketplace, there will typically be a large demand for consumer or peacetime goods—automobiles, television sets, clothing, food, housing, and so on. These demands conflict and compete with the demands of the government for resources needed to conduct the war effort. In short, the government must do something to ensure that the economy operates at a point on its production possibilities frontier where more wartime goods and fewer peacetime goods are produced than would occur if the civilian labor force were allowed to spend its wages freely.

One solution is to impose heavy income taxes on these wages and thereby divert some of the civilian spending power into the hands of the government for use in buying wartime goods. If this is the only method used to achieve this objective, however, a major war effort may require such high taxes that there will be a negative impact on workers' incentives to put in the extra hours required for the war effort. To avoid the necessity of having such high taxes, price ceilings and rationing are also used to aid in diverting resources to the war effort.

Price Ceilings Divert Resources

How do price ceilings divert resources? This is illustrated in Figure 6–2. If market forces were allowed to operate freely, the equilibrium price and quantity would be p_e and q_e, respectively. However, with the imposition of a price ceiling at p_c (which is below p_e), suppliers would only be willing to produce and supply a quantity of the good equal to q_c—for the reasons already discussed. Since q_c is less than q_e, fewer of the economy's resources will be devoted to producing this good. The resources that would have been used to produce the additional units of the good between q_c and q_e are now available for the production of wartime goods.

However, we know that at the price ceiling of p_c, buyers will demand an amount q_d that is greater than the amount q_c actually supplied. Obviously, since there is less of the good available than buyers want, demands of all buyers cannot be satisfied. There is now a shortage equal to the difference between q_d

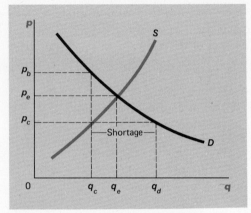

FIGURE 6-2 A Price Ceiling Causes a Shortage

A freely working market with demand curve *D* and supply curve *S* determines an equilibrium price p_e and quantity q_e. If a price ceiling of p_c is imposed on the market, suppliers are only willing to supply the quantity q_c, while buyers demand the larger quantity q_d. Market forces are prevented from eliminating the resulting shortage because buying and selling at prices above the ceiling price is illegal and prohibited.

and q_c. Since the rationing mechanism of a rising price is not allowed, some nonprice rationing device is needed to portion out the limited supply. One possibility would be to distribute the quantity q_c on a first-come-first-served basis. This would mean some of those, possibly many, who are willing to pay the ceiling price p_c would end up getting none of the good. Another possibility would be to let suppliers distribute the available quantity as they see fit. This would most likely favor the suppliers' close friends, family, and long-time customers. The rest of those willing to pay the price p_c for the good would again go without.

Rationing with Ration Coupons

Since these kinds of solutions to the problem seem inequitable and unjust, the government has often resorted to the use of the **ration**

coupon. Each coupon is a claim to a unit of the good. The government prints up just the amount of coupons that will lay claim to q_c units of the good, and then distributes them among those who want to buy the good on the basis of so many per person. If the good were bacon, for example, a family of four would be entitled to a certain number of coupons, and a family of two could have half that amount. Hence, all who want to buy the good at price p_c would be assured of getting some, though often not as much as they might want. They present their coupons to the supplier, pay the price p_c per unit of the good, and receive no more than the amount of the good their coupons allow.

Note that a price ceiling's effectiveness in cutting back on the quantity of a good produced, and thereby releasing resources for use in a war effort, depends on the elasticity of the supply curve. The less elastic the supply curve is, the less effective a price ceiling will be in achieving this objective. Indeed, if the supply curve were perfectly inelastic (or vertical), the quantity supplied would not be reduced at all.

Black Markets

So far, we have been looking at the way in which a system of price ceilings and ration coupons should work in theory. How close it comes to this ideal in reality will depend on how vigorously the system is policed. The demand curve in Figure 6–2 tells us that there are many buyers who are willing to pay more than the ceiling price in order to get some of the good. Hence there are profits to be made by those suppliers who are willing to risk breaking the law by selling the good at prices above the ceiling price. Even if they don't expand output beyond q_c, which they might well do, there is a great temptation to charge a price as high as p_b and reap large profits. *A market where goods are traded at prices above their ceiling prices is known as a* **black market**.

It should also be noted that some consumers may profit from the existence of ration-ing. There will typically be consumers who don't want any of a commodity at the ceiling price or as much of the commodity as their coupon allotments would entitle them to. On the other hand, there will be other consumers who would like to buy more than their coupon allotment of a commodity at or above the ceiling price. Those with unneeded coupons will sell them to those who want more of the commodity. This doesn't violate the spirit of a rationing system, however, because each consumer is at least given the option to have some of the commodity. It is when suppliers sell a commodity at a price above the ceiling price to individual buyers in amounts exceeding those buyers' coupon allotments that the spirit of the system is violated. Then other buyers will not be able to get all of the good that their coupon allotments entitle them to at the ceiling price.

Given the incentive provided by the above-normal profits from black market activity, a system of price ceilings without "teeth," in the form of an adequate task force for enforcement, may end up being more fiction than fact. The large bureaucracy needed to administer the price ceilings and coupon-rationing system in the United States during World War II testifies to this. The ceilings often proved "leaky," and black markets were not uncommon—a testimony to the predictability of human behavior in economic matters.

Rent Control

Rent control puts a price ceiling on the rent that may be charged tenants of rental housing. It has been estimated that approximately one-eighth of all American rental units are subject to some sort of rent regulation. Those who advocate rent control often argue that it ensures a minimum standard of housing for everyone. Whether rent control is the *best* way to achieve this objective is debatable, however.

Most rent control laws fall under the domain of local and municipal governments. The main reason there are rent controls in these areas appears to be somewhat different from the argument for ensuring a minimum standard of housing. Rent control provides an interesting example of the politics of an economic issue. Most tenants would naturally prefer that their rent not go up, whether they rent a "minimum standard of housing" or a luxury apartment. Since tenants outnumber landlords, politicians count heads and vote accordingly. Would you believe that the residents of Washington's plush Watergate complex are protected by rent controls?

Rent controls cause rental housing shortages in the areas where they apply. On the supply side, since rents are not allowed to rise above the price ceiling, there is no incentive to expand the quantity of existing rental units to alleviate this shortage. On the demand side, families are encouraged to consume more housing services than they would if the housing market were free of rent controls. For example, a couple may retain a four-bedroom apartment after children are grown because it is cheap and alternative housing may not be rent controlled. Furthermore, when rents are kept artificially low, the return on the investment in existing rental buildings is below market levels prevailing in other lines of productive activity. This discourages the flow of new financial capital into these buildings for upkeep and maintenance, and thereby leads to neighborhood decay. The result is a fall in property values and hence in property taxes that can be collected from rental buildings. This increases the tax burden on commercial and industrial property and owner-occupied single-family dwellings. To the extent that this discourages the location of new businesses and families in the area and encourages those already there to leave, the process of neighborhood decay continues and further erodes the tax base.

The financial plight of New York City in recent years, where rent controls have been extensive, is often attributed at least in part to this process. There are other areas where the same problem appears to exist, though none has captured the headlines to the extent New York City has. The history of rent control well illustrates how a price ceiling imposed on one market can have wide-ranging social and economic implications for other areas of the economy. It also shows how a policy supposedly aimed at achieving the objective of helping the poor may in fact only create conditions, in this case slums, that are at odds with that objective. Moreover, there are ways to evade rent controls, so that poorer people may not be able to afford housing legally subject to rent control anyway. For example, a rent-controlled apartment may be available only if the prospective tenant agrees to buy the existing furniture or to make some other type of side payment.

CHECKPOINT* 6-1
Suppose that when the energy crisis first hit, the government had immediately put a price ceiling on gasoline so that its price could not have risen above the pre-crisis level. What would you predict the length of the lines of motorists at gas stations would have then looked like—would they have been longer or shorter than those actually formed? Demonstrate your answer diagrammatically. Describe a scheme that might be used to deal with the problem of distributing gasoline under such circumstances.

* Answers to all Checkpoints can be found at the back of the text.

PRICE REGULATION— PRICE SUPPORTS

A governmentally imposed price support has just the opposite effect of a price ceiling. *A **price support** imposes a lower level, or floor, below which a price is not allowed to fall.* The most common reason for imposing a price support on a good or service is to bolster the income of suppliers above the level that would otherwise prevail in a freely operating market. This is the main motivation for government price supports for farm products—namely, to bolster farm incomes. Similarly, proponents of minimum-wage legislation argue that the incomes of the poor are raised by putting a floor under wages—a price support that applies to the sale of labor services.

The effect of a price support on a market is illustrated in Figure 6–3. When the market forces created by buyers and sellers are allowed to operate freely, the equilibrium price p_e and quantity q_e will prevail. Suppose, however, that the government decides to establish a price support p_s above the equilibrium price p_e. At the price p_s buyers will demand the quantity q_d, corresponding to point c on the demand curve D. However, sellers will supply a larger quantity q_s, corresponding to point a on the supply curve S. Hence supply will exceed demand, giving rise to excess output, or a surplus, equal to the horizontal distance between points a and c (also repre-

sented by the distance between q_s and q_d on the horizontal axis).

How can price supports be maintained? There are basically five schemes or ways for establishing price supports. Let's consider each in turn.

Price-Support Schemes

Scheme 1: Government purchase. One way to establish a price support is for the government to buy up the surplus. At a price level of p_s, suppliers would want to supply a quantity of the good equal to q_s, while buyers would demand the smaller quantity q_d. This would create an unsold surplus equal to the amount by which q_s exceeds q_d. The government steps in and buys up this surplus at a price p_s per unit and thereby takes it "off the market." Unless the government buys up the surplus, it will be impossible to maintain the price at the level p_s. Price would have to fall to p_g before buyers in the market would be willing to purchase the quantity q_s. But then suppliers would suffer a loss equal to p_s minus p_g per unit of output. By standing ready to buy and store the surplus at a price of p_s, the government ensures that the price will prevail in the marketplace. The government must spend an amount equal to the rectangular area $q_d q_s ac$ to do this.

Scheme 2: Output restriction. Another way the government can maintain the price floor p_s is to make it illegal for suppliers to produce any more than the quantity q_d. It might do this by assigning each individual supplier a production quota such that the sum of all suppliers' quotas does not exceed q_d. Given the demand curve D, buyers would be willing to pay suppliers a price of p_s per unit for this quantity. Such a scheme would require an elaborate administrative and enforcement apparatus. This apparatus would be needed because the temptation for suppliers to exceed their quota would be great, given that a price of p_s lies above the supply curve at an output level of q_d.

Scheme 3: Demand promotion. Yet another way to maintain the price level at p_s would be

FIGURE 6-3 Price Supports Cause a Surplus

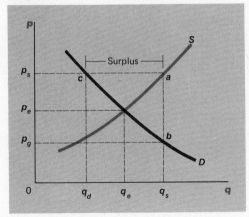

A freely working market with demand curve D and supply curve S determines an equilibrium price p_e and quantity q_e. However, if price is supported at the level p_s, buyers will demand the quantity q_d, while suppliers will supply the larger quantity q_s. The result will be the indicated surplus.

to somehow get the demand curve D to shift out until it intersected the market supply curve S at point a. This would result in a market equilibrium price of p_s and quantity q_s. For example, a food stamp program has the effect of shifting the demand curve for food outward in this fashion.

Scheme 4: Direct payment. Another alternative is for the government to tell producers it will guarantee them a price of p_s per unit of output. They would then be allowed to produce accordingly and sell the output for whatever price the market will bear. The government then simply pays producers the difference between the price they receive in the market for each unit sold and the higher price p_s guaranteed by the government. Knowing that they are guaranteed a price p_s for every unit sold, producers will supply the amount q_s. In the marketplace buyers will be willing to pay a price of p_g to purchase this quantity. The total revenue received by suppliers from the market will then be p_g times the number of units sold q_s. This is represented by the rectangular area $0q_sbp_g$ in Figure 6–3. When the government pays suppliers the difference between the market price p_g and the support price p_s per unit sold, suppliers will receive an additional amount of revenue from the government. This additional amount is equal to the rectangular area p_gbap_s in Figure 6–3.

Scheme 5: Legislative prohibition of lower-price transactions. The government makes it illegal for a service to be bought or sold at a price below p_s. At price p_s the quantity q_s will be supplied to the market, corresponding to point a on supply curve S. But only the smaller quantity q_d will be purchased, corresponding to point c on demand curve D. Hence there is a surplus, as indicated in Figure 6–3. Minimum-wage legislation is an example of this scheme. A minimum wage of p_s would give rise to a surplus of labor. This surplus represents workers who would be willing to work at the minimum wage p_s but who would not be hired at this wage.

Note that the size of the surplus that results from the establishment of a price support above the equilibrium price is larger the more elastic are demand and supply.

Agriculture and Price Supports

Price-support schemes like those outlined above have been used extensively by the government in agricultural markets to deal with the "farm problem."

United States agricultural policy over the past 50 years has been shaped, at least in part, by strong political pressures in favor of price supports. Agricultural interest groups have lobbied for the idea that farmers should be paid prices for their products that bear the same relationship to other prices that farm prices did in the 1909–1914 era, the "golden age" of agriculture. This concept is known as **parity**. Simply put, it means that if the price received for a bushel of wheat in 1909 was such that a farmer could buy a shirt with that amount of money, then he should be able to buy a shirt with the money he receives for a bushel of wheat now. We know, however, that in a dynamic, changing economy it is unrealistic to expect the prices of different goods to bear the same relationship to one another over long periods of time. This is particularly true of the relationship between the prices of farm products and the prices of other goods.

Productivity Growth Exceeds Demand Growth

Agriculture has experienced a much larger rate of productivity growth than the rest of the economy—twice the rate of the industrial sector since 1930. On the other hand, the growth in demand for agricultural products has not been as great as the growth in demand for most other goods and services. In an economy that has reached the level of affluence that the United States has over the last 50 or 60 years, the demand for basic necessities such as food and fiber does not grow at a rate as high as that for industrial products and other services. (A person can only eat so many good meals a day.) Increases in

POLICY PERSPECTIVE

Farm Support Programs and the Surplus Problem

The first serious attempts to support agricultural prices were made in the early part of Franklin D. Roosevelt's presidency. The emphasis then was on output restriction, after the fashion of the quota system described in connection with Figure 6–3 (Scheme 2). Instead of telling farmers how much they could produce, however, they were told how many acres they could cultivate. But farmers worked this reduced acreage more intensively. The result was that crop output continued to grow at such a rate that a parity price level such as p_s could not be maintained. Agricultural policy then turned to outright government purchase of the surplus (Scheme 1). While this succeeded in maintaining price-support levels, government storage bins soon bulged and storage costs skyrocketed as the process shown in Figure 6–4 continued and surpluses grew. This led the government to rely more on a program where suppliers were simply paid the difference between a guaranteed support price and whatever the market would bear (Scheme 4).

Programs Compared

Such a guaranteed-price program (Scheme 4) doesn't involve the storage costs of buying up a surplus (Scheme 1) or the difficulties of restricting output (Scheme 2). It also provides farm products to the consumer at a lower price than either of the other two plans (Scheme 1 or 2), p_g in Figure 6–3 as opposed to p_s. Consumers also buy a larger amount of the good under a guaranteed-price program (Scheme 4 rather than Schemes 1 or 2), q_s as opposed to q_d in Figure 6–3. However, the fact remains that whichever of these three schemes is used to maintain the price level at p_s, there is inefficiency of resource allocation. Government purchases of surplus (Scheme 1) and a guaranteed-price program (Scheme 4) produce more than the freely functioning market would provide, while a quota system (Scheme 2) provides less.

Demand-Promotion Programs

Policies oriented toward shifting the demand curve outward (Scheme 3) also have been pursued. The food stamp program, school lunch programs, and the Department of Agriculture's support of research aimed at finding new uses for agricultural products all promote this objective.

One particularly significant demand-promoting act was the passage of Public Law 480 (1954). This law allows underdeveloped countries to buy an assortment of grains from the United States without using dollars—that is, they use their currencies (rupees, drachmas, etc.). Since the United States does not have a great need for these currencies, the government handles these exchanges and pays American farmers in dollars out of general tax proceeds. In effect, the demand for U.S. agricultural products is increased by what amounts to a foreign-aid program.

At odds with the objective of alleviating excess supply, however, are the many activities conducted by the Department of Agriculture that increase agricultural productivity and thus push supply curves rightward. For example, the department employs county agents who teach farmers better methods of farm management, crop rotation, and soil conservation. In addition, agricultural land-grant colleges and agricultural experiment stations do much to promote growth in agricultural productivity.

The Surplus Problem

The main argument against government price supports over the long run is that they give rise to surplus production, requiring the use of productive resources that could otherwise be used in alternative activities. In short, price supports encourage too many farmers and too much land (and other inputs) to stay in agriculture—resources that unregulated market forces would otherwise encourage to leave. Thus the release of resources to other productive activities made possible by the tremendous growth in agricultural productivity is not fully realized. Over the long run this productivity growth has no doubt been passed on to consumers in the form of lower food prices to some extent. However, price-support programs keep such

price reductions from being as large as they might be.

Because of the ever growing surpluses and expenses associated with attempts to maintain farm product prices at a parity with 1909–1914 nonfarm prices, price-support levels have been lowered in recent decades. In recent years the surplus problem has also been relieved by larger sales to Western Europe, Japan, and the Soviet Union. If these trends continue, the farm surplus problem may be a thing of the past.

Questions

1. If a decision was made to eliminate price supports, do you think it would be better to do it in 1 year, or over a 5-year period? Why?

2. How would the effectiveness of a demand-promotion scheme to support a price depend on the elasticity of supply?

---

income levels are spent more than proportionally on other goods and services. And the rate of growth of the population, or new mouths to feed and bodies to clothe, has not been large enough to offset this fact.

The result has been that the capacity to supply the typical agricultural product has grown more rapidly than the demand for it. Hence, over the long run, its freely determined market price would be expected to fall in the manner depicted in Figure 6-4. There the market price falls from p_s to p_b to p_c over time because the demand curve shifts rightward from D_0 to D_1 to D_2 at a less rapid rate than the supply curve shifts from S_0 to S_1 to S_2. Meanwhile, the demand and supply curves for other goods and services typically have shifted rightward at rates that have caused their freely determined market prices either to rise or at least to fall less rapidly.

In order to maintain agricultural prices at a parity level with the prices of other goods, it has been necessary for the government to

support agricultural prices at levels above those that would prevail in a freely working market. Given that the demand curve for agricultural goods is shifting rightward at a less rapid rate than the supply curve, the surplus resulting from such a policy can be expected to become ever larger, as shown in Figure 6-4.

Perspective on Policy

Probably no industry in the economy has had research and development subsidized with public funds more than agriculture has. Political pundits and others have wryly observed that it's a shame the tremendous growth in agricultural productivity that resulted has not given the public the lower food prices their taxes have made possible.

Often there seems to be a confusion between the problems of agriculture and those of rural poverty. Ironically, price-support programs have benefited the efficient, larger

FIGURE 6-4 Long-Run Growth in Supply and Demand in Agriculture

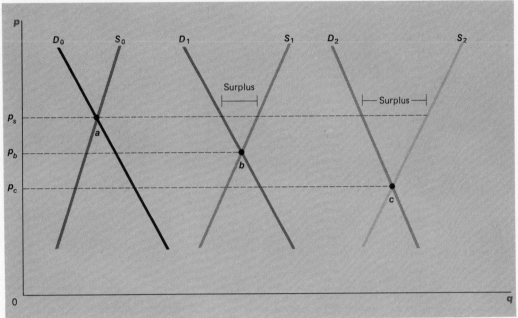

The rapid rate of growth of productivity in agriculture has caused production capacity to increase at a faster pace than the rate of growth of demand. The supply curve for agricultural products has, therefore, shifted rightward over time at a more rapid rate than the demand curve has. Hence, over the long run the freely determined market price would be expected to fall—say from p_s to p_b to p_c, as the demand curve shifts rightward from D_0 to D_1 to D_2 at a less rapid rate than the supply curve shifts from S_0 to S_1 to S_2. Under these conditions, maintenance of a price support at p_s will result in an ever growing surplus as indicated.

   At the time of the so-called golden age of agriculture, about 1909–1914, the demand and supply curves for an agricultural product might have appeared as D_0 and S_0. Support of the price at the level p_s in order to maintain parity with nonagricultural prices has led to larger and larger surpluses as the demand and supply curves of recent decades have shifted to positions such as D_1 and S_1. In even more recent years, these curves have shifted to D_2 and S_2.

farmer who least needs help much more than those farmers who are counted among the rural poor. Prudent policy would seem to suggest that the problem of rural poverty be dealt with as an issue separate from agricultural policy.

CHECKPOINT 6-2
Suppose the government wants to maintain a price support for wheat.

You are called on for your advice as to what type of price-support program would cost taxpayers the least amount of money to run, a Scheme 1 or a Scheme 4 type program. Analyze this issue, first assuming the demand and supply curves for wheat are relatively inelastic, and then assuming they are both relatively elastic. Remember to consider storage costs in your analysis.

SALES AND EXCISE TAXES

Sales and excise taxes are levied on goods in the markets where they are bought and sold. **Sales taxes** apply to a broad range of goods, while **excise taxes** are levied on particular goods. Sales taxes are used extensively by state governments as a source of revenue and are applied to a wide variety of goods (sometimes all goods) sold within the state. Excise taxes are imposed by the federal government on specific goods such as tobacco and liquor. States may also impose excise taxes, but the federal government does not impose a general sales tax.

Sales taxes are typically calculated as a flat percentage of the retail price of a good. Excise taxes are sometimes calculated as a flat percentage of the retail price, and sometimes as a fixed amount of money per unit of the good sold. If a sales or excise tax is calculated as a flat percentage of price, it is called an **ad valorem tax**. If either is calculated as a fixed amount of money per unit of the good sold, it is called a **specific tax**. Hence we can have a specific sales tax or an ad valorem sales tax, and similarly a specific excise tax or an ad valorem excise tax.

Sales and excise taxes amount to the government's legal claim on a portion of the price paid for each unit of a good sold. They may be thought of as driving a wedge between the price buyers pay for a unit of the good and the amount that suppliers receive for it. Because of this wedge, the price paid for the good by the buyer is higher and the amount received by the supplier is lower than is the case in the absence of the tax. The way in which the burden of these taxes is divided is called **tax incidence**: that is, what portion of the tax or wedge is paid by the buyer in the form of a higher price per unit, and what portion is paid by the supplier in the form of a lower revenue received per unit of the good sold.

Tax Incidence and Elasticity of Demand and Supply

Who bears the greater incidence or brunt of the tax? The answer to this question depends on the elasticity of the demand and supply curves.

Elasticity of Demand

Suppose the market supply and demand curves for the red table wine described in the Policy Perspective in Chapter 5 are S and D_e in Figure 6-5, part a. Their intersection gives an equilibrium price of $20 per case and an equilibrium quantity of 5,300 cases per month. Now what would happen if the government decided to impose a specific excise tax of $10 on each case of wine sold? Would the price of a case of wine rise from $20 to $30? The answer is no. Here's why.

Suppose the tax is collected from suppliers. Now in addition to the costs of producing a case of wine, the supplier must also pay the government $10 on each case produced. This effectively means that the cost of supplying a case of wine is now $10 more than before the tax was imposed.

Suppliers in part a of Figure 6-5 were willing to supply 5,300 cases per month at a price of $20 per case before the tax was imposed. This $20 was just sufficient to compensate them for the cost of producing a case of wine. But now when suppliers have to pay a tax of $10 per case, they will have to receive a price of $30 per case in order to be willing to supply 5,300 cases of wine per month—$20 in order to receive the same per unit price as before plus an additional $10 compensation for the tax they now pay. Similarly, whatever quantity of output we consider, suppliers must now receive $10 more per case for them still to be willing to supply that quantity after the imposition of the $10 tax. The supply curve is therefore shifted upward by $10 from its before-tax position S to its after-tax position S_a.

How does this affect the market equilibrium price and quantity of wine bought and sold? Given the supply curve, it depends on the elasticity of demand. In part a of Figure 6-5 demand is more elastic than in part b. Consider the case shown in part a. The new equilibrium point now occurs at the intersection of S_a and D_e. This means that the new

FIGURE 6-5   Demand Elasticity and the Incidence of an Excise Tax

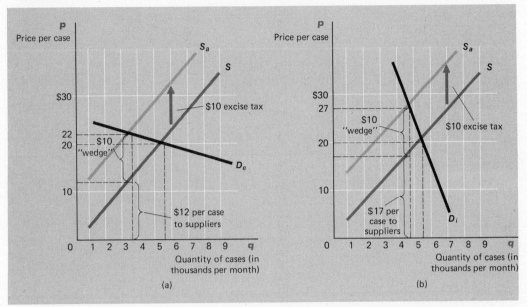

(a)

(b)

When demand is elastic, as in part a, the imposition of an excise tax forces the price to buyers up by less than it forces down the amount suppliers are able to keep after the government has been paid the tax. In part b, the supply curve is the same as in part a, but the demand curve is inelastic. The imposition of the same excise tax forces the price to buyers up by more than it forces down the amount suppliers are able to keep after tax payment. The incidence of the tax bears heaviest on suppliers when demand is elastic (part a) and heaviest on buyers when demand is inelastic (part b).

equilibrium price is $22 per case and the new equilibrium quantity is 3,300 cases per month. The price paid by buyers has risen by only $2, from $20 to $22. Of this $22, $10 goes to the government to pay the excise tax. After this "wedge" is paid, suppliers receive $12 per case—$8 less than previously. Therefore, the incidence or burden of this tax is such that buyers pay $2 of it per case and suppliers $8. The incidence of the tax bears heaviest on the suppliers.

What if demand were less elastic? In Figure 6–5, part b, the supply curve is the same as in Figure 6–5, part a, but the demand curve D_i is less elastic than the demand curve D_e in part a. The initial equilibrium price and quantity determined by the intersection

of S and D_i is the same as before ($20 and 5,300 cases per month). However, now when the government imposes the $10 excise tax, shifting the supply curve up to S_a, the new equilibrium price is $27 per case and the new equilibrium quantity is 4,600 cases per month. In this instance the price paid by buyers has risen by $7 (from $20 to $27). Out of this $27, $10 once again goes to the government to pay the excise tax. This time, the wedge between the price paid per case by buyers and the amount received by suppliers leaves suppliers with $17 per case—$3 less than before the tax was imposed. Hence in this instance, where demand is less elastic, the incidence of the tax is such that buyers are burdened with $7 of it per case and sup-

Can Excise Taxes Stop People from Smoking?

In Great Britain smoking is singled out as the biggest cause of premature deaths, killing at least 50,000 Britons a year, mainly through heart disease and lung cancer. Since the mid-1960s the British health department has been cranking out statistics and alarming reports on the health risks of smoking. The government has imposed compulsory health warnings on cigarette packs and obtained "voluntary" agreements from tobacco companies to curb advertising, including a ban on television ads. However cigarette consumption fell only gradually until 1981.

In that year the government imposed two successive increases in excise taxes on cigarettes, sending the tax up 30 percent in 6 months and the price of a pack to the equivalent of about $2.50. At that point, the British treasury took 75 percent of the retail price of a pack of cigarettes in excise tax. Britons were paying up to three times more for cigarettes than other Western Europeans. Subsequent to the 30 percent increase in the excise tax tobacco companies reported a 10 percent drop in sales. *The Guardian* newspaper described it as "the biggest and most abrupt change in national smoking habits since cigarettes were introduced at the turn of the century," and reported that a survey estimated that 2 million of Britain's 17 million adult smokers have quit.

Questions

1. Suppose that prior to the 1981 increases in the excise tax on cigarettes the price of a pack was $2.00. Is the demand for cigarettes in Britain elastic or inelastic?

2. On the basis of the survey reported by *The Guardian,* give a rough estimate of how high the price of a pack of cigarettes would have to be pushed by an excise tax in order to completely eliminate smoking in Britain.

pliers with only $3. The incidence of the tax now bears heaviest on the buyers. In sum, the example of Figure 6–5, parts a and b, illustrates the following fact about the tax incidence of an excise tax or a sales tax. In general, *given the elasticity of supply, the less elastic is demand, the greater is the burden of the incidence of the tax on buyers and the smaller is the burden of the incidence on suppliers.*

Finally, note also that the greater the elasticity of demand (compare parts a and b of Figure 6–5), the larger is the reduction in the quantity of the goods produced and sold due to the imposition of the tax, given the elasticity of supply. Hence, if the government's primary purpose is to raise revenue from such taxes, it should impose them on goods and services that have the most inelastic demands. For example, the total tax revenue obtained from the imposition of the $10 tax in Figure 6–5, part a, is $33,000 per month ($10 × 3,300 cases per month). In Figure 6–5, part b, it is $46,000 per month ($10 × 4,600 cases per month).

Elasticity of Supply

How does the elasticity of supply affect the way in which the incidence of the tax is distributed between buyers and suppliers? *Given demand, the less elastic is supply, the greater is the burden of the incidence of the tax on suppliers and the smaller is the burden of the incidence on buyers.* This is illustrated in

FIGURE 6-6 **Supply Elasticity and the Incidence of an Excise Tax**

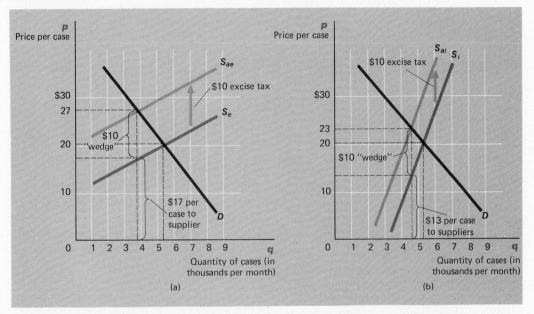

(a)

(b)

When supply is elastic, as in part a, the imposition of an excise tax forces the price to buyers up by more than it forces down the amount suppliers are able to keep after the government has been paid the tax. In part b, the demand curve is the same as in part a, but the supply curve is inelastic. The imposition of the same excise tax forces the price to buyers up by less than it forces down the amount suppliers are able to keep after the tax payment. The incidence of the tax bears heaviest on buyers when supply is elastic (part a) and heaviest on suppliers when supply is inelastic (part b).

Figure 6–6. The supply curve in Figure 6–6, part a, is more elastic than that in Figure 6–6, part b. Of the total excise tax of $10 per case in Figure 6–6, part a, buyers pay $7 while suppliers pay only $3. However, in the case of the less elastic supply curve in Figure 6–6, part b, suppliers bear the heaviest incidence of the tax, paying $7 per case while buyers pay only $3.

Subsidies

The same analysis used to examine the effects of an excise tax in Figures 6–5 and 6–6 can be applied to a study of the effects of government subsidies. A **subsidy** can be thought of as the reverse of an excise or sales

tax. While such taxes take money away from buyers and suppliers, a subsidy gives them money.

For example, suppose the government wanted to encourage wine production because it would promote economic development and help alleviate poverty in certain parts of the country suited to grape growing. Let's assume that the market supply curve is initially S_a in Figure 6–5, part a, with the equilibrium price and quantity determined by its intersection with D_e. Now suppose the government decides to pay suppliers a subsidy of $10 per case. This effectively reduces suppliers' costs by $10 per case of wine. The supply curve is therefore shifted down by this amount from S_a to S. The price of a case of wine falls to $20 per case, and the quantity supplied and sold rises from 3,300 to 5,300 cases per month, as determined by the intersection of S and D_e. *A subsidy typically has the effect of reducing price and increasing quantity supplied.* The extent of the price reduction and the quantity increase depends on the elasticity of the demand and supply curves. This can be seen by examining Figures 6–5 and 6–6.

CHECKPOINT 6-3

Suppose the supply curve is perfectly elastic (that is, horizontal) and the demand curve is like any of those shown in Figures 6–5 and 6–6. If an excise tax of $10 per case is now imposed, how will the incidence of this tax be distributed between buyers and sellers? Suppose the demand curve is perfectly elastic and the supply curve is like any of those shown in Figures 6–5 and 6–6. If an excise tax of $10 per case is imposed, how will the incidence of this tax be distributed between buyers and sellers? Suppose the demand curve is perfectly inelastic (that is, vertical) and the supply curve is like any of those shown in Figures 6–5 and 6–6. If an excise tax of $10 per case is imposed, how much will the price of a case of wine increase? Sometimes those who push for the imposition of excise taxes on liquor and tobacco do so because of a desire to reduce the consumption of these "socially harmful" goods. For any given size of the excise tax imposed, how will the elasticity of demand affect the degree to which consumption of these goods will be reduced? Do you think an excise tax on the red table wine mentioned in the Policy Perspective in Chapter 5 would produce much tax revenue, given the elasticity of the demand curve suggested by the numbers cited?

EXTERNALITIES—EXTERNAL COSTS AND BENEFITS

We have already seen in Chapter 4 how the intersection of the demand and supply curves for a good determines the equilibrium price and quantity. This is shown in Figure 6–7. To the right of the intersection, the supply curve is above the demand curve. This means that if suppliers produced an amount q_1 that is larger than the equilibrium quantity q_e, buyers would not be willing to pay a price high enough to cover the costs of supplying the additional units of output from q_e to q_1. That is, buyers do not value the additional benefits, represented by the area aq_eq_1b under the demand curve over the units of output from q_e to q_1, as highly as the value of the resources needed to produce them. The value of these resources is measured by their opportunity cost as represented by the area aq_eq_1c under the supply curve over the units of output from q_e to q_1. Resources would be overallocated to this activity in the sense that the cost to society of producing the units of output from q_e to q_1 exceeds their value to society by an amount represented by the triangular area abc. Therefore it would be economically inefficient to produce the output beyond q_e.

On the other hand, if suppliers produced an amount q_2 that is less than the equilibrium quantity q_e, buyers would be willing to pay a price that is more than enough to cover the costs of supplying additional units of output beyond q_2. This is reflected by the fact that the demand curve is higher than the supply curve to the left of the intersection. Producing the smaller quantity of output q_2 would mean an underallocation of resources to this activity. This is so because buyers value the additional benefits from the extra units of output from q_2 to q_e (represented by the area dq_2q_ea under the demand curve) more than the value of the resources needed to produce them. (Once again, the value of these resources is measured by their opportunity cost as represented by the area fq_2q_ea under the supply curve.) If suppliers produce no more

FIGURE 6-7 **The Optimum Quantity of Output**

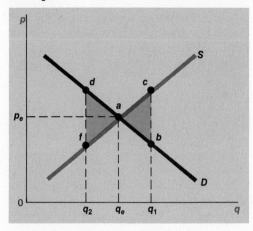

If suppliers produced an amount q_1 that is larger than the equilibrium quantity q_e, buyers would not be willing to pay a price high enough to cover the costs of supplying the additional units of output from q_e to q_1. To produce these extra units would be a waste of society's resources because buyers do not value the additional benefits as highly as the resources needed to produce them. Resources would be overallocated to this activity. If suppliers produced an amount q_2 that is less than the equilibrium quantity q_e, buyers would be willing to pay a price that is more than enough to cover the costs of supplying additional units of output from q_2 to q_e. To produce the smaller quantity of output q_2 would be an underallocation of resources to this activity. The optimum quantity is therefore q_e.

than the quantity q_2, society forgoes the excess of the value of the benefits over the costs represented by the triangular area *dfa*. In sum, the equilibrium quantity q_e determined by the intersection of the demand and supply curves is the only one for which buyers are just willing to pay a price p_e sufficient to cover the cost of the last unit produced. The value of the benefits of this last unit are just equal to the value of the resources needed to

produce it. The equilibrium quantity q_e is therefore the optimum quantity.

However, what if all the costs associated with producing the good are not paid by the firms who supply it? For example, when air and water are polluted by the production process, society at large typically bears the cost of either cleaning it up or suffering the higher health care and other costs that it may lead to. In such cases these costs are not reflected in the market supply curve for the good.

Similarly, what if the benefits associated with a good extend to others besides the buyers of the good? In this case, the total benefits may not be fully reflected in the demand curve for that good. Consider, for example, the purchase by farmers of fencing to keep their livestock from wandering. The fencing protects their investment in livestock, a private benefit that they derive directly. Society at large also benefits, however. There is a reduction in safety hazards, such as livestock wandering onto highways, and a reduction in crop loss caused by livestock wandering onto other farmers' wheat and corn fields. However, the market demand curve for fencing reflects only the value of the private benefits to the buyers of fencing, in this case the owners of the livestock.

Costs and benefits that fall on others besides the buyers and sellers of a good are often called **externalities**, or *external costs* and *benefits*. Frequently they are also referred to as *spillovers*, or *neighborhood effects*, or *external economies* and *diseconomies*. *All these terms refer to the fact that these costs and benefits fall on others besides the buyers and sellers directly involved in the transactions of the particular market for the good.*

External Costs

Suppose a particular industry pollutes the environment when it produces its product, but the cost of cleaning up the environment or suffering the consequences is borne by others. Since the firms in the industry do not

FIGURE 6-8   Externalities and the Allocation of Resources

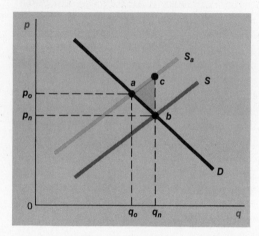

The presence of externalities in the form of spillover costs means the *market* supply curve S lies below the supply curve S_a, which includes all costs associated with production of the good. As a result, there is an *overallocation* of resources to the production of this good. Therefore the market equilibrium quantity q_n exceeds the optimum quantity q_o. Because buyers and suppliers don't pay all the costs of production, the market equilibrium price p_n is below the price p_o, which covers all costs.

give the market supply curve S_a, which includes all costs. Because of this, S_a lies above S. The equilibrium quantity produced and sold when firms pay all costs associated with production would be q_o, an amount smaller than q_n. The equilibrium price would be p_o, which is higher than p_n. The incidence of this added cost would be distributed between suppliers and buyers of the good in the same way as an excise tax, rather than falling on other parties who do not buy or sell the good.

Hence, when there are external costs associated with a good, costs not paid for by the buyers and suppliers of a good (sometimes called spillover costs), a greater quantity of output is produced and sold than is optimum. This is shown in Figure 6–8, where the supply curve S_a, which includes all costs, lies above the demand curve D for all units of the good from q_o to q_n. This means that the value of the benefits to buyers of this additional quantity of the good is less than the value of all the resources used to produce it by an amount represented by the triangular area abc.

In sum, *when there are external costs—costs of production not borne by the immediate buyers and suppliers of a good—there is an overallocation of resources to the production of that good. Therefore, more of it is produced and sold than is optimum.*

External Benefits

The market demand curve for a good reflects the value of the benefits of that good that accrue directly to those who buy it. If the good also provides externalities in the form of benefits to others who do not buy the good, these spillover, or external, benefits are not reflected in the market demand curve. The market demand curve for fencing reflects the value of its benefits to the farmers who buy the fencing to protect their investment in their livestock. It does not reflect the benefits of this fencing to motorists who drive on highways adjacent to cattle fields or

have to pay the cleanup cost, this cost is not included in the market supply curve S shown in Figure 6–8. It is an external cost borne by others not directly involved in the purchase or sale of the product. Given the market demand for the product, represented by the demand curve D, the equilibrium quantity produced and sold would be q_n and the equilibrium price p_n.

However, what if the firms in the industry had to pay the cleanup costs associated with the production of each unit of output? These costs would be added in just like an excise tax along with the other production costs to

FIGURE 6-9   Spillover Benefits and Resource Allocation

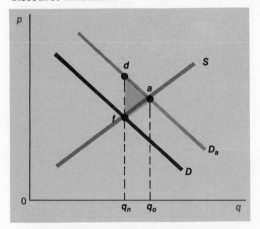

The presence of externalities in the form of spillover benefits means the market demand curve D lies below the demand curve D_a, which reflects all benefits associated with the consumption of a good. As a result, there is an *underallocation* of resources to the production of this good, so that the market equilibrium quantity q_n is less than the optimum quantity q_o.

to farmers who raise crops next door to cattle farms. Similarly, those who buy health care to protect their own well-being also generate benefits for others. For example, they reduce the spread of contagious diseases.

Since the market demand curve for these kinds of goods and services does not reflect the value of these social, or spillover, benefits, it must lie below a demand curve that is drawn to include them. Figure 6–9 shows a hypothetical market demand curve D and supply curve S for flu shots. If the value of the spillover benefits to society at large from these shots is added on, we get the demand curve D_a, which includes the value of all benefits and therefore lies above D. The market equilibrium quantity of flu shots supplied and purchased is q_n (determined by the intersection of S and D). However, the existence

of externalities in the form of social benefits means that this is less than the optimum quantity q_o (determined by the intersection of S and D_a). As a result, the demand curve D_a lies above the supply curve S for the additional flu shots from q_n to q_o. This means that the value of all the benefits to society from having these additional flu shots is greater than the cost of supplying them by an amount represented by the triangular area *adf*.

In general, *when there are external, or spillover, benefits associated with a good, too few resources are allocated to the production of that good and less of it is produced and sold than is optimum.*

Externalities and Government Policy

How can the external costs that arise in the markets for certain kinds of goods be internalized to those markets? That is, how can we ensure that such costs are borne by the buyers and sellers directly involved in the transactions in those markets, rather than by others? Similarly, what might be done to encourage a greater production of goods that have external benefits? We cannot give an exhaustive account of all the possible proposals for dealing with these questions. However, the following are often used or suggested by policymakers.

Policy and External Costs

Policies must be devised to make the suppliers and buyers in the market, rather than third parties who are not the immediate buyers and sellers of the good, bear the external costs. Corrective policy must somehow internalize these costs in the market where they occur. When the externalities associated with a good are external, or spillover, benefits, policies are needed that will encourage the production of a quantity of the good more in line with a demand that takes account of the value of all its benefits to society.

POLICY PERSPECTIVE

Acid Rain—A Spillover Cost or What?

As a practical matter of public policy it is not always easy to identify an external, or spillover, cost. An example is provided by the recent concern that acid rain is causing major damage to the lakes and forests of the northeastern United States and eastern Canada.

Those who are urging the government to take action to cut down the acidity of rain water are convinced that it is caused by sulfur-dioxide emissions from heavily industrialized regions in the Midwest and Northeast. The sulfur-dioxide emissions are thought to interact with moisture in the air to form sulfuric acid which then falls on lakes and forests whenever it rains or snows. If sulfur-dioxide emissions are indeed the culprit then it is a clear case of identifiable industries creating spillover costs for society at large. Government could mandate and enforce sulfur-dioxide emission controls and thereby internalize the costs to the polluters and those who buy their products. However, it is not certain that sulfur-dioxide emissions are the primary cause of acid rain, or even that the environmental problems noted are due to acid rain.

From 1965 to 1978, sulfur-dioxide emissions were reduced 38 percent in the Environmental Protection Agency's New England region and 40 percent in the New York and New Jersey region. Along with these emission changes, there was a 33 percent drop in sulfate concentrations in the rain measured at Hubbard Brook, New Hampshire (according to a 1983 National Academy of Sciences Report) and about a 30 percent drop in New York State (according to the U.S. Geological Survey). However the acidity of the rain showed no long-term changes in either place, suggesting that sulfate does not determine the acidity of rain. A 1982 report by New York's Acid Precipitation Research Needs Conference and the 1983 reports of Connecticut's Acid Rain Task Force and the National Acid Precipitation Assessment Program all claimed that they found no evidence of environmental problems that could be clearly linked to the acidity of precipitation. Parties on all sides of the issue do agree on one thing—more research on acid rain and its environmental impact is needed.

Questions

1. Suppose research does eventually show that sulfur dioxide is the primary causal factor in acid rain and that acid rain is harmful to the environment. Do you think it would be better to levy an excise tax on polluters to cover costs of environmental damage or to impose limits on measured sulfur dioxide emitted from smokestacks, thereby requiring business firms to incur the cost of installing smokestack scrubbers? Why?

2. Suppose those who believe sulfur dioxide is the culprit in acid rain are wrong, but nonetheless succeed in getting the government to take either one of the policy actions mentioned in question 1. How would you represent the cost to society of their being wrong in terms of a supply and demand curve diagram?

One way to deal with external costs is to pass laws that make them illegal. For example, a state or municipal government might pass laws against dumping untreated industrial wastes in rivers or pouring toxic smoke or particulate matter into the air. If the laws are backed up by sufficiently stiff fines and court actions against offenders, producing firms will take it on themselves to incur directly the costs of installing waste treatment and smoke abatement equipment as part of their production facilities. This means that the market supply curves in industries where there are external costs would shift upward as in Figure 6–8. The firms or suppliers in those industries are forced to pay those costs directly. The incidence of these additional costs would be distributed among the buyers and suppliers in proportions determined by the elasticities of demand and supply just as in the case of an excise tax.

Laws against external costs may not always be easy to enforce, however. Detection of offenders and a determination of the extent of their violation of the law can be difficult. Many different firms using a number of different production processes typically add to air pollution over a metropolitan area. Simply checking the air quality rarely gives a clear picture of who contributed what and how much to the situation. The condition of the water in rivers downstream from these areas raises the same kinds of problems for detection. How often do you read or hear of oil spills and oil slicks where the source is unknown? There may be many smokers but none willing to step forward and lay claim to the cigar and cigarette butts, especially when a fine is to be levied.

In such situations, it may be easier and more effective to simply levy excise taxes on those goods the production of which is known to give rise to spillover costs. This effectively shifts the market supply curves for these goods upward as in Figures 6–5 and 6–6. The tax revenues collected in this fashion can then be used by the government to finance cleanup operations such as waste treatment plants. In any event, such taxes have the effect of making the buyers and sellers in those markets bear the cleanup costs, while at the same time adjusting output so that it is closer to the optimum level.

Policy and External Benefits

How might the government encourage an increase in the production of those goods that give rise to external benefits? That is, how can it encourage the market depicted in Figure 6–9 to increase output from q_n to q_o? One way is to increase demand by giving buyers purchasing power in a form that can only be used to buy the particular good.

The food stamp program is an example of this strategy. It provides food stamps to people whose income falls below a certain level. The stamps may be used only to buy food. Food stores accept the stamps from buyers, and the government gives the stores money in exchange for the stamps. This effectively increases the demand for food on the part of people eligible to receive the stamps. This increase is reflected in the shift of the demand curve from D to D_a in Figure 6–9.

There may be many reasons for having such a program. Among them, it might be argued that by ensuring a better diet for poor people their state of health can be maintained or improved. This may make it possible for poor children to perform better in school and may increase the employability of adults in the job market. In short, to the extent it helps poor people to become productive members of the economy instead of indefinitely unemployed or handicapped (due to poor health) recipients of welfare, there are spillover benefits to society at large from such a program.

Another way the government might increase the output of a good would be simply to pay a per unit subsidy to suppliers (the reverse of an excise tax). This would shift the supply curve downward and increase output in the manner already discussed above in connection with subsidies.

CHECKPOINT 6-4

Suppose Senator Claghorn says that requiring pollution control equipment in a certain industry will result in costs that will be "passed on" entirely to consumers. What must the senator be assuming (probably unknowingly) about the elasticity of supply and demand in that industry? If strict pollution control laws were imposed on an industry, what combinations of supply and demand elasticities would result in severe reductions in employment in that industry?

Given your own impressions of the elasticity of demand for cigarettes, how do you think imposing an excise tax of $.20 per pack would affect the frequency of lung cancer?

Many states have laws requiring that all automobiles pass a safety inspection once a year. The inspections are typically made by privately owned service stations certified by the state to make the inspections and certify whether a car is safe or not. What does this law do to the demand for service maintenance? If you always keep your car in tip-top shape, why might you still favor this law despite the fact that the inspection costs you $10?

Given the information on the red table wine in the policy perspective of the previous chapter, do you think an excise tax on that wine would have much of an effect on its sales? Given the availability of substitutes, do you think this would do much to alleviate the spillover cost of drunk driving?

SUMMARY

1. Government-imposed price ceilings result in an excess of demand over supply, or a shortage, at the legal ceiling price. Because of this, strict enforcement measures are needed if the product is not to be traded in the black market at prices above the ceiling price. Government-managed rationing schemes are often used to ensure that all buyers who are willing to pay the ceiling price are able to get some of the good. Price ceilings are often used to affect resource allocation during wartime. Rent control is an example of how peacetime price ceilings can have wide-ranging economic and social implications.

2. Government-imposed price supports result in an excess of supply over demand, or a surplus, at the support price. In order to support the price at a level above that of market equilibrium, the government must do one of the following: buy and store the surplus, impose limitations on production, pursue policies that promote demand, or pay producers the difference between the support price and the lower price that producers receive in the market. In the case of services, such as labor services, the government may make it illegal to buy or sell them at a price less than a certain minimum price. Such policies have been used to support agricultural prices at various times.

3. Sales and excise taxes are the government's legal claim on a portion of the price paid for a unit of a good. They affect the equilibrium price and quantity in the market where they are imposed. The more elastic is the demand for a good, the smaller is the portion of the tax paid by buyers and the larger the portion paid by suppliers—the tax incidence is shifted onto suppliers. The more elastic is the supply for a good, the smaller is the portion of the tax paid by suppliers and the larger the portion paid by buyers—the tax incidence is shifted onto buyers.

4. Whenever the production and purchase of a good gives rise to costs or benefits that fall on parties other than the immediate buyers and sellers of the good, external, or spillover, costs and benefits are said to exist. When there are external costs associated with the production of a good, a greater than optimum quantity of the good is produced.

When there are external benefits, a less than optimum quantity of the good is produced. Policies are needed to internalize external costs in the markets where they occur and to encourage a greater production of goods that have external benefits.

KEY TERMS AND CONCEPTS

ad valorem tax
black market
excise tax
externalities
parity
price ceiling
price support
ration coupon
rent control
sales tax
specific tax
subsidy
tax incidence

QUESTIONS AND PROBLEMS

1. If an effective price ceiling were imposed on butter, what would happen to the price of margarine?

2. Suppose that during a war price ceilings were imposed on certain consumer goods industries in order to shift workers away from the production of peacetime goods and into the production of war goods.

a. What would have to be true of supply elasticities in consumer goods industries to make this a very effective way of achieving this objective?

b. What sort of demand elasticity conditions would make such a policy easier to administer for those responsible for the enforcement and administration of a rationing scheme?

c. What would be the sort of supply-and-demand conditions that would cause you

as a policymaker to shy away from imposing price controls on certain industries to achieve your objective?

3. It has been observed that when rent controls are imposed, owners of apartment buildings often convert them to condominiums (apartments that are owned by the occupant rather than rented). Can you explain this phenomenon?

4. Some have observed that in a way it is fortunate that the demand for agricultural products is relatively inelastic. They point out that the cost to government (and hence the taxpayer) of trying to support agricultural prices might otherwise have been larger than it has been all these years. Can you explain what these observers have in mind?

5. In 1965, many federal excise taxes were removed or sharply reduced. At the time, President Johnson stated that he wanted the American consumer to be the full beneficiary of the tax cut. He assigned several investigators to verify that this was the case—that is, to verify that prices were reduced by the full amount of the tax cut. In order for the president's desires to have been fulfilled, what would have had to be true in the industries where the excise taxes were cut?

6. Suppose an excise tax is levied on the output of television sets. What effect do you think this would have on the prices charged by movie theaters and the prices of tv dinners?

7. Suppose Congress decides it wants to formulate a tax policy that will "kill two birds with one stone." It wants to eliminate spillover costs in the markets where they occur and significantly increase tax revenues at the same time. Suppose it decides to impose excise taxes on those markets. What would have to be true in those markets if Congress is to be reasonably satisfied with the results?

8. Suppose antipollution laws are passed and effectively enforced in a certain region. In those markets where there are externalities in the form of spillover costs, what must be true of the elasticities of supply and demand curves if it is correctly claimed that the incidence of the burden, or cost of "cleaning up," bears heaviest on buyers? What must be true if the incidence of the burden falls heaviest on suppliers?

9. In 1919 Congress passed the Volstead Act prohibiting the production and sale of alcoholic beverages in the United States. What were the supporters of the act implicitly saying about their estimate of the size of the external costs associated with the production of liquor, wine, and beer? Draw a diagram of the market supply curve and demand curve for alcoholic beverages in the United States (nothing fancy—just a typical-looking demand and supply curve). Where do you think supporters of the Volstead Act would place the supply curve S_a that includes *all* costs? That is, where do you think the supply curve would hit the vertical axis in relation to where the market demand curve hits that axis?

7

The Firm and Its Costs of Production

AFTER READING THIS CHAPTER, YOU WILL BE ABLE TO:

1. Define the three legal forms of the firm—the proprietorship, the partnership, and the corporation—and state the differences between them.

2. Define the nature of the firm's explicit and implicit costs and the distinction between short-run and long-run costs.

3. Formulate the law of diminishing returns and show how it affects the behavior of variable costs as output changes.

4. Distinguish between fixed and variable costs and between total, average, and marginal costs.

5. Explain the relationship between the firm's short-run and long-run average total cost curves and how the shape of the latter is explained by economies and diseconomies of scale.

In the last two chapters we strengthened our understanding of the essential concepts of supply and demand and of the way they interact to form a market. However, in order to understand the way our economy is organized to produce goods, the underpinning of supply, we need to study the basic unit of production, the firm. In fact you may well spend most of your working life working for, managing, or even owning and running a firm. In that case you will have to become very familiar with the subjects of this chapter—the way firms are organized, the nature of production processes, and the costs of production. Subsequent chapters will analyze the way firms decide how much to produce and what price to charge for their product on the basis of their costs of production and the demand for their product.

THE FIRM

In Chapter 1, we said that a firm uses factors of production to produce goods that are sold. We need to expand on this definition here. *A* **firm** *is a business organization that owns, rents, and operates equipment, hires labor, and buys materials and energy inputs. It organizes and coordinates the use of all these factors of production for the purpose of producing and marketing goods and services.*

The concept of a plant is related to but distinct from that of a firm. *A* **plant** *is a facility where production takes place.* A factory, a store, a mine, a car wash—each of these is a plant. A firm owns and operates one or more plants. Some firms own several plants, each of which does the same thing. For example, Sears Roebuck and A&P are firms that own many retail stores. Firms that consist of such combinations are sometimes said to be **horizontally integrated**. On the other hand, a firm may own several plants, each of which handles a different stage in the production process. Automobile companies such as Ford and General Motors own iron mines, ore-carrying freighters, steel mills,

stamping plants, and assembly plants. A firm that combines plants in this way is said to be **vertically integrated**. Of course, firms can be horizontally and vertically integrated at the same time. Each of the automobile companies has a number of assembly plants located around the country, for example.

Another kind of firm, which you probably have heard a lot about in recent years, is the conglomerate. A **conglomerate** is a firm that produces a wide variety of different goods and services for sale in a number of largely unrelated markets. A conglomerate is usually formed by a parent firm that acquires a number of already existing firms. Often these firms keep their original trade names and are referred to as subsidiaries of the controlling parent firm. Gulf and Western Industries is a conglomerate that produces paper, sugar, and auto parts. It is also in the financial services business and even distributes motion pictures through its subsidiary, Paramount Pictures Corporation.

The diversity of firms in size and organization is astounding. At one extreme there are giants such as American Telephone and Telegraph and General Motors, which may realize sales of $40 billion annually and employ nearly a million people. At the other extreme are numerous small barbershops, restaurants, and corner groceries. It is not uncommon in the United States for a half million new businesses to be started in a single year and almost as large a number to fail. These large numbers testify to the strength of the urge to "make a buck," as well as the risk of losing that buck and more, that is inherent in business enterprise.

Legal Forms of the Firm

So far, we have been concerned with the firm in terms of what it does, how it is organized, what it produces, and how big it is. But a firm is also a legal entity that operates subject to certain obligations and constraints under the law. Just what these are depends on the legal form the firm takes. There are three basic legal forms for a firm: the proprietorship, the partnership, and the corporation.

The Proprietorship

In this form of organization, which is sometimes called the **sole proprietorship**, there is a single owner or proprietor who makes all decisions and bears full responsibility for everything the firm does. There are around 12 million firms of this type in the United States. Farms, small retail stores, barbershops, accounting firms, and medical and law practices are very often sole proprietorships.

The main advantage of this type of firm is that the owner is the only boss and therefore has full control over the firm. There are three main disadvantages, however. One is that the resources of the firm are limited by the amount of financial capital the owner either possesses or can borrow. Second, the owner has unlimited liability. This means that he or she is fully liable for all debts and obligations of the firm. If the firm gets into financial difficulty and does not have adequate funds to pay its debts, the owner's personal property and funds may be seized by the firm's **creditors** (i.e., those to whom the firm owes money). The third disadvantage is that the proprietor must be able to do the many different tasks necessary for managing the firm's operation. This also puts severe limits on the size of the firm.

The Partnership

A **partnership** is formed whenever two or more individuals get together and agree to own and operate a business jointly. The partnership has two potential advantages over a proprietorship. First, because there is more than one owner, the partnership's financial resources may be larger and its ability to borrow greater than is typically the case for a proprietorship. Second, management and other tasks may be divided up among partners, thereby permitting greater specialization and efficiency of operation than is possible for a proprietorship.

There are some important disadvantages to a partnership, however. First of all, the partners have unlimited liability. Therefore, each risks all personal as well as business assets on the management decisions of the others. Sometimes in order to get more money in the firm without forcing the investor to bear the full risks of partnership, a limited partnership status is granted. A **limited partner** risks only the money directly invested in the firm. A limited partner's personal assets cannot be seized to satisfy the firm's debts and obligations. In return for this arrangement, a limited partner does not participate in the management of the firm or engage in business on behalf of the partners.

Another disadvantage of a partnership is that if a partner dies or leaves, the partnership arrangement must be dissolved and reorganized. This can interrupt the business operations of the firm for a time.

There are about a million partnerships in the United States. They are common in law and investment banking. In these areas, the client's trust is a large factor in doing business. The partners' unlimited liability for one another's actions is thought to promote the client's trust in the firm.

The Corporation

Unlike proprietorships and partnerships, a **corporation** has a legal identity separate and distinct from the people who own it. In contrast to proprietorships and partnerships, a corporation can, in the course of doing business, enter into all manner of contracts that are legal obligations of the corporation but not of its owners. The owners are therefore said to have **limited liability**. In essence this means that a corporation can be sued but not its owners. In the event of failure to meet its debts, pay its bills, or deliver goods and services it has contracted to produce, the limits of financial liability extend only to the assets of the corporation. They do not extend to the personal assets of its owners, those who own shares of stock in the corporation.

A stockholder's financial liability is limited to only the amount of money that is invested in the firm through the purchase of stock.

Advantages of the Corporation

The chief advantage of setting up a firm as a corporation instead of as a proprietorship or partnership is that it makes it much easier to raise money for investment in the firm. Because their liability is limited, numerous investors, both large and small, are willing to invest their money in an incorporated firm. Such firms are therefore able to raise the large amounts of money needed to finance the large plants and complex production processes used in a highly industrialized economy. In exchange for their money, investors receive ownership shares, or stock, in the firm. These shares entitle them to vote for a board of directors who are responsible for the overall supervision of the firm and the hiring of its top-level managers. They are also entitled to share in the company's profits, which are called **dividends** when paid out. Profits not paid out, called **undistributed profits**, also belong to the shareholders. They are usually reinvested in the firm's operations.

Organized stock exchanges make it relatively easy for investors to acquire or sell shares in corporations. They can diversify risks by owning shares in several firms that are engaged in widely different businesses without having to become directly involved in the management of any of them. All of these considerations make it easier for investors to share in the monetary returns from enterprise without having to bear the risks and shoulder the management responsibilities associated with either a proprietorship or a partnership.

Because the shares in a corporation can be easily bought and sold, change of ownership does not cause disruptions in operations the way it does in either a proprietorship or a partnership. This gives the corporation a life of its own apart from its ownership. This continuity of existence makes long-range planning easier and also increases the ability of the incorporated firm to borrow money.

Disadvantages of the Corporation

Despite all these positive features, there are some disadvantages. While considering them, bear in mind that there are roughly 2 million corporations and that they account for over 60 percent of the output produced by all firms in the United States. This emergence of the corporation as the dominant form of organization suggests that its advantages far outweigh its disadvantages.

Compared to a proprietorship or partnership, the stockholder in a corporation often has little meaningful influence over the board of directors and management policy. Even though each share of stock entitles the owner to one vote, a large corporation may have so many shares outstanding that most investors can't hope to own enough of them to have a significant voting bloc. As a result, ownership and control can become separated to a much larger extent than is typically possible in a partnership. In a proprietorship, of course, the two functions are one and the same.

The personal income that a proprietor or the members of a partnership receive as the profit from their business can be taxed as high as 50 percent. Profits of corporations may be taxed as much as 46 percent. However, dividends to stockholders, which are paid out of the profit remaining after payment of this tax, are then taxed at personal income tax rates. Corporate profits are thus subject to double taxation, while those of proprietorships and partnerships are not. Some argue this constitutes an unfair discrimination against the owners (stockholders) of corporations.

Costs of the Firm

In Chapter 2 we saw that all costs are opportunity costs due to the fact that resources are scarce and have alternative uses. The production possibilities frontier shows that if resources are used to produce one good, they are not available to produce other goods. The **economic cost** of a good is therefore the alternative goods that must be forgone in order to produce it. This notion of cost is directly applicable to the individual firm.

The resources that a firm needs in order to produce its product have costs attached to them because they have alternative uses in the production of other products by other firms. Economists generally divide these costs into two groups, *explicit* costs and *implicit* costs. Added together, they make up the opportunity costs for the firm.

Explicit Costs

Some of the resources the firm needs must be purchased or hired from outside the firm and must be obtained by a direct monetary payment. Such resources include electricity, fuel, materials, labor, insurance, and so forth. The payments that must be made for these resources are considered **explicit costs**. If we consider the case of a mom-and-pop grocery store, for example, explicit costs would include property taxes, maintenance costs, payments to wholesalers for goods to be sold in the store, and the salary of a stock clerk.

Implicit Costs

Some resources needed by the firm are actually owned by the firm itself. Such resources include the managerial skills and financial resources of the owners. In the case of managerial skills, the cost of such resources is the payments they could have received were they employed in their next best alternative. Similarly, the cost of financial resources is the return they would have received were they invested in their next best alternative. Since these resources are not obtained by direct monetary payments, their costs are considered to be **implicit costs**.

Returning once again to the mom-and-pop grocery store, let's assume that the grocers own the store outright, use their own funds to finance inventories, and put 80 hours a week into running the store. The implicit cost of such resources would include the rent the grocers could receive if they leased the building to another firm, the interest or dividends their money could earn if invested elsewhere, and the salaries they could earn if they were employed in another business.

Accounting Profit, Economic Profit, and Normal Profit

There are three distinct notions of profit, each of which is based on a different way of measuring the costs of the firm in relation to its revenues. These three types of profit are *accounting profit*, *economic profit*, and *normal profit*.

Accounting profit is determined by subtracting the firm's explicit costs from its total sales receipts. This notion of profit does not consider any implicit costs.

Economic profit is the difference between the total revenue obtained from the firm's sales and the opportunity costs of all the resources used by the firm. (As we have already seen, the opportunity costs of all the resources used by the firm are the total of all explicit and implicit costs.) If this calculation results in a value of zero, then these opportunity costs are just being covered by sales receipts. Since all resources are therefore receiving just the amount they could get in their best alternative uses, there is no incentive for any of them to move to another firm. If economic profit were zero for each and every firm in the retail grocery industry, there would be no firms going out of business and leaving the industry.

What if our calculation of economic profit for the grocery store resulted in a negative value? That is, what if the sum of explicit and implicit costs were larger than sales receipts? In this case, we would say that the business was operating at an economic loss. It would now be impossible for all the resources used in the grocery business to be compensated by the full amount of their opportunity costs. *Negative economic profit, therefore, causes resources to move to alternative lines of productive activity where markets value their services enough to pay their opportunity costs.* If economic profit were negative for one or more firms in the retail grocery industry for any length of time, we would see firms going out of business and resources leaving that industry.

On the other hand, what would happen if our calculation of economic profit resulted in a positive value? This would mean that sales receipts are more than adequate to cover the sum of explicit and implicit costs. In other words, sales receipts cover more than the opportunity cost of all resources used. *Positive economic profit, therefore, attracts resources away from other lines of productive activity into those where they can earn more than their opportunity cost.* If economic profit were positive for one or more firms in the retail grocery industry for any length of time, we would see new firms opening up and resources moving into that industry.

The size of economic profit determines whether resources will be moving into or out of particular lines of productive activity. If economic profit is positive in a particular line of productive activity, resources will be drawn into that activity. If it is negative, they will tend to move out of that activity. If economic profit is zero, there will be no incentive for resources to move into or out of that activity. In this way, economic profit allocates resources among alternative productive activities in the economy.

Normal profit is what the firm is said to earn when economic profit is zero. In that case, all resources employed by the firm are just earning their opportunity costs. In particular, *when the financial capital and the entrepreneurial skills used by the firm are being compensated just enough to keep them from leaving and going into some other line of productive activity, it is said that they are earning a normal profit.* In the case of the grocery store, the grocers' entrepreneurial skills, their own funds invested in the business, and the building they own and use for the store are receiving a normal profit. That is, sales receipts are just sufficient to pay all explicit costs with enough left to just cover the implicit costs of entrepreneurial skills and financial capital.

Note that in this instance financial capital includes the grocers' own funds put directly into the business, to purchase inventories, say, *plus* the money value of the building they own and use in the business. Whether these funds are tied up in inventories or in buildings, they constitute the financial capital required to run a retail grocery business. The inventories and building necessary to do business are merely the physical capital counterpart to the financial capital. The grocers did not need to use their own funds in this way. Instead, they could have rented the building from someone else and borrowed the funds necessary to acquire inventories. It makes no difference whether the grocers provide the financial capital or whether they borrow and rent it from other parties. If the financial capital is not compensated at a rate of return equal to that which it could earn in its next best alternative, it will not be made available for use in the grocery business.

When economic profit is positive, the entrepreneurial skills and financial capital used by the firm are earning more than a normal profit. Similarly when economic profit is negative, these resources are earning less than a normal profit.

The Short Run and the Long Run

In Chapter 5 we noted that in economic analysis it is frequently useful to make a distinction between the short run and the long run. *By the* **short run** *we typically mean a period of time short enough so that the amounts of at least one or more of the factors of production used by the firm cannot be changed.* In a barbershop it takes little time, perhaps a week, to install another chair and find another barber to increase the production of haircuts. For a barbershop, therefore, the short run may be as little as a week. It may also take only a week or two to lease some space and get started in many small businesses. U.S. Steel, on the other hand, needs considerably more time to add another rolling mill or more blast furnaces and hire a work force to run them. The short run for U.S. Steel may be months or even years. Obviously, the actual length of time of the short run will depend on the kind of firm and industry we are talking about.

By the **long run** *we mean a period of time long enough so that the amounts of all factors of production used by the firm can be changed.* In other words, the long run is the amount of time it takes for a new firm to get started and operating or for an existing firm to shut down, dispose of its assets, and go out of business. For a barbershop the long run may be any time period longer than a week or two. For U.S. Steel it may be any time period longer than 2 or 3 years. The difference between the behavior of the firm's costs in the short run and the long run is very significant in the analysis of the firm, as we shall see.

CHECKPOINT* 7-1

How is a stockholder's status in a corporation different from a limited partner's status in a partnership? In what sense is a normal profit really an economic cost? Suppose there are two grocery stores that are sole proprietorships, that each has the same level of sales, and that each realizes zero economic profit. Can you think of reasons why their accounting profits might be different?

*Answers to all Checkpoints can be found at the back of the text.

PRODUCTION AND COSTS IN THE SHORT RUN

In the short run, as we have just noted, some of the firm's factors of production are fixed. Therefore, the firm's level of output during this period can be altered only by changing the quantities of the factors of production that are not fixed—the variable factors. We

need to examine the way output typically changes when these variable factors change. This in turn will allow us to examine how the firm's costs vary when output is changed in the short run.

To simplify matters somewhat, we will analyze the output and costs of a firm that has only two factors of production—capital and labor. In the short run, we will assume that capital (plant and equipment) is the **fixed factor**. Labor (number of laborers) will be the **variable factor**. Our analysis would be more complicated if we considered a firm that had several fixed factors and several variable factors. Since the conclusions would be the same, however, we will choose the simpler case for analysis.

Let's suppose that our firm makes chairs. Given its fixed stock of capital, the firm can vary the quantity of chairs produced only by changing the quantity of labor it uses. The data on quantity produced and laborers employed are given in Table 7-1. From this table, we can see that the total quantity of chairs produced (column 2) gets larger as more laborers are employed (column 1). At first glance, we might be tempted to assume that the way to expand the quantity of output indefinitely is simply to keep adding more workers. A closer look will show us that this is not the case, however.

Law of Diminishing Returns

Let's begin by assuming that the firm's fixed capital stock is idle and no labor is employed—hence there is no output. Now consider how total output changes with the addition of each successive laborer. The increase in output per each additional laborer is called the **marginal product**. The employment of the first laborer (where none had been working before) increases total output from zero up to 1 chair (column 2). Thus the marginal product of the first laborer is 1 (column 3). Adding a second laborer increases total output by 2 chairs, from 1 up to 3 chairs (column 2). The marginal product of the second laborer therefore equals 2 (column 3). The

TABLE 7-1 Chair Production and the Law of Diminishing Returns

(1)	(2)	(3)	(4)
Number of Laborers Used	Total Quantity of Chairs Produced per Week	Marginal Product (Change in Output of Chairs)	Average Product
0	0		—
		+1	
1	1		1
		+2	
2	3		1.5
		+3	
3	6		2
		+4	
4	10		2.5
		+3	
5	13		2.6
		+2	
6	15		2.5
		+1.5	
7	16.5		2.3
		+1	
8	17.5		2.2
		+ .5	
9	18		2
		0	
10	18		1.8

marginal product continues to increase until 4 laborers have been hired, the marginal product of the fourth laborer being equal to 4 (column 3). Hence up through the employment of 4 laborers, the addition to total output attributable to each successive laborer gets larger and larger—in other words, the marginal product (column 3) increases as the first laborers are employed. This occurs because the plant and equipment are difficult to operate effectively with just a few laborers. As more are added, each is able to specialize at fewer tasks and the production process runs more smoothly.

However, once 4 laborers are employed, the marginal product of each successive laborer employed after that gets smaller. Total output continues to get larger (column 2), but by smaller and smaller amounts (column 3). For instance, while the fourth laborer has

a marginal product of 4, the fifth laborer's marginal product is 3, the sixth's is 2, and so on. Why is this so? As more laborers are added, but the fixed stock of capital remains the same, crowding becomes a problem. Some laborers are idle part of the time while waiting for others to finish using a piece of equipment. Eventually, there is simply not enough equipment to go around. In the extreme, if enough laborers were crammed into the plant, production would be halted completely as movement became impossible.

In Figure 7-1, part a, the total quantity of chairs produced (Table 7-1, column 2) is plotted on the vertical axis. The number of laborers employed in the production process (Table 7-1, column 1) is plotted on the horizontal axis. This graph showing the relationship between the number of laborers employed and the total quantity of output produced, given the fixed quantity of capital, is the **short-run production function.** In Figure 7–1, part b, the marginal product (Table 7–1, column 3) is plotted on the vertical axis and, as in part a, the number of laborers is plotted on the horizontal axis. (Note that the marginal product data are plotted midway between the labor levels for which they are computed.) The marginal product graph clearly shows how the marginal product rises until 4 laborers are employed and then begins to decline as laborers are added beyond this point. Its shape illustrates the **law of diminishing returns.** *This law states that as more and more of a variable factor of production, or input (such as labor), is used together with a fixed factor of production (such as capital), beyond some point the additional, or marginal, product attributable to each additional unit of the variable factor begins to fall.*

Comparison of parts a and b of Figure 7–1 clearly shows that total output is increasing as long as marginal product is positive. When marginal product falls to zero, total output reaches its peak. There are increasing returns when marginal product is rising, and diminishing returns when it is declining.

Another measure that also reflects the law of diminishing returns is **average product,** or output per laborer (Table 7–1, column 4). The average product equals total output (column 2) divided by the corresponding quantity of labor (column 1). Average product is also plotted in Figure 7–1, part b, along with marginal product. Note that as long as marginal product is greater than average product, average product must rise, and when marginal product is less than average product, average product must fall. It necessarily follows that the marginal product graph crosses the highest point on the average product graph (corresponding to 5 units of labor, part b of Figure 7–1). This is simply a property of the mathematics of averages. If the additional, or marginal, product of one more laborer is greater than the average product of all previous laborers, then the additional laborer's contribution will raise average prod-

uct. On the other hand, when the additional, or marginal, product of one more laborer is less than the average product, the additional laborer's contribution will cause average product to fall. The same principle causes the average height of the people in a room to be raised whenever an additional (marginal) person enters who is taller than the average of those already in the room. Similarly the average height is lowered whenever someone enters whose height is below the average.

Total Cost in the Short Run

Table 7–2 shows the chair firm's short-run cost schedule. That is, the table indicates the various measures of the firm's costs (columns 3, 4, and 6–9) that are associated with each level of output (column 2) and the corresponding input of labor (column 1). First consider the relationship between the total output of chairs (column 2) and total cost (column 5) and its two components, total fixed cost (column 3) and total variable cost (column 4).

Total Fixed Cost (TFC)

In the short run the firm is saddled with its **total fixed cost,** *the cost of its unchangeable, or fixed, factors of production.* The property tax on its land and buildings, the interest payments on the money it borrowed to finance purchase of plant and equipment, and the opportunity cost of its own money invested in such facilities, measured as the return that money could earn if it were invested elsewhere, are all fixed costs in the short run. (Total fixed cost is often referred to as "overhead.") In the short run, total fixed cost is always the same no matter what level of output the firm produces—which is what is meant by the term "fixed."

Suppose that for the firm making chairs the total fixed cost attributable to its fixed factor, capital, amounts to $50 per week. This cost (column 3) is the same no matter

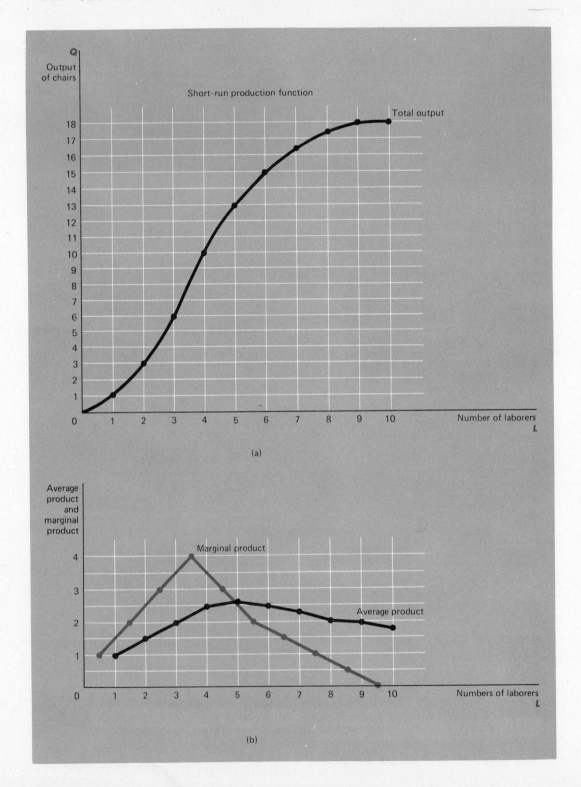

(a)

(b)

TABLE 7-2 Short-Run Cost Schedules for a Firm Producing Chairs (Hypothetical Data)

(1)	(2)	(3)	(4)	(5)	(6)	(7)	(8)	(9)
Number of Laborers (L)	Quantity of Output per Week (Q)	Total Fixed Cost (TFC)	Total Variable Cost (TVC)	Total Cost (TC)	Average Fixed Cost (AFC)	Average Variable Cost (AVC)	Average Total Cost (ATC)	Marginal Cost (MC)
			$TVC =$ wage $\times L$ (wage = $50 per week)	$TC =$ $TFC +$ $TVC =$ (3) + (4)	$AFC =$ $\frac{TFC}{Q} =$ $\frac{(3)}{(2)}$	$AVC =$ $\frac{TVC}{Q} =$ $\frac{(4)}{(2)}$	$ATC =$ $\frac{TC}{Q} =$ $\frac{(5)}{(2)}$	$MC =$ $\frac{\text{change in } TC}{\text{change in } Q}$ $\frac{\text{change in (5)}}{\text{change in (2)}}$
0	0	$50	$ 0	$ 50				$ 50.00
1	1	50	50	100	$50.00	$50.00	$100.00	25.00
2	3	50	100	150	16.66	33.33	50.00	16.66
3	6	50	150	200	8.33	25.00	33.33	12.50
4	10	50	200	250	5.00	20.00	25.00	16.66
5	13	50	250	300	3.84	19.23	23.07	25.00
6	15	50	300	350	3.33	20.00	23.33	33.33
7	16.5	50	350	400	3.00	21.20	24.20	50.00
8	17.5	50	400	450	2.80	22.80	25.70	100.00
9	18	50	450	500	2.77	25.00	27.77	

what quantity of chairs is produced per week (column 2). It is plotted in Figure 7–2 to give the total fixed cost curve TFC.

Total Variable Cost (TVC)

The costs that the firm can vary in the short run by changing the quantity of the variable factors of production and hence the quantity of output produced make up the **total variable cost.** Payments for natural gas, fuels, electricity, materials, and labor are all variable costs.

In the case of the chair firm, the only variable cost is that due to the variable factor labor. Suppose each laborer is paid $50 per

---

FIGURE 7-1 The Law of Diminishing Returns

Part a, based on the data from columns 1 and 2 of Table 7–1, shows how larger quantities of total output (vertical axis) can be produced by using larger quantities of labor, the variable input (horizontal axis), given a fixed amount of capital. As more labor is added, total output at first rises by ever larger amounts, up to 4 laborers, and then rises by ever diminishing amounts until it reaches a maximum at 9 laborers. Further additions of labor would actually reduce total output. This is further illustrated in part b (using the data of columns 3 and 4), where the graph of marginal product shows how the increase in total output associated with each additional laborer at first rises and then declines as more labor is used. Average product rises as long as marginal product exceeds it and declines when marginal product is below it. Hence marginal product intersects average product where the latter is a maximum.

FIGURE 7-2   Total Cost Equals Total Variable Cost Plus Total Fixed Cost

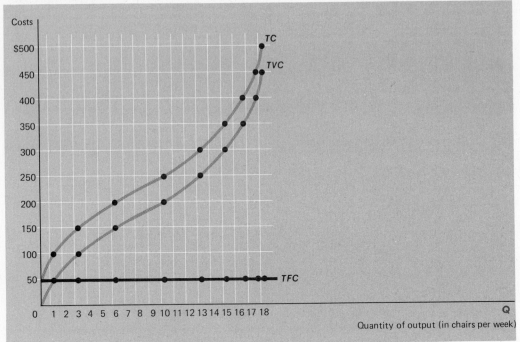

Total fixed cost *(TFC)* is the cost of the firm's fixed factors and is the same no matter what the level of production. Hence, the *TFC* curve is horizontal. Total variable cost *(TVC)* is the cost of the firm's variable factors. This cost varies with the level of production and is zero at zero level of output. The shape of the *TVC* curve shows that variable cost rises at a decreasing rate up to some point and at an increasing rate beyond. This reflects the law of diminishing returns. The total cost *(TC)* is the sum of total variable cost and total fixed cost. The *TC* curve is therefore parallel to the *TVC* curve and lies above it by the amount of the total fixed cost. The points on the curves shown here are plotted from the data of Table 7–2.

week. Multiplying the number of laborers *(L)* in column 1 by this wage therefore gives the *TVC* in column 4 associated with each quantity *(Q)* of chairs produced (column 2). The total variable cost is plotted in Figure 7-2 to give the total variable cost curve *TVC*.

Note that if the graph in Figure 7–1, part a, is turned around so that the vertical axis measuring *Q* becomes the horizontal axis and the horizontal axis measuring *L* becomes the vertical axis, we get the *TVC* curve of Figure

7-2 by simply multiplying the number of laborers by their weekly wage of $50 per laborer. Hence we see that the *TVC* curve reflects the law of diminishing returns in that it first rises at a decreasing rate and then at an increasing rate as the production of chairs is increased.

Total Cost (TC)

The firm's **total cost** *is the sum of its total fixed cost and its total variable cost at any*

given level of output. For the chair firm, total costs *TC* (column 5) are the sum of *TFC* (column 3) and *TVC* (column 4).

The total costs are plotted to give the *TC* curve of Figure 7–2. It is parallel to the *TVC* curve. For each output level *Q*, the associated point on the *TC* curve lies directly above the associated point on the *TVC* curve. The distance between these points is equal to the amount of the total fixed costs. This reflects the fact that because total fixed costs are constant, the variation in total costs is due entirely to the changes in total variable costs when the level of output is changed.

It can also be seen from Table 7–2 and Figure 7–2 that when output is zero, *TFC* and *TC* are one and the same. This simply reflects the fact that when nothing is produced, no labor is used and so there are no variable costs.

CHECKPOINT 7-2

How would the curves in Figure 7–2 be affected if total fixed cost was increased from $50 to $75? How would these curves be affected if wages rose from $50 to $75 per week? Show the effects of such changes graphically.

Average Cost in the Short Run

Now consider columns 6, 7, and 8 of Table 7–2. These columns represent average fixed cost, average variable cost, and average total cost.

Average Fixed Cost (AFC)

The **average fixed cost** at any given output level is calculated by dividing total fixed cost by that output level. In symbols this becomes

$$AFC = \frac{TFC}{Q}$$

This equation may also be interpreted as the firm's total fixed cost per unit of output produced. For the firm of Table 7–2, the *AFC* shown in column 6 is obtained by dividing the *TFC* of column 3 by the *Q* of column 2. Looking at column 6, we can see that *AFC* falls as *Q* is increased. This happens because *TFC* is the same no matter what the output level. Therefore the larger the output level, the more these overhead costs are spread out. This is clearly shown in Figure 7–3, where the *AFC* data of column 6 are plotted to give the *AFC* curve.

Now we can understand what is meant by a news item commenting on declining business profits with the statement: "When a company's volume of sales for the year turns out to be lower than was budgeted, its fixed costs, which include such items as depreciation, interest, and overhead, must be spread over a smaller volume of sales. This cuts into the company's profits per unit of sales." The lower the level of output, the larger is average, or per unit, fixed cost. Given the price at which a unit of output is sold, the larger is the portion of the price that must go to cover the per unit fixed costs. Hence the smaller is the portion of the price left over for profit.

Average Variable Cost (AVC)

The **average variable cost** at any given output level is calculated by dividing total variable cost by that output level. In symbols this becomes

$$AVC = \frac{TVC}{Q}$$

In Table 7–2 the *AVC* shown in column 7 is obtained by dividing the *TVC* of column 4 by the *Q* of column 2. The figures from column 7 are plotted in Figure 7–3 to give the *AVC* curve.

Notice that *AVC* at first falls as *Q* increases and then rises. This happens because the *AVC* data are derived from the *TVC* data, and since *TVC* reflects the law of diminishing returns so does *AVC*. When output falls to low enough levels, *AVC*, or average variable cost per unit, rises in the same manner as *AFC*, or average fixed cost per unit. This can be seen clearly in Figure 7–3.

FIGURE 7-3 **The Average and Marginal Cost Curves**

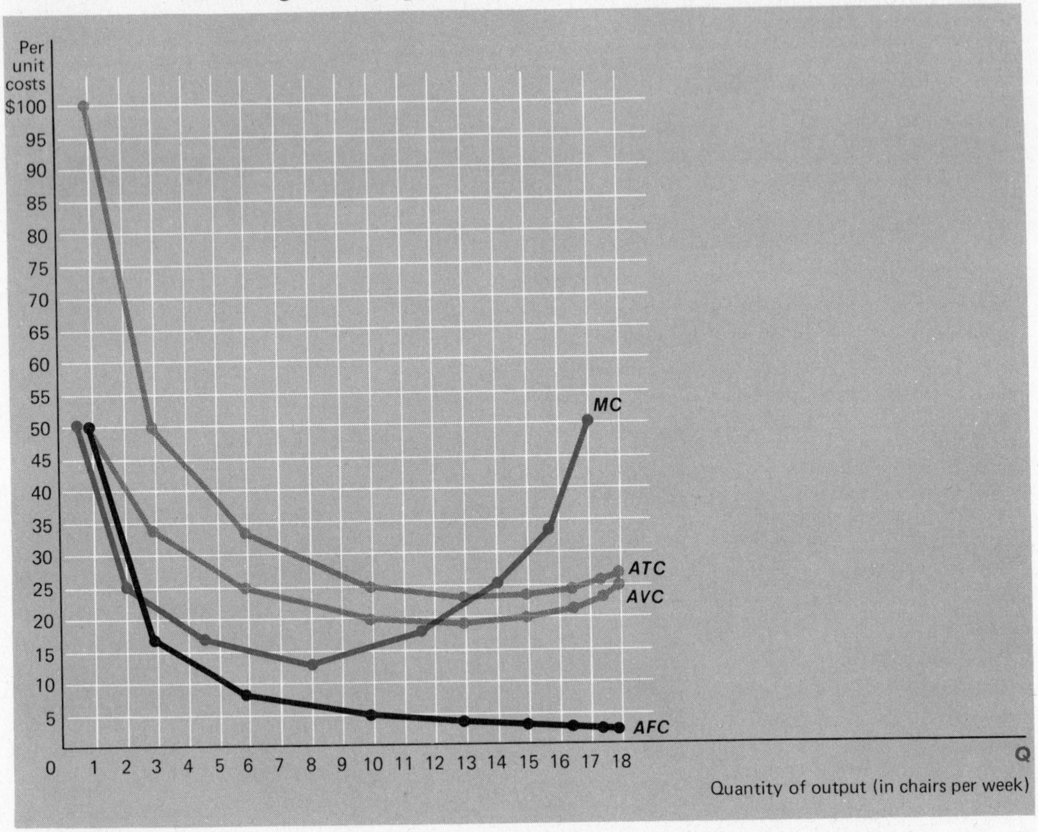

Quantity of output (in chairs per week)

Average fixed cost *(AFC)* is equal to total fixed cost *(TFC)* divided by output *(Q)*. The *AFC* curve here is plotted from the data in column 6 of Table 7–2. *AFC* falls as *Q* is increased because *TFC* is the same no matter what the output level. Hence the overhead costs are spread out.

Average variable cost *(AVC)* is equal to total variable cost *(TVC)* divided by output *(Q)*. The *AVC* curve is plotted from the data in column 7 of Table 7–2. *AVC* first falls as *Q* increases and then rises, reflecting the law of diminishing returns.

Average total cost *(ATC)* is equal to total cost divided by output *(Q)*. The *ATC* curve is plotted from the data in column 8 of Table 7–2. Since *ATC* equals *AFC* plus *AVC,* the *ATC* curve may be viewed as the sum of the *AFC* and the *AVC* curves. Hence at any output level the distance between the *ATC* curve and the *AVC* curve equals *AFC*.

Marginal cost *(MC)* is the change in total cost associated with the production of an additional unit of output *(Q)*. Equivalently, marginal cost is the change in total variable cost associated with the production of an additional unit of output. The *MC* curve is plotted from the data in column 9 of Table 7–2. Its shape reflects the law of diminishing returns. The *MC* curve always crosses the *AVC* and *ATC* curves at their bottommost points.

Average Total Cost (ATC)

The **average total cost** at any given output level is obtained by simply dividing total cost by that output level:

$$ATC = \frac{TC}{Q}$$

However, since $TC = TFC + TVC$, we see that

$$ATC = \frac{TFC + TVC}{Q}$$

And knowing that

$$\frac{TFC}{Q} = AFC$$

and

$$\frac{TVC}{Q} = AVC$$

we can say that

$$ATC = AFC + AVC$$

The data for ATC are shown in column 8 of Table 7–2. At any output level, it can be seen that the figure in column 8 can be obtained by dividing the figure in column 5 by that in column 2, or alternatively by adding the figures in columns 6 and 7. The data in column 8 are plotted in Figure 7–3 to give the ATC curve. At any output level, the distance between the ATC curve and the AVC curve equals AFC.

Because ATC is the sum of AFC and AVC, the diagnosis given in the news item referred to above could be carried even further. Observe that as output falls to low enough levels, ATC, or average total cost per unit, rises as shown in Figure 7–3. Given the price per unit of output, this means a larger portion of the price is required to cover average total cost per unit. Hence a smaller portion is left for profit. The news item most likely means accounting profit when referring to "profits per unit of sales."

CHECKPOINT 7-3
Suppose total fixed cost falls by $10. Show how this will affect average fixed cost, average variable cost, and average total cost in Table 7–2 and Figure 7–3. Suppose the weekly wage of a laborer increases from $50 to $60 per week. Show how this will affect average fixed cost, average variable cost, and average total cost in Table 7–2 and Figure 7–3.

Marginal Cost in the Short Run

Marginal cost *(MC)* is one of the most important concepts in economics. *The addition, or increment, to cost associated with producing one more unit of output is the* **marginal cost**. Since total cost changes with output only because total variable cost changes, marginal cost may be viewed equivalently as either the addition to total cost or the addition to total variable cost associated with the production of an additional unit of output. Therefore, we can say that

$$MC = \frac{\text{change in } TC}{\text{change in } Q} = \frac{\text{change in } TVC}{\text{change in } Q}$$

Marginal Cost and the Law of Diminishing Returns

Marginal cost for our hypothetical chair firm is given in column 9 of Table 7–2. Since labor is the only variable factor, TC and TVC change only because of the change in the employment of labor. Starting from a zero level of output, the marginal cost of the first chair produced is $50, which is just the change in TVC (column 4). It is also the change in TC (column 5) divided by one chair. The successive changes in total output Q (column 2) associated with the employment of each additional laborer (column 1) vary according to the law of diminishing returns, as indicated by the marginal product figures in column 3 of Table 7–1. (Note that columns 1 and 2 of Table 7–1 are the same as columns 1 and 2 of Table 7–2.) This is reflected in the data for MC (column 9 of Table 7–2), which is computed as the change in TC divided by the change in Q or the marginal product associated with the employment of each additional laborer.

Since the marginal product of labor *increases* up to the point where 4 laborers are employed, and since the increase in cost associated with each additional laborer is always the same ($50), marginal cost *decreases* over this range. However, beyond this point, the marginal product of labor begins to *decrease* with the employment of each additional laborer. Again, since the increase in cost due to each additional laborer is always $50, marginal cost *increases* from this point on.

The marginal cost data of column 9 are plotted in Figure 7–3 to give the *MC* curve. (Note that the *MC* data are plotted midway between the output levels for which they are computed.) *The shape of the MC curve clearly reflects the fact that MC falls when the marginal product of the variable factor (labor) rises, and that MC rises when the marginal product of the variable factor falls.*

The Relationship Between Marginal and Average Cost

Looking at columns 7, 8, and 9 of Table 7–2, we can see that, starting from a zero level of output, *AVC* and *ATC* fall as output increases so long as *MC* is lower than *AVC* and *ATC*. This is true up to the point where 5 laborers are employed producing 13 units of output. Beyond this point *MC* rises above *AVC* and *ATC*, and *AVC* and *ATC* then rise as output is increased. This relationship is reflected in Figure 7–3 by the fact that the *AVC* and *ATC* curves decline over the range where the *MC* curve is below them and increase over the range where the *MC* curve is above them. It follows from these observations that *the MC curve passes through the AVC and ATC curves at their minimum, or bottommost, points.*

The reason for this relationship between the marginal magnitude *MC* and the average magnitudes *AVC* and *ATC* is strictly mathematical, as we have already discussed. When the addition to total cost (the marginal cost) associated with the production of another unit of output is greater than *ATC*, *ATC* rises. Conversely, if the marginal cost of another unit is less than *ATC*, *ATC* will fall. Hence *ATC* declines as long as *MC* is below *ATC*. When *MC* is above *ATC*, *ATC* rises. Therefore, at the output level at which *MC* rises from below *ATC* to just above it, *ATC* ceases to decline and begins to rise. It follows therefore that *ATC* reaches its lowest point at the output level at which *MC* crosses *ATC*. Exactly the same argument applies to *AVC*. There is no such relationship between *MC* and *AFC*, however. This is so because *AFC* depends upon *TFC*, and since *TFC* is unaffected by changes in *TVC*, *AFC* declines continuously as output changes no matter what the behavior of *MC*.

The Significance of Marginal Cost for the Firm

The importance of marginal cost is that it tells the firm exactly how much it will cost to produce an additional unit of output. Conversely, it tells the firm the reduction in cost that will result if it reduces production by a unit of output. Average variable and average total cost do not give this kind of information because they are based on the cost of *all* output produced.

As we shall see repeatedly in the next few chapters, the firm's output decision in the short run is always made at the margin. The answer to the question, Should we produce an additional unit of output? will be found by comparing the cost of producing that additional unit (the marginal cost) with the additional revenue received from the sale of that unit.

CHECKPOINT 7-4

Notice that in Table 7–2, columns 7, 8, and 9, the *change* in average variable cost between successive output levels is always less than the change in the marginal cost. Notice also that the same is true of the change in average total cost only *after* the point at which 3 laborers are employed and 6 units of

output are produced. Why is this so? If diminishing returns are larger than is the case in Table 7–2, how would the *MC* curve of Figure 7–3 be affected?

PRODUCTION AND COSTS IN THE LONG RUN

The long run in economic analysis is a period of time long enough for the firm to be able to change the quantities of *all* its factors of production. As with the short run, the period of time called the long run is different for different firms and industries. A barbershop or a beauty parlor can change all its factors of production, go into business, or go out of business more quickly than a steel company. Hence, the long run for barbershops and beauty parlors is a shorter period of calendar time than is the long run for a steel company.

All Factors of Production Are Variable in the Long Run

When all factors of production are variable, there is, of course, no longer a distinction between variable and fixed costs. In the long run the only relevant average cost concept is the long-run average total cost, because when all factors are variable, so are all costs. In order to understand average total cost in the long run, we must first look at how changes in plant size affect costs and output.

Changes in Plant Size

The firm can change the entire plant in the long run to meet its production needs. For any given output level there is an optimum-size plant—one that entails lower per unit production cost (or average total cost) than any other. Each possible plant size can be represented by its short-run *ATC* curve.

Let's see how different plant sizes and their short-run *ATC* curves are usually related to different output levels. Starting from a zero output level, larger and larger plant sizes typically have lower and lower *ATC* curves at successively higher output levels up to some point. Beyond a certain output level, however, successively larger plant sizes give rise to successively higher *ATC* curves. This is illustrated for three possible different plant sizes in Figure 7–4. The lowest point on the *ATC* curve for the smallest plant (Plant 1) occurs at 700 units of output. For the next largest plant (Plant 2), the lowest point on its *ATC* curve occurs at a larger level of output, 1,800 units, and is obviously lower than that of Plant 1. The lowest point on the *ATC* of the largest plant (Plant 3) occurs at 2,700 units of output and is clearly higher than that of Plant 2.

Points *a* and *b* of Figure 7–4 are of particular interest. If the firm produces less than 900 units of output, Plant 1 is the best plant size to use because it has the lowest per unit costs for output levels less than 900. This is clear from the fact that to the left of point *a* the *ATC* curve for Plant 1 lies below that for Plant 2. If the firm produces between 900 and 2,400 units of output, Plant 2 is the best plant size to use because it has the lowest per unit costs for this range of output. This is reflected in the fact that the *ATC* curve of Plant 2 lies below that of Plant 1 to the right of *a*, and below that of Plant 3 to the left of *b*. If the firm produces more than 2,400 units of output, Plant 3 is the best plant size to use because it has the lowest per unit costs for this range of output. This is apparent from the fact that the *ATC* curve of Plant 3 lies below that of Plant 2 to the right of point *b*.

Long-Run Average Total Cost

The observations we have just made about the firm's selection of the optimum plant size to produce different output levels suggest the nature of the firm's long-run average total cost curve. *The long-run ATC curve, sometimes called the firm's planning curve, shows the lowest per unit cost at which it is possible to produce a given output when there is enough time for the firm to adjust its plant size.* In

FIGURE 7-4 Average Total Cost Curves for Three Possible Plant Sizes

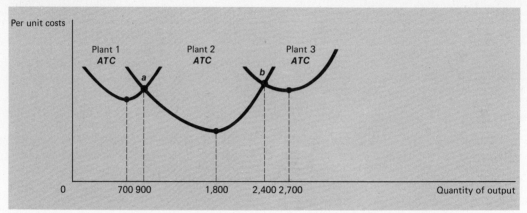

In the long run the firm can change the size of its plant. Starting from a zero output level, successively larger plants typically have lower and lower *ATC* curves up to some output level and then successively higher *ATC* curves beyond. The three representative *ATC* curves associated with the three successively larger plants shown here illustrate this.

Plant 1 is the best plant size for output levels less than 900 units because its *ATC* curve is the lowest to the left of point *a*. Plant 2 is the best plant size for output levels between 900 and 2,400 units because its *ATC* curve is the lowest between points *a* and *b*. Plant 3 is the best plant size for output levels greater than 2,400 units since its *ATC* curve is the lowest beyond point *b*.

If these are the only three possible plant sizes, the long-run *ATC* curve consists of the segment of Plant 1's *ATC* curve up to point *a*, the segment of Plant 2's *ATC* curve between points *a* and *b*, and the segment of Plant 3's *ATC* curve from point *b* on.

Figure 7–4 the long-run *ATC* curve consists of the segment of Plant 1's *ATC* curve up to point *a*, the segment of Plant 2's *ATC* curve between *a* and *b*, and the segment of the *ATC* curve for Plant 3 from point *b* on.

While only three possible plant sizes are shown in Figure 7–4, a firm may, in fact, have an almost unlimited number from which it may choose. The larger the number of possible plant sizes, the smaller will be the part of each plant's *ATC* curve used to make up the long-run *ATC* curve. This is illustrated in Figure 7–5. Here, two more possible plant sizes and their associated short-run *ATC*s have been added to the three shown in Figure 7–4. With the addition of *ATC* curves for Plants 4 and 5, it can be seen that

the segments *a′a*, *aa″*, *b′b*, and *bb″* of the three original short-run *ATC* curves are no longer parts of the long-run *ATC* curve. They are replaced by the segments *a′a″* and *b′b″* of the *ATC* curves associated with the two additional possible plant sizes.

As more and more possible plant sizes are considered, the segments of their associated *ATC* curves that are part of the long-run *ATC* curve become smaller and smaller. With an unlimited number of possible plant sizes, the long-run *ATC* curve is a smooth curve, made up of all the points of tangency with the unlimited number of short-run *ATC* curves. This curve appears as a heavy line in Figure 7–5. Only five of the unlimited number of short-run *ATC* curves that make

FIGURE 7-5 **The Long-Run Average Total Cost Curve**

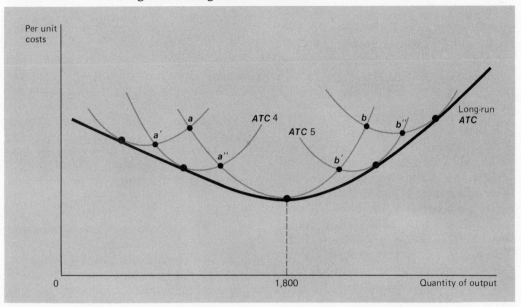

Two more possible plant sizes with short-run *ATC* curves *ATC* 4 and *ATC* 5 are shown here together with the short-run *ATC* curves for the three plant sizes shown in Figure 7–4. The segments of the plant *ATC* curves that now make up the long-run *ATC* curve are the segment of the smallest plant's *ATC* curve up to point *a'*, the segments *a'a''*, *a''b'*, *b'b''*, and the segment of the largest plant's *ATC* curve from *b''* on.

The segments *a'a*, *aa''*, *b'b*, and *bb''* of the three original short-run *ATC* curves are no longer part of the long-run *ATC* curve once we add the fourth and fifth plants. This illustrates that as more and more possible plant sizes are taken into account, the segments of their associated *ATC* curves that are part of the long-run *ATC* curve become smaller and smaller until they are no more than points. Hence, given an unlimited number of possible plant sizes, the long-run *ATC* curve is made up of all the points of tangency with the unlimited number of short-run *ATC* curves.

Only the minimum point of the long-run *ATC* curve is tangent to the minimum point of the short-run *ATC* curve (at 1,800 units of output). Below 1,800 units, the long-run *ATC* curve is tangent to the short-run *ATC* curves along their declining portions, and above 1,800 units it is tangent along their rising portions.

As output increases, the firm realizes economies of scale along the falling portion of the long-run *ATC* curve and diseconomies of scale along the rising portion.

up the long-run *ATC* curve are shown. Note that only the minimum point of the long-run *ATC* curve at 1,800 units of output is tangent to the minimum point of a short-run *ATC* curve. At output levels below 1,800 units, the points of tangency occur to the left of the minimum points on the short-run *ATC* curves. At output levels above 1,800 units, the tangency points occur to the right of the minimum points on the short-run *ATC* curves.

It is clear now why the long-run *ATC* curve is sometimes called the planning curve. At any output level the associated point on the long-run ATC curve is a point on a short-run ATC curve corresponding to that plant size that is the most efficient for producing that output level. Therefore, if the firm plans to produce a certain output level, the long-run ATC curve tells it the best-size plant to construct. It is best in the sense that the planned output level may be produced at the lowest possible per unit cost.

CHECKPOINT 7-5

It has been said that a firm's long-run ATC curve really represents nothing more than a collection of blueprints. In what sense is this true? When a plant operates at a point to the left of the minimum point on its short-run ATC curve, it is said to be underutilized. Assuming there are an unlimited number of plant sizes making up the long-run ATC curve of Figure 7–5, why is it always cheaper at any given output level less than 1,800 units to underutilize a larger plant than to overutilize a smaller one? Similarly, why is it always cheaper at any given output level greater than 1,800 units to overutilize a smaller plant than to underutilize a larger one?

Economies and Diseconomies of Scale

Why do the short-run ATC curves associated with successively larger plant sizes become steadily lower up to some output level and then begin to rise, giving the long-run ATC curve the shape shown in Figure 7–5? The reason is *not* the law of diminishing returns, which assumes that some of the factors of production are fixed. That law only explains the U-shape of the short-run ATC curve associated with a particular plant size. It does not apply here because, in the long run, all factors are variable. Hence, the reasons for the U-shape of the long-run ATC curve must lie elsewhere. We will find them by examin-

ing what economists call *economies* and *diseconomies* of scale.

Economies of Scale

Economies of scale are the decreases in the long-run average total cost of production that occur when the firm's plant size is increased, as represented by the declining portion of the long-run ATC curve. Economies of scale can occur for a number of reasons.

1. *Specialization of factors of production.* In a small firm labor and equipment must be used to perform a number of different tasks. It is more difficult for labor to become skilled at any one of them and thereby realize the gains in productivity and reductions in per unit costs that specialization permits. In the same way, management functions cannot be as specialized in a smaller firm. Supervisors may have to devote time to the screening of job applicants, a task usually more efficiently handled by a personnel department in a larger firm. Executives may have to divide their attention between finance, accounting, and production operations—functions that could be handled more proficiently by departments specializing in each of these areas in a larger firm.

Similarly, machinery and equipment cannot be used as efficiently when they have to be switched back and forth between tasks. Moreover, in many types of production processes, the most efficient types of production facilities are practicable only at high levels of output. It is very expensive to build custom-made cars by hand, but it would be equally or more expensive to use a large General Motors assembly plant to build just 100 Chevrolets per year. However, if the plant is used to build 100,000 cars per year, the highly specialized techniques of the assembly line allow the cost per car to be greatly reduced.

2. *Volume discounts on the prices of materials and other inputs used in production.* Often the suppliers of raw materials, machinery, and other inputs will charge a lower price per unit for these items if a firm buys in large

POLICY PERSPECTIVE

Economies and Diseconomies of Scale and the Number of Firms in an Industry

The number of firms in an industry is an important determinant of the degree of competition that exists among firms in that industry, a major concern of antitrust policy which we will study in Chapter 12. In general, competition will be more intense if there are more firms, other things equal. The existence of economies and diseconomies of scale is an important determining factor of how many firms there are in an industry.

Consider the three different long-run *ATC* curves shown in Figure P7–1. In part a, economies of scale are relatively small and diseconomies of scale set in relatively quickly as output is increased. In part b, economies of scale are again quickly exhausted, but there is a considerable range of output over which the long-run *ATC* curve is flat before diseconomies of scale set in. In part c, economies of scale are realized over a much larger range of output before diseconomies of scale set in.

Given the consumer demand facing an industry, there is likely to be a greater number of smaller-sized firms in the industry if the typical firm's long-run *ATC* curve is like that of part a than if it is like that of either part b or part c. On the other hand, if the typical firm's long-run *ATC* is like that of part c, the industry is more likely to be composed of a smaller number of larger-sized firms. This is so because firms will not realize minimum per unit costs until they push production to relatively higher output levels. The in-between case depicted in part b suggests the possibility of an industry composed of firms more varied in size, each of which realizes similar levels of minimum per unit costs.

Question

1. If there were a decline in demand for an industry's product, which one of the long-run ATC curves in Figure P7–1 would probably entail the least number of firms having to go out of business? Why?

FIGURE P7-1 Three Different Types of Long-Run Average Total Cost Curves

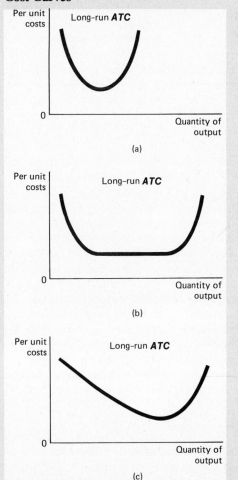

quantities. When a firm produces at high output levels, it needs a large volume of inputs and can take advantage of the associated price discounts to reduce its per unit costs.

3. *Economic use of by-products.* The production of many types of goods gives rise to by-products that also have economic value. Large-scale firms are often able to recycle "waste" by-products that smaller-size firms simply have to throw away because it is not economical to do anything else with them. For example, a small sawmill may simply throw away sawdust and old wood scraps. A large lumber-processing firm often finds the volume of these waste products large enough to make it economical to package sawdust and sell it as a sweeping compound for cleaning floors and hallways in large buildings. The wood scraps may be packaged, processed, and sold as kindling wood and artificial logs for home barbecues and fireplaces. In this way, the sale of by-products effectively reduces the per unit costs of producing lumber in large volume. For the same reasons, large oil firms often produce a host of petroleum by-products, and meat-packing firms produce fertilizers, glue, leather, and other by-products of meat production.

4. *The growth of supporting facilities and services is encouraged by the firm's large scale of operation.* As a firm's scale of operations gets larger, it often becomes worthwhile for other firms and local governments to provide it with services. If a firm builds a large plant in a particular area, an improvement in highways and expanded transportation services may soon follow. Smaller suppliers, which find a large part of their sales going to the larger firm, may move closer to the larger firm to reduce transportation costs. All of these developments result in lower per unit costs for the large firm.

Diseconomies of Scale

Diseconomies of scale refer to the increasing long-run average total cost of production represented by the rising portion of the long-run *ATC* curve. When the firm produces at output levels greater than those corresponding to the minimum point on the long-run *ATC* curve, the upward pressure on per unit costs due to diseconomies of scale more than offsets the downward pressure resulting from economies of scale.

Diseconomies of scale are largely a result of the firm's growing so large that it becomes cumbersome to manage. Once the firm gets beyond a certain size, the problems of efficiently coordinating a large number of plants and diverse operations become more complex. Central management must communicate with many more areas of the firm and process more information in order to keep tabs on what's going on. This often means that more authority must be delegated to middle- and lower-management levels. The increased chances of misguided decisions, combined with central management's difficulty in monitoring all operations, may result in inefficiencies that cause the per unit costs of output to rise.

SUMMARY

1. The three primary legal forms of the firm are the proprietorship, the partnership, and the corporation. While proprietorships and partnerships are more numerous, the corporation is the dominant form of large business enterprise. This is so mainly because it is the only legal form of business organization that affords owners the protection of limited liability. This feature enhances the corporation's ability to raise capital.

2. Whether resources are owned directly by the firm or must be hired from outside, their cost is the money payment they could have received if employed in their next best alternative use. The firm's costs include explicit costs, which are the payments to resource suppliers outside the firm, and implicit costs, which equal the compensation that resources already owned by the firm could earn in alternative uses outside the firm. Implicit costs include a normal profit from the entrepreneurial skills and financial capital supplied by a firm's owners.

3. In the short run, some of a firm's factors of production, such as its plant, are fixed. Its level of output can be varied only by changing the quantities of its variable factors, such as its labor. In the long run, there is sufficient time for the firm to vary all its factors of production, including the size of its plant.

4. In the short run, the law of diminishing returns describes the changes in output that result as increasing amounts of a variable input are applied to a fixed input. It says that the additions to total output, called the marginal product, associated with the addition of each successive unit of the variable factor will begin to decline beyond some point.

5. Total fixed cost *(TFC)* includes all the firm's costs associated with the factors of production that are fixed in the short run. The firm is saddled with fixed cost no matter what level of output it produces. Total variable cost *(TVC)* includes all the firm's costs associated with the factors that are variable in the short run. Total variable cost changes with the level of the firm's output. At any output level the firm's total cost *(TC)* equals the sum of total fixed and total variable cost.

6. Average fixed cost *(AFC)* equals total fixed cost divided by the output level. It falls continuously as the output level is increased. Average variable cost *(AVC)* equals total variable cost divided by the output level. As output is increased, *AVC* first falls and then rises, reflecting the law of diminishing returns. Average total cost *(ATC)* equals the sum of average fixed cost and average variable cost. It falls and then rises as output increases.

7. Marginal cost *(MC)* is the increment, or addition, to total cost resulting from the production of an additional unit of output. As output increases, *MC* first falls and then rises, reflecting the law of diminishing returns. It cuts the *AVC* and *ATC* curves at their bottommost points.

8. Because all factors of production are variable in the long run, so are all costs. When the firm has sufficient time to adjust the size of its plant, it will select the plant size that has the lowest short-run *ATC* curve at the desired output level. For this reason the long-run *ATC* curve is composed of segments of all the short-run *ATC* curves. It is sometimes called a planning curve.

9. The long-run *ATC* curve is U-shaped, its declining portion reflecting economies of scale and its rising portion reflecting diseconomies of scale. Economies of scale result from increased specialization of the factors of production, price discounts on volume purchases of inputs, more economical use of by-products, and the growth of supporting firms and services. Diseconomies of scale result from the increased difficulty of managing large-scale operations once the firm has grown beyond a certain size.

10. Economies and diseconomies of scale play a major role in determining the size and number of firms in an industry. In general, given the demand for an industry's product, the larger the economies of scale, the greater will be the size and the smaller the number of firms in an industry. Conversely, when economies of scale are few, in general the size of firms will be smaller and the number of firms will be larger in the industry.

KEY TERMS AND CONCEPTS

accounting profit
average fixed cost *(AFC)*
average product
average total cost *(ATC)*
average variable cost *(AVC)*
conglomerate
corporation
creditor
diseconomies of scale
dividends

economic cost
economic profit
economies of scale
explicit costs
firm
fixed factor
horizontally integrated
implicit costs
law of diminishing returns
limited liability
limited partner
long run
marginal cost
marginal product
normal profit
partnership
plant
short run
short-run production function
sole proprietorship
total cost *(TC)*
total fixed cost *(TFC)*
total variable cost *(TVC)*
undistributed profits
variable factor
vertically integrated

QUESTIONS AND PROBLEMS

1. Suppose you examined the costs of each of the firms in a random collection of sole proprietorships and compared them with the costs of each of the firms in a random collection of corporations. Among which group would you generally expect implicit costs to be a larger proportion of economic costs? Why?

2. Rank the following firms according to the maximum length of calendar time you think would constitute the short run: retail shoe store, road construction company, real estate brokerage firm, shoeshine stand, nuclear power company, and oil refinery. Suppose the demand for the goods and services produced by these businesses were to increase

tenfold. Rank the industries represented by each of these types of business according to the speed with which you think each would exhibit a complete supply response.

3. Describe how the law of diminishing returns works in each of the following situations, taking care to identify the product and classify the fixed and variable factors in each case: preparing for a final exam, insulating a house, looking for a parking spot within walking distance of a downtown store at 3:00 P.M. on a weekday, controlling crime in a big city, convincing somebody to give you a job, cleaning up the environment, protecting the population against nuclear attack, protecting yourself from heart attack, getting to the other side of town as fast as possible, discussing the weather, and increasing unemployment benefits to help unemployed people get by financially while looking for a job.

4. For each of the firms in problem 2, describe the nature of their fixed and variable costs. Is there any relationship between your cost description and how you ranked the firms in your answer to problem 2? Why?

5. Consider the fixed, variable, and total costs of an electric power company. How are its *TFC, TVC, TC, AFC, AVC, ATC,* and *MC* curves affected by the following changes:

a. an increase in interest rates;

b. an increase in wages;

c. a decrease in property taxes;

d. an increase in the price of coal, oil, and nuclear fuel;

e. a decrease in the purity of the water it takes in for use in its boilers;

f. imposition of an excise tax on electricity sales collected by the government from the company;

g. a tax on plant size to cover the city's water cleanup costs;

h. passage of an antipollution law;

i. increase in premium rates for hazard insurance.

6. Because of technological progress, there have been considerable increases in economies of scale in farming in the past 50 years. How do you think this has affected population shifts between urban and rural areas, all other things remaining the same?

7. As an economist, what do you think would be the major pros and cons of merging the Army, the Navy, and the Air Force into *one* large military organization?

THREE

Market Structure, Pricing, and Government Regulation

8

Perfect Competition

AFTER READING THIS CHAPTER, YOU WILL BE ABLE TO:

1. Define the concept of market structure.

2. Characterize the form of market organization known as perfect competition.

3. State the relationship between the perfectly competitive firm's demand curve and the demand curve of the industry.

4. Show how cost and revenue considerations lead the perfectly competitive firm to decide whether or not to produce in the short run and, if so, how much to produce using the marginal cost-marginal revenue criterion.

5. Explain the long-run adjustment process in a perfectly competitive industry and the nature of the long-run industry supply curve.

6. List the reasons why a perfectly competitive world is considered to be an ideal of efficiency in the allocation of scarce resources to satisfy consumer wants.

7. Explain some of the criticisms of perfect competition.

What is the nature of a market or industry that has more than 97,000 firms in it? How does a firm function in such a market as contrasted with one in which there are only a few firms, such as in the automobile or steel industry? For purposes of economic analysis, how is the farm in western Kansas a different firm from a retail store, a public utility such as Con Edison, or a rubber company such as Firestone?

The answers to these questions depend on considerations such as the number of buyers and sellers in the market, the similarity of their product, and the ease with which firms can enter and leave the industry. These factors have a great deal to do with determining **market structure**, or what is sometimes called industrial organization. For purposes of description and analysis, economists identify four basic types of market structure: perfect (or pure) competition, monopoly, monopolistic competition, and oligopoly. Like the aeronautical engineer's model of the real aircraft, each of these is an abstract characterization of a type of real market.

In this chapter we will focus on perfect competition. In many respects economists consider this kind of market structure an ideal form of economic organization for providing goods and services to consumers as efficiently as possible. For this reason it is often used as a standard or norm against which other forms of market structure are compared, as we shall see in the next three chapters.

PERFECT COMPETITION IN THEORY AND REALITY

Perfect competition exists only if each firm, or seller, in a market or industry is a **price taker.** Each firm is unable to affect its price because its production of output is such a small portion of total industry supply—a mere "drop in the bucket." Hence the firm can change its level of production and sales without having any noticeable effect on the price of the good it sells. The firm is there-fore a price taker because it must accept the sales price established in the market as given.

Four Market Characteristics That Promote Perfect Competition

What kind of characteristics of an industry or a market promote the existence of perfect competition? Basically there are four: (1) ease of entry into and exit from the industry by firms, (2) all firms sell an identical product, (3) there are many firms, and (4) buyers are perfectly informed about the prices at which all market transactions take place. Let's examine how each of these characteristics tends to promote the existence of perfect competition.

1. Ease of Entry into and Exit from the Industry by Firms

Firms and the resources they employ may easily enter and leave the industry. There are no significant financial, legal, technological, or other barriers to new firms entering the industry or existing firms leaving it. Low barriers to entry put pressure on firms in the industry to operate as efficiently as possible because otherwise new, more efficient firms can easily enter the industry and replace them.

2. All Firms Sell an Identical Product

The important thing here is that the product of one firm is considered by the buyer to be the same as that of any other firm. Therefore, in the mind of the buyer, each firm's product is viewed as a perfect substitute for the product of any other firm in the market. This ensures that no buyer has any economic incentive to pay any firm a higher price for the product than is charged by other firms.

An important implication of this product homogeneity in a perfectly competitive industry is that there is no incentive for firms to engage in nonprice competition. Nonprice competition is encouraged by differences in the products of different firms that can be exploited by advertising and other types of sales promotion. When no such differences exist and buyers know it, advertising by individual firms will yield them no market advantage over other firms.

3. There Are Many Firms

"Many firms" does not mean any specific number. Rather, there are enough firms so that any one firm's contribution to total industry supply is so small that whether a firm produces at full capacity or not at all, market price will not be noticeably affected.

4. Buyers Have Perfect Knowledge About Prices

When buyers have perfect knowledge about the prices at which transactions take place in the market, it is not possible for sellers to charge anyone more than the market price for the homogeneous product.

It is also assumed that there are many buyers and that not one of them is able to affect market price because each is such an insignificant part of the market. Therefore, like firms, buyers are also price takers.

Let's summarize how these four characteristics promote the existence of perfect competition, a market structure where each firm is a price taker. Because the firm's product is indistinguishable from that of any other firm in the market (characteristic 2), there is no incentive for buyers to pay a higher price for it than for that of any other firm. The existence of many other such firms (characteristic 3) and the easy entry of new firms (characteristic 1) ensures that any one firm's output is but a drop in the bucket. Because buyers are perfectly informed about the prices of all market transactions (characteristic 4), they will know if any firm tries to charge them a higher price than any other firm. Accordingly, no firm will be able to sell its product if it charges a price higher than the given price. Since a firm can effectively sell all it can produce at the given price, there is no reason for it to sell its output at a lower price.

Does Perfect Competition Exist?

By this time you may be scoffing at the notion that a perfectly competitive market exists. Your skepticism is understandable. It would be hard to find an industry that has a market structure *perfectly* exhibiting all four characteristics. However, there are industries or markets that come close and, more importantly, ones in which firms, or sellers, are price takers.

Competition in Agriculture

Agriculture is such a market. For example, there are roughly 1.2 million farms that grow corn. A survey reported in a news item "showed that the nation's farmers intend to plant 82.7 million acres of corn." Using these numbers as a rough estimate suggests that the average corn grower will plant 68.9 acres of corn. The average farm will thus contribute roughly 1/1,000,000 (or 1/10,000 of 1 percent) of the total amount of corn produced. It certainly seems reasonable to believe that whether any one farm produces or not will have little if any noticeable effect on the market price of corn. And in the market for corn it is unlikely that one farm's corn can be distinguished from another's—the product is homogeneous. These considerations (many firms and a homogeneous product) strongly suggest that the typical farmer is a price taker in the corn market.

The corn market certainly does have many characteristics of a perfectly competitive market. However, even here there is one characteristic that is missing—ease of entry into the industry. Purchasing a farm (or even a few acres for most of us) poses a rather sizeable financial barrier. Even if farmland is rented, typically one must purchase expensive farm equipment to run a modern farm. Nonetheless, perfect competition seems to be an apt description of agricultural markets in general.

A Standard for Market Structure

The concept of perfect competition provides a useful standard against which other market structures may be compared. Economists regard it as capturing the spirit of free enterprise and unbridled competition. In many respects it also exemplifies the most efficient way to allocate scarce resources among unlimited wants—a matter we will examine at the end of this chapter. In this way, perfect competition is an idealization of several important notions in economics. Perfect competition also provides the simplest starting point for studying the nature of price and output determination by the firm, and the role that the cost concepts of the previous chapter play in this process.

Market Demand and the Firm's Demand in Perfect Competition

It is important to understand the relationship between the demand curve of the individual firm and the market or industry demand curve. It is also important to understand the relationship among total, average, and marginal revenue for the perfectly competitive firm.

The Market Demand Curve and the Firm's Demand Curve

When we say that the perfectly competitive firm is a price taker, or that it cannot affect the price at which it sells its product, we are saying something about the shape of the demand curve as seen by the individual firm. Specifically, we are saying that this demand curve is horizontal (perfectly elastic) at the level of the prevailing market price over the range of output that the firm can feasibly produce.

Such a demand curve looks like the one in Figure 8–1, part a. In this example, we will assume that the firm's highest feasible output level is 1,200 units. The industry demand and supply curves for the entire competitive market are shown in Figure 8–1, part b. Their intersection determines the equilibrium market price p_e and equilibrium market quantity, which in this case is 1 million units of output.

The firm's demand curve is perfectly elastic for two reasons. First, its product is indistinguishable from that of any other firm in the industry. Hence, if the firm were to raise its price above p_e, it would sell nothing since buyers can get the identical product at the price p_e from other firms. Second, since the individual firm's output capacity is but a drop in the bucket compared to that of the entire industry, the firm can effectively sell all it can produce at the market equilibrium price p_e.

Two important points are clearly illustrated in Figure 8–1, parts a and b. First, because the individual firm provides such a small fraction of the total industry output (about $1/1,000$ in this example), it has no effect on the market-determined price p_e. The actions of all firms taken together, however, do affect market price and therefore the market demand curve D is downward sloping even though the individual firm's demand curve d is perfectly horizontal. Second, although price is *determined* by the interaction of all buyers and sellers in the market as represented in part b, this price p_e is essentially given to, and beyond the influence of, any individual firm as shown in part a. Again, this simply reflects the fact that the individual firm's contribution to total output is a drop in the bucket as far as the whole market is concerned. Indeed, the 1,200 units on the horizontal axis of part a are hardly bigger than a dot on the horizontal axis of part b.

Total, Average, and Marginal Revenue of a Perfectly Competitive Firm

A demand curve may be looked at from two different viewpoints. On the one hand, it shows the quantity of a good that consumers will purchase per period of time at different prices. On the other, it shows the price, or revenue, per unit that a seller can receive for different quantities of output per period of time. We now want to consider the second interpretation from the standpoint of the perfectly competitive firm.

FIGURE 8-1   Relationship Between a Competitive Firm's Demand Curve and the Competitive Industry's Demand Curve

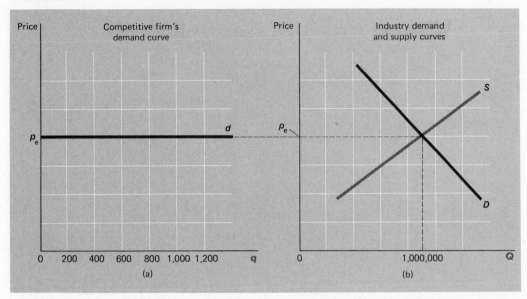

Because the industry demand curve D is downward sloping, the production of all firms taken together can affect the market price in part b. The market equilibrium price p_e is determined by the intersection of the market demand curve D and market supply curve S representing the output of all firms—in this case 1,000,000 units. Because the individual competitive firm can only contribute a small fraction (about 1/1,000) to this total, its actions cannot affect price. Therefore, its demand curve is perfectly elastic, or horizontal, at the market-determined price level p_e as shown in part a. The horizontal axis in part a represents little more than a dot on the horizontal axis in part b.

Suppose the price given to the firm by the market is $10. Since the firm's level of production does not affect this price—it can sell any amount of output it produces—**total revenue** *equals quantity sold multiplied by the selling price* of $10 per unit. The relationship between total revenue and quantity sold, for a given price of $10 per unit, is shown by the total revenue curve TR_{10} in Figure 8–2, part a. For example, when 5 units (measured on the horizontal axis) are sold at a price of $10 per unit, total revenue (measured on the vertical axis) is $50. This is represented by point a on TR_{10}. If an additional unit is sold, making a total of 6, total revenue rises by an

amount equal to the price of $10. Total revenue is then $60, as represented by point b on TR_{10}. Similarly if one more unit is sold at the given price of $10 per unit, bringing the total to 7 units, we move from point b to point c on TR_{10}, where total revenue is $70.

Suppose the price given to the firm by the market were to fall from $10 to $5 per unit. This would cause the total revenue curve to pivot clockwise about the origin from the position TR_{10} to TR_5. If the firm now sells 5 units of output, total revenue will be $25, as represented by the point a' on TR_5. The sale of 6 units would bring a total revenue of $30, point b' on TR_5. The sale of yet one more

FIGURE 8-2 **The Total Revenue Curve, Marginal Revenue Curve, and Demand Curve for a Perfectly Competitive Firm**

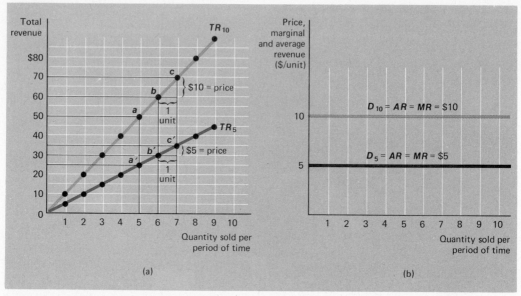

Because the perfectly competitive firm's level of production does not affect its price, it can sell any amount of output it produces for the same price. Total revenue, which is equal to the quantity sold multiplied by the selling price, therefore rises at a constant rate, equal to the price per unit, as the quantity of output sold is increased. This constant rise is represented by an upward-sloping straight-line total revenue curve. In part a, this curve would look like TR_{10} if price is $10 per unit or TR_5 if it is $5 per unit.

Since the price per unit sold is always the same no matter what quantity of output is sold, average revenue AR in part b, which is equal to total revenue divided by the number of units sold, equals price. It is therefore the same at all levels of output. It is also the same as the firm's demand curve D. Marginal revenue MR, which is equal to the change in total revenue resulting from the sale of one more unit of output, also equals price in part b. It is therefore equal to AR at all output levels in part b. Hence the perfectly competitive firm's demand curve is the same as its marginal revenue curve and is perfectly elastic (horizontal). When price is $10, the demand curve associated with TR_{10} in part a is D_{10} in part b. When price is $5, the demand curve associated with TR_5 in part a is D_5 in part b.

unit at the given price of $5 would bring total revenue to $35, point c' on TR_5.

Notice that the TR curves in Figure 8–2, part a, are straight lines—their slopes are unchanged, $10 per unit on TR_{10} and $5 per unit on TR_5, no matter what the output level. Because of this, starting from the origin, average revenue per unit sold is the same no matter what total quantity of output is sold.

For example, at point a on TR_{10}, average revenue per unit sold equals the total revenue of $50 divided by 5 units, or $10 per unit. At point b, average revenue equals $60 divided by 6 units or, again, $10 per unit. Similarly at point c, $70 divided by 7 units gives an average revenue of $10 per unit. Hence, *for a perfectly competitive firm average revenue is the same at all output levels.* **Average rev-**

enue *is always equal to the price per unit of output.* For TR_{10} the average revenue AR, which equals price per unit (or \$10), is plotted in part b. Hence, average revenue is represented by the perfectly competitive firm's demand curve D_{10} when price equals \$10 per unit. Similarly, for TR_5, the average revenue AR, which equals price per unit (or \$5), is plotted in part b. Average revenue is represented by the perfectly competitive firm's demand curve D_5 when price equals \$5 per unit.

Marginal revenue *is the addition to total revenue resulting from the sale of one more unit of output.* Since the perfectly competitive firm sells each and every unit of output at the same price, the marginal revenue associated with the sale of one more unit of output is always the same. This is reflected in the fact that the TR curves in Figure 8–2, part a, are straight lines. Along TR_{10} each additional unit sold increases total revenue by \$10. Hence, at every level of output, marginal revenue equals average revenue equals price. We see, therefore, that if the marginal revenue of \$10 per unit is plotted against output in part b, it is the same as the competitive firm's demand curve D_{10}. If price per unit were \$5, then the marginal revenue curve would be the same as the demand curve D_5 at the level of \$5 per unit in part b. *Note that $AR = MR$ at all output levels only in perfect competition.* In each of the other three forms of market structure that we will discuss—monopoly, monopolistic competition, and oligopoly—this is not true.

CHECKPOINT* 8–1

Suppose that an industry starts out being perfectly competitive, but after a while the product of each firm in the industry ceases to be identical with that of every other firm. Does this mean that each firm's product becomes more, or less, of a substitute for that of every other firm? How will this affect each firm's demand curve? Suppose the price of a competitive firm's product were to rise from \$10 to \$15.

How would this affect its *TR* curve in Figure 8–2, part a, and the associated demand curve in part b? Explain your answer.

*Answers to all Checkpoints can be found at the back of the text.

THE COMPETITIVE FIRM IN THE SHORT RUN

In the short run, the competitive firm's plant is fixed. It can only change the quantity of output it produces by changing its variable inputs, such as labor, materials, electricity, and other energy inputs. *We assume that the firm's objective is to use an amount of the variable inputs together with its fixed plant to produce and sell a quantity of output that will maximize its economic profit or, if necessary, minimize its losses.* If total revenue is greater than *total cost* (the sum of total variable cost plus total fixed cost), the firm will make an economic profit. If it is less, the firm will experience a loss. (Remember that total cost includes a normal profit.)

The way in which the firm seeks to maximize profits or minimize losses may be looked at in two ways. It may be seen either as a process of comparing total revenue and total cost or, equivalently, as a process of comparing marginal revenue with marginal cost. Both approaches will be explained here in order to demonstrate the relationship between them. However, economists typically rely on the marginal revenue-marginal cost approach. Both approaches may also be used to study the firm's behavior in the context of the other three market structures as well—monopoly, monopolistic competition, and oligopoly.

Should the Firm Produce in the Short Run?

In the short run, the firm is saddled with its fixed costs regardless of whether it produces or not. If it produces nothing, variable costs will be zero, but it will suffer a loss equal to its fixed costs. Hence, the first question the firm has to answer is whether or not it can reduce the size of this loss, or better yet make a profit, by employing variable factors to produce and sell some quantity of output. Simply put, *the firm's first question in the short run is whether to produce or not.*

The answer to this question depends on the following considerations. Variable costs are incurred only if the firm produces some quantity of output. Suppose the total revenue received from the sale of this output is greater than the total variable cost of producing it. In this case, the excess of total revenue over total variable cost will offset some or possibly all of the fixed cost. Hence, it pays the firm to produce something. Even if the excess doesn't fully offset the fixed cost, the loss realized by the firm if it produces something will be smaller than its loss, which is its fixed cost, if it produces nothing. Better yet, if the firm's total revenue exceeds its total variable cost by an amount that is greater than its total fixed cost, it will earn an economic profit. In sum, *the firm should produce in the short run if the loss it incurs is less than its fixed cost or, better yet, if it can earn an economic profit.*

There are clearly three possible situations that may arise in the short run. (1) The firm's total revenue from the sale of its output exceeds its total cost, which is the sum of its total variable and total fixed cost, and it earns an economic profit by producing. (2) The firm's total revenue exceeds its total variable cost and thus offsets some of its total fixed cost as well. The loss incurred by producing is therefore less than the firm's total fixed cost, which is the loss if the firm remains idle. (3) The firm's total revenue is not sufficient to cover the total variable cost to which production gives rise. In this case, the loss (equal to total fixed cost) of remaining idle is less than the loss of producing (which is equal to total fixed cost plus the amount by which total variable cost exceeds total revenue).

In the first two cases, *where it pays the firm to produce, the second question the firm must answer is how much to produce.* In the third case, the firm obviously should not produce at all. In the first case, the firm will answer the question by choosing that output level that maximizes economic profit. In the second case, the firm will answer by choosing that output level that minimizes losses. This is also essentially the choice it makes in the third case, when it chooses an output level of zero. Assuming given cost data for a hypothetical perfectly competitive firm, we will now consider how the answer to the question of how much to produce is determined in each of these cases. In each case we will examine how the firm can answer the question from the viewpoint of total revenue and total cost, as well as from the viewpoint of marginal revenue and marginal cost.

Maximizing Economic Profit

Table 8–1 contains the total, average, and marginal cost data, as well as the price, total revenue, and marginal revenue data, for a hypothetical perfectly competitive firm that wants to maximize its economic profit. (All data in Table 8–1 are measured per some period of time, such as a month.)

Total Cost-Total Revenue Viewpoint

The firm's total cost data and its associated output levels appear in columns 1–4. The price p at which the firm can sell its output is always $9 per unit (column 8). The firm's total revenue TR (column 9) from sales at each output level is obtained by multiplying this price by output (column 1). Profit or loss (column 10) equals the difference between total revenue TR and total cost TC (column 4).

Examination of column 10 shows that the answer to the question as to whether the firm should produce or not is yes. If the firm remains idle (output level of zero), it will incur a loss of $10, the amount of its TFC (column 2). The table shows us it can do much better than this, however. Column 10 clearly shows that the firm can realize a maximum eco-

TABLE 8-1 Output, Revenue, and Costs of a Profit-Maximizing, Perfectly Competitive Firm (Hypothetical Data)

	Total Costs			Average and Marginal Costs			Price and Revenues		
(1)	(2)	(3)	(4)	(5)	(6)	(7)	(8)	(9)	(10)
Quantity of Output (Q)	Total Fixed Cost (TFC)	Total Variable Cost (TVC)	Total Cost (TC)	Average Variable Cost (AVC)	Average Total Cost (ATC)	Marginal Cost (MC)	Price = Marginal Revenue	Total Revenue	Economic Profit (+) or Loss (−)
			$TC = TFC + TVC$	$AVC = \dfrac{TVC}{Q}$	$ATC = \dfrac{TC}{Q}$	$MC = \dfrac{\text{change in } TC}{\text{change in } Q}$	$p = MR$	$TR = p \times Q$	$TR - TC$
0	$10	$ 0	$10					$ 0	$−10
						$ 6	$9		
1	10	6	16	$6.00	$16.00			9	− 7
						4	9		
2	10	10	20	5.00	10.00			18	− 2
						4	9		
3	10	14	24	4.66	8.00			27	+ 3
						5	9		
4	10	19	29	4.75	7.25			36	+ 7
						7	9		
5	10	26	36	5.20	7.20			45	+ 9
						11	9		
6	10	37	47	6.16	7.83			54	+ 7
						23	9		
7	10	60	70	8.57	10.00			63	− 7

nomic profit of $9. This figure is achieved by producing an output of 5 units. The answer to the second question of how much the firm should produce is therefore 5 units.

The reason for this answer is demonstrated graphically in Figure 8–3, part a. Given the price of $9 per unit, the total revenue curve TR_9 is obtained in exactly the same way that we obtained the TR curves in Figure 8–2. The total cost curve TC is plotted from the data in columns 1 and 4 of Table 8–1. The total variable cost curve TVC is plotted from the data in columns 1 and 3. (This is exactly the same procedure we used to obtain the TC and TVC curves of Figure 7–2 in the previous chapter.) The shape of

the TC and TVC curves reflects the law of diminishing returns. At each output level, the vertical distance between TR_9 and TC equals the loss or profit given in column 10 of Table 8–1.

At output levels of 1, 2, and 7 units the firm realizes losses. This is reflected by the fact that the TC curve lies above TR_9. At about $2^{1}/_{3}$ units of output the firm just breaks even (TR_9 equals TC). At output levels beyond this point the firm makes a profit because TR_9 lies above TC. Another **break-even point** (a point at which total revenue TR equals total cost TC) occurs at about $6^{1}/_{2}$ units of output, beyond which the firm again experiences losses. The maximum profit,

FIGURE 8-3 Maximizing Profit in a Perfectly Competitive Firm

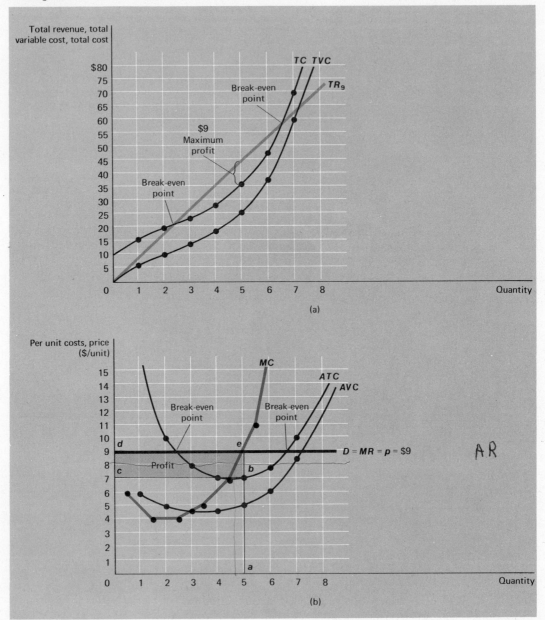

Assuming a price of $9, total revenue is plotted from the data in columns 1 and 9 of Table 8–1 to give the *TR* curve *TR*$_9$ in part a. The total cost data of column 4 and total variable cost data of column 3 are also plotted against output to give the *TC* and *TVC* curves. *TR* minus *TC* equals profit and is represented by the vertical distance between *TR*$_9$ and *TC* at equal to $9, is represented by the maximum vertical distance between TR_9 and TC, which occurs at 5 units of output.

Marginal Cost-
Marginal Revenue Viewpoint

An alternative way of viewing how the firm decides how much to produce is to consider the relationship between marginal cost and marginal revenue. As with the total cost-total revenue viewpoint, the marginal cost-marginal revenue viewpoint is applicable to all firms whether they are perfectly competitive, monopolists, monopolistically competitive, or oligopolists. The perfectly competitive firm is different from the others in one important respect, however. Only for the perfectly competitive firm is it true that price p always equals marginal revenue MR, as we have shown earlier in this chapter.

The marginal cost-marginal revenue viewpoint assumes that the firm has already decided to produce.

How does the firm use this method to determine how much to produce? The firm must compare the *marginal cost* (the addition to total cost) associated with the production of one more unit of output with the marginal revenue (the addition to total revenue) received from the sale of that unit. If the marginal cost is less than the marginal revenue, the firm will "make money" by producing and selling an additional unit of output because the increase in total revenue will exceed the increase in total cost. In the profit-maximizing case, this excess of marginal revenue over marginal cost is an addition to to-

tal profit. The firm should continue to increase its production so long as the marginal revenue from each additional unit exceeds the marginal cost of producing that unit. If the marginal cost of producing an additional unit exceeds the marginal revenue from that unit, the production and sale of that unit will "lose money." In the profit-maximizing case, this means that the additional unit will reduce total profit. It therefore "does not pay" to produce it. Hence, the firm should produce output up to the point where the marginal revenue of an additional unit of output no longer exceeds its marginal cost.

Consider the hypothetical perfectly competitive firm of Table 8–1. Starting from a zero output level, when the firm increases production to the successively higher output levels of column 1, it incurs the associated marginal cost MC shown in column 7. The MC of column 7 falls at first and then rises as production is increased, which reflects the law of diminishing returns. The marginal revenue MR (column 8) always equals the price of $9, for the reasons discussed earlier in connection with Figure 8–2. Note that MC is always less than MR up through the production of 5 units of output. However, if the firm produces a sixth unit of output, the associated MC will be $11. This is larger than the MR of $9 associated with the sale of the sixth unit. Hence, it will not pay the firm to produce more than 5 units of output. Similarly the firm will not maximize profit if it produces less than this amount. If it produces less, it will forgo the addition to profit associated with producing and selling addi-

any output level. The maximum distance between these two curves represents the maximum profit of $9, which occurs when 5 units of output are produced and sold.

For the perfectly competitive firm, marginal revenue MR always equals price p and is the firm's demand curve D at the level of the price of $9 per unit in part b. (These data come from column 8 of Table 8–1.) The AVC, ATC, and MC curves of part b are plotted from the average variable cost, average total cost, and marginal cost data of columns 5, 6, and 7 respectively in Table 8–1. The profit-maximizing level of output occurs at 5 units, where $MC = MR$ as represented by the intersection of the MC curve with the $D = MR = p = 9 curve at point e. The maximum profit of $9 is represented by the rectangular area $cbed$ in part b. It equals the difference between total revenue (represented by the rectangular area $0aed$) and total cost (represented by the rectangular area $0abc$).

tional units of output. Indeed, it can be seen from column 10 that the firm realizes its maximum possible profit of $9 when it produces 5 units of output. This is the same result we obtained when we took the total cost-total revenue point of view.

The marginal cost-marginal revenue viewpoint is depicted graphically in Figure 8–3, part b. The *MC* curve is plotted from the data in column 7 of Table 8–1. The firm's demand curve *D* is perfectly elastic (horizontal) at the price $p = MR = \$9$, the data in column 8 of Table 8–1. That *MC* is less than *MR* up through the production and sale of 5 units of output is demonstrated by the fact that the *MC* curve lies below the *MR* curve, or demand curve *D*, up to this point. Beyond 5 units the *MC* curve lies above the demand curve *D*.

Comparison of the Two Viewpoints

We know from the total cost-total revenue graph in Figure 8–3, part a, that the firm realizes its maximum economic profit of $9 at 5 units of output. This can also be seen in Figure 8–3, part b, by looking at the *ATC* curve, which is plotted from the average total cost data in column 6 of Table 8–1. At 5 units of output the average total cost per unit is $7.20, which is represented by the distance $0c$, which equals ab. Total cost can then be computed as the 5 units multiplied by $7.20, which gives a total cost of $36. This is represented by the rectangular *area* $0abc$ in part b. (For comparison, remember that total cost is also represented by the vertical *distance* directly above 5 units up to the *TC* curve in part a.) The price per unit of $9 is represented by the distance $0d$, which equals ae. Total revenue from the sale of 5 units of output equals 5 multiplied by $9, or $45. This is represented by the rectangular area $0aed$ in part b. (Remember that in part a, total revenue is represented by the vertical distance directly above 5 units up to the total curve TR_9.) Since total economic profit equals total revenue minus total cost, it is represented by the difference between the areas of the rec-

tangles $0aed$ and $0abc$. Hence, the total economic profit of $9 is represented by the area of the rectangle $cbed$ in part b. (Remember that in part a, total economic profit is represented by the vertical distance between TR_9 and *TC*.)

An alternative way of arriving at the total economic profit is to multiply the economic profit per unit by the number of units. Economic profit per unit is represented by the vertical distance cd, which equals be, in Figure 8–3, part b. It equals the average revenue per unit (which is the price p) minus the *ATC* per unit—$9 minus $7.20, or $1.80. Multiplying this by 5 gives the total profit of $9.

Note that the break-even points in Figure 8–3, part a, where the *TC* curve intersects the TR_9 curve, correspond to the points at which the *ATC* curve intersects the *D* curve at the same output levels in Figure 8–3, part b. At output levels in between these break-even points the firm's economic profits are positive. This is shown in part b by the fact that average total cost per unit, as represented by the *ATC* curve, is less than average revenue per unit, as represented by the demand curve *D*. (Remember that average total cost, like total cost, includes an allowance for normal profit.) At output levels less than the lower break-even point and greater than the upper break-even point, the firm realizes a loss. This is indicated by the fact that the *ATC* curve lies above the demand curve *D*.

We may summarize our results for the marginal cost-marginal revenue point of view as follows. *To maximize economic profit the firm should produce up to that level of output where marginal cost equals marginal revenue.* This is true whether the firm is perfectly competitive, a monopolist, monopolistically competitive, or an oligopolist, as we shall see in subsequent chapters. The perfectly competitive firm is a price taker and therefore price is the same as marginal revenue. Hence, the *perfectly competitive firm maximizes profit by producing up to the point where marginal cost equals price.* For most sets of data, such as those in Table 8–1, there is typically no whole-number level of output

TABLE 8-2 Output, Revenue, and Costs of a Loss-Minimizing, Perfectly Competitive Firm (Hypothetical Data)

	Total Costs			Average and Marginal Costs			Price and Revenues		
(1)	**(2)**	**(3)**	**(4)**	**(5)**	**(6)**	**(7)**	**(8)**	**(9)**	**(10)**
Quantity of Output (Q)	Total Fixed Cost (TFC)	Total Variable Cost (TVC)	Total Cost (TC)	Average Variable Cost (AVC)	Average Total Cost (ATC)	Marginal Cost (MC)	Price = Marginal Revenue	Total Revenue	Profit (+) or Loss (−)
			$TC = TFC + TVC$	$AVC = \dfrac{TVC}{Q}$	$ATC = \dfrac{TC}{Q}$	$MC = \dfrac{\text{change in } TC}{\text{change in } Q}$	$p = MR$	$TR = p \times Q$	$TR - TC$
0	$10	$ 0	$10					$ 0	$−10
						$ 6	$6		
1	10	6	16	$6.00	$16.00			6	−10
						4	6		
2	10	10	20	5.00	10.00			12	− 8
						4	6		
3	10	14	24	4.66	8.00			18	− 6
						5	6		
4	10	19	29	4.75	7.25			24	− 5
						7	6		
5	10	26	36	5.20	7.20			30	− 6
						11	6		
6	10	37	47	6.16	7.83			36	−11
						23	6		
7	10	60	70	8.57	10.00			42	−28

at which marginal cost *MC* is exactly equal to marginal revenue *MR*. In that case, the firm should produce output up to the point where the *MR* associated with the last unit produced is greater than the *MC* associated with that unit.

CHECKPOINT 8-2
Use the data in columns 1, 6, and 8 of Table 8-1 to convince yourself that profit is maximized at 5 units of output. Use these data to lightly sketch in the rectangular areas representing total profit in Figure 8-3, part b, for output levels of 3, 4, and 6 units. Can you see that the rectangular area representing total profit at 5 units of output is larger than any of these?

Minimizing Loss— "Hanging in There"

In this case the firm's total revenue is less than its total cost, but it exceeds its total variable cost and thus offsets some of its total fixed cost. Hence, the loss that results from producing is less than total fixed cost, which is the loss if the plant remains idle. The output and cost data from columns 1–7 of Table 8–1 are reproduced in columns 1–7 in Table 8–2. The firm is still perfectly competitive, but now it is assumed that the price given to the firm is $6 instead of $9. Therefore the revenue data in columns 8–10 of Table 8–2 are different from those in columns 8–10 of Table 8–1.

Total Cost-Total Revenue Viewpoint

When price is $6 per unit, the firm's *TR* (column 9) is less than *TC* (column 4) at all lev-

FIGURE 8-4 Minimizing Loss in a Perfectly Competitive Firm

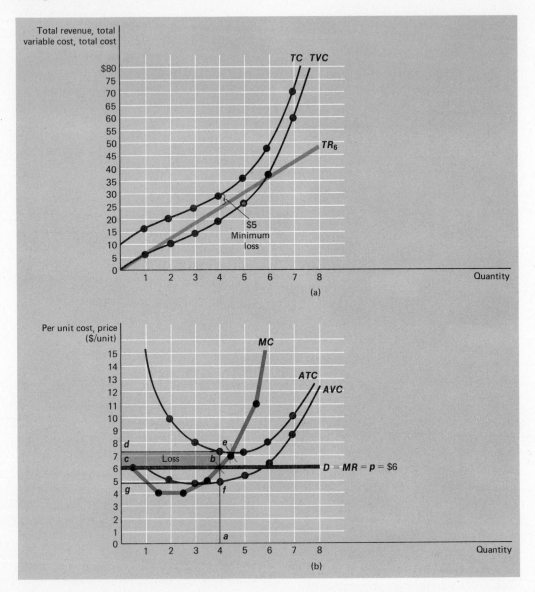

(a)

(b)

Assuming a price of $6, total revenue is plotted from the data in columns 1 and 9 of Table 8–2 to give the *TR* curve *TR₆* in part a. The *TC* and *TVC* curves are exactly the same as those in Figure 8–3. Here *TC* is greater than *TR* at all output levels, so that the firm experiences a loss represented by the vertical distance between *TC* and *TR₆* at any output level. The minimum distance between these two curves represents the minimum loss of $5, which occurs when 4 units of output are produced and sold.

The competitive firm's demand curve *D* is now at the level of the price of $6 per unit in part b. The *AVC, ATC,* and *MC* curves of part b are exactly the same as those in part b of Figure 8–3. The loss-minimizing level of output occurs at 4 units, where *MC = MR* as els of output (column 1). Therefore, the firm cannot avoid losses (column 10). If the firm were to produce nothing, the loss at a zero output level would be $10—just the amount of its *TFC* (column 2). Examination of column 10 shows that the firm can do better than this by producing. In fact, if it produces and sells 4 units of output, it will minimize its loss to $5. Another way of seeing this is to compare columns 9 and 3 and note that *TR* exceeds *TVC* by its largest amount at 4 units of output. Hence, this output level provides the largest excess of *TR* over *TVC* to offset the *TFC* that the firm is saddled with in the short run.

This situation is depicted graphically in Figure 8–4, part a. *TC* and *TVC* are plotted from the data in columns 1, 3, and 4 of Table 8–2. They are, of course, exactly the same as the *TC* and *TVC* curves of Figure 8–3. However, the *TR* curve TR_6 is less steeply sloped than TR_9. This reflects the fact that total revenue rises more slowly with output when price is $6 per unit than when price is $9 per unit. The *TC* curve now lies above the *TR* curve TR_6, reflecting the fact that total cost exceeds total revenue at all output levels. Nonetheless, the TR_6 curve lies above the *TVC* curve at output levels from 2 to 5 units, so that producing at any of these output levels will always result in some excess of *TR* over *TVC*, which offsets some part of *TFC*. The vertical distance of TR_6 above *TVC* is a maximum at 4 units of output. At this level of output the vertical distance of *TC* above TR_6 is a minimum. It equals the minimum loss of $5.

Marginal Cost–Marginal Revenue Viewpoint

Looking at the perfectly competitive firm from the marginal cost-marginal revenue

standpoint in the loss-minimizing case, we focus on columns 7 and 8 of Table 8–2. These are the *MC* and *MR* data, respectively. For the first unit of output produced, the *MR*-equal price of $6 just covers *MC*, which is also $6. However, if the firm increases output, it finds that *MC* will be less than *MR* up through 4 units of production. If it were to produce 5 units of output, the *MC* of the fifth unit would be $7, or $1 more than the *MR* of $6 received from the sale of the fifth unit. Hence, the firm should produce neither more nor less than 4 units of output. If we look at column 10 again, we can see that this corresponds to the same loss-minimizing level output we came up with by the total cost-total revenue method.

The marginal cost-marginal revenue viewpoint is depicted graphically in Figure 8–4, part b. The *AVC*, *ATC*, and *MC* curves are plotted from the data in columns 5, 6, and 7 of Table 8–2. They are exactly the same as the *AVC*, *ATC*, and *MC* curves of Figure 8–3. However, by comparison with Figure 8–3, part b, the demand curve *D* is now at the level of the lower price of $6 per unit. The *MC* curve intersects the *MR* = *D* curve at point *b*. This corresponds to the loss-minimizing output level of 4 units.

It should be noted that the loss-minimizing level of output does not necessarily correspond to the lowest level of *ATC* (the lowest point on the *ATC* curve). *ATC* at the loss-minimizing level of output of 4 units is $7.25 (Table 8–2, column 6). *ATC* at 5 units of output is in fact lower, $7.20. Similarly, in the profit-maximizing case, the profit-maximizing level of output is typically not the one associated with the lowest level of *ATC*. For example, suppose price was $12. By looking at column 7 of Table 8–2, we can see that the profit-maximizing rule of producing up to the point where $p = MR = MC$ would lead

represented by the rectangular shaded area *cbed* in part b. It equals the difference between total revenue, represented by 0*abc*, and total cost, represented by 0*aed*. Total fixed cost is represented by *gfed*. The amount by which total revenue exceeds total variable cost, and thus offsets some of the fixed cost, is represented by *gfbc*.

the firm to produce 6 units of output. But by looking at column 6 we can see that this does not correspond to the lowest level of *ATC*.

Comparison of the Two Viewpoints

Total revenue can be calculated by multiplying the output of 4 units (the distance 0*a* in Figure 8–4, part b) by the price of $6 (the distance 0*c* = *ab*) to give a *TR* of $24. This is represented by the rectangular area 0*abc* in Figure 8–4, part b. (This area corresponds to the vertical distance up to the TR_6 curve at 4 units of output in Figure 8–4, part a.) To get total cost, multiply 4 units of output by the *ATC* of $7.25 (from Table 8–2, column 6), which is the distance 0*d* = *ae*. The resulting *TC* of $29 is represented by the rectangular area 0*aed* in Figure 8–4, part b. (This corresponds to the vertical distance up to the *TC* curve at 4 units of output in Figure 8–4, part a.) The firm's loss of $5 is represented by the shaded rectangular area *cbed*, which is the difference between 0*aed* and 0*abc* in Figure 8–4, part b. (This area corresponds to the vertical distance between the *TC* curve and the TR_6 curve at 4 units of output in Figure 8–4, part a.)

The firm chooses to produce rather than shut down in the loss-minimizing case because *TR* exceeds *TVC*, as represented by the vertical distance of the TR_6 curve above the *TVC* curve at 4 units of output in Figure 7–4, part a. *TVC* can be calculated by multiplying 4 units of output by the *AVC* of $4.75 (from Table 8–2, column 5), the distance 0*g* = *af* in Figure 8–4, part b. This gives the *TVC* of $19, which is represented by the rectangular area 0*afg*. Therefore in Figure 8–4, part b, the amount by which *TR* exceeds *TVC* is represented by the difference between 0*abc* and 0*afg*, which is the rectangular area *gfbc*. If the firm produces nothing, it incurs a loss equal to the total fixed cost. Since *TFC* = *TC* − *TVC*, this loss is represented by the difference between the rectangular areas 0*aed* and 0*afg*. This difference is the rectangular area *gfed* in Figure 8–4, part

b, which is equal to $10. (This area corresponds to the vertical distance between the *TC* and *TVC* curves in Figure 8–4, part a.) Figure 8–4, part b, makes it clear that the loss, represented by *cbed*, that results when the firm produces 4 units of output, is less than the loss, represented by *gfed* (equal to *TFC*), that results if it remains idle. This is so because the amount by which total revenue *TR* exceeds total variable cost *TVC* offsets total fixed cost *TFC* (equal to *gfed*) by the amount *gfbc*.

In sum, *when the firm's total revenue is at least as great as total variable cost but not larger than total cost, it should produce up to that level of output where marginal cost equals marginal revenue in order to minimize its losses.* This is true whether the firm is perfectly competitive, a monopolist, monopolistically competitive, or an oligopolist. Since price equals marginal revenue in the case of the perfectly competitive firm, it should produce up to the point where price equals marginal cost when the object is to minimize losses.

Finally, summing up both cases, *as long as the firm has decided to produce, it will maximize profit or minimize loss by producing up to that output level where marginal cost equals marginal revenue. For the perfectly competitive firm this means producing up to the point where marginal cost equals price.*

CHECKPOINT 8-3
Use the data in columns 1, 6, and 8 of Table 8–2 (which assume that price equals $6) to convince yourself that loss is minimized at 4 units of output. Use these data to lightly sketch in the rectangular areas representing loss in Figure 8–4, part b, for output levels of 2, 3, and 5 units. Can you see that the rectangular area representing total loss at 4 units of output is smaller than any of these? Also, use the data from columns 1, 5, and 8 to lightly sketch in the rectangular areas representing the

excess of *TR* over *TVC* in Figure 8-4, part b, for output levels of 2, 3, 4, and 5 units. Can you see that the rectangular area representing this excess at 4 units of output is larger than any of these?

Deciding to Shut Down—Closing the Doors

When the firm's total revenue is not even large enough to cover its total variable cost, it will minimize its loss by producing nothing at all. Its loss will then equal its total fixed cost. Note that in the short run this does not mean that the firm goes out of business, but rather that it simply remains idle. (Of course, in the long run all factors are variable and therefore so are all costs. So if demand does not improve, the firm will go out of business.)

The shutdown case for a perfectly competitive firm is depicted in Table 8-3 and Figure 8-5. The cost data in columns 1–7 are the same as those in Tables 8-1 and 8-2. All the cost curves in Figure 8-5 are the same as in Figures 8-3 and 8-4. However, the firm can now only sell its output at a price of $4 per unit (column 8).

Total Cost-Total Revenue Viewpoint

By looking at column 10, we can see that the firm's loss is clearly minimized by producing nothing. This is represented in Figure 8-5, part a, by the fact that the *TR* curve TR_4 (plotted from the data in columns 1 and 9) now lies below the *TVC* curve at all levels of output above zero. The vertical distance be-

TABLE 8-3 Output, Revenue, and Costs of a Perfectly Competitive Firm in the Shutdown Case (Hypothetical Data)

	Total Costs			Average and Marginal Costs			Price and Revenues		
(1)	(2)	(3)	(4)	(5)	(6)	(7)	(8)	(9)	(10)
Quantity of Output (Q)	Total Fixed Cost (TFC)	Total Variable Cost (TVC)	Total Cost (TC)	Average Variable Cost (AVC)	Average Total Cost (ATC)	Marginal Cost (MC)	Price = Marginal Revenue	Total Revenue	Profit (+) or Loss (−)
			$TC = TFC + TVC$	$AVC = \frac{TVC}{Q}$	$ATC = \frac{TC}{Q}$	$MC = \frac{\text{change in } TC}{\text{change in } Q}$	$p = MR$	$TR = p \times Q$	$TR - TC$
0	$10	$ 0	$10					$ 0	$−10
						$ 6	$4		
1	10	6	16	$6.00	$16.00			4	−11
						4	4		
2	10	10	20	5.00	10.00			8	−12
						4	4		
3	10	14	24	4.66	8.00			12	−12
						5	4		
4	10	19	29	4.75	7.25			16	−13
						7	4		
5	10	26	36	5.20	7.20			20	−16
						11	4		
6	10	37	47	6.16	7.83			24	−23
						23	4		
7	10	60	70	8.57	10.00			28	−42

FIGURE 8-5   Shutdown Case, Perfectly Competitive Firm

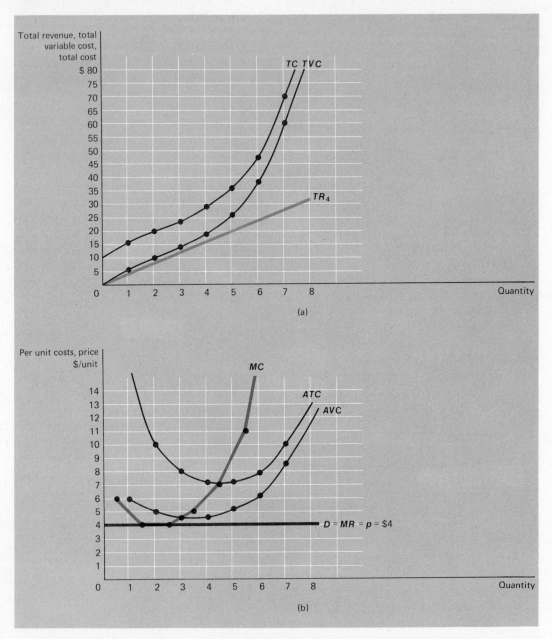

(a)

(b)

The cost curves in parts a and b are exactly the same as those in Figures 8–3 and 8–4. Assuming a price of $4, total revenue is plotted from the data in columns 1 and 9 of Table 8–3 to give the TR curve TR_4 in part a. The vertical distance between the TC and TVC curves is the same at all output levels because it equals TFC. The distance by which the TVC curve lies above the TR_4 curve at all output levels represents the additional loss the tween TVC and TR_4 at each output level represents the loss in addition to that due to the total fixed cost, which is represented by the vertical distance between TC and TVC. The sum of these two sources of loss at each output level is represented by the vertical distance between TC and TR_4, which equals the amounts shown in column 10 of Table 8-3.

Marginal Cost–
Marginal Revenue Viewpoint

The data in columns 7 and 8 of Table 8-3 tell us that MC is greater than MR at all levels of output, except 2 and 3 units of output, where $MC = MR$. However, for the first unit of output MC is greater than MR. This means that the firm would not cover its AVC per unit (column 5) even if it did produce 2 or 3 units of output. This is so because the average revenue per unit (column 8), which is its price (also equal to MR the perfectly competitive firm), is less AVC (column 5) at all levels of output. This is clearly demonstrated in Figure 8 part b, by the fact that the demand cur lies below the AVC curve at all l of output.

Summing up all three now, *if price exceeds average variab , the perfectly competitive firm sho duce that output order to maximize . If price is less than average variable cost, it will minimize loss if it produces nothing.*

CHECKPOINT 8-4
For 4 units of output, sketch in the rectangle in Figure 8-5, part b, that corresponds to the vertical distance

between the TVC and TR_4 curves in Figure 8-5, part a. What does this rectangle represent? Also for 4 units output, sketch in the rectangle in Figure 8-5, part b, that correspo to the vertical distance between TC and TR_4 curves in Figure 8- art a. For 4 units of output, ske the rectangle that represent C.

The Firm's Ma al Cost
and Short-R upply Curve

We have se t the perfectly competitive firm maxi s profit or minimizes loss by adjustin production to that level of output marginal cost equals price. (This w wn in Figures 8-3, part b, 8-4, part 8-5, part b.) In other words, as long as ce is equal to or greater than average variable cost, the perfectly competitive firm adjusts output by moving along that part of its marginal cost curve that lies above its average variable cost curve. This part of that curve conforms precisely with the definition of a supply curve. As you may recall from our earlier definition of such a curve, a supply curve indicates the amount of a good a supplier is willing to provide per period of time to the market at different possible prices.

The relationship between the supply curve and the marginal cost curve for a hypothetical perfectly competitive firm is shown in Figure 8-6, part a. At a price of p_1 the firm is just able to cover its average variable cost. It therefore produces 60 units of output, the level of output at which its MC curve intersects its MR curve MR_1. MR_1, of course, is

---

firm incurs if it produces. It can be seen that this additional loss is eliminated and the total loss minimized only when the firm produces nothing. The minimum loss will then be the TFC of $10.

This situation is represented in part b by the fact that the demand curve D is at the price level, or average revenue level, of $4, which is below the AVC curve at all output levels. Average revenue per unit is not sufficient to cover AVC per unit at any output level. The difference will represent a loss in addition to that due to TFC if the firm produces.

FIGURE 8-6   Short-Run Equilibrium for a Perfectly Competitive Firm and Industry

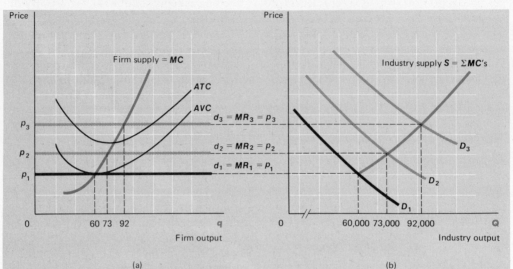

The perfectly competitive firm's supply curve is that part of its *MC* curve that lies above its *AVC* curve, as shown in part a. The industry supply curve *S* shown in part b is obtained by summing up the quantity of output that each firm will produce at each price in part a. Since there are 1,000 firms like the one shown in part a, industry supply at each price in part b is equal to 1,000 times the amount supplied by the typical firm in part a at each price. Three such prices, p_1, p_2, and p_3, and the associated output levels for an individual firm (part a) and the whole industry (part b) are shown here.

The intersection of the industry demand curve and supply curve in part b determines the equilibrium market price and output level. Since each firm supplies a fraction equal to 1/1,000 of this output, the firm cannot significantly affect market price. The firm's demand curve is therefore horizontal at the market-determined price. The position of the firm's demand curve corresponding to three different positions of the industry demand curve D_1, D_2, and D_3 (part b) is d_1, d_2, and d_3 (part a). The associated level of price is p_1, p_2, and p_3.

Because p_1 and p_2 lie below the firm's *ATC* curve, but at or above its *AVC* curve, the firm minimizes losses by producing to the point where $MC = MR_1$ or MR_2 for each of these price levels. Since p_3 lies above the *ATC* curve, the firm maximizes profit by producing to the point where $MC = MR_3$.

---

the same as its demand curve d_1 at the price level p_1. If price were to rise to p_2, the firm would increase its production to 73 units, the point at which its *MC* curve intersects $MR_2 = d_2$. And if price were to rise to p_3, *MC* would equal *MR* at the point where the *MC* curve intersects $MR_3 = d_3$. The firm would then produce 92 units of output.

In sum, *that part of the perfectly competi-*

tive firm's marginal cost curve that lies above its average variable cost curve is its short-run supply curve.

The Industry Supply Curve

Suppose there are 1,000 firms like that in Figure 8–6, part a, which together make up the perfectly competitive industry. The industry supply curve S is the sum of all the individual firms' supply curves. These supply curves are the same as their marginal cost curves (Σ may be read "sum of"), as shown in Figure 8–6, part b. For example, in Figure 8–6, part a, at a price of p_1 each individual firm supplies 60 units of output. Therefore, the total amount supplied by 1,000 such firms is 60,000 units at a price of p_1, as shown in Figure 8–6, part b. At a price of p_2, each individual firm supplies 73 units of output (Figure 8–6, part a). The total amount supplied by the industry is 1,000 times this amount or 73,000 units (Figure 8–6, part b). Finally, if price were p_3, each individual firm would supply 92 units (Figure 8–6, part a), and the total industry supply would be 92,000 units (Figure 8–6, part b).

We conclude that *at each price level the industry supply curve is constructed by summing the amounts each individual firm will supply, as indicated by its marginal cost curve above its AVC curve.* At a price below p_1, firms are not able to cover their average variable costs and therefore will produce nothing. Hence, the industry will supply nothing at a price below p_1, as indicated by the fact that the industry supply curve in Figure 8–6, part b, does not extend below this level.

Firm and Industry Equilibrium

We have seen in earlier chapters how market supply and demand interact to determine equilibrium price and quantity for an industry. Earlier in this chapter, when looking at Figure 8–1, we saw that in a perfectly competitive industry the perfectly competitive firm contributes such a small fraction of total industry supply that it cannot affect the market price. The competitive firm's demand curve is therefore perfectly elastic (horizontal). Putting these considerations together with the perfectly competitive firm's cost curves and the industry supply curve, we can examine the relationship between the com-

petitive industry equilibrium and the competitive firm equilibrium in the short run.

This relationship can be seen by examining the relationship between parts a and b of Figure 8–6. When the market demand for the industry's output is given by the market demand curve D_1 in part b, its intersection with the industry supply curve S determines the equilibrium price level p_1 and industry output of 60,000 units. A typical firm (part a) in the industry therefore faces the horizontal demand curve d_1 at the price level p_1 and supplies 60 units of output. (These 60 units are equal to 1/1,000 of the industry total.) Since the firm is just covering its AVC at this price (the demand curve d_1 is tangent to the AVC curve at its lowest point), if the industry demand curve were to shift to a position lower than D_1, firms would decide to produce nothing at all. On the other hand, if the industry demand curve shifted to D_2 in part b, the intersection of industry supply and industry demand would determine a price of p_2, and the industry would supply 73,000 units of output. The typical firm, part a, would now face a demand curve d_2. It still would not be able to cover its total costs because d_2 lies below the ATC curve. But it would minimize losses by producing to the point where marginal cost equals marginal revenue. This point is indicated by the intersection of its MC curve with its $d_2 = MR_2 = p_2$ curve at 73 units of output. Hence, in the short run, when the industry demand curve is at positions such as D_1 or D_2, firms in the industry are operating at a loss.

What happens if industry demand shifts outward to a position such as D_3 in part b? Equilibrium price is now p_3, and industry output is now 92,000 units. The typical firm's demand curve in part a would now be shifted up to the position d_3. To equate marginal cost and marginal revenue, the typical firm would increase output to 92 units. Since p_3 is above the ATC curve at this point, the firm would be maximizing profit. Hence, with industry demand at D_3, firms in the industry are now realizing profits instead of losses.

CHECKPOINT 8-5
Suppose there is a rise in the cost of raw materials used by the firms in the industry depicted in Figure 8-6. How would this affect the firm's cost curves in part a? How would it affect the industry supply curve in part b? If the industry demand curve were at D_1, what would happen to firm and industry output? If the demand curve were D_3, what would happen to price? What would happen to firm and industry output?

THE COMPETITIVE FIRM AND INDUSTRY IN THE LONG RUN

In the long run, all factors of production are variable. It is possible for new firms to enter the industry and for existing firms to leave the industry or go out of business. What is the nature of this adjustment process and how does it determine the long-run industry supply curve?

Long-Run Adjustment

We will first examine the long-run adjustment process by considering what happens when there is an increase in industry demand. We will then look at what happens when there is a decrease in demand.

Demand Increases: Excess Profit Induces Firms to Enter Industry

Suppose initially that the demand and supply curves for the perfectly competitive industry are in the positions D_1 and S_1 as shown in Figure 8-7, part b. Their intersection determines the equilibrium price p_1 and equilibrium industry output of 80,000 units. Suppose there are initially 1,000 firms in the industry, each like that shown in Figure 8-7, part a. The firm's demand curve is d_1 at the price level p_1, which of course is also its mar-

ginal revenue MR_1. MC equals MR_1 at the point where the MC curve intersects the demand curve d_1. The desire to maximize profit will therefore lead each firm to produce 80 units of output. Notice that initially each firm is just earning a normal profit. This is so because at a price of p_1, each is just covering its average total cost, as represented by the tangency of its ATC curve with the demand curve d_1 in Figure 8-7, part a. (Remember that ATC includes a normal profit.)

Now suppose that there is an increase in industry demand as represented by the rightward shift in the industry demand curve from D_1 to D_2, as shown in Figure 8-7, part b. The supply curve S_1 is the short-run industry supply curve. It is therefore the sum of the 1,000 marginal cost curves of each firm (above AVC), such as MC in Figure 8-7, part a. Initially price rises to p_2 and industry output to 100,000 (the intersection of D_2 and S_1 in part b) because each firm in the industry expands output to 100 units, as determined by the intersection of its MC curve and its now higher demand curve d_2 (part a).

However, at the now higher price of p_2, each firm will be earning a profit per unit in excess of the normal profit. This excess is represented by the vertical distance between the demand curve d_2 and the ATC curve at 100 units of output. It will serve as a signal to other resource suppliers in the rest of the economy that above-normal profits can be earned by starting new firms and entering this industry.

As new firms enter the industry, the total number of firms like that in Figure 8-7, part a, increases. This increase causes the short-run industry supply curve in part b to shift rightward. *New firms will continue to enter the industry as long as excess profits exist, since in the long run all factors of production are variable.* As the short-run supply curve shifts rightward, its intersection with D_2 in part b will occur at lower and lower prices until it has reached the position S_2. At this point, price will have fallen back to the initial level p_1, and each firm's demand curve will once

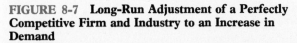

FIGURE 8-7 **Long-Run Adjustment of a Perfectly Competitive Firm and Industry to an Increase in Demand**

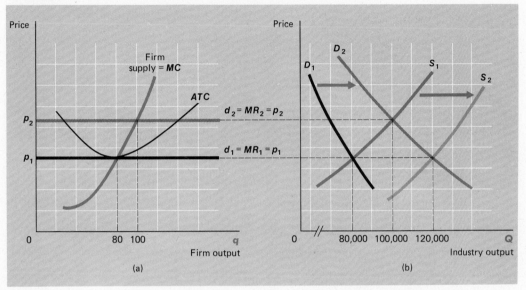

The initial equilibrium position of the perfectly competitive industry is determined by the intersection of the industry demand curve D_1 and short-run supply curve S_1 in part b. The associated equilibrium position of the representative firm is determined by the intersection of the firm's MC curve and its demand curve d_1. Initially each firm is just earning a normal profit because at price p_1, each is just covering its average total cost.

When the industry demand curve (shown in part b) shifts rightward to D_2, price initially rises from p_1 to p_2 as firms already in the industry respond by increasing output. An increase in output means each firm moves up along its MC curve to the point of intersection with its now higher demand curve d_2 (shown in part a). At this point, firms are making a profit in excess of normal profit. This attracts other firms into the industry, causing the industry supply curve shown in part b to shift rightward.

When enough firms have entered so that the short-run industry supply curve has shifted to S_2, price will return to p_1. A larger number of firms will now be in the industry in the new equilibrium, each earning a normal profit and facing a demand curve d_1 as in the original equilibrium position in part a.

again be in the position d_1. Each firm will once again produce and sell 80 units of output, as shown in part a. Each firm will again just be earning a normal profit. However, there will now be 1,500 firms in the industry ($120{,}000 \div 80 = 1{,}500$) producing and selling a total of 120,000 units of output at the price p_1 (part b).

Demand Decreases: Losses Induce Firms to Exit

Suppose we start from the same initial equilibrium we did in Figure 8–7, only now, in Figure 8–8, we will assume that industry demand falls. This is represented by the leftward shift of the industry demand curve

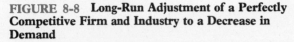

FIGURE 8-8   Long-Run Adjustment of a Perfectly Competitive Firm and Industry to a Decrease in Demand

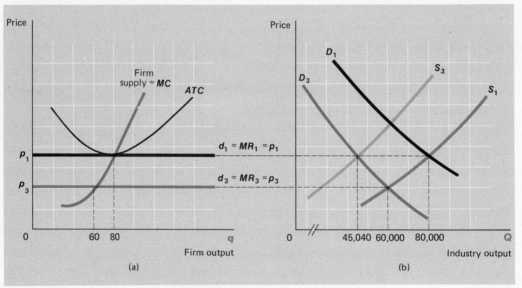

The perfectly competitive industry is initially in the equilibrium position determined by the intersection of the industry demand curve D_1 and the short-run industry supply curve S_1 in part b. The associated equilibrium position of the representative firm is determined by the intersection of the firm's MC curve and its demand curve d_1 in part a.

When the industry demand curve shifts leftward to D_3, part b, price initially falls from p_1 to p_3 as firms already in the industry respond by reducing output. This means they are moving down along their MC curves to the point of intersection of their now lower demand curves d_3, part a. At this point firms are incurring losses and some begin to go out of business. This causes the short-run industry supply curve in part b to shift leftward.

When enough firms have left so that the short-run industry supply curve has shifted to S_3, price will return to p_1. A smaller number of firms will now be in the industry in the new equilibrium, each again earning a normal profit and facing a demand curve d_1 as in the original equilibrium position in part a.

from D_1 to D_3, as shown in Figure 8–8, part b. The 1,000 firms in the industry each see this decline in demand as a fall in their demand curves from d_1 to d_3 in Figure 8–8, part a. The typical firm reduces output by moving down its marginal cost curve to reduce output from 80 units to 60 units. That is, it reduces output until marginal cost again equals marginal revenue at the point where the firm's MC curve intersects its demand curve $d_3 = MR_3 = p_3$. This lower level of output for each individual firm is reflected at the industry level by a fall in industry output from 80,000 to 60,000 units along the industry supply curve S_1, shown in part b.

Remember, however, that *in the long run all factors are variable and therefore so are all costs. Hence, unlike the short-run situation, if price is not high enough to cover average total cost, the firm will go out of business.* Since p_3

lies below the *ATC* curve in Figure 8–8, part a, the typical firm is now operating at a loss. Firms will therefore begin to leave the industry because the resources they use can no longer earn their opportunity cost. These resources will move to other lines of activity in the economy where they can be paid their opportunity cost.

As firms leave the industry, the short-run industry supply curve will shift leftward until it reaches the position S_3. Here, price once again is p_1 at the intersection of D_3 and S_3 (Figure 8–8, part b), and industry output is 45,040 units. The typical firm in the industry will once again face a demand curve d_1. Marginal cost will equal marginal revenue at the point where the *MC* curve intersects the $d_1 = MR_1 = p_1$ curve at an output level of 80 units (part a). In the new equilibrium, firms are once again just covering their average total cost—that is, they are again earning a normal profit. There will now be 563 firms in the industry (45,040 ÷ 80 = 563) as compared to 1,000 before the fall in demand. Losses have caused 437 firms to go out of business in this industry.

Let us summarize these results. When a perfectly competitive industry is in long-run equilibrium, each firm is operating at the bottommost point on its *ATC* curve. This is the point of tangency with its horizontal demand curve. Hence, *when the perfectly competitive firm is in long-run equilibrium, price equals marginal cost equals marginal revenue equals average total cost.* Each firm is just earning a normal profit. That is, economic profit is zero in long-run equilibrium. An increase in demand causes a rise in price, which leads to excess profits (above-normal profits). This attracts new firms into the industry, causing the short-run industry supply curve to shift rightward until price falls back to the level of minimum average total cost. Once again, each firm operates at the minimum point of its average total cost curve, just earning a normal profit. A decrease in demand causes a fall in price and leads to losses. Firms, therefore, leave the industry, causing the short-run supply curve to shift

leftward until price rises back to the level of minimum average total cost for the remaining firms in the industry. Each again is just earning a normal profit.

Long-Run Industry Supply Curve

The supply curves S_1, S_2, and S_3 in Figures 8–7 and 8–8 are *short-run* industry supply curves. Along any one of them, the number of firms in the industry is assumed constant, or fixed. For S_1 in Figures 8–7, part b, and 8–8, part b, there are 1,000 firms, for S_2 in Figure 8–7, part b, there are 1,500 firms, and for S_3 in Figure 8–8, part b, there are 563. Since we have been considering the long-run adjustment, what is the *long-run* industry supply curve for a perfectly competitive industry? To answer this question, we must consider three distinct situations that may arise—one in which costs are constant, one in which costs are increasing, and one in which costs are decreasing.

The Constant-Cost Case

This is the case we have described in Figures 8–7 and 8–8. Throughout our analysis of the long-run adjustment process, we assumed that the prices of all the factors of production purchased by the firms in the industry remained unchanged, no matter what level of output was produced by the industry. This means that when new firms enter the industry or existing ones leave it, the *ATC* and *MC* curves of all firms in the industry remain at the same level—that shown in Figures 8–7, part a, and 8–8, part a.

We observed three different possible positions of the industry demand curve, D_1, D_2, and D_3 in Figures 8–7, part b, and 8–8, part b, each of which had an associated long-run industry equilibrium. Although the number of firms in the industry associated with each long-run equilibrium varied, the long-run equilibrium position of each firm in the industry was always the same. Namely, each produced 80 units of output at the lowest point on its *ATC* curve where its *MC* curve

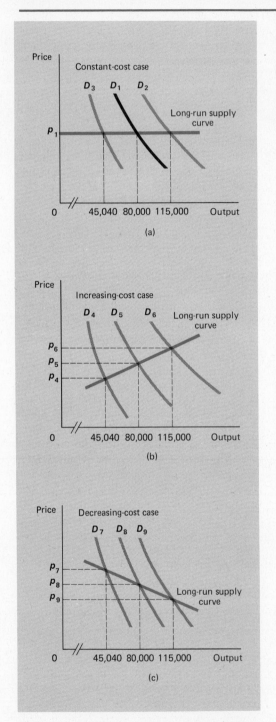

(a)

(b)

(c)

FIGURE 8-9   Long-Run Supply Curves for a Perfectly Competitive Industry—Constant-, Increasing-, and Decreasing-Cost Cases

When the prices of inputs to the industry are constant (that is, unaffected by the level of the industry's production), the per unit costs of production, and hence the level of the ATC and MC curves of the firms in the industry, are the same at all levels of industry output in long-run equilibrium. Therefore, the long-run industry supply curve is perfectly elastic (horizontal) at the same long-run equilibrium price level no matter what the level of demand in the constant-cost case as shown in part a.

When the prices of inputs to the industry rise with increases in the level of the industry's production, the per unit costs of production, and hence the level of the ATC and MC curves, of the firms in the industry rise. Therefore, the long-run industry supply curve is upward sloping in the increasing-cost case as shown in part b.

When the prices of inputs to the industry fall with increases in the level of the industry's production, the per unit costs of production, and hence the level of the ATC and MC curves, of the firms in the industry fall. Therefore, the long-run industry supply curve is downward sloping in the decreasing-cost case as shown in part c.

intersected its demand curve $d_1 = MR_1$ at the price level p_1 (Figures 8-7, part a, and 8-8, part a).

Suppose we considered all other possible positions of the industry demand curve D. In each case, after all adjustments are completed in the long run, there would be just enough firms in the industry so that total industry supply would equal industry demand at the price p_1. Therefore, the long-run industry supply curve for the perfectly competitive industry in the constant-cost case is just the horizontal line at the equilibrium price level p_1, as shown in Figure 8-9, part a. If you like, you may think of it as consisting of all the points formed by the intersections of all possible industry demand curves with the associated short-run industry supply curves, such as the intersections of D_1 and S_1, D_2 and S_2, and D_3 and S_3 in Figures 8-7, part b, and 8-8, part b.

The Increasing-Cost Case

If the resources used by the competitive industry constitute a large enough portion of the total supply of such resources, their prices may rise as the competitive industry purchases more of them. This is particularly true if the supply of these resources is not easily increased. Conversely, when the competitive industry reduces its level of production, and therefore buys fewer of these resources, their prices may fall. For each individual firm in the industry, such as that in Figure 8-8, part a, a rise in the prices of its inputs, and hence its unit costs, will be reflected in an upward shift in its ATC and MC curves. Conversely, a decline in input prices, and hence unit costs, will be reflected in a downward shift in the ATC and MC curves.

Suppose we were to consider successively higher levels of industry demand, for example, as represented by the industry demand curve shifting rightward to positions such as D_4, D_5, and D_6 in Figure 8-9, part b. When the demand curve shifts from D_4 to D_5, new firms will enter the industry in response to

the above-normal profits that are initially realized. As new firms enter, these excess profits will now be eliminated in two ways. First, as we have already seen, excess profits will be reduced by the fall in price that takes place during the adjustment process because of the expanding level of industry output. Second, excess profits will be further reduced by the upward shift of the typical firm's ATC and MC curves, which results from the rise in the price of inputs as industry expansion increases the demand for them. Once the excess profits have been eliminated by these two effects, the industry will be in a new long-run equilibrium position producing a larger output with more firms. Each will again be operating at the minimum point on its ATC curve, but now the typical firm's ATC curve will be higher than before. Hence, the larger long-run equilibrium level of industry output is supplied at a higher price.

Suppose the industry demand curve shifts rightward again. After the adjustment process has worked itself out once more, there will be an even larger level of long-run equilibrium output supplied at a yet higher price. Hence, the long-run perfectly competitive industry supply curve is upward sloping in the increasing-cost case, as shown in Figure 8-9, part b. As a result, the long-run equilibrium price associated with the successively larger levels of demand represented by D_4, D_5, and D_6 is successively higher—p_4, p_5, and p_6 respectively—at output levels of 45,040, 80,000, and 115,000 units.

The Decreasing-Cost Case

It is also possible as a perfectly competitive industry increases output that the prices it pays for inputs, and hence its per unit costs of production, may decline. This could occur, for example, if some of the industries supplying the inputs to the perfectly competitive industry experienced economies of scale as they produced larger quantities of the inputs. The resulting lower costs of pro-

POLICY PERSPECTIVE

Is Perfect Competition an Ideal?—The Pros and Cons

The concept of perfect competition has often been held up as an ideal or standard for judging other kinds of industry or market structures. Indeed, it might be said that the principal objective of antitrust policy (to be discussed in Chapter 12) is to see to it that the economy's various industries perform to the greatest possible extent according to standards exhibited by perfect competition. However, while perfect competition has many desirable economic attributes, it has shortcomings as well. We should sharpen our perspective by taking a look at both sides of the picture.

The Case for Perfect Competition

The economic case for perfect competition is largely based on the contention that it is the most efficient form of market structure for allocating resources to satisfy consumer wants. At another level, the concept of perfect competition has an appeal that is emphatically more political than economic. Like most issues in economics, these two types of appeal cannot, of course, be entirely separated. (In fact, for a great many years, the subject of economics was typically referred to as "political economy.") But for the purpose of understanding the issues here, we'll consider these two aspects separately.

Perfect Competition as an Efficient Allocator of Resources

What does it mean to say that perfect competition is the most efficient way for allocating resources to maximize consumer satisfaction? There are two basic points underlying this argument.

1. *When the perfectly competitive industry is in long-run equilibrium, competition forces firms to use a technology that yields the lowest possible ATC curves and to operate at the lowest point on their ATC curves, and consumers pay a price equal to this minimum ATC.* Any firm that doesn't operate in this fashion will be forced out of business. This follows because the existence of many firms producing an identical product means that if any firm tries to charge a higher price, consumers will simply buy from its competitors—the firm will have zero sales. Therefore each firm is forced by competition to produce at the lowest point on its *ATC* curve if it wants to stay in business. Hence, the industry produces the good at the lowest possible per unit cost and distributes it to consumers at a price that just covers this cost. Because each firm must use the least-cost technology to survive, there is no way to improve on this situation given the prevailing state of technical know-how.

2. *In a perfectly competitive equilibrium (short run or long run), price equals marginal cost, and hence for the last unit of a good purchased, consumers pay a price that just covers the cost of producing it.* Given that the industry demand curve is downward sloping, let's suppose that production is not pushed to the point where marginal cost equals price for good A. In other words, consumers are willing to pay a price for additional units of A that is greater than the cost of producing these units. The marginal cost of the additional units of A is the opportunity cost of using the resources needed to produce them, that is, the value of the resources in some alternative use. The fact that consumers are willing to pay a price greater than this

opportunity cost for the use of these resources in the production of A suggests that society values additional units of A more highly than the alternative goods that these resources could produce. Hence, if production of A is not pushed to the point where marginal cost equals the price of A, there will be an underallocation of resources to the production of A.

On the other hand, let's suppose that the production of A were pushed beyond the point where marginal cost equals price. Because marginal cost rises as output increases, the price received for the additional units will be less than their marginal cost. This would indicate that the value society places on these additional units is less than the opportunity cost of the resources needed to produce them, or society's valuation of alternative goods that could otherwise be produced with these resources. Hence, there is an overallocation of resources to the production of good A.

What are the implications for consumer satisfaction? When *all* industries in an economy are in a perfectly competitive equilibrium, each will produce just that quantity of its product so that price will equal marginal cost. Therefore, *in a perfectly competitive equilibrium, there will be no misallocation of resources between the production of different goods, and consumer satisfaction will be as large as possible.* Why is this so? If production of good A were pushed beyond the quantity at which $p = MC$, so that the marginal cost of the additional units exceeded their price, society would have to relinquish some amount of alternative goods that it values more highly than the additional units of A. Consumer satisfaction would thus be reduced. To produce an amount of A less than the quantity where $p = MC$, so that p is greater than MC, means society is forgoing an amount of A that it values more than the alternative goods these resources are producing elsewhere. Again, consumer satisfaction is less than it might be.

Finally, because there is ease of entry to and exit of firms from perfectly competitive industries, a perfectly competitive economy will quickly reallocate resources to meet changing consumer preferences or supply conditions. This will serve to preserve allocative efficiency over time.

The Political Appeal of Perfect Competition

The notion of an economy characterized by perfectly competitive markets has a special appeal for those who view concentration of power in a few hands as dangerous. Anyone who believes that power groups, whether governmental or private, pose a potential threat to individual rights and personal freedom finds much to recommend the perfectly competitive world.

Markets composed of many buyers and sellers, not one of which is large enough to have a significant impact on price and output, lead to about as much diffusion of power as one could imagine. The forces of keen competition that characterize such markets put a premium on performance. For example, firms that discriminate among workers on grounds other than their ability to perform a job will find themselves at a competitive disadvantage vis-à-vis firms who hire workers solely on the basis of ability. Indeed, they will soon be out of business. When consumer demands shift, resources will move quickly to those production activities that will satisfy them. Resources will be efficiently allocated to society's needs without being compelled by any force other than the impersonal signals of the market—the "invisible hand" of the marketplace, as Adam Smith called it.

Criticisms of Perfect Competition

Perfect competition is not without its critics. The most common criticisms levied against it are that (1) it provides little incentive for innovation, (2) it does not capture spillover costs and benefits, (3) it leads to a lack of product variety, and (4) the accompanying distribution of income may be "inequitable." All of these charges raise doubts about whether perfect competition is the best form of market organization for maximizing consumer satisfaction.

Let's look at these criticisms individually.

Perfect Competition Provides Little Incentive for Innovation

In a perfectly competitive world, information about technology is readily available to all. In an agricultural market, for example, it would be hard for a farmer to keep a newly developed production technique a secret from competitors for long. As a result, a firm cannot expect to gain much competitive advantage over other firms by developing new technology. The higher than normal profits that the firm might realize would be short lived as other firms quickly adopted the new technique and once again competed on an equal footing. Therefore, with little prospect of reaping much gain from technological innovation, there is little incentive for a perfectly competitive firm to devote much effort to such activity.

Since technological innovation is considered essential to the dynamics of economic growth (measured as the rate of increase of output per capita), it is often argued that a perfectly competitive world is lacking in this respect. The existence of *patent laws* that give inventors the legal right to exclusive use of their inventions for a stipulated period of time is in large part justified by this consideration. Of course, the existence of perfect competi-

tion is precluded in industries where there are patents held by certain firms, as we will see in subsequent chapters.

Perfect Competition Fails to Capture Spillover Costs and Benefits

We discussed spillover costs and benefits in Chapter 6 (you may need to go back and review these concepts at this point). Clearly when spillover costs exist, such as water and air pollution, the firm's marginal cost curve does not include them. Producing to the point where marginal cost equals price will therefore mean producing some goods that, in fact, cost more than the value society places on them. In this case, it can no longer be argued that the existence of perfectly competitive markets leads to the maximization of consumer satisfaction. The same argument holds when there are spillover benefits such as those associated with keeping one's automobile in safe working condition or those associated with the purchase of flu shots.

Perfect Competition Leads to a Lack of Product Variety

This criticism of perfect competition alleges that because a perfectly competitive firm produces a product indistinguishable from that of the other firms in the industry, there may be a dull sameness about a perfectly competitive world. While this may be true, economists are generally not in favor of solving this problem through attempts to create distinctions between the products of different firms when in fact no real difference exists. For example, there is no difference between beet sugar and cane sugar despite advertising to the contrary. Such advertising uses resources that could be used in other activities, with the result that the products advertised cost the consumer more than necessary. This is not to say that all advertising in a perfectly competitive market is a waste of resources. "Drink milk for good health" is an ad that may well be informative and increase the sales of all milk products, unlike an ad that says, "Sunny Farm's milk is more wholesome than any other."

The Distribution of Income Associated with Perfect Competition May Be Inequitable

A perfectly competitive world provides for an efficient allocation of resources, *given* the existing distribution of wealth or income among members of the economy. If that distribution were different, the allocation of resources provided by the perfectly competitive markets would be different as well—though still efficient by the criterion that price would equal marginal cost in each and every market. However, society's opinions about an equitable distribution of income are a separate consideration from that of the efficient allocation of resources. *The "fairness" of a particular income distribution is a normative issue—disputes over this cannot be settled* *by an appeal to facts alone.* Hence, one may have no quarrel with the efficiency with which resources are allocated in a perfectly competitive world (price equals marginal cost in each market). However, it is at the same time possible for one to feel that the prevailing distribution of income is "unfair." If Jones feeds his dog steak while Brown cannot even afford to feed his children beans, many observers may feel that this reflects an inequitable distribution of income. We will examine the subject of income distribution in greater detail in Chapter 17.

Question

1. Critics claim that perfect competition is not good for economic growth because it doesn't offer enough incentive for innovation. Does the example provided by the agricultural sector of our economy (discussed in Chapter 6) tend to support or refute this claim? Why?

---

ducing these inputs might then be passed along to the perfectly competitive industry in the form of lower input prices. Then the long-run supply curve of the perfectly competitive industry would be downward sloping, as shown in Figure 8–9, part c. For the successively larger demands D_7, D_8, and D_9, the long-run equilibrium prices are the successively lower p_7, p_8, and p_9.

An example of a decreasing-cost industry might be the development of agriculture in a typical frontier area in nineteenth-century America. As the farming industry got larger in such a region, a more extensive railway network could be supported. The resulting economies of transporting a larger volume of agricultural commodities to market, as well as supplies to farmers, would lower the per unit costs of agricultural production.

CHECKPOINT 8-6
What does the notion of opportunity cost have to do with long-run equilibrium in a perfectly competitive industry? What does it mean when we say that firms are just earning a normal profit in long-run competitive equilibrium?

SUMMARY

1. Perfect competition exists when the firms, or sellers, in a market are price takers. A perfectly competitive industry is made up of many firms producing an identical product. Because no firm is large enough to affect price, each faces a perfectly elastic (horizontal) demand curve, so that price equals marginal revenue. Barriers to the entry and exit of firms to and from the industry are insignificant.

2. In the short run, the perfectly competitive firm must decide whether or not to produce, and if it does decide to produce, how much. This decision process may be viewed from the standpoint of comparing total revenue and total cost or from that of comparing marginal revenue and marginal cost. The firm will produce as long as total revenue exceeds total variable cost or, equivalently, as long as price per unit exceeds average variable cost.

3. If the firm decides to produce, it will maximize profits by producing that quantity of output at which total revenue exceeds total cost by the greatest amount. If total cost exceeds total revenue but total revenue exceeds total variable cost, the firm will minimize losses by producing that output level where total revenue exceeds total variable cost by the maximum amount.

4. From the marginal cost-marginal revenue point of view, the firm will be able to maximize profit, or minimize loss, by producing to the point where marginal cost equals marginal revenue. Following this rule, it will maximize profit whenever price exceeds average total cost, or minimize loss whenever price is less than average total cost but greater than average variable cost. When price is less than average variable cost, the firm will shut down.

5. The segment of the perfectly competitive firm's marginal cost curve that lies above the average variable cost curve is the firm's short-run supply curve. Summing the supply curves of all firms gives the short-run industry supply curve.

6. In long-run equilibrium, a perfectly competitive firm receives a price just equal to its minimum average total cost, the lowest point on its *ATC* curve, so that it just earns a normal profit (economic profit is zero). The existence of greater than normal profit (an economic profit) would attract new firms into the industry, increasing industry supply until competition has forced price to the minimum average total cost level. Conversely, economic losses would lead firms to leave the industry, decreasing industry supply until price has risen to the minimum average total cost level. This long-run adjustment process implies that the long-run industry supply curve is horizontal in the constant-cost case, upward sloping in the increasing-cost case, and downward sloping in the decreasing-cost case.

7. It may be argued that an economy consisting entirely of perfectly competitive markets leads to a maximization of consumer satisfaction. This follows because in long-run equilibrium, competition forces firms to produce with the least-cost technology available, at the lowest possible average per unit cost, and sell to consumers at a price that just covers this cost. In addition, price equals marginal cost, so that consumers pay a price that just covers the cost of the last unit of each kind of good produced. Because of the ease of entry and exit of firms to and from industries, a perfectly competitive economy will quickly reallocate resources to meet changing consumer preferences or reflect changing supply conditions. Hence, resources are always efficiently allocated in accordance with consumers' tastes.

8. There are several reservations about whether perfect competition will ensure maximum consumer satisfaction. It is felt that perfect competition provides little incentive for technological innovation, spillover costs and benefits are not captured, there is a lack of product variety, and income distribution may not be "equitable."

KEY TERMS AND CONCEPTS

average revenue
break-even point
marginal revenue
market structure
price taker
total revenue

QUESTIONS AND PROBLEMS

1. Rank the following industries according to how closely they approximate a perfectly competitive industry—that is, judge them according to the four characteristics of a perfectly competitive industry: automobile manufacturing, electric utilities, barbering, dry cleaning, residential construction, wallpapering, soft drinks, airlines, orange growing, stereo manufacturing, retail shoe stores, and television set manufacturing.

2. The following industries have some characteristics of a perfectly competitive industry but lack others. In each case, determine what perfectly competitive characteristics they have and what ones they seem to be lacking: petroleum refining, shoeshining, steel production, hairdressing, medical care, sewage disposal, portrait painting, and cattle farming.

3. Suppose a perfectly competitive industry is in short-run equilibrium. Suppose the industry demand curve shifts rightward. Thinking in terms of Figure 8–1, what difference does the elasticity of the industry demand curve make to the individual firm?

4. Suppose the costs of the individual firm in a perfectly competitive industry are those given in columns 1–7 of Table 8–1. Suppose you are told that the industry is in short-run equilibrium with total industry production and sales equal to 2,200 units at a price of $8 per unit.

    a. How many firms are there in the industry? $\frac{2,200}{5} = 440$

    b. Are they making a profit or are they operating at a loss? What is the amount of the profit or loss per unit? $(P-ATC)Q$

    c. How will each firm adjust if price falls to $4.60? Why? *Less than 4.66*

    d. Given your answer to part a, derive the points on the industry supply curve corresponding to each of the following prices: $6, $8, $12, and $23.

5. Will the short-run equilibrium position stipulated for the firm in Table 8–2 be consistent with a long-run equilibrium position for the perfectly competitive industry made up of such firms? Why or why not? *firms go out*

6. Consider the short-run equilibrium position of the firm in Table 8–3.

    a. Describe the process of long-run adjustment that this implies for the perfectly competitive industry made up of such firms initially in such positions. *firms will exit until $P = ATC$*

    b. What would the long-run equilibrium price be in this industry? *7.20*

    c. Suppose the industry demand curve is downward sloping starting from a price level of $6.80 on the vertical axis. Would *No* this affect your answer to part b? What would be the long-run equilibrium level of output for the industry, given this industry demand curve? *0 Supply would move to left until $P = ATC$*

7. One of the concerns often expressed about perfect competition is that it may not provide enough incentive for technological innovation, which is a key to economic growth, measured as growth in income per capita. But we know that in long-run equilibrium, perfectly competitive firms are earning a normal profit. How can it be that there is not "enough incentive for technological innovation"?

9

Monopoly

AFTER READING THIS CHAPTER, YOU WILL BE ABLE TO:

1. Explain the characteristics of the form of market organization known as monopoly.

2. Define the conditions that make a monopoly possible.

3. Explain the relationship between a downward-sloping demand curve and its associated marginal revenue curve.

4. Demonstrate how the monopolist's profit-maximizing price and output levels are determined by equating marginal cost and marginal revenue.

5. Give the reasons why monopoly is considered inefficient as an allocator of resources, inequitable as a distributor of income, and controversial as a promoter of innovation and technological change.

6. Explain the nature of natural monopoly and public utility regulation.

7. List the conditions necessary for price discrimination and the reasons why it pays firms to discriminate.

We may think of **monopoly** as a form of market structure in which the entire market for a good or service is supplied by a single seller, or firm. Because of this complete dominance of the market, the single seller—called a monopolist—is not subject to competition from rival firms. If we classify market structures according to the degree to which individual firms are subject to vigorous competition from rival firms, monopoly would be at the very opposite end of the spectrum from perfect competition.

Because it is generally felt that monopoly so completely lacks the desirable attributes of perfect competition, discussed in the previous chapter, it has become public policy in the United States to eliminate or curb it where possible, or to regulate it where its existence is unavoidable. The Antitrust Division of the U.S. Department of Justice has authority to investigate whether a monopoly exists in a particular market. The Federal Trade Commission also has such authority. If it is felt that the evidence is strong enough, either of these arms of the government may attempt to establish its case in a court of law. Legal action may then be taken in order to promote the existence of a more competitive situation. This may go so far as to "break up" the firm into several smaller firms.

An industry in which the entire output is controlled by a single firm is almost as rare in the real world as perfect competition. This illustrates how the concept of monopoly, like that of perfect competition, is often used as a benchmark against which an actual, real-world market may be compared. The more closely an actual market approximates a monopoly market structure, the greater is the cause for concern by either the Department of Justice or the Federal Trade Commission. There are many industries, sometimes called oligopolies, where there are a few dominant firms who are in a position to exert monopoly-type power to varying degrees. Examples that come to mind are the automobile industry dominated by the "big three" (GM, Ford, and Chrysler), the computer industry dominated by IBM, and professional basketball and football, where the NBA and the NFL might be argued to be monopolies. It will aid our understanding of the functioning of these types of industries, which we will explore in detail in Chapter 11, to study that form of market structure in which there is only one firm. Indeed, in some economic activities, such as the provision of electricity, water, and gas, outright monopolies do exist. In the two chapters following this one, we will see that oligopoly and, to a much lesser extent, monopolistic competition are market structures in which firms have some of the characteristics of a monopoly.

WHAT MAKES A MONOPOLY?

There are three conditions that can give rise to a situation in which one seller, or firm, is able to have sole control over the output of an entire industry—that is, to be the only supplier for an entire market. These are (1) the firm's exclusive ownership of a unique resource, (2) the existence of economies of scale, and (3) the legal granting of a monopoly by the government.

Exclusive Ownership of a Unique Resource

A seller, or firm, that has exclusive ownership of a unique resource is in a monopoly position. The unique singing style and voice of a Barbra Streisand or the unique artistic talent of a Picasso give the exclusive owner in each case a monopoly over the market for an unusual but much demanded product. Around the turn of the century, the Standard Oil Company controlled almost all sources of oil in the United States, thereby effectively eliminating the possibility of competition from any new firms in the industry. Similarly, the Aluminum Company of America at one time was able to maintain a monopoly position in the aluminum market because it controlled most of the known reserves of bauxite, the ore necessary for the production of aluminum.

Economies of Scale

We saw in Chapter 7 that large economies of scale cause the firm's long-run average total cost curve to fall over a sizeable range as output is increased. In industries where the technology of production leads to economies of scale, the long-run average total cost curve for a single firm may fall over almost the entire range of output covered by the industry demand curve. When long-run average total cost falls in this fashion, it is possible for a firm that gets into this market ahead of others to obtain a competitive advantage. The ever lower per unit costs it realizes at higher and higher levels of output permit the firm to charge a price lower than the average per unit costs that prevail at lower levels of output. In this way, the firm is able to satisfy the entire market demand at a price below that which potential new rival firms must charge when getting started. These new firms would not be able to charge a price low enough to compete for sales with the established firm because they must cover the higher average costs that accompany the low levels of output they produce when getting started in the industry. Therefore, the established firm is able to keep rivals out of the market and maintain a monopoly position.

An industry in which economies of scale are large enough to lead to such a situation is often called a **natural monopoly**. Natural monopolies are common in the markets for electricity, telephone service, and water and sewage treatment—the public utilities that we will discuss in more detail later in the chapter. There are other industries in which economies of scale may not result in monopoly but nevertheless will result in industry domination by a few large firms. The steel, petroleum, and auto industries are examples.

Government-Granted Monopoly

It is sometimes said that the only really secure monopolist is one whose monopoly position is permitted by law or granted by the government. This type of monopoly is another form of exclusive ownership—the exclusive ownership of the right to produce and sell a product or service. The government can grant such monopoly power by issuing patents, licenses, copyrights, or exclusive franchises, as in the case of public utilities.

Patents, Copyrights, and Licenses

As we noted in our discussion of perfect competition, when efforts made in the area of technological innovation and invention stand small chance of reward, there is little incentive to use resources in such activities. This situation will exist whenever the results of creative effort by one party can be easily adopted or copied and marketed by others. Nevertheless, it has generally been felt that society as a whole benefits economically and in other ways from technological innovation and creative effort. In order to stimulate such activity, it is government policy to grant **patents** to those who develop new inventions and technological processes of all kinds. In the United States, patents grant inventors the exclusive right to market their products for 17 years from the date the patent is granted. This is almost the same as granting the inventor a monopoly, at least for a period of time. Of course, profits earned from a patent monopoly over one product can be used to develop other patentable products. This may lead to the growth of a firm with an ongoing monopoly position in certain markets. IBM, AT&T, Du Pont, Xerox, Polaroid, and Syntex, the inventor of the birth control pill, have all benefited in this way from the many patents they hold.

The government also grants copyrights to writers and composers. **Copyrights** are similar in effect to patents in that they give composers and writers exclusive legal control over the production and reproduction of their work for a certain period of time. (Without the protection of such copyright laws, it is doubtful that many textbooks, including this one, would ever be written.)

State, local, and federal governments grant **licenses** in a large number of areas of economic activity. It is therefore illegal to operate in these areas without such a license. It is certainly not true that very many of these licenses give monopoly control over a product or service to any one producer, but they do have the effect of limiting the number of producers in those areas where it is necessary to have a license to operate.

For example, it is necessary to have a state license to practice medicine or law. While it may well be true that it protects the public interest to have licensing requirements in these fields, it is also true that the smaller the number of licenses issued, the larger will be the incomes earned by those to whom they are issued. In order to operate a radio or television station, for example, it is necessary to have a license from the federal government. If only one license is issued in a locality, the effect is to give the radio or television station a monopoly on broadcast advertising in that area—a very profitable situation. Obviously, if you already have a license to sell a particular service, such as medical or legal services, or a particular good, such as liquor, it is in your own economic interest to see that licensing boards set high standards, which has the effect of keeping down the number of competing rivals. Have you ever wondered why in some areas barbers must pass a licensing exam that, among other things, requires them to answer questions about tonsils?

Public Utilities

When economies of scale are so great in an industry that it is a natural monopoly, the monopolist who ultimately has sole control over output in that industry is often (but not always) in a position to charge the public a high price and reap large profits. As a matter of public policy, this is considered an undesirable situation—for reasons that we will consider in detail later in the chapter.

On the other hand, it would not be efficient in such cases for several competing firms to supply the market, because the technology of production naturally gives rise to declining per unit costs as output is increased. If several firms shared the market, none would be able to sell enough output to realize the lower per unit cost. Hence, it is desirable to have one firm supply the entire market in order to realize the low per unit costs. But somehow a natural monopoly must be forced to pass such economies on to consumers in the form of lower prices. This is something a freely operating monopolist cannot be expected to do, given the temptation to reap large profits if consumer demand is large enough.

Attempts to deal with natural monopolies have led to the creation of the **public utility**. The technology of providing telephone service, electricity, water, and natural gas is characterized by large economies of scale. In addition, can you imagine having multiple water pipes, gas lines, electric lines, and telephones all hooked up to your home by several different waterworks, gas companies, electric utilities, and telephone companies each competing to sell you their services? In an attempt to give consumers the benefit of economies of scale and at the same time protect them from the undesirable aspects of natural monopolies, the government gives these companies a franchise guaranteeing them the exclusive right to provide their good or service in their region of operation. In return for this legally granted monopoly position, the public utility must agree to allow the price of its product to be regulated and its operations monitored by a government regulatory commission. The purpose of government regulation is to ensure that the legally granted monopoly position is not used to take advantage of the consumer.

Barriers to Competition

Anything that makes it more difficult for a new firm to enter any industry is a **barrier to competition**. The conditions we have been discussing—exclusive ownership, economies of scale, and government-granted monopoly—are such large barriers that they exclude competitors from the industry. In effect, they ensure the existence of a monopoly.

There are other barriers to competition that by themselves are not usually enough to make an industry into a monopoly, but that nonetheless can contribute to that end. Such barriers tend to keep down the number of firms in any industry in which they occur and thereby reduce competition. As we shall see in the next two chapters, they typically occur in oligopoly-type market structures, and some may even be found in monopolistically competitive markets. Of course, there are no barriers to competition in perfectly competitive industries.

A little reflection suggests that a firm already established in almost any industry has an advantage over one trying to get started. Accumulated know-how, a labor force that is already experienced and trained, and a management organization that has been molded into a well-coordinated team all tend to give an existing firm an advantage over a newcomer in the industry. An existing firm's proven record of performance and established lines of credit make it easier to get loans from banks and other financial markets. An existing firm typically benefits from consumer familiarity with its product and brand name recognition resulting from past advertising efforts. All these things usually have to be developed from scratch by a new firm entering the industry.

CHECKPOINT* 9-1

A news story reported that the Justice Department was conducting a "monopoly investigation into the photographic film distribution and marketing area of Kodak." What sorts of things do you think might contribute to a possible monopoly situation in this instance? The automobile industry is dominated by General Motors, Ford, and Chrysler. An otherwise unusually successful industrialist, Henry Kaiser,

*Answers to all Checkpoints can be found at the back of the text.

tried to gain a toehold in the auto industry in the late forties and early fifties by establishing a new automobile company called Kaiser-Frazer. The company failed. At the time Kaiser said, "I expected I might lose $50 million in the beginning, but I didn't think it would disappear without a ripple." What do you think was the nature of some of the barriers to competition that Kaiser-Frazer was unable to overcome?

HOW A MONOPOLIST DETERMINES PRICE AND OUTPUT

How does a monopolist decide how much output to produce? Or alternatively, how does a monopolist decide what price to charge? In fact, it turns out that the answer to either one of these questions necessarily gives the answer to the other. In this discussion, we will assume that potential rivals are kept out of the market and that the monopolist is not governed by any regulatory commission.

Demand and Marginal Revenue for a Monopolist

We saw in the previous chapter that a firm in a perfectly competitive industry cannot affect the price at which it sells its output. It can, however, sell as little or as much as it wants at the same, given price. As a result, it is a price taker, and therefore its demand curve is perfectly horizontal. By contrast, a monopolist is the only firm in the industry. Therefore, the industry demand curve and the monopolist's demand curve are one and the same. As a result, a monopolist's demand curve is downward sloping from left to right, and the monopolist can affect price by changing the amount of output.

It should be emphasized that this is not a characteristic unique to a monopoly. Whatever the market structure of an industry, so long as an individual firm in that industry can affect price by changing its level of output, that firm faces a downward-sloping demand curve. Later, we shall see that this is true of firms in monopolistically competitive as well as oligopolistic industries. In fact, it is only the firm in a perfectly competitive market that faces a perfectly horizontal demand curve. So bear in mind that the following discussion of a downward-sloping demand curve and its associated marginal revenue curve also applies to firms in other market contexts besides monopoly.

Table 9–1 contains hypothetical data on demand and revenue for a monopolist. Observe that the monopolist can sell a larger quantity Q of output (column 1) only by charging a lower price p, or average revenue AR, per unit (column 2). Total revenue TR (column 3) equals the price p (column 2) multiplied by the quantity Q (column 1). Starting from a zero output level, total revenue TR (column 3) initially gets larger as price is lowered. It reaches a maximum when 6 units of output are sold at a price of $7, or when 7 units are sold at a price of $6, and declines thereafter. This merely reflects a characteristic of a downward-sloping demand curve, which we have already discussed. (For review, reread the discussion of the demand for Rose Bowl tickets in Chapter 5.)

Marginal Revenue Declines for a Monopolist

At this point, however, we note a very important difference between a monopoly firm and a perfectly competitive firm. Remember, a perfectly competitive firm can sell each additional unit of output at the same price because its demand curve is perfectly horizontal. Hence, the marginal revenue (equal to the change in total revenue) associated with the sale of one more unit of output is always equal to price for a perfectly competitive firm. Since price doesn't change, neither does marginal revenue. This is not true for a mo-

TABLE 9-1 Demand and Revenue Data for a Monopolist (Hypothetical Data)

(1) Quantity of Output (Q)	(2) Price = Average Revenue $p = AR$	(3) Total Revenue (TR) $TR = p \times Q$	(4) Marginal Revenue (MR)
0	$13	$ 0	
			$ 12
1	12	12	
			10
2	11	22	
			8
3	10	30	
			6
4	9	36	
			4
5	8	40	
			2
6	7	42	
			0
7	6	42	
			− 2
8	5	40	
			− 4
9	4	36	
			− 6
10	3	30	
			− 8
11	2	22	
			−10
12	1	12	
			−12
13	0	0	

nopolist because a monopolist's demand curve is downward sloping. *In order to sell an additional unit of output the monopolist must lower price. And the monopolist not only must accept a lower price for an additional unit sold, but for all the units sold—units that otherwise could have been sold at a higher price.*

This means that for a monopolist marginal revenue is less than price at every level of output, except when it produces a total output of only one unit. The reason is that when price is lowered to sell an additional unit of output, the resulting change in total revenue equals the sum of two parts, one a plus and the other a minus. One part is the *increase* in total revenue equal to the price received for the additional unit sold. The other part equals the *decrease* in total revenue due to the reduction in price on all other units that was necessary in order to sell the additional unit. Thus, *for a monopolist marginal revenue (the change in total revenue) equals the price of the additional unit less the amount of the price reduction on the other units multiplied by the quantity of the other units. Therefore, marginal revenue is less than price at every level of output, except the first unit. And it follows from this that, since price declines as output increases (because the demand curve is downward sloping), marginal revenue must also decline as output increases.*

These relationships between price, total revenue, and marginal revenue are illustrated in Table 9-1. Only for the first unit of output sold is it true that price (column 2) equals marginal revenue (column 4), in this case $12. To sell two units, price must be lowered to $11. Not only is the second unit sold for $11, but now so is the first. Otherwise the first unit could have been sold for $12—if the monopolist had been satisfied to sell just one unit. Therefore, to sell two units of output, the monopolist has to give up $1 on the first unit, while getting an additional $11 from the sale of the second. The change (increase) in total revenue is therefore $10 ($11 minus $1), the marginal revenue shown in column 4. The marginal revenue of $10 is the increase in total revenue from $12 to $22 (column 3) resulting from the sale of the second unit of output. If the monopolist wanted to sell 3 units, price would have to be lowered to $10 per unit. This means that the first two units would have to be sold at $10 per unit as well, instead of the $11 per unit received when only 2 units were sold. The marginal revenue would be equal to the $10 received from the sale of the third unit less $1 per unit given up on each of the first two units, or $8. You should now be able to con-

vince yourself of the validity of the marginal revenue data in Table 9-1. Note that when output exceeds 7 units, marginal revenue becomes negative. Negative marginal revenue is associated with the range over which increases in total output lead to decreases in total revenue.

Relationship Between the Total Revenue, Demand, and Marginal Revenue Curves

The data from Table 9-1 are plotted in Figure 9-1. For each output level in column 1, the associated price is plotted to give the demand curve *D* in parts b and c. (Demand curves are not necessarily straight lines—we use them for simplicity.) Total revenue (Table 9-1, column 3) is plotted in part a to give the *TR* curve.

Comparison of parts a and b clearly shows that total revenue *TR* for the monopolist reaches its maximum at 6 units of output with a price of $7 per unit. Observe that if price is reduced from $7 to $6 (part b), the quantity of output sold increases from 6 to 7 units, but *TR* remains unchanged at $42 (part a). Why is this so? Part b shows us that when price is lowered from $7 to $6, there is a loss in *TR* of $6 ($1 per unit on the first 6 units). This loss is represented by the shaded horizontal rectangle. However, this loss is just offset by the gain in *TR* of $6, realized from the sale of the seventh unit. This is represented by the vertical shaded rectangle. Putting it another way, we can say that the marginal revenue *MR* (the change in total revenue *TR*) associated with the sale of the seventh unit of output is zero. This is borne out in part c, where the *MR* curve, plotted from the marginal revenue data (column 4) of Table 9-1, crosses the horizontal axis at 7 units of output.

Note in part a that at levels of sales less than 6 units *TR* can always be increased by lowering price (part b) and selling an additional unit. Therefore, marginal revenue is always positive up to the sale of the seventh unit. This means that the *MR* curve in part c

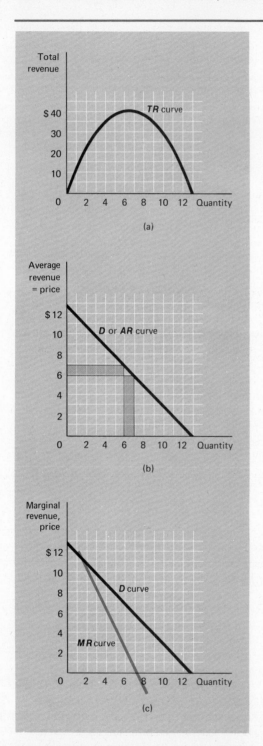

FIGURE 9-1   Relationship Between the Total Revenue Curve, the Demand Curve, and the Marginal Revenue Curve

The total revenue curve *TR* in part a is plotted from the data in columns 1 and 3 of Table 9-1. The demand *D*, or average revenue *AR*, curve in parts b and c is plotted from the data in columns 1 and 2 of Table 9-1. The marginal revenue curve *MR* in part c is plotted from the data in columns 1 and 4 of Table 9-1.

Because the *TR* curve rises at a decreasing rate up to 6 units of output in part a, the *MR* curve is downward sloping and lies above the horizontal axis up to 7 units of output in part c. It crosses the axis at this point, reflecting the fact there is no change in total revenue (part a) resulting from the sale of the seventh unit of output. This is also represented by the fact that the horizontal shaded rectangle in part b, representing the loss in total revenue on the first 6 units, is just equal to the vertical shaded rectangle, representing the gain in total revenue from the sale of the seventh unit. Because the *TR* curve falls at an increasing rate beyond 7 units of output in part a, the *MR* curve is downward sloping and lies below the horizontal axis beyond 7 units in part c.

The *MR* curve always lies below the demand curve *D* after the first unit of output, part c. This is so because the marginal revenue from the sale of an additional unit of output is less than the price received for that unit by the amount of the sum of the price cuts on all previous units sold.

lies above the horizontal axis at all output levels less than 7 units. Furthermore, starting from a zero level of output, note that *TR* (part a) rises less and less steeply as price is lowered and the number of units sold is increased (part b). This is reflected in the fact that the *MR* curve (part c) is downward sloping left to right.

Observe that only when one unit of output is sold is it true that marginal revenue equals total revenue, or $12. Therefore, the *D* curve meets the *MR* curve at 1 unit of output at a price of $12 (part c). Since at higher levels of output price is always greater than marginal revenue, the demand curve *D* always lies above the *MR* curve at output levels greater than 1 unit. Note that at output levels greater than 7 units the *MR* curve lies below the horizontal axis. This reflects the fact that the sale of each additional unit beyond this level results in a decrease in *TR*—that is, *MR* is negative.

Relationship Between Demand and Marginal Revenue Curves: Further Comments

For purposes of illustrating the basic relationship between total revenue, demand, and marginal revenue, we have used rather small numbers when talking about quantity in Table 9–1 and Figure 9–1. However, it would be more realistic in general to assume that we are dealing with much larger quantities of output. This changes the scale on the horizontal, or quantity, axis so that the number of units is so large that the distance equal to one unit is no larger than a dot. This means that the demand curve and the marginal revenue curve will meet at the same point on the vertical axis because we cannot distinguish the first unit of output, as we can in part c of Figure 9–1.

There is another relationship that follows when the scale on the horizontal axis is such that a single unit is no larger than a dot. For any downward-sloping, straight-line demand curve it will then be true that at any price

level, the horizontal distance between the vertical axis and the marginal revenue curve will be exactly half the distance to the demand curve. Note that this means the marginal revenue curve will cross the horizontal axis exactly halfway between the origin and the point where the demand curve crosses the horizontal axis.

One way to see why this is so is to recall our discussion of elasticity in Chapter 5. There we observed in Figure 5–5 that a straight-line demand curve is unit elastic exactly at its midpoint. Corresponding to this point on the demand curve, we also observed that total revenue is a maximum. In other words, just to the left of this point, marginal revenue is positive, while just to the right of it, marginal revenue is negative. Therefore, exactly at that point marginal revenue is zero. Hence, where total revenue is a maximum, the marginal revenue curve cuts the horizontal axis. This can be seen by comparing parts a and c of Figure 9–1. Suppose the scale on the horizontal axis is such that a single unit of output corresponds to a dot. It follows that the marginal revenue curve associated with a straight-line demand curve will cut the horizontal axis exactly halfway between the origin and the point where the demand curve meets the horizontal axis.

Monopoly Pricing Policy and the Downward-Sloping Demand Curve

Finally, it is very important to be clear about what a downward-sloping demand curve does and does not say about the monopolist's pricing policy. Contrary to the usual belief of the person in the street, it *does not say* that the monopolist can sell a given output at any price desired. It *does not say* that a monopolist can set price at some desired level and *independently* decide how much output to sell at that price, or vice versa. This fallacy is just a variation on the first fallacy. The downward-sloping demand curve does say that the monopolist can affect price by changing output or, equivalently, that the

TABLE 9-2 Output, Revenue, and Costs of a Monopolist
(Hypothetical Data)

(1)	(2)	(3)	(4)	(5)	(6)	(7)	(8)
Quantity of Output (Q)	Price = Average Revenue	Total Revenue	Marginal Revenue (MR)	Average Total Cost (ATC)	Total Cost (TC)	Marginal Cost (MC)	Profit (+) or Loss (−)
	$p = AR$	$TR = p \times Q$					$TR - TC = (3) - (6)$
0	$13	$ 0			$10		$−10
			$12			$ 6	
1	12	12		$16.00	16		− 4
			10			4	
2	11	22		10.00	20		2
			8			4	
3	10	30		8.00	24		6
			6			5	
4	9	36		7.25	29		7
			4			7	
5	8	40		7.20	36		4
			2			11	
6	7	42		7.83	47		− 5
			0			23	
7	6	42		10.00	70		−28

monopolist affects output by changing price. But the level of one automatically determines the level of the other due to the shape of the demand curve. Hence, the monopolist's pricing policy is not free of the constraint that selling more means accepting a lower price, or that selling a certain level of output means charging no more than a certain price level.

CHECKPOINT 9-2
Use the numbers from Table 9–1 to demonstrate the relationship between the elasticity of the demand curve in Figure 9–1, parts b and c, and its associated marginal revenue curve. (You may find it helpful to review briefly the concept of elasticity in Chapter 5.)

Bringing Together Costs and Revenues

In order to see how a profit-maximizing monopolist determines what output level to produce and what price to charge, we must bring the cost side of the picture together with the demand and marginal revenue side. To make it easier to compare the profit-maximizing behavior of the monopolist with that of the perfectly competitive firm discussed in the previous chapter, we will assume that the monopolist's costs, shown in Table 9–2, are the same as those we looked at in Table 8–1. For each output level in column 1 of Table 9–2, the monopolist's average total cost, total cost, and marginal cost data are shown in columns 5, 6, and 7, respectively. Columns 2, 3, and 4 repeat the revenue data from columns 2, 3, and 4 of Table 9–1.

**The Total Revenue–
Total Cost Viewpoint**

The monopolist's procedure for choosing that output and price level that maximize profit may be viewed from the standpoint of total revenue *TR* and total cost *TC*. Subtracting *TC* (column 6) from *TR* (column 3) at each level of output (column 1), we get the profit or loss (column 8) associated with producing and selling that output at the price given in column 2. Column 8 tells us that the monopolist realizes a maximum profit, which equals $7, when 4 units of output are produced (column 1) and sold at a price of $9 (column 2).

This is shown graphically in Figure 9–2, part a. The *TC* curve is plotted from the total cost data (column 6) of Table 9–2 and the *TR* curve is plotted from the total revenue data (column 3). The maximum vertical distance by which the *TR* curve exceeds the *TC* curve occurs at 4 units of output. This distance equals the maximum profit of $7.

The Marginal Revenue-
Marginal Cost Viewpoint

The marginal revenue-marginal cost point of view is by far the commonest way of viewing the determination of that output and price that maximize the monopolist's profit. The basic principle behind this selection is exactly the same as that described in the case of the perfectly competitive firm. The monopolist also continues to expand output as long as the marginal cost of producing an additional unit is less than the marginal revenue associated with its sale. The monopolist will produce up to that output level where the marginal cost of the last unit produced is just covered by, or is equal to, its marginal revenue.

Note, however, that the case of the monopolist differs from that of the perfect competitor in two respects. First, marginal revenue for the monopolist is always less than price (except for the first unit). For the perfectly competitive firm, marginal revenue always equals price. Second, marginal revenue for the monopolist falls as output is increased. For the perfectly competitive firm marginal revenue is the same at all levels of output because price is the same at all levels.

Compare the marginal revenue data (column 4) of Table 9–2 with the marginal cost data (column 7). Observe that *MR* exceeds

MC at all output levels up to and including 4 units. If a fifth unit is produced, however, its *MR* of $4 is less than its *MC* of $7. Therefore, according to the marginal cost-marginal revenue principle, profit will be at a maximum, which equals $7 (column 8), when 4 units of output are produced and sold at a price of $9 (column 2). This is, of course, the same answer we found from the total cost-total revenue point of view.

The marginal cost-marginal revenue point of view is shown graphically in part b of Figure 9–2. The *ATC* and *MC* curves are plotted from the data in columns 5 and 7 of Table 9–2. (Note that the points on the marginal cost curve are plotted exactly halfway between successive output levels.) The demand curve and its associated *MR* curve are plotted from the data in columns 2 and 4 of Table 9–2.

That it pays the firm to increase output up through and including 4 units is indicated by the fact that the *MR* curve lies above the *MC* curve up to that point. Beyond 4 units of output, the *MC* curve lies above the *MR* curve, indicating that marginal cost exceeds marginal revenue. Hence, the monopolist maximizes profit by producing and selling 4 units of output at a price of $9 per unit. The profit-maximizing price is the point on the demand curve that lies directly above the intersection of the *MC* and *MR* curves. We have labeled this point *c*. The profit-maximizing output level of 4 units is the point on the horizontal axis that lies directly below the intersection of the *MC* and *MR* curves.

The vertical distance $ad = bc$, which equals $1.75, is the average profit per unit, so that 4 units times $1.75 gives the total profit of $7, represented by the shaded rectangular area *abcd*. Note that according to Table 9–2, the average profit per unit at 3 units of output is $2, the difference between a price of $10 per unit (column 2) and an *ATC* of $8 per unit (column 5). However, total profit for 3 units of output at a price of $10 per unit is only $6 (3 units times an average profit per unit of $2). This illustrates the fact that the level of output that maximizes total profit

FIGURE 9-2   The Relationship Between Revenues and Costs for a Monopolist

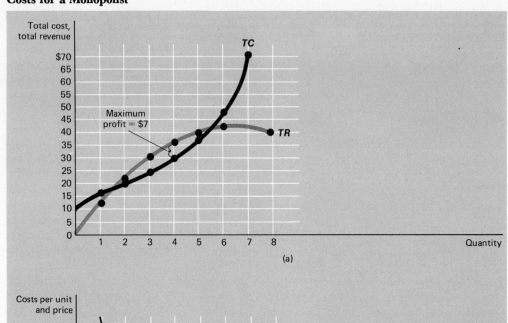

(a)

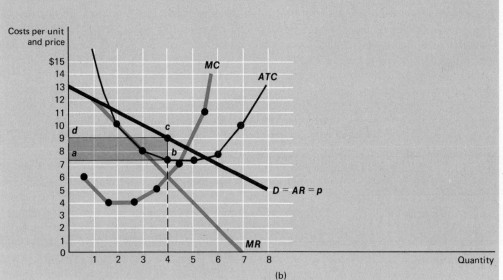

(b)

In part a the *TC* curve is plotted from the total cost data of column 6 in Table 9–2, while the *TR* curve is plotted from the total revenue data in column 3. The profit-maximizing level of output occurs when 4 units of output are sold at a price of $9. This is where the vertical distance between the *TR* curve and the *TC* curve, which equals total profit, is a maximum.

In part b the demand curve *D* and its associated *MR* curve are plotted from the price-equals-average-revenue data in column 2 and the marginal revenue data in column 4 of Table 9–2. The *MC* and *ATC* curves are plotted from the marginal cost data of column 7 and the average total cost data of column 5 in Table 9–2. The profit-maximizing level of output occurs where the *MC* curve intersects the *MR* curve, corresponding to 4 units of output sold at a price of $9. The maximum profit of $7 is represented by the rectangular area *abcd*.

does not necessarily correspond to the one that maximizes average profit per unit.

Suppose the firm with the cost curves depicted in Figure 9–2 were perfectly competitive instead of a monopolist. Let us assume that its perfectly elastic (horizontal) demand curve is at a level of $9—that is, as a price taker it is given a price of $9. Then by the $MC = MR = p$ rule we discussed in the previous chapter, it would maximize profit by producing 5 units of output. This is one more unit than would be produced by the monopolist at the same price of $9. The reason for this difference, given that the two firms have identical cost curves, is that marginal revenue equals price is constant at $9 for all levels of output for the perfectly competitive firm but not for the monopolist. For the monopolist, price, and therefore marginal revenue, falls as output increases. Therefore, at a price of $9 marginal revenue is lower for the monopolist than it is for the perfectly competitive firm. This reflects the fact that the monopolist's marginal revenue takes into account the reduced price on all prior units sold.

CHECKPOINT 9-3
If the monopolist shown in Figure 9-2 maximized profit by producing 7 units of output and selling them at the equilibrium price of $6, what would have to be true of marginal cost? Would you ever expect to see a monopolist sell at an equilibrium price in the inelastic portion of the demand curve? Why or why not?

Losses and Small Profits

Probably the most common image brought to mind by the term *monopoly* is that of a firm making large, even "rip-off," profits. This isn't necessarily the case, however.

Consider the monopolist depicted in part a of Figure 9–3. Marginal cost equals marginal revenue at the output level Q_n, as indicated by the intersection of the MC and MR

curves at that point. Producing this level of output and selling it at the price p_n, the monopolist's total revenue is equal to the rectangular area $0Q_n b p_n$. However, this area also represents the monopolist's total cost, since b is also the point at which the demand curve D is just tangent to the ATC curve. Remember that a point on the ATC curve represents total per unit cost at that level of output and therefore includes a normal profit. Hence in this case the monopolist just earns a normal profit, and economic profit is zero. This is the best the monopolist can do given the demand curve D. To produce at any other output level would entail losses, since at any other output level the demand curve D lies below the ATC curve.

Consider the monopolist in part b. The intersection of the MC and MR curves occurs at the output level Q_l. However, this is a loss-minimizing position. There is no way the monopolist can cover all costs in this case, since the ATC curve lies above the demand curve D at all output levels. Producing the output Q_l and selling it at the price p_l, the monopolist incurs a loss per unit equal to the vertical distance ab. The total loss is represented by the shaded rectangular area. The monopolist is only willing to operate at a loss like this in the short run, and then only so long as it is possible to cover average variable cost. Note that in the case depicted in part b, p_l lies above the AVC curve at the output level Q_l.

The monopolist depicted in Figure 9–2, in contrast to those of Figure 9–3, is earning more than a normal profit. The positive economic profit earned is represented by the shaded rectangular area $abcd$ in part b of Figure 9–2. The basic distinction between earning positive economic profit in a monopoly situation and earning it under perfect competition is that such a profit will attract new firms into the perfectly competitive industry in the long run but not into the monopoly industry. Output will be expanded in the competitive industry and rivalry among firms will cause price to fall until economic profit for each and every firm is driven to zero. In the case of the monopoly, however, barriers

FIGURE 9-3   **Monopoly Equilibrium Without Economic Profit**

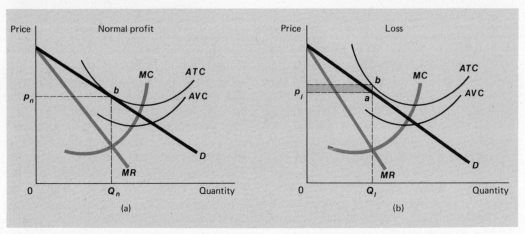

The monopolist in part a is earning a normal profit—a zero economic profit. Producing the output Q_n where marginal cost equals marginal revenue, total revenue, represented by the rectangular area $0Q_nbp_n$, is just equal to total cost. The equilibrium price p_n is just equal to total cost per unit, including a normal profit, since the demand curve D is just tangent (point b) to the ATC curve at that price.

The monopolist in part b is operating at a loss—a negative economic profit. The intersection of the MC and MR curves dictates the production of Q_l units of output to be sold at the price p_l. This is a loss-minimizing position, with the total loss represented by the shaded rectangle. Given that the demand curve D lies below the ATC curve at all output levels, this is the best the monopolist can do. Even though there is a per unit loss equal to ab, the monopolist is willing to operate at this position in the short run because the price p_l is above the AVC curve—average variable cost is more than covered.

to competition prevent this from happening. The monopoly is therefore in the position, provided costs are low enough and demand high enough, to earn positive economic profit—in this case called monopoly profit—almost indefinitely.

Why do we say "almost indefinitely"? Even a monopolist is not protected from long-run advances in technology or changes in consumer demand that may weaken its advantage. A firm that had a monopoly over the buggy-whip market a hundred years ago would have been in an enviable position. But advancing technology and the shift of consumer preferences away from horses and buggies and toward the automobile changed all that. A monopoly over the sale of whale

oil would have been more lucrative before the advent of the kerosene lamp, and a monopoly on kerosene lamps would have been more profitable before the development of the electric light. Research and changing technology, the development of substitute products and the expiration of patents on old ones, and the discovery of new resource supplies and materials can all lead to the weakening of a monopoly market.

The Marginal Cost Curve Is Not a Supply Curve for the Monopolist

We observed in the previous chapter that in the short run the part of the perfectly competitive firm's marginal cost curve MC that lies above its average variable cost curve AVC constitutes its supply curve. That is, at each possible price above the minimum point of the AVC curve, the MC curve tells us the quantity of output that the perfectly competitive firm is willing to produce. A supply curve is a unique relationship between price and output. At any given price there is one, and only one, quantity of output that the firm is willing to supply. Conversely, at any given output level, there is one and only one price that makes the firm willing to supply that output level.

In the case of a monopolist, or any other firm that faces a downward-sloping demand curve, there is no such unique relationship between price and quantity. This is illustrated in Figure 9–4. Suppose the demand curve is D_1, with the associated marginal revenue curve MR_1. The intersection of the MC curve and the MR_1 curve dictates that in order to maximize profit the monopolist should produce the output level Q and sell it at the price p_1. If the demand curve were D_2, with the associated marginal revenue MR_2, the intersection of MC and MR_2 would still occur at the same place as that of MC and MR_1. The same quantity Q of output would be produced, but it would be sold at the lower price p_2. Obviously it is possible for the same level of output to be sold at different prices, depending on the shape of the demand curve.

In fact, it is possible to construct an unlimited number of demand curves, each with an associated MR curve that intersects the same point on the MC curve. Hence, there are an unlimited number of prices at which a given level of output may be sold, depending on which demand curve actually prevails.

It is also true that at any given price it is possible for there to be an unlimited number of equilibrium output levels. You can convince yourself of this by constructing a graph. Plot two different demand curves shaped such that their associated MR curves intersect a given MC curve at two different points, so that each dictates a different output level to be sold at the same price.

FIGURE 9-4 A Firm with a Downward-Sloping Demand Curve Has No Unique Supply Curve

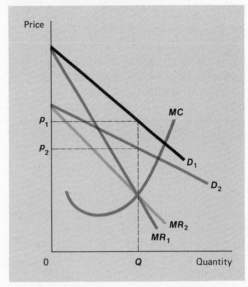

Two possible demand curves, D_1 and D_2, shaped such that their associated MR curves, MR_1 and MR_2, intersect the firm's MC curve at the same point, are shown here. If the prevailing demand curve is D_1, the profit-maximizing firm will produce the output Q and sell it at price p_1. However, if the prevailing demand curve is D_2, the profit-maximizing firm will produce the same output but sell it at the lower price p_2. It is possible for an unlimited number of such demand curves with associated MR curves to intersect the MC curve at the same point. Hence, a given output level may be sold at an unlimited number of possible prices, depending on the shape of the particular demand curve.

You should sketch two different demand curves and their associated MR curves in such a way as to convince yourself that it is also true that there are an unlimited number of possible output levels that may be sold at the same price.

CHECKPOINT 9-4

How would an increase in fixed costs affect the equilibrium price and output levels in Figure 9-3? How would such an increase affect economic profit? If the monopolist had to pay a license fee to the state to operate and the fee were doubled, how would that affect the short-run equilibrium price and output combination of the monopolist? Suppose that, without a decrease in costs, a monopolist is observed to produce and sell a certain output level at a lower price than previously was charged. What would you say to someone who claims that the monopolist must no longer be acting as a profit maximizer? Suppose the government imposes a price ceiling on a monopolist's product. How might this affect output?

MONOPOLY VERSUS PERFECT COMPETITION

In our study of perfect competition in the previous chapter, we focused on certain questions that are relevant to any market structure. How efficiently does it allocate resources? What sort of incentives does it provide for innovation and technological change? What implications does it have for income distribution? All these questions can be asked about monopoly as well. Since, as we noted in the previous chapter, perfect competition is regarded as a useful standard for market structure, it will be helpful to compare the answers for monopoly with those for perfect competition.

Resource Allocation

Consider a perfectly competitive industry such as that shown in Figure 9-5, part a. Here, the industry demand curve D and the short-run supply curve S determine the equi-

librium price p_c and quantity Q_c. Remember that the perfectly competitive industry's short-run supply curve S is the sum of the marginal cost curves of the individual firms in the industry.

Suppose now that a single firm comes along and buys up all the firms in the competitive industry without affecting the cost curves of any of them. Thus the single firm has a monopoly, and its marginal cost curve MC, shown in part b of Figure 9-5, is exactly the same as the supply curve S shown in part a. (The cost side of the picture for the industry is assumed to be the same whether it is perfectly competitive or a monopolist.)

The industry demand curve D is unchanged as well, but there will be an important difference between the way the monopolist views D and the way it was viewed by the perfectly competitive firms, each of which was a price taker. The monopoly firm is well aware that it affects price when it changes output. Hence, the profit-maximizing monopolist will use the MR curve associated with D, together with the MC curve, to determine the equilibrium output level Q_m and the price p_m in part b. *We see, therefore, that when an industry is a monopoly, consumers pay a higher price for the product and receive less of it than would be the case under perfect competition.*

But why do economists generally consider this monopoly equilibrium position to be less desirable than the perfectly competitive one? Economists say there is an inefficient allocation of resources where there are consumers who are willing to pay a price that covers the marginal cost of producing more of the good, but who will not be able to have more at those prices. Under perfect competition, output is produced up to that point, Q_c, where the price, p_c, paid for the last unit produced is just equal to the cost of producing that last unit. In other words, price per unit is equal to marginal cost. *In a perfectly competitive market, each and every consumer who is willing to pay a price sufficient to cover the marginal cost of producing the good will have some of the good.*

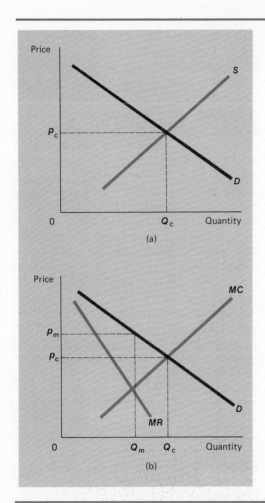

(a)

(b)

FIGURE 9-5   Effect of Monopolizing a Competitive Industry

The supply curve S and demand curve D for a perfectly competitive industry are shown in part a. They determine an equilibrium price p_c and quantity Q_c.

In part b it is assumed that a single firm takes over all the firms in the competitive industry of part a without affecting costs and becomes a monopoly. The MC curve of the monopolist of part b is therefore the same as the supply curve S of part a. The profit-maximizing monopolist uses the MR curve associated with D, together with the MC curve, to decide to produce the lower output Q_m to be sold at the higher price p_m.

Under perfect competition, every consumer who is willing to pay a price that covers the marginal cost of producing the good will have some of it. If the market is monopolized, the part of the demand curve over the range from Q_m to Q_c will lie above the MC curve. Thus, there will be consumers willing to pay a price that covers the marginal cost of producing the good who will not be able to get any at that price.

By contrast, if the market is organized as a monopoly, the portion of the demand curve D over the range Q_m to Q_c lies above the MC curve. Hence, there are consumers who are willing to pay a price for the units of output from Q_m to Q_c that exceeds the marginal cost of producing them, but are unable to do so because the monopolist will not produce and sell them at such a price. *Whenever there is a monopoly, there will be consumers who are willing to pay a price that equals the marginal cost of producing the good, but who will not be able to have any of the good at that price.*

Market Structure and Industry Cost

The above discussion assumes that costs are not affected when the perfectly competitive industry becomes a monopoly. It may well be that certain kinds of organizational and technological efficiencies are realized when all the perfectly competitive firms are combined to make a monopoly. If so, the monopolist's MC curve in part b of Figure 9–5 will not be the same as the perfectly competitive industry supply curve S in part a.

This is illustrated in Figure 9–6. When the

FIGURE 9-6   Monopolization May Lead to Lower Price and Higher Output

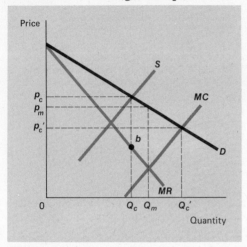

It is possible that monopolization of a perfectly competitive industry will lower per unit costs of production.

The perfectly competitive industry's supply curve S and demand curve D determine equilibrium output Q_c and price p_c. If monopolization of the industry results in a sufficiently large reduction in per unit production costs, the monopolist's marginal cost curve may assume a position such as MC. Given MC and the marginal revenue curve MR, the monopolist in this case will charge a lower price, p_m, and produce a larger output, Q_m, than occurs when the industry is perfectly competitive.

Note, however, that with lower per unit costs, it is still possible to improve on the profit-maximizing monopolist's price and output combination. A price-equals-marginal-cost solution would provide consumers with the yet lower price p_c' and greater output Q_c'.

industry is perfectly competitive, equilibrium price p_c and quantity Q_c are determined by the intersection of the industry supply curve S and the industry demand curve D. Suppose that when all the perfectly competitive firms are combined together to form a monopoly, the increased efficiencies of operation result in a lowering of the per unit costs of production. Hence, the monopolist's marginal cost curve MC lies below the perfectly competitive industry's supply curve S. If the per unit cost reductions resulting from monopolization of the industry are great enough, the monopolist's equilibrium price p_m may be lower than p_c and its equilibrium output Q_m greater than Q_c (corresponding to the intersection of MC and MR), as shown in Figure 9–6. If, on the other hand, the per unit cost reduction is not great enough to cause the MC curve to intersect MR to the right of point b, corresponding to output level Q_c, monopolization of the industry will result in a higher price and lower output level than would exist under perfect competition.

Given that monopolizing the industry may lower per unit production costs, it is entirely possible that consumers may be able to purchase more output at a lower price (as in Figure 9–6) than is the case when the industry is perfectly competitive. This is a question that can only be answered by examining the facts for a particular industry. As discussed above, such a situation occurs most often in the case of public utilities, where economies of scale make it more efficient for one firm rather than several to supply the industry.

Shortly we will examine the economics of public policy toward utilities in greater detail. For the moment, consider an industry where a reduction in per unit costs is only possible if the industry is a monopoly, such as in Figure 9–6. Then even though the profit-maximizing monopolist may provide consumers more output at a lower price, there will still be consumers who are willing to pay a price for the good greater than the marginal cost of producing it, but who are unable to get any. This is represented by the fact that the demand curve D over the range from Q_m to Q_c' lies above the MC curve. For this reason, it can be argued that some public policy, or regulation, is needed to promote a result where output Q_c' is produced and sold at a price p_c'.

Incentives for Innovation

In the previous chapter we saw that a perfectly competitive firm must use the most efficient available technology to compete effectively with the multitude of other firms in the industry. But using the best *available* technology is not the same thing as product innovation and development of new, more efficient production techniques. The incentive for a perfectly competitive firm to innovate is small because the prospect of reaping above-normal profits from such activity for any length of time is slight. Firms in the industry can all too readily adopt the innovations of others, thereby quickly eliminating any competitive advantage otherwise realized by the innovating firm. As evidence that perfect competition does not promote innovation, it is often observed that in agriculture most research and innovation comes from large manufacturers of farm machinery as well as government-supported experiment stations and land-grant colleges. Relatively little seems to be initiated by the multitude of farms that make agriculture so closely resemble perfect competition.

For a monopoly, the situation would seem to be almost the reverse. Since there are no competing firms in the industry, the monopolist, unlike the competitive firm, is not forced by the existence of many rivals to use the most efficient available technology. This is not to say that it isn't in the monopolist's best interest to do so—lower costs mean larger monopoly profits. On the other hand, for the more dynamic activity of product innovation and the development of new production techniques there would seem to be just the incentive for the monopolist that is lacking for the perfectly competitive firm— the prospect of above-normal profit for a prolonged, possibly indefinite period of time. In addition, the existence of such profit provides the monopolist with a source of funds to finance technological change and product innovation, a source unavailable to the perfectly competitive firm.

It is sometimes argued, however, that be- cause the monopolist doesn't face the strong competitive threat of rival firms, there is a tendency to stand pat and simply reap the profits from the existing situation. In fact, it has been argued that it is in a monopolist's best interest to protect the existing monopoly situation from the threat of new products and technological change introduced by potential rivals. Therefore, the monopolist may buy up and stockpile patents, effectively putting a stop to technological changes and product innovation.

In sum, there is a wide variety of opinion on the pros and cons of monopoly as a market structure that either promotes or inhibits the advancement of product change and production technology. The thrust of public policy, at least that of antitrust policy, leans toward the view that monopoly most likely inhibits innovation.

Income Distribution

Most economists believe that the existence of unregulated, profit-maximizing monopoly contributes to income inequality. In long-run equilibrium under perfect competition a great many firms earn a normal profit and the payments to productive factors, including labor, are just sufficient to cover their opportunity costs. By contrast, monopoly gives rise to a much greater concentration of economic power. Therefore, the potential exists for above-normal, even extraordinary, profit for a prolonged or even indefinite period of time. Hence, the owners of a monopoly are potentially in a position to earn much more than what their time and financial capital could earn in the next best alternative use.

If the monopoly is a corporation, the stockholders reap the above-normal, or monopoly, profits. Some economists argue that since stockholders tend to be from middle- to upper-income brackets to begin with, monopoly profit distributed to stockholders only tends to widen the gap between them and those who belong to lower-income groups.

We hasten to emphasize that the issue of income inequality, and whether a particular

POLICY PERSPECTIVE

The Monopoly as Cartel—Why Taxi Rides Can Be Expensive

Monopolies sometimes take the form of a group of firms who effectively agree to collude together to set the price and/or output level of a particular product or service. The group, often referred to as a cartel, essentially tries to behave as if it were one large monopoly firm. In the United States antitrust laws make it illegal for firms to engage in collusive agreements to fix prices or share markets. Nonetheless such monopoly, cartel-like practices do exist in the taxicab business in some cities. Why do such monopoly-type arrangements exist and what is being done about them?

How Can There Be a Taxicab Monopoly?

To answer this question it must be recognized that the crucial ingredient in a taxicab cartel is a city government that has the power to issue licenses, often called medallions, for operating taxicabs. By restricting the number of medallions issued, the city government can effectively restrict the number of cabs (hence taxicab firms) serving the city market for taxicab rides. In the absence of taxicab licensing requirements the market for taxicab rides would be very much like a perfectly competitive industry in the constant-cost case (see previous chapter), as there would be unrestricted entry into the industry of firms (taxicabs) producing an essentially homogeneous product (taxicab rides).

This is illustrated in Figure P9–1. The short-run industry supply curve of passenger miles of taxicab service S_c intersects the market demand curve D at point c so that Q_c passenger miles are bought and sold at a price (fare) of p_c per mile. Taxicabs would earn no more than a normal profit, characteristic of a perfectly

competitive market. The long-run industry supply curve is the horizontal line passing through points b and c. (Recall the discussion in the previous chapter of the long-run industry supply curve in the constant-cost case for a perfectly competitive industry, as illustrated in Figures 8–7 and 8–8.) However, when the city government has the authority to issue medallions (taxicab licenses) it is in a position to restrict output (passenger miles) and set prices like a monopolist. This entails restricting the issuance of medallions so that the short-run perfectly competitive industry supply curve is shifted leftward to the position S_m. S_m is just the horizontal summation of the marginal cost curves of the individual firms (taxicabs), as shown in the previous chapter. It is therefore the marginal cost curve of the industry when organized as a monopoly. The intersection of the marginal cost curve S_m with the marginal revenue curve MR at point b determines the equilibrium monopoly output Q_m and price p_m, corresponding to

---

FIGURE P9–1   Monopolizing the Taxicab Market

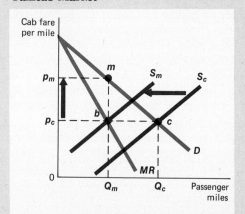

point *m* on the demand curve *D*. The cab industry now earns a monopoly profit given by the area $p_c bmp_m$. (Recall from the previous chapter that any point on the long-run perfectly competitive industry supply curve given by the horizontal line passing through points *b* and *c* represents both the marginal and the average total cost in the long run.) The monopoly cab fare p_m per passenger mile exceeds the perfectly competitive cab fare p_c by the amount *bm*, equal to the monopoly profit earned per passenger mile by taxicabs in the industry when entry is restricted by city-managed licensing.

Obviously taxi owners stand to gain when the government restricts the issuance of taxicab medallions—at least those taxi owners who have an "in" at city hall which will assure them a medallion. In several cities owners have successfully lobbied city officials, through political contributions, for *legal* restraints on trade. The supposed legal status of such restraints (limiting entry into the business) allegedly rests on the fact that a local government body, the city, is granting the right to operate a taxicab.

Policy Response

The Federal Trade Commission (the FTC has the authority to investigate pos-sible monopoly practices) has taken issue with a city government's right to exercise such restraints in the market for taxicab services. In 1984 the FTC filed antitrust suits against the cities of Minneapolis and New Orleans charging that they had colluded with special interests to fix prices, restrict entry, and otherwise form cartels in restraint of trade. The FTC action, combined with the Supreme Court's 1982 decision in *Community Communications Co. Inc. v. City of Boulder, Colo.* allowing antitrust suits against municipalities, has put local governments on notice that their aid in setting up taxicab cartels is viewed as a violation of antitrust laws. The FTC's battle is far from won however as taxicab interests have exercised their clout in Congress to attempt to thwart FTC enforcement efforts.

Questions

1. What area in Figure P9–1 represents the loss to society that results from restricting the provision of taxicab service to the quantity Q_m?

2. Why do the taxi owners need city hall to establish their cartel? Why couldn't taxi owners simply agree among themselves to collude to restrict output and charge the monopoly price p_m?

---

income distribution is "good" or "bad," typically generates controversy and deeply felt opinions. It is a normative issue and differences of opinion on the subject are rarely settled by an appeal to facts.

CHECKPOINT 9-5

It has been claimed that monopolists are in a better position than perfectly competitive firms to discriminate against minority groups in their hiring practices. What economic basis is there for this view? If you were a supplier of some input to an industry, would you expect that wining and dining your customers would do more for your sales if they were perfect competitors or if the customers were monopolists? Why? The restaurant business has many characteristics of a perfectly competitive market. In recent years we have seen the emergence of large fast-food chains such as McDonalds and Burger King. What economic explanation can you offer for this phenomenon?

REGULATION OF NATURAL MONOPOLY: PUBLIC UTILITIES

We have already pointed out that where natural monopolies exist, public policy has sought to ensure that the consumer benefits from the low per unit costs of production by regulating the price the monopolist can charge. This has resulted in the creation of public utilities. Public utilities are regulated natural monopolies that provide such products as electricity, gas, telephone service, water and sewage treatment, and certain kinds of transportation. How in principle should regulators decide what price a public utility should be allowed to charge?

Difficulty with Marginal Cost Pricing

The cost and demand curves for a natural monopoly are depicted in Figure 9–7. The firm's average total cost curve ATC and its marginal cost curve MC fall throughout the range of output covered by the market demand curve D. Of course, as long as the ATC curve is falling, the MC curve must lie below it. (If you can't remember why, reread the section on marginal and average cost in Chapter 7.)

We have seen before that the most efficient allocation of resources—that which maximizes consumer satisfaction—occurs when output is produced up to the point where price equals marginal cost. It is most efficient in the sense that output is produced up to the point where the price paid for the last unit produced just covers the cost of producing it. For the natural monopolist of Figure 9–7, this occurs where the MC curve intersects the D curve at point b to determine the price p_c and output level Q_c.

This is a much larger output and lower price than the monopolist would choose if left unregulated and allowed to maximize profit. The unregulated, profit-maximizing monopolist would produce the amount Q_m to be sold at a price p_m, as determined by the intersection of the MC and MR curves. Monopoly profit would equal the rectangular area $efgh$. However, if regulators force the monopolist to produce the amount Q_c to be sold at the price p_c, the monopolist will operate at a loss because the average total cost per unit of output sold will be greater than the price per unit sold by the amount bc. The total loss incurred by the monopolist is represented by the rectangle $abcd$. If regulators insist on a marginal-cost-equals-price solution, it will be necessary to somehow subsidize, or pay the monopolist back, by this amount. Otherwise, the firm will go out of business.

"Fair-Return" or Average Cost Pricing

In some countries regulators enforce a marginal-cost-equals-price solution and the government subsidizes the monopolist to cover losses. In the United States utility commissions typically try to enforce a **fair-return** or average cost pricing rule. The fair-return concept may be seen as a compromise between the profit-maximizing price-output combination chosen by the unregulated monopolist and the marginal-cost-equals-price solution. It is a compromise in the sense that the resulting price and output levels under a fair-return solution will lie somewhere between these two extremes. Hence, the consumer still realizes benefits from the lower per unit costs resulting from the economies of scale of the natural monopoly, while the monopolist is allowed to charge a price sufficient to cover all costs of production including a normal profit, or a fair return on capital.

The fair-return or average cost pricing solution is given by the intersection of the ATC curve with the demand curve D. In Figure 9–7, this determines that the output Q_f will be produced and sold at the price p_f. The price p_f received for each unit sold is just sufficient to cover the average total cost per unit, including a normal profit, or fair return on capital. (Remember that a normal profit is included in the average total cost curve.)

FIGURE 9-7 **Fair-Return and Marginal Cost Pricing for a Public Utility**

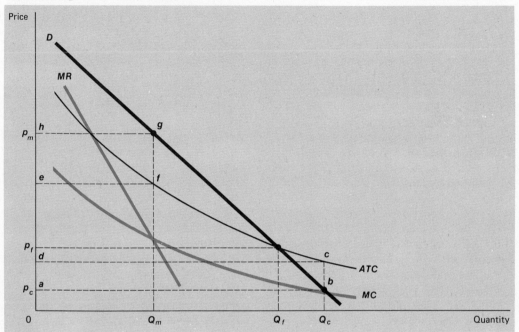

A natural monopoly has continuously declining *ATC* and *MC* curves over the entire range of output covered by the market demand curve *D*. In the absence of any regulatory constraints, the profit-maximizing monopolist would produce an output Q_m and sell it at a price p_m as determined by the intersection of the *MC* and *MR* curves.

If the natural monopoly is turned into a public utility, its price and output policy is subject to regulation by a utility commission. If the commission enforces a marginal-cost-equals-price rule, the utility will have to produce an output Q_c to be sold at a price p_c as determined by the intersection of the *MC* and *D* curves at point *b*. However, in that case the monopolist will operate at a loss represented by the rectangle *abcd*. The monopolist will go out of business unless this loss is made up for by a government subsidy.

If the commission enforces a fair-return or average cost pricing rule, the utility will produce an output Q_f to be sold at a price p_f as determined by the intersection of the *ATC* and *D* curves. In this case, the monopolist will receive a price just sufficient to cover all costs, including a normal profit. In this sense, the monopolist earns a fair return on capital.

Recall that in long-run competitive equilibrium, price also equals average total cost. While the average cost pricing solution is similar to the perfectly competitive outcome in this respect, it differs in that price does not equal marginal cost as in perfect competition. As a result, there will still be consumers who would be willing to pay a price that is greater than marginal cost for additional units of output, but these units will not be produced. This is represented in Figure 9-7 by the fact that the demand curve *D* lies above the *MC* curve over the range of output from Q_f to Q_c.

POLICY PERSPECTIVE

How Do You Keep Costs Down?—Fooling the Utility Commission

What appears easy in principle often turns out to be more difficult in practice. Such is the case with utility regulation, whether regulators attempt to enforce a marginal-cost-equals-price rule or a fair-return price rule.

While utility commissions try to enforce a solution that comes close to that provided by market forces in more competitive industries, it has been observed that regulators are probably more easily fooled than the marketplace. Regulatory commissions are almost invariably at a disadvantage vis-à-vis the firm's management when it comes to knowing what all of the firm's true costs are. They typically have to take management's word for it. No doubt there is a natural temptation for the management of a utility to inflate costs and, as it were, "hide the profits in the costs." More elaborate offices and executive perquisites, padded expense accounts, and trips of questionable necessity are a few examples of how this might be done.

A closely related problem is how to define costs. Let us say, for example, that the regulatory commission took a position that output should be priced to ensure the utility a fair return of 7 percent on capital. This 7 percent would be calculated as the ratio of profit to invested capital. The question now arises as to how to place a dollar value on the invested capital in order to calculate the rate of return. Should the allowable capital cost be measured in terms of the original purchase price or in terms of the price of replacement today? If its value is given at today's prices, then there is the further question of whether

technological change might dictate replacement with somewhat different equipment. This makes cost comparisons even more difficult.

If management is to receive 7 percent calculated on the basis of whatever the allowable capital cost figure is, sometimes called the **rate base**, then for its part there is little incentive to work to keep the allowable capital cost figure down. In fact, there is a temptation to pad the capital cost figure—allowable dollar earnings are larger when calculated as 7 percent of a larger number. Consequently regulatory commissions are under a heavy burden to formulate allowable cost accounting procedures, equipment procurement practices, and enforceable operating efficiency standards—all in the interest of keeping down the costs of the utility's service to customers.

Questions

1. If the utility commission regulates the public utility (natural monopoly) in Figure 9–7 by trying to enforce a fair-return pricing rule, where will the utility's managers like the commission to think the *ATC* curve intersects the demand curve, given that the true cost curves are as shown in Figure 9–7?

2. Do you think that the way a fair return is actually calculated by a regulated utility company will result in the use of more, or less, capital per unit of labor than would be the case if the utility were unregulated?

MONOPOLY AND PRICE DISCRIMINATION

We have seen why a monopolist may be able to earn more than normal profit. Under certain conditions a monopolist may be able to practice price discrimination and thereby realize even greater profit. **Price discrimination** *is possible whenever the same good or service can be sold at different prices for reasons not associated with cost.* We should emphasize that price discrimination can also be practiced by firms that are not monopolists. However, a monopoly firm is often in a better position to engage in price discrimination by virtue of the fact that it is the only supplier of a particular product.

Price discrimination is fairly common in our economy. For example, airlines and movie theaters charge different prices for children and adults, doctors often charge different patients different fees for the same kind of operation, and utility companies charge different rates for businesses and residences. Why? Because it is more profitable to do so. Let's explore some of the reasons as well as the conditions that make price discrimination possible.

The Ingredients for Price Discrimination

The following conditions contribute to a firm's opportunities to engage in price discrimination.

1. *Resale not possible.* The firm must be able to prevent one buyer from selling any of its product to another buyer, or the nature of the firm's product must be such that it is not resalable. For example, it would be almost impossible to charge different prices for bread to different customers. Imagine the grocer charging Jones $1 per loaf and Smith $.75 per loaf. Then Jones could simply have Smith buy enough bread for both of them at $.75 per loaf. However, if a doctor charges Jones more than Smith for an appendectomy, there is nothing Jones can do about it. Jones cannot buy Smith's appendix operation. Ob-

viously, whether a good can be sold from one buyer to another depends on the nature of the good. Services typically cannot be resold. I cannot buy your haircut and you cannot buy my dental work.

2. *Segmentation of the market.* It must be possible for the firm to segment the market by classifying buyers into separate, identifiable groups. For instance, it is relatively easy to charge one price for adults and another for children. Similarly, utilities charge one price for commercial users of electricity and another for residential users. Often a monopoly can sell its product in country A at one price and in country B at another.

Sometimes it is possible to segment a market according to which unit of output is sold—the first, second, or tenth. An electric utility keeps track of the amount of electricity you use in your home simply by reading your electricity meter. It can then charge you a different price for the first hundred kilowatt-hours than it charges you for the second hundred. Often you see advertisements for sales that say "buy one gismo from us and you can have a second one at half price."

3. *Monopoly control.* If there is only one supplier of a good or service, it is easier for that supplier to engage in price discrimination. Buyers charged discriminatory prices by the monopolist cannot turn to an alternative supplier who might sell to them at a lower price.

4. *Differing demand elasticities.* Different buyers have different degrees of willingness to buy a good. Since people are usually as unique in their tastes and preferences for goods as they are in their fingerprints, the shapes of their individual demand curves for a particular good are typically different. Assume individual A's demand curve for a good is inelastic and individual B's demand curve is elastic. From our discussion of elasticity (Chapter 5), we know that we will get more sales revenue from A by charging A a high price and more sales revenue from B by charging B a low price. Assuming the good cannot be resold, it clearly pays to charge A and B different prices for the good—to price

discriminate between them. Wherever a market can be segmented according to differing demand elasticities, price discrimination will generate larger total sales revenue than if the good is sold at the same price to all.

A Price-Discriminating Monopolist: Maximizing Profit

Assume that a firm is a monopolist, is able to identify different buyers according to the price they are willing to pay for its product, and is able to prevent resale of its product.

Examination of the monopolist's downward-sloping demand curve suggests that more profit can be made if the monopolist is able to charge each buyer the full amount he or she is willing to pay, rather than charging all buyers the same price. To see why, in the simplest way, suppose the monopolist has a constant marginal cost equal to average total cost. That is, the $MC = ATC$ curve is represented by a horizontal line as shown in Figure 9–8. Now if the monopolist charges a single price for all output produced, that profit-maximizing price would be p_s and the quantity sold Q_s, as determined by the intersection of the MR and MC curves at point b. The monopoly profit is thus represented by the rectangular area $abcd$.

Alternatively, suppose that the monopolist is able to charge each buyer of the good the maximum price that each is willing to pay for the good. That is, assume that all the conditions necessary for price discrimination, as discussed before, are satisfied. The maximum price that each and every buyer is willing to pay for the good is therefore represented by all the points on the demand curve D. For example, if the monopolist charges the single price p_s, all the buyers represented by the demand curve over the range from f to c are getting the good at a price below that which they would be willing to pay for it (except for the last unit sold at point c). If instead the monopolist were to charge each and every buyer just what each is willing to pay for the good, the monopolist would make the added profit represented by the area dcf.

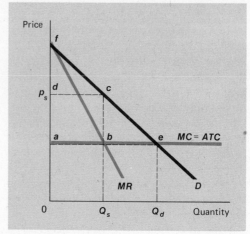

FIGURE 9-8   A Price-Discriminating Monopolist

The monopolist depicted here is assumed to have constant marginal cost MC equal to average total cost ATC. If the monopolist charges the same price for all units sold, profits are maximized by producing Q_s and selling it at the price p_s as determined by the intersection of the MC and MR curves at point b. Monopoly profit is then the rectangular area $abcd$.

If the monopolist is able to price discriminate by charging the maximum price buyers are willing to pay for each additional unit sold, the demand curve D is also the marginal revenue curve. The monopolist would then maximize profit by producing the output Q_d, determined by the intersection of the MC and D curve at point e. The monopolist's profit is then the triangular area aef, which is clearly larger than the rectangle $abcd$.

Carrying this further, if the monopolist charges for each additional unit sold the maximum price that buyers are willing to pay, the addition to total revenue will always be equal to the price received for the last unit. There now will be no offsetting reduction in total revenue as before when charging a single price for all units, which requires reducing the price on all previous units in order to sell an additional unit. Thus, selling each unit for the maximum price buyers are willing to pay means that the demand curve D will also be the marginal revenue curve MR. The monopolist will therefore expand output to Q_d, the point where the MC curve intersects the demand curve D at point e—the point at which marginal cost equals marginal revenue. The total profit is now represented by the triangular area aef. This is clearly larger than the rectangle $abcd$, the profit earned when the monopolist does not discriminate but rather charges the same price p_s for all units sold.

If an electric utility company were not subject to public regulation, it is conceivable that it might be able to behave just like the price-discriminating monopolist of Figure 9–8. By keeping tabs on customers' electricity meters, it could get a pretty good idea how much electricity each customer would purchase at different prices. Resale of electricity from one customer to another is difficult because customers would have to rig up wiring between their different homes and businesses, something that the electric utility company could easily check on. Given these conditions, the utility company could charge different customers different prices for electricity.

CHECKPOINT 9-6
Suppose all buyers have identical demand curves for a good that is not resalable. If you are the monopoly producer of the good, would it pay to price discriminate? Why or why not?

SUMMARY

1. Monopoly is a form of market structure in which the entire market for a good or service is supplied by a single seller, or firm.

2. For a monopoly to exist there must be large, in effect insurmountable, barriers to competition from potential firms seeking entry to the industry. Such barriers may take a number of different forms, such as exclusive ownership of a unique resource; economies of scale possibly even large enough to create a natural monopoly; and government-sanctioned protection in the form of patents, licenses, copyrights, and franchises. No barrier, with the possible exception of those that are government sanctioned, is as insurmountable in the long run as it is in the short run.

3. The monopolist's demand curve slopes downward and lies above the marginal revenue curve, unlike that of a perfectly competitive firm, whose demand curve is horizontal and the same as the marginal revenue curve. The profit-maximizing monopolist produces that output and sells at that price at which marginal cost equals marginal revenue. This does not mean that the monopolist always makes an above-normal or positive economic profit, however. If costs are high enough or demand falls, a monopolist may even operate at a loss in the short run. Unlike a perfectly competitive firm, the monopolist's marginal cost curve is not always identical with its supply curve.

4. Compared to a perfectly competitive firm with the same costs, a monopolist will always produce less and sell at a higher price.

5. Because an unregulated monopolist's profit-maximizing price always lies above marginal cost, there are always consumers who are willing to buy additional units at a price greater than the marginal cost of producing them. However, because the monopolist restricts output, these consumers cannot have these additional units. Compared to a perfectly competitive market, where demand is satisfied for all who are willing to pay a price that covers marginal cost, monopoly results in an inefficient allocation of resources.

6. While many economists agree that monopoly tends to contribute to income inequality, there is far less agreement on whether it promotes or inhibits product innovation and technological advancement. Some argue that the existence or potential of large profit, protected by barriers to competition, provides a great incentive to innovation and the use of improved production methods. Others argue that barriers to competition and the consequent lack of rivals causes the monopolist to be lethargic and disposed to preserve the status quo.

7. Where natural monopolies exist, as in the provision of utility services, franchises are often granted to monopolists in exchange for submitting to public regulation, thereby creating a public utility. Either marginal cost pricing or average cost pricing (fair-return) regulations may then be imposed on the utility in order to pass the low per unit cost benefits on to consumers.

8. Where a monopolist can conveniently classify buyers and effectively prevent resale of output, it is possible to price discriminate by selling a good or service at different prices to different buyers. Because different buyers almost always exhibit different degrees of willingness to buy a product, price discrimination is usually more profitable than selling the product at the same price to all.

KEY TERMS AND CONCEPTS

barrier to competition
copyright
fair return
license
monopoly
natural monopoly
patent
price discrimination
public utility
rate base

QUESTIONS AND PROBLEMS

1. What is the nature and source of monopoly power in each of the following cases: Con

Edison, Muhammad Ali, Wrigley's Spearmint Gum, the Mafia, *Gone With the Wind,* CBS, IBM, the American Medical Association, Golden Gate Bridge, and your local police department?

2. It is often said that in a spectrum of competitive characteristics, monopoly and perfect competition are the extreme opposites. Arrange the following industries according to where you feel they fall on that spectrum: electrical appliance manufacturers, automobile manufacturers, electric power production, dry cleaners, airlines, taxicab service, automotive repair shops, movie theaters, steel production, newspapers, canned goods, and professional baseball.

3. If you were a monopolist, in what portion of your demand curve would you set price—the elastic or the inelastic? Why?

4. If we observed a monopolist who always set price at that point on the demand curve where the elasticity is 1, what might we conclude about the monopolist's variable costs? If this monopolist's fixed costs were cut in half, how would this be reflected in the monopolist's price and output behavior?

5. Is normal profit part of monopoly profit?

6. Suppose the government levies a tax on a monopolist equal to 50 percent of all profit in excess of normal profit. How would this affect the profit-maximizing monopolist's choice of price and output combination? Why? How would the price and output combination be affected if such a tax were increased to 75 percent?

7. If all of a monopolist's profit in excess of normal profit were taxed away, would it improve the monopolist's performance as an allocator of resources? Why or why not? Do you think such a tax could be used to reduce income inequality? How?

8. Instead of having public utility regulators enforce either a marginal cost pricing or an average cost pricing rule, what do you think of having them allow a public utility determine price and output like any profit-maximizing monopolist and then tax away the monopoly profit and distribute the proceeds to consumers in proportion to the amount of output they bought from the utility? From the standpoint of efficient resource allocation, do you think this would be better or worse than enforcing an average cost pricing rule? Why? Would this be better or worse from the standpoint of income distribution?

9. Once a natural monopoly is turned into a public utility subject to price and output regulation, it is always a difficult task for regulators to keep costs down by enforcing average cost pricing.

a. Show how this problem would be reflected in the natural monopoly's average and marginal cost curves over time.

b. In view of your answer to part a, at which point might it be wiser to drop enforcement of average cost pricing and simply allow the utility to set price like a profit-maximizing monopolist, and then tax away the monopoly profit, redistributing it to consumers in proportion to the quantity each buys from the utility? Demonstrate your answer graphically.

10. For each of the following goods or services, tell why you think price discrimination is or is not possible and why: railroad passenger tickets, custom-tailored clothes, shoeshines, college educations, monogrammed clothes, haircuts, landscaping services, and telephone service. What role do monopoly considerations play in your answers?

10

Monopolistic Competition

AFTER READING THIS CHAPTER, YOU WILL BE ABLE TO:

1. Define the characteristics of a monopolistically competitive market.

2. Demonstrate how a monopolistically competitive industry adjusts in the long run to eliminate short-run profits or losses.

3. Discuss the efficiency of resource allocation under monopolistic competition as compared to perfect competition and understand the significance of product differentiation for this comparison.

4. Explain the role of nonprice competition in the form of advertising and the economic arguments for and against it.

5. Evaluate the incentives for innovation and technological change under monopolistic competition and consider its effects on income distribution.

A monopolistically competitive industry is one in which there are many firms, as in perfect competition, but each of them produces a product that is slightly different from that produced by its competitors. Drugstores, barbershops, dry cleaners, restaurants, gas stations, and many service industries are examples of monopolistic competition. On a spectrum of types of industry structure with perfect competition at one extreme and monopoly at the other, monopolistic competition may be thought of as the one that comes closest to perfect competition.

CHARACTERISTICS OF MONOPOLISTIC COMPETITION

Four general characteristics distinguish **monopolistic competition** from other forms of market structure: (1) there are a very large number of firms; (2) each firm's product is slightly different from the others in the industry, so that each firm has a slightly downward-sloping demand curve; (3) there is freedom of entry to and exit from the industry; and (4) the firms engage in nonprice competition.

1. *Large number of firms.* The number of firms that make up a monopolistically competitive industry may be about the same as that in a perfectly competitive industry. As a result, none of them is large enough to dominate the market. In the garment industry, for example, there are about 11,600 firms. As an indication of the size of the typical firm, there is an average of about 47 workers per shop. The average annual sales for each is slightly less than $1 million. This means the average firm accounts for only about 1/10,000 of total industry sales. Thinking about it in another way, consider the number of barbershops, drugstores, dry cleaners, restaurants, and newsstands that are found in the typical large city. Finally, think how often you pass an intersection with gas stations on two or more corners.

2. *Product differentiation.* Unlike perfect competition, in which firms produce an identical product, in a monopolistically competitive industry each firm's product is slightly different from every other's. Why do you usually go to the same barber or eat at a favorite restaurant? Most likely you think your barber "produces" a better haircut or your favorite restaurant serves better food than the others. Some gas stations have better mechanics than others. Some drugstores have a better magazine selection, others a greater variety of cosmetics, and some are simply more conveniently located. In the garment industry, some firms are considered to make certain clothing items better than others. Product differentiation is the factor that most distinguishes monopolistic competition from perfect competition.

Because of product differentiation, each firm has a slightly downward-sloping demand curve. Since each firm's product is a close, but not perfect, substitute for every other firm's product, demand is quite elastic, but not perfectly so. In perfect competition, on the other hand, each firm produces exactly the same product. Consequently, the perfectly competitive firm's demand curve is perfectly elastic (horizontal).

Because the monopolistically competitive firm's demand curve is downward sloping, the firm uses the associated marginal revenue curve to select its optimum price and output level in the same fashion as a monopolist. This is the "monopolistic" aspect of monopolistic competition. "Competition" results from characteristics 1 and 3.

3. *Freedom of entry and exit.* In a monopolistically competitive industry firms have the same kind of freedom to enter into and exit from the industry as they do in a perfectly competitive industry. We will explore in greater detail how this characteristic makes for keen competition among firms. For the moment, note that it ensures that in the long run no monopolistically competitive firm is able to make a greater than normal profit. Freedom of entry and exit means that there are no barriers to competition in a monopolistically competitive industry.

4. *Existence of nonprice competition.* Since each firm produces a similar but somewhat different product from every other firm in

the industry, there is an incentive for each firm to play up the difference in its product in order to boost its sales. This is known as **nonprice competition** and takes many forms. "Service with a smile," or, "If we forget to clean your windshield, you get a full tank free" are common examples. Beauty parlors may compete with one another by having background music, better magazine selections, and fancy interior decorating. Anything that may serve to distinguish a firm's product from that of its competitors in this way might be tried—so long as the firm feels that the cost of such promotional activity is more than made up for by the resulting increase in sales. Advertising in local newspapers, shoppers' guides, and other media outlets is common. You only have to drive down a typical main street in any town to observe fancy signs beckoning you to come in and try this or buy that.

This type of competition is common among monopolistically competitive firms. By contrast, there is no incentive for this activity in a perfectly competitive industry because one firm's product is indistinguishable from any other's.

CHECKPOINT* 10-1

Can you list the industries that might be considered to be monopolistically competitive? By way of review, explain why the slope of a demand curve is a reflection of the existence of substitutes.

*Answers to all Checkpoints can be found at the back of the text.

EQUILIBRIUM IN A MONOPOLISTICALLY COMPETITIVE INDUSTRY

Examination of the above characteristics clearly indicates that the most important difference between monopolistic competition and perfect competition is product differentiation. It is this factor that causes the monopolistically competitive firm's demand curve to be slightly downward sloping, and it is this factor that gives rise to nonprice competition.

In terms of the concept of elasticity, the less product differentiation there is between firms in the industry the more elastic will be the individual firm's demand curve. This follows from our earlier study of the determinants of demand. The more a firm's product is similar to that of other firms in the industry, the more willing consumers will be to switch to that firm's product if it lowers its price, and away from that firm's product if it raises its price. Thus the greater the degree of similarity, and therefore substitutability, between a firm's product and those of its competitors, the greater will be the change in its sales resulting from any given change in price. (In the extreme case of perfect substitutability, the firm's demand curve is perfectly horizontal, or infinitely elastic, and we are back in a perfectly competitive world.)

Since the monopolistically competitive firm is able to affect its level of sales by changing its price, it is in this respect similar to a monopoly. It knows that in order to sell an additional unit of output it must lower price, not only on the additional unit, but on all previous units as well. Therefore, like the monopolist but unlike the perfect competitor, at any output level price is always greater than marginal revenue for the monopolistically competitive firm. This is reflected in the fact that the monopolistically competitive firm's demand curve lies above its associated marginal revenue curve, just exactly as in the case of the monopolist.

Short-Run Equilibrium

The short-run equilibrium position of a monopolistically competitive firm looks just like that of a monopolist. Of course, the difference is that there are many firms in the monopolistically competitive industry, rather than just one, as in a monopoly.

One such firm is shown in Figure 10-1. Two possible short-run equilibrium positions are shown in parts a and c. Whatever the position of the firm's demand curve and

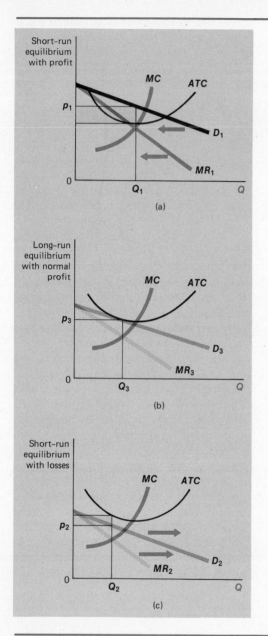

FIGURE 10-1 Equilibrium for a Monopolistically Competitive Firm

The monopolistically competitive firm in part a is in short-run equilibrium, producing output Q_1 and selling it at p_1, as determined by the intersection of the MC and MR curves. It is earning a profit equal to the shaded area. Assuming it is representative of the many firms in the industry, the above-normal profits will attract new firms into the industry in the long run, causing each firm's demand curve to shift leftward. This process will continue until above-normal profits are eliminated and each firm in the industry is in a long-run equilibrium position like that shown in part b.

Alternatively, suppose firms in the industry are realizing losses, equal to the shaded area for the representative firm in part c. Some firms will leave the industry, and those that remain will have a larger share of the market, as represented by the rightward shift in each of their demand curves. This process will continue until the remaining firms are just making a normal profit, as represented by the long-run equilibrium position shown in part b.

its associated marginal revenue curve, the firm adjusts price and output so that marginal cost equals marginal revenue. This is determined by the intersection of the MC and MR curves (assuming it can cover its average variable costs). In part a, the firm's demand curve D_1 is such that it produces Q_1 to be sold at the price p_1. The resulting profit is represented by the shaded area. In part c, demand for the firm's product is weak, and so the entire demand curve D_2 lies below its ATC curve. Assuming it can cover average variable cost, the best the firm can do is produce Q_2, sell it at the price p_2, and minimize its losses, which are represented by the shaded area.

Adjustment to Long-Run Equilibrium

For a monopolist, part a of Figure 10-1 could represent a long-run equilibrium position. However, for a monopolistically competitive firm, it can only be a short-run equilibrium position. This is so because, unlike the monopoly situation, there is free entry of new firms into the monopolistically competitive industry in the long run. There are no barriers to competition.

Above-Normal Profits— Entry of New Firms

If each of the many firms in a monopolistically competitive industry is realizing above-normal profits like the one in Figure 10-1, part a, new firms will be attracted to the industry in the long run. As more firms open up for business, the total market for the industry will have to be divided up among more and more firms. Therefore, each firm's share of the whole market will get smaller. This means that the typical monopolistically competitive firm's demand curve and associated marginal revenue curve will shift leftward during this process, as indicated by the arrows in part a. New firms will continue to enter the industry as long as above-normal economic profits exist. Hence, the demand curves of firms already in the industry will continue to shift leftward until the above-normal profits of each have been eliminated.

The typical monopolistically competitive firm will finally be in the long-run equilibrium position shown in part b. It will produce output Q_3 and sell it at price p_3 as determined by the intersection of MC and MR_3. The price p_3 will just be equal to the average total cost per unit, as indicated by the fact that the demand curve D_3 will be tangent to the ATC curve at this point. The typical firm's total revenue will just equal its total

cost, including a normal profit. There will be no incentive for any new firms to enter the industry.

Why is it that in long-run equilibrium the monopolistically competitive firm's demand curve D_3 is tangent to ATC at just that output level Q_3 where $MC = MR$? Note that for any output level greater than Q_3 the price received per unit would be less than the average total cost per unit, as represented by the fact that the demand curve D_3 lies below the ATC curve. The same is true for any output level less than Q_3. Only at output level Q_3 does price just cover average total cost per unit. Given the demand curve D_3 and associated marginal revenue curve MR_3, the best the firm can do is produce and sell Q_3 at price p_3. (It is best in the sense that it is the only output level where the firm does not realize a loss.) Hence it must be the output level corresponding to the point where marginal cost equals marginal revenue, as represented by the intersection of MC and MR. At any output level greater than Q_3, marginal cost exceeds marginal revenue, represented by the fact that the MC curve lies above the MR curve. Therefore it does not pay for the firm to produce output beyond Q_3. For any output level less than Q_3, marginal revenue exceeds marginal cost—the MC curve lies below the MR curve. Hence, it pays for the firm to expand output up to the level Q_3.

Losses—Exit of Existing Firms

Alternatively, suppose each of the many firms in the monopolistically competitive industry is realizing losses, such as the typical firm shown in Figure 10-1, part c. In the long run, if a firm continues to realize losses like this, it will be forced out of business. Therefore, firms will leave the industry. As this process continues, the share of the market left for each of the firms remaining in the industry will grow. Their demand curves and associated marginal revenue curves will shift rightward, as indicated by the arrows in part c. This process will continue until enough firms have left the industry so that those remaining are just able to cover costs, including a normal profit. The industry will then be in long-run equilibrium, with the typical firm again in the equilibrium position depicted in part b.

CHECKPOINT 10-2
The International Ladies' Garment Workers' Union's (ILGWU) difficulty in getting higher wages from the garment industry is due to the fact that "profit margins aren't great enough to pay higher wages," according to Arthur J. Goldberg. Using graphs like parts b and c of Figure 10-1, explain what would happen in the garment industry if the ILGWU were to gain large wage increases. Make sure you explain what would happen to the typical firm, and describe the resulting adjustment the industry must make. What would happen to price and output levels? What effect do you think this would have on the size of the union?

ECONOMIC EFFECTS OF MONOPOLISTIC COMPETITION

We can evaluate the economic effects of monopolistic competition by answering some of the same questions we considered in analyzing perfect competition and monopoly. How efficiently does monopolistic competition allocate scarce resources to fill consumer wants? What are the pros and cons on the economic effects of advertising, that often controversial form of nonprice competition? How much does monopolistic competition promote innovation and technological advancement? What about the effects of such a market structure on income distribution?

Efficiency of Resource Allocation

It is often claimed that monopolistic competition is inefficient because it results in too many firms in an industry, each operating with excess capacity and selling output at a

price that exceeds marginal cost.[1] This is illustrated by the monopolistically competitive firm shown in Figure 10-2.

Monopolistic Competition Versus Perfect Competition

Because of the downward-sloping demand curve and free entry into the industry, the market forces the typical firm to produce Q_1 and sell it at the price p_1. This corresponds to point a, at which the downward-sloping portion of the ATC curve is tangent to the demand curve D. Attracted by above-normal profits, so many firms have entered the industry that the typical firm has excess capacity. If the typical firm were able to use this idle capacity, it could produce the larger output Q_2, corresponding to the lowest possible average total cost per unit. In sum, *the normal profit, long-run equilibrium position of a monopolistically competitive firm occurs at an output level less than that at which average total cost is a minimum.* It is often argued that consumers' needs could be satisfied at a lower cost with fewer firms if somehow each firm could be forced to operate at the larger output level. This is the level at which average total costs are lowest, and corresponds to the minimum point on the ATC curve. There would be fewer corner grocers, barbershops, and gas stations, and each would be more fully utilized.

There are other implications of monopolistic competition that are closely related to the excess capacity issue. In long-run equilibrium, the monopolistically competitive firm produces the output Q_1 and sells it at the price p_1 in Figure 10-2. If you look to the right of this point, you will see that there is a range of the demand curve that lies above the marginal cost curve. This means that *un-*

---

[1] By convention, we say that a firm is operating at capacity when it is at the lowest point on its ATC curve. When the firm is operating on the downward-sloping portion of the ATC curve, at a point to the left of the lowest point, we say that the firm has excess capacity. When the firm is operating on the upward-sloping portion of the ATC curve, at a point to the right of the lowest point, we say that it is overutilizing its capacity.

FIGURE 10-2 Efficiency and Equilibrium in Monopolistic Competition

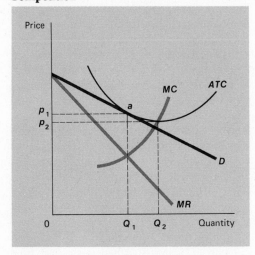

In long-run equilibrium, the monopolistically competitive firm is forced to operate at a point along the declining portion of its ATC curve. We have labeled such a point a. At this point the firm is producing Q_1 to be sold at a price p_1. Hence, average total cost per unit is above minimum ATC. If the resulting idle or excess capacity were used, the output level Q_2 could be produced at minimum ATC.

Over a range to the right of Q_1, the demand curve D lies above the MC curve. This means there are consumers willing to pay a price greater than marginal cost to have some of the product, but who are unable to get it.

If a perfectly competitive firm had the same cost curves, in long-run equilibrium it would produce the output Q_2 and sell it at the price p_2. By comparison to the monopolistically competitive firm, price for the perfectly competitive firm is lower and output higher. Moreover, price equals MC, which equals the minimum ATC.

der monopolistic competition there are consumers willing to pay a price for the product that exceeds the marginal cost of producing it but who are unable to buy it at such a price. This follows from the fact that for a monopolisti-

cally competitive firm the long-run equilibrium price is above marginal cost.

Suppose the cost curves shown in Figure 10–2 were those of a typical firm in a perfectly competitive industry. In long-run equilibrium the perfectly competitive firm would produce the output Q_2 and sell it at the price p_2. Price would equal MC as well as the minimum level of ATC. Why? Because, as we saw in Chapter 8, the perfectly competitive firm's demand curve is perfectly horizontal. This means that the demand curve and the marginal revenue curve are one and the same. Moreover, in long-run equilibrium the perfectly competitive firm's demand curve is tangent to the ATC curve at its bottommost point. The firm produces the output level corresponding to this point because here price equals marginal cost. It is also the output level where the firm produces at the lowest possible level of average total cost.

In terms of Figure 10–2, the perfectly competitive firm would produce output right up to the point where the marginal cost of the last unit produced is just covered by the price consumers are willing to pay for it. Here p_2 equals MC equals the lowest possible level of ATC. Consumers would pay a price for the good that just covers the lowest possible average total cost of producing it. By contrast, the monopolistically competitive firm produces the smaller output level Q_1 and sells it at the higher price p_1. This price is higher than marginal cost and higher than the lowest possible level of average total cost (the bottommost point on the ATC curve).

If the perfectly competitive long-run equilibrium position is taken as the ideal of economic efficiency (for the reasons discussed in Chapter 8), then monopolistic competition falls short of this standard.

Implications of Product Differentiation for Economic Efficiency

In the above comparison with perfect competition, monopolistic competition comes out on the short end of the stick. But let's carry the comparison a bit further. After all, under monopolistic competition, it is true that in long-run equilibrium no more than a normal profit is earned—just as in perfect competition. But in addition, it can be argued that monopolistic competition offers the consumer more product variety in the forms of quality, service, information, and other aspects of nonprice competition.

Are the added costs of the product variety and production at less than full capacity necessarily "bad"? The fact that consumers are willing to pay for product differentiation suggests that they think it is a benefit. If consumers want variety, who are economists to say that this is "inefficient and undesirable"? If it were decreed that the garment industry should produce only one standard outfit of clothes in order to ensure that price equals MC equals minimum ATC, the dreary sameness of everyone's appearance would be dull indeed. In a society where consumers prefer variety over sameness and are willing to pay the extra cost to have it, it is simply a value judgment (a normative statement) to say that "product differentiation is less desirable than product homogeneity." Comparisons between sameness and variety are like comparisons between apples and oranges. They are different goods.

In order to make the claim that monopolistic competition is inefficient, one must have a standard for comparison, an alternative that is "better." But can monopolistic competition really be compared with the alternative of perfect competition and marginal cost pricing? Perfect competition may be more efficient, but it can only be achieved at the cost of reducing the variety of available products. Is it therefore "better"? Any answer is open to debate.

The Pros and Cons of Advertising

If the monopolistically competitive firm is able to differentiate its product from that of its competitors in the right way, it may be able to gain a competitive advantage. Successful product differentiation amounts to tailoring the product to best suit consumer demands. Nonprice competition in the form of advertising serves this goal to the extent that it informs the consumer about differences between products. However, advertising may go beyond the simple conveying of facts when it attempts to tailor consumer demands to goods, rather than simply making consumers aware of the nature of a product. (Much of what we will say here about advertising also applies to oligopolistic market structures, the subject of the next chapter.)

There is a gray area in all this, of course. It is often difficult to distinguish informative advertising from that which simply urges consumers to buy for reasons only superficially related to the product, or even on the basis of claims that may be entirely false. Sometimes the difference between real information and pure hype is pretty obvious. What has "Marlboro country" really got to do with a cigarette? When is the last time you had a beer and then a bull came crashing through the door? There are some 15,000 to 20,000 parts in the typical automobile. What does the similarity between a mountain lion and an automobile tell you about the quality of those parts?

Since any form of advertising costs something, the question is whether the benefits justify the use of scarce resources in this kind of activity. Is it worth it? This issue is as much debated as it is unsettled.

Is Advertising Informative?

To the extent that advertising provides consumers with knowledge about product prices, quality, alternatives (substitutes), and where particular products can be purchased, it can save the consumer the costs of searching and shopping. Newspaper advertising, particularly classified ads, and shoppers' guides appear to serve this end well. On the other hand, television and radio often provide relatively noninformative types of advertising pitched along lines such as you will be more of a man if you buy this or more of a woman if you buy that. The "hidden persuaders" of this type of advertising often bear little relation to the realities of the product.

It has been argued that the prohibition of advertising by some trade groups is a practice intended to reduce information that would promote competition and lead to lower product prices. In recent years there have been various court rulings and legislative actions making some of these prohibitions illegal. Removal of such prohibitions has led to increased advertising and lower prices for eyeglasses and dentures, for example. It has also resulted in more advertising by lawyers, providing the public with greater information about the fees charged for different legal services. Such advertising is informative and very likely promotes competition among sellers that results in lower prices to consumers.

Can Advertising Reduce the Costs of Goods?

It is sometimes argued that by increasing sales and therefore revenue, advertising allows firms to introduce new products at lower costs to consumers. This argument is illustrated in Figure 10–3.

Suppose that in the absence of advertising the monopolistically competitive firm has average total cost represented by the ATC curve. Given the demand curve D_1, the long-run equilibrium occurs at point a, where output Q_1 is produced and sold at price p_1.

Now suppose the firm advertises. Let's say that advertising costs push the ATC curve upward to the position ATC'. If the advertising is effective, it should result in increased demand for the firm's product, represented by a rightward shift in the demand curve. If the demand curve shifts to a position such as D_2, then in the new long-run equilibrium the firm will operate at point b, producing output Q_2 and selling it at price p_2. This price, which is equal to average total cost, will indeed be lower. The lower price is due to the production of the larger output Q_2, which allows the firm to realize some economies of scale. But what if advertising causes the demand curve to shift rightward to a position such as D_3? The new long-run equilibrium will occur at point c. Although a larger out-

FIGURE 10-3 The Effect of Advertising on the Monopolistically Competitive Firm

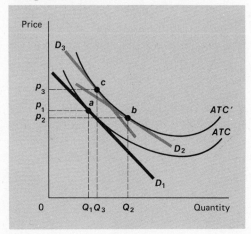

Before making any expenditures on advertising, the monopolistically competitive firm's average total cost curve is ATC. Its long-run equilibrium position is at point a, the point of tangency with its demand curve D_1, where it produces output Q_1 and sells it at price p_1.

The cost of advertising causes the ATC curve to shift upward to the position ATC'. If the effect of advertising increases consumer demand for the firm's product in such a way as to shift the demand curve outward to D_2, the new long-run equilibrium position is at point b. In that case the firm will produce Q_2 and sell it at the lower price p_2. However, if the demand curve is shifted outward to D_3, the new long-run equilibrium will be at point c. Output will then be Q_3 and price will rise to p_3.

Either outcome is possible. But since advertising tends to increase product differentiation, product substitutability will likely decrease. This will result in the somewhat steeper demand curve. Hence, point c may be the more likely outcome—advertising gives rise to the higher price p_3.

POLICY PERSPECTIVE

How Important Is Advertising to Economic Prosperity?

Total advertising expenditures in the United States usually amount to around 2 percent of GNP, the broadest measure of the total of final goods and services produced by the economy during a year. However, some economists argue that the importance of advertising to the well-being of the economy is much greater than the 2 percent figure would suggest. Basically, they contend that much advertising has the effect of molding consumer tastes to form new demands for new products, often doing this by effectively making existing products appear obsolete.

No doubt the almost steady year to year growth in demand experienced by the garment industry is a result of the industry's efforts to bring about fashion changes and new fads in clothing styles. Messages such as "Last year's dresses are simply passé this spring" or "Double-breasted suits are coming back" are part of this effort. In the auto industry, the new models produced every year are usually pushed by advertisement in all possible media outlets. Henry Ford I used to say, "You can have any color Ford you want, as long as it's black." The auto industry seems to have learned long ago that it's much better for sales to have a lot more change and variety than this.

Some economists, such as John Kenneth Galbraith, have argued that such "contrived obsolescence," aided and promoted by advertising, is a waste of resources—resources that might be better used to provide improved school systems and other public goods. It is charged that advertising creates a social imbalance between private and public goods because it is used to push private, or consumer, goods "disproportionately" more than public goods.

But who should be the arbiter of consumer tastes and preferences—consumers, advertisers, economists, government regulators? The idea of consumer sovereignty, that in the final analysis consumers decide what and how much, still has its advocates. As evidence in support of this position, cases are often cited where products were rejected by the market, despite large advertising campaigns. Similarly, products that became a market success with little or no assistance from advertising provide further evidence along this line. The maxi dress flopped despite heavy advertising. The rotary engine Mazda made only a modest and short-lived splash, despite its advertisements. The Volkswagen "bug" was one of the largest successes in automotive history, and for years this sales success came without the aid of any advertisement in the United States at all.

Questions

1. Do you see any potential conflicts between Galbraith's position and certain rights guaranteed by the U.S. Constitution?

2. Can you think of examples of attempts by the government to offset the demand expanding effects of advertising?

put Q_3 is produced, price p_3, which is equal to average total cost, is now higher than initially.

In sum, while it is possible that advertising can lead to reduced costs of production and lower product price, it is obviously possible for just the opposite to happen. Furthermore, the monopolistically competitive firm typically advertises with the intent of making the firm's product more distinguishable or different from those of other firms in the industry. This will decrease the degree of substitutability between its product and those of other firms. Therefore, the demand curve will become less elastic, or more steeply sloped, like D_3 rather than D_2. This makes it less likely that advertising will lead to a lower price.

Is Advertising Wasteful?

Advertising that is informative can certainly improve a firm's competitive position. However, much advertising aimed at improving the firm's competitive position is not informative. It merely claims brand X to be superior to brands Y and Z on the basis of doubtful allegations and meaningless comparison tests. In order to defend their market shares, brands Y and Z respond in kind with similar advertising campaigns.

As a result of such competitive advertising efforts, the total market for the industry's product may hardly increase at all. Even the market shares of the individual firms may remain unchanged because their efforts merely offset one another. But the *ATC* curves of each will be higher, reflecting the increased advertising costs. A typical participant in such a competitive advertising "war" may simply end up in a position such as point c instead of point a in Figure 10–3. Some firms may be producing a little more, others a little less. In the end, all that seems certain is that consumers will be paying higher prices for the industry's output to cover the costs of competitive advertising, which may have very little "hard" information content.

However, this may be an unduly harsh judgment. It may be that to the extent that this type of advertising (however "hokey") persuades consumers to try different brands, they will be exposed to the "true facts" of each firm's product through their own sampling activity. "Try it, you'll like it" may, at least, result in a "try it and see." Such advertising may result in the acquiring of hard information after all.

Through the use of radio, television, and outdoor signs and billboards, competitive advertising accounts for about a quarter of total advertising expenditures in the United States. The more directly informative type of advertising, roughly measured as ad expenditures in newspapers, magazines, and direct mail efforts, accounts for a little more than half of all advertising expenditures.

How Significant Is Advertising in Monopolistic Competition?

It should be recalled at this point that in long-run equilibrium the monopolistically competitive firm can only earn a normal profit, just like a perfectly competitive firm. And this is true no matter what form of nonprice competition the firm may engage in. Nonprice competition, such as advertising, can only result in above-normal profits in the short run. We have seen how the competitive force of free entry leads to an adjustment process that eliminates them in the long run. The fact that competitive advantage obtained through expenditures on advertising is fleeting no doubt puts a limit on just how much of this activity is "worth it" to the monopolistically competitive firm. Your barber probably advertises little—perhaps no more than an occasional ad in the neighborhood paper. The same is true of service stations, dry cleaners, florists, and car washes.

Much of what we have said about advertising applies equally, perhaps even more so, to oligopolistic market structures—the subject of the next chapter.

CHECKPOINT 10-3

A magazine called *Consumer Reports* is devoted entirely to objective comparisons among products of all kinds. The articles are written in a matter-of-fact manner and are usually based on scientific tests. Sold on newsstands throughout the country, this magazine has been a successful product in its own right. What do you think the popularity of this magazine says about advertising? What would be the constitutional problems in setting up a government agency to regulate advertising so that only informative advertising would be permitted?

Innovation and Technical Change

Does monopolistic competition provide much incentive for innovation and change? Remember that in a perfectly competitive market free entry of new firms makes it difficult for any firm to reap above-normal profits for any length of time. Any above-normal profit earned by the perfectly competitive firm as a result of innovation is eliminated by rivals who quickly copy and adopt the new development, thereby keeping themselves on the same competitive footing with the original innovator. Long-run equilibrium entails nothing more than a normal profit. Since a monopolistically competitive industry is also characterized by free entry and a normal profit in long-run equilibrium, it might be expected that the incentive to innovate is no greater than in perfect competition.

On the other hand, it is possible that product differentiation provides an added spur for monopolistically competitive firms to innovate. Nonprice competition may stimulate product development aimed at further distinguishing the firm's product from those of other firms in the industry. If nothing else, a firm may gain some additional, above-normal profits in the short run through such activity.

Here again, however, because such profits are short-lived, the incentive to innovate is definitely limited. For this reason, some economists argue that in monopolistically competitive industries, product innovation and technological change is more cosmetic than real. Since cosmetic change is cheaper, the development of more eye-catching packaging techniques may substitute for substantive product improvement. Given the prospect of additional short-run profit but nothing more, such changes may appear to be "worth it," while the greater expense of real innovation does not.

Some evidence suggests that this is the case. The construction industry is made up of a large number of independent contractors and might well be characterized as monopolistically competitive. Compared to other areas of the economy, the technology of constructing residential housing does not appear to progress very rapidly. (Some might argue that union work rules and outdated building codes have had more to do with unchanging techniques in residential construction than the market structure has.) True, more power tools and motorized equipment are used today. But these were developed by other industries more oligopolistic in structure—the automotive, heavy machinery, and electrical equipment industries. According to a news item on the garment industry, lack of technological innovation and progress appears to be one of that industry's acute problems: "At a recent seminar sponsored by the ILGWU for New York-area producers, ILGWU president Sol C. Chaikin told them how their industry can be brought 'kicking and screaming into the twentieth century' by using new assembly-line techniques to cut costs."

Income Distribution

In terms of its implications for income distribution, monopolistic competition is very similar to perfect competition. The absence of above-normal profit in long-run equilibrium means that all factors are just earning their opportunity costs. The presence of a large number of firms means that these normal profits are spread over a large number of people. Many economists argue that this is conducive to a more equal distribution of income.

A news item reports that in the garment industry "average hourly earnings of apparel workers are still only two-thirds of the average for all manufacturing employees." Many of the other industries in the manufacturing sector of the U.S. economy are much more oligopolistic than the garment industry. That is, there are fewer but larger firms. In these industries higher barriers to competition are no doubt a contributing factor to higher wages and larger profits.

SUMMARY

1. Monopolistic competition is very similar to perfect competition in that it is a market structure with many firms and an absence of financial, legal, or other barriers to entry into or exit from the industry. It differs from perfect competition in that each firm in a monopolistically competitive industry produces a slightly different variation of the same product. Product differentiation means each firm's product is a close but not perfect substitute for that of every other firm. This is reflected in the fact that each firm's demand curve is slightly downward sloping.

2. Because of its downward-sloping demand curve, a monopolistically competitive firm makes its price and output decisions in a manner that appears the same as for a monopolist. It produces where marginal cost equals marginal revenue and sells at a price above that at which marginal cost equals marginal revenue. However, because of low barriers to competition, the entry and exit of firms to and from the industry allows them to earn only a normal profit in the long run.

3. Compared to perfect competition, monopolistic competition is considered inefficient because in long-run equilibrium price exceeds minimum average total cost of production as well as marginal cost. Hence, consumers are not getting the product at the lowest price permitted by cost conditions, and there are consumers who are willing to pay a price greater than the marginal cost of the product but who are unable to have any of it. However, these alleged shortcomings of monopolistic competition may be offset by the benefits of product differentiation.

4. Product differentiation is the primary means by which monopolistically competitive firms engage in nonprice competition. An important but controversial form of nonprice competition is advertising. To the extent that advertising provides consumers with hard information about prices, factual characteristics of products, and where they can be purchased, it provides them with benefits in the form of reduced search and shopping costs. To the extent that it misleads consumers by distorting facts or making false claims, it only confuses them, wastes resources, and leads to higher product prices.

5. Under monopolistic competition innovation and technological advancement are limited by the fact that the above-normal profits that may reward such activity are limited to the short run. Furthermore, nonprice competition may lead to innovation in the form of product differentiation that is more cosmetic than substantive.

6. Many, but not all, economists argue that monopolistic competition may be conducive to a more equal distribution of income because in long-run equilibrium there are many firms, each earning only a normal profit.

KEY TERMS AND CONCEPTS

monopolistic competition
nonprice competition

QUESTIONS AND PROBLEMS

1. Do you think a monopolistically competitive industry is composed of many firms selling slightly differentiated products at the same price, or each at slightly different prices? Why? Do you think the cost curves of all the firms must necessarily be identical?

2. Rank the following products according to the degree to which they may be truly differentiated, as opposed to "artificially" differentiated through advertising and packaging: toothpaste, sugar, apparel, gum, aspirin, coffee.

3. Suppose the government forced all monopolistically competitive firms to set price equal to marginal cost. What sort of difficulty would this create in long-run equilibrium? What would you suggest the government do if it insists on enforcing such a policy? (Figure 10–2 will help you to answer this question.)

4. Do you think advertising makes the long-run equilibrium position of monopolistically competitive firms more, or less, like that of perfectly competitive firms? Why?

5. Rank the following goods according to the degree to which you think their advertising is informative: heavy machinery (advertised in trade journals), perfume, used cars, cigarettes, apartments, new cars, apparel, dairy products, dogs, patent medicine. Give reasons for the rankings you select.

11

Oligopoly and Market Concentration

AFTER READING THIS CHAPTER, YOU WILL BE ABLE TO:

1. List and explain the characteristics of an oligopoly market.

2. Explain the concept of industrial concentration.

3. Evaluate the current evidence on the occurrence and extent of oligopoly characteristics in American industry.

4. Explain how mutual interdependence among oligopolistic firms can lead to price rigidity in oligopolistic industries and to collusive behavior among oligopolistic firms.

5. List the conditions that affect the possibilities for collusive behavior.

A large part of our economy is made up of industries that are dominated by a few large firms. An industry of this type is called an **oligopoly**, a word of Greek origin that loosely translated means "few sellers." In terms of sheer volume of economic activity, oligopolistic industries are usually considered the most representative form of market organization in the United States.

Our analysis of oligopoly will complete our examination of types of market structures. If we were to order these structures along a spectrum according to their similarities with one another, they would line up as follows: perfect competition, monopolistic competition, oligopoly, and monopoly. Oligopoly is like monopolistic competition in that there are several firms typically (but not always) producing a differentiated product. It is like monopoly in that there are barriers to entry of new firms to the industry. In addition, the existence of only a small number of firms may result in collusive behavior, such as firms mutually agreeing to fix prices. These conditions may give rise to above-normal profits for firms in the industry for a prolonged, even indefinite, period of time. In the extreme they may give rise to a market situation that very closely approximates that of a monopoly. For these reasons, you should bear in mind that oligopoly is the most complicated and varied form of market organization that we will study.

Oligopolies may be divided into two major types. Those that produce undifferentiated, or homogeneous, products are often called perfect or **undifferentiated oligopolies**. One firm's product is no different from that of the other firms in the industry. The metals industries, producers of aluminum, steel, and copper, are examples. A manufacturer who uses one of these metals usually orders by exactly specifying characteristics such as tensile strength and carbon content. There is little, if any, room for product differentiation. Oligopolies that produce differentiated products, so-called imperfect or **differentiated oligopolies**, are more numerous. These include the electrical appliance, automobile, and aircraft industries, among many others.

Some oligopolies, such as the petroleum industry, often produce identical products but attempt to differentiate them through advertising. But since all gasolines are characterized by lead content, octane rating, and other such specified traits, there is little room for true product differentiation.

CHARACTERISTICS OF OLIGOPOLY

There are several identifying characteristics of oligopoly that are always present, although to different degrees in different industries. These are (1) economies of scale that lead to a small number of dominant firms, but not necessarily a small total number of firms; (2) recognized mutual interdependence among firms; (3) nonprice competition and price rigidity; (4) temptation for firms to collude; (5) incentive for firms to merge; and (6) substantial barriers to entry. As we proceed through this chapter, it will be apparent that all of these characteristics and their implications are interrelated.

1. *Economies of scale* are often so large relative to the size of the total market that it only takes a few firms to supply the whole market. In the case of a natural monopoly, we saw that one firm could supply the entire market because its long-run average total cost curve declined over the entire range of output covered by the market demand curve. An oligopolistic industry is a less extreme form of this situation.

This is illustrated in Figure 11–1, where D represents the industry demand curve for an undifferentiated oligopoly. Given this industry demand curve, the individual firm with the long-run average total cost curve ATC realizes sizeable economies of scale. This is represented by the fact that its ATC curve reaches its minimum point at output level q, which is a sizeable share of the total quantity Q demanded at the industry-wide price p. Hence, at a price that just covers per unit costs when firms are operating most efficiently, total market demand will only support a small number of such firms.

FIGURE 11-1   Economies of Scale Can Lead to Oligopoly

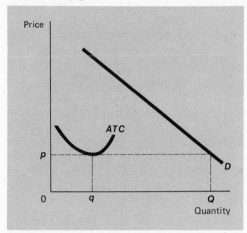

The demand curve D represents the total market demand for the output of an undifferentiated oligopolistic industry. The typical firm in the industry realizes significant economies of scale, as represented by the long, downward-sloping portion of its ATC curve. When it operates at its minimum per unit cost level of production, it produces an output level q that is a sizeable portion of the quantity demanded by the total market. At a price p that would just cover per unit costs when firms are operating most efficiently, total market demand is Q and only a few such firms can be supported by the market.

For example, in the auto industry there are only four domestic producers, but these firms are of very different sizes. It is often pointed out that there are sizeable economies of scale inherent in the production and sale of cars. It is argued that General Motors, with almost 50 percent of the U.S. market (including sales of domestic and foreign makes), is able to realize these economies of scale more fully than Chrysler and Ford, which between them account for about 25 percent of the market (foreign imports account for slightly more). And the Big Three are clearly in a better economies-of-scale position than

AMC, which usually has around 2 percent of the market.

2. *Recognized interdependence among firms* of the effects of their individual price and output decisions on one another's sales is a hallmark of oligopoly.

Since the number of firms that typically make up an oligopolistic industry is relatively small, price changes and any other kind of competitive behavior by any one of them will have noticeable effects on the rest. Each firm in an oligopolistic industry is aware of this, and each has to consider the reaction of the other firms to any price change or other competitive action it might take. A price cut by one firm will usually cause the others to cut prices in order not to lose their shares of the market. Similarly, an advertising blitz by one firm in an oligopolistic industry will usually lead to countercampaigns by the others. Such actions initiated by one firm can result in costly price wars and advertising campaigns that leave all firms worse off, including the firm that started it all.

The fewer the number of firms in an oligopolistic industry the more significant are the consequences of their actions for one another. One analyst of oligopoly behavior put it this way: "When two big guys start a fight in an elevator, the other passengers get pushed around."

3. *Nonprice competition and price rigidity* are characteristics of oligopoly closely related to the recognized interdependence among firms. Because attempts to induce customers away from competitors by cutting price can often lead to price wars and lower profits for all, firms have a strong incentive to avoid price competition if possible. This reluctance to engage in price competition causes firms to compete in other ways—to engage in nonprice competition. Consequently, oligopolistic industries are typically characterized by price "stickiness," or even price rigidity.

Nonprice competition among oligopolists often relies heavily on advertising and product differentiation. The competitive advantage that a firm may realize through these activities cannot be as easily matched by rivals as is a price cut. For example, in the automobile industry model design, pushing the "right size" car, and skillful advertising are all key elements of nonprice competition.

4. *The temptation for firms to collude* in setting prices is an understandable aspect of oligopoly behavior, given that competitive price cutting can so easily lead to lower profits for all. This is particularly true for undifferentiated oligopolists because the absence of product differentiation shuts off an important avenue of nonprice competition. It thereby tends to put more pressure on firms to engage in price competition. Recognizing that their mutual interests are best served by avoiding price wars, the firms in an oligopoly may jointly agree to charge a price that maximizes their collective profits.

An explicit agreement of this nature is illegal in the United States. However, firms may still act in a manner that amounts to the same thing by having sub rosa (secret) agreements to collude. It can be very difficult to tell whether firms are changing their prices at the same time because they are competing with one another or because they are acting in collusion.

5. *The incentive for firms to merge* is in a way a logical extension of the motives for collusion. If all firms in an oligopolistic industry colluded perfectly together, each would be, in effect, a division of a monopoly. Perfect collusion for joint profit maximization is almost the same as profit maximization for a monopolist. And as Joseph Spengler (a past president of the American Economic Association) once said, "At heart, most businessmen, like most lovers, are monopolists." An oligopolistic industry in which all the firms attempt to collude to coordinate price and output decisions is sometimes called a **shared monopoly.** The more successful their efforts to collude, the more the industry behaves like one giant monopoly firm.

When two firms in an oligopolistic industry merge to become one larger firm, they effectively enter into a perfect collusion. The new, larger firm has a larger share of the total

industry market and is therefore a more substantial competitor with the other firms in the industry. In addition, the merger may result in lower per unit production costs. This happens because the larger size of the new firm may enable it to realize economies of scale not attainable by each of the two original firms operating separately. Hence, the new firm's profits may be larger than the sum of those earned by the two original firms for two reasons: (1) a perfectly collusive pricing policy takes the place of what may have been a very competitive price relationship between the two original firms; and (2) lower per unit costs unattainable by the two original firms may be realized by the new, larger firm.

'6. *Substantial barriers to entry of new firms* into oligopolistic industries is the major factor in any explanation of the existence of oligopoly. In general, the larger these barriers are, the fewer will be the number of firms in an industry. Because barriers to entry are so crucial to the existence of oligopoly, we will examine them in greater detail in the next section. Then we will examine some of the evidence pertaining to the existence of oligopoly in the United States. After that we will examine in greater depth some of the explanations of characteristics 2 to 5 and their implications for oligopoly behavior.

BARRIERS TO ENTRY IN OLIGOPOLY

Substantial barriers to entry of new firms into oligopolistic industries can take many forms. Among the most important are economies of scale, cost differences, product recognition, and product complexity and proliferation.

Economies of Scale

Economies of scale can be a serious barrier to entry into an oligopolistic industry. This is illustrated in Figure 11–2. Suppose a firm already in the industry has a demand curve that looks like D_e in part a. Since a potential

FIGURE 11-2 Economies of Scale as a Barrier to Entry in Oligopoly

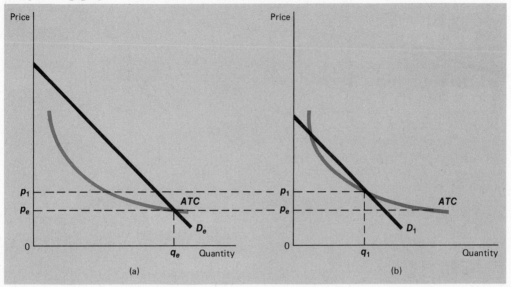

An established firm in the industry has a demand curve D_e, part a. It has an average total cost curve *ATC*, which declines over a large range of output, reflecting the presence of substantial economies of scale. Suppose a potential entrant to the industry can expect to have the same costs and therefore the same *ATC* curve, but it also expects to have a much lower level of demand, represented by the demand curve D_1, part b. If the established firm sets price anywhere below p_1 but above p_e, it can still cover costs and make an above-normal profit. However, because D_1 lies below *ATC* in this price range, the new firm would incur losses and is therefore discouraged from entering the industry.

new firm would be unfamiliar to consumers in the industry at first, let us say that its demand curve would look like D_1 in part b. But let's suppose that both the new firm and the old firm have the same average total costs, represented by *ATC*. In order to make a go of it, the new firm would have to charge a price no lower than p_1 and produce an output no greater than q_1, part b. If it tried to produce more, it would have to sell it at a price lower than per unit production costs, as represented by the fact that D_1 lies below *ATC* to the right of q_1. If the new firm did so, it would incur losses.

If the new firm enters, the firm already in the industry knows that its share of the total market will be diminished. Its demand curve D_e, part a, would therefore shift leftward. To keep the new firm out, the existing firm can take advantage of its economies of scale by charging a price below p_1. In fact, the existing firm can still make a profit at any price below p_1 so long as it doesn't charge a price below p_e and produce more than q_e. Though the existing firm might be able to maximize its profits for a time by charging a price above p_1, it might feel that such gains would not be worth it given the likely loss in market share to a new entrant attracted by the large profits. By pricing below p_1, the existing firm effectively discourages the new firm from entering the industry.

Suppose that there were no economies of scale beyond q_1, and that instead the ATC curve either became horizontal or began to rise. Then the firm already in the industry would not be able to charge a price below p_1 without incurring a loss. It would therefore not be able to charge a price low enough to keep out the potential new entrant.

Cost Differences

A potential new entrant into an industry may not have the same ATC curve as a firm already in the industry. Even putting aside economies of scale, the costs of production for a new entrant may well be higher than those of established firms for a host of reasons.

Existing firms can have lower costs because of know-how gathered from long experience in the industry. Their management organizations have had time to "shake down" into more coordinated and effective units. Their labor forces may be more experienced and production problems may be fewer. Established firms often can get better credit terms from bankers and suppliers. They also may have patents on production processes that reduce costs. Some new firms may be able to overcome these barriers eventually, but this takes time. As a result, these barriers can discourage the entry of many potential rivals.

A simple example of the potential entrant's problem is shown in Figure 11–3. The potential entrant's ATC curve, represented by ATC_n, is higher at all levels of output than that of an existing firm, represented by ATC_e. For simplicity, we will suppose that the new firm's demand curve can be just like that of an established firm, once it gets going. This curve is represented by D_e. If the established firm didn't have to worry about a possible reduction in its market share as a result of the new entry, it might well charge a price such as p_1 and produce q_1 in order to maximize profits. However, the threat of a potential new entrant leads it to

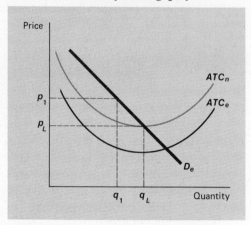

FIGURE 11-3   Cost Differences as a Barrier to Entry in Oligopoly

An established firm's ATC curve, ATC_e, is lower than that of a potential new entrant, represented by ATC_n. The established firm can effectively discourage entry of the new firm by setting price below the limit price p_L. This is because the new entrant would have to operate at a loss while the established firm could still cover costs and earn an above-normal profit, as represented by the fact that D_e lies below ATC_n and above ATC_e over a range to the right of q_L. Were it not for the threat of entry, the established firm might make a larger profit by setting price at p_1 and selling q_1.

never charge a price greater than or equal to p_L. At any price lower than p_L the potential new entrant is not able to cover per unit costs and is therefore discouraged from entering the industry. The established firm, on the other hand, can still earn a profit at a price below p_L. This is represented by the fact that the demand curve D_e still lies above ATC_e to the right of q_L.

The price p_L is often called a **limit price** because if an established firm never charges a price greater than or equal to p_L, the entry of new firms to the industry will be limited.

In sum, *when a potential new firm is at a disadvantage relative to established firms because of economies of scale, cost differences, or both, existing firms can turn these disadvantages into barriers to entry by keeping product price low enough. Yet this price may still be high enough to ensure existing firms more than a normal profit.*

Other Barriers to Entry

In oligopolistic industries, capital requirements, control of input supplies, government regulation, product recognition, product complexity, and product proliferation often constitute formidable barriers to entry. The cost of overcoming these barriers can cause the *ATC* of a potential new entrant to be higher than that of an established firm.

Capital Requirements

To operate a firm at its most efficient size in an oligopolistic industry can require many millions, even billions, of dollars of capital. A potential entrant into the airline, automobile, chemical, electrical appliance, petroleum, railroad, or steel industries, to name but a few, needs large amounts of capital. Such capital requirements are a substantial barrier to entry.

Control of Input Supplies

When existing firms in an industry control important inputs to the production process, potential new firms may face an almost insurmountable barrier to entry. For example, for many years the Aluminum Company of America controlled most of the known reserves of bauxite (aluminum ore), thus making it very difficult for other firms to establish much of a market position in the production of aluminum ingots.

Government Regulation of Entry

Government (state, local, or federal) sometimes regulates entry into various industries by granting exclusive franchises and by requiring and issuing licenses. The Federal Communications Commission, for example, controls entry into radio and television broadcasting—a station must have a license to operate in any given region of the country. In order to start a commercial bank a charter must be obtained from the federal government or from a state banking authority, depending on whether it is to be a national or state bank. There are numerous other such examples where the force of law is a barrier to entry.

Product Recognition

A potential new firm typically must introduce its product into a market where the products of existing firms are already well known and established in the minds of consumers. To overcome this "new kid on the block" problem usually requires a sizeable advertising campaign. The cost of this campaign may well be higher than the cost of advertising that is needed to maintain the market positions of already established firms.

Product Complexity

Closely related to the problem of product recognition is that of product complexity. For products such as automobiles, television sets, refrigerators, stereo equipment, and many others, the very complexity of the item requires that consumers have more information about the product than that provided by mere recognition if they are going to be convinced to buy. Product complexity often extends to such areas as the availability and quality of product service. For example, one of the major hurdles that must be bridged by a new entrant to the auto industry is the establishment of an extensive dealer network through which major service and other product problems can be handled.

Product Proliferation

Product proliferation has proven to be an effective barrier to new entrants in a number of oligopolistic industries. General Motors makes five basic automobiles—Chevrolet, Pontiac, Oldsmobile, Buick, and Cadillac. Ford makes three—Ford, Mercury, and Lincoln—and so does Chrysler—Plymouth, Dodge, and Chrysler. Yet when all the variations on these models are considered the degree of product proliferation is enormous.

Why is this? One reason may well be that product proliferation helps each of the Big Three to preserve its respective share of the auto market from the inroads of rivals and the entry of new firms into the industry. A potential entrant is not confronted with the prospect of competing with just one kind of automobile, but many. If the entrant successfully takes sales away from Ford's Mercury Cougar, these sales may amount to a small fraction of 1 percent of the automobile market. This is hardly enough to allow the new firm to realize the economies of scale enjoyed by GM, Ford, and Chrysler. In the 1920s Ford dominated the auto industry by producing the model T, which offered only slight variations in models and colors, mostly black. GM took a sizeable share of the market away from Ford in later years in large part because it offered consumers a greater variety of models.

CHECKPOINT* 11-1

Every time the automobile industry changes models, which is about once a year, plants must be equipped with new tools ("jigs and fixtures") in order to deal with new body and engine designs. This retooling is very costly. Some estimates suggest that production costs might be reduced 20 to 30 percent if the industry did not change models. Hence, it would seem firms could enjoy larger profits if they refrained from model changes. So why do you think there are model changes? If GM, Ford,

Chrysler, and AMC collude in an agreement not to change models, wouldn't each be better off?

THE EVIDENCE ON OLIGOPOLY IN THE UNITED STATES

What evidence do we have that oligopolistic market structures are widespread in the United States? Basically, we have three measures of the extent to which oligopoly exists. The first is known as the **concentration ratio**, a measure of the extent to which a few firms dominate an industry. Second, there is some sketchy evidence on the degree of price rigidity in different industries. Finally, there is the extent and nature of merger activity in the U.S. economy.

Concentration Ratios

There is a variety of types of concentration ratios used by economists to measure the extent to which a few firms dominate an industry. One of the most commonly used concentration ratios is the sales ratio. *The sales ratio for a given industry is computed on the percentage of total industry sales accounted for by the four, or eight, largest (in terms of sales) firms in the industry.* In principle the ratio can be based on whatever number of the largest firms an investigator may think is most revealing. Concentration ratios for selected manufacturing industries in the United States are given in Table 11–1.

The closer the concentration ratio of an industry is to zero, the more likely is it that the industry takes on more of the characteristics of monopolistic competition. The closer the ratio is to 100, the more we might expect to find giant firms and barriers to entry nearly as insurmountable as those of a monopoly. This interpretation should not be taken too literally, however. It is obviously tempting to suppose that higher concentra-

*Answers to all Checkpoints can be found at the back of the text.

tion ratios are indicative of less competitive conditions. However, the numbers are only based on dollar sales figures and therefore may conceal some fundamental differences between industries.

Shortcomings of Concentration Ratios

Suppose that two different industries each have identical concentration ratios. If one is a differentiated oligopolistic industry and the other is undifferentiated, there is bound to be some difference between the two in terms of the nature and extent of nonprice competi-

tion that takes place in each. (For example, think about the possible differences in this regard between the aircraft industry and the metal can industry, each of which has a concentration ratio of 59 percent according to Table 11-1.) Competition among firms in the differentiated oligopoly may be more directed toward emphasizing the differences between the products of the different firms, through advertising for instance. Therefore price competition (who charges the lowest price) may not be as important a factor as in the undifferentiated oligopoly. When buyers perceive less difference between the products

---

TABLE 11-1 Sales Ratios for Selected Manufacturing Industries

Industry	Concentration Ratio (Share of Industry's Shipments Made by Four Largest Firms)
Motor vehicles and car bodies	93
Cigarettes	NA
Aircraft engines and engine parts	74
Photographic equipment and supplies	72
Tires and inner tubes	70
Malt beverage	64
Aircraft	59
Metal cans	59
Soap and detergents	59
Radio and television sets	51
Construction machinery	47
Farm machinery and equipment	46
Blast furnaces and steel mills	45
Electronic computing equipment	44
Refrigeration and heating equipment	41
Toilet preparations	40
Hardware	39
Petroleum refining	30
Food preparation (potato chips, tea, peanut butter, etc.)	28
Periodicals	22
Newspapers	19
Fluid milk	18
Bottled and canned soft drinks	15
Machinery (except electrical)	2

SOURCE: U.S. Bureau of the Census, Census of Manufacturers, 1981, *Concentration Ratios in Manufacturing.* Data are for the year 1977.

NA = Not available

of different firms, they may well be more interested in who sells the product at the lowest price. Hence price competition may be
keener in the undifferentiated oligopoly industry than in the differentiated. The two industries could have the same concentration
ratio, but the nature of their competitive behavior would be very different, a fact not revealed by a comparison of concentration ratios.

It should also be noted that the industry
sales figures used to compute concentration
ratios exclude foreign firms' sales competing
in this country. For instance, the four largest
firms producing motor vehicles and car bodies in this country (GM, Ford, Chrysler, and
AMC) account for 93 percent of sales *by domestic producers* according to Table 11–1.
Yet this figure neglects entirely the keen
competition from foreign automobile producers. At times in recent years foreign cars
have accounted for over 25 percent of *all*
auto sales (domestic plus foreign makes) in
the United States.

In many oligopolistic industries there are a
large number of firms that are much smaller
in size than the few large firms. This competitive fringe of smaller firms is unavoidably forced to dance to the tune of the few
dominant firms. Concentration ratios typically do not reveal the existence or extent of
this fringe very well. For example, the concentration ratio in the cigarette industry in
1972 was 84 percent, while the concentration
ratio for aircraft engines and engine parts
was 77 percent, not all that different—apparently. Yet in the cigarette industry there were
only 9 other firms besides the 4 largest, while
in the aircraft engines and engine parts industry there were 185 firms in addition to the
4 largest.

Another qualification on the use of the
concentration ratio is that in some industries
the concentration ratio calculated on a nationwide basis is low. However, the market
may be regional or metropolitan in nature,
and the concentration ratio measured for the
more local market may be high. An example
is the market for daily newspapers.

Interpreting Concentration Ratios

Despite the shortcomings of concentration
ratios, they do give us a *rough* indication of
the extent to which the few largest firms
dominate an industry. And such a measure is
useful in assessing the existence and extent of
oligopoly. Indeed, dominance by a few large
firms is what basically distinguishes oligopoly from perfect competition and monopolistic competition.

In this regard note that the industries in
Table 11–1 are ranked in descending order
of concentration. In the most concentrated
industry listed, motor vehicles and car bodies
(concentration ratio equal to 93 percent), the
largest firms are also the first and second
largest manufacturing corporations in the
world—GM and Ford, respectively. In the
least concentrated industry listed, machinery
(concentration ratio equal to 2 percent), there
are about 16,000 firms. Even if the concentration ratio had been calculated on the basis
of the 50 largest firms, it would still have
been only 13 percent. Most economists
would consider the machinery industry to be
much more an example of monopolistic competition than of oligopoly.

Toward the middle of the table there is a
gray area in which attempts at classification
could lead to endless (and pointless) debate.
This, however, should bring home what is
meant when we speak of a spectrum of market structures extending from perfect compe-

**TABLE 11-2 Changes in Price and
Output in Selected Industries: 1929–1933**

Industry	Percentage Change in Price	Percentage Change in Output
Farm products	−63	− 6
Agricultural implements	−15	−80
Steel	−20	−83

SOURCE: Gardner C. Means, *Industrial Prices and Their Relative Inflexibility*, Senate Document 13 (Washington, D.C., 1935).

tition through monopolistic competition and oligopoly to monopoly.

Finally, it should be noted that concentration ratios tell us nothing about possible changes in the composition of the groups of firms constituting the four largest in an industry. For example, it's entirely possible that some (or all) of the firms among the four largest at one point in time may not be among the four largest at another point in time. Such possible turnover is not evident from a comparison of concentration ratios over time.

Price Rigidity

Just how much more rigid are prices in oligopolistic industries than they are in either monopolistically competitive or perfectly competitive industries?

During the Great Depression of the 1930s economic activity, as measured by GNP, fell roughly 50 percent between 1929 and 1933. This period provides us with the most drastic drop in the demand for goods in U.S. history. From an economist's viewpoint, it is one of those events that can yield much information about "the way the system works." In particular, it provides us with some interesting evidence on the degree of price flexibility exhibited in some concentrated oligopolistic industries compared to that exhibited in the perfectly competitive markets for agricultural products.

This is shown in Table 11–2. From 1929 to 1933, farm prices fell 63 percent, while farm output fell 6 percent. Prices in the oligopolistic markets for agricultural implements and steel fell far less, by 15 and 20 percent, respectively, while output fell far more, by 80 and 83 percent, respectively. This suggests that competitive industries such as agriculture responded to lower demand by reducing prices and maintaining output, while oligopolies such as steel and farm implements tended to maintain price and reduce output. While this evidence is limited, it is consistent with the view that the degree of industrial concentration plays an

important role in price changes, and that price is less responsive to changes in demand in oligopolistic industries than in more competitive industries.

Merger Activity

Merger of two firms, or the acquisition of one firm by another, can contribute substantially to the increased concentration of market power among a few firms in an industry. Some indication of the extent of merger activity in the United States is provided in Figure 11-4. Examination of this figure shows that merger activity has occurred in four great waves: 1897–1900, 1924–1930, 1940–1947, and 1947–1975. During the first three waves, mergers were usually horizontal (among producers of a similar product) or vertical (among buyers and sellers in different stages of the production process). Since the 1960s many mergers have been of the conglomerate form (combining firms in wholly unrelated lines of production).

How much does this activity contribute to increased industrial concentration? Some evidence is presented in Table 11-3. The data in this table suggest that the largest firms, measured by asset size, are the most active in acquiring other firms. And to a greater extent, it is the smaller firms that are most often acquired. At least on the basis of the evidence for 1978 and 1979, these facts suggest it is just those firms that might most closely approximate perfectly competitive or monopolistically competitive firms that are most often being absorbed by larger firms. And furthermore, it seems it is the largest firms that are most often getting yet larger as a result of acquisition activity.

The data on acquisitions tend to hide some important considerations from view. For example, the product line of the acquiring firm compared to the product line of the acquired firm is an important consideration for economists. Competition in the auto industry would certainly be reduced if GM acquired Ford, and economists would be unhappy

FIGURE 11-4 Merger Activity in the United States

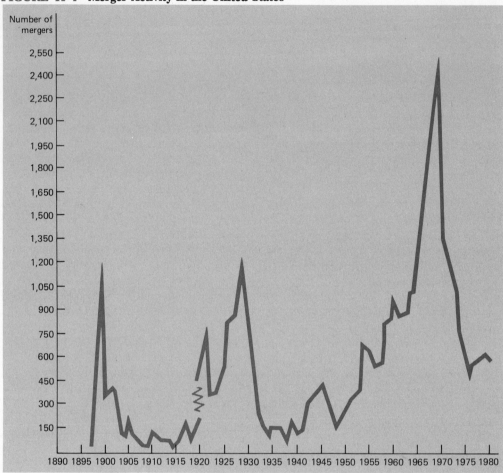

SOURCE: Data for 1895–1918 from Ralph L. Nelson, *Merger Movements in American Industry,* table 14, p. 37, Princeton University Press, 1958 (copyright, National Bureau of Economic Research, New York); Data for 1919–1980 from U.S. Federal Trade Commission.

about this. Little, if any, concern was expressed when ITT acquired Canteen Corporation, however, because the implications for competition appeared nowhere near as dire.

CHECKPOINT 11-2
It has been pointed out that concentration ratios provide no information on the relative positions of firms or the amount of turnover among firms at the top. How might such information aid in assessing the implications for competition in industries with high concentration ratios? What do you think are the implications of merger activity for price flexibility? Suppose a perfectly competitive industry has a perfectly horizontal long-run supply curve and

TABLE 11-3 Companies Acquired, by Asset Size of Acquiring and Acquired Companies: 1977 and 1978

Asset Size	Acquiring Company		Acquired Company	
	1978	1979	1978	1979
Under $1 million	197	138	895	746
$1 million to $9.9 million	44	38	119	123
$10 million to $49.9 million	220	133	157	213
$50 million to $99.9 million	148	146	46	57
$100 million and over	670	759	62	75

SOURCE: U.S. Federal Trade Commission, *Statistical Report on Mergers and Acquisitions*, 1978 and 1979.

the usual downward-sloping demand curve. Suppose the demand curve shifts leftward slowly over time. What does this suggest about the possible shortcomings of drawing inferences about the degree of observed price flexibility from the degree of concentration in an industry, as measured by the concentration ratio?

PRICE AND OUTPUT DETERMINATION

The variety of market structures that come under the concept of oligopoly is clearly much wider than that spanned by perfect competition, monopolistic competition, or monopoly. An oligopoly can be a market consisting of only two firms or of many small firms dominated by a few large ones or of several large firms. There can also be wide variation in the degree to which the market exhibits each of the six characteristics discussed above. There may be much product differentiation as in the automobile industry or relatively little as in the metal can industry.

These considerations, coupled with the existence of a recognized interdependence among firms, make it all but impossible to present *the* model of price and output determination for oligopoly as we did for perfect competition, monopoly, and monopolistic competition. Instead we will examine some of the explanations economists have offered for the existence of price stickiness and of the tendency for firms to move their prices together when they do change them. We will also examine why it pays firms to collude and the conditions that are favorable and unfavorable for collusive price behavior.

Interdependent Price Behavior

Each firm in an oligopolistic industry is aware that any price change it makes will affect the sales of the other firms in the industry. If a firm lowers price, it will take customers away from its competitors. If it raises price, it will lose some of its own customers to competitors. Other firms typically will not remain passive if they are losing customers to a price-cutting firm, but will react to defend their market positions. Hence in order to know how its sales will be affected by any price change it initiates, a firm has to be able to predict the reactions of its competitors. In short, the true demand and marginal revenue curves of a firm must take into account the reactions of rivals. But the ability to predict such reactions accurately is limited at best. What are the implications of this for price and output determination in an oligopoly?

The Firm's Demand Curve and Rival Reaction

Figure 11–5, part a, shows an oligopolist's demand curve D_n based on the assumption

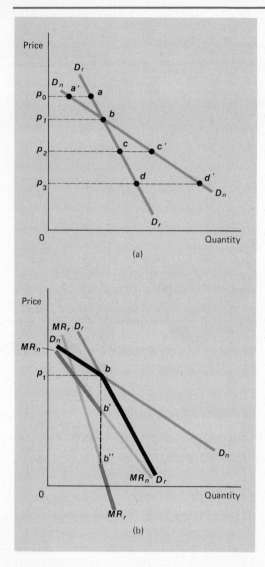

(a)

(b)

FIGURE 11-5 Rivals' Reaction to Price Change and the Kinked Demand Curve

In part a, D_n is the firm's demand curve when rivals in the industry do not react to its price changes but keep their own prices unchanged. D_r is the firm's demand curve drawn on the assumption that rivals match any price change the firm makes.

Starting from an initial position such as point b, if the firm lowers its price from p_1 to p_2, it will end up at c' on D_n if other firms do not react by lowering their prices. If other firms do react by matching the price cut, the firm will not be able to induce customers away from rivals and its increase in sales, therefore, will be less, putting it at point c on D_r. Similarly, if the firm raises its price from p_1 to p_0 and rivals raise theirs as well, the firm will end up at point a on D_r. However, if rivals do not raise prices, the firm will lose customers to rivals and end up at point a' on D_n.

The demand curves D_r and D_n of part a are reproduced in part b. If it is assumed that rivals will match any price cut that the firm initiates, but they refrain from matching any price increase, then the relevant parts of the firm's demand gives the kinked demand curve represented by the highlighted part of D_n above point b and the highlighted part of D_r below point b. The marginal revenue curve associated with D_n is MR_n, and the relevant part of MR_n associated with that part of the kinked demand curve above point b is the highlighted part of MR_n above point b'. The marginal revenue curve associated with D_r is MR_r and the relevant part of MR_r associated with that part of the kinked demand curve below point b is the highlighted part below point b''. Thus the marginal revenue curve associated with the kinked demand curve has a gap, or vertical segment, from b' to b''.

that there is no reaction from rivals when the firm changes price. D_r is the oligopolist's demand curve based on the assumption that rivals will react to any price change initiated by the firm. Suppose that initially price is p_1, so that the firm is at point b on its demand curve. If the firm reduces price to p_2 and rivals do not react by reducing their prices, the relevant demand curve is D_n, and the firm will sell an output level given by the point c'. Its increase in sales will be made up in part of purchases by customers who switch to it and away from other firms in the industry. The rest of its sales increase will be due to the substitutability of its product for similar products of other industries that are now relatively more expensive.

If instead other firms in the industry react by cutting their prices, the relevant demand curve will be D_r and the firm will move to point c as price is reduced from p_1 to p_2. The firm experiences a smaller increase in sales, reflecting the fact that its rivals in the industry have matched its price cut and therefore have not lost any customers to it. Nonetheless, the firm does experience some increase in sales, as do the other firms in the industry, because the industry's product is now cheaper relative to the substitute products of other industries. By the same line of reasoning, if the firm had reduced price to p_3 and the other firms in the industry hadn't reacted, the firm would have moved to point d' on demand curve D_n. On the other hand, if the other firms match the price cut, the firm's sales will increase less as it moves to point d on D_r.

Let's go the other way. Suppose the firm were to raise price from p_1 to p_0. If the other firms in the industry don't raise their prices, the firm will lose customers to them and will be at point a' on D_n. However, if the other firms in the industry also raise price, the firm will end up at point a on D_r and will not lose customers to them. Its loss in sales, which is now less, will only be to other industries that produce substitute products.

The Kinked Demand Curve

Given that a firm in an oligopolistic industry is initially at a position such as point b in Figure 11–5, part a, it is only reasonable to assume that its demand curve for price *decreases* will be D_r. This is the curve that assumes that rivals will react and match any price cuts in order to avoid losing customers to the initiator of the price cut. What about a price *increase* to a level above p_1? Rivals might well refrain from reacting to any price increase the firm initiates. The firm will then

lose customers to its rivals in the industry because its product becomes more expensive relative to theirs. Therefore, starting from the initial position at point b, price level p_1, the relevant demand curve for any price increase will be D_n.

The demand curves D_r and D_n are reproduced in Figure 11–5, part b, with the relevant parts highlighted. It is clear that if the firm is initially at point b, its demand curve is the kinked demand curve formed by the highlighted parts of D_r and D_n, with the kink occurring at point b. MR_n is the marginal revenue curve associated with D_n. The part of the marginal revenue curve associated with the highlighted part of D_n is the highlighted part of MR_n extending down to b'. Similarly, MR_r is the marginal revenue curve associated with D_r. The part associated with the relevant section of D_r is the highlighted part of MR_r starting at point b'' and extending downward. Hence, the marginal revenue curve associated with the kinked demand curve has a gap, or a vertical segment, extending from b' to b'' (indicated by the dark broken line) and lying directly below the kink in the demand curve at point b.

The kinked demand curve offers some possible insights as to why prices in oligopolistic industries appear to be slow to change, or "sticky." If the existing price is p_1, the firm may be reluctant to lower price because its rivals will follow suit and resulting gain in its sales will be modest. In fact, it is entirely possible that the segment of its kinked demand curve below point b is inelastic. In that case any cut in price to a level below p_1 would result in a fall in total sales revenue and any profit the firm might be making. (Note that in this case the point b'' would be at or below the horizontal axis. Why?)

Remember, although we can draw the kinked demand curve and talk as if the firm knows its shape exactly, in reality the firm may be quite uncertain as to the curve's exact shape because it may be uncertain about the extent of rivals' reactions. Cutting price below the existing level is "chancy" given that the segment below point b may in fact turn out to be inelastic. Why run the risk of "upsetting the applecart" by possibly starting a price war that could be disastrous, especially if demand is inelastic below point b.

For similar reasons the firm is reluctant to increase price to a level above p_1. The segment of the kinked demand curve above point b is elastic, as indicated by the fact that the associated marginal revenue curve above point b' lies well above the horizontal axis. Hence, if the firm raises price but rivals do not follow suit (the kinked demand curve above point b is based on the assumption that they will not), the firm will lose sales to rivals, and total revenue and any profit it may be making will fall.

The other reason why price may be "sticky" at the level p_1 has to do with the gap, or vertical segment, of the marginal revenue curve from b' to b''. Let's assume that the firm arrived at the price p_1 by equating marginal cost with marginal revenue, and that its marginal cost curve is MC_0, as shown in Figure 11-6. Suppose production costs rise, so that the marginal cost curve shifts upward. Unless costs rise enough to shift the marginal cost curve up above the position MC_2, the firm will have no incentive to change price or output. Similarly, if production costs fall so that the MC curve shifts downward, the firm will have no incentive to change price or output unless the MC curve falls to a position below MC_1. As long as the MC curve lies in the gap in the MR curve, between b' and b'', the firm will not change its level of production or its selling price.

The kinked demand curve provides one possible explanation of why firms in an oligopolistic industry are reluctant to change an established price.

FIGURE 11-6 Price Rigidity and the Kinked Demand Curve

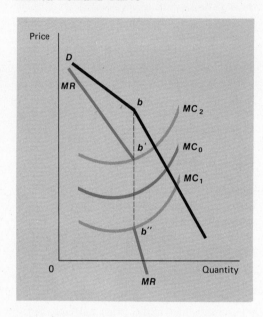

An oligopolistic firm is producing output and selling it at the price associated with point b. Its kinked demand curve is D, its associated marginal revenue curve is MR, and its marginal cost curve is MC_0. If production costs increase, the firm will have no reason to change price or output level as long as the increase is not large enough to push the MC curve above MC_2. On the other hand, if costs decrease, the firm will still have no reason to change price or output level as long as the decrease is not large enough to push the MC curve below MC_1. The existence of the vertical segment of the marginal revenue curve associated with the kinked demand curve therefore provides one explanation for price rigidity in oligopoly.

CHECKPOINT 11-3

What would cause a firm to move price to a level above the kink in the demand curve, even though the demand curve is elastic above this point and a price rise results in a fall in total revenue? Under what conditions would the firm never reduce price below the level of **the kink, no matter what happened to costs?**

Price and Output Collusion

Given an oligopolistic firm's uncertainty about rivals' reactions to any price change it might initiate, the firm is naturally fearful that it may start a price war if it lowers price or price itself out of the market if it raises price. This sort of situation, often referred to as noncollusive oligopoly, is precarious at best. We will give a simple example that illustrates why firms prefer to collude if at all possible. We will then examine conditions both favorable and unfavorable to collusion, as well as a common form of collusion known as price leadership.

Why Collusion Pays

The simplest possible form of oligopoly to analyze is the case where there are only two firms in the industry, often called a duopoly. The production of steam turbine generators in the United States, in which General Electric and Westinghouse are the only two competitors, is an example of a duopoly.

Consider a duopoly in which both firms have identical costs of production and both produce exactly the same product. To make matters even easier, we will assume that marginal cost is the same at all levels of production and that it always equals average total cost. All these assumptions are shown in Figure 11-7. Parts a and b represent the individual firms, and part c represents the entire industry.

Total industry demand is represented by the demand curve D_m. Its associated marginal revenue curve is MR_m, as shown in part c. Since each firm produces exactly the same product, it is reasonable to assume that when each charges the same price, each will have exactly half of the total industry demand given by the demand curve D_m. This is shown in parts a and b of Figure 11-7, where the total industry demand curve D_m is shown for comparison with each firm's demand curve D_f. At any price note that D_f lies halfway between the vertical axis and the total market demand curve D_m. Hence, at any price the sum of the quantities demanded from each firm equals the total industry demand. For example, at the price p_4 the quantity demanded from firm X is q_4 and the equivalent quantity, q_4, is demanded from

firm Y. The sum of these two quantities, or 2 times q_4, equals the total quantity demanded from the industry at the price p_4—the quantity Q_4 shown in part c.

Also note the following. Recall that at any given price the marginal revenue curve always lies exactly halfway between the vertical axis and the straight-line demand curve. Hence, each firm's demand curve D_f, parts a and b, is in exactly the same position as MR_m, the marginal revenue curve associated with the industry demand curve D_m in part c. The marginal revenue curves associated with each firm's demand curve D_f are shown as MR_f, parts a and b.

Suppose initially that each firm is charging the price p_1. This is the price that corresponds to the point where $MC = MR_f$ for each firm, as represented by the intersection of the MC and MR_f curves in parts a and b of Figure 11-7. At this price each firm produces and sells q_1. The sum of their outputs, $2q_1$, equals total industry output Q_1, as shown in part c. Note that this result is exactly the same as it would be if both firms colluded to act like a monopoly, or if both firms had in fact merged to form a monopoly firm. In the latter case the intersection of the curve $MC = ATC$ with MR_m determines the profit-maximizing output Q_1 and price p_1 in part c. Here the monopoly profit equals the shaded rectangle *abcd*. Producing output q_1 and charging the price p_1 is the best that each firm can do, subject to the existence of the other selling at the same price. Each realizes a profit equal to that represented by the rectangular areas *abcd* in parts a and b, which added together equal the shaded rectangle *abcd* in part c.

However, if the firms are not colluding in any way, either may be tempted to undercut the price of the other and take the whole market. That is, when one cuts price below that charged by the other, the price-cutting firm's demand curve becomes the industry demand curve D_m. Suppose firm X tries this by cutting price to p_2. Since the firms produce an identical product, firm Y, still charging p_1, loses all its customers to firm X, which now supplies the entire market the

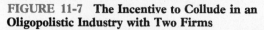

FIGURE 11-7 **The Incentive to Collude in an Oligopolistic Industry with Two Firms**

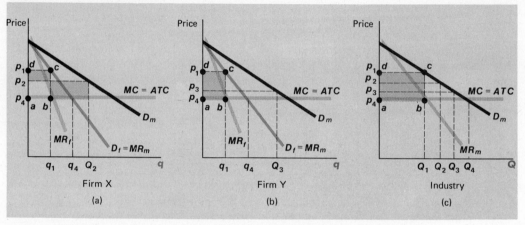

The two oligopolistic firms, X and Y, produce an undifferentiated product and have identical production costs with marginal cost MC and average total cost ATC equal to each other and the same at all levels of output, as indicated by the horizontal $MC = ATC$ curves. Total industry demand is given by the demand curve D_m with its associated marginal revenue curve MR_m in part c. Each firm's demand curve D_f in parts a and b is the same as the MR_m curve.

If each oligopolist charges a price p_1 and sells an output q_1, they split the total market sales Q_1, and each earns a maximum possible profit (represented by the rectangular area $abcd$, parts a and b) equal to half the shaded rectangle $abcd$ in part c. In effect if they collude to maintain price at p_1, they act as if they were a monopoly firm producing output Q_1 and setting price p_1, where MC intersects MR_m to give the maximum monopoly profit represented by the shaded rectangle $abcd$ in part c.

Instead of colluding, suppose firm X cuts price to p_2 and takes all market sales equal to Q_2. As a result, firm Y loses all its sales and therefore reacts by cutting price to p_3, whereupon it takes all market sales, equal to Q_3, and firm X loses all its sales. This process of price cutting continues until price is driven down to p_4, where it just covers all costs of each firm including a normal profit and each firm produces and sells q_4. The price war is over, and each firm is worse off than when price was initially p_1. It obviously pays for the firms to collude and jointly maximize profit by charging the price p_1, splitting industry sales of Q_1 so that q_1 is sold by each.

quantity Q_2. For the moment, firm X is making a larger profit than it was initially since the gain in profit, represented by the larger shaded rectangular area, exceeds the loss in profit, represented by the smaller shaded rectangular area in part a of Figure 11–7. Indeed, this was firm X's motive for cutting price. Firm Y now has no sales at all. Consequently, it reacts by cutting price to p_3, thereby undercutting firm X's price of p_2. Total industry sales Q_3 now go entirely to

firm Y, and firm X's sales fall to zero. Firm X now reacts by cutting its price to p_4, and firm Y must do likewise if it is not to lose all its sales. However, neither can cut price below this level because at p_4 both firms are just covering all costs including a normal profit.

At this point the price war is over, each firm selling q_4, or half the total market sales of Q_4 (which is equal to $2q_4$). Each firm is now just making a normal profit. Each is worse off than before the price war started because at the initial price p_1, each was making a profit (in excess of normal profit) represented by the rectangle *abcd* in parts a and b. The outcome of the competitive price war is a marginal-cost-equals-price solution, just like that in perfect competition. Consumers are better off, but each firm considers itself worse off. At this point the firms may sit down together at a "peace table" and mutually agree not to get involved in any more "shoot-outs" with each other. Both can see that it is in their own best interest to collude and jointly maximize profits by agreeing to keep price at p_1. In effect they agree to split total market sales of Q_1, with q_1 going to each. The moral of the story? Collusion pays, price wars don't.

CHECKPOINT 11-4

Is it necessary for both, or just one, of the firms in Figure 11–7 to misjudge the likely reactions of the other in order for events to lead them to the price level p_4?

Conditions for and Against Collusion

It is not usually as easy for firms in an oligopolistic industry to collude as it was in the above example. The following conditions are important determinants of whether or not successful collusion is possible.

1. *Barriers to entry* serve to keep out potential new firms that are attracted by the above-normal profits resulting from collusion among established firms in the industry. The greater the threat of entry by new firms, the more skittish established firms may be about sticking to a collusive agreement because they fear they will lose out in the long run to market inroads made by new firms. The larger the barriers to entry, the smaller is this threat, and therefore the easier it is to keep a collusive arrangement together, jointly maximizing profits.

2. *The number of firms* is a most crucial determinant of the possibility of collusion. You are no doubt well aware that the larger the number of people involved, the more difficult it is to reach a consensus on anything. The firms in an oligopolistic industry often do not have identical production costs and products. Each really wants to maximize its own profit, and this goal is usually not consistent with the role other firms want to give it in a particular collusive arrangement.

When "push comes to shove," *each firm in an oligopoly typically sees collusion as a compromise between an arrangement of price and market share it would prefer for itself and that which the other firms are willing to go along with. The more firms there are, the more difficult it is to arrive at a compromise collusive arrangement satisfactory to all.* Because of this there is incentive for each to shade price, or give "under the table deals," to get customers away from competitors. Each firm is willing to do anything that will improve its sales, so long as the other firms in the collusive arrangement don't find out. The larger the number of firms, the harder it is to police such activities and prevent competitive deviations from the agreement. Too many firms can simply make collusion impossible. This is why attempts at collusion invariably fail in perfectly competitive and monopolistically competitive markets.

3. *Product differentiation* makes collusive price arrangements more difficult. With differentiation, there is more room for disagreement on the appropriate price for one firm's product vis-à-vis the price of another firm's similar, yet somewhat different, product. A Ford and a Chevy are close competitors, yet they are different in many respects, however small. In addition, product complexity makes for nonprice competition in a number of ways, such as "extras" and "add-ons." On the other hand, the more similar each firm's product is to the others', the less room there is for nonprice competition. Each has a more difficult time getting a competitive advantage over the other, and the danger of price competition leading to a price war is greater. This increases the incentive for collusion. Lack of product differentiation in the steel industry is one of the main reasons why steel

producers are so concerned about keeping their prices in line with one another.

4. *Economic conditions in general* affect the willingness of firms to collude. When the industry or the whole economy is experiencing a recession, firms are often stuck with excess capacity and fixed costs that are spread over an unusually low volume of output. In an effort to relieve this situation, and avoid the necessity of laying off workers, each firm may be more tempted to engage in price cutting to increase sales volume. The perceived advantages of collusion are reduced during such periods, and an attitude of "every man for himself" is more likely to prevail. By contrast, during an expansionary period, the incentives for price cutting are reduced and collusion on prices and market sharing is more attractive.

5. *Antitrust legislation* in the United States forbids collusive agreements among firms to fix prices or share markets. If the duopolists of our example in Figure 11–7 were to agree to set price p_1, they would be acting illegally. (We will look at antitrust legislation more closely in the next chapter.) However, open collusion among firms, agreed to either verbally or in writing, is legal in many other countries. A group of firms colluding to set prices or share markets in this fashion is known as a **cartel**. (OPEC, the Organization of Petroleum Exporting Countries, is a cartel that agrees on setting a price at which it will sell oil to the rest of the world.) It is one thing to outlaw collusive agreements and another to keep firms from acting collusively. Firms may enter into sub rosa, or secret, collusive agreements whose existence is difficult to prove. Rather than getting together in boardrooms or executive offices, executives can make such arrangements during a round of golf or on any other "social" occasion.

Price Leadership

Given that open collusion is illegal in the United States, firms in oligopolistic indus-

tries often seek other ways to coordinate their market activities. Each usually has something to gain from any scheme that will reduce the uncertainties that might trigger competitive price cutting. Collusive sub rosa agreements are one answer. Another method that seems prevalent in many industries in the United States is the practice of **price leadership**.

In the absence of any collusive arrangement, firms find it difficult to adjust to changes in overall industry demand. If industry demand is expanding, each firm may want to increase price to take advantage of the potential for higher profit, but each may be fearful that if it does, other firms may not follow and it will lose sales. Suppose, however, there is some implicit agreement among them that one firm, possibly the largest, will always initiate or lead such moves, and that the rest will follow, on cue as it were. Then when market conditions dictate that all might benefit by increasing prices together, an "orderly" adjustment can be made. Similarly, the price leader can signal an orderly reduction of prices when industry demand decreases and each would be better off charging a lower price. The price leader not only signals the timing and direction of such moves, but the appropriate size of each firm's price change may be gauged by the size of the price leader's move.

At one time or another, the practice of price leadership has been common in such oligopolistic industries as steel and other metals industries, cigarettes, petroleum products, and coal, among others. It is certainly not always clear to an outsider whether observed pricing behavior in an industry is the result of price leadership or not, especially if the firm acting as price leader changes from time to time. In fact, prices charged by firms in an industry may well move together because they are "locked in competition." Industry representatives would certainly have us believe so.

In the next chapter we will consider the pros and cons of oligopoly as a desirable, or undesirable, form of market structure. We

POLICY PERSPECTIVE

The OPEC Cartel—International Collusion in Oil

In 1960 the world's major oil producing countries banded together to form the Organization of Petroleum Exporting Countries (OPEC).[1] Their goal was to collude in the pricing and production of oil—to act as a cartel or monopoly. However OPEC was unable to raise the price of oil during the 1960s because the OPEC countries had conceded too much control over oil production and pricing to American oil companies drilling on OPEC soil. Regaining control of their oil supplies was essential for running a successful cartel so between 1969 and 1973 the OPEC countries began to withdraw first some and then all of these concessions. They were then able to set world oil prices by acting together to exercise their monopoly-like control over the production of OPEC oil. The 1973 Arab-Israeli war further strengthened the unity and resolve of the Arab OPEC countries. Many believe it provided the spark that led OPEC in October 1973 to impose a 6-month oil embargo on the United States and other nations considered sympathetic to Israel. The abrupt halt in the supply of foreign oil caused the price of oil to quadruple. Prior to the first OPEC embargo of oil exports to the United States and the rest of the world in 1973, oil sold for about $2 per barrel. By the early 1980s the price had risen to over $35 per barrel.

Cartel Collusion and Time

The length of time needed to adjust to increased oil prices and the short-run in-

[1] The Organization of Petroleum Exporting Countries (OPEC) consists of the Arab countries of Algeria, Iraq, Kuwait, Libya, Quatar, Saudi Arabia, and the United Arab Emirates and the non-Arab countries of Ecuador, Gabon, Indonesia, Iran, Nigeria, and Venezuela.

elastic demand for oil served to strengthen the OPEC oil cartel during the 1970s. When the cartel raised the price of oil, its total revenues increased (because demand was inelastic). Under these conditions each cartel member was better off as a result of their mutual cooperation. Each had a strong incentive to remain united with the others to coordinate production plans and set oil prices. However the elasticity of demand for oil, like that of other goods, is larger in the long run than in the short run (see Chapter 5). As time passed oil substitutes were found and more energy-efficient durable goods were produced. Consequently OPEC's total sales revenue ceased growing by 1980.

Generally when the individual members of a cartel see their revenues decline, each may be tempted to cut prices to grab sales from the others and preserve its share of the market. Such behavior can destroy the unity of the cartel. By the early 1980s the OPEC cartel was beginning to experience just such problems.

Cracks in the Cartel

World oil demand began dropping by 1979. In addition, consumers began buying more oil from non-OPEC countries such as Mexico, Malaysia, Norway, Canada, and Angola. In 1979, the non-Communist countries consumed an average of 52 million barrels of oil per day, of which 31.6 million came from OPEC. By 1983 OPEC accounted for only about 14 million barrels of the estimated 43 million barrels a day being consumed by non-Communist countries. Finally, responding to this drastic reduction in demand, on March 14, 1983, OPEC announced the first price cut in its 23-year history, slashing the price of oil by $5 per barrel—from $34 to $29.

More recently, as demand for OPEC oil has continued to diminish, there have been coordinated production cuts among OPEC members in order to shore up oil prices. Such coordination is becoming more difficult to achieve however, and certain OPEC countries are cutting price while refusing to cut production as the cartel dictates. Nigeria, for example, is increasingly going her own way, declaring that she will not return to the collusive fold until other OPEC members stop cheating on production and pricing agreements.

Questions

1. What kind of barriers to entry into the oil production business were probably most important for the existence of OPEC?

2. What characteristics of the OPEC cartel were conducive to collusion, and which characteristics were not?

also will take up the subject of antitrust legislation and public policy toward market organization and industrial concentration.

SUMMARY

1. An oligopoly is an industry dominated by a few large firms. The market share of each is large enough that its actions cause reactions among the others. The competitive behavior of each firm reflects its awareness of this situation.

2. The occurrence of oligopoly depends heavily on the existence of economies of scale and substantial barriers to entry. Oligopoly also tends to be characterized by nonprice competition and price rigidity, the temptation for firms to collude, and the presence of incentives for firms to merge.

3. Concentration ratios, which measure the percent of total industry sales attributable to the largest firms in an industry, indicate oligopoly is fairly prevalent in the American economy. Comparison of price behavior among concentrated industries with that among more perfectly competitive industries suggests prices are noticeably less flexible in more concentrated industries. Evidence sug-

gests that merger and acquisition activity is a significant contributing factor to increased industrial concentration.

4. Given the many possible types of interdependent behavior among firms in a wide variety of oligopolistic industries, it has not been possible to put forward a unique theory of oligopoly. The kinked demand curve and its associated marginal revenue curve is one possible explanation of price rigidity in oligopolistic industries in which there is no collusion.

5. Firms in oligopolistic industries have an incentive to reduce uncertainty about rivals' reactions and to avoid profit-reducing price wars. Therefore, they may collude to set prices and share markets in a manner that maximizes profits for all.

6. Collusion is made difficult by lower barriers to entry, a larger number of firms, greater product differentiation, weaker market demand, and a greater likelihood of prosecution for violation of antitrust laws. Because explicit collusion is illegal in the United States, firms may enter into sub rosa agreements to collude. Another method of coordinating their actions is the practice of price leadership.

7. Given the reluctance to engage in price

competition, oligopolistic firms rely heavily on product differentiation, product proliferation, and advertising. It takes rivals more time and it is more difficult for them to match efforts along these lines than it is to match price cuts.

KEY TERMS AND CONCEPTS

cartel
concentration ratio
differentiated oligopoly
limit price
oligopoly
price leadership
shared monopoly
undifferentiated oligopoly

QUESTIONS AND PROBLEMS

1. In what ways is oligopoly similar to monopolistic competition? In 1977 there were about 550 companies producing photographic equipment and supplies, yet the industry is definitely considered an oligopoly. Why?

2. We often hear a lot about price leadership in the steel industry (four-firm concentration ratio of 45 percent, 1977). When one of the steel firms raises (or lowers) prices, the news media typically carry several stories about what the other firms have done by way of reaction on subsequent days. Why do you suppose we hear very little about this kind of price behavior in the computer industry (four-firm concentration ratio of 44 percent, 1977)?

3. Using the diagram depicting the oligopolistic firm of Figure 11–6, demonstrate the likely effects if the firm steps up its advertising. Demonstrate the likely effects if the firm's rivals step up their advertising.

4. Rank the following industries according to how difficult you think it would be for firms to collude in each of them (the concentration ratio for each is given in Table 11–1): cigarettes, metal cans, tires and inner tubes, radio and tv sets, periodicals, and fluid milk. In each case be careful to take into account all the characteristics of oligopoly mentioned in this chapter as well as the nature of the product, and give the reasons for your ranking.

5. It is sometimes claimed that collusive price behavior actually stimulates technological change and innovation. What arguments would you offer to support such a claim?

6. The Antitrust Division of the Justice Department took action to deal with a duopoly situation that it considered to be in effect a shared monopoly. In the case of General Electric and Westinghouse Electric, the only U.S. competitors in the steam turbine generator market, the government ordered each company to "blind" itself to the details of the other's pricing activities. What are the economic merits of this order? Do you think the order is realistic? What reasons are there for expecting that it will or will not be followed?

7. The following statement was made by Roger Blough, former board chairman of U.S. Steel, before the Senate Subcommittee on Antitrust and Monopoly (1957):

> Mr. Chairman, my concept is that a price that matches another price is a competitive price. If you don't choose to accept that concept, then, of course, you don't accept it. In the steel industry, we know it is so.

What are the pros and cons regarding the truth of Mr. Blough's statement?

12

Market Structure, Public Policy, and Regulated Markets

AFTER READING THIS CHAPTER, YOU WILL BE ABLE TO:

1. Assess the evidence on the efficiency of oligopolistic industries, their impact on technological change and innovation, and the relationship of these considerations to the degree of industrial concentration.

2. Outline the major antitrust laws and the procedures for their administration.

3. Briefly sketch the evolution of judicial interpretation of the antitrust laws.

4. Delineate the various schools of thought on the "proper" role of antitrust policy.

5. Briefly describe the regulated industries, the pros and cons of such regulation, and the consequences of deregulation.

Previous chapters have examined how market competition helps to provide an efficient allocation of resources to maximize consumer well-being. Where monopoly is unavoidable, we have seen how government regulation is used to try to enforce a price and output solution more consistent with a competitive outcome. In the last chapter we saw how oligopolistic industries may possess pronounced elements of monopoly power, particularly when there is a high degree of industrial concentration. In this chapter we will examine the case for government intervention in these industries with the aim of establishing more competitive conditions.

First we will look at some evidence on the economic effects of oligopolistic market structures and the existence of large firms in the United States. We will then consider how antitrust legislation has evolved and been used to deal with monopoly-type power and other anticompetitive practices in the American economy.

Before we begin, a word on terminology. We are concerned with the issue of the existence of monopoly-type power and how public policy deals with it. Strictly speaking, monopoly means that one seller supplies a whole market. We have already seen how public policy regulates that situation by use of the public utility concept. As a practical matter, most of the industries where monopoly-type power becomes a matter of concern are oligopolies. Because these industries exhibit many monopoly traits, they are often loosely referred to as monopolies in the press and even occasionally in economics textbooks. **Antitrust policy** *is largely concerned with deciding when and where monopoly characteristics are pervasive enough in an oligopolistic industry to warrant some kind of legal action to eliminate or at least curb them.*

ECONOMIC EFFECTS OF OLIGOPOLY AND INDUSTRIAL CONCENTRATION

How well does oligopoly allocate scarce resources to unlimited wants? The criteria we have used to try to answer this question for the market structures discussed in previous chapters are relevant here as well. Because oligopolistic industries account for such a large share of the economy's output and typically represent large concentrations of economic power, economists have spent a good deal of effort trying to determine how well oligopoly measures up by these criteria. We will try to summarize some of these findings and their implications in the next few pages.

Efficiency

Clearly oligopolies do not produce at that level of output for which marginal cost equals price. Even if an oligopoly had exactly the same cost curves as a perfectly competitive firm producing the same product, nothing ensures that it would produce at the minimum point on the ATC curve as the perfectly competitive firm would. If it does not produce that level of output at which per unit costs are lowest, it would not be efficient by this criterion.

This comparison is largely a fiction, however, because of the significant role that economies of scale play in oligopoly. These economies make it unreasonable to suppose that if an oligopolistic industry were reorganized to be perfectly competitive, the resulting perfectly competitive firms would have the same cost curves as the oligopolist. If the steel industry were reorganized in this fashion, it would take thousands of small firms to produce the amount of steel currently produced by a handful of large firms. And none of these small firms would be able to realize the economies of scale that are attained by large firms such as U.S. Steel, Bethlehem, and the other dominant firms that presently make up the industry. Therefore, per unit costs of production would be higher under perfect competition, even though each firm would be operating at the minimum point on its ATC curve.

But now we have to ask the following question: Do firms in oligopolistic industries tend to be just large enough to take advantage of economies of scale so that per unit production costs are at a minimum, or do they tend to be so large that inefficiencies in production and distribution are encountered?

Research on this question tends to suggest that most firms in the industries studied are larger than the need to realize economies of scale would warrant. It appears that economies of scale are realized in the plant in manufacturing and that multiplant operation seldom lowers costs further. Large manufacturers typically have large plants and many plants, not all of optimum scale. Large manufacturers tend to grow past the point of maximum efficiency and encounter rising per unit costs of production and distribution. The largest multiplant firms realize economies in borrowing funds, purchasing supplies, and advertising, rather than in production and distribution. Overall, however, concentration ratios in most industries studied seem considerably higher than economies of scale would justify.[1]

Technological Change and Innovation

Does oligopoly encourage technological change and innovation? Some economists would say "most definitely." They argue that oligopoly may well be the most progressive of all types of market structure because it comes closest to the "ideal" combination of the carrot of profits and the stick of competition.

The possibility of above-normal profits, protected by substantial barriers to entry, provides an incentive for innovation as well as a ready source of funds to finance innovative activity. In this respect, oligopoly is much the same as monopoly. However, in an oligopolistic industry the existence of rival firms, coupled with a reluctance to engage in price competition, creates unusually heavy pressures to engage in nonprice competition. Such competition takes the form of product development and innovation to spur sales, and advances in production techniques to lower production costs. It is argued that

since firms are leery of price competition as a means of capturing a larger share of the market and increasing profits, there is more emphasis on technological change and innovation. The competitive advantages that a firm may realize through these activities are not as easily or quickly matched by rivals as is a price cut.

In sum, it may be argued that technological change and innovation are encouraged in an oligopoly because of the existence of potentially high profits, as in monopoly. However, unlike monopoly, in an oligopoly technological change and innovation are also stimulated by the competitive pressures created by rival firms. Similarly, it may be argued that technological change and innovation in oligopoly benefit from the competitive pressures created by rival firms as in perfect and monopolistic competition, but unlike these forms of market structure oligopoly does not suffer from a lack of profit incentive.

The preceding paragraph sums up briefly the arguments of some economists in support of oligopoly as the form of market structure most favorable to technological progress and innovation. However, other economists argue that to the extent oligopolistic industries are characterized by collusive arrangements of one kind or another, a "live-and-let-live" mentality may develop. As a result, they claim, there is less progressive and innovative behavior than the existence of several "apparently" competitive rivals would seem to suggest. It may be that collusive behavior among oligopolistic firms results in a sort of shared-monopoly situation. In that case the implications for innovation and technological change are much more like those of monopoly than those of an oligopoly characterized by the existence of vigorous competition. What does the evidence suggest?

The Evidence[2]

It does not appear that invention has been particularly dependent on the activities of

[1] F.M. Scherer, A. Beckenstein, E. Kaufer, and R.J. Murphy, *The Economics of Multiplant Operation* (Cambridge, Mass.: Harvard University Press, 1975), p. 339.

[2] This section draws from D.F. Greer, *Industrial Organization and Public Policy* (New York: Macmillan, 1984), Chapter 9.

large firms. Studies to date suggest that inventive efforts, inventive output, and the efficiency of inventive efforts (measured, say, by the inventive output per dollar of research and development expenditure) tend to increase with firm size only among small- to medium-sized firms. Beyond that, no further gains from size are evident and, if anything, losses are more likely than gains. A study of case histories for 70 major twentieth-century inventions found only one-third of them came out of corporate research laboratories.[3] More than half were due to individuals working on their own. However, over the course of the twentieth century the relative importance of individual inventors seems to be shrinking.

What about the process of turning new inventions into mass-produced products? Here it would seem that costs of engineering, testing, tooling, and marketing, along with the inherent risks of bringing a new product to market, would tend to favor the larger firm. However, researchers find that innovative activity typically rises with size only from small- to medium-sized firms. Beyond that, larger firm size does not generally seem to be associated with greater innovative zeal.

A cross section of industry studies shows that some innovations do require financial resources that exceed those of small firms in some industries. A distinguished researcher on this issue sums up the evidence: "All things considered, the most favorable industrial environment for rapid technological progress would appear to be a firm size distribution which includes a preponderance of companies with sales below $500 million, pressed on one side by a horde of small technologically oriented enterprises bubbling over with bright new ideas and on the other by a few larger corporations with the capacity to undertake exceptionally ambitious developments."[4]

[3] J. Jewkes, D. Sawers, R. Stillerman, *The Sources of Invention,* 2nd ed. (New York: Norton, 1969), p. 28.
[4] F.M. Scherer, *Industrial Market Structure and Economic Performance,* 2nd ed. (Chicago: Rand McNally, 1980), p. 422.

Is there any relationship between market structure and the speed with which a new technique developed by one firm is adopted by others in an industry? The evidence on this seems consistent with the theory advanced by economists that imitation is stimulated more by a less concentrated market structure.[5]

What about the effects of market structure on economic growth? It seems that invention, innovation, and imitation play a large role in economic growth. Here the evidence seems to suggest that large size and concentration are associated with higher growth in labor productivity up to very high levels of concentration, beyond which just the opposite seems to be the case. [6]

To sum up, studies suggest that for a large portion of invention and innovation, high concentration ratios and obstructive barriers to entry seem to stifle progress. At the other extreme, very low concentration ratios and high firm turnover in an industry do not appear conducive to technological progress either. Intermediate market structures, tending to the competitive side of the spectrum, seem best. The exception might be for productivity growth.

Profits, Advertising, and Concentration

Economic theory suggests that oligopoly is likely to give rise to above-normal profits, particularly when firms engage in collusion. There are several aspects to this issue and a certain amount of evidence to support this theory. In our analysis of monopolistic competition in Chapter 10, we discussed the pros and cons of advertising. We pointed out (and you might wish to reread that section at this time) that advertising may play an even larger role in oligopoly than in monopolistic competition. In oligopolistic industries advertising may well contribute to excess (above-normal) profits because it stimulates

[5] Edwin Mansfield, *Industrial Research and Development* (New York: Norton, 1968), Chapter 7.
[6] Greer, *Industrial Organization,* p. 529.

POLICY PERSPECTIVE

Is the U.S. Economy Becoming More, or Less, Competitive?

A recent study by William G. Shepherd looks at trends in industry concentration ratios in the United States in an attempt to answer this question.[1] Specifically, Shepherd has charted changes between 1958 and 1980 according to the following categories of competition:

1. *Pure Monopoly* (PM): situation where a single firm has nearly 100 percent of the market, where entry to the market by other firms is blocked, and where there is evidence of price control.

2. *Dominant Firms* (DF): situation where there is a dominant firm which has 50 to over 90 percent of the market, with no close rival, with high barriers to entry,

[1] William G. Shepherd, "Causes of Increased Competition in the U.S. Economy, 1939–1980," *Review of Economics and Statistics* (November 1982), pp. 613–626.

with strong price control, and with excess profit.

3. *Tight Oligopoly* (TO): situation where the four largest firms have more than 60 percent of the market, where market shares are stable, where there are medium to high barriers to entry, and where there is a tendency toward cooperation or collusion.

4. *Effective Competition* (EC): situation where the four largest firms have less than 40 percent of the market, where market shares are unstable, pricing is flexible, there is little collusion, and profit rates and barriers to entry are low.

The first three categories may be regarded as relatively noncompetitive markets, with pure monopoly (PM) being the least competitive, followed by the dominant firms (DF) market structure, and

FIGURE P12-1   Trend in Competition, Summary of U.S. Competition, 1958–1980.

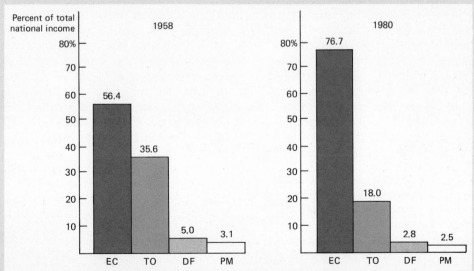

SOURCE: William G. Shepherd, "Causes of Increased Competition in the U.S. Economy, 1939–1980," *Review of Economics and Statistics* (November 1982), p. 619.

then tight oligopoly (TO). The last category, effective competition (EC), has characteristics which tend to promote vigorous competition.

Shepherd's results, shown in Figure P12-1, indicate that the share of economic activity occurring in effectively competitive (EC) industries increased from 56.4 to 76.7 percent between 1958 and 1980, while the shares of the noncompetitive categories declined.

Questions

1. In distinguishing between categories 3 and 4, (TO) versus (EC), why is the criterion "stable" versus "unstable" market shares important?

2. What role do barriers to entry play in distinguishing between categories 1 through 4?

---

product differentiation and proliferation. As we said in Chapter 11, product differentiation and proliferation can be formidable barriers to entry and thereby help exclude potential competitors from an industry. This makes it easier for established firms to charge higher prices and realize monopolistic profits.

On balance, studies of this issue seem to suggest that the ratio of advertising expenditures to sales is highest in those industries where concentration ratios are neither extremely high not especially low, but somewhere in the middle or upper-middle region.[7] One of the most consistent findings reported by different studies is that: "The higher the advertising/sales ratio was in an industry, the higher industry (or in some cases, firm) profits tended to be."[8] In addition, numerous studies find that in industries where concentration ratios are high, profit rates tend to be relatively high as well.[9]

An Evaluation of Oligopoly

Looking at the great variety of industries that have pronounced oligopoly characteristics, all observers might agree on one point. Namely, all could cite a few oligopolistic industries to support the claim that oligopoly is an ideal combination of the carrot of profit,

[7] Scherer, *Industrial Market Structure*, p. 390.
[8] Ibid., p. 391.
[9] Ibid., Chapter 9.

which provides incentive, and the stick of competition, which enforces efficiency. At the same time one could point to a few oligopolistic industries that bear a disturbing resemblance to an unregulated monopoly situation—a shared monopoly. Where the latter situation occurs, or where there are strong overtones of it, economists raise the same kind of concerns about the efficiency of resource allocation, technological progress, income distribution, and the concentration of economic power that we have discussed in the case of unregulated monopoly.

The evidence does suggest that generally in those industries where concentration ratios are high, profit rates (measured as either the ratio of after-tax profit to sales, or to the market value of the firms' common stock) tend to be somewhat higher as well. It also suggests that for most industries studied, concentration ratios seem higher than can be justified by economies of scale. This finding implies the existence of production and distribution inefficiencies.

With regard to invention and innovation, the evidence that has been gathered so far generally does not support the contention that high industrial concentration and very large firm size provide a definite increase in benefits in this direction.

Advertising outlays tend to be large in increasingly concentrated consumer goods industries and also to bear a distinct relationship to above-average profits in those industries. Much of the money goes for television advertising, which has a dubious information value. (According to a recent survey, about 46 percent of the public thinks television commercials are misleading; only 28 percent feels that way about newspaper and other printed ads.)

It should be emphasized that this somewhat negative appraisal is not a blanket evaluation of all oligopolistic industries. Rather it is directed at those that appear to fall into the gray area in which the complex of oligopolistic characteristics becomes more noticeably shaded by overtones of monopoly. We will now look at how public policy deals with these problem areas.

CHECKPOINT* 12-1

The evidence cited above suggests that in industries where concentration ratios are high, profit rates tend to be relatively high as well. How would the implications you might draw from this conclusion be affected by information about the degree to which the identity of the four largest firms in such an industry changes over time? If an industry was found to have a concentration ratio that could be justified by economies of scale, what do you think its profit rate would be like compared to that associated with a finding that the concentration ratio was larger than could be justified by economies of scale? Why? Would the nature of an industry's product have an effect on the implications you might draw from a finding that its advertising outlays are large and its concentration ratio is high? Why? Compare the automobile and the cigarette industries in this regard.

*Answers to all Checkpoints can be found at the back of the text.

PUBLIC POLICY TOWARD SIZE AND MARKET POWER

By means of a series of antitrust laws, public policy has been directed toward maintaining competition in the large unregulated part of the economy consisting of manufacturing, mining, distribution, services, and construction. Agriculture is exempt from antitrust laws. So are public utilities, those natural monopolies whose structure, rates, finance, and other aspects are regulated by state and federal agencies. Governmental agencies also supervise banking and insurance, sectors of the economy that are also largely exempt from the antitrust laws. Nonetheless, that part of our economy that is subject to antitrust laws produces roughly two-thirds of the GNP.

The small number of firms that dominate an oligopolistic industry have market power—they are the major suppliers and their decisions largely determine price and output for the entire industry. The smaller the number of firms that dominate, the more their market power takes on shades of monopoly-type power. We will now consider some of the ways firms achieve and exercise market power. We will then examine major antitrust laws aimed at curbing such power and promoting competition. Some antitrust legislation has not had this intended effect, and we will look at a few of the shortcomings. Finally, we shall examine how some of the major antitrust laws are administered.

The Nature and Exercise of Market Power

Market power can be realized and exercised in many ways in an oligopolistic industry.

1. A more dominant firm may result from the merger of existing firms or as a result of the acquisition by one firm of the stock or assets of another.

2. Firms may collude to maximize profits for all by fixing prices and output at mutually agreed upon levels. Such price fixing is a

practice that works to the advantage of all parties to the agreement, as we saw in the previous chapter.

3. A firm may engage in so-called **predatory behavior** against competing firms. Slashing a rival's packages in the cereal industry, as has been reported on occasion, is an extreme example. Another type of predatory behavior is **predatory pricing,** a practice whereby a large firm, operating in many markets, can afford to sell at prices below costs in some markets until smaller competitors in those markets are driven out of business. Once the competition is eliminated, the larger firm is in a monopoly position in those markets.

4. Firms may use exclusive dealing agreements and tying contracts to restrict competition and increase their domination over the market. Many manufacturers enter into **exclusive dealing agreements** with dealers and distributors that restrict the purchase, sale, or use of competing products. The idea is that if a distributor or dealer concentrates on selling one product line—Goodrich tires, Ford cars, or Chevron petroleum products—the result will be a more effective job of selling the manufacturer's product. This practice is *sometimes* regarded as a way of increasing market power.

A firm wishing to expand sales may resort to the use of a **tying contract**. A large firm selling several products that are typically used in conjunction with one another is sometimes in a position to force a buyer wanting product X to buy products Y and Z as well.

Each of these four methods of achieving and exercising monopoly-type power has been the object of some form of antitrust legislation, which we will examine in the next section.

Major Antitrust Legislation Promoting Competition

During the 1880s and 1890s there was a great deal of merger activity in the United States. Small and large firms alike combined to form "trusts," in which they colluded to restrict output and raise prices. In some industries huge firms assumed monopoly-type dominance, often as a result of openly predatory behavior toward rivals. It became increasingly clear that some form of antitrust legislation was needed if the growth of monopoly was to be curbed and more competitive markets were to be maintained.

The major cornerstones of antitrust law passed by Congress are the Sherman Act (1890), the Clayton Act (1914), the Federal Trade Commission Act (1914), and the Celler-Kefauver Antimerger Act (1950).

Sherman Act (1890)

This act declared illegal "every contract, combination in the form of a trust or otherwise, or conspiracy, in restraint of trade or commerce among the several states, or with foreign nations. . . ." In short, this section made it *illegal to monopolize trade.* The act went on to declare that "every person who shall monopolize, or attempt to monopolize, or combine to conspire with any person or persons, to monopolize any part of the trade or commerce among the several states, or with foreign nations, shall be deemed guilty of a misdemeanor. . . ." The act stipulated that "person" or "persons" was meant to include corporations. The act named the Justice Department as prosecutor in antitrust cases and gave jurisdiction to the federal courts. While the act clearly came out against monopoly, it was not clear as to what specific acts constituted violation of the law.

Clayton Act (1914)

Congress passed the Clayton Act in order to clarify further the intent of the Sherman Act. It was designed to nip monopoly in the bud by preventing practices that tended to lessen competition or led to the creation of a monopoly. Congress intended this statute to deal with monopolistic tendencies well before they took on such proportions as to justify use of the Sherman Act. The Clayton Act is more of a "preventative," while the Sherman Act is more like a "cure" for monopoly-type power.

The Clayton Act outlawed any form of price discrimination deemed to lessen competition. Exceptions to this feature of the act allowed for were (1) differences in grade, quality, or quantity, (2) differences in cost of selling, and (3) lower prices set "in good faith to meet competition." The Clayton Act also banned exclusive, or tying, contracts, acquisition of the stock of a competing corporation, or anyone serving as director of competing corporations. One of the controversial features of the Clayton Act was that it exempted labor unions from the antitrust laws.

Federal Trade Commission Act (1914)

This act created the Federal Trade Commission (FTC) to administer the Clayton Act and to investigate, hold hearings, and issue cease-and-desist orders in cases of "unfair methods of competition" and "unfair acts or practices," which were prohibited under section 3 of the act. Section 5 of the act was designed to protect competitors, not consumers. The Wheeler-Lea Act (1938) amended this act to extend protection to consumers as well as competitors, declaring "unfair or deceptive acts or practices" to be illegal. This established the FTC's main role in policing deceptive advertising practices.

Celler-Kefauver Antimerger Act (1950)

Section 7 of the Clayton Act prohibited one firm from acquiring shares of stock in another if this lessened competition. However, sharp lawyers noted that nothing was said about one firm purchasing outright the assets (plant, equipment, etc.) of another. This loophole became a major merger route in the 1920s and in the years immediately after World War II. As a result, Congress amended section 7 of the Clayton Act by passing the Celler-Kefauver Act, which pro-

hibited one firm from purchasing the assets or stock of another where "the effect of such acquisition may be substantially to lessen competition, or to tend to create a monopoly."

Questionable Antitrust Legislation

Most economists would agree that the antitrust statutes outlined above should in principle effectively promote competition. Two pieces of antitrust legislation, the Robinson-Patman Act and the Miller-Tydings Act, are often criticized by economists as examples of antitrust legislation "run amuck"—acts that have tended to curb competition rather than promote it.

Robinson-Patman Act (1936)

This act sought to curb the buying power of mass distributors, which allowed them to purchase their supplies at lower costs and pass these savings on in the form of lower prices at the retail level. Smaller competitors were not able to match these lower prices and still cover costs. The basic thrust of the act was to forbid suppliers from giving large buyers, such as A&P and Sears, extra services not equally available to all buyers and to forbid quantity discounts to such buyers that lessened competition or created a monopoly.

Supporters of the act ignored an FTC study that found operating efficiencies responsible for 85 percent of a large chain's ability to undersell the small retailer, with buying advantages claiming only 15 percent of the price differential. Economists have mainly criticized the act because it tends to protect less efficient firms from competition itself.

Miller-Tydings Act (1937)

This act had the effect of curbing price competition by greatly increasing the power of manufacturers to enforce **resale-price maintenance contracts** with retailers. Such contracts are agreements whereby the retailer is bound not to resell below a stated price fixed by the manufacturer. Laws that sanction such agreements are called **fair-trade laws**. The Miller-Tydings Act exempted resale-price maintenance contracts from federal antitrust laws in states where fair-trade laws existed, thereby denying the consumer the benefits of retail price competition. A 1951 Supreme Court decision rendered the act ineffective.

Administration of the Laws

Practices that violate antitrust laws may be either criminal or civil offenses. Under criminal law a firm found guilty may be fined, its officers fined or given jail sentences, or both. If a firm is found guilty in a civil case, the court may force it to desist from practices that violate the law, or require the firm to be broken up into a number of smaller firms.

If a firm is found guilty in a case brought by another firm (a private case), the offending firm may be required to pay the complainant an amount as much as three times the total damages—**treble damages**. Treble damage is designed to provide firms with an incentive to report situations that violate antitrust laws.

The Sherman Act subjects violators to possible criminal liability and private suits for treble damages if convicted. In addition, it authorizes the Justice Department to bring civil suits aimed at restraining and prohibiting violations. Such suits allow the Justice Department to obtain court orders for the **dissolution** of a firm (breaking it up into smaller firms) convicted of monopolization, or the **divestiture** of properties (selling off assets) obtained through merger.

The Federal Trade Commission follows a more informal procedure in administering the Clayton Act and other laws under its jurisdiction. Acting on a complaint or on its own initiative, the FTC investigates any alleged violation of the law or reported merger. Often it simply contacts the alleged violator and seeks assurance of voluntary compliance with the law. In the case of a merger, the FTC may notify the parties that it will challenge the merger and ask for divestiture.

CHECKPOINT 12-2
Some supporters of the Robinson-Patman Act agree that it may protect smaller, less efficient competitors, but they ask what the eventual consequences would be of allowing larger firms to eliminate competition by driving smaller firms out of business. What do you think might be some undesirable consequences?

EVOLUTION OF ANTITRUST POLICY

How have the laws drawn up by Congress been enforced by the Justice Department and the FTC? How have they been interpreted by the courts? How have they been used to regulate industrial concentration and market structure and to curb anticompetitive business practices or market conduct?

Regulation of Industrial Concentration and Market Structure

Naturally enough, the antitrust laws have largely been administered and interpreted by prosecuting attorneys and judges. Until the late 1930s, monopoly-type *behavior*, rather than the *existence* of the type of market structure that gives rise to such behavior, tended to be the target of antitrust action. The legal mind seems to have more inclination to look for *bad market conduct* than for *bad market structure*, structure that leads to monopolistic practices.

Judicial Interpretation Up to the 1930s—The Rule of Reason

In 1911 the Standard Oil Company of New Jersey and the American Tobacco Company were found guilty of violating the Sherman Act, and both were ordered to be dissolved into smaller companies. However, despite the fact that Standard Oil had 85 percent of the market for refined petroleum and American Tobacco controlled 93 percent of cigarette output, the decisions rested on the finding of restrictive and predatory practices aimed at monopolizing. Their behavior, *not* their almost complete control of the market, was the reason they were found guilty. These two cases established the so-called **rule of reason**, *the concept that market conduct rather than share of market control would determine guilt or innocence under the Sherman Act.*

Subsequent cases showed that the rule of reason in effect continued to grant large market share immunity from prosecution. The U.S. Steel case (1920) narrowed judicial interpretation of antitrust laws even further. At that time U.S. Steel was the nation's largest firm and controlled 50 percent of the market. Moreover, it was well known that U.S. Steel worked out cooperative agreements on prices and other industry matters with other steel companies. However, the Supreme Court claimed that this only demonstrated that U.S. Steel had failed to establish a monopoly! The Court said: "The law does not make mere size an offense. It requires . . . overt acts." This stretched the rule of reason so far as to raise the question of how "bad" bad conduct had to be before it violated the law.

For all intents and purposes, these developments in judicial interpretation of antitrust laws effectively removed them as barriers to monopolistic tendencies up until the late thirties. During much of this period there was a generally favorable public attitude toward big business. As Calvin Coolidge said, "The business of America is business." This was a time of limited government intervention, a public policy stance that was re-flected in the Supreme Court. The Great Depression of the 1930s spawned a less sympathetic public attitude toward big business. By the late 1930s the Justice Department initiated moves to reduce concentration in entire industries.

Overturning the Rule of Reason

A landmark case, begun just before World War II and concluded in 1945, was that of the Aluminum Company of America (Alcoa). Alcoa accounted for 90 percent of aluminum ingot production. The Court found Alcoa to be in violation of the Sherman Act even though it acknowledged that the company was not abusing its power at the time of the trial. The Court said that in passing the Sherman Act Congress "did not condone 'good trusts' and condemn 'bad ones'; it forbad all." The decision reversed the precedent set by the U.S. Steel case (1920) and appeared to overturn the rule of reason. Now market structure rather than market conduct became the major criterion. Highly concentrated oligopolistic industries were now suspect simply by virtue of being highly concentrated. Subsequent antitrust actions somewhat modified the strong antibigness position taken in the Alcoa case.

Importance of Market Definition

The Alcoa case raised an important question. If market dominance itself violates the Sherman Act, then how is the relevant market defined? Obviously the greater the number of substitute goods included in the definition of a market, or the broader the geographic area, the smaller will be the market share of any one firm. In the Alcoa case the court ruled that Alcoa was a monopoly because substitutes for aluminim (copper, various kinds of steel, scrap and imported aluminum, and other metals) should not be included in Alcoa's market.

In the Du Pont cellophane case (1953) the Supreme Court defined the market to include all flexible wrapping materials, and cellophane accounted for 18 percent of this market. The Court ruled in favor of Du Pont arguing that its share was insufficient to establish monopoly-type power. Economists and the Court's minority opinion argued that cellophane should be considered a separate market because of its transparency. By that definition, Du Pont had nearly 75 percent of the market for transparent wrapping material and would probably have lost the case.

More recently (1982), the Justice Department dismissed its 13-year-old suit against IBM. Again the deciding issue was, what was IBM's market? The suit accused IBM of monopolizing the "general-purpose computer and peripheral-equipment industry." When the suit was initiated in 1969 IBM supplied almost 40 percent of the office equipment market and roughly 70 percent of the large mainframe computer market. However during the 13 years of litigation competition in the computer industry increased to the point where IBM controlled only 5 percent of the telecommunications and computer-services markets, 18 percent of the word-processor market, and 20 percent of the minicomputer market. Though IBM still controlled 70 percent of the domestic market for mainframe computers, in 1982 the Justice Department dropped its suit against IBM on the grounds that IBM no longer dominated the computer market broadly defined. Since the Alcoa case (1945) judicial interpretation of what defines a market has broadened.

In 1982 American Telephone and Telegraph (AT&T) reached an agreement with the Justice Department settling a suit charging AT&T with violating the Sherman Act. The Justice Department argued that AT&T shouldn't be allowed to extend its regulated (public utility) monopoly power over telephone service into related, but potentially competitive, markets. The intent was to prevent AT&T from using its monopoly power in regulated markets to subsidize its activities and gain competitive advantage in unregulated markets. The Justice Department agreement compelled AT&T to divest itself of its local public utility phone companies and fairly join battle with the competition (such as IBM) in the information systems market. Here again the crucial concept of market played an important role in the settlement.

Superior Performance Versus Unfair Business Practices

There is legitimate concern that antitrust policy runs the risk of punishing firms that have achieved market dominance through superior innovation and efficiency, rather than by use of restrictive or unfair business practices. The Alcoa ruling fueled this concern since it seemed to declare market dominance illegal regardless of the way dominance came about. However subsequent test cases have resulted in rulings that turned on precisely how market dominance was realized.

The Eastman Kodak case (1972) was notable in this regard. A competing firm filed an antitrust suit charging Eastman Kodak gained unfair advantage over other film processors by virtue of the method Kodak used to introduce its pocket-sized instamatic camera and film. But higher courts ultimately decided in Kodak's favor, ruling that the advantages resulted from superior innovation. In a similar case Du Pont was charged with using unfair practices to gain advantage over smaller competitors in the titanium dioxide market. The antitrust charges against Du Pont were dismissed by the FTC, which claimed that the advantage gained was the result of Du Pont's efficiencies.

Mergers and the Celler-Kefauver Antimerger Act (1950)

Section 7 of the Clayton Act (1914) banned firms from acquiring stock in competing companies, and the Celler-Kefauver Antimerger Act (1950) amended section 7 to prohibit the acquisition of real assets as well if such acquisition "substantially" lessens competition. Nevertheless, there has been a large merger movement since World War II (see Figure 11–4 in preceding chapter), with a pronounced increase in conglomerate mergers relative to horizontal and vertical mergers.

A **horizontal merger** is a merger between two firms selling the same, or very similar, products in the same market. The merger of two grocery stores would be a horizontal merger. A **vertical merger** is a merger between a supplier and its customer. For example, an oil refining company might merge with an oil pipeline company so that the refining and shipping operations are vertically integrated under one company. A **conglomerate merger** is a merger of companies that operate in completely different markets and produce largely unrelated products. An example would be the merger of a sporting goods company with a computer company and a cosmetics company.

In the case of horizontal mergers, the Supreme Court has taken the unyielding position that they lessen competition. While antitrust policy has been quite successful in blocking vertical and horizontal mergers, it has had little effect on the surge of conglomerate mergers that started after World War II and peaked in the late 1960s.

From the standpoint of antitrust policy, conglomerate mergers are a relatively new and unfamiliar phenomenon. Part of the difficulty stems from a relative lack of knowledge about their impact on competition and market structure. Though they probably have increased concentration in manufacturing, there is little evidence that conglomerate mergers have lessened competition in individual markets. Because of their relatively large size and the wide range of their activities, they would seem to gain advantages in dealing with suppliers and customers on a reciprocal basis. ("Our branch X will buy supplies from you if you will buy the nuts and bolts you need from our branch Y.") While fears of such arrangements were once a matter of some concern to the Antitrust Division, investigations have not turned up evidence that they are all prevalent or significant.

Before 1973 the government could fight proposed conglomerate mergers by arguing that the merger would pose a *potential* threat to competition. Since 1973 it has been required that the government demonstrate that a proposed merger *actually* would reduce competition. Not surprisingly, government attempts to stop conglomerate mergers have been stymied since 1973.

Since their heyday in the 1960s, it seems the "bloom is off the rose" for conglomerates. It appears that in many instances their rapid earnings growth was the product of clever, but misleading, accounting practices. It appears that economic reality caught up with many conglomerates in the early 1970s. It may be the case that managing a conglomerate whose products and markets have very little in common often gives rise to serious problems of management and organization. Nonetheless, there is little doubt that conglomerate mergers have contributed significantly to the increase in the share of corporate assets held by the nation's largest corporations since World War II. In 1945 the nation's 200 largest manufacturing concerns owned 45 percent of all assets in U.S. industry. Today they own over 60 percent.

Regulation of Market Conduct and Business Practices

In addition to regulating industrial concentration and market structure, the antitrust laws specifically ban certain kinds of market conduct and business practices. Let's briefly examine some of these and a few of the instances in which they have brought about important court decisions.

Collusive price-fixing agreements among firms are illegal under the Sherman Act. In 1961 the electric equipment industry was found guilty of colluding to fix prices, allocating business among themselves, and rigging bids on contracts to utility companies. Ensuing treble-damage suits cost GE and Westinghouse over 300 million dollars. Several high-level executives were jailed on criminal charges—the first time this had ever happened under the antitrust laws. This example no doubt has served as a deterrent to potential price fixers in other industries.

Price discrimination is outlawed by section 2 of the Clayton Act whenever its effects reduce competition. This section of the law is concerned mainly with the effects of discrimination on competitors of the firm offering the lower price. In particular it is aimed at the practice of producers charging very low prices in markets where rival firms competed and higher prices in markets where competition was less or had been eliminated.

In a case that involved both price fixing and price discrimination the FTC ruled in 1983 that Du Pont and Ethyl Corporation illegally "signaled" price changes for lead-based gasoline antiknock compounds. The FTC also found that the companies illegally set one price for delivered shipments of the product regardless of destination and wrote contracts that guaranteed favored companies the lowest prices available. The ruling was important because it was the first decision ever to forbid price signaling, or informal practices that effectively set prices. The companies were said to have signaled price increases by announcing new prices several days in advance of the 30–day notice they had agreed to give customers. The early warning allowed Ethyl and Du Pont and their two smaller competitors to reach the same price level by the day notice was required.

Copyrights and *patents,* while meant to encourage innovation and invention, may also be used to suppress competition. For example, in 1953 General Electric was found guilty of using its patents to fix the retail prices of light bulbs.

Licensing is a practice that is frequently used to restrict competition. Where a license is required to practice a particular occupation or profession—medicine, law, driving a cab, hairdressing, and so forth—there is always the possibility that the licensing procedure will be used to control entry in order to restrict supply and thereby keep wages up. While licensing is typically advocated in principle as necessary for the "public's protection," in practice it is often nothing more than a convenient way of limiting competition. The use, or abuse, of licensing in this fashion has been largely untouched by antitrust policy.

Unfair and *deceptive practices* that are harmful to consumers are banned under section 5 of the Clayton Act. Enforcement by the FTC has not been easy. Nonetheless, it has issued thousands of orders to sellers to stop false advertising that misrepresents goods as to their quality, curative power, real price, composition, and origin. For example, after a long struggle, the FTC was finally able to require a label on cigarette packages alerting consumers to the health hazards of cigarette smoking.

Current Thought on Antitrust Policy

Antitrust activity has been greater since the late thirties than it was during the 40 years following the passage of the Sherman Act (1890). When President Theodore Roosevelt (the "trustbuster") set up the Antitrust Division of the Justice Department in 1903, it employed only a few lawyers and prosecuted 2 or 3 cases a year. Today, it employs several hundred lawyers and prosecutes upward of 50 or more cases a year. Yet economists continue to differ considerably on the merits of antitrust policy.

What are the main schools of thought about antitrust policy and the direction it should take in the future? Basically there are three: (1) large firms and highly concentrated oligopolistic industries are our best hope for future progress and should be left alone, (2) antitrust laws should be revised to promote "workable competition," (3) we need more active enforcement of current antitrust laws and changes in other policies that tend to lessen competition. Let's consider each of these in turn.

Bigness Means Progress

The distinguished economist Joseph Schumpeter (1883–1950) argued that economists were wrong to place so much emphasis on perfect competition as a model of ideal efficiency. He claimed that the incentive for technological change and product innovation comes from the prospects for above-normal, or monopoly, profit. These prospects are greater when there is monopoly power, not where competitive conditions prevail.

Some proponents of this point of view go on to argue that in many industries modern technology and the efficiencies realized from economies of scale do not go along with a market structure of many firms, the basic ingredient of a highly competitive market. To use antitrust laws to impose such a market structure in these cases would only result in a loss of efficiency due to a decrease in economies of scale and technological innovation.

Antitrust Laws Should Promote "Workable Competition"

This school of thought is somewhat related to the first. According to this view, the concept of perfect competition is an idealization that has few counterparts in real-world market structures. Furthermore, given the existence of mass production technologies and the associated economies of scale, antitrust policy and laws based on the notion that there must be many firms engaged in fierce price competition may be misdirected.

Proponents of **workable competition** argue that it would be both realistic and more promising to recognize that vigorous competition can take many forms in an oligopolistic industry, including product differentiation and development, innovations in production technology, better customer service, and informative advertising. They say it would be wiser if antitrust policy focused more on these dimensions of nonprice competition. They say that workable competition exists where competition along these lines is vigorous among existing firms and where there is the potential threat of new entrants to the industry should prices and profits rise too much. Moreover, they claim that workable competition may exist in oligopolistic industries where firm size is large, the number of firms is few, and industry concentration is high.

However, critics of the workable competition concept say that it puts too much stress on judging an industry by its market performance. They argue that in effect it would return antitrust policy to something like its earlier "rule of reason" philosophy.

Antitrust Policy Should Promote Competition More Actively

Proponents of this point of view argue that more resources ought to be devoted to the investigative activities of the Antitrust Division of the Justice Department as well as those of the Federal Trade Commission. In addition, they argue that policy changes are needed in several related areas.

Markets Untouched by Antitrust Policy. There are groups in our economy that are currently exempt from antitrust law and that, it is claimed, indulge in monopolistic practices. Labor unions, which are exempt under the Clayton Act, are among these groups. Some argue that the market power of large unions far exceeds that of all but the largest corporations—and maybe even that as well. The restrictions imposed by unions on entry of new trainees into the skilled trades is often cited as evidence of this. Trade and professional associations, such as the American Medical Association and the American Dental Association, are often accused of similar practices aimed at restricting entry and limiting the supply of practitioners, thereby keeping their incomes high. Trade practices among lawyers, doctors, dentists, real estate agents, and architects typically bar competitive determination of fees. Yet these groups have remained largely immune from antitrust policy. All these groups are usually cited as targets for some form of action by those who advocate more vigorous antitrust policy.

More Dissolution, Divorce, and Divestiture. Those who favor a more active antitrust policy often argue that there has been too much reluctance to use the three *D*'s of antitrust—dissolution, divorce, and divestiture—to break up large firms. These are cited as the most effective ways to break up monopoly power because they attack market structure directly. Once in a great while courts have decided in favor of the separation of the units of a vertical combination (divorce) or the selling of assets (divestiture). The breaking up of a larger firm into several smaller firms (dissolution) is even rarer. The reluctance to do this stems largely from the legal and financial problems involved—the difficulty of "unscrambling an omelet." There is also the fear that the resulting smaller units might not succeed. There have only been about 30 cases of dissolution, divestiture, and divorcement in 9 decades of antitrust activity.

Public Policy Bias Toward Big Business. There is a tendency for government policy to lend a helping hand to large businesses in trouble while many small businesses fail every day with little notice. In a competitive marketplace, some less efficient competitors are bound to fail. Why inefficient large firms should be saved from failure by government protection while small firms are not is a hotly debated question. In recent years, for example, controversy over this issue was spurred by the government's rescue of Penn Central, Lockheed, and Chrysler from bankruptcy. Critics of such policy argue that it encourages the notion that there is an added safety feature in bigness—government protection from failure. This may encourage merger activity and management policies that are riskier and less efficient than would be the case without the safety of a government backstop.

Removal of Barriers to Foreign Trade. One way to increase competition and provide the consumer with a greater variety of products at lower prices is to remove barriers to foreign competition. Such barriers include import tariffs (taxes on imported goods) and quotas (volume limits on the quantity of imported goods). In those areas of the economy in which industrial concentration is high and oligopoly market structure has strong overtones of monopoly power, removal of barriers to direct foreign competition may be the most effective public policy for the maintenance of vigorous competition.

A Final Comment

It may well be that the mere existence of antitrust laws serves as a significant deterrent to the exercise and growth of monopoly power. For example, it is sometimes said that General Motors, which currently has nearly 50 percent of the auto market, would take over a good deal more of that market if it were not afraid of the antitrust action that would likely be taken against it. The deterrent effect of antitrust laws is difficult to measure. Nonetheless, many economists feel that it is of significant importance to the maintenance of competition and the restraint of monopoly-type power and practices.

CHECKPOINT 12-3
Why might it be argued that market structure is a more important criterion than market conduct for judging an industry when enforcing antitrust laws? What aspect of the Sherman Act did the Supreme Court seem to ignore when it handed down its decision in the U.S. Steel case (1920)? In what way did the Alcoa case (1945) reverse the judicial interpretation of the antitrust laws given earlier in the U.S. Steel (1920) case.

THE REGULATED INDUSTRIES—PROTECTING CONSUMERS OR THE REGULATED?

Certain industries such as airlines, trucking, railroads, radio and television broadcasting, and banking are (or have been) regulated by government commissions. More often than not it seems such regulation protects the regulated from competition instead of assuring the benefits of competition to the consumer. Some economists argue that the regulatory agency is often "captured" by the regulated firms and used to fix prices (rates), allocate market shares among firms, restrict entry into the industry, and promote other anticompetitive practices. This is done under the guise of legitimate government regulation, and is otherwise in violation of the antitrust laws from which these industries are mostly exempt. This type of criticism of regulated industries has given rise to a movement toward *deregulation* in recent years.

The Pros and Cons of Industry Regulation

Those critical of industry regulation generally argue that it tends to create resource misallocation, inefficiency, and therefore higher costs to the public. Regulation critics question the ability of bureaucratic intervention to improve on the market-guided decisions of individual firms where the potential for competition exists. Regulation proponents argue that regulation is required in some markets to protect vulnerable consumers. In addition they claim that regulation is sometimes necessary to protect firms from periodic bouts of cutthroat competition that threaten their ability to provide reliable service to the public. The examples provided by the industries regulated by the ICC (Interstate Commerce Commission), the CAB (Civil Aeronautics Board), and the FCC (Federal Communications Commission) illustrate both sides of the debate.

The ICC—Regulation of Railroads and Trucking

When the ICC was established in 1887 it was supposed to protect the public from possible railroad price collusion and the railroads from rate-cutting wars among themselves. The advocates of such regulation were concerned about the threat of railroad cartels and monopoly-type power on the one hand, and "excessive" competition on the other. By the mid-1930s, ICC regulation extended to all commercial surface transportation in the country. Up until the late 1970s the ICC controlled the number of products railroads and truckers could haul, what routes they used, what cities they could operate between, the shipping rates charged, route abandonment and service discontinuance, as well as carrier layoffs of labor. ICC control even covered mergers and financial issues. The ICC also permitted railroads and truckers to operate rate bureaus to fix prices.

A host of critics argue that the ICC used its regulatory powers to limit the number of truckers and rail carriers that could operate in interstate commerce—in effect, to limit entry into the transport industry. Critics claim that entry restriction, rate-setting regulations, and other ICC controls served to protect established concerns and labor unions from competition. And consumers ended up paying higher prices due to higher transport costs.

The CAB—Regulation of Air Transport

The CAB had the same sort of regulatory control in the air as its ICC counterpart had on land. Advocates of the regulation of airline routes and fares argue that without such controls rate-cutting competition might invite cost-cutting practices that endanger public safety. It is also frequently claimed that regulation is necessary to assure air service to smaller communities.

Critics point out that CAB regulations prevented airlines from charging fares on different routes to reflect differences in costs per passenger mile (due to cost efficiencies associated with time in the air and route travel density). Routes were also assigned by CAB administrators on the basis of noneconomic considerations ("such-and-such community needs air service," says its influential congressman).

The FCC—Regulation of the Airways

The FCC regulates radio and television use of the airwaves and effectively restricts the number of radio and television stations in local areas across the country. Limiting entry to the radio and television industry in this way effectively jacks up profits from advertising revenues and has led to dominance by three major networks—ABC, CBS, and NBC. Advocates of radio and television regulation say that regulation is necessary to protect the public interest. Opponents argue that it mainly serves to generate above-normal profits for the radio and television industry while restricting the program menu available to the public. In recent years the advent of cable television networks has brought more competition to the industry.

Movement Toward Deregulation

Since the late 1970s there has been some significant deregulation, reducing controls exercised by the ICC, CAB, and FCC, as well as some controls on banking and finance (removal of deposit interest ceilings and restrictions on the provisions of financial services, for example). The deregulation movement has had remarkably wide public and bipartisan political support. Yet it has also met resistance (perhaps increasing) from affected special interests, typically the established firms and unions feeling the pinch of increased competition.

Deregulation of Railroads

The Railroad Revitalization and Regulation Reform Act of 1976 (the 4-R Act) and the Staggers Rail Act of 1980 provided the first efforts at railroad deregulation. The 4-R Act committed the ICC to greater price flexibility in rate setting, giving railroads more freedom to set their own rates rather than working under ICC imposed rates. The act also eased restrictions on abandoning low-revenue and loss-producing operations while encouraging railroad mergers. Though the number of operating railroads has declined under the 4-R Act, competition seems to have increased as stronger merged railroads are more effectively challenging other modes

of transportation such as trucking. The Staggers Act (1980) further extended the 4-R deregulation. It freed railroads to make most rate changes without prior ICC approval and gave them permission to contract directly with shippers at less-than-market rates for long-term bulk shipments. It is estimated that previous prior approval requirements had cost railroads up to $1 billion per year due to ICC delayed inflation adjustment of rates.

Deregulation of Trucking

The Motor Carrier Act of 1980 initiated gradual deregulation in the trucking industry. The act gave greater rate-setting freedom to individual truckers and eased entry restrictions into long-haul, interstate trucking. Competition in the industry increased rapidly. During the first 18 months of deregulation 5,200 new trucking firms entered the industry, average freight bills dropped 10 to 20 percent, and the ICC received 20,000 new route applications. As with the railroads, trucking deregulation is by no means total. The ICC still has final authority over many areas of rate making and maintenance of service.

Deregulation of Airlines— The CAB's Demise

The Airline Deregulation Act of 1977 and 1978 relaxed many CAB controls over the airline industry. The practice of granting virtual monopoly power to certain carriers over some routes was ended. Air carriers were also given greater freedom to enter or exit from airline markets and to set rates. Consequently many existing carriers altered their routes (both expanding and contracting service on specific routes). At the same time, a number of new long-distance carriers entered the industry bringing most long-distance air fares down. Loss-producing routes were abandoned to new specialized commuter lines (especially in smaller communities on low-industry routes) or the larger carriers adjusted fares upward to reflect real operating costs. Deregulation seems to have resulted in lower fares as the airlines have been allowed to price and operate in response to actual supply-and-demand conditions.

The CAB was shut down altogether on December 31, 1984, as mandated by the Airline Deregulation Act of 1978. Remaining CAB functions have been transferred to the Transportation Department. The CAB's demise came despite once considerable pressure from airlines to keep the agency alive to limit competition. One former CAB chairman remarked, "If there were no CAB, the airlines would have created it, and in fact they did."

SUMMARY

1. Some economists contend that oligopoly provides an ideal combination of the opportunity for profit, which gives incentive to innovation, and the existence of competition, which encourages efficiency. However, evidence suggests that concentration ratios are higher in some industries than can be justified by economies of scale, and that high industrial concentration and large firm size are not consistently related to inventive and innovative activity. There also tends to be a positive relationship between industrial concentration and above-average profit rates, and between industrial concentration and the amount of advertising, a large part of which is of dubious information content.

2. Public policy, expressed in a series of antitrust laws, has sought to maintain competition and curb monopoly power in the unregulated part of the economy that accounts for roughly two-thirds of GNP. The keystone of antitrust policy is the Sherman Act of 1890. This act made it illegal to monopolize trade and stipulated that any firm or firms that did so would be guilty of a misdemeanor. Unfortunately, the act was vaguely written and did not spell out what specific acts constituted violation of the law.

3. In 1914 Congress passed the Clayton Act to clarify the intent of the Sherman Act. The Clayton Act declared that price discrimination, tying contracts, intercorporate stockholdings, and interlocking directorates are illegal whenever their effect is to lessen competition. It also exempted labor from antitrust laws.

4. The Federal Trade Commission Act of 1914 created the Federal Trade Commission (FTC) to administer the Clayton Act. Empowered to investigate, hold hearings, and issue cease-and-desist orders, the FTC's main role today is to police false or deceptive advertising practices and other forms of product misrepresentation.

5. Economists generally agree that the Robinson-Patman Act (1936) and the Miller-Tydings Act (1937) tended to inhibit competition rather than promote it. The Robinson-Patman Act sought to curb the buying power of mass distributors (chain stores), which allowed them to purchase their supplies at lower costs and pass these savings on in the form of lower prices at the retail level. The Miller-Tydings Act empowered manufacturers to enforce resale-price maintenance contracts with retailers.

6. The evolution of judicial interpretation of the antitrust laws has proceeded from judgments based on an evaluation of market conduct (the rule of reason doctrine) to judgments based on an evaluation of market structure. The rule of reason doctrine was initiated with the Standard Oil and American Tobacco Company cases of 1911 and held sway until the late 1930s, when the Alcoa case (settled in 1945) set the course for a new judicial interpretation based on market structure.

7. The Celler-Kefauver Antimerger Act (1950) prohibited one firm from acquiring the assets of another firm if the effect was to lessen competition. While antitrust policy has been quite successful in blocking vertical and horizontal mergers, it has had little effect on the wave of conglomerate mergers that began after World War II and peaked in the late 1960s.

302 THREE: MARKET STRUCTURE, PRICING, AND GOVERNMENT REGULATION

8. There are basically three schools of thought on the proper role of antitrust policy: (1) large firms and highly concentrated industries should be left alone, (2) antitrust laws should be revised to promote "workable competition," and (3) current antitrust laws should be more actively enforced and changes should be made in other policies that currently dampen competition.

9. There has been a movement toward deregulation in the regulated industries—railroads, trucking, airlines, broadcasting, and banking. Legislative action has substantially reduced the regulatory commissions' powers over such matters as rate setting, route assignments, entry of new firms, and broadcast rights. Deregulation appears to have resulted in increased competition, greater product selection, and lower prices—all to the benefit of the public.

KEY TERMS AND CONCEPTS

antitrust policy
conglomerate merger
dissolution
divestiture
exclusive dealing agreement
fair-trade laws
horizontal merger
predatory behavior
predatory pricing
resale-price maintenance contract
rule of reason
treble damages
tying contract
vertical merger
workable competition

QUESTIONS AND PROBLEMS

1. To what extent do you think the rule of reason doctrine would rely on industrial concentration ratios when examining an industry for possible antitrust law violations? Suppose an industry has a much higher concentration ratio than can be justified by economies of scale. How might this manifest itself in ways that would violate antitrust laws under the rule of reason doctrine? Why?

2. What is the relationship between the Sherman Act and the Clayton Act?

3. Consider the following news item.

> The American Bar Association said it will fight a civil antitrust suit by the Justice Department challenging the ABA's ban on advertising by lawyers. Last February the ABA moved to permit limited advertising if state bar associations approve, but several state bars have rejected the code-of-ethics change.

What aspects of antitrust law do you suppose the ABA's practices may violate?

4. A *Fortune* magazine editorial (June 1965) observed that "The U.S. economy might end up completely dominated by conglomerates happily trading with each other in a new kind of cartel system." What is your assessment of this statement?

5. Compare and contrast vertical and horizontal mergers in terms of their likely effects on market structure and the growth of monopoly power. How do the three *D*'s of antitrust policy deal with these types of merger activity?

6. In the electrical equipment industry price-fixing case of 1961, it was found that the executives of GE and Westinghouse met secretly with smaller producers to rig bids, fix prices, and allocate business among themselves. It was established that the conspirators used false names and blank stationery to correspond, and phases of the moon to signal which company would put in a "low" bid on a contract. Why was it necessary to dig up all this evidence on collusive activity when it would seem that simple observation of the prices charged would indicate that prices moved together?

7. What would each of the various schools of

thought on antitrust policy have to say about the following statement by Edmund Burke:

> One of the finest problems in legislature [is] to determine what the State ought to take upon itself to direct by the public wisdom, and what it ought to leave, with as little interference as possible, to individual exertion.

8. A distinguished authority on the economics of antitrust policy, E. S. Mason, once said: "Market power is the central problem which any effective antitrust policy must confront." What do you think the proponents of the various schools of thought on antitrust policy would have to say about this?

9. "The ICC is now primarily a forum at which private transportation interests settle their disputes. . . . As a passive forum the ICC has failed to provide for any useful . . . representation of the public interest" (Ralph Nader Study Group, 1970).

Explain what is mean by this quote.

13

Government Regulation: Dealing with Market Shortcomings

AFTER READING THIS CHAPTER, YOU WILL BE ABLE TO:

1. Explain why market outcomes may not be optimal due to the existence of public goods, externalities, imperfect information, and nonmarket goals.

2. Explain why it is important to assess the trade-offs between the benefits and costs of government regulation.

3. Show how benefit-cost analysis can be used to determine the optimal amount of government regulation.

4. Explain why the total elimination of pollution is not necessarily optimal and describe the government's role in environmental protection.

5. Describe and evaluate government efforts in regulating working conditions, product safety, and consumer advertising and labeling.

The U.S. economy is a mixed economy—one in which the questions of what and how much to produce, how to organize production, and for whom to produce are answered by a mixture of government regulation and control in some areas of the economy, coupled with a reliance on private enterprise and free markets in other areas. We have already examined government intervention in areas of the economy where monopoly, oligopoly, and collusion have threatened to diminish competition—a problem that has been attacked through antitrust legislation and government regulation (often controversial) of some markets. We have also seen how government has attempted to provide a minimum standard of living for all citizens through social security, minimum-wage legislation, and various welfare programs. All such forms of government intervention give recognition to the fact that some outcomes of pure market, laissez faire capitalism are undesirable—that indeed government intervention is sometimes necessary to improve on the results.

In this chapter we extend our analysis of the ways in which freely operating markets may not give satisfactory results. We will consider whether or not government regulation can be expected to improve matters and whether the costs of regulation are justified by the potential benefits. We will then examine the kinds of government regulation that attempt to correct shortcomings of the market mechanism. In particular, we will consider government regulation to protect the environment and to promote better working conditions, product safety, and consumer protection.

SHORTCOMINGS OF THE MARKET

We may identify four major problem areas for the market. First, markets cannot be depended on to provide certain products (such as national defense and lighthouses), called *public goods*. Second, markets do not always capture the full costs and benefits associated with the production of a particular good or service—these are the so-called *external* or *spillover* costs and benefits. Third, while markets convey information about prices, they sometimes suffer from a lack of other kinds of *information*—for example, information about the possible hazards of a complex product such as a new drug. Finally, some goals such as an equitable income distribution or equal employment opportunities often cannot be achieved through the market mechanism; these are the so-called *nonmarket goals*. Let us consider each of these market shortcomings in turn.

Public Goods

We briefly introduced the concept of a public good in Chapter 3. Here we will elaborate on this concept by distinguishing between a *pure public good* and a *near-public good*.

Pure Public Goods

A **pure public good** *is a good that cannot be provided to one person without being provided to others. That is, it is impossible to prevent joint consumption.* The beacon from a lighthouse is an example. If one ship in the vicinity can see the beacon, so can others. Suppose a shipping company were to buy and operate a lighthouse. There is no way it could exclude other shipping companies' ships from benefiting from the beacon, even though they contributed nothing to the purchase of the lighthouse. The other shipping companies would be so-called *free riders. A* **free rider** *is anyone who receives the benefits from a good or service without having to pay for it.*

Markets will fail to supply pure public goods precisely because of the free-rider problem. Since anyone can have all the benefits provided by a pure public good without paying, no one will pay for it. Therefore private producers will have no incentive to produce it. Hence despite the fact that a pure public good yields valuable benefits to society, the market mechanism will not provide such a good. Pure public goods must be provided by the government and paid for with tax money or with revenues from the sale of government bonds.[1]

In sum, a pure public good is *not* subject to the **exclusion principle.** *Any good whose benefits accrue only to those who purchase it is said to be subject to the exclusion principle.* Those who do not pay for the good are excluded from its benefits. If you buy a car, your neighbor is excluded from its benefits, unless you choose to allow him or her to use it.

What are some other examples of pure public goods? Our legal system is one. Laws that protect you also protect me, but neither of us would be willing to finance the system alone. Another example is national defense. Even if I am on welfare and pay no income taxes, our national defense system protects me as much as any multimillionaire who pays hundreds of thousands of dollars in income taxes. Neither I nor the multimillionaire would have any incentive to pay voluntarily for national defense, and, since it is provided, we are both free riders. (If it were not provided, neither of us individually could really make a significant contribution to it anyway, even though we both may value national defense highly.) The quality of the air we breathe is also a pure public good. If it is clean and free of pollutants for one, it is so for all. If many pay taxes to finance the costs of antipollution efforts, those who don't pay taxes share equally in the benefits as well—they are free riders.

If the legal system, national defense, and environmental protection were not provided by government, they would not be provided at all. For why should any individual producer of these services provide them, knowing that it is not possible to charge free riders for consuming the benefits—and why should any individual pay if he or she can be a free rider? In short, since no one would voluntarily pay for these services, no private producer would find it profitable to provide them. Yet they are important to our society, and so government is authorized to provide them.

Near-Public Goods

Near-public goods *are goods that are consumed jointly, though it is possible to exclude nonpaying customers.* Pure public goods are consumed jointly too, but it is *not* possible to exclude anyone from consuming them. Examples of near-public goods are athletic events, plays, movies, television and radio broadcasts, parks, and highways (toll roads). Government provision of pure public goods is necessary because of the free-rider problem. However, near-public goods are subject to the exclusion principle. Hence it is feasible for them to be provided by private producers responding to market demand.

In our economy we see near-public goods provided both publicly and privately. There is Public Radio and Public Television produced and supported by the government, while at the same time there are private broadcasting companies such as the major radio and television networks. There are government owned and operated parks, such as Yosemite National Park, and privately run parks such as Disneyland. There are also publicly provided as well as privately provided zoos.

Since near-public goods may be produced privately, why should the government ever produce them? Critics of government provision argue that since consumers get the good at a zero price, there is no way of knowing how much of it to provide. Is the cost of providing more of the good covered by what consumers would be willing to pay if they had to? This question suggests that government provision may result in either over- or underproduction of near-public goods. Society may end up devoting too many or too few resources to such goods, which is economically inefficient in either event. Hence, the case for government provision of near-public goods is not as persuasive as the case

---

[1] Note that the government may simply contract with private firms to have the good produced.

for government provision of pure public goods.

Externalities

We previously discussed externalities in Chapter 6. Here we will briefly review the concept to provide a basis for our discussion of government regulation.

Recall that **externalities** *are any costs or benefits that fall on others besides the buyers and sellers of a particular good or service.* Externalities are often referred to as *external costs* or *benefits, spillovers, neighborhood effects,* or *external economies* and *diseconomies.*

There are numerous examples of external costs. Nonsmokers trapped in a meeting room with smokers cannot avoid inhaling some of the smoke. The health hazard of the smoke is an external cost to the nonsmoker. Similarly, residents in the vicinity of a steel mill bear an external cost when smoke from the mill corrodes the paint on their houses, pollutes the air they breathe, and stunts the growth of the surrounding plant life. If residents feel they must move, then they bear an external cost in the form of moving expenses. When Uncle Jake cleans his false teeth ultrasonically, it may cause static on his neighbor's radio. The radio static is an external cost borne by the neighbor. Some electronic heating machines used to make plywood and plastic goods can cause serious interference with frequencies used by airport flight-control towers. The resulting reduction in air passenger safety, possibly leading to airline crashes, is an external cost borne by airlines and their passengers.

Examples of external benefits are not hard to find either. You may invest considerable time and money caring for your yard. Your neighbor reaps the external benefit of viewing a beautiful lawn and garden without spending a cent. If you buy a flu shot, you protect yourself from sickness, an obvious benefit to you. However, others get an external benefit because they are less likely to catch the flu from you. Similarly, if you spend money maintaining the brakes on your car, you bestow an external benefit on other drivers because your car is now less likely to run into them. A pure public good is an extreme example of a good that provides external benefits to parties not directly involved in the purchase or sale of the good. A shipping company may pay you to provide a lighthouse beacon. But nonpaying shippers receive an external benefit because they can use the beacon free of charge—they are free riders, as are all recipients of external benefits.

Society's Loss Due to External Costs

Recall our discussion of external costs in Chapter 6. There we considered an industry (any industry) that pollutes the environment while producing its product. The cost of cleaning up or suffering the consequences is an external cost borne by others. Hence this cost is not included in the industry or market supply curve S shown in Figure 13-1. Given the market demand curve D, the equilibrium quantity produced and sold without regard for this external cost is q_n and the equilibrium price is p_n.

Suppose the firms in the industry had to pay some or all of the environmental cleanup costs associated with the production of each unit of output. These costs would be added to the firms' other production costs to give the market supply curve S_a, which includes all costs and hence lies above S. The equilibrium quantity produced and sold would now be q_0, an amount smaller than q_n. The equilibrium price would be p_0, which is higher than p_n. In this new equilibrium, the cost of pollution would be borne entirely by the buyers and sellers of the product—it is no longer borne by nonconsenting third parties.

The new equilibrium is optimal from society's standpoint; the old equilibrium is not. Why? Because the external costs associated with a good—costs not borne by the buyers and sellers of the good—foster the production of additional units of output that are not valued as much as the cost of producing them. This can be seen in Figure 13-1 from the fact that the supply curve S_a (which in-

FIGURE 13-1 Society's Loss Due to External Costs

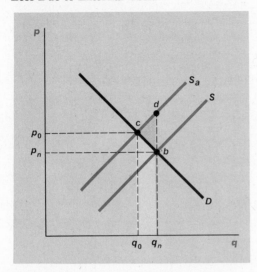

The presence of external costs means that the actual market supply curve S lies below the supply curve S_a that includes all costs associated with production of the good. The external (or spillover) costs lead to the production of additional units of the good (equal to $q_n - q_0$) that are not valued as much as the cost of producing them. The dollar amount of this excess of costs over value equals the area cbd; it represents society's loss due to external costs when the amount q_n is produced.

cludes all costs) lies above the demand curve D for all units of the good from q_0 to q_n. The dollar value of the total benefits to buyers of this additional quantity $q_n - q_0$ of the good is represented by the area q_0q_nbc. The cost, or dollar value, of the resources used to produce these additional units is represented by the area q_0q_ndc. The dollar amount by which the costs of the additional units *exceed* their benefits is represented by the area cbd. This is society's loss due to external costs (spillover costs).

This loss is a consequence of the fact that output q_n exceeds the optimal output level q_0—resources are overallocated to the pro-

duction of this good. The price per unit of the good p_n fails to cover the costs of producing the good. Society's loss due to external costs is the result of a market shortcoming— namely, a failure to prevent some of the costs of the good from being borne by nonconsenting third parties.

Society's Loss Due to Missed Opportunities: External Benefits

In our discussion of external benefits in Chapter 6 we saw that if a good provides benefits to others who do not buy the good, these spillover, or external, benefits are not reflected in the market demand curve. For example, the market demand curve for flu shots reflects the value of their benefits to the people who buy them to prevent themselves from contracting the flu. It does not reflect the benefits of the flu shots to those who don't buy them, but who are nonetheless better off due to the reduction in the spread of a contagious disease.

Since the market demand curve for goods and services providing external benefits does not reflect the full value of these benefits, it must lie below a demand curve that is drawn to include them. Figure 13–2 shows a hypothetical demand curve D and supply curve S for flu shots. The market equilibrium quantity of flu shots supplied and purchased is q_n, and the equilibrium price is p_n. If the value of the external (or spillover) benefits to society at large from these flu shots were added on to D, we would get the demand curve D_a. Since D_a includes the value of all benefits, it lies above D. The equilibrium quantity produced and sold would now be q_0, an amount larger than q_n, and the equilibrium price would be p_0, which is higher than p_n.

Why is the new equilibrium, q_0 and p_0, optimal from society's standpoint? Because when external benefits are associated with a good—benefits that accrue to others who don't pay for it—the market will not produce enough of the good. When only q_n units of the good are produced, society forgoes a quantity of goods ($q_0 - q_n$) that it values

FIGURE 13-2   External Benefits: Society's Loss Due to Missed Opportunities

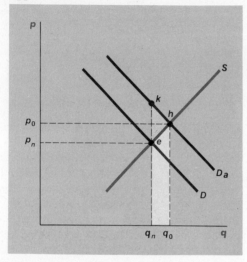

The presence of external benefits means that the market demand curve D lies below the demand curve D_a that includes the value of all benefits associated with the good. Because of the external (or spillover) benefits, the market fails to produce additional units of the good (the quantity $q_0 - q_n$) that are valued more than the cost of producing them. The dollar amount of this excess of benefits over costs equals the area ehk; it represents society's loss because the market produces less than the optimal amount of the good.

more than the cost of producing them. This can be seen in Figure 13–2 from the fact that the demand curve D_a (which includes the value of all benefits) lies above the supply curve S between output quantities q_n and q_0. The dollar value of the benefits to society of the additional quantity $q_0 - q_n$ of the good is represented by the area q_nq_0hk. The cost of the resources used to produce these additional units is represented by the area q_nq_0he. The dollar amount by which the total benefits of these additional units *exceed* their cost is represented by the area ehk. This represents society's loss due to the missed oppor-

tunity of not having the additional output from q_n to q_0—a loss caused by the failure of the market to capture external benefits.

The loss reflects the fact that output q_n falls short of the optimal output level q_0. Resources are underallocated to the production of this good because the price per unit of the good p_n fails to reflect the full value of the good.

In summary, *where there are external costs, the market mechanism tends to encourage overproduction, the provision of goods whose costs exceed the value of their benefits. Where there are external benefits, the market mechanism gives rise to underproduction, the failure to provide goods even though the value of their benefits exceeds their costs.*

Imperfect Information

The market mechanism may fail to provide adequate information. Information is an economic good; it has value. Consumers spend time and money seeking information about products—how good is the product, how safe, what are the alternatives, how much does the product cost in one store as compared to another? Sometimes the information desired is prohibitively expensive or perhaps unavailable at any price. For example, a new drug may have side effects that are as yet unknown. Buyers must always make decisions to varying degrees on the basis of imperfect information. To what extent is there a conflict between producer and consumer interests where product information is concerned? To what extent is product information a public good? To what extent is the lack of perfect information fit cause for government market intervention?

Conflict Between Consumer and Producer Interests

A buyer who purchases a product repeatedly will become quite familiar with its characteristics by trial and error. Foods, beverages, clothing, haircuts, hair permanents, restaurant meals, and dry cleaning are all examples of goods and services whose producers are very dependent on repeat sales if they are to stay in business. Producers have a considerable incentive to ensure consumer satisfaction, because consumers will become fairly well informed about their products in a short period of time. If brand A soap causes a skin rash or brand B toothpaste tastes bitter, sales will drop off fairly rapidly. However, even repeat-purchase items can have characteristics that consumers may not learn about on their own. For example, it is typically not in the producer's best self-interest to inform consumers about possible health hazards associated with long-run use of a product. Cigarette companies were certainly not pleased when the Surgeon General forced them to print health-hazard warnings on cigarette packages. There is, then, often a disparity between what consumers would like to know about a product and what producers want them to know.

Products that are only purchased infrequently, or that are too complex for the typical consumer to evaluate knowledgeably tend to allow greater scope for conflict between consumer and producer interest. Suppose you hire a contractor to build a house. Suppose 10 years later you discover that faulty foundations are cracking, giving rise to basement flooding during heavy rains. The contractor may have long since become wealthy building subdivisions of homes like yours. The market's failure to provide information that protects home buyers from such calamities is one reason most local governments establish building codes. Drugs provide another good example of product complexity that is beyond the information-gathering ability of the consumer. Imperfect information concerning these products has given rise to significant government regulation. And sometimes the cost of gathering information is so high that the use of standards set by government regulatory agencies may be a cheap substitute for other, expensive information.

At its worst, the conflict between consumer and producer interests can lead to producer attempts to deceive consumers deliberately. Such deception may take the form of false advertising claims and misleading labeling of products. Subtle manipulation of demand through advertising that appeals to the consumer's ego or emotions is common. Deceptive advertising and labeling amount to attempts to misinform the consumer. Over the years increasing government regulation has been used in an attempt to curb such practices. At the same time, a good deal of government activity has been devoted to the provision of additional product information.

Is Product Information a Near-Public Good?

As we already noted, information is an economic good. There is a market for it. Sellers spend money on advertising to spread information about their wares in trade journals, in newspapers, and on radio and television. Consumers spend money to get information from shoppers' guides, newspapers, and magazines. (Recall our discussion of the information content of advertising in Chapters 10 and 11.) There are private organizations that specialize in selling information to consumers.

One example is *Consumer Reports,* a magazine that contains reports on the results of its own extensive testing of hundreds of products. *Consumer Reports* provides this information for the price of the magazine; to avoid conflicts of interest, it accepts no advertising. The information provided by *Consumer Reports* is very much in the nature of a near-public good. It cannot be provided to the initial purchaser without possibly providing it to others who do not pay—it is not entirely subject to the exclusion principle. Only the original purchaser must pay the price of the magazine. Anybody can read a copy at the public library for nothing. Obviously many people could read a single copy, yet the publisher would receive only the purchase price of that one copy. The publishers of such information are unable to capture the full value of the service provided, because they cannot keep those who don't pay for the information from getting it.

In short, the external benefits from *Consumer Reports* are probably considerable. As we saw in Figure 13–2, this means that the market produces less of this information than is optimal from society's standpoint. Hence, it may be argued that government action is appropriate to provide additional product information. Indeed, as will be discussed below, there has been a good deal of government activity in this area.

Nonmarket Goals

Certain of the goals and values of any society are either ill-served or not served at all by the marketplace. For instance, markets do not keep people from harming themselves and each other in ways that society considers unacceptable. Also, freely working markets will reward some and penalize others to extremes that may conflict with society's sense of fairness and justice.

Protecting Individuals from Themselves and Others

Markets are capable of providing many kinds of goods and services that society at large considers harmful to the buyer. The government may declare the production and sale of such products illegal or limit their distribution in some way. For example, the government prohibits the sale of hard drugs such as heroin. Some states ban the sale of firecrackers. Other states essentially require the purchase of crash helmets because they have laws requiring motorcycle riders to wear them. Often there is considerable controversy about whether the government is too overbearing in such regulation. One of the most notable examples of controversial legislation was the Volstead Act (1919), which banned the production and sale of alcoholic beverages in the United States. This law proved to be so unpopular and difficult to enforce that it was repealed in 1933.

People also have to be protected from one another. (Of course, this is a major reason why governments and the rule of law exist in the first place.) Government intervention in the marketplace for this purpose includes child-labor laws that protect children from exploitation by establishing a minimum working age. Laws requiring children to have a minimum amount of schooling tend to restrain parents from extracting full-time labor services from their children in the home or on the farm. The Equal Employment Opportunity Commission attempts to prevent discrimination against minorities in the labor market. Of course, in a broader sense, antitrust laws, welfare policies, and regulations governing product safety, working conditions, and environmental quality are all intended to protect individuals from one another. All such laws, policies, and regulations may be regarded as responses to market shortcomings.

Income Redistribution

Freely working markets will reward some and penalize others. Those who are hardworking, able, and lucky may live handsomely by the market. Most people have little sympathy for the able-bodied but lazy whom the markets treats sternly. But the impersonal forces of the market are indifferent to the disabled, the handicapped, and others beset by misfortune beyond their control. Society generally takes the attitude that, in such cases, private charitable organizations, government policies, or both should be used to redistribute income from the more fortunate to the less fortunate. (We will examine a number of policies with this goal in Chapter 17, where we will focus on the problems of poverty.)

Some argue that antipoverty efforts are a public good. When you give money to private charity to help alleviate poverty, you bestow external benefits on nongivers. That is, the benefits that stem from poverty reduction (a decline in disease, slums, and so forth) accrue to society at large. Hence each would-be giver is tempted to be a free rider—let the other person do the giving. As illustratated in Figure 13–2, whenever there are external benefits associated with a good, there will be underproduction of the good—in this case, antipoverty efforts.

CHECKPOINT* 13–1

Some machines used to make plywood are as powerful as large AM radio stations. If not contained by shields, the machines' signals can cause serious interference with frequencies used by airport flight-control towers. Some machine owners are reluctant to install the shields because of their high cost. But a letter from the FCC informing them they may be liable for airline crashes usually gives them an incentive. How is the FCC's letter to the plywood makers likely to affect the price and quantity of plywood bought and sold? Why? The Nevada Highway Patrol sought FCC help to stop interference with mobile radio signals caused by video amusement machines. How would you describe the nature of the external costs caused by the video amusement machines that the Nevada Highway Patrol complains about? How would you measure such costs?

*Answers to all Checkpoints can be found at the back of the text.

GOVERNMENT REGULATION: A RESPONSE TO MARKET SHORTCOMINGS

When markets perform inadequately in the ways we have discussed, should government regulations be used in an attempt to attain perfection, or are there trade-offs between the reduction of shortcomings and its costs? How do we know how much government regulation is needed? And what about the possibility that government regulation will make matters worse? We now turn to these questions. In addition we will also briefly ex-

amine four areas of government regulation: protection of the environment, working conditions, product safety, and consumer protection—the last through regulations aimed at preventing deceptive advertising and labeling.

How Much Government Regulation Is Appropriate?

How do we know how much government regulation is needed to correct the undesirable consequences of market shortcomings? Attempts to answer this question are a source of continual, often heated debate among politicians, policymakers, and citizens and special interests affected by regulation. The kind of regulation called for can vary greatly from one type of market shortcoming to another. But in all cases, in determining the appropriate amount of regulation, we must recognize that there is a trade-off between the benefits and costs of regulation. Moreover, we should be aware that any regulation can have perverse effects, outcomes quite the opposite of those intended.

Trade-offs Between the Costs and Benefits of Regulation

Economics is a study of trade-offs. To have more of one thing we have to give up a certain amount of something else. The cost (or opportunity cost) of having more of one thing is the value of the other things that must be given up. *Intelligent decisions about the appropriate amount of regulation require recognition of the fact that regulation has a cost too, and that there is a trade-off between the costs and benefits of regulation.*

Consider government regulation to promote safety. Some argue that it is impossible to put a dollar value on human suffering or human life. However, any decision concerning the imposition of safety regulations unavoidably makes such a valuation. For example, advocates of the 55-mile-per-hour speed limit argue that the regulation saves lives. They judge the saving of those lives (along with any fuel savings) to be more valuable than the time that is lost through slower travel. On the other hand, those who advocate increasing the speed limit to 70 miles per hour imply that the time saved is worth more than the reduction in suffering and loss of life that results from fewer traffic accidents at the lower speed. Each of the two groups implicitly argues that there is a trade-off between the value of human lives and the value of time.

If human life were priceless, people would not travel in airplanes, work on skyscrapers, build bridges, drive motorcycles, mine coal, or go to war. The question, then, is not whether or not a value can be placed on human life; when society sets any policy or takes any action, it implicitly decides on such a value. The only question is whether that value is acceptable. Most automobiles can go 80 miles per hour. But society values life too highly to make 80 the acceptable speed limit.

Regulation and Perverse Results

It has been said that the road to hell is paved with good intentions. Sometimes, regulations that are motivated by the best of intentions can actually make matters worse.

For example, most people would agree on the desirability of some minimum level of qualifications for doctors and health care facilities. Regulations in most states stipulate that many medical services may be provided only by a licensed physician. Nurses and paramedics could provide some of these services equally well, but regulations prevent them from doing so. Such regulations tend to restrict the supply of medical care and thus drive up its price. The result is that people who otherwise would seek professional care now resort to home remedies: bandages instead of stitches, over-the-counter medicines instead of more effective prescription drugs, birth at home instead of in hospitals. Thus, as regulation aimed at improving the quality of health care drives up its price, the consumption of professional medical services

(and perhaps the overall quality of health care) declines.

Benefit-Cost Analysis

The optimal amount of regulation should be determined in the way we determine the optimal amount of any other good or service. That is, *regulation should be extended up to the point where the dollar value of the last unit of benefit just equals the cost of obtaining it.* A determination of the optimal amount of regulation according to this principle requires a benefit-cost analysis. We will illustrate how benefit-cost analysis can be used to determine the appropriate amount of regulation for environmental protection.

Environmental Protection

Environmental pollution is an earmark of industrialized societies. It plagues capitalist, socialist, and communist countries alike. It is an inevitable consequence of economic growth, the increase in the output of goods and services per capita. Industrialization and increased production of goods and services also mean increased production of "bads" and "disservices": noxious waste products that pollute air and waterways; junkyards, slag heaps, smokestacks, derricks, and mining and industrial sites that spoil the landscape; and urban and suburban congestion and noise that cause tension and stress.

The costs imposed on society by these bads and disservices take the form of health and property damage and, generally, an impaired quality of life. Moreover, these costs are external, or spillover, costs—they are borne by parties other than the producers and buyers of the goods whose production causes them. These costs cannot be eliminated, but they can be shifted to the parties who cause them. This is done by internalizing such costs to the markets where they occur.

For example, suppose the residents in the vicinity of a steel mill incur property damage and health-care costs as a consequence of air pollution caused by the mill. If the steel mill is required to purchase equipment that eliminates its emission of air pollutants, then the cost of the pollution is shifted to those directly involved in the production and sale of steel. Those who buy and use steel now pay all the costs of producing steel; none of the cost is imposed on people living near the steel mill. The supply curve of steel is shifted leftward as discussed in connection with Figure 13–1. Those who buy steel now pay a higher price, which includes the cost of pollution. (For a discussion of how this cost is distributed between buyers and sellers, see Chapter 6.)

Environmental pollution occurs because clean air and clean rivers, lakes, and oceans are public goods. It is impossible to keep the air or water clean for some in a region and not for others. The exclusion principle does not apply.

A firm that *voluntarily* invested in equipment to reduce the amount of pollutants emitted from its smokestacks would not be able to charge for this service. Why? Because those who won't pay will have clean air just the same as those who do. Everyone has an incentive to be a free rider and "let the other guy pay." If the firm charged a higher price for its product to cover the cost of its antipollution efforts, it would lose sales to competitors who did not incur such costs and who therefore could charge lower prices. Environmental protection thus seems to require government regulation. The tough questions are, How much and in what form?

How Much Pollution Control: Benefits Versus Costs

Regulation, like any "product," provides certain benefits and gives rise to certain costs. These benefits and costs vary as the amount of regulation varies. A **benefit-cost analysis** is an examination of the benefits and costs associated with differing levels of output (here the output is regulation) to determine the most effective level according to some criterion.

To illustrate, let's consider a hypothetical benefit-cost analysis of pollution control in a particular region, as illustrated in Table 13–1. Suppose that as a by-product of its production process, a large company is polluting the air, giving rise to external, or spillover, costs. In the absence of government regulation requiring the company to control its pollution, suppose the company's smokestacks annually emit 100,000 units of pollutant (row 1, column 1 of Table 13–1), causing external costs equal to $1 million of damage (external costs) to the surrounding area (row 1, column 2 of Table 13–1). The government decides to take action to regulate this pollution. Should government regulators force the company to stop polluting entirely, or should they require only that some portion of the pollutant be removed from smokestack emissions?

The answer is that *regulators should require the company to remove pollutants from smokestack emissions up to the point where the marginal cost of pollution reduction equals the marginal benefit of pollution reduction.*

Suppose the company is required to reduce pollution from 100,000 to 90,000 units (column 1, rows 1 and 2). Pollution damage would be reduced from $1 million to $900,000 (column 2, rows 1 and 2), so that the marginal benefit of pollution reduction is $100,000 (column 3). The total cost to the company of reducing pollution this much is $10,000 (column 4, row 2), which is also the marginal cost (column 5) since the company starts from a level of zero pollution expenditures. Total benefits from pollution reduction amount to $100,000 (column 6, row 2). This amount of pollution reduction is clearly worthwhile since the marginal benefit of $100,000 (column 3) certainly exceeds the marginal cost of $10,000 (column 5). In fact, examination of columns 3 and 5 indicates that the marginal benefits of increasing pollution reduction continue to exceed the marginal cost of such reduction until pollution

TABLE 13-1 Benefit-Cost Analysis for Pollution Control (Hypothetical Data)

	(1) Annual Units of Pollution (Thousands)	(2) Annual Pollution Damage (Thousands of Dollars)	(3) Marginal Benefit of 10,000 Units of Added Pollution Reduction (Thousands of Dollars)	(4) Annual Total Costs of Pollution Reduction (Thousands of Dollars)	(5) Marginal Cost of 10,000 Additional Units of Pollution Reduction (Thousands of Dollars)	(6) Total Benefits Equal Total Reduction in Pollution Damage (Thousands of Dollars)	(7) Net Gain Equals (6) Minus (4) (Thousands of Dollars)
1.	100	$1,000		$ 0		$ 0	$ 0
2.	90	900	$100	10	$ 10	100	90
3.	80	750	150	25	15	250	225
4.	70	575	175	50	25	425	375
5.	60	460	115	90	40	540	450
6.	50	350	110	150	60	650	500
7.	40	250	100	235	85	750	515
8.	30	160	90	355	120	840	485
9.	20	80	80	555	200	920	365
10.	10	35	45	905	350	965	60
11.	0	0	35	1,405	500	1,000	-405

has been reduced to a level of 40,000 units (column 1, row 7). Reducing pollution from 50,000 to 40,000 units gives rise to marginal benefits of $100,000, which exceeds the marginal cost of $85,000 associated with reducing pollution by another 10,000 units.

It would not be worthwhile to force the company to reduce pollution to 30,000 units (column 1, row 8). Why? Because the required additional, or marginal, cost of $120,000 (column 5) would exceed the additional, or marginal, benefit of $90,000 (column 3). This would amount to an overallocation of resources to pollution control.

In sum, *the marginal benefit-marginal cost rule implies that pollution control should be expanded as long as marginal benefits* (column 3) *exceed marginal costs* (column 5). According to this criterion, the most effective amount of control is at, or as close as possible to, that point where marginal benefits equal marginal costs. Note that *this rule maximizes the excess of total benefits over total costs* (column 7); *that is, it provides the greatest net gain from pollution control* (equal to $515,000, column 7, row 7). In our example, government pollution regulations should require that the company not emit more than 40,000 units of pollution annually.

Three important observations should be made at this point.

1. The Optimal Level of Control. The total elimination of pollution is not necessarily optimal. We know it is not optimal to reduce speed limits to the point where there are no traffic accidents. The benefit-cost analysis of our pollution control problem (Table 13-1) shows why it is not optimal to eliminate pollution completely. The total annual cost of reducing pollution to zero is $1,405,000 (column 4, row 11). The total benefits resulting from the complete elimination of pollution damage equal $1 million (column 6, row 11). The net gain is *minus* $405 million (column 7, row 11), a loss! In other words, the cost of completely eliminating pollution exceeds the value of the benefits—it isn't worth it. Com-

plete elimination of pollution would be optimal only if the marginal cost of pollution reduction were always less than the marginal benefits. While this is not true for our example in Table 13-1, it could be the case for certain kinds of pollution problems. In any event, a benefit-cost analysis is necessary to determine the optimal amount of pollution control. More generally, *a benefit-cost analysis is required to determine the optimal amount of any form of government regulation.*

2. Enforcing Pollution Control. With the benefit-cost data of Table 13-1, government regulators could calculate the optimal pollution level as we have. They could use either of two alternative schemes to enforce pollution control: (a) adopt legislated standards, or (b) levy pollution emission taxes.

(a) *Legislated standards.* The government could pass laws empowering government regulators to establish minimum allowable levels of pollution. For instance, regulators could declare it illegal for the company of Table 13-1 to emit pollutants in excess of 40,000 units per year (row 7). If the law were backed by sufficiently stiff fines and possible court action, the company could be compelled to incur the $235,000 cost of abiding by the 40,000 units per year pollution limit.

(b) *Pollution emission taxes.* The government could also achieve the optimal pollution level by placing a tax on pollution. For example, if the government levies a pollution tax of $90,000 for each 10,000 units of pollutants, the company in Table 13-1 would have an incentive to keep pollution down to the optimal level of 40,000 units. To see why, note that the marginal cost of reducing pollution by another 10,000 units is less than $90,000 (column 5, rows 1-7) all the way to the point where pollution has been reduced to a level of 40,000 units. To this point it is cheaper for the company to pay the cost of reducing pollution than to pay the pollution tax. However, the company will find it cheaper to pay the pollution tax on the remaining 40,000 units of pollution. Why? Because the marginal cost of eliminating each successive 10,000 units of pollution once the pollution level has been reduced to 40,000 units is always greater than the $90,000 tax per 10,000 units of pollution. (That is, the last four entries in column 5 are all greater than $90,000.)

You would find it instructive at this point to answer questions 4 and 5 at the end of this chapter.

3. Problems of Measurement. In our discussion to this point, we have assumed that government regulators know the dollar value of the pollution damage associated with each level of pollution. It also has been assumed that they can measure the quantity and nature of the pollution as well as the benefits and costs of preventing it. In other words, we have assumed that the government regulators know all the data in Table 13–1. In reality this is rarely the case. Deciding what is the optimal level of pollution regulation is therefore very difficult in practice. Nonetheless, *a benefit-cost analysis forces the analyst to ask the right questions and to seek the information needed for wise decision making.*

Government's Role in Environmental Protection

The U.S. government has a long history of involvement in environmental protection, although such activities have not always been labeled as such. This history dates at least from the late nineteenth century, when the first national forest area was set aside to prevent destruction by loggers and commercial developers. At about this time the government also became engaged in water resource management aimed at the reclamation of arid and semiarid lands in the West. Government involvement in land and water resource management was extended significantly with the formation of the Tennessee Valley Authority (1933) and the Bureau of Land Management (1946). During the 1960s and 1970s, growing concern about air and water pollution gave rise to new legislation and new government

agencies intended to establish and enforce air and water quality standards. Table 13–2 summarizes the purposes and functions of the more important legislative acts and government agencies concerned with environmental protection.

In recent years the Environmental Protection Agency (EPA) has had the major responsibility for setting standards and enforcing legislation for environmental protection. While the EPA has brought about pollution reduction in some areas of our economy, it has frequently been criticized for not paying enough attention to the costs of these reductions. Most critics believe the EPA should put more emphasis on benefit-cost analysis in assessing the effectiveness of its regulations.

CHECKPOINT 13-2
In the benefit-cost analysis example of Table 13–1, suppose the marginal cost of pollution reduction were $70,000 higher at every level—that is, assume every entry in column 5 is larger by $70,000. What would be the optimal level of pollution?

Working Conditions

Can the market effectively deal with problems of occupational health and safety? Those who say yes argue as follows. Workers will take hazardous jobs only if they are offered higher wages to compensate for the increased risk of injury. Employers will reduce work hazards if it costs less than paying higher wages. On the other hand, if paying higher wages is cheaper than reducing hazards, then workers will be compensated for the hazards.

Those who disagree with this argument claim there are factors that hamper the labor market's ability to deal effectively with problems of occupational health and safety. They argue that often there is inadequate information on the relationship between job conditions and health and safety hazards. For example, the effects of many health risks, such

TABLE 13-2 U.S. Government Agencies and Legislation for Environmental Protection

Agency or Legislation	Date	Purpose or Function
Bureau of Reclamation, Department of the Interior	1902	Constructs, operates, and maintains works for the storage, diversion, and development of waters for the reclamation of arid and semiarid lands in the West.
Forest Service, Department of Agriculture	1905	Manages the national forests and grasslands of the United States.
Tennessee Valley Authority (TVA)	1933	First direct government involvement in energy production and marketing; also involved in flood control, recreation improvement, and forestry and wildlife development.
Bureau of Land Management, Department of the Interior	1946	Manages public land, mainly in the West and Alaska.
Federal Maritime Commission	1961	Among other things, ensures that financial responsibility for cleanup of spills of oil or hazardous substances is assigned.
Motor Vehicle Pollution Control Act	1965	First major environmental law authorizing auto emissions standards.
Environmental Protection Agency (EPA)	1970	Develops and administers standards for air and water quality as well as strategies for controlling toxic substances.
Clean Air Amendments	1970	Directed EPA to establish minimum ambient standards for air quality.
Water Pollution Control Act	1970	Authorized grants to demonstrate new methods and techniques and to establish programs to train people in water management.
Water Pollution Act Amendments	1972	Authorized EPA to set effluent standards for both privately and publicly owned plants.
Office of Surface Mining, Department of the Interior	1977	Establishes standards for regulating strip mining.

as exposure to cancer-causing substances, may not show up for years, or such hazards may not be known during the term of employment. Unsafe or unhealthy working conditions also may give rise to external costs—costs borne by parties other than the employer and employee. For instance, workers exposed to certain substances subsequently may have children with birth defects attrib-utable to this exposure—the children are the injured third parties. Imperfect information and the presence of external costs will tend to inhibit workers from demanding wages adequate to compensate for health and safety hazards. Therefore employers will not have adequate incentive to incur the costs of reducing work hazards, and consequently there will be an underallocation of resources to the maintenance of health and safety in the workplace. It can be argued that these considerations make a case for government regulation of occupational health and safety.

Government Regulation of Workplace Safety Standards

The accident rate in U.S. manufacturing increased by over 25 percent between 1960 and 1970. An alarmed Congress passed the Occupational Health and Safety Act of 1970 to deal with the "on-the-job health and safety crisis." The legislation was intended "to assure so far as possible every working man and woman in the nation safe and healthful working conditions." The act created the Occupational Safety and Health Administration (OSHA) and authorized it to set and enforce occupational health and safety standards.

OSHA regulations are enforced by unannounced inspections (though firms may require a search warrant) triggered by employee complaints, serious or fatal accidents, or above-average injury frequencies in a particular industry or workplace. Firms in violation of regulations may be warned, cited, or fined, depending on the severity and number of violations. How well has OSHA worked, and how might it be improved?

OSHA's Performance. OSHA has encountered a good deal of ill will from the business community. No doubt this is somewhat unavoidable, given OSHA's mission. However, OSHA's critics have raised issues that merit serious concern.

One common complaint is that OSHA's health and safety regulations are often complex and arbitrary. This problem is largely due to the fact that within 1 month of the agency's establishment it adopted 4,000 standards based on prior regulations and industry codes. Few of these were carefully reviewed. In 1978 OSHA responded to the "complex and arbitrary" charge by eliminating nearly 1,000 standards deemed more nuisance than helpful.

OSHA has also been criticized for not giving enough consideration to the cost of complying with its standards. The cost burden on firms may take the form of increased record keeping, decreased labor productivity due to required changes in work practices, and the purchase or modification of capital equipment to meet OSHA standards.

Some of OSHA's critics charge that it has not really reduced injuries. Their studies conclude that OSHA has not had a statistically significant effect on injury rates.[2]

Improving OSHA's Performance. Most critics agree that OSHA's performance would be considerably improved if the agency were required to carry out benefit-cost analyses of its regulations. Such analyses should be done before imposing a regulation, and they should be applied on a continuing basis to existing regulations to monitor their effectiveness. In a decision completely counter to this point of view, the Supreme Court ruled in June 1981 that OSHA must protect workers from toxic substances to the greatest extent feasible, regardless of how large the cost or how small the benefit.

Another recommendation frequently made by critics is that OSHA change the nature of its regulations from prescriptive standards to performance standards. OSHA's safety regulations are usually in the form of prescriptive standards; that is, they tell a firm *what* it must do to avoid violations. For example, a prescriptive standard would indicate exactly what kind of equipment a firm must install to avoid a certain kind of injury, whereas a performance standard would indicate the desired safety objective and allow the firm to decide what to do to meet that objective. For example, a performance standard would tell a firm that the occurrence of a certain kind of injury must be kept to some minimum level.

[2] See A. L. Nichols and R. Zeckhauser, "Government Comes to the Workplace: An Assessment of OSHA," *Public Interest* (Fall 1977), pp. 36–69; and W. K. Viscusi, "The Impact of Occupational Safety and Health Regulation," *Bell Journal of Economics,* vol. 10, no. 1 (Spring 1978), pp. 117–140.

Controversy Over Benefit-Cost Analysis— How Much Is Human Life Worth?[1]

When benefit-cost analysis is applied to regulation of working conditions there is typically a conflict of interest between the firms, or industry, regulated and the intended beneficiaries, the workers. The firms who bear the direct costs may try to discourage regulation by overstating the costs and understating the benefits. The workers who reap the benefits have an incentive to understate the costs and overstate the benefits. OSHA's attempts to curb brown lung disease among cotton-mill workers provide an interesting example of the controversial issues involved.

Controlling Cotton Dust

Brown lung (known medically as byssinosis) is a crippling respiratory disease affecting cotton-mill workers who are exposed to high cotton dust levels. One way to reduce the risk of brown lung at all stages of production is improving the ginning process to remove more trash (twigs and bract that grow at the base of the cotton boll). Ginning is performed by different firms than milling. When OSHA proposed weak regulations on ginning in 1977, the ginner's lobby prevented their adoption. However, when OSHA was created in 1970, cotton dust exposure regulations had been imposed on mills. These regulations were tightened in 1976 and 1978.

The American Textile Manufacturers Institute challenged the 1978 standard, arguing that OSHA had not justified it on the basis of a benefit-cost analysis. This line of argument had implications for potential regulation of thousands of other hazardous substances.

[1] Adapted from "OSHA Hits Brown Lung Rules," *Dollars and Sense,* May/June 1982.

Application of Benefit-Cost Analysis

How do you come up with a dollar figure for the benefit of a long healthy life, or retirement with dignity? Complicating the problem is the difficulty of adding up the benefits of regulation when the full health impact of brown lung is not known. And where do you get reliable numbers on the costs of regulation to the industry?

One way to figure the benefits to workers is to calculate how much more income a worker who dies or is forced to retire would have made if he or she had worked a normal lifetime. When adding up these income figures each year's income is discounted more (given less weight) the further it is in the future. This method of putting a value on human life strikes some people as inhumane, but courts are increasingly accepting such a standard when settling liability claims in all kinds of cases involving injury and death. In the case of cotton-mill workers it has also been argued that since about half the labor force is female, and one-fifth is black, calculating the value of a worker's life on the basis of prevailing wage levels reflects sex and racial discrimination, and thus unfairly "biases" the value of benefit calculations downward.

As for costs to the industry, the manufacturers insisted during the 1977 OSHA hearings that compliance with new standards would cost as much as $2.3 billion. However they refused to release information about the cost of new equipment that would meet OSHA's standards. The Textile Workers Union responded by producing data from Treasury Department documents that showed industry estimates of the cost of the new machinery to be $450 million, not $2.3 billion.

The Supreme Court Ruling of 1981

The manufacturers' challenge to the 1978 regulations was finally denied by the Supreme Court in 1981. The Court argued that the Occupational Safety and Health Act of 1970 "places the benefit of worker health above all other considerations except the feasibility of achieving that benefit." This was a serious setback for the use of benefit-cost analysis in determining the optimal amount of regulation of working conditions.

Questions

1. If benefit-cost analysis were used to determine the optimal amount of regulation to control brown lung, what would ultimately happen to the incidence of death from brown lung if cotton-mill worker wages fell, other things being equal?

2. When making a benefit-cost calculation for regulation to control brown lung, how and why might you want to take account of the incidence of cigarette smoking among cotton-mill workers?

It would be left to the firm to decide the most efficient way to do this. The reasoning behind a performance standard is that the firm has a greater incentive than an outsider (the government regulator) to find the least costly way of achieving a given safety objective.

Government Regulation of Other Working Conditions

We noted earlier that any society has certain goals and values that are either ill-served or not served at all by the marketplace. For example, the market does not prevent people from exploiting one another in ways that society considers unacceptable. Some government regulation of working conditions is motivated by just such concerns.

The Fair Labor Standards Act (1938) sought to enforce minimum-wage laws, to establish 40 hours as the standard workweek, with premium pay for overtime, and to restrict the manner and use of child labor. Such an act expresses society's sense of fairness and decency and its awareness that an unfettered labor market can ignore such concerns. (Whether a minimum wage really helps workers is of course a much debated issue—see Chapter 17.)

During the 1960s society became acutely concerned that people could suffer economic hardship because they were discriminated against in the labor market for reasons beyond their control—race, sex, religion, or nationality. The Equal Pay Act (1963), the Civil Rights Act (1964), and the establishment of the Equal Employment Opportunity Commission (1965) attacked such discriminatory practices in the job market. A summary of important agencies and legislation aimed at regulating working conditions is given in Table 13–3.

Product Safety

Government regulation of product safety is based on the contention that many products are too complex for consumers to make informed purchase decisions. Moreover, as we observed earlier, information is like a near-public good in that the market tends to produce less than the optimal amount of information. Product complexity, together with inadequate market provision of information, may lead consumers to underestimate the hazards associated with certain products.

The legal position of the consumer relative to that of the seller has changed substantially during the last century. That position has

TABLE 13-3 Agencies and Legislation for Working Conditions

Agency or Legislation	Date	Purpose or Function
Railroad Retirement Board	1935	Administers pension, unemployment, and sickness benefit plans for railroad workers.
Fair Labor Standards Act	1938	Provided for minimum wage, 40-hour workweek, overtime pay, and control of child-labor practices.
Equal Pay Act	1963	The first key antidiscrimination act.
Civil Rights Act	1964	Banned discrimination in private employment on account of race, sex, or national origin.
Equal Employment Opportunity Commission (EEOC)	1965	Investigates charges of job discrimination on the basis of age, sex, religion, race, color, or national origin; brings suits to end discrimination unless acceptable conciliation or agreement is reached.
Occupational Safety and Health Administration (OSHA)	1970	Develops and promotes occupational safety and health standards, develops and issues regulations, conducts investigations and inspections to determine compliance with regulations and standards, issues citations and proposes penalties for noncompliance.
Pension Benefit Guarantee Corporation	1974	Provides mandatory insurance coverage for most private pension programs, which must meet certain legislated standards.
Mine Safety and Health Administration	1977	Develops and promotes mandatory mine safety and health standards; ensures compliance and assesses penalties for noncompliance.

shifted from one of *caveat emptor*, "let the buyer beware," to one of *caveat venditor*, "let the seller beware." Under the doctrine of *caveat emptor*, buyers bore responsibility for the consequences of their purchase decisions. They could not claim damages from sellers for faulty products. Gradually, legal rules of fraud evolved that allowed buyers to recover damages if they could prove that sellers had misrepresented their products. In addition, negligence rules evolved that held the seller responsible for the costs of injuries caused by product defects that the seller either knew about or should have known about. Recent years have seen a dramatic upsurge in product liability actions against sellers. Judges and juries are increasingly deciding that sellers are responsible for the goods they market.

Paralleling the emergence of the doctrine of *caveat venditor* has been an expansion of government regulation to ensure product safety. Two particularly important and powerful agencies established for this purpose are the Consumer Product Safety Commission and the Food and Drug Administration.

The Consumer Product Safety Commission (CPSC)

Prior to 1972, federal regulation of product safety consisted mainly of isolated statutes intended to protect consumers from specific hazards. Examples are the Flammable Fabrics Act (1953), the Federal Hazardous Substances Labeling Act (1960), and the Child Protection Act (1966). The purposes and functions of these acts are described in Table 13–4. A number of other acts also gave the

TABLE 13-4 Agencies and Legislation for Product Safety

Agency and Legislation	Date	Purpose and Function
Food and Drug Act	1906	Prohibited the adulteration and misbranding of goods in interstate commerce.
Food and Drug Administration (FDA)	1906	Enforcement agency for the Food and Drug Act.
Food, Drug, and Cosmetics Act	1938	Established predistribution safety and clearance of new drugs. Strengthened the Food and Drug Act.
Food Safety and Service, Department of Agriculture	1953	Inspects meat, poultry, and related products processed by plants engaged in interstate or foreign commerce; inspects liquid, dried, and frozen egg products; sets grading standards for food and farm products.
Flammable Fabrics Act	1953	Authorized control of sale of dangerously flammable fabrics and apparel.
Federal Aviation Act	1958	Centralized regulation of air safety.
Food Additives Amendment	1958	Extended predistribution clearance requirement to food as well as drugs.
Federal Hazardous Substances Labeling Act	1960	Authorized the FDA to require warnings on labels of potentially hazardous substances.
Drug Amendments	1962	Required proof of effectiveness as well as safety before marketing of new drugs.
Highway Safety Act	1966	Set uniform safety standards for state highways.
Child Protection Act	1966	Gave FDA power to prohibit sale of toys and other products potentially harmful to children.
National Traffic and Motor Vehicle Safety Act	1966	Established vehicle and equipment safety standards.
Federal Aviation Administration, Department of Transportation	1967	Issues and enforces rules regarding aircraft, aviators, and airports.
National Highway Traffic Safety Administration, Department of Transportation	1970	Sets safety standards for motor vehicles and equipment, develops and promotes mandatory fuel economy standards for automobiles.
Consumer Product Safety Act	1972	Provided for mandatory product safety standards and for banning of hazardous substances.
Consumer Product Safety Commission	1972	Sets mandatory safety standards for consumer products, can act to ban hazardous consumer products, conducts research on safety standards.
Motor Vehicle and School Bus Safety Act	1974	Established criteria and procedures for auto recall and defect notification.
National Transportation Safety Board	1975	Makes recommendations on transportation safety; evaluates safety programs of other government agencies, including those concerned with the transport of hazardous substances; investigates accidents in civil aviation, railroads, pipelines, highway transportation, and waterways.
Nuclear Regulatory Commission	1975	Licenses and regulates nuclear power to protect public health, safety, and the environment.

Federal Drug Administration regulatory authority over drugs (see Table 13–4).

A new strategy was conceived when the Consumer Product Safety Act created the Consumer Product Safety Commission (CPSC) in 1972. The act created a mechanism intended to provide comprehensive regulation of consumer product safety. The CPSC is empowered to ban or require the recall of hazardous products, issue mandatory safety standards, force producers to notify consumers of particular hazards, require industry-financed product testing, seize and destroy dangerous products, specify labeling requirements, and require manufacturers to provide performance data. The commission also has authority to seek civil or criminal penalties against firms that violate its regulations. (Certain products that are regulated by other federal agencies are excluded from the CPSC's jurisdiction. These are motor vehicles, aircraft, boats, foods, drugs, fuels, nuclear materials, pesticides, tobacco products, medical devices, cosmetics, firearms, and ammunition.)

Has the CPSC been effective? The commission has been criticized for doing less than was anticipated. For instance, it has somewhat neglected its responsibility to give consumers comparative information on the safety of specific products. Similarly, the commission has done little to get manufacturers to provide technical and performance data on their products. The commission has also been criticized for paying more attention to industry interests than to consumer groups when determining standards. Another criticism is that the commission has often adopted labeling requirements instead of the standards or laws recommended by its staff. Others view this favorably, on the grounds that labeling aids consumer choice by providing information, while regulations simply restrict consumer choice.

On the plus side, the commission has the best injury surveillance system in the country. Its hazard identification data have been useful in correcting problems in several million products. Its injury data are used by private attorneys to strengthen product liability suits. And businesses have an incentive to design safer products as the cost of liability suits increases. Indeed, the very possibility of CPSC action probably has caused industries to raise standards of product safety on their own.

The Food and Drug Administration (FDA)

A strong case can be made for government regulation of the food and drug industries. The average consumer does not have the resources to check the sanitary conditions at food processors or to examine the ingredients that go into the vast variety of packaged foods found in a typical supermarket. It is probably even more difficult to evaluate drugs. A wrong choice in either case could mean serious illness or death.

Around the turn of the century there was a burst of publicity about unsanitary conditions in the food industry. At the same time there was an increase in illnesses and deaths caused by products of the developing patent-medicine industry. Congress responded in 1906 by passing the Food and Drug Act. This act prohibited the adulteration and mislabeling of food sold in interstate commerce and created the Food and Drug Administration (FDA) to enforce the law. The act had shortcomings that limited its effectiveness, and adulterated and mislabeled drugs continued to be a problem through the 1930s. To bolster the original act, Congress passed the Food, Drug, and Cosmetic Act of 1938, which strengthened the definitions of adulteration and misbranding. The act was further strengthened in 1962, when Congress passed amendments giving the FDA authority to regulate the testing of drugs. The amendments also required that manufacturers must show that new drugs are effective as well as safe—that they satisfy all the claims made for them. The amendments also gave the FDA the power to remove immediately from the market any drug considered to pose a substantial risk to public health.

In recent years, critics have contended that the FDA's drug evaluation procedures are so

POLICY PERSPECTIVE

Air-Traffic Controller "Burnout"—Working Conditions Versus Product Safety[1]

Sometimes the objectives of one set of government regulations conflict with those of another. Government attempts during the mid-1970s to compensate air-traffic controllers for "burnout" caused by on-the-job stress seem to have jeopardized airline safety, ordinarily an area of product safety regulated by the Federal Aviation Administration (FAA). A study of the problem suggests that changes in federal law made it easier for controllers to prove job-related disability. The study also suggests that, in order to prove these claims, some controllers let airborne planes get closer to each other than federal rules allow.

The Suspect Change in the Law

The Federal Employees Compensation Act entitles government workers to tax-free payments of as much as 75 percent of their salary if they are unable to work because of a job-related disability. A claim to such compensation must be supported by a doctor and must show loss of income because of a decline in job performance. In 1974 the law was modified so that, for the first time, a federal worker could choose his or her own doctor (instead of a government doctor) to support a claim. The modification also let the worker choose, for the first time, psychologists and psychiatrists.

The study reported that this change had a special effect on controllers because most controller claims of job disability are "mental," presumably caused by stress. Proof often consists of subjective judgments about depression or nervous conditions. A report produced by the FAA's Office of Aviation Medicine shows that 52.8 percent of all controllers medically disqualified between January 1972 and December 1978 were disqualified for psychological or psychiatric reasons. Such reasons are difficult to deny if endorsed by a doctor, and after 1974 controllers could "shop around" for a sympathetic doctor. Labor Department statistics show that controllers made about 370 disability claims in the last months of 1974 (there are no statistics on controllers before that). The volume rose to 887 claims for 1975, and jumped 42 percent to 1,257 in 1976.

The Effect on System Errors

A controller commits a system error if the planes being monitored get closer than the minimum separation standards set by the FAA. After the 1974 law change, according to the study, some controllers had an incentive to commit system errors because an error afforded proof that a controller's job performance had slipped, thereby strengthening a disability claim.

FAA data in Figure P13–1 show that system errors were generally just under 300 a year nationwide from 1969 to 1973 (except for 1972). However, in 1974 they increased about 18 percent to 340, another 25 percent to 420 in 1975, and about 17 percent to 491 in 1976. The study found a "significant" correlation between the increase in system errors and the increase in ease of obtaining disability compensation. According to the study, other factors don't explain the error surge. For example, the FAA says air traffic (measured in take-offs and landings) increased an average of only 4 percent a year from 1973 to

[1] Adapted from "Doubts Arise in 'Burnout' of Controllers," *Wall Street Journal,* August 27, 1981.

FIGURE P13-1 System Errors Committed by Air Controllers

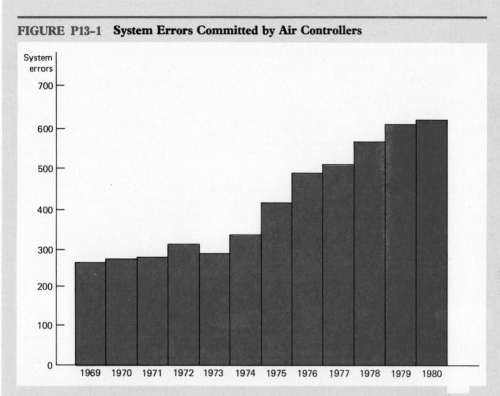

System errors are defined as occurring when the planes a controller monitors violate minimum separation standards.

SOURCE: Federal Aviation Administration.

1976. Similarly, the number of controllers rose an average of only about 3 percent during that period.

Subsequent Changes

The study doesn't claim any significant statistical correlation after April 1976 between the increase in system errors and the increase in ease of obtaining disability compensation because other factors came into play. For one thing, air traffic increased greatly after mid-1976. For another, a program was initiated that offered partial immunity from punishment to controllers who reported system errors. Both factors could explain why system errors continued to climb after 1976. Meanwhile, the Labor Department reports that

controller disability claims have gradually fallen, citing more careful scrutiny of claims. Also, a department spokesman argues that controller incentives to file claims fell after 1978 because Congress cut allocations for a "second career program" that, after 1972, had paid disabled workers for 2 years of retraining.

Questions

1. Do you think that more careful scrutiny of disability claims is likely to increase or to reduce system errors, other things being equal?

2. It might be said that there is a supply curve for disability claims. What would be measured on each axis of such a diagram?

strict that they hinder the development of new drugs. It is estimated that in the United States, it costs $50 to $60 million and an average of 10 years is required to introduce a new drug that meets all the FDA requirements. But is this good or bad? On the plus side, caution—even extreme caution—on the part of the FDA reduces the chance of a mistake that could cost lives or cause injury. Unfortunately, the cost of caution is the lives that might have been saved, and the illnesses cured, if the drug had been approved sooner. Because it is hard to know how many lives might be saved if a drug were available sooner, it is very difficult to say whether drug regulation is excessive or not.

A related criticism of the FDA is that it evaluates drugs and food additives according to an absolute risk standard—a substance suspected to be a health risk will not be approved. Critics contend that it would be more sensible to weigh relative risks, that is, to weigh the risk of using the drug against the risk involved in not using the drug.

Safety Regulation in Transportation and Nuclear Power

Table 13–4 includes the important agencies and legislation aimed at regulating safety in transportation and nuclear power. The case for government regulation of these industries is twofold. First, the products (motor vehicles, aircraft, and nuclear reactors) that provide transportation and nuclear power are far too complex for the average consumer to evaluate. Second, use of these products gives rise to significant external, or spillover, costs. If the car I buy is hazardous to operate, you also bear the risk when I drive on the same street you do. If an airplane crashes in a congested area, the damage costs are borne by third parties on the ground as well as by the airline company and fare-paying passengers. When a nuclear reactor in a power-generating plant breaches its radiation shield and spews radioactive fallout on the surrounding countryside, the health and property damage to third parties can be enormous. Such damage caused by the accident at the Three Mile

Island nuclear power plant in Pennsylvania has been estimated to be in the hundreds of millions of dollars.

Deceptive Advertising and Labeling

The complexity of many products, coupled with the producer's obvious self-interest in selling them, often gives rise to the use of deceptive advertising and labeling practices. Government regulation of advertising and labeling is intended to curb such practices and to motivate producers to provide more accurate consumer product information.

The Federal Trade Commission

Congress passed the Federal Trade Commission Act in 1914. The act created the Federal Trade Commission (FTC) and gave it the authority to prevent firms or persons from engaging in unfair methods of competition in commerce. The original act was primarily concerned with improving competition among firms and was not very effective at protecting consumers from deceptive advertising and labeling. To bolster the act for this purpose Congress passed the Wheeler-Lea Amendment in 1938. The amendment explicitly gave the FTC responsibility to protect consumers from false or misleading advertising. Since the Wheeler-Lea Amendment, Congress has passed a series of acts that have increased FTC authority to require accurate information about products. These acts are described in Table 13–5.

deceptive advertising and labeling is the difficulty of distinguishing between harmless exaggeration and harmful deception. Another problem stems from the fact that consumers receive no monetary awards for damages caused by firms successfully prosecuted by the commission. Consequently, consumers have little incentive to report unfair practices to the FTC. By contrast, competing firms have a strong incentive to point fingers at one another, since their complaints result in unfavorable publicity for competitors. As a result, the FTC gets more complaints from

TABLE 13-5 Agencies and Legislation to Control Deceptive Advertising and Labeling Practices

Agency and Legislation	Date	Purpose and Function
Federal Trade Commission (FTC)	1914	Among other things, acts to "prevent unfair or deceptive acts or practices" such as deceptive packaging and labeling and false advertising; requires true credit-cost disclosure by lenders.
Securities Act	1933	Required full disclosure of nature and financial status of companies wishing to sell securities to the public.
Securities and Exchange Act	1934	Extended full disclosure requirements to all companies listed on security exchanges, provides for registration of securities, regulates insider trading and stock exchange trading practices.
Wheeler-Lea Amendment	1938	Gave the FTC explicit responsibility for protecting consumers against fraudulent or misleading advertising.
Wool Products Labeling Act	1939	Gave FTC power to regulate labeling of wool goods.
Fur Products Labeling Act	1951	Gave FTC power to regulate labeling of furs.
Textile Fiber Products Identification Act	1958	Gave FTC power to regulate labeling of textiles.
Cigarette Labeling and Advertising Act	1965	Required a health hazard warning on cigarette packages.
Fair Packaging and Labeling Act	1966	Broadened scope of FTC's authority to regulate labeling.
Consumer Credit Protection Act	1969	Required complete disclosure of credit terms before a credit transaction is completed and regulated advertising of credit terms.
Public Health Cigarette Smoking Act	1969	Prohibited the advertising of cigarettes on radio or television.
Consumer Product Warranty Act	1975	Set minimum disclosure standards for written consumer product warranties. Gave FTC additional powers to deal with unfair or deceptive practices at the state and local levels.

firms than from the consumers it is supposed to protect. However, the FTC does not rely solely on complaints from firms and consumers; it has a staff that continually monitors labeling and printed advertising, as well as radio and television commercials.

Financial Disclosure

Corporate stocks and bonds are ownership claims on the assets of corporations. A corporation is typically a very complex business, often producing a variety of products and services. Consequently, a good deal of *accurate* information about a corporation's financial health, management ability, and sales prospects is required for even an informal assessment of the value of its stock or bonds. The Securities Act of 1933 and the Securities and Exchange Act of 1934, described in Table 13–5, were intended to protect the public from misrepresentation concerning the securities and business prospects of corporations issuing securities. The Securities and Exchange Act created the Securities and Exchange Commission (SEC) and gave it authority to enforce the laws regulating the purchase and sale of stocks and bonds.

CHECKPOINT 13-3

Compared to regulations for product safety, do you think regulation of deceptive advertising serves to enhance or restrict consumer choice?

SUMMARY

1. The market mechanism has several problem areas: it does not provide pure public goods, it gives rise to external costs and benefits in providing certain goods, it provides inadequate amounts of certain kinds of information, and its results are incompatible with some of society's goals. Government intervention, in the form of regulation, may be used in an attempt to correct such faults.

2. Government provision of pure public goods, such as national defense, is necessary because such goods are not subject to the exclusion principle. Near-public goods are jointly consumed, like pure public goods, but they are subject to the exclusion principle and hence they will be provided by the market.

3. Whenever external costs are associated with the market for a good, society suffers a loss because too much of the good is produced. Whenever there are external benefits, a loss occurs because too little of the good is produced. In either case government regulation may be used to achieve the optimal output level.

4. Imperfect information is usually a problem in the purchase and sale of products that are not purchased repeatedly or that are complex. The market probably provides less product information than is optimal because such information is like a near-public good.

5. Society has goals and values that are sometimes at odds with market outcomes. Government may ban products that markets will provide but that society deems harmful to those who would buy them. Government regulation is also used to prevent people from exploiting one another in ways society considers unacceptable. And the government plays an ever increasing role in the redistribution of income to modify the income distribution otherwise provided by market outcomes.

6. Any determination of the appropriate amount of government regulation must recognize that there is a trade-off between the costs and benefits of regulation, and that it is possible for regulation to make matters worse rather than better. Benefit-cost analysis is a useful tool for determining the optimal amount of regulation.

7. Environmental pollution imposes external, or spillover, costs, because clean air and clean rivers, lakes, and oceans are public goods. Benefit-cost analysis suggests that total elimination of pollution is usually not optimal. Legislated standards and pollution emission taxes can be used to regulate the amount of pollution and internalize its costs to the markets that cause it. Since 1970 the Environmental Protection Agency (EPA) has been primarily responsible for setting and enforcing environmental standards. The EPA has been criticized for not paying enough attention to benefit-cost guidelines.

8. Imperfect information about job hazards and the presence of external costs in the labor market suggest that there is an underallocation of resources to maintaining health and safety in the workplace. In 1970, Congress created the Occupational Safety and Health Administration (OSHA) to regulate working conditions. OSHA has been criticized for not reducing injury rates significantly, for not relying more on benefit-cost analysis, and for using prescriptive rather than performance standards. Government regulation of working conditions also extends to the enforcement of minimum-wage laws and child-labor laws and to the elimination of discriminatory hiring practices.

9. The case for government regulation of product safety is based on product complexity and inadequate provision of product information by the market. In 1972 Congress created the Consumer Product Safety Commission (CPSC) to provide comprehensive regulation of consumer product safety. The CPSC has been criticized for heeding industry interests more than consumer interests. However, the CPSC's hazard identification data, the threat of product liability suits, and the possibility of CPSC action probably foster greater product safety.

10. The Food and Drug Administration (FDA) is the main vehicle for government regulation of food and drug safety. The FDA has been criticized for allegedly slowing the introduction of new drugs and for using an "idealized" absolute risk standard in evaluating them. Government safety regulation has also been extended to transportation and nuclear power, where it is deemed necessary because of product complexity and significant external costs.

11. The complexity of many products, coupled with the producer's motivation to sell them, often gives rise to deceptive advertising and labeling practices. Government intervention to prevent such practices rests mainly with the Federal Trade Commission (FTC). FTC efforts in this area are hampered by the difficulty of distinguishing between harmless exaggeration and harmful deception, as well as the lack of incentives for consumers to report violations.

12. The Securities and Exchange Commission (SEC) enforces financial disclosure laws that are intended to protect the investing public from the misrepresentation of securities issued by business firms.

KEY TERMS AND CONCEPTS

benefit-cost analysis
exclusion principle
externalities
free rider
near-public good
pure public good

QUESTIONS AND PROBLEMS

1. What is the distinction between a pure public good and a near-public good? Classify each of the following as either a pure public good, a near-public good, or neither: a movie, a radio program, a symphony concert, a clean ocean, a haircut, a cable television program, a quiet neighborhood, a baseball game, a clean lake, a keg of beer, the spectrum of radio waves, international relations.

2. It has been observed that community-owned property (such as a public park, roadside, or stadium) tends to be more littered with wastepaper and empty bottles than private property (such as people's yards and driveways). How would you relate this observation to each of the following concepts: public good, external costs, the free-rider problem? Suggest some product regulations that might reduce this litter. Illustrate the nature of the problem for bottled beverages in terms of either Figure 13–1 or 13–2, indicating how you would measure the size of the external costs on such a graph and the effect of regulations to eliminate the external costs.

3. Why does the market provide less product information than is optimal? Do you think that information in general is likely to be underproduced or overproduced?

4. Suppose the total amount of pollution damage in Table 13–1 were $1 million greater at every level of pollution (that is, add $1 million to each entry in column 2). A public outcry about the problem leads the local government to hire you as an economic consultant to advise them what to do. Assume that prior to the $1 million jump in pollution damage the government already taxed pollution emissions at the rate of $90,000 per 10,000 units of pollutants. What would you advise the government to do now? _same_ Is it possible for pollution damage to get worse even though you always follow an optimal environmental protection strategy?

5. Suppose there are two firms in a neighborhood, each emitting 5 units of pollutants in the absence of regulation. Suppose their marginal costs of eliminating each unit of pollution are as shown in the following table.

Emissions Without Regulation	Marginal Cost of Eliminating Each Successive Unit of Pollution				
	1st	2nd	3rd	4th	5th
Firm A 5	$100	200	300	400	500
Firm B 5	$200	400	600	800	1,000

Assume regulators wish to reduce neighborhood pollution by a total of 6 units. You are called in as a consultant and asked whether they should set a maximum emission limit of 2 units of pollution per firm or, alternatively, use a pollution emission tax to accomplish their goal. What would you tell them, and why? What does this indicate about the relative merits of maximum emission standards and pollution emission taxes as tools for pollution control?

6. Suppose a plant has a number of safety hazards. How should the plant manager allocate available resources to eliminate these hazards? That is, how should the manager decide the amount of resources to allocate to each problem area?

7. Suppose employees were allowed to waive their right to work in an "OSHA acceptable" work environment in return for a wage increase. Do you think the wage increase they would ask for would be greater than or less than the increase that the firm would be willing to grant in return for exemption from OSHA standards? Why?

8. What effect would a more vigorous enforcement of consumer product safety standards have on consumer product prices? Why?

9. Suppose the FTC were considering more vigorous enforcement of regulations against deceptive advertising of the following products: barbells, diet pills, glue, automobiles, cigarettes, wheat, detergents, eggs, cosmetics, toothpaste, air conditioners, shoes, and thumbtacks. Rank the products according to the size of the effect such vigorous enforcement would be likely to have on sales. Then rank the products according to complexity, and finally according to the degree to which they are repeat-purchase items. What kind of relationships do you observe among the three rankings?

FOUR

Price Determination of Economic Resources

14

Production and the Demand for Productive Resources

AFTER READING THIS CHAPTER, YOU WILL BE ABLE TO:

1. Explain why the demand for a productive factor is a derived demand.

2. List and explain the determinants of the elasticity of a factor demand curve.

3. Summarize the marginal productivity theory of factor demand.

4. Delineate the causes of shifts in a factor demand curve.

5. Set forth the principles underlying the firm's determination of the optimum combination of several productive factors that it uses.

Up to now we have focused on the way prices are determined in the markets for the goods and services produced by firms, the markets where households are on the demand side and businesses on the supply side. We have said little about the determination of the prices of the economic resources, or factors of production, that the firm must use to produce these goods and services, the markets where firms are on the demand side and households on the supply side. The prices of such economic resources as land, labor, capital (plant and equipment), energy, and raw materials are matters of major significance. In this chapter we will look at some of the basic considerations that enter into the determination of these prices.

WHY RESOURCE PRICING IS IMPORTANT

Resource pricing is important basically for two reasons. First, it determines how the economy's limited supply of economic resources is allocated to the various production activities necessary to produce the multitude of goods and services that society wants. Second, it determines how income earned from productive activities is distributed among the citizens of the economy.

Allocation of Economic Resources to Productive Activities

Resource prices are the signaling devices that direct resources to the different industries, firms, and governmental activities that constitute the economy's productive capacity. If the wages paid to machinists in the auto industry rise relative to those paid to machinists in the aircraft industry, this type of labor resource will tend to move away from aircraft production and into auto production. If the price of land for residential use rises relative to that for agricultural use, the rate at which farmland is converted into suburbs will tend to increase. If the rate of return on financial capital invested in physical capital

(plant and equipment) in the computer industry rises relative to the rate earned in the steel industry, the rate of new physical capital formation in the computer industry will tend to rise relative to that in the steel industry. If the wages paid to government employees rise relative to those paid to workers in the private sector, labor will tend to flow into the government sector and away from the private sector.

Determination of Income Distribution

All productive resources in our economy are owned by somebody. The owners sell the services of their resources and the payments received in exchange constitute their incomes. There are two variables that make up this exchange: the quantity of resource services sold, and the price at which a unit of the service is sold. A laborer's income depends on the number of labor hours sold and the price (or wage rate) of a labor hour. A landlord's income depends on the number of acres of land or square feet of floor space rented out and the rental rate per unit. The income that a stockholder in a corporation receives depends on the number of shares owned and the dividends and capital gains earned per share.

Whether we are talking about laborers, landlords, or stockholders, it is obvious that the prices received per unit of the resource service sold enter into the determination of the income they receive. This income in turn determines the share of the economy's output of goods and services that each of them may purchase. Given the implications for the welfare of different groups in the economy that follow from this, it is little wonder that the determination of resource prices is frequently a matter of considerable controversy. What is a "just" wage or a "fair" return? Questions such as these go to the heart of the often emotional issue of income distribution, a subject fraught with normative judgments. We will delve more deeply into various aspects of the roles of labor unions, business, and government, and explore other institutional characteristics of this subject over the course of the three following chapters.

Our discussion in this chapter is concerned with the analysis of factor demand from the viewpoint of the firm. We will be concerned with how it works rather than with the normative questions of its implications for the distribution of income among different groups in the economy, a subject to be taken up in a subsequent chapter. The demand for economic resources, or factors of production, is really just a special application of the general principles of demand with which you are already familiar.

FACTOR DEMAND IS A DERIVED DEMAND

The basic characteristic of factor demand is that it is a **derived demand**. *This means that the demand for any productive factor ultimately depends upon, or derives from, the demand for the final product or products that the factor is used to produce.*

The demand for steelworkers derives from the demand for steel. The demand for steel derives from the demand for the many products that contain steel. The demand for farmland derives from the demand for agricultural products, as does the demand for farm machinery and other capital equipment needed in agricultural production. The demand for high-technology space scientists and engineers is derived from the demand for space vehicles and their support facilities. Examples of derived demand are almost endless.

The demand for any particular productive factor may well derive from its use in the production of several different products. The more narrowly we define a productive factor, the fewer the products its demand will be derived from. Labor is used in the production of all goods. Barbers are used only in the production of haircuts. Similarly, drill presses are a general category of capital equipment needed in many production processes, but only certain types of presses are used to produce wristwatches. The complexity of explaining *the* derived demand for a productive factor will therefore depend on how broadly or narrowly we define that factor.

MARGINAL PRODUCTIVITY THEORY OF FACTOR DEMAND

The nature of the demand for a productive factor can be made more precise by determining the productive factor's specific contribution to the making of the final product. Common sense suggests that the larger the contribution the factor makes to the output of a product, the greater will be the demand for the factor. The **marginal productivity theory of factor demand** provides an explanation of why this is so.

To understand the basics of this theory, it is easiest to begin by considering a firm that sells its product in a perfectly competitive market. Hence the firm is a price taker. As we have seen, this means that the firm can sell as little or as much of its product as it wants at the given market price because it provides such a small portion of total supply that its effect on market price is insignificant. We will also assume that the firm uses one fixed factor (such as capital) and one variable factor (such as labor) of production. That is, the quantity of one factor is fixed and unchangeable while the quantity of the other factor can be varied. The firm also buys the variable factor in a perfectly competitive market, which means that it can buy as little or as much of that factor as it wants at a given price. In other words, the firm's purchases of the variable factor represent such a small fraction of the total supply of the factor that the firm cannot affect the factor's market price.

Marginal Revenue Product

Suppose the firm has a certain quantity of the fixed factor. Table 14–1 illustrates the way in

TABLE 14-1 Relationship Between Productive Factor and Marginal Revenue Product, Assuming Perfect Competition in Both Factor and Product Markets

(1)	(2)	(3)	(4)	(5)	(6)
Quantity of Productive Factor (F)	Total Output of Final Product (Q)	Marginal Physical Product (MPP)	Price of Product (p)	Total Revenue (TR)	Marginal Revenue Product (MRP)
		$MPP = \dfrac{\text{change in } Q}{\text{unit change in } F}$		$TR = p \times Q$	$MRP = \dfrac{\text{change in } TR}{\text{unit change in } F}$
0	0			$ 0	
		12			$120
1	12		$10	120	
		10			100
2	22		10	220	
		8			80
3	30		10	300	
		6			60
4	36		10	360	
		4			40
5	40		10	400	
		2			20
6	42		10	420	
		1			10
7	43		10	430	

which the quantity of the variable factor F contributes to the production of the firm's final product and therefore to the revenue the firm realizes from the sale of that product.

As more of the factor F is used (column 1), the quantity of output of final product Q increases (column 2). The increase in total output associated with the addition of one more unit of the factor F to the production process is the **marginal physical product** MPP (column 3). Columns 2 and 3 of Table 14-1 measure total output and marginal physical product in terms of physical units, such as the number of bushels of wheat or the quantity of widgets. Because of the law of diminishing returns, the MPP decreases as more and more of the factor F is added and used together with the given quantity of the fixed factor. The relationship between the quantity

of the factor F and the total quantity of output of final product Q (column 2) is the short-run production function, a concept that we looked at in Chapter 7. Figure 14-1, part a, plots the data in columns 1 and 2 of Table 14-1 on a graph. The relationship between the factor F and the marginal physical product MPP is illustrated in Figure 14-1, part b, using the data in columns 1 and 3 of Table 14-1. (Note that the marginal physical product data are plotted midway between the integers on the horizontal axis. This is so because they represent the changes in total output and total revenue respectively from one unit of the factor to the next.)

In order to arrive at the relationship between the quantity of the factor F and the sales revenue it helps to produce, it is necessary to multiply the output of column 2 by

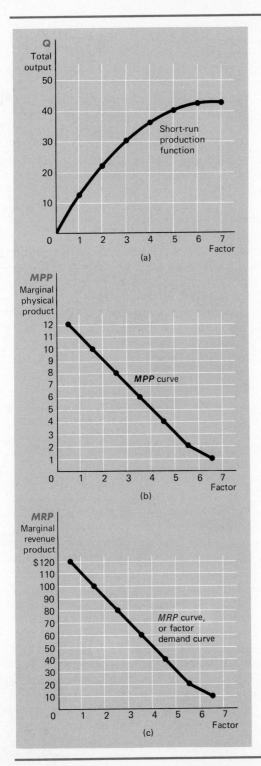

(a)

(b)

(c)

FIGURE 14-1 Relationship Between Short-Run Production Function, Marginal Physical Product, and Marginal Revenue Product, Assuming Perfect Competition in Both Factor and Product Markets

Part a shows the perfectly competitive firm's short-run production function plotted from the data in columns 1 and 2 of Table 14–1. The law of diminishing returns is reflected in the fact that the curve rises less and less as more and more of the variable factor is added to the production process and used together with the given quantity of the fixed factor.

Part b is a graph of the marginal physical product, the increase in total output attributable to each additional unit of the variable factor. It is plotted from the data in columns 1 and 3 of Table 14–1. Its downward slope reflects the law of diminishing returns.

Part c is a graph of the marginal revenue product, the increase in total revenue attributable to each additional unit of the variable factor, plotted from the data in columns 1 and 6 of Table 14–1. It is an image of the *MRP* curve of part b because *MRP* may be obtained by multiplying the given final market price *p* (equal $10 in this case) by *MPP*.

The marginal curves of part b and c are plotted at the midpoints of the integers on the horizontal axes. This is because they represent the change in total output and total revenue respectively from one unit of the factor to the next.

the price at which it is sold. Since the firm sells its product in a perfectly competitive market, this price is the same no matter what the output level. Assuming that the price p is $10 (column 4), total revenue TR, which equals $p \times Q$ (column 4 times column 2), is given in column 5. *The increase in total revenue associated with each 1-unit increase in the variable factor F is called the* **marginal revenue product** MRP. This figure is given in column 6. It may be computed either by determining the difference between the successive total revenue figures in column 5 or by multiplying the MPP of column 3, which is the addition to total output Q, by the price p of column 4. The marginal revenue product curve MRP is plotted in part c of Figure 14-1 from the data in column 6 of Table 14-1. Note that it mirrors the MPP curve of part b. This is so because MRP may be obtained by multiplying the given final market price p (which does not change with the firm's output under perfect competition) by MPP.

Determining the Quantity of a Factor to Employ

How does the firm decide how much of the variable factor to employ? The principle that is used to answer this question is very similar to the marginal-cost-equals-marginal-revenue rule used to decide how much output to produce.

Employ the Factor Until MCF = MRP

In Chapter 7, we found the question, How much output should be produced? was answered as follows: Produce that level of output at which *the marginal cost of the last unit produced is just equal to the marginal revenue obtained from the sale of that last unit.* The answer to the question, How much of the variable factor should be employed? is really just a slight variation on the answer to the question, How much output should be produced? This is not surprising if we remember that when the firm produces its optimum

output level (the one that maximizes profit), it must of necessity use a certain amount of the variable factor to produce it. This amount is the answer to the question, How much of the variable factor should be employed? In short, we may view the firm's profit-maximizing level of activity either from the vantage point of input or from the vantage point of output.

From the vantage point of input (how much of the variable factor should be employed?)—*the firm should employ the variable factor up to the point at which the marginal cost of the factor MCF is just equal to the marginal revenue product MRP.* In other words, it should employ the variable factor up to the point at which the cost of the last unit of that factor employed is just equal to the additional revenue realized from the sale of the additional output produced by that last unit of the factor.

This may be illustrated by use of the data in Table 14-1. Suppose the price of the factor, its per unit cost to the firm, is $50. Since the firm is a price taker in the factor market, it must pay $50 per unit of the factor no matter how much or how little of the factor it buys—the firm's MCF equals $50 at every level of output. At this price the firm will employ 4 units of the factor. Why is this so? Because the MRP (column 6) exceeds MCF (equal $50) for every unit of the factor up through 4 units, and falls below it for every additional unit of the factor beyond 4 units. Each additional unit of the factor employed up through the fourth adds more to total revenue than it costs to purchase the factor. Hence, it is profitable for the firm to employ each of these units of the factor. For instance, the addition of the fourth unit of the factor increases total revenue by $60. The marginal cost of the factor MCF is $50, which is less than the marginal revenue product MRP of $60 (column 6). The firm realizes $10 profit. However, if the firm were to add a fifth unit of the factor, the MCF of $50 would exceed the MRP of $40 realized from the sale of the fifth unit. Hence, the firm would lose $10 on the production and sale of the additional output realized from the employment of the fifth unit of the factor. Similarly, the firm would lose money on each additional unit of the factor employed beyond the fifth. Thus, the firm should employ no more or less than 4 units of the variable factor.

Factor Demand Curve Is MRP Curve

The *MRP* curve of part c of Figure 14–1 is reproduced in Figure 14–2. According to the data in column 6 of Table 14–1, the first unit of the factor *F* has an *MRP* of $120. If the price of 1 unit of *F* is less than this, the firm will hire the factor. The *MRP* of a second unit of the factor is $100. If the price of the factor is $110, say, then the firm will hire 1 unit but not a second. On the other hand, if the price of 1 unit of the factor is $90, the firm will hire 2 units of *F*. We can continue this line of reasoning by considering successively lower prices for the factor. Assuming that the factor is divisible into fractional units (so many hours, minutes, and seconds of labor services, for example), the result will be the smooth *MRP* curve that in effect constitutes the firm's demand curve D_F for the factor. It tells us how much will be demanded at each possible price of the factor.

For example, if the price of the factor is $50 and the firm can buy as much as it wants of the factor at that price, the *MCF* of the factor is $50 at every level of output. The supply curve of the factor is then S_F as shown in Figure 14–2. The firm will employ 4 units of the factor as determined by the intersection of S_F and D_F, the point where $MCF = MRP$.

Variable Product Price and Factor Demand

The data in Table 14–1 and Figures 14–1 and 14–2 assume that the firm sells its product in a perfectly competitive market. Therefore the price at which it sells each unit of output is the same no matter how much the firm produces, as indicated in column 4 of Table 14–1. Since $MRP = MPP \times p$, the

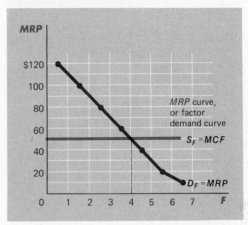

FIGURE 14-2 Marginal Revenue Product Curve Is the Firm's Demand Curve for a Productive Factor

The marginal revenue product curve *MRP* shown here is the same as that shown in part c of Figure 14–1. Since the price of a productive factor is the marginal cost of the factor *MCF* to the firm, and since the firm will purchase the factor up to the point where $MCF = MRP$, the curve tells us how much of the factor the firm will demand at each price. Therefore, the *MRP* curve is the firm's factor demand curve D_F.

If the firm can purchase as much as it wants of the factor at a price of $50, the marginal cost of the factor, or *MCF*, to the firm is $50 and the supply curve of the factor to the firm is S_F. The firm will purchase 4 units of the factor, as determined by the intersection of D_F and S_F, the point where $MRP = MCF$.

Since $MRP = MPP \times p$, the factor demand curve D_F will be steeper, or less elastic, the more rapidly *MPP* declines as the firm expands its output by using more of the factor.

only reason the factor demand, or *MRP*, curve of Figure 14–1, part c, and Figure 14–2 slopes downward is that *MPP* falls, reflecting the law of diminishing returns. (The fall in *MPP* is shown in column 3 of Table 14–1 and in Figure 14–1, part b.) However,

TABLE 14-2 Relationship Between Productive Factor and Marginal Revenue Product, Assuming Imperfect Competition in Product Market and Perfect Competition in Factor Market

(1)	(2)	(3)	(4)	(5)	(6)
Quantity of Productive Factor (F)	Total Output of Final Product (Q)	Marginal Physical Product (MPP)	Price of Product (p)	Total Revenue (TR)	Marginal Revenue Product (MRP)
		$MPP = \dfrac{\text{change in } Q}{\text{unit change in } F}$		$TR = p \times Q$	$MRP = \dfrac{\text{change in } TR}{\text{unit change in } F}$
0	0		$10	$ 0	
		12			$108
1	12		9	108	
		10			68
2	22		8	176	
		8			34
3	30		7	210	
		6			6
4	36		6	216	
		4			-16
5	40		5	200	
		2			-32
6	42		4	168	
		1			-39
7	43		3	129	

if the firm were an imperfectly competitive firm—a monopolist, an oligopolist, or a member of a monopolistically competitive industry—the price at which it sells its product would vary with the quantity of output it produces. That is, the demand curve for the firm's product would slope downward, reflecting the fact that the price p the firm receives for its product falls as more of that product is supplied to the market. Hence both MPP and p fall as the firm increases output.

The combined effect of the fall in both MPP and p on total revenue and marginal revenue product is illustrated in Table 14-2. The firm is the same as that in Table 14-1 so that columns 1, 2, and 3 remain unchanged. However, it is now assumed that the demand curve for the firm's product is downward sloping, so that the firm must accept a lower price in order to sell larger quantities of its product, as indicated in column 4 of Table 14-2. Because of this, total revenue and marginal revenue product (columns 5 and 6) fall more rapidly in Table 14-2 than is the case in columns 5 and 6 of Table 14-1.

Using the data in column 6 of Table 14-2, the marginal revenue product curve, which is the same as the firm's factor demand curve for the variable factor, is plotted as D_F' in Figure 14-3. The D_F curve from Figure 14-2 is reproduced in Figure 14-3 for comparison.

Clearly the factor demand curve D_F' lies to the left of D_F and is more steeply sloped. This is so because D_F' reflects the decline in the price of the firm's product *in addition to* the decline in MPP when more of the factor is used to increase the imperfectly competitive firm's output. The result, as can be seen

FIGURE 14-3 The Factor Demand Curves of an Imperfectly Competitive Firm and a Competitive Firm Compared

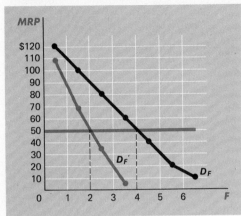

The factor demand curve of the perfectly competitive firm of Table 14–1 and Figures 14–1 and 14–2 is shown again as D_F. The factor demand curve D_F' of the imperfectly competitive firm of Table 14–2 is plotted from the data of column 6. The two firms are the same in all respects except that the demand curve for the *final product* of the imperfectly competitive firm is downward sloping and that of the perfectly competitive firm is horizontal.

The factor demand curve D_F of the perfectly competitive firm is downward sloping only because *MPP* falls as more of the variable factor is used, a reflection of the law of diminishing returns. The factor demand curve D_F' of the imperfectly competitive firm lies to the left of D_F and is more steeply sloped because in addition to the fall in *MPP*, the price of the firm's product falls as more of the factor is used to produce more output. The less elastic the demand curve for the firm's product, the more rapid will be the fall in price, and therefore the steeper, or less elastic, will be the factor demand curve.

in Figure 14–3, is that at any price of the factor the imperfectly competitive firm will demand less of the factor than the perfectly competitive firm, all other things remaining the same. For example, at a factor price of

$50, the imperfectly competitive firm will demand 2 units of the factor, while the perfectly competitive firm will demand 4 units.

Finally, note that the less elastic is the demand curve for an imperfectly competitive firm's product, the more rapid is the decline in product price as the firm increases output. Therefore, the less elastic the demand curve for the firm's product, the less elastic will be the factor demand curve.

Market Demand Curve for a Factor

Recall that we get a market demand curve for a good by summing up all the individual demand curves for the good. Similarly, we could obtain the market demand curve for a productive factor by summing up all the individual firms' factor demand curves. As with any demand curve, a movement along the market demand curve for the factor assumes that *only* the price of the factor and the quantity of the factor demanded change. All other things are assumed to remain the same, or unchanged. However, this assumption will not hold for the market demand curve for the factor obtained in the usual way we have just described. Let's consider why.

If the price of the factor is lowered, for example, all of the firms in an industry (suppose it is perfectly competitive) that use the factor to produce their product will now be able to get it cheaper. This means that the cost of production for the firms in the industry will be lower. The industry supply curve will therefore shift rightward (equivalently it may be viewed as shifting downward). Therefore the industry's output will increase and the price of its product will decline. But this is one of the prices, along with all others, that was assumed to remain unchanged when we move down the market demand curve for the factor.

Hence, when we lower the price of the productive factor, our assumption that all other things remain unchanged is no longer valid. In particular, the price of the product the factor helps produce is changed. The fall in product price means that each firm's *MRP*, or factor demand curve, will fall both because *MPP* falls and because product price *p* falls. This is exactly the case we have just examined for the imperfectly competitive firm. But it applies as well to the firms in a perfectly competitive industry that use the factor when we allow for the fact that the industry product price falls as they all expand output. Because of the fall in product price, each firm's demand curve for the factor will be steeper, like D_F' rather than D_F in Figure 14–3. Summing up all such D_F' curves, we would get the market factor demand curve. Because it takes account of the fall in product price, it will be steeper than the market demand curve that would be obtained by summing up the individual firm demand curves D_F, which do not take account of the fall in product price.

CHECKPOINT* 14-1
Suppose the variable factor *F* on the horizontal axis of Figure 14-2 is labor, that D_F is a firm's demand curve for labor, and that S_F is the horizontal supply curve of labor whose level is determined by the wage rate. Using this figure, show why if "the cost of labor is soaring" it could "trigger increasing layoffs."

*Answers to all Checkpoints can be found at the back of the text.

SHIFTS IN THE DEMAND CURVE FOR A FACTOR

Up to this point we have only considered movements along a factor demand curve. What causes shifts in the position of a factor demand curve? There are essentially four major reasons for the curve to shift: (1) changes in the demand for the final product, (2) changes in the quantities of other productive factors, (3) technological improvements, and (4) changes in the prices of other factors. Let's consider each in turn.

Changes in the Demand for the Final Product

If there is an increase in demand for the final product that the factor helps produce, firms will need to use more of the productive factor in order to increase production of the final product to meet this demand. This will cause the demand curve for such a factor to shift rightward. Similarly, a decrease in demand for the final product will ultimately result in a leftward shift of the factor demand curve. As demand for the final product decreases, firms will produce less and therefore use smaller amounts of the productive factor. Looking back to Table 14–1, suppose there is an increase in demand for the final product that causes product price *p* to rise from $10 to $15 in column 4. If you redo the calculations, you will find that for each quantity of the productive factor in column 1, the *MRP* in column 6 will now be larger. Consequently, the factor demand curve in Figure 14–1, part c, and Figure 14–2 will be shifted rightward.

Changes in the Quantities of Other Productive Factors

If the amounts of other productive factors used by a firm are increased while the quantity of one factor remains the same, the marginal productivity of the unchanged factor will increase. For example, suppose we give one laborer a half-acre of land and some seed but no capital equipment such as a shovel or a hoe. He or she then produces a certain quantity of output. The laborer's productivity will rise considerably if he or she is provided with some capital equipment; it will rise even more if another half-acre of land is added. If the laborer is given more capital equipment in the form of a tractor and plow plus another 100 acres of land, the laborer's productivity will rise still higher. In terms of Table 14–1, if the firm were to get more of the factor that was assumed to be fixed, the *MPP* (column 3) of the variable factor would be larger for every amount of that factor shown in column 1. This would mean that the factor demand curve of Figure 14–1, part c, and Figure 14–2 would be shifted rightward.

Technological Improvements in Productive Factors

If there is an increase in the productivity of some factors due to technological changes specific to those factors, the productivity of other factors used in conjunction with those factors will be increased as well. For example, if a woodcutter's handsaw is replaced by a power saw, the woodcutter's productivity will increase. Of course, the woodcutter's productivity may be increased even more by added education in the art of woodcutting. In sum, the *MPP* of a factor may rise either because of improvements in other factors or because of improvements in the factor itself. If the *MPP* figures in column 3 of Table 14–1 are increased, the *MRP* figures of column 6 will also be increased. As a result, the factor demand curve of Figure 14–1, part c, and Figure 14–2 will be shifted rightward.

Changes in the Prices of Other Factors

We have already noted that there is a certain amount of substitutability among the productive factors used in most production processes. We also know from our study of demand curves that if the price or prices of goods *other* than the one for which the demand curve is drawn change, then the demand curve for that good will shift. We learned that the direction of the shift in the demand curve will depend on whether the other good whose price changes is a substitute or a complement for the good for which the demand curve is drawn. Similar principles apply when we consider a factor demand curve.

Substitute Factors

Given the demand curve for a factor *F*, let's suppose that the price of a substitute factor *S*

falls. The effect on the demand curve for factor *F* must be broken into two parts. *First,* because the substitute factor *S* is now cheaper relative to the factor *F*, there will be a tendency to substitute factor *S* for factor *F* in the production process. This happens because firms desire to produce their output in the least costly manner. This **substitution effect** alone will reduce the demand for factor *F* and thereby cause factor *F*'s demand curve to shift leftward. *Second,* the reduction in the price of factor *S* means that the cost of producing the final product whose production requires the use of factors *F* and *S* is now lower. This means the supply curve of the final product will be shifted rightward. Hence, there will be an increase in the production of the final product, which will require the use of more of both factors *F* and *S*. This **output effect** alone will shift factor *F*'s demand curve to the right. Since the output effect and the substitution effect push factor *F*'s demand curve in opposite directions, the final position of the factor demand curve after a fall in the price of *S* will depend on which effect is larger. This can only be established on a case-by-case basis.

Complementary Factors

Just as there is complementarity among some final products, such as between coffee and sugar or ham and eggs, there is complementarity among some factors of production. These are called, logically enough, **complementary factors** of production. Two factors are complements in production if an increase in the amount of one of them used in production requires an increase in the use of the other one as well. Conversely, a decrease in the use of one factor will lead to a decrease in use of the other. For example, to produce cargo transportation service in a city requires trucks (capital) and drivers (labor). If the price of trucks falls, it will be cheaper to provide cargo transportation service. It can be sold at a lower price and more of it will be used. The demand curve for the factor trucks will therefore shift rightward. Since each truck needs a driver, a complementary factor, the demand curve for drivers will also shift rightward. In the case of complementary factors there is only an output effect, since complementary factors are not substitutes for one another and so cannot be used in place of one another.

CHECKPOINT 14-2

How do changes in the firm's final product price affect D_F? Why? Use Figure 14–2 to illustrate the effect on employment of the fact reported in a news item that "firms generally have managed to boost their prices even more rapidly than labor costs have risen." How do "productivity gains" affect the position of the factor demand curve in Figure 14–2? Explain your answer.

ELASTICITY OF FACTOR DEMAND

The elasticity of the derived demand curve for a particular productive factor is determined by the nature of the demand for the final product produced with the aid of the factor, as well as by the nature of the production process and costs associated with producing the final product.

Determinants of the Elasticity of Factor Demand

When we consider the effect of a change in the price of a productive factor, we want to know how much the quantity demanded of that factor will change as a result of the change in its price. That is, we want to know the shape of the derived demand curve. This requires an examination of four links between the demand curve for the productive factor and the demand curve for the final product it helps produce. These links are four of the basic determinants of the shape of the derived demand curve for the productive

factor. These determinants are (1) the elasticity of the demand curve for the final product, (2) the ratio of the cost of the productive factor to the total cost of producing the final product, (3) the degree of substitutability of the productive factors used to produce the final product, and (4) the rate of decline in marginal physical product MPP that occurs as the firm expands its output by using more of the factor. We will consider each determinant separately.

1. Elasticity of Final Product Demand

Suppose the price of a productive factor is reduced. The price of that factor is a cost to the firms that use the factor to produce a final product. Hence, the reduction in the factor's price means that the cost of producing the final product will be reduced as well. This in turn will lead to a fall in the price of the final product. Consequently there will be an increase in the quantity of the final product demanded. The extent of that increase will depend upon the elasticity of the demand curve for the final product. The more elastic the demand, the greater the increase will be. The larger the increase in the quantity demanded, the larger the quantity of the final product that will be produced. The larger the quantity of the product produced, the larger will be the increase in the quantity of the inputs needed to produce it. In sum, *the greater the elasticity of the demand curve for the final product, the more elastic will be the derived demand curve for a factor used to produce it, all other things remaining the same.*

2. Ratio of Factor Cost to Total Cost

The meaning of this determinant will become clear if we consider a case in which only one productive factor is used to produce a final product. If the price of this productive factor is reduced by 50 percent, the cost of producing the product will also be reduced by 50 percent, since that cost is exactly the same as the cost of the productive factor. Alternatively, let us suppose that the cost of this one productive factor accounts for only 2 percent of the cost of producing the final product, with the cost of other productive factors accounting for the remaining 98 percent of the total cost of production. A 50 percent reduction in the price of this one productive factor will result in only a 1 percent reduction (50 percent of 2 percent) in the cost of producing the final product. Given the shape of the demand curve for the final product, the resulting decrease in the price of the good that results from the reduction in the cost of production will be greater in the first case than in the second. It follows, then, that the increase in production of the final product that results in the first case will be greater than in the second. Consequently, the increase in the demand for the productive factor will be greater as well. In general, *the larger the ratio of the cost of a productive factor to the total cost of producing the final product, the greater will be the elasticity of the derived demand curve for the productive factor, all other things remaining the same.*

3. Degree of Factor Substitution

The production of most products typically involves the use of several different productive factors. However, it is often true that there are a number of different combinations of these productive factors that might be used to produce a given amount of a product. A thousand bushels of wheat may be grown by use of a number of different combinations of land, labor, and capital equipment. Many labor hours can be combined with a modest amount of capital equipment (such as hoes and sickles) and a certain amount of land. Alternatively, a few labor hours may be combined with more sophisticated capital equipment (such as tractors, combines, and harvesters) and a different amount of land. Generally, if we reduce the amount of one productive factor, we must increase the amounts of one or more of the other productive factors in order to be able to produce the same amount of a product. In other words, there is a certain amount of substitutability between factors used in any production process.

The particular combination of productive factors used to produce a given quantity of a product will depend on the prices of the factors. If the price of one factor falls, it becomes cheaper relative to other productive factors and the firm will tend to use more of it in place of other productive factors. The degree to which this will take place will depend on the degree of substitutability between factors, and this varies with the kind of product produced. For example, the degree of substitutability between labor and capital equipment in the production of wheat is greater than that between these two factors in the production of hothouse orchids. The degree of substitutability between steel and aluminum is greater in the production of automobiles than in the production of airplanes, and greater in either of these than in the production of railroad flatcars. In general, *the greater the degree of substitutability of a factor for other factors in the production of a final product, the greater will be the elasticity of the derived demand curve for the productive factor, all other things remaining the same.* That is, the greater the degree of substitutability of a factor for other factors, the larger will be the increase in the quantity demanded of that factor in response to a given reduction in its price.

4. Rate of Decline in Marginal Physical Product MPP

Finally, note that since $MRP = MPP \times p$, the elasticity of the MRP curve (see Figure 14–2), or factor demand curve D_F, also depends on how much the marginal physical product MPP of the variable factor declines as output is increased by using more of the factor. If MPP tends to decline rapidly, then the factor demand curve will decline rapidly, and if MPP tends to decline slowly, the factor demand curve will decline slowly. In sum, *the MRP curve, or factor demand curve, will be less elastic the more rapidly MPP declines as the firm expands its output by using more of the factor, and it will tend to be more elastic the less rapidly MPP declines.*

Summary of Determinants of Elasticity of Factor Demand

In summary, the elasticity of the derived demand curve for a productive factor depends upon the following:

1. *The elasticity of the demand curve for the final product.* The greater the elasticity of the demand curve for the final product, the greater the elasticity of the factor demand curve.

2. *The ratio of the cost of the productive factor to the total cost of producing the final product.* The larger the ratio of the cost of the productive factor to the total cost of producing the final product, the greater the elasticity of the factor demand curve.

3. *The degree of substitutability of the factor for other factors in the production of the final product.* The greater the degree of substitutability, the greater the elasticity of the factor demand curve.

4. *The rate at which marginal physical product MPP declines as the firm expands its output by using more of the factor.* The slower the decline in *MPP*, the greater the elasticity of the factor demand curve.

=====

CHECKPOINT 14-3

Describe what you think the demand curve for rubber looks like in terms of the first three basic determinants listed above that link it to the final products in which it is used. Take care to think about the likely relative importance of these final products in terms of the proportion of total rubber output that each uses. List five examples of factor inputs that you think would have very inelastic demand curves, and in each case explain your selection in terms of the first three basic determinants that link it to the goods in which it is used. Which do you think has a more elastic demand curve, farm tractors or Ford farm tractors? In general, do you think anything can be said about the relationship between the breadth of the definition of a factor and its elasticity of demand?

=====

OPTIMUM USE OF SEVERAL FACTORS

Our discussion up to this point has assumed that there is only one variable factor of production. In reality a firm typically uses several variable factors of production. How in principle does a firm decide how much of each of these factors to employ? In other words, what determines the optimum (or best) combination of inputs of factors to use in the production process? The answer may be arrived at by two closely related methods: the least-cost combination and the maximum-profit combination. For simplicity we will assume that there are two variable factors of production, both of which are sold in perfectly competitive markets. The analysis, however, readily extends to cases where there are several factors.

The Least-Cost Combination of Factors

In previous chapters whenever we have used the concept of a cost curve, it has always been *assumed* that at any output level the corresponding point on the cost curve represents the least possible cost at which that output level can be produced. But how does the firm select that particular combination of factors that minimizes the cost of producing a given output level? Or in other words, for any given output level, how much of each of the factors should the firm employ if it wants to produce that output level at the least possible cost? The answer is that *the firm produces a given output level at the least possible cost when the marginal physical product per dollar spent on each factor is the same.*

To convince yourself that this is true, suppose there are two factors—labor and capital. Suppose a firm is producing a given level of output with a quantity of capital and a quantity of labor such that

$$\frac{MPP \text{ of capital}}{\text{price of capital}} = \frac{60 \text{ units of output}}{\$10}$$

and

$$\frac{MPP \text{ of labor}}{\text{price of labor}} = \frac{30 \text{ units of output}}{\$10}$$

With the price of a unit of labor and the price of a unit of capital each being $10, the firm could produce more output for the *same* total cost by spending $10 less on labor and $10 more on capital. The cutback of 1 unit of labor would reduce total output by 30 units, while the increase of 1 unit of capital would increase total output by 60 units. Hence, by simply shifting $10 away from expenditure on labor and toward expenditure on capital, there will be a net increase in total output of 30 units.

As long as there is a difference between the marginal physical product of capital MPP_c per dollar and the marginal physical product of labor MPP_L per dollar, the firm can always increase the total output produced for a given total dollar expenditure by reallocating this expenditure away from the factor with the lower MPP per dollar and toward that one with the higher MPP per dollar. As the quantity of labor is reduced and capital increased, we would move up along labor's downward-sloping MPP_L curve while moving down capital's downward-sloping MPP_c curve. In our example we would continue to reduce the quantity of labor used and increase the quantity of capital until

$$\frac{MPP_L}{p_L} = \frac{MPP_c}{p_c} \qquad (1)$$

(p_L and p_c are respectively the price of a unit of labor and capital.) Once a combination of capital and labor is employed such that this equality holds, it is not possible to increase total output further by reallocating the given total expenditure between the two factors. At this point the maximum possible output is being produced given the total dollar expenditure on factors. Stated the other way around, but equivalently, the quantity of output is being produced with the least costly combination of factors whenever the equality in Equation 1 holds.

Any given output level that a firm might choose to produce typically can be produced with a variety of different possible combinations of factors. However, only that combination which satisfies the equality in Equation 1 allows the firm to produce the given output level at the least possible cost. If the quantities of both the factors of capital and labor are variable, it follows that whenever we say that a firm is producing and selling that level of output that *maximizes* profit, we are implicitly assuming that the equality in Equation 1 holds. If this were not true, it would mean there exists a less costly combination of the factors that could be used to produce that output level, in which case profit could be made larger.

The Maximum-Profit Combination of Factors

Looking at the employment of two or more factors of production from the standpoint of the maximum-profit combination is really just a straightforward extension of the marginal revenue product principle that we have already examined in the case of one variable factor.

Recall that so long as the cost of an additional unit of the factor (the marginal factor cost) is less than the addition to total revenue (the marginal revenue product) resulting from the sale of the additional product produced with the help of that unit, the firm will be able to increase profit by using more of the factor to increase output. The firm will expand output until a point is reached at which the marginal factor cost of using one more unit of the factor is equal to the marginal revenue product realized from the sale of the additional output produced with the aid of that unit. If the factor were labor and it cost the firm p_L per unit, the firm would hire labor up to the point where this price was equal to the marginal revenue product of labor MRP_L, or $p_L = MRP_L$.

The same principle applies if there are two or more variable factors of production. If the firm is a price taker in the market for these factors (it can't affect the prices of these factors), it will be able to increase its profit as long as the MRP of any factor still exceeds the price of that factor. If the firm has two factors, capital and labor, it will maximize profit by employing that quantity of each factor such that

$$p_L = MRP_L$$

and

$$p_c = MRP_c$$

Note that these two expressions may be rewritten as

$$\frac{MRP_L}{p_L} = 1$$

and

$$\frac{MRP_c}{p_c} = 1$$

or

$$\frac{MRP_L}{p_L} = \frac{MRP_c}{p_c} = 1 \qquad (2)$$

Relationship Between Least-Cost and Maximum-Profit Approaches

How is the least-cost combination of factors viewpoint, expressed by Equation 1, related to the maximum-profit combination of factors viewpoint, expressed by Equation 2? Recall that the marginal revenue product of a factor equals its marginal physical product multiplied by the price p of the product that it helps to produce. That is, we know that $MRP_L = p \times MPP_L$ and $MRP_c = p \times MPP_c$. Hence, if we multiply both sides of Equation 1 by p we get

$$\frac{MRP_L}{p_L} = \frac{MRP_c}{p_c} \qquad (3)$$

This looks very much like Equation 2 *except that* this equality can hold even if the ratio of the marginal revenue products of the factors to their factor prices does not equal 1, as is required by the maximum-profit combination of factors point of view expressed in Equation 2. In other words, if the equality in Equation 2 holds, then the equality in Equation 1 must hold as well, but if the equality

in Equation 1 holds, it does not necessarily mean that the equality in Equation 2 holds.

What is the meaning of this distinction? Recall that when both labor and capital are factors that the firm can vary in its production process, the equality in Equation 1 must be satisfied at all points along the firm's cost curve. This is so because each point on the cost curve represents the least possible cost for which the associated output level can be produced. However, it is entirely possible for the firm to produce and sell a quantity of output that does not maximize profit according to the marginal-cost-equals-marginal-revenue criterion that we studied in previous chapters. Nonetheless, it can still be producing that quantity of output at the least possible cost. That is, the equality in Equation 1 will be satisfied and so will the equality in Equation 3, which is simply obtained by multiplying both sides of Equation 1 by the product price p. However, the ratio of the marginal revenue product of each factor to its respective price will not equal 1. The equality in Equation 2 is satisfied *only if* the firm is also producing and selling that level of output that maximizes profit.

Example of Distinction Between Least-Cost and Maximum-Profit Approaches

In sum, the equality in Equation 2 says that in order to maximize profit, the firm should use that least-cost combination of productive factors such that the marginal revenue product per dollar spent on each factor equals 1. For example, suppose p_L and p_c each equal $1 and that a firm is producing a level of output such that $MRP_L = MRP_c = \$5$. The equality in Equations 1 and 3 is satisfied— the firm is producing output at the least possible cost. However, Equation 2 is clearly not satisfied. The firm is not maximizing profit. Since the firm can buy an additional unit of each factor at $1 apiece, and since the *MRP* of each factor exceeds its price by $4 ($5 − $1), the firm can increase profit by hiring more of the factors and increasing its level of

Will Robots Replace Workers?

During the 1980s a strange new word became more commonplace in our vocabulary—"robotics," a new field dealing with the technology and use of robots in all sorts of practical applications. No longer a science-fiction fantasy, robots are beginning to replace workers in a wide variety of manufacturing operations. They promise greater automation of the office as well. It is becoming so apparent that robots will take over an increasing share of the American workload that both labor leaders and their rank and file are concerned about job losses due to robots.

Why hire robots? There are lots of reasons. A robot doesn't have good or bad days—only perfect days. Robots don't belong to unions. A robot does the same task over and over again without mistakes. A robot will work all night without complaint. A robot doesn't require a salary, fringe benefits, or pension. Robots don't go on vacation and they don't call in sick. A robot never talks back or asks for a raise.

The Economics of Robots

About half the robots used in the United States are employed in the auto industry. This is not surprising given that the hourly cost of an auto worker (including all fringers as well as wages) is the highest among all blue-collar workers in U.S. manufacturing. General Motors alone plans to have more than 14,000 robots in place by 1990.

When rising wage demands make it more and more difficult to run a manufacturing plant at a profit, robots are increasingly seen as an alternative. Reports suggest that typically an industrial robot purchased for $50,000 can be paid for and operated for about $6 per hour, compared to an average minimum cost in excess of $20 for a human worker. It is not hard to see why it has been predicted that by the year 2,000, 45 million factory and office jobs could be affected by automation in some way. Robots simply seem to be a sensible alternative to human workers from a "bottom-line" standpoint.

Displaced Workers and Fears of Unemployment

The prospect of robots replacing millions of humans in the workplace worries a lot of people. Even the most profit-minded management is concerned that greater efficiency might not mean much if millions of people are thrown out of work by robot technology. There is particular concern that unskilled workers, who have traditionally worked on the lowest rung of American industry, will be lost in the shuffle as businesses rush to buy robots to increase efficiency and match the competition.

There is an old and familiar ring to all this however. The history of rising living standards is one of technological change eliminating certain kinds of jobs while creating new ones, and improving labor productivity in the process. Candlemakers were replaced by makers of kerosene lamps, who in turn were replaced by electricians. Blacksmiths and carriage makers were replaced by auto workers. One farmer today can produce the equivalent of what 50 produced at the turn of the century. The other 49 are now working in other sectors of the economy which, in fact, were able to develop and expand precisely because labor was released from the farm. Automation of manufacturing assembly lines and the office place has been going on for decades—machines replacing laborers. The advent of robots is just a continuation of that process. They too are just another kind of capital, a new type of machine. Their development is no more ominous for jobs and employment than the development of the steam shovel for ditch digging, the printing press for reproducing manuscripts, or the automatic cash teller for dispensing money.

Questions

1. How does the development of robots affect the marginal physical product of capital? Illustrate your answer in a graph.

2. Are robots likely to affect the marginal physical product of labor and, if so, how? Are robots likely to affect labor productivity, defined as the average product of labor? If so, why?

---

output and sales. It should continue to hire capital and labor until the *MRP* of each falls to $1. At that point, the equality in Equation 2 will be satisfied and the firm will produce and sell that quantity of output that maximizes profit.

SUMMARY

1. There are two basic reasons why resource pricing is important: (1) it determines how the economy's limited supply of productive resources, or factors, is allocated to the various production activities necessary to produce the multitude of goods and services society wants, and (2) it is a major determinant of how income earned from productive activities is distributed among the economy's citizens.

2. The demand for a productive factor ultimately derives from the demand for the final product or products that it helps to make.

3. The marginal productivity theory of factor demand says that when a firm is a price taker in a factor market, it will hire the factor up to the point at which the price of the factor just equals its marginal revenue product. Because of this, the marginal revenue product curve of the factor constitutes the firm's demand curve for the factor.

4. Because of the law of diminishing returns, the marginal physical product of a factor falls as additional units of it are used. Consequently, the marginal revenue product curve, or factor demand curve, is downward sloping for this reason alone if the firm is a price taker in the product market. However, if the firm's product demand curve is also downward sloping, the factor demand curve will be downward sloping not only because of the decline in marginal physical product with the use of additional units of the factor but also because of the decline in product price.

5. The factor demand curves of individual firms can be summed to obtain the market demand curve for a factor. However, when doing so, it should be recognized that it is not realistic to assume that the price of the product the factor helps produce remains constant when we change factor price and thereby move along the factor demand curve.

6. Shifts in a factor demand curve are caused by (1) changes in demand for the final product; (2) changes in the quantities of other productive factors; (3) technological improvements in the factor for which the factor demand curve is drawn or in the other factors with which it is combined in the production process, or both; and (4) changes in the prices of other factors.

7. If two factors X and Y are substitutes in production and there is a change in the price of X, there will be a substitution and an output effect, each of which pushes the factor demand curve for Y in a direction opposite to the other. The ultimate direction of the shift depends on which effect dominates. On the other hand, if X and Y are complements in production and the price of X rises (falls), then the factor demand curve for Y will shift leftward (rightward) since there is only an output effect among complementary factors.

8. The elasticity of a factor demand curve depends on (1) the elasticity of the demand curve for the final product, (2) the ratio of the cost of the productive factor to the total cost of producing the final product, (3) the degree of substitutability of the productive factor for other productive factors used to produce the final product, and (4) the rate at which the marginal physical product declines as the firm expands output by using more of the factor.

9. To produce any given level of output, the firm's least-cost combination of productive factors is determined by employing that quantity of each such that the marginal physical product per dollar spent on each factor is the same for every factor.

10. To produce that level of output that maximizes profit, the firm should use that least-cost combination of productive factors such that the marginal revenue product per dollar spent on each factor equals 1.

KEY TERMS AND CONCEPTS

    complementary factors
    derived demand
    marginal physical product
    marginal productivity theory of factor
      demand
    marginal revenue product
    output effect
    substitution effect

QUESTIONS AND PROBLEMS

1. Specify how each of the following would affect the demand curve for a productive factor X that is used in the production of a product Y. Where there is uncertainty, explain why.

  a. an increase in the demand for Y;

  b. a decrease in the number of substitute products for Y;

  c. a change in production technology that has the effect of reducing the amount of X used relative to other factors;

  d. a technological improvement in one of the other factors that is used with X in the production process;

  e. a fall in the price of one of the other factors that is used with X in the production process;

  f. a decrease in the price of X;

  g. a natural disaster that destroys some of the other factors used with X in the production process.

2. "It would be just awful for the kids if they (Congress) raise the minimum wage again. It's bad enough, but if the floor goes up again, the kids simply won't ever get hired" (Betty Jackson, social worker, Dade County, Florida). Using the marginal productivity theory of factor demand and the aid of a diagram like Figure 14–2, explain the nature of the problem that concerns Betty Jackson.

3. How is the derivation of the demand curve for a factor by an imperfectly competitive firm similar to the derivation of the market demand curve for a factor?

4. Sometimes it is argued that the way to help poor people is to educate and train them in ways that will increase their productivity. Assuming a perfectly competitive industry, how might this point of view be refuted or buttressed by the marginal productivity theory of factor demand? (Remember that while each firm in the industry is a price taker in the labor market, this does not rule out the possibility that the supply curve of labor to the industry may be upward sloping—even though to the individual firm it appears horizontal as in Figure 14–2.) In assessing this point of view, what difference does it make whether the supply curve of labor to the industry is horizontal or upward sloping?

5. Consider the production and sale of automobiles. Suppose that the price of each of the following items falls by 5 percent: safety glass, copper, aluminum, steel, rubber, synthetic fiber, plastic, and wood.

    a. Rank the items according to the degrees of impact that you think the 5 percent price reduction in each has on the price of automobiles. Explain the reasoning underlying your ranking.

    b. Rank the items according to their degree of substitutability in the production of automobiles. Explain your ranking.

    c. Rank the items according to the elasticity of the automobile industry's demand curve for each of them, and explain the reasons underlying your ranking.

6. Explain why it is possible for a firm to use a least-cost combination of factors and yet still not maximize profit.

7. Consider a firm that uses labor and capital to produce a good for which these two factors have the productivity shown in the following table. Suppose that the good is sold at a price of $1 per unit, and that the price of

labor is $1 per laborer and the price of capital is $2 per unit of capital. Assume the firm is a price taker in both the factor market and the product market.

Number of Laborers	MPP of Labor	Units of Capital	MPP of Capital
1	12	1	20
2	10	2	17
3	8	3	14
4	7	4	7
5	4	5	2
6	2	6	1
7	1	7	0

a. If the firm wanted to produce 88 units of output, what combination of the two factors would allow it to do so for the least cost? Explain the principle by which you arrived at your answer.

b. If the firm wanted to maximize profit, what quantity of output should it produce and what combination of the two factors should it use to produce it? Explain the principle by which you arrived at your answer.

c. If your answers to parts a and b are both least-cost combinations, why are they different?

d. Suppose the price of a laborer rises to $8. How would this change your answer in part b of this question?

15

Wage Determination, Labor Market Structure, and Unions

AFTER READING THIS CHAPTER, YOU WILL BE ABLE TO:

1. Distinguish between money wages and real wages.

2. Summarize the reasons why wages differ across occupations and between workers.

3. Explain the role of market structure in the determination of the wage and employment level in a labor market.

4. Explain the origins and nature of the growth of the union movement in the United States.

5. Describe the institutional framework of today's labor markets and the nature of collective bargaining.

6. Assess the record of achievement of unionism.

In the last chapter we examined the marginal productivity theory of factor demand. We saw that it provides a convenient starting point for thinking about the demand for labor. However, there is much more to be explained about the nature of wage determination in today's labor markets. The existence of large unions confronting large corporations to hammer out agreements on wages, fringe benefits, working conditions, hiring, layoffs, grievance procedures, and management-versus-union prerogatives tends to conjure up images of war games more often than the cut-and-dried interaction of supply and demand curves.

For most households wages and salaries are the primary source of income. They are therefore a major determinant of most people's aspiration for a decent standard of living, or perhaps even a claim on "the good life." They are the payment to our most important resource—people, or what economists often refer to as human capital. Little wonder that real-world wage determination has often been accompanied by hostile confrontations and even violence.

In this chapter we will look more deeply into the nature of wage determination, and in particular the role played by unions and other important institutional factors that have fashioned the modern-day collective bargaining process used by management and labor.

WHAT ARE WAGES, SALARIES, AND EARNINGS?

The terms wages, salaries, and earnings are familiar to all of us. Loosely speaking, they refer to the payments made in exchange for labor services. More particularly, the term *wage* is commonly used to refer to the hourly rate of payment made to blue-collar workers, while *salary* customarily refers to the weekly, monthly, or annual payments made to white-collar workers. The term *earnings* may refer to either wages or salaries, but most often it is used to designate the sum of payments received from the sale of any kind of labor service over some considerable length of time. The term *labor* may refer to any kind of worker, from the floor sweeper to the chairperson of the board, or to doctors, dentists, mechanics, proprietors of self-owned businesses, fire fighters, and even entertainers and professional athletes. In general, **wage** *is the price per unit of labor service,* such as the price per labor hour, for example.

Money Wages Versus Real Wages

It is very important in any discussion of wages always to keep in mind the distinction between money wages and real wages. *The* **money wage** *is simply the size of the wage measured in dollars and cents. The* **real wage** *is the size of the wage measured in terms of the quantity of goods that can be purchased with it.* The real wage is a more meaningful measure of a worker's wage because it indicates the standard of living that the wage makes available to the worker in terms of purchasing power.

For example, suppose you were offered a job paying a money wage of $20 per hour. Sounds pretty tempting, doesn't it? However, suppose you find out that the price of a loaf of bread has risen to $10, a pair of shoes to $200, and a gallon of gas to $7. Similar price increases have also taken place for a host of other commodities. You would probably decide that an hourly money wage of $20 is not much of a real wage—it simply doesn't allow you to buy very much. Almost unconsciously, we tend to think of a dollar in terms of what it will buy. In other words, we think of its real value, measured in terms of the goods it enables us to have. We do the same thing when quoted a money wage. That is, we convert it to a real wage by envisioning the quantities of various goods that it will buy.

Converting a Money Wage to a Real Wage

How do we convert a money wage to a real wage? Let's take a simple example. Suppose the only good in the economy is bread. Also, suppose your money wage is $6 per hour and that the price of bread is $1 per loaf. Since the real wage is the size of the wage measured in terms of the quantity of goods that can be purchased, your real wage must be 6 loaves of bread. It is the money wage of $6 divided by the price of a loaf of bread, which is $1. Suppose that next year the price of a loaf of bread rises to $2 per loaf. If the money wage remains at $6 per hour, the real wage must fall to 3 loaves of bread per hour, or $6 divided by $2. Since the money wage of $6 only buys half as many loaves as previously, the real wage has been halved.

In reality there are many goods in our economy. So when economists want to convert a money wage to a real wage, they usually divide the money wage by an index of the general price level. The index of the general price level is constructed in such a way as to measure the cost of the "basket" of goods purchased by a "typical," or "representative," household. The real wage obtained in this fashion is a measure of the money wage's purchasing power in terms of such a basket of goods.

For example, the consumer price index had a value of 100 in 1967, a value of roughly 72 in 1950, and a value of roughly 311 in 1984. This index may be interpreted to mean that the price of a basket of goods in 1950 was about 30 percent lower than the price of that same basket of goods in 1967. By 1984, however, the price of that basket had risen until it was over three times as expensive as it was in 1967. Another completely equivalent interpretation is that $1 in 1967 had exactly the same purchasing power in 1967 as $.72 did in 1950. Similarly, it would take $3.11 in 1984 to have the same purchasing power that $1 had in 1967. Using 1967 as a base year, we can convert a money wage in any year to its equivalent expressed in 1967 dollars. (The selection of 1967 as the base year is arbitrary.) We would then have a measure of the real wage expressed in terms of 1967 dollars. For example, suppose we convert a money wage of $6 per hour to a

real wage expressed in terms of 1967 dollars for each of the years 1950, 1967, and 1984. This customarily would be done by dividing $6 by the consumer price index, expressed as .72 for 1950, 1 for 1967, and 3.11 for 1984. The real wage for 1950 expressed in 1967 dollars would be $8.34 (equal $6 ÷ .72), for 1967 it would be $6 (equal $6 ÷ 1), and for 1984 it would be $1.93 (equal $6 ÷ 3.11). Hence if your hourly money wage (the number of dollars actually paid to you for an hour of work) remained the same at $6, your real wage would have fallen over the years from 1950 to 1984. The amount of purchasing power given to you in exchange for 1 hour of work in 1984 would have been less than one-quarter of what it was in 1950.

Money Wages and Real Wages Since 1955

An index of the "representative," or average, hourly money wage earned in the private sector of the U. S. economy for each of the years 1955–1984 is shown in Figure 15-1. Also shown is an index of the average hourly real wage in each of these years. The average real wage index is obtained by dividing the index of the money wage for each year by an index of the general price level for that year. Clearly the money wage has risen at a faster rate than the real wage. This reflects the fact that the general price level also has been rising throughout these years, so that the purchasing power of the money wage, as measured by the real wage, has not risen as fast. Nonetheless, the rise in the real wage does indicate that the rise in the money wage has been more rapid than the rise in the general price level, except during 1974, 1979, 1980, and 1981.

In 1974 our economy had a severe recession. At the same time, however, it also experienced more inflation than at any time since the Korean War in the early 1950s. In the face of this recession and the accompanying rise in the unemployment rate, labor was not in a position to command increases in the money wage rate sufficient to keep ahead of

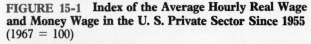

FIGURE 15-1 Index of the Average Hourly Real Wage and Money Wage in the U. S. Private Sector Since 1955 (1967 = 100)

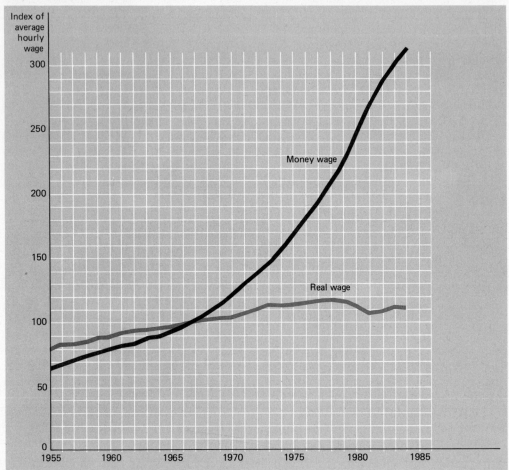

The index of the average hourly real wage shown here is obtained by dividing the index of the average hourly money wage for each year by an index of the general price level for that year. Observe that the average hourly money wage has risen at a faster rate than the average hourly real wage. This reflects the fact that the general price level has also been rising throughout these years, which means that the purchasing power of the money wage, as measured by the real wage, has not risen as fast. The rise in the real wage does indicate that the rise in the money wage has been more rapid than the rise in the general price level up through 1972. In 1974, 1979, 1980, and 1981, money wage increases did not keep up with the rise in the general price level, and the real wage fell.

SOURCE: U.S. Department of Labor, Bureau of Labor Statistics.

the general rise in prices. Consequently, real wages fell. The rate of inflation in the 1979–1980 period exceeded that of 1974. Money wages increased less rapidly than the general price level in 1979, and real wages fell once more. A mild recession in 1980 again made it difficult for labor to obtain money wage increases sufficient to keep up with rising prices. Again, real wages fell in 1980 and 1981.

Real Wages and Productivity

In the last chapter we saw how the demand for a factor such as labor depends on its productivity. In particular, the marginal productivity theory of factor demand tells us that if a firm purchases labor services in a perfectly competitive market (the firm can buy as many labor hours as it wants at the given wage rate), it will hire labor up to the point where the marginal revenue product MRP of labor equals its money wage w. Recall also that the MRP of labor is equal to the marginal physical product of labor MPP multiplied by the price p of the product that the labor is used to produce. This may be written

$$w = p \times MPP = MRP \qquad (1)$$

Equivalently, by dividing both sides of the equation by p, this may be expressed as

$$\frac{w}{p} = MPP \qquad (2)$$

The left side of Equation 2 is the real wage, which is the money wage w divided by the price p. Note that since p is the price of a unit of the firm's product, $w \div p$ is the real wage in that it measures the compensation of labor in terms of the number of units of the firm's product.

We know from the last chapter that technological progress and an increase in other factors used in combination with labor lead to increases in labor productivity. This in turn is reflected in increases in MPP and rightward shifts in the demand curve for la-

bor. From Equation 2 we can see that such increases in MPP mean that labor's real wage, $w \div p$, will rise when labor productivity increases. This suggests that the rise in the real-wage index for the private sector of the U.S. economy shown in Figure 15–1 reflects the growth in demand for labor due to the growth in labor productivity. Of course, the supply of labor has been growing over these years, and we know from supply-and-demand analysis that this factor by itself would tend to push money wages and real wages down.[1] But since the real wage has been rising, it seems that the growth in labor productivity has been great enough to cause the demand for labor to grow at a faster rate than the supply of labor. This is illustrated in Figure 15–2.

A rough measure of the growth in productivity in our economy is provided by the behavior of output per labor hour. If labor productivity increases, then the quantity of output produced per labor hour increases, all other things remaining the same. An index of output per labor hour in the private sector of the economy is shown in Table 15–1 for each of the years since 1960. For comparison, the data for the index of the real wage plotted in Figure 15–1 are also shown in Table 15–1. Notice how closely these indices move together over time, supporting the view that the real wage has increased with the growth in productivity.

Sources of Productivity Growth

In the last chapter we noted that increases in labor productivity, or the MPP of labor, may be due to a number of factors. The most obvious is increased years of schooling and job-specific training, so-called investment in hu-

[1] You may convince yourself of this by turning back to Figure 14–2. The marginal cost of the factor MCF in that figure shifts down along D_F. Given the price level p, from Figure 14–1, part b, we can see that this means that the MPP of labor falls. From Equation 2, this means that the real wage, $w \div p$, falls.

FIGURE 15-2 **Effect of Growth in Labor Supply and Demand on Real Wage**

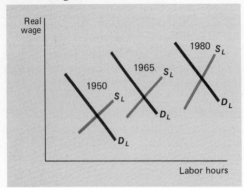

The increase in productivity in the United States has caused the demand for labor to increase at a faster rate than the increase in the supply of labor. Hence, over time the demand curve for labor has shifted farther rightward than the supply curve, thereby causing the real wage to rise.

TABLE 15-1 **Index of Output per Labor Hour and Real Wage in United States Private Sector Since 1960** (1967 = 100)

Year	Output per Labor Hour	Real Wage ($w \div p$)
1960	78.0	81.5
1961	80.6	83.7
1962	84.6	86.5
1963	87.6	88.6
1964	91.2	92.0
1965	94.2	94.0
1966	98.2	97.6
1967	100.0	100.0
1968	103.0	103.4
1969	103.3	105.2
1970	104.4	106.6
1971	108.4	108.9
1972	112.3	111.9
1973	115.2	113.4
1974	112.1	111.2
1975	112.2	112.2
1976	116.4	115.5
1977	118.2	117.4
1978	119.2	118.3
1979	118.1	116.3
1980	117.5	112.7
1981	119.7	108.3
1982	120.0	109.3
1983	123.2	110.9
1984	127.6	110.8

SOURCE: U.S. Department of Labor, Bureau of Labor Statistics, *Handbook of Labor Statistics*, 1985.

man capital that improves labor productivity directly. In addition, labor productivity increases when labor is combined with new capital equipment embodying the latest advances in technology and scientific know-how. Output per labor hour on the farm increased greatly when the tractor, with its much greater pulling power, replaced the horse. Somewhat less obvious at first thought, but nonetheless of great importance to the growth of labor productivity, are the improvements in economic organization and other institutional arrangements in our society. The improvement of traffic flows through and around metropolitan areas makes the transport of goods to markets and labor to jobs easier, thereby contributing to increased productivity. Effectively enforced antitrust laws may well promote the quest for more efficient operation of firms trying to get a competitive edge on rivals. Similarly, the more competitive environment may provide greater incentive to develop and adopt more productive technologies.

Does Technological Progress Create Unemployment and Make Labor Worse Off?

One thing is clear. It is very difficult to disentangle, identify, and separate out the individual sources of growth in labor productivity. With this in mind it is interesting to consider the common allegation that new machines and technology eliminate jobs and create unemployment, thereby making labor worse off. It is true that this kind of progress may well eliminate certain jobs and cause certain workers to seek other employment. But this is typically, though not always, a short-run adjustment process. In the long run, new machines and technology increase labor productivity and thus increase output per labor hour and make possible an increase in real wages. The jobs eliminated release a certain amount of labor and make it available to produce more goods and services previously unavailable. Hence, for a given size of the economy's labor force, it is possible to produce a larger total output. Over the long run it is this process that allows the real wage of all workers to rise and thereby results in an increase in the general standard of living.

For example, even if all of India's labor force were fully employed, the total output of the Indian economy would be minuscule compared to that of the United States. Because labor productivity in India is low, so are real wages. The low productivity is due to a number of factors: a generally high rate of illiteracy and poor health due to low investment in human capital (in the form of education, job training, and medical care); an insufficient quantity of modern physical capital (machines, paved highways, and so forth) to complement the labor force and make it possible to engage in modern production activities; and, of course, political and cultural institutions that are often not conducive to a change in these conditions. Yet if India's labor force were fully employed, this would amount to several hundred million jobs! This example points out that jobs are not the source of an economy's wealth. Rather it is the high productivity and the high real wages that high productivity makes possible. It is differences in productivity that explain the differences in real wages between nations.

CHECKPOINT* 15-1

In 1977 the United Steelworkers of America negotiated a contract with steel companies calling for a "guaranteed annual wage increase of at least 3 percent in addition to a cost-of-living rise." Describe this contract in terms of its impact on the money wage as compared to its impact on the real wage. Suppose someone is concerned that the introduction of new capital equipment will eliminate jobs. To be logically consistent with this point of view, what should this person's position be on a plan to introduce a more efficient traffic flow pattern in and around a large city? Why? What jobs might be eliminated? How will output per labor hour be increased?

*Answers to all Checkpoints can be found at the back of the text.

Why Wages Differ

Why do wages differ from one occupation to another and between individuals in the same occupation? Doesn't it seem unfair that some professional athletes are paid several hundred thousand dollars a year for playing a game while a coal miner makes but a small fraction of that sum for performing a dangerous, grimy job providing an essential source of energy for the economy?

These differences can be explained in terms of supply and demand. Hardly anyone can play golf as well as Jack Nicklaus or run with a football like Tony Dorsett. The supply of that kind of talent is extremely limited and the public's demand to see it displayed is large. While the demand for coal and consequently the derived demand for coal miners is also large, many people possess the ability and willingness to be coal miners. In short, the difference in wages between great professional athletes and coal miners is due to the difference between the size of the supply *relative* to the demand for the services provided in each of these occupations. The supply of great professional athletes *relative* to the demand to see them perform is much smaller than the supply of coal miners *relative* to the demand for their services in producing coal.

But what are the factors underlying such differences in demand relative to supply in various labor markets, both within and across occupations? Perhaps the best way to identify these factors is to envision the nature of an economy in which there are no wage differences.

Suppose all members of the labor force were exactly alike in ability, skills, and educational background. Each worker could therefore do any job as well as any other worker, whether it were brain surgery, plumbing, playing professional football or the violin, or collecting garbage. If in addition each laborer were completely indifferent as to choice of job or occupation, the wage would be the same for each and every laborer in a competitive economy. For example, if the wage were higher in one occupation relative to that prevailing in the others, laborers would tend to move into that occupation and out of the others. Then the increased supply of labor to that occupation would push its wage rate down and the decreased supply to the others would push theirs up until a uniform wage prevailed once again. Conversely, if the wage in one occupation were lower than that prevailing in others, workers would move from that occupation and into the others until the wage difference was similarly eliminated. Of course, the elimination of wage differences requires that labor be perfectly mobile. If members of the labor force are *not* perfectly mobile, are not indifferent as to job preference, and are not exactly alike in ability, skills, and educational background, wage differences will exist between occupations, between workers in the same occupation, and between geographic locations. We will now look at each of these factors in turn.

Labor Mobility

One has only to look at the persistently high unemployment rates and low wages in Appalachia to see that low wages and a lack of jobs do not necessarily cause labor to move. Family ties, old friends, a sense of "roots," the costs of searching for a new job, the costs of moving, ignorance about alternatives, and a fear of the unfamiliar are all factors that may inhibit labor mobility. These factors do not mean, however, that labor is immobile "at any price." They lead to labor immobility

only when the alternatives to the status quo as perceived by a worker are not felt to be worth the cost of change. Often these factors contribute more significantly to immobility among older workers. Given that their working-life horizon is shorter than that of younger workers, they have less chance to recoup the costs of searching out and moving to a new job. This is even more the case when costs of retraining and acquiring new skills are required in order to successfully make such a move.

Labor immobility can also foster high wages. For example, there are institutional constraints on labor mobility that tend to keep wages high in some occupations. Law, medicine, dentistry, and a number of other occupations require participants to be licensed before they may legally practice their trade in a given state or locality. Those already licensed typically exercise firm control over the local licensing board. Obviously they are not eager to issue more licenses that would permit an influx of practitioners from other areas of the country and thereby push their wages down. Similarly, craft unions restrict the mobility of tradespeople. An electrician is going to have a tough time finding a job in most big cities without a union card. If an electrician desires to move to such a city in order to realize a much larger wage, the possibility of doing this typically rests with the local electricians' union.

Of course, in addition to all these considerations there is the fact that demand for different kinds of labor in different parts of the economy is always changing. Indeed, the resulting differences in wage rates between occupations and regions are signals that tell the labor force where more lucrative opportunities exist and when local ones may be drying up. In a dynamic economy where this allocation mechanism is at work, we would naturally expect to see wage differences for this reason alone. Since labor is not perfectly mobile, it takes time for it to move in response to these signals.

Another factor that impedes labor mobility is discrimination by race and sex. This takes many forms, from an employer not being willing to hire a member of a particular minority group (black, Mexican, Indian, or immigrant) or sex to barriers to training and education necessary to gain admittance to a particular occupation.

Job Preference and Nonpecuniary Considerations

Even if each laborer were exactly like every other laborer in ability, skills, and educational background, there might be considerable variation in how much each enjoys, or does not enjoy, doing a particular job. Hence, two equally able workers might have to be offered considerably different wages in order to induce them to take a given job.

For example, a great many people feel the death penalty is an unconscionable punishment for the state to impose, no matter what the crime. Yet states where the death penalty exists have no trouble finding executioners when they pay them a wage of around $100 to $200 per execution. It takes no special training or talent to turn the gas valves or throw the electrical switch. What wage would it take for you to be willing to do this job? Some of you may say there is no wage that could induce you to do it. Others of you may feel it would require a lot more than $200. Though reluctant to admit it, a few might pay (accept a negative wage) to be given the job depending on the nature of the particular case. In a technical sense all are equally able to do the job, but because of the great differences in feelings about doing it, the necessary wage may vary greatly from one potential executioner to the next.

Many jobs in the economy may differ in the wages they pay in part because of these so-called nonpecuniary advantages or disadvantages associated with them. Working conditions, the degree of danger associated with doing the job, the location, and even the degree of pride or humiliation one may feel in having a particular kind of job are all nonpecuniary considerations. *The* **nonpecuniary considerations** *surrounding a job are the characteristics associated with it that will cause labor to require either a higher or a lower wage, depending on whether the particular characteristics make the job either less or more attractive.* Welders who work on skyscrapers get higher wages than welders who work at ground level. The difference is necessary as compensation for the greater danger associated with working at such heights.

Ability, Skills, and Education

The marginal productivity theory of factor demand tells us that the greater the productivity of a factor such as labor, the greater will be the demand for it. Labor's productivity can be enhanced by vocational training, formal education, on-the-job experience, improved health care, and any other form of investment in human capital. Of course, such factors as innate ability and motivation play a large role in determining just how much productivity can be improved by education and specialized training. Very few of us will ever play tennis like John McEnroe or Chris Evert, or be scientists like Einstein or Marie Curie, no matter how much training and education we receive.

In general, the greater one's productivity in any given occupation, the greater will be one's earnings. The more skilled house painter, the more motivated salesperson, and the more competent manager all have an edge over their less capable coworkers. Their greater productivity will typically mean that the demand for their services is larger. If you can do a job more efficiently and quickly than the next person, your output per unit of time is greater and you can expect to earn more. A barber who can give more haircuts per hour than other barbers will usually earn a higher wage. Unusual talent or skills will not necessarily result in high wages, however. Again, it depends on the relationship between supply and demand. The supply of blacksmiths is less today than a hundred years ago, but so is the demand for their services. Thus, wages are not particularly high for the few that remain.

FIGURE 15-3   **The Relationship Between Education, Age, and Earnings**

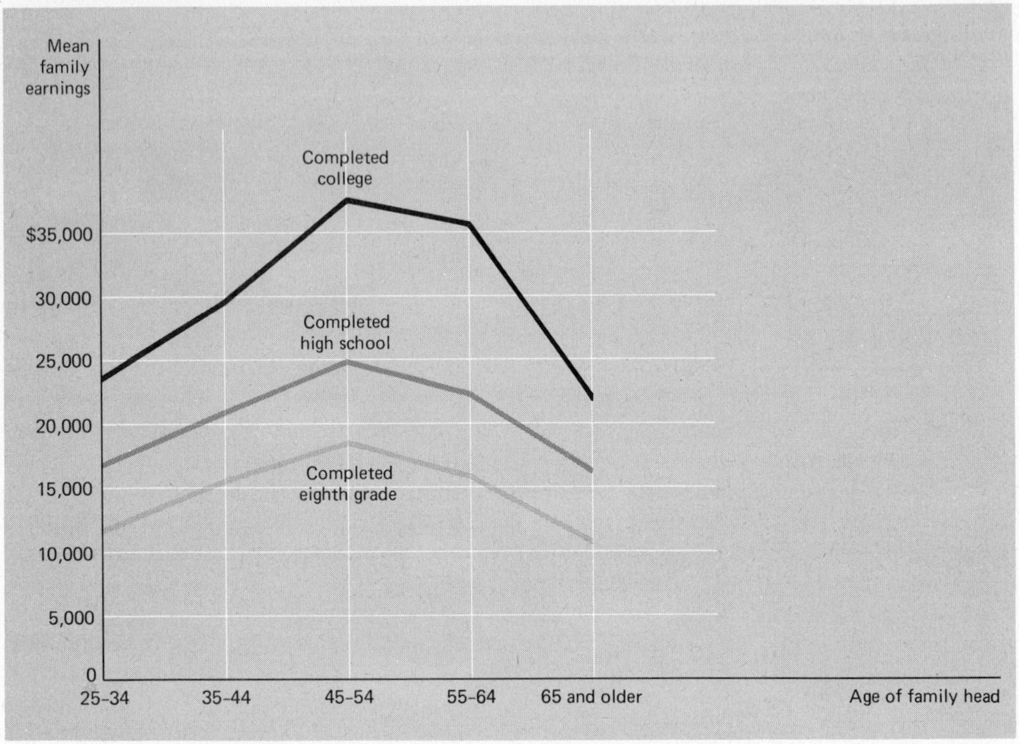

Over a lifetime, the earnings of college graduates tend to exceed those of high school graduates, which in turn tend to exceed the earnings of those who have only completed the eighth grade. (These data refer to heads of families for the year 1978.)

SOURCE: U.S. Department of Commerce, *Current Population Reports,* Series P-60, 1980.

Many occupations require a person to have a considerable amount of education in order to become successfully employed in them. In general, the more rigorous the training and the more prolonged and expensive the required educational process, the higher the level of wages required to induce people into that particular occupation, other things remaining the same. Surgery and architecture are examples of such professions. This consideration, together with the fact that increased training and education tend to increase labor productivity, suggests that higher earnings should be related to higher educational levels. The available evidence, as indicated in Figure 15–3, seems to bear this out.

CHECKPOINT 15-2

Rank the following jobs according to your preference for them, assuming each pays an hourly wage of $5 per hour: mail carrier, garbage collector, dogcatcher, night watchperson, traffic cop. If the night watchperson's job pays $5 per hour, what hourly wage would each of the other jobs have to pay for *you* to feel indifferent as to which job you take? (The necessary wage of each will typically be different from that of

every other.) Now have a friend answer these same questions and compare answers. If I wanted to fill one garbage collector job *and* one traffic cop job, what would be the minimum hourly wage I would have to offer to pay for each of these two jobs if I want to get each of you to fill one of them? Explain what factors determined which one of you took which job.

MARKET STRUCTURE AND WAGE DETERMINATION

In previous chapters, we have seen how the equilibrium quantity and price of a final product depend on the structure of the market in which it is bought and sold. Similarly, the wage rate and the quantity of labor services bought and sold in a particular labor market also depend on market structure. We will now consider several important types of labor market structure and the significant role played by unions in some of them.

Wages and Competitive Markets

In a perfectly competitive labor market, there are so many laborers competing with one another for jobs that no one of them individually is able to affect the wage that he or she receives. The same is true on the buyers' side of this market. There are so many employers that each represents but a small fraction of the entire market. So small in fact that no one of them can affect, by their individual hiring and firing decisions, the wage that must be paid for labor services. In aggregate, however, employers in such a labor market will have to pay a higher wage if they want to increase the quantity of labor they hire.

As long as workers have alternative employment opportunities, it will be necessary to pay a wage high enough to induce them away from their next best employment opportunity in some other area of the economy. As more workers are hired, employers can only compete for those with other employment opportunities by paying them a higher wage.

Figure 15–4 depicts equilibrium in a perfectly competitive labor market (part b) and the associated equilibrium position of a typical firm hiring labor in that market (part a). This figure might be the market for farmhands in Kansas, for example. The market demand curve D_m in part b is the sum of the individual firms' demand curves for labor, such as d_f in part a. These demand curves are the marginal revenue product curves MRP for labor for each firm. The demand curve d_f is a factor demand curve like those studied in the previous chapter (D_F in Figure 14–2, for example). The market supply curve S_m in part b is upward sloping, reflecting the fact that if all firms want to hire more labor in this market, they will have to pay a higher wage. The market equilibrium money wage w_0 is determined by the intersection of the market demand and supply curves, D_m and S_m respectively, in part b.

The supply curve of labor for the individual firm (part a) is perfectly horizontal at the money wage rate w_0. This reflects the fact that the individual firm cannot influence the wage no matter how little or how much labor it hires. Because of this, the supply curve of labor for the individual firm is the same as the marginal cost of labor MCL for the firm. (Each additional unit of labor service adds its price per unit, the wage rate w_0, to the firm's total costs.) As we saw in the previous chapter, the firm will hire labor up to the point at which the marginal cost of that factor equals its marginal revenue product. In this instance, the quantity of labor L_f is determined by the intersection of MCL and d_f in part a. This amount represents but a tiny fraction of the total amount hired, L_M, in the entire market, part b.

Unions and Wages in Competitive Markets

The laborers in the perfectly competitive labor market we have just described compete

FIGURE 15-4 A Perfectly Competitive Labor Market

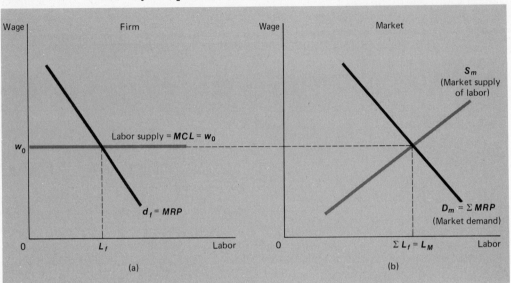

(a)

(b)

In a perfectly competitive labor market, there are many firms and laborers, each one constituting such a small fraction of the total that none can affect the wage rate by its individual actions alone. The supply curve of labor to the typical firm (part a) is therefore horizontal (or perfectly elastic) at the money wage w_0. This wage is determined by the intersection of the market demand curve for labor D_m and the market supply curve of labor S_m in part b.

According to the marginal productivity theory of factor demand, the typical firm hires the quantity of labor L_f (part a) determined by the point where the marginal cost of labor MCL equals its marginal revenue product MRP.

The market supply curve of labor S_m (part b) is upward sloping because if the aggregate of all firms buying labor in this market want more labor, they must bid it away from its alternative employment in other areas of the economy. The market demand curve D_m (part b) is the aggregate of all the individual firm demand curves for labor, $d_f = MRP$—that is, $D_m = \Sigma MRP$. The total amount of labor services bought and sold in the labor market shown here is L_M.

The labor market for farmhands in Kansas is an example of the type of labor market depicted here.

with one another for jobs, and each deals directly with his or her employer on all matters concerning the terms of employment. Suppose, instead, that the laborers band together to form a union. *A* **union** *is an organization that all laborers agree will represent them collectively in bargaining with employers over wages and other terms of employment.* Laborers agree to this arrangement because in unity there is strength. It is still assumed that there are a large number of employers on the

buyers' side of the market, all competing with one another in the hiring of labor.

The usual objective of the union, but typically not the only one, is to put labor in a stronger bargaining position in order to secure higher wages for its members. There are basically three different ways for a union to do this: restrict the supply of labor, impose a wage above the equilibrium wage, and support policies that promote increased demand for labor.

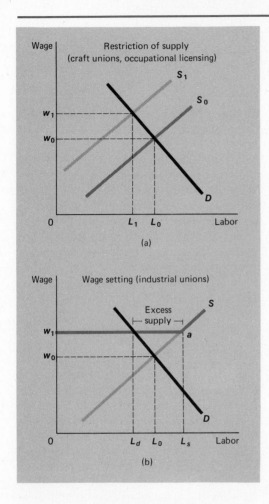

(a)

(b)

FIGURE 15-5   The Effect of Craft Unions and Industrial Unions on Wages and Employment

Craft unions directly restrict the supply of skilled labor by controlling apprenticeship programs and limiting union membership. As shown in part a, this effectively shifts the supply curve leftward from S_0 to a position such as S_1, causing employment to fall from L_0 to L_1 and wages to rise from w_0 to w_1. Many occupations, such as law and medicine, have licensing requirements, which also have the effect of shifting the supply curve leftward and raising wages. Child-labor laws, immigration quotas, compulsory retirement at a certain age, and a shorter workweek also have this effect on the general labor supply.

In contrast to craft unions, industrial unions attempt to organize all the hourly paid workers, skilled and unskilled, in a given industry. As shown in part b, the union then uses the resulting bargaining power to set the wage rate at a level such as w_1, which is above the equilibrium wage rate w_0 that would otherwise prevail in a perfectly competitive labor market. Because the demand curve D is downward sloping and the supply curve S is upward sloping, the amount of labor demanded and employed is L_d, while the amount supplied is L_s. There is thus an excess supply, or quantity, of unemployed union members, represented by the difference between L_s and L_d. The supply curve of labor to the industry is effectively w_1aS.

Restriction of Supply: Craft Unions, Occupational Licensing

In certain occupations that require the development of special skills, training in a craft, or extensive education before one can "do the job," it is possible to restrict the supply of labor and thereby increase wages. This is much more difficult in labor markets for unskilled labor because, by comparison, lower educational and skill requirements allow a great many more workers to enter the market to compete for jobs.

For example, workers in the skilled trades, such as bricklayers, electricians, and printers, have often banded together to form **craft unions**. By controlling the length of apprenticeship programs and restricting membership (which is often necessary to get into such programs), unions are able to control the supply of skilled labor in these trades. The more effectively they can do this, the easier it is to force employers to agree to hire only union members. This in turn further strengthens the craft union's ability to restrict the labor supply. The effect of this on the wage rate and the level of employment in such a trade is shown in Figure 15-5, part a.

Before formation of the craft union, the equilibrium wage is w_0 and the equilibrium level of employment is L_0, as determined by the intersection of the labor demand curve D and supply curve S_0. When the craft union is formed and operating effectively, less labor will be supplied at every wage rate. This causes the supply curve to shift leftward from S_0 to S_1. The new equilibrium wage is now increased to w_1 and the level of employment is reduced from L_0 to L_1.

To work in a number of occupations and professions, it is necessary to have a license—no license, no job. The medical and legal professions are examples. To get a license to practice medicine one must go through 4 years of medical school (preceded by a college education), and as many as 7 to 8 more years of internship and residency are required in some specialized fields. While such extensive training is often defended as being in the public interest, it is nonetheless true that it makes entry into the practice of medicine difficult and therefore restricts the supply of doctors. This tends to push up doctors' wages, as shown in Figure 15–5, part a. The average income of doctors in the United States is over $50,000 per year. While entry into the legal profession is less restrictive, a college education followed by 3 years of law school and a passing performance on the bar exam likewise tends to push the supply curve of lawyers leftward, as in Figure 15–5, part a. In general, any occupation for which licensing is required will have this effect, whatever the merits of "in the public interest" arguments.

In addition to restricting their own membership levels, almost all unions at various times have supported legislation that serves to restrict the supply of labor generally. Such legislation includes child-labor laws, immigration quotas, compulsory retirement at a certain age, and a shorter workweek.

Wage Setting: Industrial Unions

Industrial unions, unlike craft unions, do not restrict their membership to only those workers in a particular trade. On the con-

trary, they attempt to organize all the hourly paid laborers, skilled and unskilled, in a given industry. Indeed, given the easy substitutability of readily available nonunion semiskilled and unskilled labor, it would be foolish for the union to restrict membership. In effect, by maximizing the size of its membership and getting complete control of the labor supply needed by the industry, an industrial union forces firms in the industry to bargain exclusively with the union over wages and other conditions of employment. Firms unwilling to reach mutually agreeable terms with the union face the threat of being closed down by a walkout or **strike**—the loss of their labor supply—at least until one or the other side gives in.

Armed with this kind of bargaining power, an industrial union is able to set wages above the level that would otherwise prevail in a perfectly competitive labor market. This situation is illustrated in Figure 15–5, part b. Without the union, the equilibrium wage would be w_0 and the quantity of labor bought and sold would be L_0, corresponding to the intersection of the demand curve D and the supply curve S. Using its bargaining power, the union is able to push the wage up to w_1. Because the demand curve is downward sloping and the supply curve is upward sloping, the quantity of labor demanded falls to L_d while the quantity of labor supplied increases to L_s. This gives rise to an excess supply of labor, which is represented by the distance from L_d to L_s. These are workers who would like to have jobs in the industry at this wage but can't—they are involuntarily unemployed.

Obviously, *the higher the union pushes the wage, the larger will be the pool of unemployed workers among its membership. This fact limits the union's ability to push up the wage rate.* A large pool of unhappy, unemployed members may lead to defection within the ranks and threaten the very solidarity on which union bargaining strength is based. The more inelastic (steeply sloped) the demand and supply curves, the smaller the rise in such unemployment as the wage is pushed up. Thus there will be less of an unemployment constraint on the union's ability to push up the wage.

With the wage rate at w_1, the supply curve of labor to the industry is represented by w_1aS. The industry can hire as much labor as it wants up to the quantity L_s. If it wants more than this, it will have to raise the wage, as indicated by the upward-sloping portion of the curve aS.

While both the craft union and the industrial union reduce the level of employment as a result of their efforts to raise members' wages, their methods differ. *The craft union pursues policies aimed at directly restricting the supply of labor. This is represented by the fact that the craft union causes the supply curve to be shifted leftward (Figure 15–5, part a), which then leads to a rise in the wage rate. By comparison, the industrial union uses its bargaining power directly to set the wage rate higher (Figure 15–5, part b), which then leads to a fall in employment.*

Increasing Labor Demand

When labor unions succeed in raising the wages in a particular labor market either by restricting supply or by direct bargaining, the level of employment in that market is reduced. If instead unions are somehow able to bring about an increase in the demand for the labor services of their members, they will be able to have the "unmixed blessing" of *both* higher wages *and* higher employment. Particularly in the case of industrial unions, this avoids the conflict between getting higher wages for most members while creating unemployment for the rest. This is illustrated in Figure 15-6. If the demand curve for labor can be shifted from D_0 to D_1, the equilibrium wage and level of employment will rise from w_0 and L_0 to w_1 and L_1, respectively.

How can unions cause the demand curve for their labor services to shift rightward? The marginal productivity theory of labor demand tells us that anything that increases labor productivity will cause the demand curve to shift rightward. The International Ladies' Garment Workers' Union (ILGWU)

FIGURE 15-6 **Increased Labor Demand Leads to Higher Wages and Increased Employment**

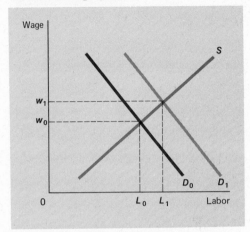

If unions can somehow increase the demand for their labor services, they can have the best of both worlds—higher wages and more employment. A shift in the demand curve for labor from D_0 to D_1 results in an increase in the wage from w_0 to w_1 and a rise in employment from L_0 to L_1.

The marginal productivity theory of labor demand tells us that when unions promote policies that increase labor productivity, a rightward shift in the labor demand curve will take place. Tariffs and import quotas will also have this effect.

has actually conducted seminars to instruct employers on how assembly-line techniques may be used to increase productivity in the garment industry. Another way to increase labor demand in specific industries is to put tariffs and import quotas on imported goods that compete with domestically produced goods, thereby raising the prices of the foreign goods. This tends to increase the demand for domestically produced goods, which are substituted for the now more expensive imported goods. The derived demand for the labor used to produce the domestic goods is thereby increased. Because of this it is not surprising that labor unions frequently join with employers to support tariff legislation that protects their industry from import competition.

Monopsony: The Monopoly Employer

A **monopsony** *is a market structure in which one buyer purchases a good or service from many sellers.* It may be thought of as the opposite of a monopoly, in which one supplier sells to many buyers. A labor market in which one employer, the monopsonist, confronts a nonunionized group of laborers competing with one another for jobs, may be characterized as a monopsony. Many mill towns in the South, where the labor supply is not unionized and where the major employer in town is the local textile mill, may be characterized as monopsony labor markets. In fact, any "company town" usually provides an example of a monopsony.

Table 15–2 and its graphical representation in Figure 15–7 illustrate how wages and employment are determined in a monopsony labor market. Being the only buyer of labor services in the market, the monopsonist firm must pay a higher and higher wage to employ more and more labor. This is indicated in columns 1 and 2 of Table 15–2, and de-

picted by the supply curve S in Figure 15–7. The higher wage, or average cost of labor, must be paid not only to the last unit of labor hired but to all those units of labor already employed as well. If this were not done, previously employed laborers would become unhappy, quit, and have to be rehired at the higher wage paid the last worker employed. (This is very similar to the way a monopolist who wants to sell an extra unit of output in the product market must be willing to take a lower price not only on the extra unit sold but on all previous units as well.) Therefore, the additional, or marginal, cost of hiring one more unit of labor is the sum of the wage paid to the additional laborer *plus* the increase in the wage that must be paid to all previously employed laborers, multiplied by the number of such laborers. Equivalently, the marginal cost of labor MCL (column 4) is simply the increase in the total cost of labor TCL (column 3) due to the employment of one more unit of labor. Figure 15–7 shows clearly that MCL rises faster than the wage rate, which is governed by the supply curve S.

How much labor will the monopsonist hire? According to the marginal productivity theory of factor demand, the firm will hire

TABLE 15–2 Wage and Employment Determination in a Monopsony Labor Market

(1) Number of Units of Labor Service (L)	(2) Wage Rate = Average Cost of Unit of Labor Service or Supply Price of Labor (w)	(3) Total Cost of Labor (TCL)	(4) Marginal Cost of Labor (MCL)	(5) Marginal Revenue Product of Labor (MRP)
1	$3	$ 3	$ 3	$15
2	4	8	5	13
3	5	15	7	11
4	6	24	9	9
5	7	35	11	7
6	8	48	13	5

FIGURE 15-7   Wage and Employment Determination in a Monopsony Labor Market

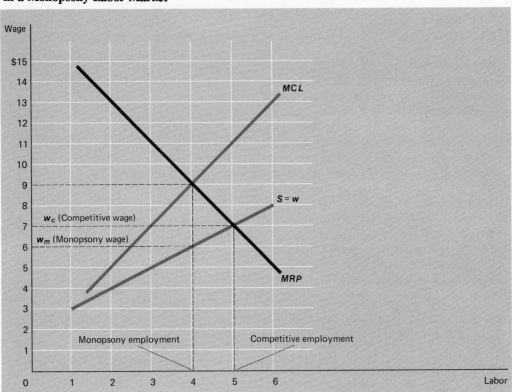

The monopsonist's demand curve for labor is the marginal revenue product curve *MRP* plotted from the data in column 5 of Table 15–2. The supply curve of labor *S* is plotted from the data in column 2, while the marginal cost of labor curve *MCL* is plotted from the data in column 4.

The *MCL* curve lies above the *S* curve, reflecting the fact that to hire an additional labor unit, the monopsonist must pay a higher wage not only for the additional unit but for all previously hired units of labor as well. The monopsony firm hires the factor labor up to the point at which its marginal cost equals its marginal revenue product, $MCL = MRP = \$9$, as determined by the intersection of the *MCL* and *MRP* curves. The monopsonist thus hires 4 units of labor at a wage w_m of $6 per unit of labor.

By contrast, if the labor market were perfectly competitive, the equilibrium wage w_c would be $7 and the quantity of labor hired would be 5 units, as determined by the intersection of the *MRP* and *S* curves. Clearly the monopsonist pays a lower wage and hires less labor.

labor up to the point at which the marginal cost of the factor equals its marginal revenue product. That is, it will hire labor up to the point at which $MCL = MRP$. Columns 4 and 5 of Table 15–2 tell us that this point is reached when 4 units of labor are hired. At

that point, the marginal cost of labor and its marginal revenue product both equal $9. This corresponds to the point at which the *MCL* and *MRP* curves in Figure 15–7 intersect. Here the monopsonist will pay labor a wage w_m of $6, the amount necessary, according to the supply curve S (and columns 1 and 2 of Table 15-2), to induce 4 units of labor to offer their services. Note by comparison that if the labor market were perfectly competitive, the equilibrium level of employment would be 5 units of labor at a competitive wage rate w_c of $7, as given in columns 1, 2, and 5 of Table 15-2 and as represented by the intersection of S and MRP in Figure 15-7.

In summary, *when laborers compete with one another for jobs offered by a monopsonist employer, the resulting equilibrium wage and level of employment will be lower than would be the case if the particular labor market were perfectly competitive.*

Finally, it should be noted that while the monopsonist firm is a monopoly buyer in the labor market, it may be selling its product in any kind of market structure, ranging over the entire spectrum from perfect competition to monopoly.

Bilateral Monopoly

So far, we have considered a labor market in which the supply of labor is controlled by an industrial union and a monopoly seller of labor and the demand for labor consists of many employers (firms) competing with one another in the hiring of labor. In that case, we saw that the wage is set by the union as shown in Figure 15-5, part b. At the other extreme, we have considered the case of a monopoly buyer of labor services, a monopsonist, and laborers who are not unionized but instead compete with one another for jobs. These laborers receive the monopsony wage as shown in Figure 15-7.

But what happens when there is monopoly power on both sides of the market—that is, when there is a **bilateral monopoly**? Suppose a large industrial union represents the labor force in the sale of labor to a monopsonist. The monopsonist, or monopoly buyer of labor, may be one large firm or several firms acting in a collusive, oligopoly fashion in the hiring of labor services. A situation very similar to the latter occurs when the United Automobile Workers (UAW) con-

fronts the Big Three—Chrysler, Ford, and General Motors—to bargain over auto worker wages and other terms of their employment. A similar example is provided by the steelworkers' union and the several large firms that make up the steel industry.

In order to characterize such a situation, we combine the analysis of the industrial union shown in Figure 15-5, part b, with that of the monopsonist shown in Figure 15-7. This is illustrated in Figure 15-8. Given a labor supply curve S and the associated marginal cost of labor curve MCL, the monopsonist would like to hire L_0 units of labor service at a wage of w_m. On the other hand, the industrial union would like to set the wage at w_u when L_0 units of labor services are sold. The union may wish to set the wage higher than this but then, of course, the employer will hire less than L_0 units of labor service.

There is obviously a discrepancy between the desired wage objective of the union and that of the monopsonist when L_0 units of labor service are employed. This discrepancy is equal to the difference, or gap, between w_u and w_m. When "push comes to shove" and the monopoly hiring power of the employer is set against the monopoly selling power of the union, what mutually agreeable wage level in this gap will finally prevail? The bargaining power of the union typically depends on the willingness and financial ability of its membership to endure the hardship of a strike. Similarly, the bargaining power of the employer depends on the willingness to incur the loss of business that will result from a shutdown. The greater the bargaining power of the union relative to that of the employer, the closer we would expect the ultimate wage settlement to be to w_u. Conversely, the greater the bargaining power of the employer relative to that of the union, the closer we would expect the ultimate wage settlement to be to w_m.

If the union prevails completely on the issue of wages, the supply curve of labor is $w_u a S$. If the employer prevails completely, it is $w_m c S$. Indeed, it is possible for the relative bargaining power of the two sides to be such

FIGURE 15-8   A Bilateral Monopoly Labor Market

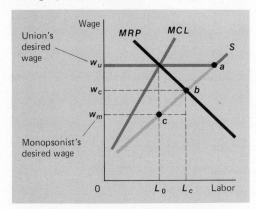

A situation in which there is a monopsonist on the employer side of the labor market and an industrial union on the seller's side may be represented by combining the analysis of the industrial union in Figure 15–5, part b, with that of the monopsony in Figure 15–7, as shown here.

The monopsonist would like to hire L_0 units of labor service at a wage of w_m. The industrial union would like to set the wage at w_u when L_0 units of labor service are sold. The wage that will be mutually agreeable to both sides will lie somewhere between w_u and w_m, depending on the relative bargaining power of the industrial union versus that of the monopsonist. The greater the strength of the monopsonist relative to that of the union, the closer the wage will be to w_m. Conversely, the greater the strength of the union relative to that of the monopsonist, the closer the wage will be to w_u.

If the union prevails completely, the supply curve of labor is $w_u aS$, while if the monopsonist prevails completely, it is $w_m cS$. Indeed, it is possible that their relative bargaining power might be such that the equilibrium wage is w_c and employment level L_c, the same as the perfectly competitive outcome. The supply curve of labor is then $w_c bS$.

that the wage settlement occurs at w_c with an amount of labor employed equal to L_c. This is the same outcome as would result in a perfectly competitive labor market! The supply

curve of labor would then be $w_c bS$. In sum, the level of the ultimate wage settlement depends on the bargaining power of the union relative to that of the employer, and this varies from one industry and time to the next.

In general, *in a bilateral monopoly labor market, at the level of employment corresponding to the intersection of MCL and MRP, the wage level mutually agreeable to the monopoly employer and monopoly union will lie somewhere between the most desired wage w_u of the union and the most desired wage w_m of the employer.*

CHECKPOINT 15-3
What difference does it make in the position of the *MRP* curve in Figure 15–7 whether the monopsonist is a monopolist or a perfect competitor in the product market? In a news item it was reported that union leaders in the construction industry were going to push for higher wages despite the recession in the industry. Using a diagram like that in Figure 15–5, part b, for the industrial union analysis, show why the union leaders' objective is more difficult to achieve during a recession than during more normal times. Suppose it were reported that, "To forge a more united management front, one industry group, the Contractors Mutual Association, is seeking to bring significant numbers of contractors together." How would you explain the economic rationale for this move? In another case, the UAW leadership sent out a letter to its 1,600 local unions trying to persuade them that the union should join forces with the giant labor federation, the AFL-CIO. They argued that the move would be "in the best interests of the entire labor movement" because "antiunion forces" are united, while labor is divided. Characterize and explain why such a move may well be in the best interests of the labor movement.

GROWTH OF UNIONS IN THE UNITED STATES

The history of unions in the United States has been characterized by a long struggle for employer recognition and public acceptance. This struggle has often been marked by violence and disruptive confrontation. But since World War II confrontation has by and large given way to a spirit of mutual accommodation between management and labor that now generally typifies the widespread practice of collective bargaining. The union-management disputes that make headline news today represent but a very small portion of the many negotiations and settlements that only merit notice on page 8, if they make the newspaper at all.

The Struggle for Recognition

From the early 1800s to the 1930s, the struggle to establish unions in the United States was uneven in its successes and frequent in its failures.

Incentives for Unionization

The advent of the Industrial Revolution in the late 1700s set in motion a fundamental change in the nature of working conditions for an ever increasing portion of the labor force. Before the Industrial Revolution the labor force was largely engaged in agricultural pursuits. What little industry existed could be characterized as "cottage industry"—spinning, weaving, and other handicrafts typically carried out by households otherwise engaged in farming on the same premises. Such activity, carried out along with farm chores, was usually aimed at satisfying the immediate needs of the family. While the average family was poor by present-day standards, the purpose and rewards of such work were direct and obvious. Moreover, the working conditions and relationships were personal and family oriented, and the work regimen, if long on hours, was loose and varied, involving work indoors as well as in the open air. The boss and arbiter was the head of household, usually oneself or one's parents.

The growth of mass production and factories caused labor to move away from such rural settings and into rapidly expanding towns and cities. There workers typically found themselves tied to the strict and tedious regimen of machines set on mass production schedules. They worked long hours in the close confines of poorly ventilated, crowded shops ("sweatshops") and factories, turning out a product at the command of impersonal market forces. They typically felt themselves oppressed and abused by an authoritarian boss who at best often appeared as nothing more than an unpleasant, unsympathetic stranger to be feared. Monopsony was an apt characterization of many of the labor markets spawned by the new industries. Wages were low and 12- to 14-hour workdays, six days a week, were common. Living conditions in crowded tenements in sooty, smoke-filled cities were usually as unhealthy and gray as working conditions. It was one thing to be poor in a cottage industry setting, quite another in a nineteenth-century city.

Spurred by these conditions, workers began to recognize that by acting together they could confront monopolistic employers much more forcefully. In a real sense, the whole could be much greater than the sum of its parts. In unity there could be strength and "solidarity," an oft-used term in the history of the labor movement. Improved working conditions could be demanded of employers and wages pushed higher, as indicated by our analyses of craft unions, industrial unions, and bilateral monopoly in Figures 15–5 and 15–8.

Early Local Craft Unions

In the late eighteenth and early nineteenth century, local craft unions were the only kind of labor union that seemed able to survive for any length of time in the United States. Skilled workers, such as printers, carpenters, and shipwrights, were relatively few in number. When they formed unions they were usually able to control their own numbers, and hence the supply of their services, by making union membership a necessary condition for admission to apprenticeship in the trade. By contrast, the supply of unskilled labor was much more plentiful and fed almost continually by immigrants. Therefore the durability of a union of unskilled labor was easily undercut by employers' ability to hire from the large pool of nonunionized, unskilled workers.

Because of the unique role a particular craft might play at a certain stage of a production process, it would be very difficult to find substitutes for it. Hence a craft union often had bargaining leverage over an employer that was great despite the fact that its members might represent only a small proportion of the employer's total labor force. By contrast, an industrial union had to have power similar to the employer's. Furthermore, since the craft union employees typically represented only a small portion of the employer's total labor force, total costs were not affected that much by giving in to a craft union's demand for higher wages. Similar concessions to unskilled labor could result in a much larger increase in total costs.

From our analysis of factor demand in the previous chapter, we know that the fewer substitutes there are for a factor and the smaller the factor's share of total costs, the more inelastic will be the demand curve for that factor. Thus, if a craft union pushes up members' wages, the possible reduction in employment of its members is likely to be much less than would be the case if a union of unskilled workers tried to do likewise. Unemployment among the rank-and-file membership serves to undermine the union's solidarity. Why be an unemployed union member at a zero wage? Why not leave the union and offer to work at a lower wage than union members are getting?

Given these considerations, it is clear that craft unions had definite advantages over unions of unskilled labor in the struggle for recognition in the early days of the labor movement. It is not surprising that craft unions were the only ones that seemed likely to last, especially in a time when there was little legal support for unions and employers were extremely hostile and combative toward the union concept.

Obstacles to Unionization

The main obstacles to unionization in the United States during the 1800s and early 1900s were the courts and a business attitude that unions infringed on employers' rights.

Since there was no specific legislation that covered the legal standing of unions until the 1930s, the courts had to deal with the issue. Unfortunately for the labor movement, American courts borrowed a piece of English common law for guidance—the **criminal conspiracy doctrine**. This doctrine held that organization of workers with the intent to raise wages constituted a criminal conspiracy and was therefore illegal! The legal status of this doctrine began to weaken in 1842 as a result of a Massachusetts court case, *Commonwealth* v. *Hunt*. The court decided that labor could form unions and bargain with employers over wages and other conditions of employment.

Nonetheless, the spirit of the doctrine reflected a general attitude toward the labor union concept that lingered right up through the 1920s. In no small part, this was due to the fact that unions were always cast in the role of trying to gain new rights for labor that could only come from a reduction in the long-established rights of employers. Against this background, the courts even interpreted the Sherman Act of 1890 as applying to unions, though Congress intended the act to be used against business monopolies. Courts also made it easy for employers to obtain injunctions against unions. (Injunctions are court orders preventing unions from striking or picketing employers to force acceptance of union demands.)

Employers had other methods for resisting unions besides the support of the courts. Employees who agitated for unionization of a firm were frequently fired and put on a **blacklist**. These lists of "troublemakers" and "agitators" circulated among employers and effectively constituted a "who's who" of the "unemployable." Sometimes employers made workers sign a **yellow-dog contract** whereby the employee, as a condition of employment, agreed not to join a union. Such contracts could be enforced in court. Refusal to sign usually meant no job.

When workers did go on strike, employers frequently hired **strikebreakers**, or scabs, workers willing to work despite the objectives of other workers. If all else failed, the employer might resort to a **lockout**, the employer's own form of strike. The employer simply shut down operations in the hope that the financial hardship imposed on workers by this unemployment would bring them around to the employer's "point of view." Whether labor went on strike or the employer imposed a lockout, the determining factor in the outcome was usually which side was best able to suffer financial losses. In the 1800s and early 1900s, **strike funds**, or money set aside by unions to tide the workers over a strike period, were meager or nonexistent. This put labor at a distinct disadvantage.

On the darker side of employer resistance, skull crackings and even killings were not at all uncommon in employer-labor conflicts through the 1930s. While employers hired "goon squads" to intimidate workers, workers often damaged or sabotaged plants and equipment. Workers sometimes used violence on fellow workers to force them to go along with union-organizing efforts and other union objectives.

The AFL and the National Labor Movement

The Knights of Labor, founded in 1869, was the first big union dedicated to organizing all workers, skilled and unskilled alike, on a national level. The Knights' objectives were as diverse as its membership, encompassing political reform and agitation as well as better wages. Although the Knights reached a peak membership of some 700,000 in 1886, "pie-in-the-sky" goals such as socialist revolution tended to dilute efforts to achieve bread-and-butter gains in wages and other terms of employment. Several unsuccessful strikes were staged by unskilled workers, and frequent fights erupted among the leadership over means and objectives. All this, combined with a feeling among skilled workers that they were better off looking out for themselves in the usual tradition of the craft union, led to the complete demise of the Knights by 1917.

The first outlines of the blueprint for modern unionism were laid down with the founding in 1886 of the American Federation of Labor (AFL) by Samuel Gompers. While early on he was interested in the type of social reform issues pushed by the Knights, Gompers decided to focus on what he felt could best be accomplished. He therefore made a commitment to unionizing the skilled trades, restricting the labor supply, and **business unionism**, the concentration of union efforts on getting higher wages and better working conditions. The AFL was organized around the principle of **federalism**, whereby each national union had the exclusive right to organize and regulate labor in its particular trade. Gompers also stressed that labor should not tie itself to any one political party, but rather allow itself the flexibility of rewarding allies and punishing enemies as dictated by the expediency of labor's best interests. Finally, Gompers supported the concept of **voluntarism**, a policy that opposed government intervention in union affairs, including organizing, collective bargaining, and union-management conflicts.

By 1920 the AFL had a membership of 4 million skilled workers, or 10 percent of the country's labor force. However, the 1920s were an era of prosperity and strong pro-business, antiunion sentiment. By the depth of the Great Depression in 1933, AFL membership had fallen until it constituted only 4

FIGURE 15-9   Total Union Membership in the United States Since 1900

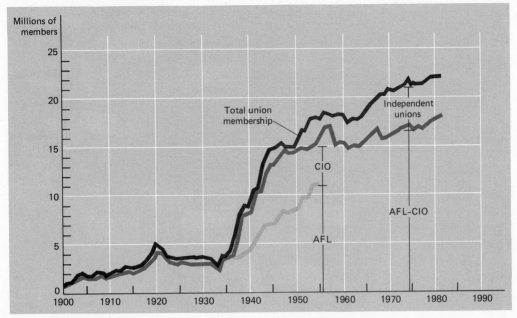

With the Great Depression of the early 1930s, the public became more sympathetic to the plight of the blue-collar worker and the aspirations of the union movement. Aided by the New Deal atmosphere and the legal sanction of the Wagner Act (1935), which guaranteed workers the right to form unions, union membership increased dramatically after 1935.

SOURCE: U.S. Department of Labor, Bureau of Labor Statistics.

percent of the labor force, or a little more than 2 million workers.

The New Deal and World War II: The Growth Years

The dramatic growth in union membership during the New Deal era of the 1930s is illustrated in Figure 15-9. What caused it?

Depression and the Wagner Act

With the onset of the Great Depression and the subsequent election of Franklin Roosevelt and his New Deal, public attitude toward big business soured. Sympathy for the worker's plight ("Brother, can you spare a dime?") was widespread. Then in 1935

Congress passed the National Labor Relations Act, or Wagner Act, the first major piece of pro-union legislation. It guaranteed workers the right to organize and to elect by majority vote in a secret ballot an exclusive bargaining agent to represent them in their wage and employment negotiations with management. The act also set up the National Labor Relations Board (NLRB) to guard against employer use of "unfair labor practices" against labor. The NLRB can issue cease-and-desist orders against employers, and it can hold elections in a firm or plant to establish what union will represent employees.

Unions now had a strong law on their side. Union membership surged upward, as shown in Figure 15-9, and the percentage of the labor force in unions rose from around 7 percent in 1935 (roughly 3.7 million members) to about 15.5 percent by 1940 (roughly 8.9 million members).

The CIO

The Wagner Act made it much easier to organize unskilled as well as skilled labor. While the AFL had several industrial unions in its federation, it had a craft union bias and had never been particularly successful in organizing all workers (skilled and unskilled) in a large industry. A dissident group in the AFL, led by John L. Lewis of the United Mine Workers (an industrial union), argued that the mass production industries such as automobiles and steel could only be effectively organized as industrial unions. They argued that craft unions, each composed of a certain type of skilled worker, were not well suited to the many vertical stages of production and different kinds of labor used in such industries. Where it would take the combined cooperation of many separate craft unions, which were often at odds with one another, to deal effectively with management, one all-encompassing industrial union would constitute a much more effective and united front.

Finally in 1936 Lewis and several other industrial union leaders and sympathizers withdrew from the AFL and formed the Congress of Industrial Organizations (CIO). The CIO's organizing efforts were amazingly successful, especially in the giant auto and steel industries, as can be seen in Figure 15-9. Convinced by the CIO's example, the AFL put more effort into organizing along industrial lines, although craft unionism remained its central theme. At last the labor movement had pushed labor markets in the large mass production industries toward more of a bilateral monopoly structure. This structure was more favorable to them than the near monopsony situation that existed previously, especially for unskilled workers.

Postwar Period: Taft-Hartley, the AFL-CIO

Public opinion was quite pro-labor and sympathetic to the strikes aimed at organizing and winning recognition in major industries during the years immediately following passage of the Wagner Act. But by the end of World War II and in the immediate postwar period, many strikes were not motivated by demands for recognition and higher wages, but rather by **jurisdictional disputes** between rival AFL and CIO unions. The work stoppages caused by such interunion squabbling over which union had the right to organize a group of workers did not arouse public sympathy, but rather alerted the public to the seeming excesses of unionism.

The Taft-Hartley Act (1947)

Supported by public sentiment, in 1947 Congress passed the Taft-Hartley Act (the Labor-Management Relations Act). While maintaining the rights given to labor under the Wagner Act, the Taft-Hartley Act defined and prohibited certain "unfair labor practices" of unions. These included **featherbedding** (requiring unnecessary tasks to make work), jurisdictional strikes (caused by disputes between two or more unions as to which does a certain job), union failure to bargain in good faith with an employer, and **secondary boycotts** (union strikes and picketing aimed at disrupting business between employers). The act also banned the **closed shop**, which required union membership as a condition of employment. But it allowed the **union shop**, which permitted a nonunion employee to be hired provided the employee joined the union within a certain time after employment. However, the act hedged on this provision by allowing states to enact **right-to-work laws**, which had the effect of banning the union shop. Such laws were passed in some 20 states. Labor has repeatedly but unsuccessfully pushed Congress to repeal this provision, largely because it has made it difficult to unionize workers in many states, especially in the South.

Other important features of the Taft-Hartley Act are aimed at forestalling strikes until all avenues of mediation and conciliation have been exhausted. Most notably in this regard, the act allows the U.S. president to intervene in labor-management conflicts by getting a court injunction prohibiting a strike during an 80-day cooling-off period whenever it is deemed a serious threat to national health or safety.

The AFL-CIO (1955)

Almost 20 years after John L. Lewis left the AFL to form the CIO, with its commitment to the industrial union concept, old rivalries had cooled and a new union leadership began to take over. Furthermore, it was becoming more difficult to sustain the expansion of union membership, especially at the pace of earlier years (see Figure 15-9). Because of this and the fact that the public's onetime pro-labor sentiments had shifted to a more critical stance, the labor movement was reminded of the need for unity.

The setting was right for the realization of a long-sought goal of the labor movement—the formation of one giant federation of unions. Thus in 1955 the AFL and the CIO joined to form the AFL-CIO. The combined strength represented by this marriage can best be appreciated by examining Figure 15-9. While there always have been and still are a number of independent unions (the Teamsters and the United Automobile Workers are prominent examples), the AFL-CIO represents more than 75 percent of all union members in the United States.

Collective Bargaining

Today the process by which labor and management interact to determine wages and other terms of employment is similar to a meeting of attorneys attempting to reconcile the interests of opposing clients. When unions were struggling to organize and gain employer recognition during the tumultuous 1930s and before, such negotiations often took the form of pitched street battles. Today's negotiating process is most accurately described as **collective bargaining**.

If the National Labor Relations Board certifies that a union has been "properly" elected by a majority of employees, management may then deal with the union as the collective bargaining agent for the employees. Union representatives meet with management to negotiate a **labor contract**, which spells out in detail mutually agreeable terms for wages, fringe benefits, hours, grievance procedures, seniority, union and management prerogatives, the length of time the contract is binding (time until it is to be renegotiated), and so forth. Initially there is usually much disagreement on many of the terms and a bargaining process is entered into, each side giving a little here to get a little there. Successful collective bargaining means that mutually agreeable terms are decided upon without resort to a strike. Such a strike costs both sides—lost wages for labor and lost production and sales for management. Which side will finally give in on disputed issues ultimately depends on who is least willing to sustain further losses.

If the collective bargaining process reaches an impasse ("talks are deadlocked") over certain disputed issues, but both sides wish to avoid a strike or to end one, they frequently make use of mediation or arbitration procedures. **Mediation**, or conciliation, brings an unbiased third party into the negotiations. The mediator tries to lead discussions into areas where conciliation is possible or to suggest alternative compromises. The mediator's role is that of a catalyst and adviser whose suggestions and advice need not be accepted. The Federal Mediation and Conciliation Service is an independent federal government agency set up to provide such service. There are private mediators who may be hired to perform these services as well.

Alternatively, labor and management may

resort to **arbitration**. In this process, both sides agree to bring in a third party, or arbiter, who acts as a judge in interpreting the terms of a contract. Both sides agree that the arbiter will decide the dispute—the arbiter's decision is binding on both parties.

One testament to how well the collective bargaining process has worked in the post–World War II era, despite what newspaper headlines might lead you to believe, is the rather small percentage of total work time that has been lost in our economy due to strikes. Since 1950 the average time lost to strikes has amounted to about two-tenths of 1 percent of the economy's total work time per year, or roughly 1 minute out of every 8-hour workday! (Most of us spend more time than this daydreaming on the job, especially when writing or reading a textbook.) In the worst year, 1959, the figure was one-half of 1 percent, which was largely a reflection of the 109-day steel strike.

Prospects for the Growth of Union Power

It is clear from Figure 15-9 that union growth has leveled off in recent years. The percentage of the total labor force belonging to unions peaked at 25.5 percent in 1953 and has declined gradually to around 20 percent in recent years. This decline is largely due to the fact that the blue-collar worker, the mainstay of union membership, constitutes only about 25 percent of the labor force today, down from about 50 percent after World War II. In addition, all the "easy wood has been cut"—blue-collar workers not yet unionized are in those industries and regions of the country most resistant to unionism, such as the textile industry in the South and the service industries throughout the economy.

Problems with Corruption in Unions

A factor that has tarnished the image of unionism has been revelations or allegations of misuse of union funds and power by the leadership of some unions. Whether true or alleged, such findings and charges, like the "squeaky wheel," have drawn much public attention that spills over adversely on many honestly managed unions as well. (A 1983 Gallup poll ranked union leaders next to last—just above car salesmen—in ethics and honesty.) To deal with some of these problems, Congress passed the Landrum-Griffin Act (the Labor-Management Reporting and Disclosure Act) in 1959. Among other things, it requires filing of union financial reports, puts restrictions on union office holding by ex-convicts and Communists, limits union loans to officials to a maximum of $2,000, requires regular secret-ballot elections of officials, guards against summary disciplining of employees by the union, and forbids nonwage payments by employers to union representatives. Despite these curbs, there continue to be problems and allegations of abuse of union-official power, of infiltration by organized crime, and of misuse of union funds. A recent example of concern is the giant central states Teamsters Union pension fund, alleged to be controlled by underworld elements that have infiltrated that union.

Sources of Future Union Growth

Further expansion of the union movement will probably be more pronounced in the service and trade sectors (retail store clerks, cashiers, etc.) of the economy. Another area where unionism seems to be gaining ground is in federal, state, and local government. There are now about 3 million unionized public employees, up from just over a million in 1960. One unusual aspect of unionism in government is the fact that strikes by public employees are usually prohibited by law. For example, it is often argued that the services provided by fire fighters, the police, and garbage collectors are too important to public health and safety to allow such workers to use the strike as a weapon for wage bargaining. Without this weapon, however, the bargaining position of these workers is consider-

POLICY PERSPECTIVE

Have Unions Increased Wages?

Figure 15–1 showed us that the average real wage of labor in the United States has risen during the postwar period. This average real wage represents an average of both union and nonunion workers. Two issues are of interest: (1) the effect of unions on their members' real wages, and (2) the effect of unions on all workers' real wages.

Effect of Unions on Members' Real Wages

Have unions brought about a greater increase in real wages for their members than would have occurred without them? After all, that is one of the major objectives of unionism—to raise members' wages higher than might otherwise be possible. Figures 15–5 through 15–8 indicate ways in which unions achieve this goal.

At first thought you might be tempted to compare the real wages of nonunion workers with those of union workers over time to answer the question about union effectiveness. But it is not as easy as that. There are too many other possible factors that enter into the determination of the behavior of real wages. For example, suppose demand for industry A's product is static, neither growing nor declining, while demand for industry B's product is expanding rapidly. As a result, suppose real wages in industry B are rising more rapidly than in A. A's workers may be unionized and B's not, but union efforts to push up wages in A are constrained by the unemployment this causes among union members in a static industry. Conversely, if B's workers are unionized and A's are not, how do we know to what extent the more rapid rise in B's real wages is due to faster demand growth for B's product

rather than to the efforts of the union? This gives some idea of the difficulties encountered when researching the union effectiveness question. Bearing this in mind, what does research tell us?

Industry studies appear to indicate that unions are often effective in raising real wages somewhat above those paid for nonunion labor. The differential between union and nonunion wages within an industry appears to be not more than 10 percent for the average organized industry. However, in a few industries, such as coal mining, commercial airlines, and construction, the differential may be as much as 25 percent, while in a number of industries there is little wage advantage at all.

Effect of Unions on All Workers' Real Wages

Have unions pushed the average real wage of all workers, union and nonunion, up to a higher level than would have been reached without them?

That unions can raise real wages in certain industries is certainly consistent with our theoretical analysis in Figures 15–5 through 15–8. Each of those figures showed how the existence of a union pushes up the money wage for its members. For a given price level p, this means the real wage $w \div p$ must also rise. However, the same type of analysis suggests that unions may not be able to do this for the average real-wage level of all workers—union and nonunion—taken together.

The reason is illustrated in Figure P15–1. Suppose labor market X, represented by Figure P15–1, part a, is unionized by a craft union. This causes the supply curve of labor in that market to shift leftward from S_X to $S_X{'}$. The money wage therefore rises from w_0 to w_1 (determined by the intersection of S_X and S_X' with demand curve D_X), so that given the price level, the real wage of union members rises also. Note, however, that the quantity of labor employed in that market falls from L_0 to L_1. The quantity of unemployed labor L_1L_0 must now find employment in some other market. To the extent that these unemployed workers seek work in a nonunionized labor market such as Y, represented by Figure P15-1, part b, they will cause the supply curve in that market to shift rightward from S_Y to a position such as S_Y'. Hence, the money wage in that market will fall from w_0 to w_2. Given the price level, the real wage of workers in this market will fall, and the level of employment will rise from L_0 to L_2. The net result is that a smaller number of workers (L_1) are now earning a higher real wage in market X while more workers (L_2) are earning a lower real wage in market Y.

It is not clear whether a weighted average of the two real-wage levels (each real wage weighted by the proportion of the labor force employed at that real wage) would be higher, lower, or the same as the weighted average of the two real-wage levels prevailing in the two markets before unionization of market X. It all depends on the shapes of the supply and demand curves in the two markets, as well as the number of workers employed in each market before and after the supply curves shift.

In view of these theoretical considerations, it is not surprising that *research has generally concluded that it is difficult to say that unions have had any discernible impact on the average level of real wages received by workers as a whole.*

In some instances union policies may even have inhibited technological change and retarded productive efficiency. This seems to be the case in coal mining, construction, and railroads. To this extent unions have held back improvements in real wages for the entire labor force. Yet unions often contribute to industrial disci-

FIGURE P15-1   Effect of a Union on the Average Real Wage of Union and Nonunion Workers

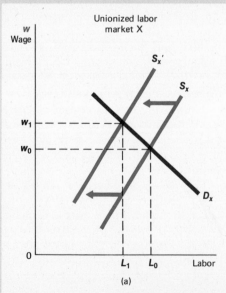

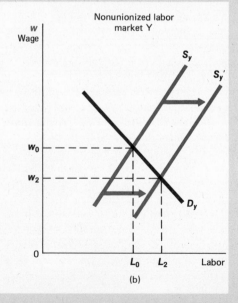

(a)

(b)

pline (reduce labor turnover and absenteeism) and cooperate with management to improve productivity, thereby contributing to raising real wages. On the national level, while there is little evidence that unions have had much effect in causing money wages to rise more rapidly than they otherwise would have during times of prosperity, they do seem to have been successful in resisting wage reductions during recessions.

Questions

1. Given the initial equilibrium positions and the indicated shifts in the supply curves shown in Figure P15–1, what kinds of shapes of the demand curves would assure that the weighted average real wage would fall as a result of unionization of market X?

2. Given the shapes of the demand curves indicated by your answer to question 1, how difficult do you think it would be to maintain union solidarity as compared to a situation where the demand curves are shaped as shown in Figure P15–1?

---

ably weakened. How this issue will be resolved remains unclear.

Do Unions Have Too Much Monopoly Power?

A frequent complaint against unions is that they can exert monopoly-type power in certain industries because they are exempt from antitrust law.

The Clayton Act (1914) specifically exempted unions from antitrust law. Since the merger of the AFL and the CIO, there has been increasing concern that unions may have monopoly power that far exceeds that of the largest corporations, which unlike unions are the object of antitrust law. Some critics argue that unions should also be subject to the antitrust laws against monopoly. Union supporters respond that unions and business corporations are not comparable entities, and that it would be a misuse of antitrust laws to apply them to unions. Both sides would most likely agree on two points: (1) application of antitrust principles to unions would probably require some reworking of existing antitrust laws or the passage of some additional antitrust laws tailored to unions, and (2) applying antitrust laws to unions would most likely reduce union power. This, of course, is precisely why unions oppose such laws while antiunion forces advocate them.

SUMMARY

1. Wage is the price of a unit of labor. The money wage is the size of the wage measured in dollars and cents. The real wage is the size of the wage measured in terms of the quantity of goods that can be purchased with it. The real wage is usually obtained by dividing the money wage by some index of the general price level. The level of real wages is a reflection of labor productivity, which in turn is determined by the amount of capital and other resources, the state of technology, the amount of education and training invested in human capital, and the institutional, social, and political structure of the economy. Real wages have risen in the United States because these factors have caused the demand for labor to grow faster than the supply of labor.

2. Wage differentials exist because labor is not perfectly mobile; workers differ in their job preferences; jobs have nonpecuniary considerations associated with them; and workers differ in ability, skills, and education.

3. The structure of a labor market is as important to an explanation of wage determination as the structure of a product market is to explaining price determination. In a perfectly competitive labor market, a large number of employers compete with one another to hire labor from among a large number of workers competing with one another for jobs. The intersection of the market demand and supply curves for labor determines the equilibrium wage rate and quantity of labor employed. If workers organize a union in such a market, they can push the wage level above the equilibrium level.

4. A craft union is an organization of skilled workers in a particular craft or trade. It raises competitive wages by controlling the supply of labor. An industrial union is an organization that attempts to encompass and represent all workers, skilled and unskilled, in a given industry. It uses its bargaining power to set the wage rate higher than the competitive level. It is limited in its ability to do this by the unemployment that this causes among its membership. The main bargaining weapon of a union is the strike.

5. A monopsony labor market is one in which there is a monopoly buyer of labor services confronting unorganized workers competing with one another for jobs. Because the monopsonist must bid up wages to hire additional laborers and pay the higher wage to all workers employed, the marginal cost of labor curve will lie above the labor supply curve. When the monopsonist hires labor up to the point at which the marginal cost of labor equals its marginal revenue product, less labor will be employed at a lower wage than would be the case if the structure of the market were perfectly competitive.

6. When a monopsonistic employer buys labor services from a union that is a monopoly supplier of labor, the structure of the labor market is that of a bilateral monopoly. The level of the wage that prevails in such a market depends on the bargaining strength of the union relative to that of the employer. No more definite statement can be made about the effect of such a market structure on wages and labor supply.

7. In the late eighteenth and for most of the nineteenth century, attempts to unionize la-

bor were largely unsuccessful due to the criminal conspiracy doctrine and the antagonism of employers. With the exception of certain craft unions, employers were able to check the growth of unionism by the use of the yellow-dog contract, strikebreakers, blacklisting, lockouts, skull cracking, and the support of the courts. The formation of the American Federation of Labor (AFL) by Samuel Gompers in 1886 marked the beginnings of the modern union movement on a national level with its emphasis on better wages and working conditions.

8. The AFL, with its emphasis on craft unionism, dominated the labor movement until the 1930s, although total union membership in the United States fell during the 1920s and the worst years of the Great Depression. With the New Deal and the passage of the Wagner Act (1935), which guaranteed labor the right to organize, total union membership experienced its most rapid period of growth, which lasted right through World War II. This growth was greatly aided by the formation of the Congress of Industrial Organizations (CIO) with its emphasis on industrial unionism, a form of union ideally suited to unionization of the large mass production industries such as automobiles and steel.

9. With the end of World War II, the public became concerned with the seeming excesses of unionism as a result of frequent work stoppages caused by jurisdictional disputes among different unions. The Taft-Hartley Act (1947) brought stricter control over "unfair union practices" and set up procedures aimed at forestalling strikes, in particular allowing the president to prohibit a strike for an 80-day cooling-off period if it might threaten national health or safety.

10. The union movement strengthened its solidarity with the merger of the AFL and the CIO in 1955 to form the AFL-CIO. The percentage of the total labor force in unions peaked at around 25 percent in 1953 and has gradually slipped to around 20 percent since then.

11. Modern-day collective bargaining between management and labor is a highly professionalized process for negotiating mutually acceptable wages and other conditions of employment, all carefully spelled out in a labor contract.

12. The main problem hampering union growth today is the fact that the blue-collar worker represents about 25 percent of the labor force, down from about 50 percent at the end of World War II. It has also proved more difficult to organize those sectors of the economy that are not yet unionized, particularly in those states having right-to-work laws. Union corruption has tarnished the union image somewhat in the postwar era and still remains a problem, despite the passage of legislation aimed at policing union-management practices (Landrum-Griffin Act, 1959). Unionization in the government sector has been a major source of union growth in recent years and promises to be so in the future.

13. The evidence from industry studies suggests that unions have been successful in raising the real wages of union workers about 10 percent over those of nonunion workers. However, research has generally concluded that it is difficult to say that unions have had any discernible impact on the average level of real wages received by workers as a whole.

KEY TERMS AND CONCEPTS

arbitration
bilateral monopoly
blacklist
business unionism
closed shop
collective bargaining
craft union
criminal conspiracy doctrine
featherbedding
federalism

industrial union
jurisdictional dispute
labor contract
lockout
mediation
money wage
monopsony
nonpecuniary considerations
real wage
right-to-work laws
secondary boycott
strike
strikebreakers
strike fund
union
union shop
voluntarism
wage
yellow-dog contract

QUESTIONS AND PROBLEMS

1. The index of the general price level is constructed in such a way that it measures the cost of the "basket" of goods purchased by a typical, or representative, household. Suppose two workers are paid the same money wage, and suppose this money wage rises by the same percent as the general price level year in and year out. Why might you expect that the real wages of each of these workers are, in fact, changing at different rates?

2. Explain why the level of real wages is a reflection of labor productivity. How do you think each of the following would affect real wages?

a. passage of a law allowing taxpayers an income tax deduction for expenditures on schooling and vocational training;

b. raising restrictions on immigration quotas;

c. reducing the length of the workday;

d. increasing the size of the reward paid workers who have their suggestions, which they place in the employee suggestion box, chosen for adoption by the plant;

e. increasing the tax on oil;

f. discovery of a new oil field;

g. passage of laws restricting the use of coal.

3. In the field of news reporting—radio, television, newspapers—average reporter salaries are quite low compared to the salaries of many other occupations requiring a comparable educational background. Earnings of interstate truck drivers (teamsters), for example, are two or more times as high, yet far less schooling is required to do this job. What factors do you think explain these earnings differentials?

4. It is sometimes said that while unions usually oppose automation and the adoption of new capital equipment, ironically they may be a major cause of such technological development. Explain this point of view and its possible relation to the fact that the proportion of blue-collar workers in the labor force has fallen from about 50 percent at the end of World War II to about 25 percent today.

5. Compare and contrast the advantages and disadvantages of craft unions and industrial unions as ways of organizing labor. How are the concepts of craft unions and occupational licensing related?

6. How would you characterize the structure of the following labor markets: professional football players, teamsters, household help, the police in a town or city, blue-collar workers in the rubber industry, shoe salespersons, fortune tellers, dentists?

7. What relation do you see between the Wagner Act, monopsony, and bilateral monopoly? How would you describe the possible effects of the Taft-Hartley Act on a labor market that was characterized as a bilateral monopoly?

8. Suppose a monopsonist hires nonunion labor. Under what conditions would the monopsonist be able to realize the greatest advantage: when the labor supply curve is more elastic or when it is less elastic? Under what conditions would labor potentially be able to realize the biggest wage gains from unionization: when the monopsonist's demand curve for labor is more elastic or when it is less elastic?

a. If the mobility of nonunion workers in a monopsony labor market is very low, how do you think their incentive to unionize would compare to that in a situation where their mobility is very high?

b. The United Mine Workers has been very successful in gaining higher wages for its union members. Labor costs make up about 70 percent of total costs in coal production. About 60 percent fewer coal miners are employed now than were employed at the end of World War II. How might you explain this?

16

Rent, Interest, and Capital

AFTER READING THIS CHAPTER, YOU WILL BE ABLE TO:

1. Define the concept of economic rent.

2. Explain how economic rent can be viewed as both a cost and a surplus.

3. Explain how capital may be viewed as a roundabout process of production.

4. Explain the meaning of the net productivity of capital and its relation to the rate of return on capital.

5. State the relationship between saving, capital formation, and interest rate determination.

6. Give the reasons why there are many different interest rates, and explain their role in resource allocation and the important distinction between real and nominal interest rates.

The wages of labor, which we looked at in the previous chapter, constitute by far the largest source of income in our economy. They amount to about 80 percent of total income when we consider not only the wages of hourly and salaried workers, but also that form of labor income earned in the professions (by doctors, lawyers, etc.) and by the proprietors and partners in the many forms of unincorporated businesses. In this chapter we will examine two other main sources of income—rent and interest.

No doubt, the terms rent and interest are already familiar to you from everyday conversation. In this chapter, however, we will see how the economic concept of rent applies to the pricing of all resources, not just land and buildings. The theory of interest rate determination and its relation to the concept of capital is a complex subject. We will touch only on some of its more elementary aspects here.

ECONOMIC RENT

For most people the term rent brings to mind the monthly payment due on their apartment or the payment made to Avis or Hertz for the use of an automobile. Although we think of rent as a simple payment, we can easily see that it covers a host of costs. The rent on an apartment goes to pay property taxes, insurance, heat, maintenance, and other costs connected with the apartment building. Car rental payments go toward all the costs associated with operating a car rental business.

In economics the term rent, or economic rent, has a much more definite meaning than that often associated with the term in everyday usage. **Economic rent** *is any amount of payment a resource receives in excess of its supply price when there is market equilibrium.* The supply price of any resource is the price that the resource must be paid in order to cover its opportunity cost. In other words, it is the price the resource must receive in order to keep it from going into its next best

alternative use. If a buyer is willing to pay the supply price, the resource will be supplied to that buyer. The qualifier "when there is market equilibrium" is necessary because resources will often receive *temporarily* higher payments while markets are adjusting to shifts in demand and supply curves.

Economists first developed the concept of economic rent in connection with the nature of the payments received by landlords for the use of their land. Subsequently, it came to be recognized that other factors and resources also receive economic rent. First we will illustrate the meaning of economic rent in the case of land, and then we will examine its meaning more generally for any resource.

Land

The most prominent characteristic of land is that there is a fixed supply of it. It is true that in some parts of the world it has been possible to reclaim land from the ocean, such as in the Netherlands, and it is also true that its fertility can be depleted by some crops, such as cotton. Aside from these qualifications, *it is an essential characteristic of land that its supply is fixed and exhaustible.* In economic terms, the supply curve of land is vertical, or perfectly inelastic.

Economic Rent and Land

Economists first used the term economic rent to refer to the payments for the use of land. In early nineteenth-century England the price of corn (the term used to refer to all grains at that time) rose to such levels that it became a matter of heated public debate as to what to do about it.

On one side were those who claimed that it was the fault of the landowners. It was argued that they charged farmers such high rents for the use of their land that the farmers in turn had to charge a high price for corn in order to cover these costs. Proponents of this point of view proposed that the government should control the amount of rent that landlords could charge farmers. Central to their position was the belief that high rents *caused* high corn prices.

On the other side of the debate were those who claimed just the opposite—high corn prices *caused* high rents. Perhaps the most lucid proponent of this position was David Ricardo, the renowned classical economist. Ricardo's analysis is illustrated in Figure 16-1. Essentially, he argued that the supply of land available for growing corn was fixed, say at the amount Q, and that it had no other use except the growing of corn. In modern economic terms its supply curve S was perfectly inelastic, or vertical. As with any factor of production, the demand for the land is a derived demand. In this case, the demand curve D is derived from the demand for corn, the final product that the land produces. It was argued that as a result of the Napoleonic Wars, there was a shortage of corn and therefore the price of corn was high. Farmers thus found it very profitable to produce corn. In competing with one another to obtain the use of the fixed supply of cornland, they bid up its price, or rent.

In modern economic terms we know that the price of the final product determines the position of the derived demand curve for a factor of production (as we discussed in Chapter 14). Hence, the higher the price of corn, the higher the position of the derived demand curve D for land in Figure 16-1. The price, or rent, p_0 per acre paid by farmers to landlords for the use of their land, is determined by the intersection of D and S.

But what did Ricardo mean when he claimed that high corn prices caused high rents? Essentially, Ricardo assumed that the land had no other use, that it was simply there and the quantity of it available was completely unresponsive to any change in the price, or rent, paid for its use. Landlords simply rented their land to the highest bidder, and they would certainly rather earn something from it than let it lie idle. If the demand curve fell to a position such as D_1 in Figure 16-1, landlords would be offered nothing for the use of their land—its price, or rent, would be zero—yet the amount sup-

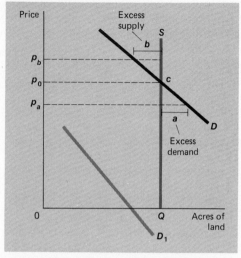

FIGURE 16-1 Economic Rent for Cornland

When there is a fixed supply Q of a factor or resource such as cornland, its supply curve S is perfectly inelastic (vertical). Since the demand for corn is a derived demand, the position of the demand curve for cornland depends on the price of corn. If the price of corn is high, the demand curve for cornland is D and the rent per acre of cornland is p_0, which is determined by the intersection of D and S. On the other hand, if the price of corn is low enough so that the demand curve for cornland is D_1, landlords will receive a zero rent per acre for their land.

Since the cornland is assumed to have no other use, landlords passively accept whatever rent demand dictates, renting their land to the farmers who bid highest for it (however little this might be) rather than leaving it idle and earning nothing. For this reason Ricardo argued that high corn prices *cause* high rent.

This argument gave rise to the concept of economic rent, which is defined as the surplus, or amount of payment a factor or resource receives in excess of its supply price, or opportunity cost, when there is market equilibrium. Since cornland has no other use, its supply price is zero and the rent, or price, received per acre, p_0, is its economic rent. The total economic rent received by cornland is represented by the rectangular area $0Qcp_0$.

plied would still be the same, Q. If the price, or rent, was p_a and the demand curve was D, there would be an excess demand for land equal to the distance a. In their attempts to obtain land, farmers would bid the rent up to p_0 as landlords rented it out to the highest bidder. If on the other hand rent per acre was p_b and the demand curve was still D, there would be an excess supply of land equal to the distance b. Rather than leave this land idle and therefore earning nothing, landlords in competition with one another to rent their land out would lower rent to p_0. In short, land receives whatever rent the demand for it dictates. The price of corn determines ("causes") the position of the derived demand curve for land, and landlords react—accordingly. The landlords' role is passive. *Hence, Ricardo claimed, the price, or rent, of cornland was high because the price of corn was high, not the other way around.* Advocates of this point of view argued that the solution to the problem of high corn prices was not to control landlords but rather to lower restrictions on the import of foreign corn. This would increase the supply of corn and lower its price, thereby lowering the demand for cornland and reducing its rent.

Ricardo's analysis generally came to be accepted by economists as correct. It gave rise to the concept of economic rent. Economic rent, once again, is defined as the surplus, or amount of payment to a factor over and above its supply price, or opportunity cost, when there is market equilibrium. In the case of Ricardo's cornland in Figure 16–1, the economic rent per acre is p_0, the entire rent, or price, paid for the use of an acre of cornland. This is so because the cornland is presumed to have no other use (its supply price is zero) and therefore can be kept in the activity of corn production even at a zero rent. The total economic rent received by cornland is equal to the rectangular area $0Qcp_0$.

Taxing Land's Economic Rent

Land's economic rent has struck many, both economists and laypeople alike, as an "un-

earned surplus." When population and incomes grow, the demand for the fixed quantity of land increases. The good fortune of landowners is to sit back and effortlessly watch the economic rents they receive grow accordingly as the demand curve for their land shifts rightward. How many times have you heard of someone who bought a corner lot on some sleepy country crossroads 20 years ago that is now worth a small fortune as commercial property on a busy suburban intersection? It has always appeared to many that economic rent is more a product of good fortune than the fruits of "honest" work. It is little wonder that land rents should have become a ready target for taxation.

In the latter half of the nineteenth century, Henry George, a printer with a penchant for economics, gathered a large following of supporters behind his **single-tax movement**. Running on this platform, he was almost elected mayor of New York in 1886. The main objective of George's movement was to finance government by taxing away the "unearned increment" that landowners receive as economic rent on their land. George and his followers argued that in a growing economy, particularly in urban areas, these economic rents were an ever growing "surplus" obtained by landowners without effort. To them it seemed only just that government should be financed by taxing away this surplus—that economic rent rather than the wages of the working person should bear the burden of taxation. Since the land was there as the bounty of nature, George argued that these economic rents rightfully belonged to the public and should be used for public purposes. This position was forcefully advanced in his popular book *Progress and Poverty* (1879).

Aside from its compelling appeal to the public's sense of justice, *a single tax on land has another advantage over most other forms of taxation—it is neutral in its effects on production incentives and resource allocation.* We know, for example, from our discussion of excise and sales taxes in Chapter 6, that taxes typically affect the prices and the quantities bought and sold of the goods and services on which they are levied. The reason this does not happen when a single tax is levied on the economic rent of land is illustrated in Figure 16-2.

The supply of land Q, being fixed, is inelastic, as indicated by the vertical supply curve S. This, together with the demand for the use of land, represented by the demand curve D, determines an economic rent received by landowners equal to p_0. Now suppose the government levies a tax amounting to 50 percent of the economic rent received on all land. In other words, 50 percent of any rent payment made for the use of a piece of land must go to the government. This tax is just like the sales or excise taxes we studied in Chapter 6. In particular, recall that when the supply curve is perfectly inelastic, as in Figure 16-2, the entire burden of the tax is borne by the supplier—in this case the landowner.

The position of the demand curve D and its intersection at point a with the supply curve S are unaffected by this tax. It thus follows that the price, or rent, p_0 paid for the use of a unit of land remains the same as before the imposition of the tax. However, after the government has taxed away 50 percent, the portion actually received by the landowner per unit of land is p_n—the rent net of (or minus) tax. This is represented by the intersection of the net demand curve D_n with the supply curve S at b. The net demand curve D_n is the one effectively facing the landowners after the government has taken its cut out of the economic rent. Any point on the demand curve D_n lies one-half the distance below the point vertically above it on D, a reflection of the 50 percent tax.

In sum, *the full burden of the tax falls entirely on the landowners and there is nothing they can do about it,* despite the fact they don't like it. The quantity of land is fixed and they must take whatever is given to them by demand. *Since the quantity of the land Q and the rent paid for it p_0 are the same as before the tax, there is no distortion of resource allocation.* This is true because if the rent p_0 paid by

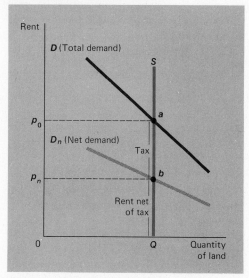

FIGURE 16-2 Landowners Bear the Entire Burden of a Tax on Land's Economic Rent

Suppose the economic rent on land is initially p_0, as determined by the intersection of the demand curve D and the perfectly inelastic supply curve of land S. If the government levies a 50 percent tax on economic rent, D and S are unchanged and so is the rent p_0 paid by farmers and other land users. However, landowners now only receive half of this rent after the government takes its cut. From the landowners' viewpoint, the demand curve for land is effectively D_n, which is the demand after tax, or net demand. The economic rent p_n received by the landowners corresponds to the intersection of D_n and S at b.

Because the supply of land is fixed, landowners bear the full burden of the tax. Since the rent p_0 paid by land users remains unaffected by the tax, the prices and quantities of products that use land as a factor of production (corn, for example) are similarly unaffected. Hence, a single tax on land is neutral in its effects on production incentives and resource allocation.

farmers or other users is unchanged, it means that the tax does not affect the prices and quantities of any products that use land as a factor of production. This would be true whether the tax is 10 percent, 75 percent, or any other percent.

Difficulties with a Land Tax

Taxing the economic rent earned by land appeals to many in theory, but it is difficult to carry out in practice. The problem is that rent payments cover the costs of other things in addition to the land itself, as we noted at the outset of our discussion of economic rent. For example, how do you separate out that part of the actual rent payment for agricultural land that is made because the land is more productive due to investment in land clearing, drainage canals, and other such productivity-increasing activities? Indiscriminate taxation of land rents would discourage landowners from spending money to make such improvements, because unlike the land itself, the supply of such activities is dependent upon the return they bring in. To the extent such indiscriminate taxation of actual rent payments applies to the portion that goes to pay for other factors besides the land itself, production incentives and resource allocation will be disturbed.

The same problem arises when we consider rent payments made on urban and suburban properties. A part of such payments covers the services of the buildings and facilities that stand on the land. How do you separate this part from the part that is the economic rent for the land? Is it really possible to do so? Rent payments cover the costs of the building and a host of other factors that have to be sorted out to get at the economic rent attributable to the land. To the extent that attempts to tax the economic rent of land in urban and suburban areas also apply to the rent for the buildings on this land, the construction of new buildings and the maintenance of existing ones will be retarded. Again, production incentives and resource allocation will be disturbed.

Economic Rent on Other Factors

The concept of economic rent first arose in connection with land. The supply of land was usually assumed to be unchangeable and to have but one use, such as corn growing. Given these assumptions, the supply curve of land is vertical. It is more realistic, however, to recognize that a given piece of land typically has more than one use. For example, farmland can be converted to residential and urban use. The greater the demand for housing, the larger the portion of available farmland that is converted to such use. Hence, the supply curve for land for residential use is upward sloping, left to right, rather than vertical. Because they have alternative uses this is true of most resources that are used as factors of production. When a factor's supply curve is upward sloping, part of the payment to the factor is economic rent and part is the factor's supply price.

This is illustrated for the factor labor in Figure 16–3, part a. Labor is a factor whose supply is responsive to price, as reflected by the fact that its supply curve is upward sloping, left to right. In the perfectly competitive labor market of Figure 16–3, part a, the intersection of the labor demand curve D and supply curve S determines the equilibrium wage w_0 and level of employment L. In equilibrium each and every laborer is paid the wage w_0. However, only for the last laborer employed is w_0 just the amount necessary to induce that laborer to work in this line of activity instead of some other. That is, w_0 just equals the last laborer's supply price, represented by the point at which the supply curve S is intersected by the demand curve D. The supply price of each laborer hired prior to the last one is represented by a point on the supply curve to the left of this intersection.

For example, the supply price of the first laborer employed is w_1, the point at which the supply curve meets the vertical axis. In equilibrium, the first laborer's economic rent is represented by the difference between w_0, the wage actually received, and w_1, the labor-

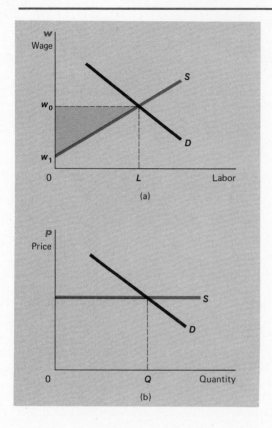

(a)

(b)

FIGURE 16-3 Economic Rent Results When Factor Owners Differ in Willingness to Supply Them

In a perfectly competitive labor market (part a), laborers differ in their willingness to supply labor and therefore have different supply prices. The upward-sloping supply curve reflects this fact. The equilibrium wage and level of employment in such a market are w_0 and L respectively, determined by the intersection of the demand curve D and supply curve S. The supply price of the last laborer hired is just equal to the market wage w_0, so that this last laborer earns no economic rent. However, the supply price of the first laborer hired is w_1, so that in market equilibrium the first laborer earns an economic rent equal to the difference between w_0 and w_1. The supply price of each succeeding laborer is higher, but below the market-determined wage w_0 that each receives. Hence, each earns economic rent (except the last laborer hired). The total economic rent earned by labor in this market is represented by the shaded area. There are many factors of production besides labor that have such supply curves and therefore earn economic rent.

If, unlike the situation in part a, all owners of a factor have the same supply price, no economic rent will be earned. In that case the supply curve of the factor is horizontal, or perfectly elastic, as shown in part b.

er's supply price. The supply price of each successive laborer hired after the first is progressively higher, as represented by the upward-sloping supply curve. Consequently, the economic rent received by each successive laborer becomes progressively less until the last laborer hired receives a zero economic rent. The total economic rent received by labor in this market is represented by the shaded area. Other factors with upward-sloping supply curves also receive economic rent that is represented in this manner.

There are many factors of production that have upward-sloping supply curves because owners differ in their willingness to supply the factor. Therefore part of the price received for these factors by their owners is economic rent. No economic rent will be earned only if all owners of a factor have the same supply price. In that case the supply curve of the factor is horizontal, or perfectly elastic, as shown in Figure 16–3, part b.

Economic Rent as Cost and Surplus

Whether we are talking about resources with perfectly inelastic supply curves, such as any

POLICY PERSPECTIVE

Subsidized Job Training Versus Labor's Economic Rent

In the early days of the auto industry, Henry Ford foresaw that the growing industry would need a large and increasing supply of skilled labor—tool- and die makers, layout designers, and so forth. One way to get more labor into these trades would be simply to allow the increasing demand for such services to raise wages—that is, let the usual market forces of supply and demand solve the problem. Another way would be to subsidize training in these areas and thereby increase the supply of skilled workers. Ford tried the latter route and opened the Ford Trade School.

The Alternatives Compared

The two alternatives just mentioned have different implications for employer costs and skilled labor's wages. The difference turns on the issue of economic rent. This is illustrated in Figure P16-1. Suppose the objective is to increase the quantity of skilled labor from L_1 to L_2. Given the supply curve S for skilled labor, this could be done by raising the wage from w_1 to w_2, a movement from point c to point d on S. Note that this results in a considerable increase in the economic rent paid labor, which is represented by the shaded area w_1cdw_2. Note also that a large part of this increase in economic rent has to be paid to the quantity of skilled labor L_1 that was already willing to work at the previous wage of w_1. This part of the economic rent increase is represented by the shaded area to the left of the vertical hatched line between points c and e—that is, the area w_1cew_2.

Now let's look at the other alternative—subsidizing the training of skilled labor, as Henry Ford did by setting up the Ford Trade School. This subsidy has the

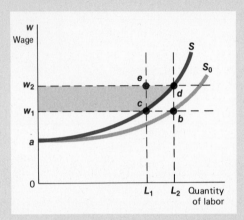

FIGURE P16-1 Employers' Costs Versus Labor's Economic Rent

effect of increasing the quantity of skilled labor that is available at any wage level, as represented by the rightward shift of the supply curve from S to S_0. This means that the required increased supply of labor L_2 can now be had at the same wage w_1 as before.

Compare the costs of the two alternative ways of increasing the quantity of labor from L_1 to L_2. It can be seen that increasing the labor supply simply by raising the wage from w_1 to w_2 along supply curve S means that the employer will have to pay more in total wages than if the employer subsidizes the training of workers. The additional amount of total wages is represented by the rectangular area w_1bdw_2, the largest portion being the additional economic rent represented by the shaded area w_1cdw_2. Remember that this market is the demand and supply of labor services per some unit of time, such as a month or year. If the additional amount of total wages per unit of time is greater than the costs per that same unit of time of subsidizing the operation of the trade school, it will be cheaper for the employer to obtain L_2 laborers by operating the trade school rather than paying a higher wage w_2. If the reverse is true, it will be cheaper for the employer to simply pay the higher wage.

Choosing the Best Alternative

Obviously, the best alternative from the employer's standpoint depends on the elasticity of the labor supply curve. The more inelastic it is, the greater will be the increase in total wages and in labor's economic rent if the payment of a higher-wage alternative is followed. Hence, the greater the likelihood that it is better for the employer to take the subsidization of the trade school approach. Organized labor, such as craft unions, always prefer the higher-wage alternative because it gives labor higher wages and therefore higher economic rents.

Henry Ford operated the Ford Trade School up through the 1930s. Then, with the great surge in the labor union movement after 1935, organized labor in the auto industry recognized what the school was costing them in terms of lower wages,

in particular their forgone economic rents. Labor pressure led to the closing of the school.

Policy Implications

The same type of issue is still very much alive today. Policymakers often advocate various sorts of government-subsidized job-training programs to deal with high unemployment among teenagers and other hard-core unemployment problem areas in the economy. One can understand why union members might have mixed feelings about such programs. One can also see why big business often seems eager to cooperate with and lend support to these programs.

Questions

1. How would you explain the fact that there are many fellowships and scholarships available for graduate students in physics, chemistry, and other basic scientific disciplines, while there are comparatively very few available for medical students?

2. Why do you think some economists favor high inheritance taxes?

type of land that has only one use, or those with upward-sloping supply curves, such as labor, the nature of economic rent depends on whether you are a buyer or seller. If you are a farmer renting land to grow corn, the economic rent you must pay is a cost of production as far as you are concerned. Similarly, if you are a firm hiring labor, that part of the wages you pay that is economic rent is still a cost to you. From the standpoint of the owner of the productive factor, the economic rent is an excess above supply price, the price at which the owner would be willing to supply the factor anyway. From the owner's vantage point, economic rent is "gravy"—a surplus above that needed to engage the fac-

tor in the particular line of productive activity.

Explicit and Implicit Economic Rent

In Chapter 7 we made a distinction between explicit and implicit costs. (You might want to look back over that section at this point.) That distinction is also relevant for economic rent. Landowners might use their land themselves rather than rent it out, as is the case with farmers who farm their own land. Such farmers would be kidding themselves as to how well they are doing if their calculations didn't include the cost of using their own land—that is, its implicit cost, or rent. The implicit rent equals the economic rent the farmers would receive if they were to rent the land out to someone else.

Similarly, an owner who personally manages his or her business would make the same kind of mistake if the wages he or she could make managing someone else's business weren't included as costs. Moreover, the owner should not calculate the opportunity cost of these services as the price for which he or she would be willing to work somewhere else—his or her supply price. Rather, the cost should be calculated as the wage the market would pay for this work. It may well be that this market wage is greater than the owner's supply price. To use the supply price rather than the market wage would leave out the economic rent the owner could earn and therefore understate his or her opportunity costs.

CHECKPOINT* 16-1

It is sometimes said that movie stars and great professional athletes earn large economic rents. Explain this observation. As a proportion of their earnings, how do you think the economic rents earned by presidents of major corporations compare with those of movie stars and great professional athletes? Why? If Henry George were alive today, what do you think his position would be on the taxation of economic rent of individuals with unique or unusual skills? Comparing landowners and such individuals, what do you think would be a "just" position?

*Answers to all Checkpoints can be found at the back of the text.

INTEREST AND CAPITAL

When you borrow money to pay your tuition, to buy a car or house, or simply to make ends meet until the next paycheck, you must pay a special price called **interest** for the use of such funds. This aspect of interest is quite familiar to most people. What is not so obvious is the intimate relationship between interest and capital. In Chapter 1 we observed that businesses need capital—plant, equipment, inventories—to produce goods and services, and that they need money, or financial capital, to purchase this productive factor. It is the productivity of the capital that allows businesses to pay the interest necessary to obtain this money.

Why There Is Capital

Recall that capital, or capital goods, are all man-made goods used in production, or goods used to produce other goods. Factories, trucks, drill presses, and computers are but a few examples. The economy has limited resources and therefore can only produce so much output per period of time. Thus if a portion of that output is to take the form of new capital goods, the economy will have to forgo a certain amount of goods that could otherwise be produced for current consumption. We know this from our discussion of the production possibilities frontier in Chapter 2. Moreover, if society is to be persuaded to sacrifice some current consumption goods in order to produce capital goods, it must perceive some gain or return from doing so.

Capital Productivity and Roundaboutness

The gain from the production of capital goods today essentially derives from the fact that it will make possible a greater production of goods (of all types) tomorrow than would be otherwise possible without those capital goods. Ranking in importance with the invention of the wheel was the realization that the most direct way of producing goods was not necessarily the most efficient.

Stone Age people discovered that it was usually more productive to take some time off from hunting game and tilling a plot of ground with bare hands or sticks and use this time to fashion stone hatchets and crude stone hoes to use in these activities. The first hunting and growing season they did this they had less game and food to consume than usual because of the hunting and crop-tending time lost to toolmaking. But in the next season, aided by their new tools, they were able to kill more game and grow more food than before when they were hunting and producing only with the aid of sticks. This is a simple example of a roundabout process of production. *A* **roundabout process** *involves taking time and effort away from the direct production of goods for current consumption and instead producing capital goods that will provide a larger subsequent production of goods than would be otherwise possible.*

Just as in a Stone Age economy, modern economies, whether centrally planned like that of the Soviet Union or more market-oriented like that of the United States, use the same principle of roundaboutness to increase their productivity. By devoting a portion of this year's production to the formation of capital goods instead of consumption goods, the total output of the economy in future years will be larger than if those capital goods were not produced this year. The current sacrifice of consumption to produce capital is rewarded by the gain in future production that it makes possible. The larger the prospective gain, the more willing society is to sacrifice current consumption to this end.

Net Productivity of Capital and Its Rate of Return

The expenditure for a new unit of capital is typically referred to as investment in capital, or simply **investment**. You may think of capital as an investment in a roundabout process. How do we calculate the net productivity of capital and its rate of return?

First, since capital is only one of the factors of production, we need to know the portion of the total dollar value of the sales of the final product attributable to it. By deducting the costs of the other factors of production (including allowance for a normal

profit) from total sales, we obtain the dollar receipts of capital. The sum of these receipts over the life of a capital good minus (or net of) the cost of the capital good is a dollar measure of its net productivity. If this calculation doesn't yield a positive dollar value, there is no net productivity. If net productivity is positive, we are usually interested in determining whether the net productivity is large enough to justify investment in the capital good.

In order to do this, we determine the ratio of the dollar measure of the capital good's net productivity to the cost of the capital good and express it as a percentage per year, or **rate of return**. We may then say that *the* **net productivity of capital** *is the annual percentage rate of return that can be earned by investing in it.*

For example, in a large, bustling city a taxicab might last a year (after that it becomes scrap). Suppose you buy a cab for $8,000, employ a cabdriver for $11,000 per year, spend $7,000 on gasoline, $2,000 on maintenance, $1,000 on insurance, $1,000 for a license, and $1,000 in taxes. Also suppose you take $1,000 per year as a normal profit compensating you for your management services and the entrepreneurial risks of running your cab business. Suppose total receipts from cab fares for the year come to $32,800. Total costs exclusive of the cost of the cab, which is a capital investment of $8,000, are $24,000. Subtracting this from total receipts leaves $8,800, which is what is left to cover the cost of the cab. Subtracting the cost of the cab ($8,000) from $8,800 leaves $800. That $800 is attributable to the productivity of the capital good, the cab. The net productivity, or rate of return, on this capital good is therefore $800 ÷ $8,000, which equals .10, or 10 percent.

As we noted earlier, you must pay interest in order to borrow money. Since the interest on borrowed money must be paid with money, interest is expressed as a percentage rate just like the rate of return on capital. What market interest rate would you be willing to pay to borrow the money to buy the

$8,000 cab and start your own taxicab business? Certainly not more than 10 percent, because a higher interest rate than this would exceed the rate of return on your investment in the cab and you would realize a loss. Any lower interest rate would allow you to realize a profit. Rather than borrow the money you might choose to use your own money. But the decision as to whether to invest or not would be no different. You would not be willing to invest your own money in the cab if the market interest rate exceeded 10 percent. Why? Because the opportunity cost of doing so exceeds the net productivity, or rate of return, on the cab. You would be better off lending your money out to someone else at the higher interest rate.

The Demand for Capital

The demand for capital derives from its net productivity in the production of goods. Like the demand for any factor of production, it is a derived demand. Recall that the demand curve for labor is its marginal revenue product curve. Similarly, the demand curve for capital may be thought of as its marginal revenue product curve expressed in percentage terms, or what we have called its net productivity.

This is illustrated in Figure 16–4, where for simplicity it is assumed that there is only one kind of capital. The demand curve D is made up of the points representing the net productivity of capital (vertical axis) associated with each additional unit of capital (horizontal axis). The first unit of capital has a net productivity of 14 percent. (The scale on the horizontal axis is such that one unit of capital is no larger than a point.) If the interest rate is higher than this, it will not pay to invest in this unit of capital. Note that each additional unit of capital has a lower net productivity than the previous unit—hence the demand curve is downward sloping. This reflects the fact that the law of diminishing returns applies to capital just as it does to other productive factors, such as labor. Given the fixed amounts of all other factors, the net productivity of each additional unit of capital decreases as the total quantity of capital is increased.

If the market interest rate is 10 percent, for example, it pays to invest in capital, or undertake those roundabout processes that have a net productivity greater than 10 percent. Once the economy has created the capital that has a net productivity of 13 percent, it will move on to invest in capital that has a net productivity of 12 percent, and so on until it has exploited all those opportunities to create capital that have a net productivity, or rate of return, greater than 10 percent per year. Therefore at an interest rate of 10 percent, the stock of capital demanded will equal K_0. If the market interest rate were 6 percent, the economy would desire to invest in all those capital projects with a rate of return greater than 6 percent, and the stock of capital demanded would equal K_1.

Interest and Saving

We have seen that to produce capital goods it is necessary to give up a certain amount of current consumption. Only by doing so can a portion of this period's total production take the form of capital goods. The sacrifice of current consumption to the roundabout process of capital formation must be made up for by the prospect of a future gain in order to make the sacrifice worthwhile.

Economists call this sacrifice of current consumption **saving**. *For the economy as a whole, saving is defined as not consuming all of this period's production of output.* It is the extent of saving, or refraining from current consumption, on the part of the individual members of the economy that determines the amount of total saving. This total saving is the amount of this period's total production that can be devoted to the output of capital goods, as opposed to goods for current consumption.

People save part of their incomes for many reasons—to provide for old age, to buy a home or a car, to give their children a college education, and so on. The attainment of

FIGURE 16-4 **The Demand for Capital Depends on Its Net Productivity**

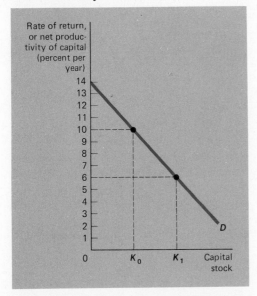

The demand for capital, like that for any other productive factor, is a derived demand.

Its demand curve D may be thought of as its marginal revenue product curve expressed in percentage terms, or what we have called its net productivity. The demand curve D is made up of the points representing the net productivity of capital (vertical axis) associated with each additional unit of capital (horizontal axis).

As shown here, the first unit of capital produced has a net productivity of 14 percent. Because of diminishing returns, each additional unit of capital has a lower net productivity than the previous one, as reflected in the fact that D is downward sloping. If the market interest rate is 10 percent, it will pay to invest only in those capital projects that have a net productivity, or rate of return, greater than 10 percent. Hence, the stock of capital demanded will equal K_0. If the market interest rate is 6 percent, it will pay to invest in all those capital projects with a rate of return in excess of 6 percent, and therefore the total demand for capital will equal K_1.

these goals is the reward they expect for the sacrifice of current consumption that saving requires. Another very tangible reward is the interest they can earn on their saving. Whatever the other reasons for saving, the higher the interest rate received, the larger the reward for saving, and therefore the more people will be induced to save part of their incomes.

The relationship between the interest rate and the total amount of saving (or refraining from current consumption) for the whole economy is illustrated in Figure 16–5. The saving curve S gives the relationship between the interest rate (vertical axis) and the economy's total saving per year, or the dollar amount of that part of the economy's total annual output that may take the form of capital goods. The higher the interest rate, the larger the amount each individual will want to devote to saving and hence the greater the total amount of saving. As a result, the saving curve is upward sloping. For example, at an interest rate of 4 percent, the total amount of saving would equal S_0, while at the higher interest rate of 7 percent, saving would be the larger amount S_1.

Interest Rate Determination

We are now in a position to lay out the basics of the traditional theory of interest rate determination. This is illustrated in Figure 16–6. Part a shows the economy's net productivity, or demand curve for capital, like that shown in Figure 16–4. Part b shows the economy's saving curve, like that shown in Figure 16–5.

It should be emphasized that it is the stock of capital that is measured (in units of capital) along the horizontal axis in part a of Figure 16–6. It takes time, often many years, for an economy to accumulate a sizeable capital stock. Suppose the economy's capital stock is K_0, the endowment from many years of accumulation that is represented by the perfectly inelastic (vertical) stock supply curve k_0. This curve intersects D at a, and the net productivity, or rate of return, on the last

FIGURE 16-5   The Relationship Between the Interest Rate and Saving

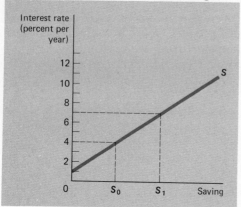

Saving is defined as refraining from current consumption. To this extent, it entails a sacrifice.

Among the possible rewards of saving is the rate of interest that can be earned. The higher the interest rate, the larger this form of reward and the greater is the incentive to save. The upward-sloping saving curve S reflects this fact. The higher the interest rate (vertical axis), the larger the economy's level of saving per year (horizontal axis). The level of saving is also the dollar amount of that part of the economy's total annual output that may be used to obtain capital goods. At an annual interest rate of 4 percent, the total amount of saving would equal S_0, while at the higher interest rate of 7 percent, total saving would be the larger amount S_1.

unit of this capital stock is therefore 10 percent. Hence, if the economy saves, that is, refrains from consuming, a part of this year's total production of output (a flow measured as so many dollars of output per year) so that this part may take the form of investment in new capital goods, the rate of return on these new capital goods will not be greater than 10 percent. Investors in new capital stock will therefore be willing to pay an interest rate up to 10 percent to induce people to lend them their savings so that the investors can buy newly produced capital goods.

But point a on D represents a short-run equilibrium. Let us see why. At an interest rate of 10 percent, people will be induced to save an amount totaling S_0 dollars per year, as shown in part b of Figure 16–6. Remember that the horizontal axis of part b measures *flow*, the dollar flow of saving out of this year's dollar flow of output. Lent out to investors it becomes the dollar flow of investment, or expenditure on new capital goods, produced in the current year. The new units of capital produced in the current year and purchased with this money are then added to the stock of capital K_0. (Assume for simplicity that there is no depreciation, or wearing out, of the existing capital stock, so that new capital isn't used for replacement of old.) Hence, over time the stock of capital will grow and the vertical stock supply curve in part a will move rightward. Its resulting intersection with the capital stock demand curve D at lower and lower points down along D means that the rate of return on capital, and therefore the interest rate, will fall.

As the interest rate becomes progressively lower, it is clear from part b that the amount of saving that makes new additions to the capital stock possible will also decline. Finally, when the capital stock has grown to the size K_1, so that the vertical stock supply curve of capital k_1 intersects D at b, the rate of return on capital and the interest rate will be 1 percent. The flow of saving will be zero (part b) and new capital formation will cease. The economy will consume its entire annual production of output, and nothing will be devoted to capital formation. Point b on D (part a) therefore corresponds to its long-run equilibrium position.

In sum, *the existing stock of capital, together with the net productivity or demand curve for capital, determines the interest rate, which in turn determines the amount of saving. The amount of saving is the amount of total output produced that is not devoted to current consumption and that is therefore available for the production of new capital goods, which increase the size of the capital stock. The long-run equilibrium interest rate is that interest rate at which saving becomes zero and new capital formation therefore ceases.*

FIGURE 16-6 **The Determination of the Interest Rate**

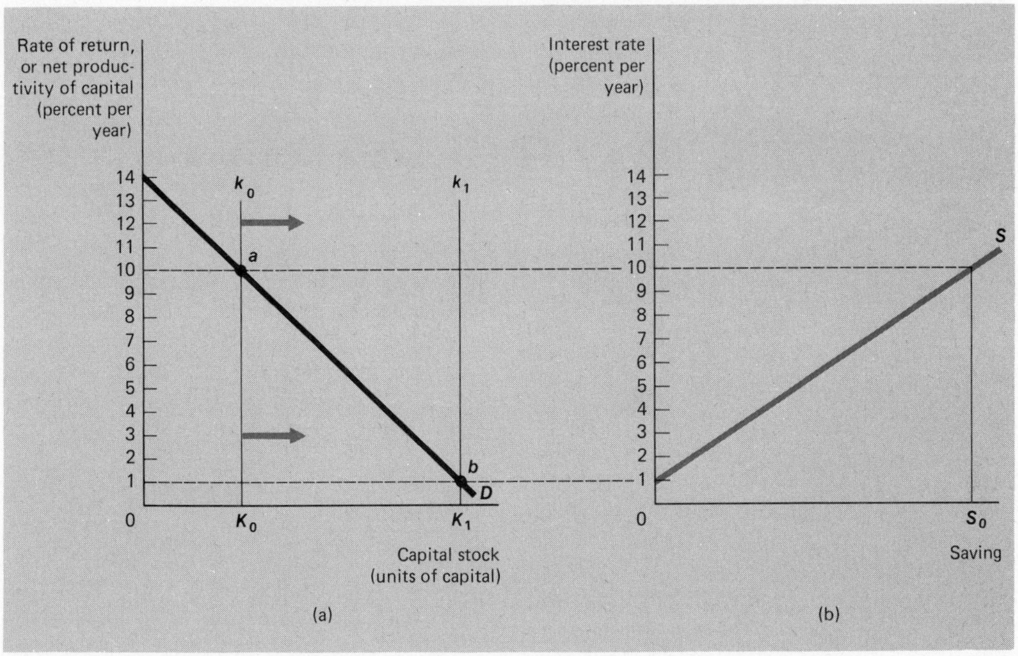

The net productivity, or demand, for capital curve D in part a is the same as in Figure 16–4. The saving curve S in part b is the same as in Figure 16–5.

Given the economy's stock of capital, which has been accumulated over time, the vertical stock supply curve of capital k_0 intersects D at point a, where the rate of return on capital, and therefore the interest rate, is 10 percent. At this interest rate the economy is willing to save (refrain from consuming) S_0 dollars worth of the economy's annual production of output. Lent out to investors, this becomes the dollar flow of investment, or expenditure, on new capital goods produced in the current year. Point a on D is therefore only a short-run equilibrium position because this new capital formation will increase the size of the capital stock. This is represented by the rightward shift of the vertical stock supply curve of capital (part a).

As long as the interest rate is high enough to induce saving, capital formation will continue. This will eventually drive down the rate of return on capital, and hence the interest rate, to the point where saving becomes zero. This occurs with a capital stock of K_1, where the supply curve k_1 intersects D at b (part a) to determine an interest rate of 1 percent. At this point saving becomes zero (part b), and investment in capital formation ceases. This is the point of long-run equilibrium.

Why We Never See Long-Run Equilibrium

To reach long-run equilibrium, we must move down the demand curve D and realize diminishing returns because all other things are assumed constant. In reality, of course, the other things, such as technology and population, do not remain unchanged. New inventions and technological progress cause the net productivity of capital to increase. This causes the demand curve D for capital to shift rightward. We know from our discussion in Chapter 14 that when the supply of one factor of production increases, the marginal productivity of other factors is increased. Therefore increases in the labor supply resulting from population growth also increase the net productivity of capital and, likewise, cause the demand curve D to shift rightward. In a dynamic, growing economy the demand curve for capital will be continually shifted rightward as a result of such ongoing changes. Consequently, the rate of return on capital, and hence the interest rate, never falls to the extent necessary to reach the long-run equilibrium position.

In our discussion of the demand curve D in Figure 16-6, part a, it was implicitly assumed that the net productivity, and hence the rate of return on capital, is known to investors in capital with certainty. This is, of course, not true in reality. Any assessment of the net productivity of capital goods or roundabout processes undertaken today can at best only be based on educated guesses about the demand for the goods that they will produce in the future. Given this, the demand curve for capital is subject to changes in such guesses, and changes in events will lead to a continual revision of these guesses. Shifts in business optimism about the future, which often occur rapidly, cause sporadic movement in the demand curve D and therefore its intersection with the vertical stock supply curve of capital. The interest rate will move about accordingly.

Historically, the saving habits of the economy have been much more stable than investor willingness to undertake new capital formation. This is not surprising given that saving is a decision made about the disposition of income already in hand (how much of it to save and how much to spend on current consumption), while investment in new capital is based to a much greater extent on guesses about events yet to happen. Nonetheless, the saving curve in part b of Figure 16-6 can shift around and thereby affect the rate of capital formation. This in turn will

affect the amount of change in the interest rate over time.

Consumption Loans

From time to time some people want to spend more than their total income on current consumption. To do so, they may borrow from others in the economy who save a part of their income. In this case the amount of such borrowed funds that the borrower spends on current consumption is just equal to the amount the lender must refrain from spending on current consumption in order to make the loan. What one consumes, the other doesn't. The aggregate, or sum, of all such consumption loans in the economy therefore does not affect the amount of total expenditure on current consumption. Hence, it does not affect the position of the economy's saving curve in Figure 16-6, part b. At any interest rate above 1 percent, total saving is positive. This means that the total amount saved by those not spending all their incomes exceeds the total amount spent by individuals on current consumption in excess of their incomes.

Why There Are So Many Different Interest Rates

Up to now we have talked about "the" interest rate. Economists find this convenient in order to spell out the basic elements of the traditional theory of capital formation. However, a casual observer of the financial pages of any newspaper or the behavior of the numerous financial institutions in our economy knows that there are, in fact, many different interest rates. These rates correspond to the many different debt instruments issued by borrowers to lenders. *These* **debt instruments** *are the written contracts between borrower and lender specifying the terms of a loan, such as its expiration or maturity date, its size, and the rights of the borrower and lender under the agreements.* Bonds, bank deposits, commercial paper, common and preferred stocks, credit union shares, and mortgages are all examples of debt instruments. Interest rates on debt instruments differ because of differences in risk, length of loan, marketability of the loan, and the structure of financial markets.

Risk essentially depends on the likelihood that the borrower will default on (be unable to pay back) the loan. The greater this likelihood, the larger the interest rate that will have to be paid to induce lenders to make the loan. A small company in a highly competitive space age technology industry will typically have to pay a higher interest rate to borrow money than General Motors does because there is a higher risk of the small company defaulting on its loan.

Loan length, or maturity, refers to the duration of time until the loan must be repaid. Naturally the greater the length of time over which the money is borrowed, the greater the possibility that the lender may run into financial difficulty somewhere down the road. Therefore, the interest rate is usually higher on longer-term loans to compensate the lender for this risk.

Marketability, or the liquidity of a loan, refers to the ease with which the lender may sell the debt instrument to someone else before the loan matures. If you write me an IOU for a gambling debt, I will probably be able to sell it to someone else only if I am willing to take considerably less for it than the amount owed. By comparison, the market for an IBM bond is much more extensive and well developed. The chances of selling it for what I paid for it are much greater. Interest rates on less marketable debt instruments tend to be higher, all other things remaining the same, to compensate the lender for their lower marketability.

Financial market structure plays much the same role in determining the level of interest rates as product market structure considerations play in determining the price level of goods. A monopoly lender is in a better position to charge a higher interest rate than many lenders competing with one another to make loans.

Interest Rates and Resource Allocation

The existence of many different interest rates on the many different kinds of debt instruments in the economy serves the same kind of resource allocation function as does the existence of many different prices on the many different kinds of goods the economy produces. There is in reality a large variety of capital investment projects, ranging from building dams and ships to starting up a mom-and-pop grocery store. Capital projects differ in their riskiness and life expectancy, as well as in their size. Shifts in the demand for the products that capital goods help produce will cause changes in the capital goods' relative net productivity and thus in the interest rates they can pay to attract financial capital.

For example, during the last 50 years the increased demand for airline passenger service relative to that for railroad passenger service increased the net productivity of capital used in the former industry relative to that used in the latter. The interest rates that could be paid to attract financial capital into the building of airplanes and airports thus rose relative to those that could be paid to finance railways, passenger cars, and depots. Consequently, the rate of capital formation in the airline industry rose relative to that in the railroad passenger industry.

The problem of capital allocation has to be solved by every economy. Centrally planned economies like that of the Soviet Union must resort to some sort of interest rate structure to do this just as do market-oriented economies like that of the United States. The institutional structure surrounding the determination of interest rates, and even the terminology used, differs, reflecting the differences in political and ideological orientation between the two countries.

Nominal and Real Interest Rates

Suppose there is no inflation occurring in the economy. (Inflation is defined as an ongoing increase in the general price level at some percentage rate per year.) Suppose also that lenders are lending money at an interest rate of 5 percent, based on the expectation that there will continue to be no inflation. A lender just willing to lend out $1 worth of purchasing power today is induced to do so by the promise of getting back $1.05 worth of purchasing power tomorrow, or 5 percent more purchasing power than originally loaned. In terms of goods, or "real" terms, the lender will be able to obtain 5 percent more goods tomorrow than today. The annual percentage rate of increase in the lender's purchasing power on money loaned is the **real interest rate**.

Now suppose for some reason lenders come to expect a rate of inflation of 4 percent per year. They no longer will be willing to lend at an interest rate of 5 percent, but will now charge an interest rate of 9 percent. Why? Because the dollars they lend out today will be worth 4 percent less in terms of their purchasing power in a year—4 percent less in real terms. Hence, lenders must charge an additional 4 percent in interest to ensure that they still get back 5 percent more purchasing power than they originally loaned. In short, in order to continue to realize an increase in purchasing power, or a real rate of interest, of 5 percent, it is necessary to charge a nominal rate of interest of 9 percent. *The* **nominal interest rate** *equals the real interest rate plus the rate of anticipated inflation.*

In our example, when the anticipated rate of inflation was zero, the real interest rate and the nominal interest rates were the same, 5 percent. Only when the anticipated rate of inflation equals zero is it true that the nominal interest rate and the real interest rate are equal. The quoted interest rates we observe in financial markets are nominal interest rates. To arrive at the real interest rate, it is necessary to subtract the anticipated rate of inflation from these nominal interest rates. However, as a practical matter, it is difficult to measure accurately the public's anticipated rate of inflation.

The Government and Interest Rates

The government can affect interest rates in many ways. Two major avenues of influence are the federal government's fiscal and monetary policy actions.

Fiscal policy affects interest rates through government expenditure and tax policies. For example, if government expenditures exceed tax revenues, then the Treasury Department must issue government bonds to finance the deficit. Government bonds must compete for financial capital alongside private debt instruments and will cause interest rates to rise, other things remaining the same.

Monetary policy, as implemented through the Federal Reserve System, affects the amount of money available to accommodate loan demand. If the Federal Reserve limits expansion of the money supply, interest rates will tend to rise, at least in the short run, as borrowers' demand for loans grows relative to the rate of growth in the availability of lendable funds through the banking system. On the other hand, if the Federal Reserve increases the availability of funds more rapidly than the rate of growth of loan demand, interest rates will tend to fall, in the short run at least. In the long run, if the Federal Reserve continues to expand the nation's money supply at such a rate, prices are likely to rise correspondingly and cause the public to anticipate an ongoing inflation. As we discussed above, this means that nominal interest rates will rise relative to the real interest rate as lenders attempt to protect themselves against the erosion of the purchasing power of the dollars they loan out.

State, local, and municipal governments also affect the interest rates by their issuance of bonds to finance schools, roads, and numerous other capital projects necessary to provide public services not covered by tax revenues.

CHECKPOINT 16-2
How is a college education a roundabout process? How would you

measure the net productivity, or rate of return, of such an investment in human capital? If for some reason people became less willing to save, how would this affect the saving curve in Figure 16–6, part b? How would this affect the long-run equilibrium stock of capital? Why? Suppose there is a sharp increase in the rate of population growth. How will this affect the position of the demand curve for capital in Figure 16–6, part a, and the long-run equilibrium stock of capital?

SUMMARY

1. Economic rent is any amount of payment a factor, or resource, receives in excess of its supply price when there is market equilibrium.

2. Because land is basically in fixed supply and available whether or not it receives payment, any economic rent received by land may be considered a surplus. Taking this point of view, in the late nineteenth century Henry George initiated the single-tax movement, which advocated taxing the economic rent on land to finance government. In theory such a tax would not affect resource allocation. However, in practice it is difficult to distinguish that part of economic rent attributable to land from that earned by buildings and other capital improvements on the land.

3. Any productive factor—not just land—may earn economic rent. The economic rents of productive factors are a surplus to the economy as a whole, but they are costs to firms and others who must pay to use them.

4. When factors are used by their owners, their economic rents are implicit. Implicit economic rent is equal to the explicit economic rent that could be received by a factor if its owner hired it out to its next best alternative use.

5. Interest is the price, expressed as a percentage rate, that must be paid for the use of borrowed funds.

6. When an economy saves, it refrains from consuming a portion of its current output. This allows it to undertake roundabout production processes by devoting that portion to the formation of capital goods. The gain from capital formation is the net productivity of capital, measured as the annual percentage rate of return that can be earned by investing in it.

7. Capital's demand curve may be expressed in percentage terms. Plotted on a graph, the stock of capital demanded is measured on the horizontal axis and its annual percentage rate of return on the vertical axis. Any point on the demand curve represents that market interest rate at which it just pays to invest in the associated stock of capital.

8. One of the rewards of saving, among others, is the interest people can earn by lending their savings. Hence the higher the interest rate, the more people will be induced to save.

9. The existing stock of capital together with the demand curve for capital determines the interest rate, which in turn determines the amount of saving in the economy and hence the rate of new capital formation. The long-run equilibrium interest rate, where saving becomes zero and new capital formation ceases, is never attained because of continual technological change and population growth. Uncertainty, which plays a large role in the assessment of capital's net productivity, and changes in saving habits may also cause the interest rate to fluctuate.

10. A certain amount of lending takes the form of consumption loans. Summing across all borrowers and lenders this nets out, so that the economy's total saving at any interest rate is the amount available for capital formation.

11. In our economy there is a variety of interest rates because there are many kinds of loans differing in risk, maturity, marketability, and the structure of the financial market in which the loan is made. These interest rates play the same kind of role in the allocation of resources as do prices in goods markets. Inflation's erosion of the purchasing power of money leads to a distinction between nominal and real interest rates.

12. The federal government affects interest rates through monetary and fiscal policy. State, local, and municipal governments affect interest rates through their issuance of bonds to finance the provision of local public services and the construction of public facilities such as roads and schools.

KEY TERMS AND CONCEPTS

> debt instrument
> economic rent
> financial market structure
> interest
> investment
> loan length
> marketability
> net productivity of capital
> nominal interest rate
> rate of return
> real interest rate
> risk
> roundabout process
> saving
> single-tax movement

QUESTIONS AND PROBLEMS

1. Using the marginal productivity theory of factor demand, explain why some pieces of land receive higher economic rents than others.

2. Why is it often said that the economic rent of land is demand determined, unlike the economic rent of other productive factors? In what way does the levying of a tax on the economic rent of land have different implications for resource allocation than the levying of a tax on the economic rent of other kinds of productive factors?

3. It has been argued that if the economic rent of land is an "unearned surplus" that should be taxed, then so is the economic rent received by anyone who owns an unusual natural talent, such as a great singing voice or an above-average IQ. If land is a gift of nature, then so are such unusual abilities, and if land's economic rent should be taxed, it is only just that the economic rent of these abilities should also be taxed. Would you agree with this position? What difficulties might hamper the implementation of such a policy?

4. Suppose you own some grapevines, and it costs you $20 to turn this year's grapes into grape juice. Suppose that after 1 year you can sell the juice as wine for $22. Assuming there are no other costs, what is the net productivity, or rate of return, on this roundabout process?

5. Some observers have maintained that many underdeveloped countries are held back by their low levels of saving. What do you think is the rationale for this point of view?

6. What is the relationship between the economy's willingness to sacrifice current consumption, the net productivity of capital, interest, and saving?

7. During World War II, many Americans bought war bonds sold by the U. S. government to help finance the war effort. Years later these bond owners found that the real interest rate they earned on the bonds was negative. Explain how this could have happened.

8. How would you rank the following loans according to their riskiness: college tuition loan, mortgage loan, car loan, City of New York municipal bond, Israel bond, and U.S. government bond?

17

Income Distribution, Poverty, and Welfare Policy

AFTER READING THIS CHAPTER, YOU WILL BE ABLE TO:

1. Explain the concept of income distribution and show how income inequality is measured.

2. Summarize some of the major determinants of income inequality.

3. Explain the measurement, description, and basic causes of poverty.

4. Describe the social security system, its critics, and its problems.

5. Explain how poverty may be attacked through the labor market and by use of an income tax transfer system.

Few issues generate more heated discussion and controversy than those related to income distribution, poverty, and welfare policy. These issues go to the very heart of the questions, For whom is the economy's output produced? What is a "just distribution" of income?

The kind of social order we call "capitalism," constructed on the basis of a market economy, was from its beginnings hostile to any political or "social" definition of distributive justice. Its basic premise is that a "fair" distribution of income is determined by the productive input of individuals to the economy—"productive" as determined by the marketplace. Specific talents, character traits, and just plain luck enter into the determination of such productivity. Capitalism holds that this market-based distribution of income creates economic incentives that encourage the production of goods and services. Such production provides society's material standard of living, which is not necessarily shared equally by all. And, this system may shape society in ways not everyone likes. Historically, market-oriented capitalistic societies have been reluctant to concede to any authority the right to overrule the determination of income distribution provided by the marketplace.

By contrast, noncapitalist societies historically have adhered to a very different notion of distributive justice. For them, it is based on the individual's contribution to the *society,* not merely to the *economy.* Economic rewards are "socially" justified, as distinct from economically justified. For example, in the Middle Ages the activities of the Church and the clergy were deemed to have a social significance and value that justified compelling ordinary people to provide their economic support. Similarly, the Communist party in the Soviet Union today does not have to defend its budget on economic grounds. The value of its contribution to the society as a whole is beyond question.

In today's world there are no pure forms of market capitalism, nor are there any noncapitalistic societies that do not allow some capitalistic, free-market practices to exist. All noncapitalistic societies recognize to one degree or another the need for differences in rewards, based on individual skills, as a spur to economic activity. Likewise, all capitalistic, market-oriented societies recognize to one degree or another that if the marketplace were the sole judge of the individual's claim to a piece of the economic pie, cruel hardships would befall some.

What can be said about these different concepts of a "good" society and the principles of "fairness" in income distribution by which they operate? In the abstract, the question of which principle of distribution is "better" is a normative issue. It cannot be settled by a mere appeal to facts. A society's judgment about this issue will depend on such things as its traditions, attitudes, social conventions, and history. It is pointless to argue that a society "should" be capitalist or socialist, if the vast majority of its people will not be bound by the different kinds of discipline that each of these systems requires in order to work.

In this chapter we will examine the measurement and determinants of income distribution, focusing in particular on those used in the United States. We will also study the economics of poverty, along with the social security system and other programs and proposals designed to prevent or alleviate it.

INCOME DISTRIBUTION

There are many possible ways to look at the distribution of income. Whichever way we choose, however, it is always the case that all the economy's income is ultimately received by households. This happens because households are the ultimate owners and suppliers of all resources (land, labor, and capital) used to produce the economy's output. Another fact that should be kept in mind in any analysis of income distribution is that reported income data usually do not include all the income that households receive. Unearned income (such as gifts and favors), income received in kind such as occurs in a barter transaction (I give you a cord of firewood in exchange for your cutting my lawn during the summer), and cash transactions for goods and services are all examples of income that may go unreported to tax collectors and census takers, our main sources of income data.

Keeping these limitations in mind, we will now look at the two commonest ways of analyzing income distribution. These are the functional distribution of income approach and the size distribution of income, or personal distribution of income, approach.

The Functional Distribution of Income

In preceding chapters we have examined the determinants of wages, rent, interest, and profits—the earnings of the factors of production labor, land, and capital. Since all income derives from the sale of factors of production, economists have long been interested in the distribution of income among the owners of these factors—that is, the distribution of income according to the function performed by the income receiver. *The* **functional distribution of income** *approach to the analysis of income distribution characterizes the way income is distributed according to the function performed by the income receiver.* Rent payments are the money income received by property owners, wages are the money income received by labor, and interest and profits compensate those who provide financial capital and own businesses (either incorporated or unincorporated).

Labor, landowners, and capitalists were the three major social classes in the eyes of nineteenth-century economists such as David Ricardo and Karl Marx. The relatively clear distinctions between these classes perceived in the nineteenth century are considerably more blurred today. It is now common for any given individual to receive income from ownership of at least two, and possibly all three, of these factors. For example, the rise of the corporation as the dominant form of business organization has made it possible

for large numbers of the labor force to be capitalists through ownership of shares of corporate stock and the receipts of dividend income.

The functional distribution of income in the United States for selected years is expressed in percentage terms in Table 17-1. Employee compensation consists of all salaries, wages, and supplements to salaries and wages such as bonuses and employer contributions to social insurance plans (social security and unemployment insurance). Proprietor's income represents the income earned by lawyers, doctors, farmers, the owners of unincorporated businesses, and other self-employed individuals. It is interesting to note that the share of the economy's total income going to employee compensation has increased from 60.2 percent in 1929 to 76.1 percent in 1982. Over the same period the share going to proprietor's income has fallen from 17.6 to 4.4 percent. These trends most likely reflect the declining role of agriculture and the growth of employment in corporations and the government sector, which has expanded significantly over this period. The share of rental income, relatively small even in 1929, shrank to 2 percent. Corporate profits tend to be quite volatile on a year-to-year basis, reflecting the fact that they are what is left over after all other costs have been deducted from sales revenue. The share of net interest income has increased, largely as the result of the generally rising level of interest rates in the postwar years.

Karl Marx predicted that as a capitalist society developed, the capitalist class would become relatively better off and workers relatively worse off. The trends in employee compensation, proprietor's income, and corporate profits shown in Table 17-1 do not appear to support this prediction. Adam Smith and David Ricardo predicted that landlords would become relatively better off and capitalists relatively worse off as society developed. If anything, the data in Table 17-1 seem to suggest that landlords have lost ground relative to capitalists. However, it should be reemphasized that the distinctions

TABLE 17-1 Percent Distribution of National Income by Type of Income—the Functional Distribution of Income in the United States

Type of Income	1929	1950	1960	1970	1975	1982
Employee compensation	60.2	65.5	71.6	76.3	76.9	76.1
Proprietor's income	17.6	16.3	11.4	8.2	7.5	4.4
Rental income	5.8	3.0	3.3	2.3	1.9	2.0
Corporate profits	10.8	14.3	11.3	8.5	7.6	6.7
Net interest	5.5	1.0	2.4	4.7	6.2	10.6
Total	100.0	100.0	100.0	100.0	100.0	100.0

SOURCE: Based on data from U.S. Bureau of Economic Analysis, *The National Income and Product Accounts of the United States,* 1929–1974, and *Survey of Current Business,* January and July 1976 and July 1983.

NOTE: Columns may not add up to 100 because of rounding.

between classes are not as clear today as they appeared to economists a century or more ago.

The Size Distribution of Income

The **size distribution of income** *approach to the analysis of income distribution ranks all families in the economy according to the size of the income received by each regardless of the source (wages, rent, interest, or profit) of their income.* It may then be asked what percent of total income is received by families in different income brackets. For example, what percent of total income goes to families earning less than $3,000 per year, what percent to families earning $3,000 to $6,000 per year, and so forth? The size of the income brackets is a matter of choice. Alternatively, this approach may ask what percent of total income is received by the lowest fifth (or quintile) of all families, the second fifth, the middle fifth, and so forth. (Any other fraction might be used as well.) This is illustrated for selected years in the United States in Table 17–2, along with the percent of total income received by the highest 5 percent of all families.

The size distribution of income approach is thought to be a better indicator of the de-

gree of inequality of income distribution than is the functional distribution of income approach. For example, among those receiving proprietor's income there are rich business people and poor ones, well-to-do farmers and subsistence farmers. Within each classification by type of income in Table 17–1, such income inequalities are hidden from view.

Examination of the size distribution of income over time in Table 17–2 suggests that there has been a reduction in the degree of inequality in income distribution between 1929 and the immediate post–World War II years. Most noticeable is the reduction that took place between 1929 and 1950 in the share of income going to the highest fifth of families (a drop from 54.4 to 42.7 percent). The reduction in the share of income going to the highest 5 percent was even greater (from 30 to 17.3 percent). By contrast, *each* of the other quintiles realized an increase in the share of income received between 1929 and 1950.

Several factors probably contributed to this change. The Great Depression of the 1930s wiped out many fortunes, large and small, along with the high incomes often realized from such wealth. World War II and the accompanying full-employment years of

TABLE 17-2 Percent of Aggregate Income Received by Each Fifth and Highest 5 Percent of Families in the United States

Quintile	1929	1950	1960	1970	1975	1978	1983
Lowest fifth	3.5	4.5	4.8	5.4	5.4	5.2	4.7
Second fifth	9.0	11.9	12.2	12.2	11.8	11.6	11.1
Middle fifth	13.8	17.4	17.8	17.6	17.6	17.5	17.1
Fourth fifth	19.3	23.6	24.0	23.8	24.1	24.1	24.4
Highest fifth	54.4	42.7	41.3	40.9	41.1	41.5	42.7
Total	100.0	100.0	100.0	100.0	100.0	100.0	100.0
Highest 5 percent	30.0	17.3	15.9	15.6	15.5	15.6	15.8

SOURCE: *Statistical Abstract of the United States*, 1975, 1976, and 1984 editions.

NOTE: Columns may not add up to 100 because of rounding.

the early and middle 1940s greatly boosted the average worker's paycheck. The war also brought about a sizeable increase in income tax rates. These were **progressive income tax** rates, so that the larger a household's income, the greater the percentage of that income taken away by income taxes. The income data on which Table 17–2 is based represent before-tax figures. The effect of this tax structure as an explanatory factor behind the change in before-tax income distribution between 1929 and 1950 is a subject of debate among economists. For example, is it possible that progressive tax rates tend to dampen people's incentive to work harder and make more money, thus reducing the share of before-tax income going to the highest fifth of families?

Since World War II the size distribution of income in the United States has changed very little. We can see this by comparing the size distribution of income for the years 1950, 1960, 1970, 1975, 1978, and 1983 in Table 17–2. In addition, the incomes in each quintile have grown at almost the same rates, so that the position of each relative to the others has remained about the same. This is illustrated in Figure 17–1, which shows the income range for the families in each of the first four quintiles (or 80 percent of all fam-

ilies), the next 15 percent, and the highest 5 percent in constant (1975) dollars for the years 1950, 1955, 1960, 1965, 1970, 1975, 1978, and 1983. The ratio of the income level corresponding to the upper limit of each bracket (except the highest 5 percent) to the income level at the upper limit of the lowest bracket is shown for each of these years. These ratios have remained relatively stable over this 33-year period. The decline in incomes during the postrecession year 1983 is evident in all brackets.

The Lorenz Diagram

A convenient way to represent the degree of inequality in the size distribution of income is to construct a **Lorenz diagram**. This is illustrated in Figure 17–2, part a.

The lengths of the horizontal and vertical axes are the same in the Lorenz diagram, and the units of measurement along each are percentages. The percent of total families in the economy is measured along the horizontal axis, and the percent of the economy's total income is measured along the vertical axis. Suppose income were distributed equally among all families. This would mean, for example, that 20 percent of all families would receive 20 percent of the economy's total income as represented by point *a*. Forty per-

FIGURE 17-1 Ranges of Income Received by Each Fifth and Highest 5 Percent of Families, and Ratios of the Upper Limit of Each Bracket to Upper Limit of Lowest Bracket, U.S. Data in Constant (1975) Dollars

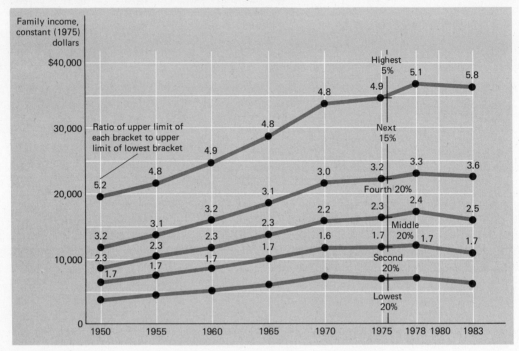

Shown here are the income ranges (in constant 1975 dollars) for the families in each of the first four quintiles, the next 15 percent, and the highest 5 percent for the years 1950, 1955, 1960, 1965, 1970, 1975, 1978, and 1983. The ratio of the income level corresponding to the upper limit of each bracket (except the highest 5 percent) to the income level at the upper limit of the lowest bracket is shown for each of these years. Incomes in each bracket have grown at almost identical rates over this 25-year period as indicated by the near constancy of these ratios over this period. Hence, the size distribution of income has been quite stable in the postwar era. The decline in incomes in all brackets is evident for the postrecession year 1983.

SOURCE: Data from U.S. Bureau of the Census, *Current Population Reports,* Series P-60, Nos. 100, 123, and 140.

cent would receive 40 percent of total income as represented by point *b,* and so on. Hence, if each family received exactly the same income as every other, this would be represented by a straight diagonal line passing through points *a, b, c,* and *d* connecting the corners of the square Lorenz diagram.

Because the straight diagonal line represents perfect equality of income distribution, it provides a benchmark against which to compare the degree of inequality in the actual size distribution of income. Using the data in Table 17-2 for 1983, the curve (called the Lorenz curve) representing the

FIGURE 17-2 Measuring Income Inequality with a Lorenz Diagram

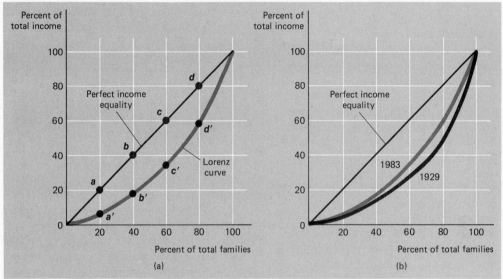

In the Lorenz diagrams shown here the percent of total families in the economy is measured along the horizontal axis and the percent of the economy's total income is measured on the vertical axis.

In part a, if total income were divided equally among all families, 20 percent of all families would receive 20 percent of total income as represented by point *a.* Forty percent would receive 40 percent of total income as represented by point *b,* and so on. Hence, the straight diagonal line in a Lorenz diagram corresponds to perfect equality in the size distribution of income.

The greater the degree of inequality in the size distribution of income, the more bowed the Lorenz curve will be toward the lower right-hand corner of the diagram. For example, the Lorenz curve based on the data given in Table 17-2 for the United States for 1983 passes through the points *a', b', c',* and *d'.* Part b compares this Lorenz curve with that constructed from the data for 1929. The greater degree of income inequality in 1929 is reflected in the fact that its Lorenz curve is more bowed than that for 1983.

size distribution of income in the United States passes through the points *a', b', c',* and *d'.* Point *a'* indicates that the lowest 20 percent of families receives 5.2 percent of the economy's total income. Point *b'* indicates that the lowest 40 percent of families receives 16.8 percent, the sum of 5.2 and 11.6 from Table 17-2. Points *c'* and *d'* are obtained in similar fashion.

The greater the degree of inequality in the

size distribution of income, the more the Lorenz curve will be bowed toward the lower right-hand corner of the Lorenz diagram. This becomes clear when we compare the size distribution of income in the United States for 1929 with that for 1983. Based on the data from Table 17-2, the Lorenz curves for these two years are drawn in Figure 17-2, part b. As noted already, the size distribution of income for 1929 shows greater income inequality than is the case in 1983. Hence, the Lorenz curve for 1929 is more bowed than that for 1983.

CHECKPOINT* 17-1
If we look at the size distribution of income for white families in the United States for the year 1983, we find that the lowest fifth received 5.2 percent, the second lowest fifth 11.5 percent, the middle fifth 17.2 percent, the fourth fifth 24.2 percent, and the highest fifth 42.0 percent. The size distribution of income for nonwhite families in 1983 is such that the lowest fifth received 3.6 percent, the second lowest fifth 8.8 percent, the middle fifth 15.6 percent, the fourth fifth 25.3 percent, and the highest fifth 46.8 percent. Using this information, construct Lorenz curves for whites and for nonwhites, and compare them. What do you conclude?

*Answers to all Checkpoints can be found at the back of the text.

Determinants of Income Inequality

What causes an unequal distribution of income? In many respects an answer to this question is as complex as an answer to the question, Why do people have different tastes and behavior patterns? Some of the primary factors economists cite as explanations of income inequality are differences in the productivity of labor, market structure, the distribution of wealth, differences in earning power with age, the tax structure, and sheer luck. Let's consider each of these.

Marginal Productivity and Factor Demand

In Chapters 14 and 15 we examined how wages are determined according to the marginal productivity theory of factor demand. We saw that, other things remaining the same, the greater a laborer's productivity, the higher the wage the laborer is likely to receive, and hence the higher the laborer's income. (Don't forget that a laborer can be anyone from a floor sweeper to the head of a giant corporation.) It follows that those things that determine a laborer's productivity are therefore important determinants of the size of a laborer's income. They are also important to any explanation of differences in income among laborers.

As we noted in our earlier discussions, natural abilities, character traits, education, and job training are all important determinants of a laborer's productivity. Therefore, we would expect different endowments of these factors among individuals to lead to differences in income. Natural ability certainly makes it possible for Barbra Streisand to earn a larger income than the typical member of the local choir. Character traits referred to by terms such as "work ethic," "grit," and "stick-to-itiveness" are difficult to measure but no doubt are very important. Tom Dempsey was born with only one hand and minus a half of one foot, but he holds the National Football League record for the longest field goal (63 yards). American history is replete with rags-to-riches stories.

Data indicate that there is a definite positive relationship between education and earning power. This relationship is illustrated in Table 17–3. It is tempting to conclude from these data that more education leads to higher income. But we should be wary of concluding that there is a definite cause-and-effect relationship—the *post hoc, ergo propter hoc* ("after this, therefore, because of this") fallacy that we discussed in Chapter 1. The figures in Table 17–3 are average relationships. There are millionaires who have had less than 8 years of schooling just as there are people on welfare who have had 4 or more years of college. Nonetheless, the data are *consistent* with the notion that education, or investment in human capital, increases labor productivity and leads to higher earnings.

TABLE 17-3 Relationship Between Years of Education of Head of Household and Median Household Income: 1981

Education of Head	Median Household Income
Less than 8 years	$12,541
8 years	14,935
1–3 years high school	18,025
4 years high school	23,864
1–3 years college	27,607
4 or more years college	35,648

SOURCE: U.S. Bureau of the Census, *Current Population Reports,* Series P-60.

Market Structure

In our previous discussions of the four basic forms of market structure—perfect competition, monopoly, monopolistic competition, and oligopoly—we touched on some of their implications for income distribution. We noted that economists generally believe that monopoly and oligopoly, with their accompanying excess, or above-normal, profits, lead to a less equal distribution of income than do market structures more aptly characterized as monopolistically or perfectly competitive. We also observed that the evidence suggests that profits tend to be higher in those industries where concentration is higher.

In our study of labor markets in Chapter 15, we saw how the level of the wages depends on market structure. In particular, if there are many firms competing with one another to purchase labor services from a large union, the wage level will be higher than if both sides of the market are perfectly competitive. The wage level will also be higher if the labor market is perfectly competitive than if there is a monopsony purchasing labor services from a large body of unorganized laborers competing with one another for jobs. Clearly the structure of labor mar-

kets will have an effect on the relative distribution of income between employers and employees.

Professional organizations, such as the American Medical Association and the American Bar Association, and craft unions, that seek higher wages by restricting the supply of labor in their respective fields, also have an effect on income distribution. The existence of these groups tends to increase the incomes of those accepted into their ranks relative to the incomes of those who are excluded. Licensing requirements, which restrict entry to many occupations, have a similar effect.

The Distribution of Wealth

Wealth includes holdings of cash, checking and savings balances, real estate, corporate stock, bonds, notes and mortgages, and life insurance. With the exception of cash, all these forms of wealth typically generate income, called property income, for their owners. The Lorenz curve for wealth distribution in the United States in Figure 17–3 shows that there is greater inequality in the distribution of wealth than in the distribution of income. Indeed, the largest incomes in the United States are earned by those families with the largest wealth holdings. While this great inequality in the distribution of wealth has shown a tendency to decline in the twentieth century, the top 1 percent of the wealth-holding families still held about 25 percent of the total wealth in 1972, down from around 35 percent in 1929. This great inequality in the distribution of wealth means that the inequality in the distribution of property income among families is greater than the inequality in the distribution of income from work (wages, salaries, and income from unincorporated businesses). Hence, the inequality in the distribution of wealth contributes to the inequality in the distribution of the economy's total income (income from all sources).

FIGURE 17-3 Inequality in the Distribution of Wealth Is Greater Than Inequality in the Distribution of Income

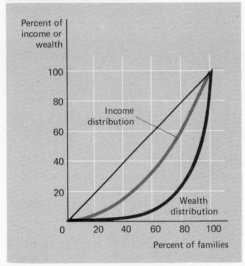

The 1983 Lorenz curve for income distribution is representative of income distribution in the United States since 1950, since there has been little change in income distribution over this period of time (see Table 17–2). Data on wealth distribution shown here are based on 1970 data compiled by the Survey Research Center of the University of Michigan.

The greater inequality in the distribution of wealth leads to a greater inequality in the distribution of property income than in the distribution of income from work. Hence the inequality in the distribution of wealth contributes to the inequality in the distribution of total income.

Differences in Earning Power with Age

It is commonly observed that earning power tends to vary over a worker's lifetime. Younger members of the labor force have the least work experience and so-called on-the-job training. In professional fields such as law and medicine, younger members simply have not put in the years necessary to develop the contacts and clientele established by their older counterparts. It usually takes business executives and managers a couple of decades to acquire the knowledge and experience that allows them to function at their full potential. The typical worker's earning power appears to increase up through the beginning of middle age and into the fifties. After that it tends to taper off until retirement age is reached. This pattern is illustrated in Table 17–4. The age structure of the population tends to change over time. Because earning power tends to vary with age, it follows that a changing age structure will cause the distribution of income in the economy to change over time, all other things remaining the same.

Tax Structure

On a par with the weather, people probably complain about few things more than taxes. Year in and year out there always seem to be some politicians seeking votes with promises to close tax "loopholes," perfectly legal aspects of the tax laws that seem to give special tax breaks to those in the highest income brackets. Many believe that such breaks tend to make it easier for those who are rich to stay rich.

It is often argued that under our present tax structure those in middle-income brackets who aspire to climb the economic ladder by work, saving, and capital accumulation have a tough time because too much of their income is taxed away. Indeed, as their in-

TABLE 17-4 Average Household Income by Age of Head of Household: 1981

Age of Head	Average Household Income
16–24 years	$15,528
25–34 years	22,855
35–44 years	29,114
45–54 years	32,070
55–64 years	29,492
65 and over	18,945

SOURCE: U.S. Bureau of the Census, *Current Population Reports*, Series P-60.

POLICY PERSPECTIVE

Who Gets Ahead?

A team of researchers led by Christopher Jencks, a Harvard sociology professor, has attempted to identify the factors that enable some people to earn more than others.[1] Based on a variety of in-depth statistical sources, the researchers identified four critical factors that play a major role in the determination of a person's future economic success. They are: (1) family background; (2) formal education (the number of years of school completed); (3) academic ability, as reflected in scores on I.Q. and aptitude tests in primary and secondary school; and (4) personality traits and behavior. Policymakers concerned about how to deal with the problems of poverty would be well advised to study these findings.

Family Background

The researchers found that being born into the "right" family is important. A child from a family in the top one-fifth in the country, as measured by income and occupational status, is likely in adult years to have earnings that are anywhere from 150 to 186 percent of the national average. A child from a family in the bottom one-fifth is likely to have earnings that are only 56 to 67 percent of the national average. The researchers stress that it is not just having *rich* parents that makes the difference. A whole cluster of family-background variables is important to a child's eventual performance. The father's occupation is the most important of these, but family size, the father's and mother's education, geographic location, and many "intangibles" are also significant. Jencks

[1] Jencks, Christopher et al. *Who Gets Ahead: The Determinants of Economic Success in America.* New York: Basic Books, 1979.

notes that, "There are many 'advantaged' families that are not rich." Some of the other findings on the effect of family background are:

(1) Even when families' overall incomes and the fathers' occupations are identical, children from small families do markedly better than those from large families. However, within families of any given size, older children *do not* do significantly better than their younger siblings.

(2) Black families still cannot expect their children to earn as much as they would if they were white, despite the progress on the civil rights front during the last generation.

(3) Income differences among white ethnic groups are relatively modest.

Number of Years of School Completed

Finishing college appears to have a dramatic effect on one's earning potential. The researchers found that completing college gives whites a 49 percent earnings advantage over those who do not. For blacks the percentage earnings advantage is even *larger*. The income advantage is due primarily to the fact that those who finish college have the credential needed to enter high-status occupations. Completing high school increased expected earnings for whites by only 4 to 6 percent, and even less for blacks.

Intelligence

The researchers found that the common belief that those who are naturally the most talented and intellectually gifted are the ones who get ahead economically is unfounded. The standard measures of intellectual ability, such as scores from I.Q. tests and other kinds of aptitude and achievement tests, turn out to be poor predictors of economic success. The data indicate that if you have high test scores but don't go to college, the odds are that your superior intelligence will not do you much good economically.

Personality Traits

Eventual earning power appears to be significantly affected by personality traits. Leadership qualities count most. Young people who lead an active social life tend not to do as well in school but do not seem to suffer any subsequent earnings disadvantage, possibly because their "social skills" compensate. Affiliations with church groups, social clubs, and school clubs (such as debating, drama, or the school newspaper) appear to have a positive effect on later economic success, while participation in sports shows no statistically significant effect. Though bookworms make better grades in school, they do not seem to make more money in later life, possibly because they sacrifice money

for personal or intellectual challenge. Perhaps more surprising, working during the school year seems to have no correlation with future success according to the researchers.

A Word of Caution About the Findings

Jencks urges a bit of caution when interpreting these findings. In particular he points out that while family background, academic ability, personality traits, and formal education all affect earnings during a person's lifetime, none of the traits stands out as the "key" to success. In fact, there are people with none of these advantages who are economically successful.

Questions

1. What might the Jencks study's findings suggest to government policymakers concerned about reducing poverty?

2. Can you think of some traits that would seem important to economic success that are not represented by this study's measures?

---

comes rise, a larger and larger percent is taken because of our marginally progressive income tax rates. On the other hand, it is often argued that families living off the income earned from inherited wealth are the beneficiaries of lenient inheritance and gift taxes. Our discussion of the evidence on the distribution of wealth in the United States seems to lend strength to this point of view. To the extent that these criticisms are valid, our tax structure may well contribute to an unequal distribution of income.

In short, one question will continue to be heatedly debated among economists and laypersons alike: "Are our tax laws such that it is too easy to stay rich and too difficult to get rich?"

Preferences, Luck, and Opportunity

Suppose everyone were born with identical talents and abilities and given equal access to training and education. It would still be true that income would differ among individuals. Although all would be equally capable of being poets and folksingers, those who preferred to be poets might well find their incomes lower than that of those who prefer being folksingers. For better or worse, society's demand for poets might be slight relative to the supply, while the demand for folksingers might be great relative to the supply. For the most part, differences in preferences will lead to differences in income, all other things being equal.

Good or bad luck, being at "the right place at the right time" or "the wrong place at the wrong time," is also a source of differences in income. Similarly, opportunity or a lack of it has the same effect, a subject we will consider in more depth later in this chapter when we look at the problem of poverty.

CHECKPOINT 17-2

Using Lorenz curves, show how a marginally progressive tax structure (one that taxes each successive dollar of income at a higher rate than the previous one) would affect the distribution of after-tax income as compared to the distribution of before-tax income. What effect do you think the "baby boom" of the late 1940s and 1950s would have on the Lorenz curves of income distribution for 1970, 1980, 1990, and 2000?

THE ECONOMICS OF POVERTY

What is poverty? Is it definable? What are its causes?

Poverty Defined: A Relative Standard

In general, a person is considered to live in **poverty** *if his or her income and other means of support are insufficient to provide for basic needs as defined according to some social norm.* Obviously different societies, and different people and groups within the same society, may disagree as to what constitutes "basic needs." In many underdeveloped countries of the world, tens of millions of people exist on a per capita income of less than $100 per year. (Income data for underdeveloped countries can be misleading, however, because in such countries much trade is carried on by barter and therefore escapes official money measures of economic activity.) In such countries a person with an annual income of $5,061 per year generally would be consid-

ered rich. In the United States, a single person with no dependents who had such an income would be considered on the poverty line according to 1983 standards set up by a federal interagency committee. Poverty is relative to what a society considers a "decent standard of living."

A family's needs depend on its size, the age of its members, and the state of its members' health. A family of four with an annual income of less than $10,178 or a family of seven with an annual income of less than $15,500 would be below the official poverty line according to the government's 1983 standards. These standards vary somewhat depending on such things as whether the head of household is 65 or older and whether certain health problems (such as blindness) are present or not. "Official" definitions of poverty are always somewhat arbitrary. The merits of any definition are open to debate.

Aside from the aged, the infirm, and those who are by nature dependent (such as children), poverty is often much more than a simple shortage of money. Mere numbers do not tell the complete story. Poverty is also a human condition, as distinct from a statistical condition. When considering the statistics of poverty, bear in mind that there is a social dimension to poverty that cold numbers cannot completely convey. The poverty population, particularly in our cities, is often demoralized, as evidenced by higher rates of crime, juvenile delinquency, drug addiction, unwanted teenage pregnancy, and alcoholism.

Identifying the Poor

According to government definitions of poverty, 15.2 percent of the total population of the United States was living in poverty during 1983. This was down from 23.4 percent in 1959 and 17.3 percent in 1965, but up from around 11 to 12 percent during the middle to late 1970s. Table 17-5 presents some selected characteristics of the dimensions of poverty in the United States for 1982 and 1983. As a benchmark for compari-

TABLE 17-5 Median Family Income in United States and Selected Characteristics of Families Below Poverty Income Level in United States

Median family income (all families, 1983)	$24,580
Poverty income level, family of four (1983)	$10,178
Percent of total population below poverty level (1983)	15.2%
Whites	12.1%
Blacks	35.7%
Families with male head	9.2%
Families with female head	40.2%
Metropolitan areas (1982)	11.1%
Nonmetropolitan areas (1982)	14.5%
Persons 65 and older (1982)	9.3%

SOURCE: U.S. Bureau of the Census, *Current Population Reports*, Series P-60, No. 104.

son, note that the median annual income for all families in 1983 was $24,580. This was about two and a half times the poverty income level of $10,178 for a family of four. While 15.2 percent of all families fell below the poverty line in 1983, the incidence of poverty varied noticeably in several ways:

1. *The incidence of poverty among blacks (35.7 percent) was about three times greater than it was among whites (12.1 percent).* Much of this difference is a result of discrimination, past and present.

2. *The incidence of poverty among families with a female head was 40.2 percent, about four and a half times the 9.2 percent incidence among families headed by a male.* Women left without a husband because of death, divorce, or desertion are typically held back by the need to look after children and a lack of marketable job skills and job opportunities.

3. *The incidence of poverty in metropolitan areas was less (11.1 percent) in 1982 than it was in nonmetropolitan, or rural, areas (14.5 percent).* (However, in inner-city areas, with their slums and ghettos, the incidence was 16.7 percent as compared to 7.5 percent in suburban areas.) The relatively higher incidence of poverty in rural areas reflects the

declining job opportunities in agriculture and the chronically depressed state of the economy in certain areas, such as Appalachia, combined with a relatively immobile labor force in these regions.

4. *The incidence of poverty among those over 65 years of age was 9.3 percent in 1982, or about 60 percent of the incidence among the total population (15.2 percent).* Older people are past their peak earning years and are often forced into retirement by ill health and labor market conventions. Those who want and are able to work typically find job opportunities very limited and wages quite low. However, increases in social security and Medicare benefits in recent years have reduced the incidence of poverty among persons 65 and over.

Of all those heads of families falling below the poverty line in 1981, 44.2 percent of the males and 18 percent of the females worked full time year round. That they were still living in poverty reflects the fact that they held unskilled, low-paying jobs, usually in the service industries such as hotels, dry-cleaning establishments, and retailing. By region, the highest incidence of poverty occurred in the South.

Causes of Poverty

As you might expect, many of the factors we have already cited as causes of inequality in the distribution of income are also important causes of poverty. A lack of natural abilities, training, education, and opportunity, as well as labor markets that restrict entry, all come immediately to mind. Several other factors should be noted, including poverty itself, lack of political influence, and discrimination.

Poverty As a Cause of Poverty

Poverty has been likened to a vicious circle. It tends to perpetuate itself from one generation of a family to the next.

Because a family is poor, it suffers from a lack of dental and medical care, adequate nutrition, and other amenities important to childhood development. A poverty-line income typically cannot provide sufficient fruit, vegetables, meat, and clothing or proper housing conditions. Newspapers, magazines, books, and other sources of cultural and educational enrichment are luxury items that must usually be forgone. All these conditions impair the ability of children in such families to perform in school and keep up with their more prosperous contemporaries. Discouraged in school, and often finding little encouragement in the home to pursue educational endeavors, these children drop out of school or attend only in a perfunctory manner, gaining little from the educational system. They are destined to have job opportunities no better than those of their parents. In short, because they are poor, they are ill-educated. Because they are ill-educated, the job market offers little opportunity for economic improvement. Because of this, they grow up to be poor and form below-poverty-line families of their own. The vicious circle is complete.

Serious students of the poverty problem find the evidence on the circle of poverty disheartening. The odds on poverty families breaking out of this circle appear to be about one in five.

The Silent Poor

Almost every segment of our society has some kind of organized political voice. Labor has its unions. Various industries have their trade associations—the Air Transport Association of America, the American Petroleum Institute, the National Association of Manufacturers, the American Bankers Association, and so forth. There are even associations and societies that look after the well-being of animals. Almost all of these special interest groups contribute to political candidates sympathetic to their causes and points of view. All such groups have resources to devote to enhancing their political visibility and clout. The political voice of the poor is generally weak by comparison.

Living in slums, ghettos, and rural backwaters where they often have little visibility, usually disorganized and unsophisticated in the art of politics, their collective voice is weak at best or most often simply mute. Organizations that collect money on behalf of the poor often divert a good share of these funds to cover their own "overhead." Naturally the public becomes suspicious. Are these organizations merely using the poverty issue and playing on public sympathy as a means of providing income for a bureaucracy of middle-class administrators? Perhaps not, but public suspicion that they are does limit their effectiveness.

Discrimination

We have already noted before that the incidence of poverty among blacks is about three times what it is among whites (see Table 17–5). The decline in the incidence of poverty generally has not led to any noticeable change in this relationship. In 1959 the incidence of poverty among blacks was 56.2 percent, while that among whites was 18.1 percent—again, the incidence among blacks was more than three times that among whites.

While the lessening of poverty overall seems to have helped nonwhites as much as whites, the persistence of the same difference in its relative incidence is largely due to discrimination. The effects of discrimination are also reflected in family income data. This is illustrated in Table 17–6, which compares the median income for white families to that for nonwhite families in the United States for selected years. According to the data, nonwhite families earned slightly more than half of what whites earned up through the middle 1960s. Then for a time the nonwhite families seem to have gained some ground. This is quite likely a reflection of the reduction in discrimination in a number of areas of the economy, possibly spurred to a significant degree by the passage of the Civil Rights Act of 1964. More recently, however, since 1970, nonwhites seem to have lost some of their earlier gains relative to whites.

TABLE 17-6 Median Income in Constant (1983) Dollars of Families by Race

| Year | Median Income | | Ratio |
	White Families	Nonwhite Families	Nonwhite to White
1950	$14,250	$ 7,733	.54
1955	17,157	9,461	.55
1960	19,621	10,862	.55
1965	22,886	12,603	.55
1970	26,252	16,711	.64
1975	26,412	16,251	.62
1980	26,484	15,324	.59
1983	25,757	14,506	.56

SOURCE: U.S. Bureau of the Census, *Current Population Reports*, Series P-60.

Discrimination affects earning power in a number of ways. Historically blacks and other nonwhites have been barred from many of the kinds of educational opportunities available to whites. This, plus other constraints and barriers, has kept them out of certain professions and trades in which whites have traditionally earned relatively higher incomes. Educational institutions, unions, professional organizations, company hiring and promotion practices, and societal attitudes generally have all conspired to constrain the upward income mobility of blacks and other nonwhites. Discrimination in these areas has lessened considerably in recent years, but it will take some time for this development to make a significant break in the vicious circle of poverty that has existed among blacks and other nonwhites for most of our country's history.

CHECKPOINT 17-3
Colleges and universities have come under fire for not having more black students. However, some have argued that institutions of higher learning may, in fact, have little control over this situation because the return on investment in the human capital represented by a college education is lower for blacks than whites. How would you explain the rationale behind this point of view? Suppose there are two occupations, A and B, each requiring the same degree of natural ability and training. Assume blacks are prohibited from entering A but not B. Use supply-and-demand analysis to demonstrate the effects of such discrimination in these two labor markets as compared to the outcome if there were no discrimination.

SOCIAL SECURITY

As a result of illness, injury, death, retirement, or unemployment, a family or individual may suffer a drastic loss of income and consequent economic hardships. The Great Depression of the 1930s dramatized this problem for large numbers of people. In an effort to provide families and individuals with some protection against such calamities, Congress passed the Social Security Act in 1935.

This act, together with its subsequent amendments, created the **social security system** of the United States. This system was intended to provide a form of social insurance and public assistance to aid the old, the disabled, the sick, the unemployed, and families financially crippled by the death of the breadwinner. First we will look at the basic structure of the insurance system and then at some of the major special assistance programs. Finally, we will examine some of the criticisms and problems of the social security system.

The Insurance System

There are two basic components of the insurance system—social insurance and unemployment insurance.

Social Insurance—Old-Age, Survivors, Disability, and Health Insurance (OASDHI)

This is basically a government-managed social insurance program paid for by a tax, the **social security tax**, on labor earnings (wages and salaries). The employee and the employer share the tax equally. Old-age, survivors, and disability insurance covers almost all jobs where people work for wages or salaries, as well as most work of self-employed persons. About 9 out of 10 workers in the United States are involved in this program. Workers receive benefits upon retirement at age 65, or somewhat reduced benefits upon retirement at 62. Disabled workers (whatever their age) and their children (up to age 18, or 22 if attending school) also receive benefit payments. Survivors (widow or widower and orphans) of a deceased worker continue to receive benefits. In 1984 the average monthly benefit received by a retired worker was about $442, while the average monthly payment to a disabled worker was $455.

The health insurance part of the social insurance system (the HI in OASDHI) is more commonly known as Medicare. Congress established this program in 1965 in order to relieve social security beneficiaries 65 and over of some of the burdensome medical costs that typically plague old age. In July 1973 coverage was extended to cover persons (of any age) who are entitled for 24 months to receive a social security disability benefit; certain persons with chronic kidney disease and their dependents; and, on a voluntary basis with payment of a special premium, persons 65 and over not otherwise eligible for hospital benefits. Except for the voluntary program, costs of Medicare are paid out of the social security taxes paid by employees and employers.

Unemployment Insurance

While old-age and survivors insurance is entirely a federal program, the unemployment insurance program is a federal-state system. It provides insured wage earners with partial replacement of wages lost during involuntary unemployment, protecting most workers in industry, but few in agriculture. Each state has its own law and operates its own program. Based on the employee's prior wages and length of employment, state laws determine the amount and duration of weekly benefits. When unemployment rises to and remains above specified state or national levels, states are required to extend the duration of benefits. These programs are financed by payroll taxes on employers.

Special Assistance Programs

Special assistance programs are the noninsurance part of the social security system intended to help special categories of needy people who are not eligible for OASDHI. These programs are charitable or welfare programs in that benefits are not based on any previous contribution payments by beneficiaries. They are administered by federal, state, and local governments but are largely financed by the federal government.

One of the largest of these programs is the Supplemental Security and Income program (SSI), intended to aid the needy aged, blind, and disabled who are unable to work. It provides both for federal payments based on uniform national standards and for state supplementary payments varying from state to state. The Social Security Administration administers the federal payments, financed from general funds of the Treasury, and state supplements for states electing to have their programs federally administered. There were about 3.9 million persons receiving an average of $224 per month in 1984 under this program.

Another important program is the state-administered Aid to Families with Dependent Children program (AFDC), which is partly funded with federal grants. About 3.6 million families, representing about 10.7 million people, received an average monthly income of $311 per family in 1983.

Medicaid relies on a combination of federal, state, and local revenues to help those eligible for SSI and AFDC benefits pay for medical care.

The food stamp program is intended to help provide an adequate diet for low-income citizens. Those with incomes below a certain level are eligible to receive food stamps, or coupons, which may be exchanged for food.

Social Security's Critics and Problems

From its inception the social security concept has always had its share of critics and more recently, of problems. One line of criticism has been directed at its basic philosophy, another at the way it is financed.

Criticisms of the Social Security Philosophy

Few people take issue with public policies directed at helping those who are simply unable to work—the disabled, the sick, and those who are by nature dependent on others for their support, such as children. That part of the social security system designed to help these groups in our society is often criticized for not doing this job as effectively as it might, but rarely for the spirit of its intent.

Criticism of the basic philosophy of social security is usually directed at that part of the system that (1) *forces* able-bodied workers and their employers to set aside a *stipulated* amount of their earnings for retirement and (2) allows them no *choice* as to who shall manage these funds—namely, they must entrust them to government management. Those who criticize social security on these grounds are usually motivated by a concern that the fabric of a free society is weakened when its citizens must unnecessarily give up freedom of choice to their government. This point of view has a long tradition in America. Abraham Lincoln put it this way: "You can-

not really help men by having the government tax them to do for them what they can and should do for themselves."

Even among the large number of people who are willing to go along with the first point (compelling workers and employers to set aside certain amounts for retirement), there are many who disagree with the second point on more practical grounds. They argue that evidence indicates that for the same amount of money contributed to social security, a worker could realize larger retirement benefits from investment in any number of annuity programs offered by private insurance companies. The alleged reason is that these companies must compete with one another to sell their programs. They are forced by competition to manage them efficiently in order to be able to offer the investor a better deal than their rivals. This brings us to the controversy over the way in which the social security system is financed.

Financing Social Security

When social security insurance was originally established in 1935, it was intended that the premiums contributed (social security tax payments by employees and employers) would be accumulated in a reserve account, or trust fund, the Old Age and Survivors Fund, which was to be just like the pension fund of a business firm or labor union. This fund was supposed to grow steadily, earning interest, until it became large enough to meet commitments to contributors when they retired. The contributors were to own the assets in the fund with the government serving merely as trustee.

How Social Security Is Actually Financed. However, as the social security system evolved over the years it has come to operate in a very different way. The trust fund has not been allowed to grow to more than a fraction of its required size. Instead, much of the money contributed by wage earners and employers has been used to pay increased benefits to people whose contributions were not enough to warrant these benefits. In short, the government didn't raise social security taxes as fast as it increased benefits. It is estimated that to build the trust fund to a size sufficient to pay beneficiaries in the manner originally intended would require more than 2 full years of our entire GNP! This is obviously not practical.

As a result of these developments, today's contributors are not building a fund at all. The taxes they pay into social security must be handed over as benefits to current beneficiaries in order to honor the system's commitments. The system's Old Age and Survivor Insurance fund now only provides a thin buffer between the taxes paid into the system and the benefits that the system is obliged to pay out to retired workers and the surviving family members of deceased workers. Similarly, the disability fund, which pays benefits to disabled workers, and the health fund, which pays Medicare benefits, are not in much better shape. In sum, *because of the inadequate size of the trust funds, the social security system has evolved more and more into an income tax transfer system.* Today's workers and employers pay taxes that are used to support yesterday's workers who are now retired, as well as those who are disabled and the dependents of those who died before retirement age. In turn, when current workers retire, they will be completely dependent on future workers for their benefits.

The Future of Social Security Financing. The "baby boom" of the 1950s, together with the low birthrates of the 1960s and early 1970s, ensure that there is going to be an unprecedented increase in the ratio of retired persons to workers. Since most of the beneficiaries are already born, it is estimated that by the year 2020 the number of social security claimants will double, while the labor force will increase by only about one-third. In the meantime the low fertility rates during the late 1920s and the 1930s will be reflected in a considerable reduction in the growth of the population over 65 during the 1990s and the first decade of the twenty-first century.

At the same time, the post-World War II baby boom generation will continue to swell the labor force. Consequently the ratio of beneficiaries to workers, which has increased continually since 1940, is estimated to remain relatively stable from now until about the year 2005.

Current financing provisions schedule an increase in the combined employee-employer payroll tax of 1 percent to take effect by 1990 (.72 percent in 1988 and .28 percent in 1990), just as costs (social security payouts) as a percent of payroll are projected to decline. With costs falling and social security tax revenues increasing, the social security program is projected to run substantial annual surpluses until 2020. These accumulated reserves are then scheduled to be drawn down to cover annual social security deficits (the excess of social security benefit payments over social security tax revenues) in the years between 2020 and 2060.

Regressive Taxation and Inadequate Benefits. The payroll tax used to finance social security is often criticized because it is a regressive tax. A regressive tax is one that takes a larger share of income from low-income taxpayers than from high-income taxpayers. The social security payroll tax is levied on an employee's wages up to some maximum yearly total wage. (Half of the tax is paid by the employee and half by the employer.) For example, the maximum yearly total wage subject to tax in 1984 was $37,800. An employee earning this amount had to pay a social security payroll tax of $2,646. Additional income beyond this amount is not taxed. For instance, an employee earning twice this amount, or $75,600, would pay the same amount of tax—$2,646. But for the $75,600 wage earner, this would amount to a smaller portion of total income (3.5 percent) than it would for the $37,800 wage earner (7.0 percent). In general, an employee earning anything less than $37,800 per year must give up 7 percent of his or her earnings in the form of social security payroll taxes. The more an employee earns above $37,800, the smaller

will be the percentage share of his or her total income that is taken by payroll taxes. Because of the regressive nature of the social
security payroll tax, many critics argue that it
unjustly burdens lower-income groups more
than higher-income groups.

Some critics of social security claim that
old-age benefits are not adequate to provide a
"decent" standard of living for people over
65. Furthermore, critics argue that because
benefits to those over 65 are reduced or lost
altogether if they work, it is difficult for this
age group to maintain a decent standard of
living through part-time work. The problem
is of course that more liberal old-age retirement benefits would increase the cost of financing social security.

CHECKPOINT 17-4

**What effect do you think the social
security system financed through use of
a trust fund as originally intended
would have on after-tax (social security
tax) income distribution? How do you
think the effect is different as a result
of the way the system has actually
come to be financed?**

ATTACKING POVERTY: WAYS AND MEANS

In addition to social security, what other
methods have been used or proposed for attacking the poverty problem? One proposal
involves attacking the problem through the
labor market, either by use of **minimum-
wage laws** that attempt to raise wages of
low-paid workers directly or by use of government-subsidized job-training programs
that attempt to increase the employability of
the hard-core unemployed and those lacking
the skills to earn a decent wage. Another
method is to use some form of a tax transfer
system that taxes the income of higher-income earners and transfers the proceeds to
those in lower-income groups.

Jobs and the Labor Market

Many of those who fall below the poverty
line are able-bodied workers. Most, however,
lack sufficient job skills and training to earn a
nonpoverty income when they can find employment or, in many instances, to gain any
employment at all. For example, the unemployment rate among those 16 to 19 years old
has typically been around 20 percent in recent years, with the rate for black youths
running about twice these levels. It is interesting to note that among all those families
below the poverty line, a large portion of the
male family heads are often employed full
time year round (44.2 percent in 1981), and a
not insignificant portion of female family
heads are also employed full time year round
(18.0 percent in 1981). That they still live in
poverty when they are fully employed reflects their inability to earn a decent wage.
Two approaches to aiding able-bodied workers below the poverty line are minimum-
wage legislation and government-subsidized
job-training programs.

The Minimum-Wage Approach

In an attempt to help those workers who are
employed yet earn wages that still leave them
poor, Congress passed the Fair Labor Standards Act in 1938. This act made it illegal
for employers to pay workers an hourly wage
below a certain statutory level often called
the minimum wage. Over the years Congress
has periodically increased this minimum-
wage level and extended the categories of labor covered. Many states have minimum-
wage laws as well, but they have generally
been less effective than the federal statute.
The minimum-wage concept has been a subject of controversy since its inception. What
are the arguments pro and con?

The Case Against Minimum Wage. Many
are of the opinion that the minimum wage
contributes to unemployment. Their argument is illustrated in Figure 17–4, part a,
which shows the labor demand curve *D*

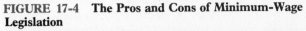

FIGURE 17-4 **The Pros and Cons of Minimum-Wage Legislation**

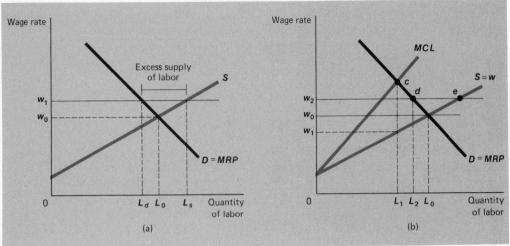

(a)

(b)

Minimum-wage legislation affects employment differently in different labor markets.

Part a depicts a perfectly competitive labor market. The equilibrium wage and level of employment are w_0 and L_0 respectively, as determined by the intersection of the labor demand curve D (which is the marginal revenue product curve MRP of labor) and supply curve S. If minimum-wage legislation sets a minimum wage of w_1, the quantity of labor employed will fall from L_0 to L_d and the quantity $L_d L_0$ will be thrown out of work.

Part b depicts a monopsony labor market. The equilibrium level of employment L_1 is determined by the intersection of the marginal cost of labor curve MCL and the labor demand curve D at point c. The equilibrium wage is w_1. If minimum-wage legislation sets a statutory minimum wage of w_2, the marginal cost of labor curve will become $w_2 e$. Employment will rise to L_2, as determined by the intersection of $w_2 e$ with D at point d. In general, if the minimum wage lies anywhere above w_1 up to the level corresponding to point c, both employment and earnings will be higher than they would be without such a minimum wage. However, if the minimum wage is set higher than point c, employment will be reduced.

Minimum-wage legislation definitely raises wages for some workers. But since its effects on employment may vary, depending on the structure of the labor market, it may not be a reliable method for fighting poverty.

(which is also labor's marginal revenue product curve MRP) and the labor supply curve S in a perfectly competitive labor market. When the market is in equilibrium, the wage is w_0 and the quantity of labor employed is L_0. However, suppose the market-determined wage w_0 is below the legislated minimum-wage level w_1. This means it is illegal for employers to pay labor a wage as low as w_0 because society feels such a wage is "substandard."

When employers are forced to pay the minimum wage w_1, they will demand less labor, the quantity L_d, because the demand curve for labor is downward sloping. On the other hand, the supply of labor will increase to the quantity L_s because the supply curve of labor is upward sloping (the higher the wage, the more workers who are willing to work). Consequently, at the minimum wage w_1, there will be an excess supply of labor equal to the difference between L_s and L_d.

The quantity of labor actually employed, L_d, is less than the quantity L_0 that would be employed in the absence of the minimum-wage law. The quantity of labor unemployed in this market as a result of the minimum-wage law equals $L_d L_s$. It is true that though a smaller quantity of labor is employed, those who are employed are better off since they earn a higher wage w_1.

In sum, *many who are against minimum-wage legislation argue that while it increases the wages of some workers, it increases unemployment among others. Therefore, they conclude, it is not a very effective method for fighting poverty.*

The Case for Minimum Wage. Those who favor minimum-wage legislation argue that the perfectly competitive model of the labor market, shown in part a of Figure 17–4, is not representative of many of the labor markets in our economy. They claim that in a large number of labor markets employers have a substantial monopoly position in the hiring of labor—they are monopsonists, a concept we discussed in Chapter 15.

The effect of minimum-wage legislation in a monopsony labor market is illustrated in Figure 17–4, part b. (This diagram is the same as Figures 15–7 and 15–8.) From our discussion in Chapter 15, you will recall that a monopsonist will hire labor up to the point at which the marginal cost of labor equals its marginal revenue product. This is represented in Figure 17–4, part b, by the intersection of the *MCL* curve and the labor demand curve D (the marginal revenue product curve *MRP*) at point c. In this situation, the monopsonist will hire L_1 units of labor and pay them a wage equal to w_1.

Again suppose society regards such a wage level as substandard, and that minimum-wage legislation makes it illegal for employers to pay a wage less than the statutory minimum. Let us say that this minimum wage is w_2. The marginal cost of labor to the monopsonist is now represented by the line $w_2 e$. Its intersection with the labor demand curve D at point d indicates that the amount

of labor the monopsonist will now hire is L_2. The level of employment in this market is now higher than before. Moreover, labor is now earning a higher wage than previously, since the minimum wage w_2 is higher than w_1.

In fact, *if the statutory minimum wage lies anywhere above w_1 up to the level corresponding to point c, both employment and earnings will be higher.* If, for example, the minimum wage were w_0, the level of employment, L_0, would be the same as that which would prevail in a perfectly competitive equilibrium. Of course, if the minimum wage were above point c, employment would be less than L_1. Minimum-wage legislation would then have the same kind of adverse effect on employment that it does in the perfectly competitive labor market of part a in Figure 17–4.

In sum, *those who favor minimum-wage legislation argue that many labor markets are monopsonistic. They therefore claim that a statutory minimum wage may not only increase workers' earnings but may increase employment as well—so long as the minimum wage is not set too high.*

Both sides of the minimum-wage debate make telling points. Obviously, whether a statutory minimum wage has beneficial or adverse effects on employment depends on the structure of the particular labor market examined. Minimum-wage legislation definitely raises wages for some workers. But given its uncertain effects on employment, such legislation may make some workers worse off. For example, most studies conclude that the minimum wage contributes to the high unemployment rate among teenagers. Therefore, it does not seem to be a reliable method for attacking poverty.

Job-Training Programs

A second approach to reducing poverty through the labor market is the use of government-subsidized **job-training programs**, sometimes called manpower programs. These are aimed at helping the young and unemployed develop the job skills they need to increase their employability. These programs also aim at improving the job skills of older workers who are below the poverty line even when fully employed because they lack the skills to hold any but low-paying jobs.

The Rationale for Job-Training Programs. The basic rationale behind this approach is that by increasing workers' skills, their productivity and hence their earning power is increased. This is illustrated in Figure 17–5. Recall from Chapter 14 that the marginal physical product of labor *MPP*, together with the price *p* of the final product that labor helps to produce, determines the position of the marginal revenue product (*MRP*) or demand curve for labor, $D = p \times MPP$. (You may want to review these concepts in Chapter 14 at this point.) Given the existing state of labor productivity, along with the price of the final product, suppose the demand curve for labor in the labor market of Figure 17–5 is *D* (which is equal to *MRP*). This, together with the labor supply curve *S*, determines the equilibrium wage w_0 and level of employment L_0. A training program that increases labor's productivity, and hence its *MPP*, causes the demand curve for labor to shift rightward to a position such as D_1 (which is equal to MRP_1). As a result, workers now receive a higher wage w_1 and in addition a larger number of workers, L_1, are employed. Unlike the minimum-wage approach, there is no question about the increase in employment. And along with this increase, workers will receive a higher wage because they are more productive and therefore have more market value in the production process, not because of a statute requiring that they receive a higher wage.

The Development of Job-Training Programs. During the 1960s and early 1970s several programs were initiated to upgrade the job skills of low-income groups. In 1973 many of these were consolidated under the Comprehensive Employment and Training Act

FIGURE 17-5 Increased Labor Productivity Leads to Increased Labor Demand and Higher Wages

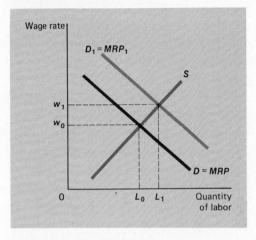

The demand curve *D* for labor is its marginal revenue product curve *MRP*. Recall that $MRP = p \times MPP$, or the price *p* of the final product labor helps to produce times the marginal physical product of labor *MPP*. The basic intent of the job-training approach to reducing poverty is to increase labor productivity, or *MPP*, by increasing workers' skills. In the labor market shown here, this causes the labor demand curve *D* (which equals *MRP*) to shift rightward to D_1 (which equals MRP_1). Given the supply curve of labor *S*, this results in an increase in employment from L_0 to L_1 and an increase in the wage rate from w_0 to w_1.

(CETA). This act set up a community manpower system intended to give people training and transitional public-service employment aimed at enhancing their employability in the private sector. The principal federal role under the system was to provide support and technical assistance to local programs. In addition, subsidized jobs for older workers were funded under the Older American Community Service Employment Act of 1973. Other federal activities have included apprenticeship programs, the Job Corps, and

POLICY PERSPECTIVE

The Negative Income Tax—Give the Money to the Poor and Cut Out the Bureaucracy

The attacks made on poverty by minimum-wage legislation, job-training programs, and the numerous forms of aid provided by the social security system have obviously not eliminated poverty. Many have argued that the sheer number of these programs has resulted in overlapping responsibilities and the proliferation of agencies employing tens of thousands of bureaucrats. The result is inefficiency and large payrolls, all of which drive up the costs of helping the poor and providing welfare. Such considerations have led policymakers and economists to propose schemes that simply take income tax revenues from higher-income groups and transfer them into the hands of the lowest-income groups with a minimum amount of bureaucratic intervention and loss of funds to bureaucracy payrolls along the way. One such income tax transfer scheme frequently contemplated is the negative income tax.

A **negative income tax** *is taxation in reverse on any income that is less than a certain statutory level. If a household's earned income falls below the statutory level, the government gives the household a subsidy, or negative income tax, equal to a certain fraction of the difference between the statutory income level and the income earned by the household.* The negative income tax is financed by income taxes on households with income above the statutory level.

Example of the Negative Income Tax

For example, suppose that the negative income tax rate is 40 percent and that the statutory income level is $9,000. The way in which the negative income tax would

work for earned income below this level is shown in Table P17–1. If a household had no earned income (column 2, row 1), its earned income of zero would be $9,000 less (column 3) than the statutory level of $9,000 (column 1). The government would give the household a negative income tax equal to 40 percent of this difference, or $3,600 (column 4). The total income received by the household therefore would be $3,600 (column 5), which is equal to the household's earned income (zero in this case) plus the amount of its negative income tax (column 2 plus column 4). A family with no earned income at all is thus ensured a minimum income of $3,600 in this example of a negative income tax scheme. If the family had an earned income of $1,000 (column 2, row 2), this would be $8,000 less (column 3) than the statutory level of $9,000 (column 1). In this case the government would give the household a negative income tax equal to $3,200 (column 4), or 40 percent of $8,000. The total income received by the household, therefore, would be $4,200 (column 5), which is again equal to the sum of its earned income and the amount of its negative income tax (column 2 plus column 4). You should check the numbers given by this calculation process for the earned income levels given in rows 3 through 10.

Note that the closer the family's earned income level is to the statutory level of $9,000, the smaller the negative income tax (column 4) that it receives. If its earned income is $9,000, it receives no subsidy from the government at all. Above this level the household pays income taxes to the government according to the regular income tax schedule. The

TABLE P17-1 A Negative Income Tax Scheme
(Hypothetical Data)

	(1)	(2)	(3)	(4)	(5)
	Statutory Income Level	Earned Income	Statutory Minus Earned = (1) − (2)	Negative Income Tax = .40 × (3)	Total Income = (2) + (4)
1.	$9,000	$ 0	$9,000	$3,600	$3,600
2.	9,000	1,000	8,000	3,200	4,200
3.	9,000	2,000	7,000	2,800	4,800
4.	9,000	3,000	6,000	2,400	5,400
5.	9,000	4,000	5,000	2,000	6,000
6.	9,000	5,000	4,000	1,600	6,600
7.	9,000	6,000	3,000	1,200	7,200
8.	9,000	7,000	2,000	800	7,800
9.	9,000	8,000	1,000	400	8,400
10.	9,000	9,000	0	0	9,000

particular negative income tax scheme shown in Table P17-1 is but one possible example. In general, the statutory income level may be set at any level and so may the negative income tax rate.

Important Features of the Negative Income Tax

There are several important features of a negative income tax scheme:

1. It provides a guaranteed minimum level of income for households that have no earned income at all.

2. At the same time that it provides financial assistance to low-income households, it also gives them an incentive to work. This can be seen by examining Table P17-1. Starting from a position of zero earned income, row 1, note that if the household is able to earn $1,000 (column 2), the amount of the negative income tax it receives falls by only $400, from $3,600 to $3,200 (column 4). Therefore, by working it is $600 better off—its total income rises from $3,600 to $4,200 (column 5). As long as the household's earned income is below the statutory income level, the negative income tax it receives falls by only $.40 for every additional $1 of in-

come it earns. It always pays to earn income under this scheme.

3. The only criterion for deciding whether a household is eligible for assistance is whether its earned income level is below the statutory income level. Other welfare and assistance programs use a multitude of criteria, some of which are so subjective as to put welfare administrators and social workers in the position of playing god to the poor. Many feel this kind of paternalism is arbitrary and demeaning to those receiving assistance. It is demeaning enough to be poor without having to justify and explain one's personal life to a stranger.

4. The negative income tax could be administered by the Treasury Department and the Internal Revenue Service using existing machinery for tax collection and income transfer. This might well be more efficient than the elaborate bureaucratic structure now used to administer welfare programs.

Criticisms of the Negative Income Tax

Despite all these positive features, the idea of a negative income tax has its critics, which is attested to by the fact that it has never made it off the drawing board:

1. There is a conflict between any attempt to provide a minimum guaranteed income level intended only for those at or below the poverty line and at the same time provide an incentive to work. Referring once again to Table P17–1, suppose the minimum guaranteed income of $3,600 were regarded as the poverty line. The negative income tax subsidies that are received for those having earned income greater than zero (rows 2–10) are putting these households above the poverty line—people who are not poor are receiving assistance. On the other hand, suppose $9,000 were regarded as the poverty line. In order to maintain the incentive-to-work feature of the negative income tax, it is unavoidable that many households with earned incomes below $9,000 will remain below the poverty line.

2. Many students of poverty argue that it is not realistic to think that by simply handing money to poor people, you can expect to break the vicious circle of poverty. If the head of household is addicted to drinking, drugs, or gambling or is simply irresponsible with money, the benefits to the rest of the household from a money handout may be slight at best. Critics argue that the negative income tax ignores these aspects of the social pathology of poverty. Money handouts without some guidance or change in habits may only reduce poverty by definition—not in fact. Again, "guidance or change in habits" gets us back into questions of subjectivity and normative issues.

3. Many citizens object to the negative income tax concept simply because it is such a blatant way of taking income away from one group and handing it over to another. Lower-middle-income workers would find themselves forced to give some of their income over to people with income only a few hundred dollars less than their own.

Questions

1. Construct a table illustrating a negative income tax scheme with a 50 percent negative income tax rate that guarantees a minimum household income of $10,178, the official 1983 poverty line for a family of four.

2. Does it seem reasonable to say such a family is poor only if its income is below this line? How does this bear on the criticism of the negative income tax that it may subsidize people who are not poor?

---

the Work Incentive Program (WIN). The federal government has also supported apprenticeship programs conducted by employers, often jointly with labor unions, to train workers on the job in a skilled trade. The Job Corps has provided training for disadvantaged youth largely at residential centers, and has also conducted nontraditional training for women. The Work Incentive Program has provided manpower, placement, and other services to help people receiving Aid to Families with Dependent Children get and keep jobs.

The Effectiveness of Job-Training Programs. How effective have these job programs been at improving employability and earnings of those below the poverty line?

The $60 billion spent by the CETA program during its 9-year existence only resulted in about 30 percent of its participants getting private sector jobs. This is not too surprising since only 18 cents of every CETA dollar was spent training people for jobs in the private sector. In some large cities, funds that were intended to be used for jobs for poor blacks, Hispanics, and welfare mothers were used to rehire municipal workers laid off in budget cutbacks. Another problem at the local level was that rather than creating new jobs, federal public-service money was diverted into supporting functions that state and local governments might have provided from their own budgets.

Vested Interest and Job Training. The experiences with WIN, its advocates, critics, and potential problems, reveal the motives behind the way different vested-interest groups react to job-training programs aimed at helping people who live below the poverty line. State and local officials see such programs as a chance to cut the welfare costs burdening their budgets. Often this means that federal efforts will merely be substituted for state and local efforts, resulting in little net reduction in the number of people below the poverty line. Unions, worried about "low-wage competition for their members," may attempt to block extension of job-program legislation. Of course, employers who see able-bodied adults on welfare as a potential pool of labor are no doubt hoping that this will help inhibit the rise of wages by curbing the bargaining power of labor unions. We examined the economics of the labor-management conflict over this issue in connection with our discussion of economic rent in the last chapter. The resolution of these kinds of conflicts will have a lot to do with the future and effectiveness of job programs.

The Private Sector and the Job-Training Partnership Act. CETA was replaced with the Job-Training Partnership Act (JTPA) of 1982 which is focused almost entirely on the private sector. JTPA uses federal funds to provide seed money for state and local governments to set up local training centers, with the help of industry, that provide training tailored to the available jobs in those communities. Under JTPA at least 70 cents of each training dollar must be used for direct training costs, as compared to CETA's 18 cents. So far the program appears to be much more successful than CETA at getting participants jobs in the private sector.

SUMMARY

1. The distribution of income in an economy goes to the heart of the question, For whom is the economy's output produced? One important measure of this distribution is the functional distribution of income, which shows how the economy's total income is divided between wages, rents, interest, and profits. Another is the size distribution of income, which shows how total income is divided between individual households, the ultimate recipients of all factor income.

2. The basic determinants of the observed inequality in the distribution of income are (a) the differences between individuals in ability, education, training, and motivation; (b) the various market structures of the many different markets in our economy; (c) the distribution of wealth among individual households; (d) the age distribution of the population; (e) the economy's tax structure; and (f) differences between individual job preferences, luck, and opportunities.

3. In the United States the inequality in the distribution of income lessened between 1929 and the end of World War II. Since that time the distribution of income has remained relatively unchanged, with the lowest one-fifth of families receiving less than 6 percent of the total income and the highest one-fifth receiving slightly more than 40 percent. The inequality in the distribution of wealth is even greater than the inequality in the distribution of income.

4. In the United States about 15 percent of the population lives below the poverty line, down from approximately 17 percent in the mid-1960s. The incidence of poverty falls heaviest among blacks, families with a female head, those living in rural areas and the inner city, and the aged. Poverty begets poverty in that families have great difficulty rising above it from one generation to the next. Relative to other groups in our society the poor suffer from a lack of political visibility. Discrimination appears to be a major cause of the higher incidence of poverty among blacks.

5. The social security system, financed by payroll taxes on employers and employees, provides a form of social insurance for the old, the disabled, the unemployed, and the dependents of deceased workers. Through its special assistance programs, the system provides welfare aid to the needy. In recent years benefit payments have far outstripped the social security trust funds' capacity to finance them, and thus benefits are increasingly financed directly out of social security payroll taxes.

6. Poverty also may be attacked through the job market. Minimum-wage legislation has established statutory minimum-wage levels. While providing higher wages for some workers, others may be forced into unemployment by this approach, which raises doubts about its overall effectiveness in combating poverty. The job-training approach attempts to increase the employability and wages of poor people by improving their productivity and labor skills. While this approach has experienced modest success and shows promise, it has proved costly.

7. Income tax transfer schemes attempt to combat poverty by taxing higher-income groups and transferring the proceeds to lower-income groups. Under one such proposal, the negative income tax, the government pays households with incomes below some statutory level an amount equal to some percentage of the difference between the statutory level and the household's earned income. While this approach may be an economically efficient way to fight poverty, some argue that simply handing money to poor people does not come to grips with the social pathology of poverty.

KEY TERMS AND CONCEPTS

functional distribution of income
job-training programs
Lorenz diagram
minimum-wage law
negative income tax
poverty
progressive income tax
size distribution of income
social security system
social security tax

QUESTIONS AND PROBLEMS

1. It has been said that if perfect equality in the distribution of income could be enforced, possibly by means of some kind of redistributive tax scheme, individuals would unavoidably be treated unequally. In what ways might this be so?

2. In the early days of the Russian Revolution, one much-publicized dictum of Communist party ideology held that income distribution would be determined according to the dictum "from each according to his ability, to each according to his need." How are workers' "needs" and "abilities" reflected in a perfectly competitive labor market? How well might the objective of the dictum be achieved in an economy where factors are employed in accordance with the marginal productivity theory of factor demand?

3. Harriet Martineau, a nineteenth-century English writer, once hypothesized that if the government redistributed income in the morning to achieve perfect income equality, by nightfall the rich would once again be back in their comfortable beds and the poor asleep under the bridges. What factors would Martineau most likely stress as the important determinants of income inequality?

4. Suppose you constructed the Lorenz curves representing income distribution in *each* of the following occupational groups: grade school teachers, gamblers, lawyers, business proprietors, and boxers. How do you think the curves would look relative to one another and why?

5. One commentator on poverty has made the following observation: Suppose we put the poverty line at one-half the median income in the United States, which is above the official poverty line recognized by the government for a family of four. In New York City a family of four on welfare receives in cash and kind (food stamps, subsidized housing, and Medicaid) an amount sufficient to place them above this more generous poverty line. On the basis of this, would you be willing to argue that we have abolished poverty in New York City? What does this say about the way we measure poverty? What are the dimensions of poverty that numbers such as these fail to capture?

6. Historically, the aged have typically had to depend on the young for their support. It was fairly traditional for older people to live with their children, often largely dependent on their offspring's sense of duty and parental respect. As originally conceived, the social security system could be said to lessen that dependence to some extent. Today some crit-

ics of the social security system say that the old are again becoming dependent on the younger generation for financial support. What is the basis of this contention, and in what sense is it correct?

7. What effects do you think minimum-wage laws would have on employment in each of the following: apple orchards, textile mill towns in the South, and dry-cleaning businesses?

8. Some argue that minimum-wage laws have effects that are the same as if the age limit on child-labor laws was increased. Why is this so and how might job-training programs get around this problem despite the presence of minimum-wage laws? Illustrate your answer graphically.

9. In what way would the size of the negative tax rate affect the incentive of those receiving a negative income tax to seek work?

Hints and Answers to Checkpoints

CHAPTER 1

Checkpoint 1-1

There is considerable leeway on what might be counted as correct in response to this question. Some statements in the news item have both positive and normative elements. What should be emphasized are the (potentially, at least) *verifiable* nature of the positive statements in the paragraph and the value-judgment nature of the normative statements. The use of "loaded language" as a prop for a shortage of factual statements should be noted.

Checkpoint 1-2

The long gas lines could have been shortened—that is, the quantity of gasoline demanded could have been reduced—if the price of gas had been increased.

Checkpoint 1-3

If the demand in the other city is less sensitive to changes in price, then the graph of its demand would be more vertical than the demand curve illustrated in Figure 1–3. This would show that a change in price would induce a smaller change in quantity demanded in the less sensitive city. Hence, the city whose demand is illustrated in Figure 1–3 would experience the greatest reduction in the quantity of electricity demanded, given an equal price change in the two cities.

Checkpoint 1-4

Some examples of cause-and-effect confusion might include:

> *People looking at the night sky for a longer time will see more shooting stars than people who look for a shorter time. But this does not mean that looking at the sky longer causes more shooting stars.*
>
> *Ships can often be seen preparing to sail before high tide. But this does not mean that preparing to sail causes high tide.*

A football game crowd illustrates the fallacy of composition in this way: If one person stands up to watch the game, he or she will be able to see the game better. But this certainly does not remain true if everyone stands up.

CHAPTER 2

Checkpoint 2-1

The opportunity cost to Clyde of choosing combination d instead of combination c in Figure 2–1 is what Clyde must give up to move from combination c to combination d, that is, 10 bushels of corn. Similarly, the opportunity cost of choosing b instead of d is what must be given up to move from d to b, namely, 10 cords of wood. The opportunity cost of choosing d instead of b is the 20 bushels of corn that must be forgone in order to move from b to d.

Checkpoint 2-2

The cost of moving from d to c is 20,000 scrubbers, the cost of moving from c to b is 30,000 scrubbers, and the cost of moving from d to a is 100,000 scrubbers. Figure 2–2 can be used to illustrate the law of increasing costs as follows: The move from e to d gains 20 million bundles of other goods (including food) at a cost of 10,000 scrubbers, the move from d to c gains 20 million bundles at a cost of 20,000 scrubbers, the move from c to b gains 20 million bundles at a cost of 30,000 scrubbers, and the move from b to a gains 20 million bundles at a cost of 50,000 scrubbers. In each step, the 20 million bundles of other goods gained has a greater opportunity cost in terms of scrubbers, thus illustrating the law of increasing costs.

Checkpoint 2-3

The questions of what to produce and for whom to produce are of a normative nature because they cannot be answered strictly by an appeal to the facts.

Checkpoint 2-4

A pure market economy would select a point on the production possibilities frontier without any government intervention, using only the price signals generated in the marketplace to determine what quantity of scrubbers and bundles would be produced and purchased. If the public desired a different quantity of scrubbers than was currently being produced, its desires would cause changes in demand for scrubbers relative to other goods, and hence would cause changes in relative prices, profits, and production of scrubbers and bundles of other goods. In a command economy, the point on the production possibilities frontier would be mandated from above, with quotas for scrubbers being assigned from a central authority in the same manner as quotas for all other goods.

For both types of economies, greater industrial development would allow greater indulgence in the "luxury" of scrubbers. Less developed economies would probably consider food, shelter, and producer goods (capital goods) necessary to survival and development rather than scrubbers.

CHAPTER 3

Checkpoint 3-1

A coincidence of wants is lacking here. If trade were to be carried on at all, one of the people would have to accept an unwanted good and later trade for the wanted good. For example, since C wants fish and has wheat, C can travel to A's island, trade wheat for corn, and then travel to B's island and trade the corn for the fish C desires. Substantial transport time and costs are involved, even if C knows in advance what the supplies and wants of the other people are. If A, B, and C used money, C could travel to A's island and sell his wheat for money and then transport only the money to B's island to buy fish. Coincidence of wants would no longer necessitate someone transporting goods they did not want.

Checkpoint 3-2

Gompers meant that a business that cannot operate at a profit is not operating efficiently. Since it wastes resources, it will eventually be driven out of business. The resulting loss of jobs will hurt working people. Also, a firm that is not able to operate at a profit cannot attract the investment capital necessary for growth and the creation of new jobs. While Marx saw capitalists' profits as a surplus value stolen from the working class, Gompers saw profits as a reward for wise management and entrepreneurship and as a return to attract financial capital.

Checkpoint 3-3

The government's power to enforce contracts contributes to the development of markets by making the process of exchanging goods and services less risky. Government's power to enforce gives all parties to a contract added assurance of its fulfillment.

The postal service is not a public good because the exclusion principle applies: only those who pay for the service can have it. Furthermore, there is a private market incentive for providing such service. Parcel Post is an example of a mail service provided by a private firm.

The military draft may be thought of as a transfer of income from those who are drafted to those outside the military services, because the draftees are paid at less than the free-market wage for military labor services (if military wages were determined in a free market, there would be no shortage of military labor and the draft would be unnecessary). Also, since the draft does not discriminate in terms of wealth or income (at least in the absence of corruption), persons who would not enter military service even at the free-market wage are forced to serve. This too constitutes a redistribution of income.

In contrast to government agencies, private businesses that don't operate very efficiently are forced out of business by experiencing losses.

There are, of course, many pro and con arguments concerning the effect of limiting the number of terms a politician can remain in office. For example, one might argue that a politician who remains in office for many terms can set up a political machine that ensures reelection regardless of his or her responsiveness to public wishes. On the other side of the fence, one might argue that it is the threat of losing an election that forces politicians to be responsive to public desires. Thus, a politician who knows he or she is ineligible for reelection might be totally unresponsive to voters' wishes once in office. There are many other arguments that could be made for either side as well.

CHAPTER 4

Checkpoint 4-1

If the price of peas were to rise, this would shift the demand curve of lima beans to the right, since the two goods are substitutes, and more lima beans would be demanded at every price. If the price of pretzels were to fall, the demand curve for beer would shift to the right, since the two goods are complements. The demand curve for pretzels would remain unchanged, since we are talking about a change in the price of pretzels and this would result in a movement along the pretzel demand curve rather than a shift in the curve. If the price of hamburger buns were to go up, the demand curve for hamburgers would shift to the left, since these goods are complements, and less hamburger would now be demanded at every price.

Checkpoint 4-2

If wages go up, then supplier costs go up and a higher price must be charged at each level of production. Hence the supply curve is shifted upward (alternatively, it can be said that at each purchase price, higher costs allow fewer units to be supplied, so that the supply curve shifts to the left). An improvement in technology, such as the improvement mentioned, will lower production costs and shift the supply curve to the right. If the price of lamb were to rise, some suppliers would begin to produce lamb instead of hamburger (since similar resources are used in producing either). This would cause a change in the supply of hamburger. Specifically, the supply curve of hamburger would shift leftward, reflecting the fact that a higher price would now have to be paid for resources that could otherwise be used to produce lamb.

Land is a resource potentially useful in both corn production and the factory production of CB radios. Suppose the land is being used in the production of corn, and an entrepreneur feels that it might be more profitably used in the production of CB radios. The entrepreneur can offer to buy the land at a price that reflects the potential profits in CB production. If this price is higher than what the farmer feels the land is worth in terms of expected potential profits from corn production, then the transaction will take place and the land will change uses.

Checkpoint 4-3

This checkpoint deals with simultaneous changes in supply and demand. If the price of hot dogs should fall, it would affect the equilibrium price and quantity of hamburger on both the demand and supply sides of the market. On the demand side, hot dogs and hamburger are substitutes, and so the fall in the price of hot dogs would reduce the demand for hamburger. This would, other things held constant, reduce both the equilibrium price and the equilibrium quantity of hamburger. But on the supply side, the same resources can be used to produce both hamburger and hot dogs, so that if the price of hot dogs falls, suppliers will tend to produce more hamburger instead, shifting the supply curve of hamburger to the right. This would, other things being equal, tend to increase

equilibrium quantity and reduce equilibrium price. Therefore, equilibrium price will decrease, since both demand and supply influences push price downward. But we cannot say which way equilibrium quantity will go without knowing the relative sizes of the supply and demand influences, since they operate in opposite directions.

If hamburger bun prices fall, demand for hamburger will increase, since hamburger buns and hamburger are complementary goods. But if the cost of labor used in hamburger production falls, the supply of hamburger will increase at any given price; equilibrium quantity will tend to increase and equilibrium price will tend to decrease. Taken together with the increased demand, the net effect will be an increase in the market equilibrium quantity, with an indeterminate change in the equilibrium price.

If the price of electricity rises, then the demand for hamburger will fall, since these goods are complements. If the office rent for hamburger producers rises, then the supply of hamburger will decrease. A decrease in both demand and supply will decrease equilibrium quantity and have an indeterminate effect on equilibrium price.

If the only information that you were given was that the price of hamburger had risen, then you could not make any statement about what had happened to quantity, since it could have either risen or declined, depending on whether a shift occurred in supply or demand or both.

If consumers' income increased, then the demand for shoes would probably increase (assuming that shoes are a normal good). This would tend, *ceteris paribus*, to increase both the equilibrium price and the equilibrium quantity of shoes bought and sold. Since the equilibrium quantity actually decreased, some other factors must have caused a leftward shift in the supply curve, which more than offset any rightward shift in the demand curve.

CHAPTER 5

Checkpoint 5-1

Using the midpoints formula, the following elasticities result: $9 to $8, 3.40; $8 to $7, 2.14; $7 to $6, 1.44; $6 to $5, 1.00; $5 to $4, .69; $4 to $3, .47; and $3 to $2, .29. As we move down the demand curve from left to right, we observe the elasticity of demand declines (in absolute value). If the Rose Bowl is filled to its 100,000-seat capacity and total revenue is at its maximum, then we could be at the unit elastic point on a demand curve that is to the right of the illustrated demand curve. However, it is also possible that the demand curve is so far to the right that the unit elastic point on the demand curve lies to the right of the 100,000-seat capacity point on the horizontal axis. In that case the point on the demand curve lying directly above the 100,000-seat capacity would be in the elastic range of the demand curve. The maximum *possible* revenue would still be obtained by charging a ticket price corresponding to that point on the demand curve—still a sellout. The point lying above the 100,000-seat capacity could not be in the inelastic range of the demand curve. If it were, the unit elastic point would lie to the left of the 100,000-seat capacity, and revenue maximization would require setting the ticket price higher (at the unit elastic point) and not filling the stadium.

Checkpoint 5-2

Supply elasticities are positive and demand elasticities are negative because supply curves are direct (positive-slope) relationships and demand curves are inverse (negative-slope) relationships.

Checkpoint 5-3

If the marginal utility per dollar of X is greater than the marginal utility per dollar of Z, then this would mean that if the consumer took a dollar away from expenditure on Z and spent it on X instead, there would be a gain in total utility. This is so because the loss in utility from consuming a dollar's worth less of Z would be more than offset by the gain in utility from consuming an additional dollar's worth of X. This reallocation of expenditure would also mean that the marginal utility of X per dollar would decrease while that of Z would increase. We know this from the law of diminishing marginal utility. As long as the marginal utility of Z per dollar is less than that of X, the consumer's total utility can be increased by shifting expenditure away from Z and toward X. Because of the law of diminishing marginal utility, we know that eventually the marginal utility of Z per dollar would be brought into equality with the marginal utility of X per dollar.

If we begin from a point where the consumer is maximizing utility, and only the price of Z rises, then we will have a situation where the marginal utility per dollar spent on Z is less than the marginal utility per dollar spent on X, which is exactly the situation in the foregoing paragraph. And as before, the law of diminishing marginal utility will cause the consumer to shift expenditure away from Z and toward X. Thus we have shown that an increase in the price of Z results in a decreased demand for it, which is a description of a demand curve that slopes downward to the right.

CHAPTER 6

Checkpoint 6-1

If the government had put a price ceiling on gasoline, then the lines at gas stations would have been longer than they already were. This could be shown diagrammatically by drawing the usual supply and demand curves and placing the price ceiling line below the market equilibrium price. The distance between the supply curve and the demand curve on the price ceiling line would be the amount of excess demand or shortage. The problem of distributing gasoline under such circumstances could be dealt with by using nonprice rationing, such as the rationing coupons used in World War II. But such techniques are of limited effectiveness if there are black markets.

Checkpoint 6-2

In terms of Figure 6-2 under both schemes the government sets a price of p_s and the farmers, true to their supply curves, supply quantity q_s. Under Scheme 1, the government buys the wheat not demanded by the public at price p_s at a cost of q_s minus q_d times p_s (an amount equal to the area of rectangle $q_d q_s a_c$). The more *elastic* the demand and supply curves, the greater the distance from q_d to q_s and the more the government's cost will be. In addition note that the government is the owner of q_d to q_s bushels of wheat, for which it must pay the storage costs, since it cannot sell it without affecting the price and quantity adversely.

Under Scheme 4, the farmers sell their wheat at the price that it will bring on the market, namely p_g. The entire quantity of wheat produced is bought by the public, and the government has no wheat to store. But the government pays the farmers the difference between the price they receive (p_g) and the support price (p_s) on each bushel of wheat sold, for a total cost of p_s minus p_g times q_s (an amount equal to the area of the rectangle $p_g b a p_s$). Now, the more elastic the demand and supply curves are, the smaller the distance from p_g to p_s will be and the less the government's cost will be. There are no storage costs associated with this scheme. Hence we see that the question of which scheme will cost less depends on the elasticity of the demand and supply curves and the costs of storage.

Checkpoint 6-3

With a perfectly elastic supply curve, the entire incidence of the $10 excise tax falls on buyers.

With a perfectly elastic demand curve, the entire incidence of the $10 excise tax falls on sellers. If the demand curve is perfectly inelastic, then the selling price will increase by the entire amount of the tax and the entire incidence of the tax will fall on the buyer. For any given size of excise tax, the more elastic the demand curve, the greater will be the reduction in quantity consumed. Since the elasticity of demand for wine in the Chapter 5 Policy Perspective was quite great, it is not likely that an excise tax would produce much revenue, since the quantity consumed would fall a great deal when the tax was imposed.

Checkpoint 6-4

The senator must be implicitly assuming that the supply for this product is perfectly elastic or that the demand for this product is perfectly inelastic.

If strict pollution control laws were imposed on an industry, employment and output would fall more the greater were the elasticities of both supply and demand.

Since the demand for cigarettes seems to be quite inelastic, a $.20 tax per pack would probably not change the quantity consumed very much and hence would have little effect on the frequency of lung cancer.

The required inspections increase the demand for service maintenance. This law might still be favored by you even though you keep your car in top shape anyway, because it would increase the safety of the other cars on the road (some of which might not be kept in top shape without the requirement). You would realize an external benefit.

Although the high elasticity of the demand for the red wine will cause its consumption to decline in the presence of an excise tax, the ready availability of substitutes for consumers of alcohol will make a wine-specific excise tax of limited usefulness in cutting down on drunken driving.

CHAPTER 7

Checkpoint 7-1

A limited partner has no say in the management of the firm, whereas a stockholder has some influence by virtue of his or her right to vote for a board of directors. Also, a limited partner's death would necessitate the reorganization of the partnership, while that of the stockholder would merely transfer his or her shares to heirs.

Normal profit is an economic cost because it represents the opportunity cost of the financial capital and entrepreneurial skills used by the firm.

In one store the proprietor might own the building outright. The opportunity cost of the owner's funds tied up in the building would not be included when calculating accounting profit. Suppose the owner of the other store has borrowed funds to buy the building. Then the interest payments (opportunity cost of the funds) would be included when calculating accounting profit.

Checkpoint 7-2

If total fixed cost increased from $50 to $75, then the fixed cost line (*TFC*) would shift upward by $25, and the total cost curve would also shift upward by $25. The total variable curve would remain unchanged.

If wages rose from $50 to $75, then the *TC* and *TVC* curves would both pivot counterclockwise about their intercepts. The *TFC* curve would remain unchanged.

Checkpoint 7-3

If fixed cost fell by $10, then average fixed cost would shift downward by $10 at 1 unit of output, by $5 at 2 units of output, and so on. Average total cost would shift downward in the same manner. Average variable cost would remain unchanged.

If weekly wages increase from $50 to $60, average fixed cost will not be affected, but average variable cost and average total cost will both increase, and the curves will shift upward. The new *AVC* and *ATC* columns are shown in Table A–1.

TABLE A-1

1	1	$60.00	$110.00
2	3	40.00	56.67
3	6	30.00	38.33
4	10	24.00	29.00
5	13	23.08	26.92
6	15	24.00	27.33
7	16.5	25.45	28.48
8	17.5	27.43	30.28
9	18	30.00	32.78

Checkpoint 7-4

The change in average total cost includes the change in average fixed cost, which falls more rapidly than marginal cost over the first six units of output. If diminishing returns are larger than is the case in Table 7–2, then the slope of the marginal cost curve would be greater to the right of its lowest point.

Checkpoint 7-5

The long-run ATC curve represents a collection of blueprints, because each point on it corresponds to a different plant—a different-size plant. In the long run a business can choose from a number of different sizes of plants in the planning stage. Hence the long-run ATC is a collection of blueprints. Selection of a plant size corresponds to the selection of a particular blueprint.

Underutilizing a larger plant when production is below 1,800 units and overutilizing a smaller plant when production is over 1,800 units is necessary if the firm is to produce a given output level at the lowest possible per unit cost in the long run—that is, if it is to operate on its long-run ATC curve.

CHAPTER 8

Checkpoint 8-1

As products cease to be identical, they become less substitutable for one another. Each firm's demand curve will begin to take on some slope instead of being perfectly horizontal. As each firm's demand ceases to be perfectly elastic, the firm ceases to be a price taker.

If the price of a competitive firm's product were to rise from $10 to $15, the TR curve in Figure 8–2, part a, would rotate counterclockwise around the origin until a slope of 15 was achieved. The firm's demand curve in part b would shift upward to $15. This is because each unit is sold at a market price of $15, making average revenue equal to $15 and total revenue equal to $15 times the number of units sold.

Checkpoint 8-2

Table 8–1 makes it clear that the difference between average revenue and average cost is greatest at 5 units produced and sold.

Figure 8–3, part b, was designed so that the number of profit squares shaded at 5 units of output is greater than the number shaded at 3, 4, or 6 units of output. At 5 units of output, approximately 10 squares are shaded, while at 3, 4, and 6 units of output, approximately 3, 8, and 6 squares respectively are shaded.

Checkpoint 8-3

Figure 8–4, part b, was designed so that the number of loss squares shaded at 4 units would be at a minimum. At 4 units of output, approximately 4 loss squares are shaded, while at 2, 3, and 5 units of output, approximately 8, 6, and 5 squares respectively are shaded.

The data in Table 8–2 show that the difference between price (= marginal revenue = average revenue) and average variable cost is at a maximum at 4 units of output.

Figure 8–4, part b, shows that the shaded area of the excess of total revenue over TVC is 5 squares at 4 units (1.25×4), while the excess is 2, 4 (= 1.34×3), and 4 (= $.80 \times 5$) squares at 2, 3, and 5 units respectively.

Checkpoint 8-4

The shaded area would represent the loss associated with producing 4 units of output as opposed to just shutting down. The area corresponding to the vertical distance between the TC and TR_4 curves would be the area between $4 and $7.25 out to 4 units of output. The area representing TFC would be the area between $7.25 and $4.75 out to 4 units of output.

Checkpoint 8-5

An increase in the cost of raw materials would shift the MC, AVC, and ATC curves upward. This would shift the industry supply curve upward. If demand curve D_1 represented the industry demand, then the firms would decide to produce nothing at all, and firm and industry output would fall to zero. If the demand curve were D_3, then the equilibrium price would increase, and firm and industry output would decline.

Checkpoint 8-6

When a perfectly competitive industry is in long-run equilibrium, all factors employed by the industry are earning just what they could earn in alternative endeavors. Hence all factors are compensated by an amount that just equals their opportunity cost. If firms are just earning a normal profit in long-run competitive equilibrium, then the financial capital and entrepreneurial skill employed by the firms are earning an amount just equal to their opportunity cost.

CHAPTER 9

Checkpoint 9-1

Kodak holds a large number of patents on products and processes related to film production and processing. It has also accumulated a large stock of customer goodwill and name recognition through extensive advertising.

Kaiser was probably not able to overcome the economy of scale barrier. In addition, Chrysler, Ford, and General Motors had established competitive advantages in the form of patents; accumulated know-how; well-integrated sales, production, and service facilities; and well-established credit lines and consumer familiarity with their products.

Checkpoint 9-2
The relationship may be most easily demonstrated in an area around the maximum point. Between 6 and 7 units of output, marginal revenue is zero and total revenue is at a maximum ($42). The (midpoint) elasticity of demand at this point is 1.0 = $(1/6.5)/(1/6.5)$. At 1 unit of output less, between 5 and 6 units of output, total revenue is $41 and marginal revenue is $2. The elasticity is 1.37 = $(1/5.5)/(1/7.5)$. At a point where output is one unit more than at the revenue-maximizing point (between 7 and 8 units), total revenue is $41, marginal revenue is −$2, and the elasticity of demand is .73 = $(1/7.5)/(1/5.5)$. This shows that where demand is inelastic, marginal revenue is negative, and where demand is elastic, marginal revenue is positive.

Checkpoint 9-3
Given the monopolist pictured in Figure 9–2, if profit was being maximized at an output of 7 units and a price of $6, then the marginal cost would have to be 0. This is because marginal revenue and marginal cost are always equal when profits are being maximized, and marginal revenue at 7 units is 0.

You would never expect a monopolist to sell at an equilibrium price in the inelastic portion of the demand curve, because marginal revenue in this region is negative and the marginal revenue and marginal cost equality would necessitate a negative marginal cost.

Checkpoint 9-4
An increase in fixed costs in Figure 9–3 would move *ATC* upward (increasing losses) but would not affect equilibrium price and output levels, since these are the loss-minimizing levels regardless of the level of fixed costs (variable costs determine loss-minimizing levels of price and output). The increase in fixed costs would increase negative economic profit (losses). Doubling a license fee paid to the state would constitute an increase in fixed cost and hence would not change price and output levels. If a monopolist changes price without changing output, then it could be in response to a change in demand (and hence marginal revenue). The demand curve could change position in such a way that the marginal revenue curve still intersects the marginal cost curve at the same point. If the government imposes an effective price ceiling, this could cause output to increase, since this would make the monopolist's effective demand curve horizontal, just like the perfect competitor's. The intersection of the marginal cost and marginal revenue curves would occur farther to the right of the original intersection.

Checkpoint 9-5
A monopolist can engage in noneconomic luxuries such as hiring discrimination, because there is no competitive pressure to force the monopolist to use the most economically efficient labor as there is under perfect competition. Wining and dining a monopolist can be effective for the same reasons. Without the rigorous competition of many rivals, a monopolist can "get away with" efforts that do less than maximize profit. Wining and dining could influence the monopolist to buy supplies from you even if your prices were higher than those of other suppliers. Competition would force the perfect competitor to use only economic reasoning to arrive at his or her choice of supplier.

One reason for the emergence of large fast-food chains in the competitive restaurant business might be economies of scale in production, construction, and advertising and the ability to buy supplies at large-volume discount prices.

Checkpoint 9-6
If all buyers have identical demand curves, then all buyers have identical demand elasticities, and the profit-maximizing monopolist will charge the same price to all of them.

CHAPTER 10

Checkpoint 10-1
A list of monopolistically competitive industries could include retail record sales, retail jewelry trade, watch repair, automobile service stations, construction contracting, computer peripherals, ice cream, ball-point pen manufacturing, furniture manufacturing, "variety store" retail trade, retail "drugstore" industry, stereo equipment manufacturing, rock-and-roll bands, and bicycle manufacturing.

The slope of the demand curve reflects the existence of substitutes because the more close substitutes there are for a given product, the more sensitive buyers will be to a change in the price of that product. That is, buyers will more readily switch to other products in response to a change in that product's price. Hence the more close substitutes there are for a product, the flatter will be that product's demand curve.

Checkpoint 10-2

If the ILGWU were to gain large wage increases, then the *ATC* curve for a typical firm in the industry would shift upward and the firm would experience losses (the typical firm's situation would look like that in Figure 10-1, part c). In the long run, firms would exit the industry, so that the demand curves of the remaining firms would shift to the right as their market shares increased. This would continue until the long-run equilibrium with normal profit was once again achieved (as illustrated in Figure 10-1, part b). Equilibrium prices would rise, and equilibrium output in the industry would fall. This would result in fewer garment workers being employed and a decrease in the size of the union's membership rolls.

Checkpoint 10-3

The popularity of a magazine such as *Consumer Reports* implies that a substantial portion of the populace doesn't believe that the bulk of advertising is informative in nature (otherwise they would not pay for a product—accurate product information—that they could get free in advertisements). If a government agency were set up to ensure that all advertising was informative, it would raise severe constitutional difficulties concerning freedom of speech and the press. Distinguishing between informative and noninformative advertising would be extremely difficult, even if such an agency's existence were to get by the courts.

CHAPTER 11

Checkpoint 11-1

The constant model changes constitute part of a policy directed at increasing product proliferation and product complexity. This helps each of the automakers to keep the others off balance and serves as a very substantial barrier to the entry of new producers. The existing auto manufacturers are quite experienced at maintaining a fairly constant stream of new and changed models. This means that a new entrant into the market must not only be able to produce autos but to produce them while constantly changing styles in order to sell to a public that has grown used to such changes. It is not at all clear that under such circumstances it would be better for the four automakers to collude in order to stop such model changes. It is even possible that the overall industry demand is being increased by this behavior, in which case ending the constant model changes would be detrimental to the sales of all four firms.

Checkpoint 11-2

Information about the relative position of the firms at the top in a concentrated industry would provide evidence of how much "infighting" is going on among the industry's dominant firms. For example, a highly concentrated industry might have vigorous competition—even including price competition—among the top two or three firms. But the concentration ratio method of measuring oligopoly power would count this industry the same as one that had the same concentration but a very stable (and possibly collusive) relationship among the top two or three firms. Clearly, equal concentration ratios do not necessarily imply equal oligopoly power.

Since a merger of two firms will enable them to engage in perfectly collusive price behavior, merger activity is almost certain to decrease price flexibility.

If a perfectly competitive industry has a horizontal long-run supply curve and a downward-sloping, leftward-shifting demand curve, price will not decline. The concentration ratio in the industry would be very low, but price flexibility would appear to be absent. Hence a low concentration ratio does not necessarily imply that one will see price change in response to changing demand conditions.

Checkpoint 11-3

A firm could move price to a level above the kink in the demand curve if its marginal cost curve shifted upward until it intersected the marginal revenue curve at a point to the left of the kink.

The firm would never reduce price below the kink if the demand were inelastic to the right of the kink—that is, when marginal revenue is negative to the right of the kink.

Checkpoint 11-4

It is only necessary for one of the firms in Figure 11-7 to misjudge the likely reactions of the other in order for events to lead them to the price level p_4.

CHAPTER 12

Checkpoint 12-1

A finding that there was very little change in the identity of the top four firms in an industry characterized by high concentration and high profits would strengthen the implication that through overt or covert collusion, the top firms were acting as a joint monopoly and reaping monopoly profits. If the top four firms were subject to frequent turnover, however, it would be much more difficult to draw such a conclusion.

If an industry is more concentrated than is justified by economies of scale, then it would experience higher costs per unit than if its concentration were more in accord with available scale economies. The too-concentrated industry would experience a lower profit rate than if its concentration ratio were more in line with available scale economies.

In an industry where both advertising outlays and concentration are high, one would be tempted to draw the conclusion that the high advertising outlays are responsible for the high concentration. But the nature of the product would certainly have a bearing on this conclusion. For example, the automobile and cigarette industries both have high advertising outlays and high concentration, but in the auto industry, scale economies would seem to be a much more plausible cause for high concentration. The differences between different brands of cigarettes are not as great or as complex as the differences between makes of automobiles. Cigarette advertising is less informative than automobile advertising but probably has more to do with establishing market dominance than automobile advertising.

Checkpoint 12-2

The supporters of the Robinson-Patman Act would say that the risk of protecting inefficient small firms from going out of business is outweighed by the risk of creating a monopoly situation if the large firms are allowed to successfully drive their small competitors out of business.

Checkpoint 12-3

Market structure might be judged a more important criterion than conduct for antitrust enforcement because even though there may not be any misconduct, highly concentrated market structures represent a potential for misconduct. The spirit of this criterion is not whether there is a smoking gun, but rather whether there is any gun at all.

The Supreme Court seemed to ignore the fact that the Sherman Act outlawed all conspiracies to restrain trade, not just overt actions. The "Gary dinners" certainly seem to be such a conspiracy.

In the Alcoa case, the Supreme Court ruled against Alcoa in spite of the absence of misconduct. The precedents set in the U.S. Steel and International Harvester cases had required proof of misconduct. The Alcoa case emphasized market structure, as opposed to market conduct, as the criterion by which a company would be judged in violation of the Sherman Act.

CHAPTER 13

Checkpoint 13-1

The FCC's letter to the plywood makers informs them that unless they put shields around their electronic heating machines, they might be held liable for airline crashes attributed to interference with communication between flight-control towers and aircraft. It is likely that the plywood makers would rather incur the costs of putting shields around their machines than run the risk of incurring the potentially much larger damage costs associated with an airline crash. Installation of the costly shields will increase the cost of making plywood. This will cause the supply curve for plywood to shift upward. Given a downward-sloping demand for plywood, the equilibrium quantity of plywood bought and sold will decline.

When video amusement machines interfere with radio communications of the Nevada Highway Patrol, there is less efficient and effective traffic and crime control. The costs of less effective law enforcement would be borne by society in the form of more traffic accidents and higher crime rates. Such costs show up in the form of increased medical expenses, higher costs of automobile insurance, and generally higher costs of crime prevention.

Checkpoint 13-2

If the marginal cost of pollution reduction were increased by \$70,000 at every level of pollution reduction shown in Table 13-1, the optimal level of pollution would be 60,000 units. If pollution were reduced below this level, the marginal benefit from pollution reduction (column 3) would be less than the marginal cost (column 5).

Checkpoint 13-3

There is no unambiguously correct answer to this question. However, it might be argued that because regulations for product safety prevent or slow down the introduction of new medical drugs to the marketplace, such regulations are more restrictive of consumer choice. Regulation of deceptive advertising is less likely to restrict the introduction of products to the marketplace because its aim is to regulate what is claimed about products rather than to prevent the sale of them altogether.

CHAPTER 14

Checkpoint 14-1

In Figure 14-2, "the cost of labor is soaring" would be modeled by shifting the horizontal supply curve of labor upward dramatically. This would cause the equilibrium quantity of labor given by the intersection of supply and demand for labor to fall—that is, it would "trigger increasing layoffs."

Checkpoint 14-2
Changes in the firm's final product price will affect the firm's marginal revenue product curve for the factor (and hence affect D_F), because the marginal revenue product of a factor at any given output level is the marginal physical product times the output price.

If firms have managed to raise their prices more rapidly than labor costs have risen, then the MRP curve of Figure 14–2 would shift upward more than the MCF curve would, and the equilibrium quantity of labor used would increase.

Productivity gains will shift both the MPP and MRP curves upward. The first unit of variable factor will now produce more units of output, valued at more dollars than before, and so on.

Checkpoint 14-3
The tire and tube industry is by far the largest user of rubber, and rubber cost is a large proportion of final cost of tires, implying a larger elasticity for the rubber demand curve of the tire industry. Rubber is not very easily substituted for in tire production, tending to decrease the rubber demand elasticity. The demand for tires is probably inelastic, and so the tire industry's demand for rubber will tend to be inelastic. Industrial hoses, belts, and tubes use rubber and probably have an inelastic demand for rubber for the same reasons. The footwear industry uses rubber, but because it can be fairly easily substituted for in many applications, the footwear demand for rubber is probably more elastic than that of the tire or hose industries. Using "armchair averaging," it would probably be correct to say that the rubber demand, overall, is fairly inelastic.

Some inelastically demanded factor inputs (and their elasticity-determining factors) might be diesel fuel (the transportation industry's product demand is fairly inelastic, substitution of other input factors is difficult and limited, and fuel is a fairly large proportion of total transport cost), transistors (the electronics industry has a fairly inelastic product demand, substitution of other factors is difficult, and the transistor cost is a small part of total product cost), nails (although demand for wood construction might be fairly elastic, substituting for nails in the production process is difficult, and nails are a small part of the cost of the final product), crude oil (although its cost is a large part of the cost of the final products, it is difficult to substitute for, and the demand for products using crude oil seems to be quite inelastic), and fertilizer (the demand for products using

it is inelastic, fertilizer is usually a fairly small cost relative to the final product cost, and it is quite difficult to substitute for).

The demand for Ford tractors is more elastic than the demand for tractors in general. The broader the definition of a factor, the more inelastic its demand is likely to be.

CHAPTER 15

Checkpoint 15-1
A guaranteed cost-of-living increase in a labor contract ensures that the real wage of labor remains constant even in periods of inflation. It works by granting automatic increases in the nominal wage of workers equal to the percentage increase in a selected price index. An additional 3 percent per year raise in the nominal wage would increase the real wage by 3 percent per year. If it is not going to increase the cost of labor per unit of output, then labor's productivity must also be increasing at 3 percent per year.

If the person is consistent, then he or she would not want to improve the traffic flow, since this would involve introducing new capital equipment such as traffic lights and new roads. It might eliminate some jobs, such as traffic policing, increase the productivity of truckers so that fewer would be needed, and perhaps eliminate some public transportation jobs as people decided the change made driving a more attractive choice. However, the change in traffic flow would also make the transportation of goods more efficient and reduce commuting time. Also, since most people view commuting as work related and not leisure, a reduction in commuting time would be likely to reduce worker fatigue and boost labor productivity on the job.

Checkpoint 15-2
The purpose of this question is to illustrate the fact that more unpleasant jobs will have to have a higher wage rate in order to induce someone to take them.

Checkpoint 15-3
As pointed out in Chapter 14, the monopolist and the perfect competitor have different demand curves for labor. The MRP curve would have a steeper slope for the monopolist—see Figure 14–3 in Chapter 14.

During a recession, the demand for labor will decline. This could be modeled in Figure 15-5 by shifting the demand curve to the left. This will further increase the excess supply at the union wage, which makes it difficult for the union to push for wage increases.

The economic rationale for the Contractors Mutual Association is to give monopsony power to the buyers of unionized labor services to combat the monopoly power of the union.

Consolidation of the various separate unions is essentially a horizontal merger and as such increases the monopoly power of the unions in the sale of labor services.

CHAPTER 16

Checkpoint 16-1

Movie stars and great professional athletes earn large economic rents because they typically do not have alternative employment opportunities that are nearly as lucrative. As a proportion of earnings, the economic rents earned by corporation presidents are most likely considerably smaller than those of movie stars and great athletes because corporate presidents have more lucrative alternatives, such as other top management positions.

To be consistent, Henry George would probably argue that the economic rents earned by individuals with unique skills should be taxed in the same way as economic rent on land.

A just position might recognize that gifted individuals must still work hard to develop their talents. As with the development of land, it is difficult to determine what is truly economic rent and what is the result of an individual's efforts to develop his or her innate abilities.

Checkpoint 16-2

A college education is a roundabout process because an individual typically gives up 4 years of full-time wages in order to acquire education and skills that will enable him or her subsequently to make higher wages than otherwise would be possible. One way to measure the rate of return on this investment would be to compare the lifetime earnings of college-educated and non-college-educated people and see what difference in earnings per year the 4-year college investment has made.

If people became less willing to save, the saving curve in Figure 16-6, part b, would shift to the left. This would decrease the long-run equilibrium stock of capital because the saving curve would intercept the vertical axis at a higher interest rate—that is, the long-run equilibrium interest rate would be higher, and therefore the long-run equilibrium capital stock would be less.

An increase in the rate of population growth would increase the rate of growth of the labor force and hence increase the potential productivity of capital. This would shift the demand for capital to the right and increase the long-run equilibrium stock of capital.

CHAPTER 17

Checkpoint 17-1

The Lorenz curves constructed should look very similar to Figure 17-2, part b. The income distribution for nonwhite families should show slightly more inequality.

Checkpoint 17-2

A marginally progressive tax structure should make the distribution of after-tax income more equal than the distribution of before-tax income.

The "baby boom" people began entering the work force in the late 1960s and have increased their experience and earning power with the passage of time. So one would expect the Lorenz curves for successive decades to show increasing income equality, other things being equal.

Checkpoint 17-3

The expected rate of return from a college education has historically been less for blacks than whites as the result of limited job opportunities due to discrimination. Hence the percentage of blacks choosing to make that investment is likely to be lower than among whites, other things being equal.

If A and B require equal skill and training and blacks and whites can enter them equally, then the equilibrium wages in the two occupations should be equal. But if discrimination prohibits blacks from entering A, then this has the effect of restricting the supply of labor to A and increasing the supply of labor to B. This will increase the wage for A and decrease the wage for B. The whites who are able to do so will get into the A market, since it now has a higher wage. This will counteract the wage effect somewhat—but not completely, since the blacks are "captive labor" for the B market.

Checkpoint 17-4

As the system was originally set up, the tax was a transfer from workers to themselves at a later age. Since the social security tax is regressive, it would make the after-tax income distribution more unequal.

The current operation of the system acts as an income tax transfer from current workers to current benefit recipients. Though the social security tax is still regressive, the intergenerational income transfer from younger to older people probably makes the after-tax income distribution more equal.

Glossary

A

absolute energy reserves The world's total stocks of energy reserves, equal to the sum of proven reserves plus unproven reserves.

accelerator principle The relationship between changes in level of retail sales and the level of investment expenditures.

accounting profit Profit obtained by subtracting the firm's explicit costs from its total sales receipts. Does not consider any imputed costs.

ad valorem tax Sales tax or excise tax calculated as a flat percentage of the sales price of a good.

antitrust policy Government policy for curbing monopoly characteristics and business practices aimed at reducing competition.

arbitration Process for settling labor-management disputes: an impartial third party, whose decision is binding on both parties, acts as a judge.

average fixed cost (AFC) Cost determined by dividing total fixed cost by the number of units of output.

average product Total output divided by the number of laborers required to produce that output.

average revenue Total revenue divided by the number of units sold.

average total cost (ATC) Cost determined by dividing total cost by the number of units of output.

average variable cost (AVC) Cost determined by dividing total variable cost by the number of units of output.

B

barrier to competition Any circumstance that makes it difficult for a new firm to enter an industry. Examples are the exclusive ownership of a unique resource; economies of scale; and government-sanctioned protection in the form of patents, licenses, copyrights, and franchises.

barter economy Trading goods directly for goods.

benefit-cost analysis An examination of the benefits and costs associated with any government program; is based on the principle that any program should be carried on to the point at which the last dollar spent (the last dollar of cost) on the program just yields a dollar's worth of benefit.

bilateral monopoly Market structure in which there is monopoly power on both the buyer's and the seller's side of the market.

blacklist List of names circulated among employers of employees considered "unemployable" because of union-organizing activity.

black market Market in which goods are traded (illegally) at prices above a government-imposed ceiling.

break-even point Point at which the quantity of output produced by a firm is such that total revenue just equals total cost or, equivalently, where average revenue (price) equals average total cost.

budget constraint Straight line representing all possible combinations of goods that a consumer can purchase at given prices by spending a given-size budget. Also called *budget line*.

business fluctuations Recurring phenomena of increasing and decreasing unemployment associated with decreasing and increasing output. Also called *business cycles*.

business unionism Concentration of union efforts on obtaining higher wages and better working conditions.

C

capital consumption allowance See *capital depreciation*.

capitalism Form of economic organization in which the means of production are privately owned and operated for profit and where freely operating markets coordinate the activities of consumers, businesses, and all suppliers of resources.

cartel A group of firms that collude to set prices or share markets.

ceteris paribus Latin expression for "all other things remaining the same."

closed shop Workplace that requires union membership as a condition of employment.

coefficient of elasticity Number obtained by dividing the percentage change in quantity by the percentage change in price.

coincidence of wants The possibility of barter between two individuals that occurs when each has a good that the other wants.

collective bargaining Process by which labor and management negotiate mutually acceptable wages and other conditions of employment.

command economy An economy in which the government answers the questions of how to organize production, what and how much to produce, and for whom to produce.

complementary factors Factors of production, the use of which always increases (decreases) whenever the use of any one of them increases (decreases).

complementary good A good that tends to be used jointly with another good.

concentration ratio Measure of the extent to which a few firms dominate an industry, computed as the percentage of total industry sales accounted for by the four (or eight) largest (in terms of sales) firms in the industry.

conglomerate A firm that produces a wide variety of goods and services for a number of largely unrelated markets.

conglomerate merger Merger of companies that operate in completely different markets and produce largely unrelated products.

consent decree Agreement with the Justice Department whereby a firm agrees to certain restrictions on the way it does business without being technically guilty of violating the law.

copyright Exclusive right granted to composers and writers that gives them legal control over the production and reproduction of their work for a certain period of time.

corporation Firm that has a legal identity separate and distinct from the people who own it.

craft union A union of skilled workers trained in a particular trade or craft.

creditor A person or organization to whom money is owed.

criminal conspiracy doctrine A doctrine from English common law that held that the organization of workers with the intent to raise wages constituted a criminal conspiracy and was therefore illegal.

D

debt instrument Written contract between borrower and lender specifying the terms of a loan.

deduction Reasoning from generalizations to particular conclusions; going from theory to prediction.

demand curve Graphic representation of the law of demand.

demand schedule Numerical tabulation of the quantitative relationship between quantity demanded and price.

derived demand Term used to characterize the demand for a productive factor because that demand is dependent upon, or derives from, the demand for the final product that the factor is used to produce.

differentiated oligopoly Oligopoly in which each firm produces a product that is somewhat different from that produced by the other firms. Also called an *imperfect oligopoly*.

diminishing marginal rate of substitution Characteristic of the behavior of the marginal rate of substitution along an indifference curve, reflecting the fact that the more of good B a consumer has *relative* to good A, the more of good B the consumer is willing to part with in order to get an additional unit of good A.

direct relationship Relationship between variables in which the value of each changes in the same way (both decrease or both increase).

diseconomies of scale Increasing long-run average total cost of production that results when a firm grows so large that it becomes cumbersome to manage.

dissolution Breaking a firm up into smaller firms.

divestiture Requiring a firm to sell some of its assets.

dividends Share of a firm's profits paid out to stockholders.

E

economic cost The alternative goods that must be forgone in order to produce a particular good. Also called *opportunity cost*.

economic efficiency Using available resources to obtain the maximum possible output.

economic policy Proposed method of dealing with a problem or problems posed by economic reality that is arrived at through the use of economic theory and analysis.

economic problem How to use scarce resources to best fulfill society's unlimited wants.

economic profit Difference between the total revenue obtained for the firm's sales and the opportunity costs of all the resources used by the firm.

economic rent Any amount of payment a factor or resource receives in excess of its supply price when there is market equilibrium.

economics A social science concerned with the study of economies and the relationships among economies.

economic theory A statement about the behavior of economic phenomena, often referred to as a law, principle, or model.

economies of scale Decrease in the long-run average total cost of production that occurs when a firm's plant size is increased.

economy A particular system of organization for the production, distribution, and consumption of all things people use to obtain a standard of living.

elastic demand Coefficient of elasticity is greater than 1.

elasticity of demand Degree of responsiveness of quantity demanded to a change in price.

elasticity of supply Degree of responsiveness of quantity supplied to a change in price.

elastic supply Coefficient of elasticity is greater than 1.

equilibrium price Price at which market equilibrium is achieved.

equilibrium quantity Quantity of the good supplied and demanded at the point of market equilibrium.

excise tax A tax levied on the sale of a particular good.

exclusion principle Distinguishing characteristic of private goods, the benefits of which, unlike those of public goods, accrue only to those who purchase them.

exclusive dealing agreement Manufacturer's agreement with dealers and distributors that restricts the latter's purchase, sale, or use of competing products.

explicit costs Direct monetary payments made by a firm to purchase or hire resources from outside the firm.

externalities Costs or benefits related to a good or service that fall on others besides buyers and sellers of that particular good or service. Also called *spillovers, neighborhood effects, external costs* or *benefits, spillover costs* or *benefits,* or *external economies* or *diseconomies.*

F

factors of production The inputs (land, labor, and capital) necessary to carry on production. Also called *economic resources.*

fair return Pricing rule under which the price of a good is determined by the intersection of the average total cost curve with the demand curve.

fair-trade laws Laws that sanction resale-price maintenance agreements.

fallacy of composition Error in reasoning that assumes that what is true for the part is true for the whole.

fallacy of division Error in reasoning that assumes that what is true for the whole is true for its individual parts.

fallacy of false cause Error in reasoning that assumes one event is the cause of another event simply because it precedes the second event in time.

featherbedding The practice of requiring an employer to hire more workers than are necessary or to continue to employ workers for jobs that are obsolete.

federalism Principle whereby each national union in the AFL-CIO has the exclusive right to organize and regulate labor in its particular trade.

financial market structure Market in which lending and borrowing take place through the exchange of debt instruments at interest rates mutually determined by lenders and borrowers.

firm A business organization that owns, rents, and operates equipment, hires labor, and buys materials and energy inputs. The firm organizes and coordinates the use of all these factors of production for the purpose of producing and marketing goods and services.

fixed factor Factor of production that cannot be changed in the short run.

free rider Anyone who receives benefits from a good or service without having to pay for them.

functional distribution of income Method of characterizing the way income is distributed according to the function performed by the income receiver.

H

high-employment budget Difference between the actual level of government spending and the level of tax revenue that would be collected if the economy were at a high-employment level of GNP.

horizontally integrated Term used to describe a firm that owns several plants, each of which performs the same functions.

horizontal merger Merger between two firms selling the same, or very similar, products in the same market.

I

ideology Doctrine, opinion, or way of thinking.

implicit costs Costs of resources actually owned by the firm itself. These costs are the payments such resources could have received were they employed in their next best alternative.

income effect A decrease in the price of a good allows the consumer to buy more of it even though the consumer's money income remains the same.

indifference curve A graphical representation of an indifference schedule—the consumer gets the same level of satisfaction at any point along the curve.

indifference map All of an individual's indifference curves taken together.

indifference schedule A listing of all possible combinations of goods that give a consumer the same level of satisfaction.

induction Reasoning from particular facts and observations to generalizations.

industrial union A union that seeks to organize all hourly paid workers, skilled and unskilled, in a given industry.

inelastic demand Coefficient of elasticity is less than 1.

inelastic supply Coefficient of elasticity is less than 1.

inferior good A good that people typically want more of at lower income levels and less of at higher income levels.

interest rate, or **interest** The price of borrowing money, or the price received for lending money, expressed as a percentage.

inverse relationship Relationship between variables in which the value of one increases as the value of the other decreases.

involuntary unemployment Occurs when workers willing to work at current wage rates are unable to find jobs.

J

job-training programs Government-subsidized efforts aimed at improving work skills among the poor. Also called *manpower programs*.

jurisdictional dispute Disagreement among unions over which one has the right to organize a particular group of workers.

L

labor contract Binding agreement between labor and management stipulating the terms of employment and the wages to be paid labor.

laissez faire ("let [people] do [as they choose]") The belief that people should be allowed to conduct their economic affairs without interference from the government.

law of demand Theory that the lower the price of a good, the greater will be the demand for it and, conversely, the higher the price, the smaller will be the demand.

law of diminishing marginal utility Given the consumer's tastes, the marginal utility associated with the consumption of any good over a given period of time eventually begins to fall as more and more of the good is consumed.

law of diminishing returns As more and more of a variable factor of production is used together with a fixed factor of production, beyond some point the marginal product attributable to each additional unit of the variable factor begins to decrease.

law of increasing costs The cost per additional good obtained, measured in terms of the good sacrificed, rises due to the different productivity of resources when used in different production processes.

law of supply Theory that suppliers will supply larger quantities of a good at higher prices than they will at lower prices.

license Right granted, usually by a state, to practice certain professions.

limited liability Characteristic of a corporation that makes it attractive to investors (the owners) in that financial liability extends only to the assets of the corporation, not to personal assets of the investors.

limited partner Member of a partnership who does not participate in the management of the firm or engage in business on behalf of the partners. A limited partner risks only his or her money directly invested in the firm (the limited partner's personal assets cannot be seized to satisfy the firm's debts and obligations).

limit price The lowest price at which a new firm can enter an industry and just cover average total cost. Existing firms in the industry with lower average total costs can set price below the limit price level and discourage new entrants.

loan length The duration of time until a loan must be repaid. Also called *maturity*.

lockout Closing down of operations by an employer in an attempt to force workers to accept employer's wage offer and terms of employment.

long run Period of time long enough so that the quantity of all factors used to produce a particular good can be changed.

Lorenz diagram Method of illustrating the extent to which actual income distribution deviates from a perfectly equal distribution of income.

M

macroeconomics Branch of economic analysis that focuses on the workings of the whole economy or large sectors of it.

marginal cost Change in total cost resulting from a unit change in output.

marginal physical product Increase in total revenue associated with each one-unit increase in a variable productive factor.

marginal product Increase in total output that results from the addition of a unit of a variable factor of production.

marginal productivity theory of factor demand Theory that states that a profit-maximizing firm will increase its use of a productive factor up to the point where the factor's marginal revenue product equals the factor's price.

marginal rate of substitution Rate at which the consumer is just willing to substitute one good for the other along an indifference curve.

marginal revenue Change in total revenue resulting from the sale of one more unit of output.

marginal revenue product Increase in total revenue associated with each 1 unit increase in a variable productive factor.

marginal utility The change in total utility that occurs with the consumption of an additional unit of a good.

market An area within which buyers and sellers of a particular good are in such close communication that the price of the good tends to be the same everywhere in the area.

marketability Ease with which a lender may sell a debt instrument to someone else before the loan must be repaid in full. Also called *liquidity.*

market demand curve The sum of all the individual demand curves for a good.

market equilibrium Equilibrium established at the price where the quantity of the good buyers demand and purchase is just equal to the quantity suppliers supply and sell.

market period Period of time so short that none of the factors of production used to produce a particular good can be changed.

market structure Characteristics of market organization, such as the number of buyers and sellers, the similarity of their product, and the ease of entry or exit from the industry. Also called *industrial organization.*

mediation Nonbinding advisory process for settling labor-management disputes in which an impartial third party attempts to reconcile differences.

microeconomics Branch of economic analysis that focuses on individual units or individual markets in the economy.

midpoints formula variation Method of calculating the coefficient of elasticity in which the averages of the two quantities and the two prices are used as base points when computing the percentage changes in quantity and price.

minimum-wage law Law that makes it illegal for employers to pay workers a wage below a certain statutory level that is often called the minimum wage.

mixed economy An economy in which what, how, and for whom to produce goods are determined partly by the operation of free markets and partly by government intervention.

money wage Price per unit of labor services measured in dollars and cents.

monopolistic competition Industry or market structure where there is easy entry and exit, and in which there are many firms, each of which produces a product that is slightly different from that of the others.

monopoly Form of market structure in which the entire market for a good or service is supplied by a single seller or firm.

monopsony Market structure in which one buyer purchases a good or service from many sellers.

N

nationalized industry An industry owned by the government.

natural monopoly Industry in which the economies of scale make it possible for an established firm effectively to prevent rivals from entering the industry.

near-public good A good that is consumed jointly, though it is possible to exclude nonpaying customers—a movie is an example.

negative income tax Tax plan through which households with incomes below a statutory level receive a subsidy from the government equal to some fraction of the difference between the statutory income level and their earned income.

net productivity of capital The annual percentage rate of return that can be earned by investing in capital.

nominal interest rate The real interest rate plus the anticipated rate of inflation.

nonpecuniary considerations Characteristics associated with a job that will cause labor to require either a higher wage (if characteristics are viewed as disadvantages) or a lower wage (if characteristics are viewed as advantages).

nonprice competition Competition among firms for sales by means other than price cutting—such as by advertising and product differentiation.

normal good A good that people typically want more of as their income rises.

normal profit Payments to financial capital and entrepreneurial skill that are just sufficient to keep them employed in a particular productive activity—that is, to keep them from leaving and going into some other productive activity.

normative statement A statement of what should or ought to be that cannot be supported or refuted by facts alone; a value judgment or opinion.

O

oligopoly A market dominated by a few sellers.

opportunity cost The cost of a unit of a good measured in terms of the other goods that must be forgone in order to obtain it.

output effect When the price of a factor falls (rises), the costs of production fall (rise), leading to a rise (fall) in the output of final product and a consequent increase (decrease) in the use of all factors.

P

parity Price of an agricultural good that gives the good a purchasing power, in terms of the goods that farmers buy, equivalent to that which it had in a base period.

partnership A firm owned and operated jointly by two or more individuals.

patent Exclusive right granted to the inventor to market a product for a certain period of time.

perfectly elastic Quantity of good demanded changes by an unlimited amount in response to a change in price.

perfectly inelastic Quantity of good demanded does not change at all in response to change in price.

plant A facility in which production takes place.

positive statement A statement of what is, was, or will be that can be verified or refuted by looking at the facts.

poverty State in which an individual's or family's income and other means of support are insufficient to provide for basic needs.

predatory behavior Actions by one firm directly intended to eliminate a rival firm.

predatory pricing Practice whereby a large firm, operating in many markets, can afford to sell at prices below costs in some markets until smaller competitors in those markets are driven out of business.

price The exchange value of a good in terms of other goods, most often expressed as the amount of money people will pay for a unit of the good.

price ceiling Government-imposed upper limit on price.

price discrimination Selling the same good or service at different prices to different buyers.

price leadership Informal agreement among firms in an industry that one, usually the largest, will always initiate or take the lead in price changes.

price support Government guarantee to suppliers that they will receive a specific price for a good even if the market will not pay this price.

price taker A firm that must accept the sales price of its product as given and beyond its control.

production possibilities frontier A curve representing the maximum possible output combinations of goods for a fully employed economy.

progressive income tax Income tax rates set such that the larger a household's income, the greater the percentage of that income that is taken away by income taxes.

proven energy reserves The quantities of oil, natural gas, and coal that producers are almost certain they can bring out of the ground given current energy prices and the state of mining and drilling technology.

public assistance programs Government programs aimed at providing help to dependent families, the sick, the handicapped, and the aged—those who for reasons largely beyond their control cannot work.

public goods Goods that will not be produced in private markets because there is no way for the producer to keep those who don't pay for the goods from using them—for example, a lighthouse beacon.

public utility Natural monopoly whose operation, including the setting of prices, is regulated by a government agency.

pure market economy An economy in which what, how, and for whom to produce goods is determined entirely by the operation of markets.

pure public good A good that cannot be provided to one person without being provided to others—national defense is an example.

R

rate base Allowable capital cost used in determining the prices that may be charged by a public utility.

rate of return Ratio of the dollar measure of a capital good's net productivity to the cost of the capital good expressed as a percentage per year.

ration coupon Coupon issued by government entitling an individual or household to buy a certain number of units of a good.

real wage Price per unit of labor services measured in terms of the quantity of goods that can be purchased—often measured as the money wage divided by an index of the general price level.

rent control Government-imposed price ceiling on the rent a tenant may be charged.

resale-price maintenance contract Agreement whereby a retailer is bound not to sell a product below a stated price fixed by the manufacturer.

resource misallocation See *underemployment*.

restrictive license Agreement under which the holder of a patent allows others to sell the product or use the process under restricted conditions (price limitations, quantity limitations, and so forth) stipulated in the license.

right-to-work laws State laws guaranteeing an individual the right to work in a unionized shop without becoming a member of the union, effectively banning the union shop.

risk The likelihood that a borrower will default on a loan.

roundabout process Taking time and effort away from the direct production of goods for current consumption and using that time to produce capital goods that will ultimately make possible a larger subsequent production of goods than otherwise possible.

rule of reason The legal view that market conduct rather than share of market control should determine guilt or innocence under the Sherman Act.

S

sales tax A tax levied on the sale of any of a broad classification of goods.

saving Refraining from current consumption.

scarce Existing in a limited amount.

scientific method Ongoing cycle of induction from observation to theory, followed by deduction from theory to prediction, and explanation and checking of predictions and explanations against new facts to see if theory is verified, refuted, or needs to be modified.

secondary boycott Union strikes and picketing aimed at disrupting business between employers.

shared monopoly An oligopolistic industry in which all the firms attempt to collude to coordinate price and output decisions so that the industry effectively behaves like one giant monopoly firm.

short run Period of time short enough so that the quantity of one or more factors of production used to produce a particular good cannot be changed.

short-run production function Relationship between the amount of a variable factor of production used and the total quantity of output produced.

single-tax movement Late nineteenth-century movement, led by Henry George, to finance government by taxing the economic rent on land.

size distribution of income The ranking of all families in the economy according to the size of the income received by each, lowest to highest, regardless of the source of their income.

slope of the demand curve Change in price over some range of the curve divided by the change in quantity demanded over that same range.

social security system A form of social insurance and public assistance to aid the old, the disabled, the sick, the unemployed, and families financially crippled by the death of the breadwinner.

social security tax Tax on wages and salaries (shared equally by employee and employer) used to finance social security benefits.

sole proprietorship A firm with a single owner who makes all decisions and bears full responsibility for everything the firm does.

specialization of labor System of production in which each worker performs only one task for which he or she is specifically trained.

specific tax Sales tax or excise tax calculated as a fixed amount of money per unit of good sold.

strike Labor's refusal to work for an employer until the employer agrees to the demand for higher wages or changes in other terms and conditions of employment.

strikebreakers Workers willing to work on jobs currently vacated by workers on strike.

strike fund Money set aside by a union to tide workers over during a strike period.

subsidy Amount of money paid to a supplier by the government per unit of a good produced.

substitute good A good that can be used in place of another good because it fulfills similar needs or desires.

substitution effect When factors are substitutable for one another in the production process, a fall (rise) in the price of one of them will to a certain extent lead to its substitution for (replacement by) the other.

supply curve Graphic representation of the law of supply.

supply schedule Numerical tabulation of the quantitative relationship between quantity supplied and price.

T

tax incidence Distribution of the burden of a tax between the buyer and the seller.

technology The production methods used to combine resources of all kinds, including labor, to produce goods and services.

total cost The sum of the firm's total variable cost and total fixed cost at a given output level; the sum of the opportunity costs of the inputs used to produce that output.

total fixed cost (TFC) Cost of the unchangeable, or fixed, factors of production in the short run.

total revenue Quantity of the good sold multiplied by the price per unit.

total variable cost (TVC) Costs that the firm can vary in the short run by changing the quantity of the variable factors of production and, hence, the quantity of output produced.

treble damages Practice under which firms found guilty of violating antitrust laws are required to pay the complaining firm three times the total damages sustained.

tying contract Contract whereby a firm agrees to sell one of its products only on the condition that the buyer purchases its other products as well.

U

underemployment A condition in which available resources are employed in tasks for which other resources are better suited or in which the best available technology is not used in a production process. Also called *resource misallocation*.

undifferentiated oligopoly Oligopoly in which each firm produces the same product. Also called a *perfect oligopoly*.

undistributed profits Profits not paid out to shareholders (but still belonging to them). Undistributed profits are usually reinvested in the firm's operations.

union An organization of workers that represents them collectively in bargaining with employers over wages and other terms of employment.

union shop Workplace that permits a nonunion employee to be hired provided the employee joins the union within a certain period of time after employment.

unit elastic Coefficient of elasticity equals 1. Also called *unitary elasticity*.

utility The service or satisfaction a good yields to the consumer.

V

variable factor Factor of production that can be changed in the short run.

vertically integrated Term used to describe a firm that owns several plants, each of which handles a different stage in the production process.

vertical merger Merger between a supplier and its customer.

voluntarism Policy opposing government intervention in union affairs.

W

wage Price per unit of labor services.

workable competition Vigorous price and nonprice competition accompanied by the significant potential for the entry of new firms into an industry—may exist even in industries where there are few firms.

Y

yellow-dog contract Signed statement whereby a worker, as a condition of employment, agrees not to join a union.

Index